FINANCIAL
ANALYSIS

Susy, thanks again for the first 21

FINANCIAL ANALYSIS

Second Edition

BILL REES

University of Strathclyde

PRENTICE HALL

London   New York   Toronto   Sydney   Tokyo   Singapore
Madrid   Mexico City   Munich

First published 1995 by
Prentice Hall International (UK) Limited
Campus 400, Maylands Avenue
Hemel Hempstead
Hertfordshire, HP2 7EZ

A division of
Simon & Schuster International Group

Typeset in 10 on 12 pt Times
by MHL Typesetting Ltd

Printed and bound in Great Britain by
Redwood Books, Trowbridge, Wiltshire

Library of Congress Cataloging-in-Publication Data

Rees, Bill.
    Financial analysis / Bill Rees.
      p. cm.
    Includes bibliographical references and index.
    ISBN 0-13-288283-3
    1. Corporations—Finance. 2. Business enterprises—Finance.
3. Managerial accounting. I. Title.
    HG4011.R42   1995
    658.15—dc20   95-13407
                                                   CIP

British Library Cataloguing in Publication Data

A catalogue record for this book is available from
the British Library

ISBN 0-13-288283-3

---

1 2 3 4 5   99 98 97 96 95

Contents

Preface   ix

1 Financial Analysis and Financial Information   **1**

  1.1 Introduction   1
  1.2 Financial analysis and analysts   2
  1.3 Theoretical developments   38
  1.4 The structure of the text   42

  Note   44
  Questions   44
  References   45

2 Financial Statements and Creativity   **46**

  2.1 Introduction   46
  2.2 The role of accounting information in financial analysis   55
  2.3 A definition of 'ideal' financial statements   56
  2.4 Measurement problems and creativity in accounting 59
  2.5 Some specific examples of measurement problems in accounting   62
  2.6 Example financial reports   69
  2.7 The implications of the efficient market hypothesis (EMH)   78
  2.8 Conclusion   80

  Questions   81
  References   82

3 Ratio Analysis: Methods and Issues   **83**

  3.1 Introduction   85
  3.2 Ratio analysis — techniques and problems   88
  3.3 Examples of ratio computation and interpretation   95
  3.4 The statistical properties of financial ratios   101
  3.5 Distributional characteristics of accounting ratios   106

3.6 Interrelationships between accounting variables 109
3.7 Conclusion 113

Note 114
Questions 114
References 116

4 Time-series Analysis and Forecasting **117**

4.1 Introduction 117
4.2 Accounting times-series 118
4.3 Evidence on the behaviour of accounting time-series 124
4.4 Forecasting accounting numbers 128
4.5 Management and security analysts' forecasts 132
4.6 Share prices, fundamentals and earnings forecasts 142
4.7 Conclusion 147

Note 148
Questions 148
References 150

5 Capital Markets and Asset Pricing **153**

5.1 Introduction 153
5.2 The capital markets 154
5.3 Risk and return 157
5.4 Asset pricing models 164
5.5 Capital market efficiency 174
5.6 Efficient market anomalies 178
5.7 Conclusion 181

Note 182
Questions 182
References 184

6 Accounting, Value and the Capital Market **186**

6.1 Introduction 186
6.2 Market reaction to accounting announcements 187
6.3 Accounting information and market efficiency 197
6.4 Accounting and valuation models 207
6.5 Conclusion 222

Questions 222
References 224

7   Links between Accounting Numbers and Economic Fundamentals   226

7.1   Introduction   226
7.2   Links between the outputs of accrual accounting and the value of
      equity capital   227
7.3   The link between accounting rate of return (ARR) and internal
      rate of return (IRR)   237
7.4   The Edwards, Kay and Mayer (EKM) analysis   242
7.5   Accounting information and risk assessment   246
7.6   Conclusion   250

Appendix 7.1   250
Notes   251
Questions   252
References   253

8   Corporate Takeovers and Allied Activity   255

8.1   Introduction   255
8.2   Background and motives for mergers   256
8.3   Performance record of merger activity   270
8.4   Characteristics of acquired firms   277
8.5   Predicting and exploiting mergers   280
8.6   Identifying, valuing and costing mergers   283
8.7   Accounting for merger activity and holding companies   284
8.8   Conclusion   286

Questions   287
References   289

9   Corporate Failure Prediction and Credit Evaluation   291

9.1   Introduction   291
9.2   Financial failure in the UK   293
9.3   Distress prediction and financial variables   297
9.4   Multivariate models of distress prediction   302
9.5   Developments of the prediction models   310
9.6   Conclusion   317

Questions   322
References   324

10   Social, Environmental and Employee Reporting   326

10.1   Introduction   326
10.2   Social reporting   328
10.3   Environmental reporting   332

10.4 Employee reporting   342
10.5 Disclosure of information for collective bargaining   347
10.6 Conclusion   353

Notes   354
Questions   354
References   355

11 Regulation of Accounting   358

11.1 Introduction   358
11.2 History of accounting standards setting in the UK   360
11.3 International comparison of accounting regulation   367
11.4 The case for the regulation of accounting practices   370
11.5 Decision criteria and accounting choice   374
11.6 The political aspects of regulation   377
11.7 Conclusion   381

Notes   381
Questions   381
References   383

Author Index   384
Subject Index   388

Preface

This book differs from most other texts concerned with financial studies as its scope is defined by the span of financial analysis — the use of publicly available financial information to assess the performance and prospects of a firm. There are many fine texts available which explain the theories and institutions of finance, a substantial number of, typically more turgid, explanations of the technical requirements of the accounting process, and a number of straightforward resumés of financial interpretation techniques. As yet, with a few notable exceptions, there is little coverage of the analysis of financial information. This is unfortunate as it is difficult to evaluate or understand the financial accounting process without a sound awareness of the uses to which accounting information is put. Also, a conceptual knowledge of finance theory is not a great deal of use to practitioners without an appreciation of the information base on which financial decisions are made. Thus I would argue that an understanding of financial analysis is an important component of understanding finance or accounting.

However, there is a further reason for writing this book. The technique of financial analysis is one of some fascination as it allows the user to observe firm performance and presents a window on the world of business. The study of financial analysis is a demanding amalgam of interdisciplinary techniques which incorporates a broad spectrum of methodologies and theories including finance, accounting, economics, statistics, strategy and sociology. Thus financial analysis is a potentially interesting and demanding discipline which is perhaps most suitable, at least at the level covered in this text, as a focus for final year undergraduate courses or masters level courses for specialist business students.

The style of this book is determined by the characteristics of the discipline covered. There are few neat theories susceptible to elegant exposition as with corporate finance, nor are detailed technical skills required as with accounting. There is, however, extensive evidence concerning the behaviour of firms, financial information and financial analysts. Therefore the content is strongly influenced by research results and methodology. This allows the reader to investigate the practicability of various analytical tasks using financial data and to assess some of the alternative procedures for approaching these tasks. These comments were included in the Preface to the first edition and I believe that they still hold true. However, there is evidence of some change. Theoretical developments as well as advances in the empirical evidence are gradually changing the subject. We can hope that the next revision of this text may allow for a much stronger reliance on theory, and, following the adage that there is nothing so practical as a good theory, rather more practical advice. As discussed in Chapter 1 the study of financial analysis can help the reader develop considerable insights but it still leaves analysts with the task of developing their own methods.

The organisation of the text remains exactly as in the previous edition. A number of sensible changes have been proposed but these were rarely in agreement and I envisage considerable change in the subject over the next few years which will no doubt occasion a substantial change in any subsequent edition. Lecturers do, of course, have the option of rearranging the order of the subjects as they wish. Thus the first chapter sets the scene discussing the uses, users and sources of financial information and the scope and potential for development of the subject. Chapters 2 to 5 cover the basic knowledge required to interpret financial information: where does the information come from, to what extent can it be relied upon, and what does it mean? Some changes from the earlier edition include increased emphasis of creative accounting, and using examples from European countries other than the UK. The use of English has been made as straightforward as possible to help students whose first language is not English. For rewriting of Chapter 5 I owe a considerable debt to my joint author: Professor Paul Draper of the University of Strathclyde. Chapters 6 to 10 consider the application of these skills to a number of analytical tasks including investment decisions, merger analysis, bankruptcy prediction and social and environmental reporting. Chapter 7, which is not as difficult as it appears, presents important theoretical developments in the link between accounting information and economic fundamentals, and I owe a considerable dept to my co-author for this chapter: John O'Hanlon of Lancaster University. The final chapter considers the regulation of accounting information which along with Chapter 10 was co-authored by Christine Cooper of the University of Strathclyde, whose help has been invaluable.

This book is intended for use by undergraduates in accounting, finance and other areas of business studies, and for MBA and other postgraduate students involved in the interpretation of financial data. Given that students will be coming from different backgrounds certain chapters may seem rather simple to some and difficult to others. The text may be used as a review of the issues and most research evidence included is explained intuitively rather than in detail. It may be also be used as the basis for more in-depth study and the citations for the original research are given wherever possible. In the same vein the questions at the end of the chapters vary from quite simple reviews to more detailed studies which will require the students to seek material and guidance from other sources. This is as it should be and I make no apology for this nor for the fact that few of the problems set will lead to definitive answers. Unfortunately that is in the nature of the subject.

In addition to my three co-authors I would like to thank Cathy Peck, and Andy Goss, her replacement at Prentice Hall, for their encouragement and patience. The responsibility for any remaining errors is mine. There still remains considerable scope for development of this subject, and, as I explained earlier, I believe that is starting to happen. I will be very grateful for any comments or suggestions.

BILL REES

CHAPTER 1

Financial Analysis and Financial Information

CHAPTER OBJECTIVES

This chapter will:

1 Define the scope and objectives of this text.

2 Outline the supply and demand for financial information.

3 Present a simple review of the firm and its managers' objectives.

4 Introduce some of the main developments in finance and accounting theory which impinge on financial analysis.

1.1 Introduction

This text is different from many other books concerning accounting or finance as it takes as its remit the scope of financial analysis. As a focus, financial analysis is a useful alternative or complement to the conventional disciplinary perspective of texts dealing with finance theory or accounting practice. It is difficult to evaluate the accounting process without a sound awareness of the uses to which accounting information is put. Also, a conceptual knowledge of finance theory is not of much practical use without some appreciation of the information base on which financial decisions are made. However, the work of financial analysts is not only an alternative approach to the study of the financial aspects of business but is also an interesting one. It presents a window onto the world of business and the theories and skills covered allow the student to appreciate the performance and prospects of the firms which make up such an important part of the modern environment.

Individuals in developed capitalist economies are employed by firms, sell goods and services to firms, invest in and borrow from firms, consume their products, are poisoned by their wastes (and sometimes their products) and are supported by the taxes which the

1

firms pay. These individuals appear to judge the performance of politicians, at least in part, by the economic performance of firms, in much the same way as football supporters judge the performance of their team's manager by the success of the players. In each case, an individual's relationship with the firm or the individual's appreciation of the firm's performance could be supported by the skills of a financial analyst.

Financial analysis requires the synthesis of a demanding mix of interdisciplinary techniques which incorporate a broad spectrum of methodologies and theories. Not all of these theories can be covered in any one text though many students will meet these other disciplines during their full program of studies and will be able to relate them to this book. However, it is intended that this book will provide sufficient guidance for those with no experience of these other studies to cope successfully with the requirements of financial analysis. Clearly, accounting and finance are fundamental disciplines for a financial analyst and the early chapters are devoted to establishing a basic understanding of these topics. Statistical and computing skills will also be called upon, while economics and econometric analysis would be helpful. Finally, behavioural and political considerations are referred to.

Section 1.2 of this chapter will review the circumstances in which the analysis of financial information is employed together with the various available sources of information. As the firm is the object of the analysis, Section 1.2 also presents a thumb-nail sketch of the activities, objectives and management of the firm and a brief explanation of investing in firms. Although investment is not the only motivation for analysis of financial information, it is perhaps one of the more important reasons. Even where it is not the objective of the analysis, an understanding of the significance of the investments in a firm will almost certainly be required for other types of analysis. Section 1.3 presents an overview of the role of theory and a review of some of the more significant recent theoretical developments. The final section of this chapter will give the reader some insight into the scope and ordering of the subjects dealt with later in the text.

1.2   Financial analysis and analysts

In this text the financial analyst is viewed as *any user of publicly available financial information concerning firms who wishes to use the information for the purpose of economic decision making and who has no access to the internal information systems of the firm*. Financial analysis is the procedure they use to interpret the information.

Clearly the skills employed by a financial analyst are also important for a firm's internal management, but the managerial aspects of decision making, accounting and information systems would require a book each, and in fact there are many such books available. The definition used here would exclude a firm's managers when they are examining problems regarding their own organisation, but not when they are examining other firms. However, the definition would include employees of a firm when they are denied the privilege of demanding information or information systems to suit their needs, as with the trade union or employee engaged in wage negotiations.

At this point it is helpful to look at the characteristics of 'good' financial analysis. Beaver (1991) in an editorial of the *Financial Analysts' Journal* listed the 'Ten Commandments of Financial Statement Analysis'. At this stage the reader may not appreciate the significance of each of the points made but few (if any) academics have made a more substantial contribution to the development of financial analysis as an academic discipline and his views are well worth bearing in mind. Somewhat paraphrased, Beaver's commandments are:

1. Only use financial statements with regard to the broader context of other available information. The meaning of financial statements is conditional on the environment.
2. Use all relevant sources of information as well as the financial statements. Not only are the financial statements conditional on the environment but they only tell part of the story.
3. Read the small print (or more precisely the notes to the accounts). It takes a great deal of time to understand a set of financial statements and some of this time includes investigating the details.
4. Do not become obsessed with earnings (or any other single dimension of the firm's performance). It is important to assess the quality of the earnings, the potential for growth, and the risk attributes of the firm, and these are only the more important among many other factors.
5. Understand the implications of the firm's characteristics as determined in the analysis. For example, whilst it might be quite easy to measure gearing (or any other single dimension), it is not so easy to decide whether the level of gearing is good or bad.
6. Don't forget that the financial statements are out of date by the time they are known and the older they are the greater the likelihood of important events occurring after the accounting year end.
7. Remember that financial statements are restricted to giving details regarding events (a) which occur within the accounting period, (b) are defined as affecting the firm (or the group) directly, (c) can be measured in monetary amounts, and (d) that these events are accounted by a set of rules which may not produce the most helpful measures.
8. A little knowledge is a dangerous thing. Whilst there is no need to be scared of financial reports it is advisable to retain a healthy awareness of most people's limited analytical skills.
9. Where the task in hand is beyond the analyst's ability seek expert help. However, it might be advisable to maintain a scepticism regarding the analytical skills of many 'expert' analysts as it seems that many of these have only a basic knowledge of financial techniques.
10. Avoid unnecessary risks. With or without expert analysis the technique of financial analysis is fallible. The process of determining the apparent financial attributes of a firm does not alter the genuine attributes. Put more simply a firm facing imminent bankruptcy may appear to have a sound balance sheet. Don't invest on the basis of financial analysis unless you can afford to lose.

Table 1.1 The users of financial information

1.	Investors in the firm	(a)	Shareholders
		(b)	Bondholders
		(c)	Banks
2.	Business contacts	(a)	Suppliers
		(b)	Customers
		(c)	Employees
3.	Other users	(a)	Taxation agencies
		(b)	Government
		(c)	Local government
		(d)	Regulators
		(e)	Competitors
		(f)	Public
4.	Intermediaries	(a)	Analysts
		(b)	Media

1.2.1 *The demand for financial analysis*

Table 1.1 lists the individuals and firms who might be expected to utilise financial analysis skills for various decisions. In many cases the user group has a right to certain specified information supplied by the firm in question, while in other circumstances it has to make do with information sources that are publicly available. For example, the directors are required by law and stock exchange rules to provide annual financial statements to the shareholders, but these statements are public documents and other users are able to exploit this information source. Conversely, banks enjoy no legal or quasi-legal rights of access but are able to impose on the directors and insist that they are provided with the required data as a condition of a loan.

In none of these cases does the user of the information make any explicit payment to the supplier, although there are considerable costs borne by the supplier. However, the firm providing the information does receive some benefits to set against the costs of disclosure. Where they are able to demonstrate that an investment or contract is reasonably secure, or that the firm is well managed, the shareholders, lenders or other business contacts are able to moderate the terms required from the firm and may be able to refrain from other costly monitoring or enforcement procedures. Consequently there are many examples where firms provide more information than is legally required of them.

The decisions to be addressed by these many different users are so diverse as to provide a great deal of variety in the sources of information and techniques used. Details of these analysts are as follows.

1. Investors in the firm

(a) Shareholders and their investment advisers will be interested primarily in measuring the current performance of the shares and in forming expectations about future performance.

Where the investor is interested in attempting to identify mis-priced shares in order to sell over-priced shares and buy under-priced shares there is a presumption of market inefficiency. Where the investor assumes that the market value of the share is a fair value other attributes of the investment such as the risk, yield, and growth relevant to the management of the investment will be the focus of attention. The many different techniques of investment analysis have been conventionally divided into two principal classifications. Technical analysis, which examines patterns and trends in the share price, and fundamental analysis, which examines all available sources of information, including financial statements, in order to establish a value for the share.

The investor will also be concerned to ensure that the management of the firm controls its resources for the benefit of the shareholders. Normally the shareholders will not be able to take an active part in the management of a firm or in monitoring the performance of their representatives. The shareholders will therefore try to arrange contracts which reward the management for results which are in the shareholders' interests and/or constrain the management from inappropriate activities. The shareholders will also monitor the firm's performance in order to dispose of ineffectual managers or those who take decisions which are not in the shareholders' interests. In either case, financial information and its interpretation will be basic to these purposes.

The level of commitment and the method of investment by the shareholders will stretch from a few hundred pounds from the small investor or a firm's employee, through to massive commitments by pension funds, unit trusts and life assurance companies. Clearly, the resources and abilities of these investors will differ as will the extent to which they rely on investment advisers and professional analysts.

(b) The investor who buys the fixed interest securities, bonds or debentures issued by a firm has different objectives from the equity investor. Under normal circumstances the financial performance of the firm is less crucial. If the firm performs better or slightly worse than the average it is unlikely to affect the payment of principal or interest due to the investor. The concern of the debt-holder is to ensure that the solvency of the firm is assured and that the security for the debt is adequate. In this instance, measures of the firm's economic performance are secondary to those concerning the value of the assets and liabilities. Financial information may play a further part in this process as many debt contracts include rights of intervention for the debt-holders. This enables them to constrain management action or to seize control of secured assets where certain specified circumstances occur. These circumstances may well be defined in financial terms.

(c) Other investors might include banks which, in the UK at least, often allow firms to operate with extensive unsecured overdrafts. As with fixed interest securities, bonds and debentures, the prime consideration here is monitoring the security of the principal and interest payments. Although UK banks tend not to take an active role in management, continental European and Japanese banks traditionally have taken a more pro-active role. This may be due to the much higher proportion of a firm's capital contributed by the banks in these countries. This requires the bank to concern itself with the economic performance of the firm rather than merely with the security of the debt. Where a bank has provided much of a firm's finance and that firm under-performs, it is unlikely that the bank's capital will be protected as there is relatively little equity to cover any shortfall.

2. Business contacts

(a) Suppliers will be interested in the financial security of their customers for much the same reason that debt-holders are. Indeed, trade creditors will often provide as much capital to firms as debt-holders. Under certain conditions the relationship between supplier and customer will be especially close. For instance a firm may find itself tied to one customer for a substantial part of its output. The supplier is still concerned for the security of the sums owing for its supplies but the future development of the supplier is also inextricably linked to the performance of the customer.

(b) Customers would typically have a more relaxed attitude to the financial standing of their suppliers. However, it might be thought that a financially distressed supplier may take short cuts with quality control. Where the goods are in short supply the continuity of supply will also be a consideration. In the case of long-term contracts the cost of a supplier failing might be considerable. In such cases the failure to deliver the product might be damaging and it would be normal for the customer to make progress payments which might be lost if the supplier were to become insolvent. At the time of writing the commercial airliner manufacturing industry appears to be struggling to meet the medium-term demand for aircraft. If an airline contracts for its future aircraft with a manufacturer which becomes insolvent, the airline will either have to cut back or pay a premium on hiring or buying planes in a sellers' market.

It is also conventional for some pricing arrangements to be dependent on financial information. Long-term contracts, especially during periods of inflation, are often based on cost-plus arrangements. Government contracts, particularly for products for which there is no normal market such as defence supplies, are frequently priced so as to allow a supplier a given return on capital. Thus financial analysis will be involved in the determination of prices, and a sceptical attitude might be merited where it is of some importance to the supplier to ensure that its capital base is inflated.

(c) Employees and trade unions in the UK are concerned principally with job security and wage negotiations. In continental Europe they are often also involved in consultation with management. In both cases the union/employee may use financial information as an input to negotiations or for predicting future employment levels. As yet there has been little development of financial analysis by employees or their representatives, though the practice of distributing simple employee reports is now widespread. In some continental European countries the employee—union—management relationship is more constructive. Employees have some influence in the management of a firm and monitor management performance in much the same way as do equity holders.

3. Other analysts of financial information

(a) The government raises a significant portion of its revenue from tax on corporate profits and considerably more from other taxes collected through corporations such as Value Added Tax, Customs and Excise duty and payroll taxes. For this fund-raising the government relies heavily on financial information and would ideally seek a system which both exhibits a degree of objectivity and measures with reasonable accuracy the factors that the revenue service is required to tax. Thus a system which is open to manipulation of the profit figure or lengthy dispute regarding the appropriate profit figure would not be ideal — save for those who make their living manipulating and disputing. It is also less than ideal if the reported profit fails to measure accurately the wealth creation by the firm if that is the subject of the tax. While it is possible to design measures of profit which display considerable certainty and also to develop approximate measures of wealth created, they are at opposite ends of the spectrum of available accounting systems. It appears impossible to combine the two aspects in one measure.

(b) Government or quasi-government organisations are charged with formulating policies to manage the economy and with supervising sections of the economy. The financial statements are an essential input to both these objectives. Aggregate financial statements allow the government to assess the health and performance of sectors of the economy and to obtain feedback on the effectiveness of its policies.

Many sectors of the economy are subject to state control, either directly or through some quasi-governmental organisation. The financial sector of the economy, and banks in particular, have long been subject to supervision regarding their financial structures. In continental Europe the supervision of takeover activity is also an issue which has been controversial in recent years. With regard to the UK the Monopolies and Mergers Commission often examines the financial standing of the parties to a proposed takeover when making its decisions.

Recently the policy of many European (and other) governments has been to privatise some public enterprises that have a monopolistic market position. In order to protect the public, and other sectors of the economy that are more constrained by market forces, a series of supervisory bodies have been established. In the UK this supervision has been operated by the Office of Fair Trading and more recently specific organisations have been created to monitor particular industries. OFTEL, OFGAS, OFWAT and OFFER, which are the watchdogs for the telecommunications, gas, water and electrical supply industries in the UK, are the first major organisations of this type and have so far relied on rather simplistic but robust financial controls. In the United States this style of supervision has been influenced considerably by more sophisticated financial measurement, especially in the case of the regulation of utilities which have local monopolies.

Supra-governmental bodies are also becoming of greater importance. In particular, the European Commission has acquired powers to investigate many aspects of firm or industry performance. This trend seems likely to continue.

(c) In most European states local government taxes are independent of financial reports but local government will still wish to monitor the performance of firms operating within its boundaries, in much the same way and for much the same reasons as does central government.

(d) Public sector supervisory agencies monitor significant sectors of the UK economy. Typically in the rest of Europe such tasks are undertaken by central government or bodies appointed by government. The motivation for this activity may be to discourage central government interference or to regulate profitable activities. Typically, such self-regulatory bodies exhibit greater flexibility and awareness than a government equivalent, but they are also liable to criticism as they may lack a mandate or adequate enforcement powers. Obvious examples of self-regulatory public sector agencies are the various European stock exchanges which have to ensure an orderly market, adequate information flows, and effective order and payment systems.

(e) Competitors have considerable cause to review the performance of a firm. The financial performance of competitors is often used as a benchmark for identifying sub-standard performance within a firm. Monitoring the performance of the competition regarding the levels of research and developments, advertising and pricing, geographical and industrial diversification of operations, the level of capital investment, and the stock market performance of the competitor's shares, may be crucial for the strategic decisions of a firm. While merger and acquisitions decisions may be driven by a variety of motives, the financial analysis of targets, potential targets and aggressors will undoubtedly be a crucial element. However, the contribution of intuitive or emotional factors may also be considerable.

(f) The general public's interest in the financial analysis of firms is modest. However, it may be awakened by specific issues, particularly when a firm is proposing or undertaking activities of which sections of the public disapprove. Politically active elements, such as environmental pressure groups or political parties, may indulge in more regular monitoring of the performance of firms, and while this is occasional rather than general it may nevertheless be important. The limited level of public interest in financial analysis may be a reflection of the characteristics of a financial reporting system which is designed for investment decision-making or creditor protection and which may be inappropriate when it is applied to political decisions. For example, financial reports may be of limited help to environmentalists when no account is taken of environmental costs which are not borne by the firm, even though they may be directly caused by the firm's activities. Equally, where social costs are ignored, for example unemployment costs or indirect subsidies, the political relevance of the financial reports is not clear.

The financial monitoring of companies may also be restrained by the low level of financial literacy of the general public and its limited access to financial information. Both of these elements are undergoing change although it is not obvious that this will induce a substantial change in the public's use of financial analysis.

4. Intermediaries

(a) Analysts who operate as independent advisers will be included in most of the categories represented above. There are obvious examples. Investment analysts offer advice to individuals and institutions as specific buy, sell or hold recommendations or as financial forecasts of earnings or dividends. Credit assessment agencies will produce trade credit assessments or a ranking of the investment standing of corporate bonds. The advantage to the investor, bank or supplier of using such 'information intermediaries' is that they can develop and employ specialist skills and information sources that would be uneconomical for the occasional user. Thus it is more efficient for an investment broker or credit rating agency to analyse the prospects of a large sample of firms and sell that information to many users, than for each user to conduct the analysis independently. The use of specialist analysts is also apparent on an irregular basis in many of the other categories mentioned above. A trade union might employ the specialist skills of a financial analyst to help prepare a case for wage negotiations, or a political party use specialist consultants to assess the viability or impact of certain policies. In less formal instances, a pressure group will often find like-minded individuals with some analytical skills who will help prepare its case for public hearings or for propaganda.

(b) It is also interesting to consider the financial media as a group of users as well as suppliers of financial information. The providers of press commentary in the city pages of newspapers, the teams which put together investigative reports into business practice, and the organisations which gather and disseminate financial information are all seeking to profit from processing the data. It is clear to even the casual observer that the prevelance of financial commentary is much greater over the last few years than it has been previously. A demand for financial information is being created and exploited. The consumers of this supply are undoubtedly getting a service which would have been inconceivable not long ago.

1.2.2 *Sources of financial information*

Just as the categories of financial analysts and their objectives exhibit a great deal of diversity there are many different sources of information available to the analyst, not all of which are financially quantified. Exhibit 1.1 (p. 10) contains the Extel card for Siemens AG, the German electronics combine. This service, which is typical of a number of other products marketed worldwide, is included as an indicator and example of the spread of information thought to be of interest to analysts. Exhibit 1.1a is the basic information set, 1.1b the graph of recent share price performance, and 1.1c the news announcements made by the firm.

Table 1.2 lists various sources of information, some of which are illustrated in Exhibit 1.1 whilst others are not, and the following text expands on them. In many cases more detailed examples of these sources are given in subsequent chapters. Another interesting way of appreciating the variety of sources that can be used is to examine the reports prepared by professional analysts. An example is given here in Exhibit 1.2, but the reader is advised to collect more. Their scope and length vary immensely.

One aspect of the supply of information not dealt with here is the impact of regulation. Corporate law, stock market and professional accounting requirements all affect the supply of information defining what information should be released, and how and when this should happen. It also affects how the information is prepared and the form and detail of the disclosure. Finally, in most developed economies there are laws or regulations which govern what information cannot be released or acted on if received: the 'insider trading' rules. All these aspects are important to the supply of information and whilst there is an argument for including these considerations here, this would introduce too many topics into the first chapter. They are dealt with in Chapter 11 but there is no reason why this chapter need be left until the end of the course.

————————————— **Exhibit 1.1a** —————————————

SIEMENS AG

Security Name	**Closing Price**
DM50(VAR)	DM622 (No change) Cum dividend
Shares in Issue	**Market Capitalisation**
55,070,425	DM34,253,804,350
Latest Dividend	**P/E Ratio***

Latest Dividend

Nett	DM13
Gross	DM18.571429
Tax	DM5.571429
Div Type	Yearly payment
Pay Date	February 24, 1995
Ex Date	February 24, 1995

P/E Ratio*

16.11

EPS*

DM32.2

*Last reported 12 month earnings

Country of Quotation

Germany

Gross Dividend Yield

N/A

Industrial Classification (SEC)

N/A

Market Codes

SEDOL	4807100
TOPIC	N/A
VALOREN	342635
CUSIP	N/A
TICKER	723600

NOTE: The information above relates to the security which is deemed to be the company's prime line.

Amendment Date

November 10, 1994

Annual Update

April 12, 1994

HEAD OFFICE

Wittelsbacherplatz 2, 80333 Munich, Germany Tel: +49 89 234-0 Telex: 52100 Fax: +49 89 234-42 42

PAYING AGENTS

Siemens Financial Services Ltd, 19 Berkeley Street, London W1X 5AE England

SUPERVISORY BOARD

CHAIRMAN: Dr-Ing Eh H. Franz JOINT DEPUTY CHAIRMAN: A. Graf; Dr jur W. Schieren MEMBERS: A. Bock; Dr jur U. Cartellieri; R. Fauroux; B. Grube; H. Hawreliuk; R. Heckmann; D. Kreyenberg; Dr rer pol H. Kriwet; G. Nassauer; W. Neugebauer; K.-H. Nolden; Dr rer pol W. Roller; Dr jur A. Schmidt; Dr iur N. Senn; P. von Siemens; H.J. Strenger; H. Wagner

MANAGEMENT BOARD

PRESIDENT AND CHIEF EXECUTIVE: Dr jur H. von Pierer MEMBERS: Dr rer oec K.-H. Baumann; Dr-Ing H. Baur; Prof Dr rer nat H.G. Danielmeyer; Dr oec publ E.N. Hardt; A. Huttl; Dr Eng hc V. Jung; E. Kill; J. Knorr; Prof Dr-Ing W. Kunerth; Dr-Ing H. Langer; W. Maly; C.-H. Thomas; G. Wilhelm

SIEMENS AG

AUDITORS

KPMG Deutsche Treuhand-Gesellschaft AG Wirtschaftsprufungsgesellschaft

COMPANY HISTORY

Established 1847 The Company's name changed from Telegraphen-Bau-Anstalt Siemens & Halske to Siemens AG in 1966. In 1890 the Company was converted into a limited partnership and in 1897 into a joint stock corporation. In 1903, the Company and Elektrizitats AG transferred their power operations into a new company, Siemens Schuckert Werke, of which the Company became the sole shareholder in 1939. In 1966, the Company absorbed Siemens Schuckert Werke and Siemens Reinigerwerke in which it had a 98.7% holding. It acquired the outstanding shares in Siemens Reinigerwerke by way of a share exchange on a one for one basis. In November 1988, the Company and the General Electric Company (GEC) PLC (United Kingdom) set up a joint subsidiary, GEC Siemens PLC with the intention of taking over Plessey PLC (United Kingdom). By September 1989, GEC Siemens had acquired over 90% of Plessey's capital. On 11-04-1990 approval was granted by the Cartel Authorities for the Company's acquisition of a majority holding in Nixdorf Computer AG. On 01-10-1990 the Company integrated its Data and Information Systems Group into Nixdorf and renamed it Siemens Nixdorf Informationssysteme (SNI) AG. On 21-10-1991 the Company made an offer to purchase publicly held outstanding shares in Siemens Nixdorf Informationssysteme (SNI) AG, at a price of DM 225 per DM 50 share between 28-10-1991 until 06-12-1991 which resulted in the acquisition of a further 17.2%. In March 1992, it was decided to fully integrate SNI into the Company. This was achieved by compensating holders of the remaining SNI shares by exchanging one Company share for six SNI shares; holdings of less than six shares were settled with a cash payment.

ACTIVITIES

The Company carries out its activities through the following divisions: Power Generation (KWU); Power Transmission and Distribution; Industrial and Building Systems; Drives and Standard Products; Automation; Private Communication Systems; Public Communication Networks; Defence Electronics; Automotive Systems; Transportation Systems; Medical Engineering; Semiconductors; Passive Components and Electron Tubes; Electromechanical Components; Audio and Video Systems; Siemens Nixdorf Informationssysteme; Osram (lamps and fluorescent bulbs); Bosch-Siemens Hausgerate (domestic electrical equipment).

SUBSIDIARIES

DOMESTIC: Siemens Nixdorf Informationssysteme AG; Osram GmbH; Vacuumschmelze GmbH; Siemens Audiologische Technik GmbH; Siemens Ubertragungssysteme GmbH; Rofin-Sinar Laser GmbH; NRG Nuklearrohr-Ges mbH; Siemens Finanzierungsges fur Informationstechnik mbH; Siemens Miet- und Portfolio-GmbH & Co OHG; Siemensstadt-Grundstucksverwaltung GmbH & Co OHG; Duewag AG (97%); Siemens Solar GmbH (51%) FOREIGN EUROPE: Siemens Beteiligungen AG (Switzerland); Siemens SA (Belgium); ATEAN NV (Belgium); Siemens AS (Denmark); Siemens Oy (Finland); Siemens SA (France); Siemens Automotive SA (France); Siemens AE Elektrotechnische Projekte und Erzeugnisse (Greece); Siemens PLC (United Kingdom); Siemens Plessey Electronic Systems Ltd (United Kingdom); Siemens Ltd (Eire); Siemens Telecomunicazioni SpA (Italy - merger with Italtel SpA, a subsidiary of STET, announced 12-05-94); Siemens SpA (Italy); Siemens Nederland NV (Netherlands); Siemens AS (Norway); Siemens AG Osterreich (Austria) (74%); Siemens SA (Portugal); Siemens-Elema AB (Sweden); Siemens AB (Sweden); Siemens-Albis AG (Switzerland)

SIEMENS AG

(78%); Siemens SA (Spain); Simko Ticaret ve Sanayi AS (Turkey) (51%); Turk Siemens Kablo ve Elektrik Sanayii AS (Turkey) (55%); Osram SA (France); Osram Ltd (United Kingdom); Osram Sta Riunite Osram Edison-Clerici SpA (Italy); Osram SA (Spain) (90%); Siemens Nixdorf Information Systems SA/NV (Belgium); Siemens Nixdorf Information Systems SA (France); Siemens Nixdorf Information Systems Ltd (United Kingdom); Siemens Nixdorf Informatica SpA (Italy) (51%); Siemens Nixdorf Informatiesystemen BV (Netherlands); Siemens Nixdorf Informationssysteme GesmbH (Austria); Siemens Nixdorf Informationssysteme AG (Switzerland); Siemens Nixdorf Sistemas de Informacion SA (Spain) NORTH AMERICA: Siemens Corpn (USA); Osram Sylvania Inc (USA); Siemens Nixdorf Information Systems Inc (USA); Siemens Electric Ltd (Canada) SOUTH AMERICA: Siemens SA (Argentina); Siemens SA (Brazil) (81%); Siemens SA (Columbia) (94%); Siemens SA de CV (Mexico); Siemens SA (Venezuela); Osram Argentina SACI (66%); Osram do Brasil-Companhia de Lampadas Eletricas SA (Brazil); Osram SA de CV (Mexico); Siemens Western Finance NV (Netherland Antilles) ASIA: Siemens Ltd (India) (51%); Siemens KK (Japan) (83%); Siemens Components (Advanced Technology) Sdn Bhd (Malaysia); Siemens Pakistan Engineering Co Ltd (64%); Siemens Components (Pte) Ltd (Singapore); Siemens Telecommunication Systems Ltd (Taiwan) (55%); Osram-Melco Ltd (Japan) (51%) AFRICA: Siemens Ltd (South Africa) (52%) AUSTRALIA: Siemens Ltd

CAPITAL at 30-09-93

	ISSUED	SHARES ISSUED
Ordinary Bearer shares of DM 50	DM 2,751,283,100	55,050,425
Registered Preference shares of DM 50	DM 46,181,700	923,634

Including 113,876 Ordinary shares held in Treasury.

CAPITAL HISTORY

1985	Jan	600,000 Ord	Issue to Staff at DM 489
	Mar	2,748,687 Ord &	Rights - 1:17 at DM 100 (xr
		51,313 Pref	05-03-85)
		126,622 Ord	Options
1986	Feb	300,000 Ord	Issue to Staff at DM 796
1987	Feb	300,000 Ord	Issue to Staff at DM 702
		267,631 Ord	Options
1988	Feb	350,000 Ord	Issue to Staff at DM 326.30
		20 Ord	Options
1988/89		800,000 Ord	Issue at DM 518.5
		46,197 Ord	Options
		1,808,808 Ord	Options
1989/90		560,000 Ord	Issue to Staff
1990/91		600,000 Ord	Issue to Staff
1991/92		2,993,583 Ord	Options
		188,410 Ord	Acquisition
1992/93		24,763 Ord	Issue to shareholders of Siemens Nixdorf Informationssysteme AG

ACQUISITION HISTORY

1987/88		approx DM 500m	Majority of Bendix Electronics Group (USA)
		approx DM 200m	Further 18% of Siemens AG Osterreich (Austria)
1988	Sep		Majority of Optilas Laser Industriel (France)
	Oct		Outstanding 40% of Alkem
	Oct		Outstanding 40% of RBU
	Nov		91.6% of Plessey PLC (United Kingdom) through GEC Siemens

SIEMENS AG

```
                                        PLC
1989    Jan                             100% of Bergmann Kabelwerke AG
        Mar         FFr 346.5m          51.75% of IN2 (France)
        Jul                             Shares in European Silicon
                                          Structures
        Aug                             Arco Solar Inc (USA)
        Aug                             Majority of assets of Rolm (USA)
        Sep                             Majority of Duewag AG
1990    Jan                             Outstanding 51% of GEC-Osram
                                          (United Kingdom)
        Apr                             51% of Nixdorf Computer AG
        May                             33.33% in Linotype AG
        Aug                             Interest in Maci Industries
                                          Group (Canada)
                                        Further stake in Nixdorf
                                          Computer AG
1991    Jan                             WSSB Signaltechnik GmbH
                                        Starkstrom-Anlagebau Leipzig
                                          GmbH
                                        Starkstrom-Anlagebau Rostock
                                          GmbH
                                        Kabelwerke Meissen GmbH
                                        Schweriner Kabelwerke GmbH
1991    Oct                             17% of Siemens Nixdorf
                                          Informationssysteme AG
1991/92                                 Outstanding 50% of ROLM (USA)
                                        Interest in A-C Equipment
                                          Services Inc (USA)
                                        Outstanding shares in Siemens
                                          Nixdorf Informationssysteme AG
```

RIGHTS OF SHARES

VOTING: Ordinary and Preference shares are entitled to one vote each. Preference shares are entitled to six votes each in a second vote that may be demanded by the holders of Preference shares.

SHAREHOLDINGS

NUMBER OF SHAREHOLDERS in the Company at 01-08-93: 607,000.

DIVIDEND PAYMENT DETAILS - ORDINARY Year end September 30

	DM Gross Per Share	Paid and Ex Date	Coupon Number
1989	12.5	23-03-90	34
1990	13	02-04-91	35
1991	13	13-03-92	36
1992	13	12-03-93	37
1993	13	11-03-94	38

DIVIDENDS OF EARLIER YEARS - ORDINARY

DM (Gross): 1984, 10; 1985, 12; 1986, 12; 1987, 11; 1988, 11

PER SHARE RECORD OF DM 50 ORDINARY - Adjusted for Capital Changes

	Sep 30 1990	Sep 30 1991	Sep 30 1992	Sep 30 1993
EARNINGS as reported by Company (DM)				
Basic	29.70	35.00	32.10	32.20

a Shares on which earnings calculated (m)

SIEMENS AG

Basic	51	53	55	56
DIVIDEND (DM)	13.00	13.00	13.00	13.00
DIVIDEND COVER	2.28	2.69	2.47	2.48
NET ASSET VALUE as reported by Company (DM) At Balance sheet date	321.50	328.10	341.50	341.60
Capital Issue Factor	-	-	-	-

(a)Including shares held in Treasury totalling 5,804 in 1990, 32,505 in 1991, 164, 560 in 1992 and 113,876 in 1993.

PRICES to December 31 - Adjusted for Capital Changes

FRANKFURT ORDINARY (DM)	1989	1990	1991	1992
High	720.00	815.50	673.00	702.40
Low	502.20	514.50	557.00	536.40

BORROWINGS at 30-09-93

BONDS 6-1/4% WITH WARRANTS 1987/94. Issued and Outstanding: DM 500,000,000. 4-3/4% 1983/93. Issued: SFr 100,000,000. Outstanding: DM 114,000,000. ZERO COUPON BONDS WITH WARRANTS 1986/2001. Issued: US$120,000,000. Outstanding DM 191,000,000. 8% WITH WARRANTS 1992/2002. Issued: US$1,000,000,000. Outstanding: DM 1,642,000,000. CREDIT INSTITUTIONS Outstanding: DM 1,764,000,000. NOTES AND OTHER LOANS Outstanding: DM 434,000,000.

CONSENSUS FORECAST

Forecast last revised July 27, 1994

			a Sep 1993	Sep 1994	Sep 1995
Cash EPS	(DMm)	LATEST	142.17	134.76	143.79
		High		156.00	169.00
		Low		116.00	127.00
		Previous		135.21	142.93
		Std. Deviation		10.58	12.75
EPS	(DM)	LATEST	38.45	35.06	40.03
		High		38.50	44.50
		Low		31.89	36.20
		Previous		35.71	40.64
		Std. Deviation		1.83	2.12
EPS Growth		LATEST		(8.80)	14.20
		Previous		(6.80)	13.80
Dividend	(DM)	LATEST	13.00	13.09	13.75
		High		14.00	15.00
		Low		13.00	13.00
		Previous		13.75	14.25
		Std. Deviation		0.29	0.80
No of brokers		LATEST		17	15
		Previous		16	11

(a)Actual figures.

SIEMENS AG

Consensus estimates and actuals provided by FIRST CALL INTERNATIONAL

INTERIM RESULTS

	Jun 30 1993 DEM m	Jun 30 1994 DEM m
Domestic sales	25,100	23,600
Foreign sales	30,700	34,100
Net profit	1,324	1,245
Domestic new orders	26,600	25,300
Foreign new orders	33,300	39,400
Fixed asset investments	4,700	3,500

CONSOLIDATED PROFIT AND LOSS ACCOUNT

	Sep 30 1989 DM m	Sep 30 1990 DM m	Sep 30 1991 DM m	Sep 30 1992 DM m	Sep 30 1993 DM m
TURNOVER	61,127.8	63,184.9	73,008.4	78,509.0	81,648.0
Cost of sales	–	–	–	(53,894.0)	(56,949.0)
GROSS PROFIT	–	–	–	24,615.0	24,699.0
Administration exps	–	–	–	(15,268.0)	(15,870.0)
Incr in stocks etc	389.2	1,396.7	1,699.6	–	–
Raw materials etc	(19,472.3)	(20,045.4)	(24,109.7)	–	–
Own work capitalised	1,155.4	1,262.9	1,600.4	–	–
Staff expenses	(25,904.2)	(26,988.1)	(31,816.9)	–	–
Other trading exps	(19,594.9)	(21,506.2)	(23,647.3)	(9,457.0)	(10,154.0)
Misc other tdg inc	3,815.5	4,372.2	5,088.7	2,333.0	2,382.0
TRADING PROFIT	1,516.5	1,677.0	1,823.2	2,223.0	1,057.0
Equity A/c profits	3.0	76.5	91.7	36.0	223.0
Interest/inv income	3,204.3	3,357.3	2,933.2	2,706.0	3,360.0
Interest payable	(1,383.0)	(1,490.1)	(1,026.2)	(1,679.0)	(1,728.0)
Other expenses net	(553.2)	(797.6)	(403.0)	(89.0)	–
PROFIT BEFORE TAX	2,787.6	2,823.1	3,418.9	3,197.0	2,912.0
Tax	(1,210.6)	(1,155.2)	(1,627.3)	(1,242.0)	(930.0)
PROFIT AFTER TAX	1,577.0	1,667.9	1,791.6	1,955.0	1,982.0
Minority interests	(104.3)	(121.1)	56.0	(160.0)	(179.0)
NET INCOME	1,472.7	1,546.8	1,847.6	1,795.0	1,803.0
Non equity dividends	(11.5)	(12.0)	(12.0)	(12.0)	(12.0)
Ordinary dividends	(610.6)	(666.1)	(673.5)	(715.0)	(716.0)
RETAINED PROFITS	850.6	868.7	1,162.1	1,068.0	1,075.0

NOTES TO CONSOLIDATED PROFIT AND LOSS ACCOUNT

	Sep 30 1989 DM m	Sep 30 1990 DM m	Sep 30 1991 DM m	Sep 30 1992 DM m	Sep 30 1993 DM m
STAFF EXPENSES BY TYPE					
Wages & salaries	(20,138.0)	(21,478.4)	(25,372.6)	–	–
Social security	(3,248.0)	(3,509.1)	(4,103.0)	–	–
Staff pensions	(2,518.2)	(2,000.6)	(2,341.3)	–	–

SIEMENS AG

	(25,904.2)	(26,988.1)	(31,816.9)	–	–
OTHER TRADING EXPS					
Depreciation	(3,838.4)	(3,761.7)	(4,117.3)	–	–
Amortn of intangibles	(218.3)	(213.7)	(282.8)	–	–
Research & dev	–	–	–	(7,554.0)	(7,698.0)
Misc other tdg exps	(15,538.2)	(17,530.8)	(19,247.2)	(1,903.0)	(2,456.0)
	(19,594.9)	(21,506.2)	(23,647.3)	(9,457.0)	(10,154.0)
INTEREST/INV INCOME					
Investment income	–	–	–	–	613.0
Interest income	–	–	–	2,706.0	2,747.0
	3,204.3	3,357.3	2,933.2	2,706.0	3,360.0
Non equity dividends	(11.5)	(12.0)	(12.0)	(12.0)	(12.0)
PROFIT BEFORE TAX is after (charging) crediting					
Directors emoluments	(37.5)	(40.9)	(40.1)	(21.1)	(19.1)
Dirs compensation etc	–	–	–	(11.0)	(11.0)
Wages & salaries	–	–	–	(27,043.0)	(28,443.0)
Social security	–	–	–	(4,392.0)	(4,546.0)
Staff pensions	–	–	–	(1,597.0)	(2,258.0)
Staff expenses	–	–	–	(33,032.0)	(35,247.0)
FA rentals etc	–	–	–	(176.0)	(185.0)
Duties & taxes	(432.0)	(475.8)	(552.5)	(477.0)	(416.0)
Research & dev	(6,875.0)	(6,980.0)	(7,892.0)	–	–
Av no of staff	361,800	374,000	406,000	417,800	403,800
No of staff at y/e	365,000	373,000	402,000	413,000	391,000

BUSINESS ANALYSIS (DM m)

SALES

	Sep 30 1990	Sep 30 1991	Sep 30 1992	Sep 30 1993
Power Generation (KWU)	5,812	4,955	6,570	8,692
Power Transmission & Distribution	4,950	5,307	5,568	5,951
Industrial & Building Systems	7,577	8,774	8,717	8,946
Drives & Standard Products	6,279	6,522	6,686	6,538
Automation	5,548	5,680	5,811	5,365
Data & Information Systems	7,690	–	–	–
Private Communication Systems	4,820	5,105	5,383	6,267
Public Communication Networks	9,071	11,260	13,165	13,549
Defence Electronics	1,073	1,679	1,460	1,238
Automotive Systems	1,819	2,127	2,540	2,580
Transportation Systems	1,158	2,141	2,718	3,580

SIEMENS AG

Medical Engineering	6,580	7,429	7,887	7,905
Semiconductors	1,983	2,029	1,881	2,145
Passive Components & Electron Tubes	1,668	1,591	1,488	1,507
Electromechanical Components	800	832	855	1,023
Audio & Video Systems	122	249	261	348
SNI	-	12,125	13,010	11,922
Osram	2,640	2,971	3,119	2,990
Hell	1,045	-	-	-
Other	1,383	1,446	1,251	1,061
Inter Group	(8,833)	(9,214)	(9,861)	(9,959)
	63,185	73,008	78,509	81,648

GEOGRAPHICAL ANALYSIS (DM m)

SALES - BY MARKET

	Sep 30 1990	Sep 30 1991	Sep 30 1992	Sep 30 1993
Germany	44,504	51,245	56,339	59,206
Rest of Europe	19,532	23,338	23,485	22,634
North America	7,543	8,517	8,716	10,160
Latin America	1,771	1,563	1,417	1,935
Asia	2,088	2,715	2,582	3,031
Other	1,011	1,100	1,178	1,184
Inter Group	(13,264)	(15,470)	(15,208)	(16,502)
	63,185	73,008	78,509	81,648

CONSOLIDATED STATEMENT OF CASH FLOWS

	Sep 30 1992 DM000	Sep 30 1993 DM000
OPERATIONS	8,654,000	9,103,000
INVESTING ACTIVITIES		
Invests acquired	(3,014,000)	(1,881,000)
Tangibles acquired	(5,560,000)	(4,793,000)
Tangibles sold	983,000	1,039,000
	(7,591,000)	(5,635,000)
FINANCING ACTIVITIES		
Share capital issued	2,505,000	16,000
Dividends paid	(686,000)	(720,000)
Misc financing inflow	(1,771,000)	(628,000)
	48,000	(1,332,000)
CASH & EQVTS INCREASE	1,111,000	2,136,000

NOTES TO CONSOLIDATED STATEMENT OF CASH FLOWS

SIEMENS AG

	Sep 30 1992 DM000	Sep 30 1993 DM000
OPERATIONS		
Profit before tax	3,197,000	2,912,000
Taxation	(1,242,000)	(930,000)
Depn & amortn incr	4,735,000	4,605,000
Decrease in stocks	(1,832,000)	1,149,000
Decrease in debtors	(1,860,000)	(1,571,000)
Incr in accrued exp	647,000	1,673,000
Increase in creditors	1,280,000	1,439,000
Other wkg cap decr	3,647,000	(53,000)
Misc tdg inflows	82,000	(121,000)
	8,654,000	9,103,000
CASH & EQVTS INCREASE		
Notes & bills	1,512,000	1,633,000
Misc cash/eqvt inflow	(401,000)	503,000
	1,111,000	2,136,000
TAXATION	(1,242,000)	(930,000)

CONSOLIDATED BALANCE SHEETS

	Sep 30 1989 DM m	Sep 30 1990 DM m	Sep 30 1991 DM m	Sep 30 1992 DM m	Sep 30 1993 DM m
FIXED ASSETS					
Intangible assets	477.5	414.1	275.3	410.0	277.0
Tangible assets	13,901.2	14,456.1	16,453.8	16,917.0	16,919.0
Financial assets	2,645.9	3,698.3	2,659.5	2,506.0	3,726.0
	17,024.6	18,568.5	19,388.6	19,833.0	20,922.0
OWN EQUITY SHARES	7.9	1.9	12.7	57.0	45.0
PREPAID EXPENSES	56.2	50.0	69.4	43.0	66.0
CURRENT ASSETS					
Stocks	6,887.6	7,314.1	8,238.8	6,282.0	5,228.0
Trade debtors	10,815.1	11,780.6	14,387.1	14,459.0	14,713.0
Misc debtors	8,373.1	7,389.7	8,817.3	10,905.0	12,740.0
Cash & equivalents	1,754.3	3,660.7	3,478.1	3,077.0	3,580.0
Securities &c	19,477.4	15,684.5	15,075.5	16,543.0	18,188.0
	47,307.5	45,829.6	49,996.8	51,266.0	54,449.0
CREDS due within 1 yr					
Debt due within 1 yr	2,410.0	2,469.8	2,538.7	1,600.0	2,308.0
Trade creditors	3,880.8	4,113.3	4,651.9	4,640.0	5,725.0
Misc creditors	4,956.0	4,787.6	5,986.3	5,931.0	6,797.0
	11,246.8	11,370.7	13,176.9	12,171.0	14,830.0
NET CURRENT ASSETS	36,060.7	34,458.9	36,819.9	39,095.0	39,619.0

SIEMENS AG

TOTAL ASSETS LESS CURRENT LIABILITIES	53,149.4	53,079.3	56,290.6	59,028.0	60,652.0
CREDS due after 1 yr					
Long term debt	1,816.6	1,588.3	2,036.2	2,931.0	2,337.0
L/T trade creditors	292.3	237.8	260.0	214.0	239.0
Misc other L/T liabs	1,451.1	1,597.8	865.0	744.0	727.0
	3,560.0	3,423.9	3,161.2	3,889.0	3,303.0
PROVISIONS	30,810.3	31,835.7	34,094.0	35,441.0	36,334.0
DEFERRED INCOME ETC	225.6	262.5	386.5	418.0	489.0
NET ASSETS	18,553.5	17,557.2	18,648.9	19,280.0	20,526.0
SHARE CAPITAL	2,489.9	2,608.4	2,638.4	2,798.0	2,799.0
Capital reserves	5,199.2	5,923.7	6,244.4	8,590.0	8,605.0
Profit for the year	622.5	678.2	686.0	727.0	728.0
Currency apprecn res	–	–	–	(1,116.0)	(966.0)
Revenue reserves	9,536.9	7,557.7	7,734.6	7,035.0	7,953.0
SHAREHOLDERS' FUNDS	17,848.5	16,768.0	17,303.4	18,034.0	19,119.0
Minority interests	705.0	789.2	1,345.5	1,246.0	1,407.0
NET ASSETS	18,553.5	17,557.2	18,648.9	19,280.0	20,526.0

NOTES TO CONSOLIDATED BALANCE SHEETS

	Sep 30 1989 DM m	Sep 30 1990 DM m	Sep 30 1991 DM m	Sep 30 1992 DM m	Sep 30 1993 DM m
INTANGIBLE ASSETS					
Misc intangible FA	477.5	414.1	275.3	410.0	277.0
	477.5	414.1	275.3	410.0	277.0
TANGIBLE ASSETS					
Property – cost	9,702.0	10,414.9	12,441.7	12,753.0	13,522.0
Property depreciation	(3,366.7)	(3,839.2)	(4,604.5)	(4,795.0)	(5,247.0)
Property NBV	6,335.3	6,575.7	7,837.2	7,958.0	8,275.0
Oth tangible FA-cost	26,859.9	28,492.8	31,218.4	31,484.0	32,252.0
Oth tangible FA depn	(19,294.0)	(20,612.4)	(22,601.8)	(22,525.0)	(23,608.0)
Other tangible FA NBV	7,565.9	7,880.4	8,616.6	8,959.0	8,644.0
Tangible assets	13,901.2	14,456.1	16,453.8	16,917.0	16,919.0
FINANCIAL ASSETS					
Invs in assoc cos	1,736.1	1,260.7	1,493.6	1,267.0	1,274.0
Other trade invs	909.8	2,437.6	1,165.9	1,239.0	2,452.0
Trade investments	2,645.9	3,698.3	2,659.5	2,506.0	3,726.0

SIEMENS AG

STOCKS					
Raw materials etc	1,955.2	2,174.4	2,512.3	2,448.0	2,402.0
Work in progress	4,102.1	4,334.3	4,798.0	4,489.0	4,348.0
Finished gds & resale	4,593.0	4,748.5	5,478.3	5,140.0	4,741.0
Payments on account	(12,183.2)	(13,474.3)	(15,604.5)	(18,393.0)	(18,312.0)
Unbilled contracts	8,420.5	9,531.2	11,054.7	12,598.0	12,049.0
	6,887.6	7,314.1	8,238.8	6,282.0	5,228.0
DEBTORS includes					
Due after one year	1,443.4	1,725.1	3,642.4	3,225.0	4,309.0
DEBT BY TYPE					
Bonds & Debentures	2,185.4	1,649.6	2,231.3	2,611.0	2,881.0
Bank loans	2,041.2	2,408.5	2,343.6	1,920.0	1,764.0
	4,226.6	4,058.1	4,574.9	4,531.0	4,645.0
DEBT BY MATURITY					
Debt due within 1 yr	2,410.0	2,469.8	2,538.7	1,600.0	2,308.0
Due after 1 year	1,816.6	1,588.3	2,036.2	2,931.0	2,337.0
	4,226.6	4,058.1	4,574.9	4,531.0	4,645.0
DEBT BY SECURITY					
Secured	133.2	134.6	167.0	181.0	123.0
Unsecured	4,093.4	3,923.5	4,407.9	4,350.0	4,522.0
	4,226.6	4,058.1	4,574.9	4,531.0	4,645.0
PROVISIONS					
Deferred taxation	-	-	-	460.0	404.0
Pension provisions	11,616.1	12,734.5	13,957.1	14,761.0	16,012.0
Misc provisions	19,194.2	19,101.2	20,136.9	20,220.0	19,918.0
	30,810.3	31,835.7	34,094.0	35,441.0	36,334.0
SHARE CAPITAL					
Ordinary shares	2,443.7	2,562.2	2,592.2	2,752.0	2,753.0
Preference shares	46.2	46.2	46.2	46.0	46.0
	2,489.9	2,608.4	2,638.4	2,798.0	2,799.0

GENERAL NOTES TO ACCOUNTS

In the consolidated financial statements for the 1993 fiscal year, the Company changed several methods in order to adjust its accounting principles to internationally recognized standards. For the profit and loss account, the presentation has been changed to the cost of sales method of accounting as opposed to the total cost method that had previously been used. The Company's foreign subsidiaries financial statements are now translated into German marks using the year-end current rate method. Goodwill resulting from the initial consolidation of subsidiaries and associated companies is no longer offset against retained earnings, but is capitalized and amortized to income.

ANNUAL GENERAL MEETING (year to 30-09-93)

Olympiahalle, Munich, 10am, March 10, 1994.

FINANCIAL CALENDAR

Annual General Meeting February.

Exhibit 1.1b

SIEMENS AG DM50(VAR)

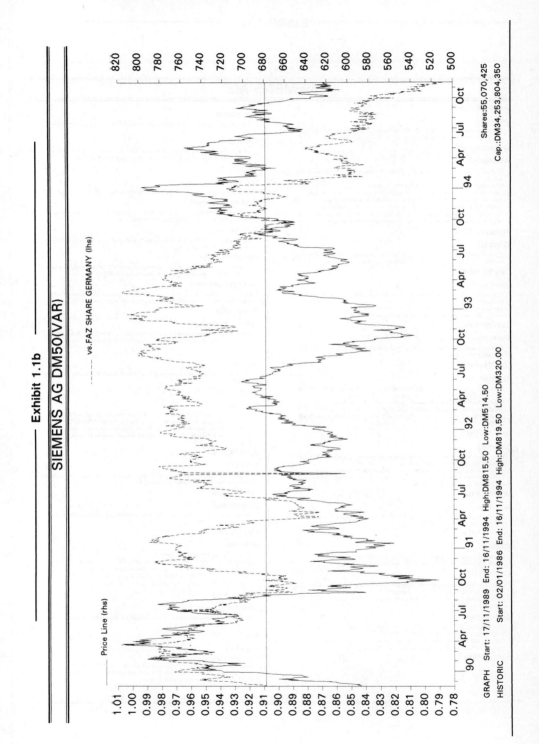

―――― Price Line (rhs)

------- vs.FAZ SHARE GERMANY (lhs)

GRAPH   Start: 17/11/1989 End: 16/11/1994 High:DM815.50 Low:DM514.50

HISTORIC   Start: 02/01/1986 End: 16/11/1994 High:DM819.50 Low:DM320.00

Shares:55,070,425

Cap.:DM34,253,804,350

—————————————— **Exhibit 1.1c** ——————————————

SIEMENS AG

August 8, 1994

Activities

Group will invest further DEM 100m in its Dresden microelectronics centre to assemble and test microchips in addition to planned operations.

August 2, 1994

Activities

Company plans to reorganise and globalise its research and development activities.
Company plans to reorganise R&D activities so that its research can be transformed into innovative and marketable products more quickly. It also plans to "globalise" its research and development activities to give more weight to international and cross-corporate cooperation. It intends to encourage international and domestic coordination of research by playing larger role in international and domestic associations and institutions.

August 1, 1994

Contract

Company received £40m contract to build and commission 14 electro-trains for Heathrow Express, new connection between Heathrow and London.

July 29, 1994

Joint Venture

Company and French car component supplier Valeo SA are holding talks on 2 possible joint ventures.
Companies want to combine technological and manufacturing resources in heating and air conditioning as well as small electrical vehicles.

July 26, 1994

Personnel

Company wants to reduce number of employees from 391,000 at 30-06-94 to 385,000 by 30-09-94.

July 25, 1994

Quarterly Results

Results for nine months to 30-06-94 were released, with sales up 3% to DEM 57.7bn (1993: DEM 55.8bn) and net profit down 6% to DEM 1.245bn. Figures in DEM m: Domestic sales 23,600 (1993: 25,100). Foreign sales 34,100 (30,700). Net profit 1,245 (1,324). Domestic new orders 25,300 (26,600). Foreign new orders 39,400 (33,300). Fixed asset investments 3,500 (4,700).

July 19, 1994

Contract

Consortium led by group's power generation division KWU has won DEM 1bn contract for construction of power station in Kazakhstan.
Group's share of contract amounts to some DEM 500m. Other partners in consortium are Babcock Lentjes Kraftwerkstechnik GmbH, Balcke-Duerr AG and US/Turkish company United BMB Group.

July 18, 1994

Activities

Group will expand telephone business in China by launching its "Hicom 100" telecommunication systems there.

July 15, 1994

Contract

Consortium of company and Alcatel SEL won DEM 100m contract to set up digital telephone network management system to start end-1995.

Contract

Company signed agreement with Bangkok Transit System Corp for DEM 2.2bn contract to construct first 2 lines of Bangkok city train network.
Construction will begin in near future and lines are scheduled to go into operation in 1997.

Joint Venture

Siemens-Nixdorf Informationssysteme AG signed joint venture with Top Victory Electronics Ltd of China from October 1994.
SNI will have majority stake in joint venture, which will produce personal computers for Chinese and south-east Asian markets.

July 13, 1994

Negotiations

Company is holding negotiations on take-over of Telefonica supplier Amper SA.

Contract

Group expects to win contract worth some DEM 2.2bn to build urban railway system in Bangkok; contract is expected to be signed on 15-07-94.

July 11, 1994

Dividend

Company expects dividend for year to 30-09-94 to be maintained at DEM 13.

Trading Statement

Chief financial officer Karl-Hermann Baumann said orders and sales in first nine months to 30-06-94 slightly down on last year.

Acquisition

Czech government has approved company's acquisition of MEZ electrical motor company in Czech Republic.

Interim Results

Company announced results for eight months to 31-05-94, showing 3% rise in sales to DEM 50.4bn and 6% rise in new orders to DEM 56.7bn.

Trading Statement

Company expects results for year to 30-09-94, showing orders to rise 3% to DEM 87bn, sales to rise 4% to DEM 84bn and net profit down 10-15%.

July 8, 1994

Trading Statement

Group values its newly booked and expected orders from China, finalised during visit by Prime Minister Li Peng to Germany, at DEM 6bn.

June 29, 1994

Assets

Co has sold its heart pacemaker activities to St Jude Medical Inc for US$500m.

June 24, 1994

Activities

Co will cut administrative expenses by DM 1bn from current DM 4.2bn.
Co will cut administrative expenses by DM 1bn from current DM 4.2bn. Savings will be in administrative activities at Co's Munich headquarters as well as in infrastructure, accounting and personnel services at various sites.

June 14, 1994

Contract

Co secures a contract with National Power to build a 1,350 megawatt combined cycle gas turbine power station in Didcot, Oxfordshire.

June 7, 1994

Share Stake

Co buys a 10% stake in Societe Rhenane de Participations et de Gestion for an undisclosed sum.

May 24, 1994

Activities

Co to build a chip factory in Dresden.
Co will receive building permission for its DM 2.7bn chip factory in Dresden on 30-05-94. Construction will begin in June with a production start-up date of 1996. Environmental pressure groups had opposed construction of the plant, which will produce 64 MB chips.

May 16, 1994

Contract

Co has won a contract from Isla Communications to develop a mobile phone network in the Philippines.

May 12, 1994

Activities

Co merges Italian Sub with Italtel SpA.
Co will pay STET SpA Lire 1 trillion as a result of the merger of Sub Italtel SpA and Co's Sub Siemens Telecommunicazioni SpA with both Co and STET holding 50% of the merged Group.

SIEMENS AG

May 6, 1994

Negotiations

Negotiations with Skoda terminated.
Co's KWU Power Generation division has terminated negotiations with Skoda to form a turbine construction joint venture.

Activities

Power station marketing agreement with Skoda.
Co has signed a marketing agreement with Skoda, whereby Skoda Sub Skoda Controls will market Co's power stations in the Czech Republic.

April 28, 1994

Contract

Co announces contract with Bell Telecommunications Inc.
Co and Alcatel-Alsthom have signed a US$1.5bn contract to supply Bell Telecommunications Inc of the Philippines with telecommunications equipment. Order is subject to government approval to operate a nationwide network.

April 25, 1994

Interim Results

Co announces results for six months to 31-03-94.
Net profit in six months to 31-03-94 was DM 879m (1993, DM 877m) on sales of DM 38bn (DM 37bn) and new orders of DM 44.4bn (DM 40.9bn). Domestic sales were down 9% to DM 15.6bn, while foreign sales rose 13% to DM 22.4bn. Domestic new orders fell 6% to DM 17.5bn, while foreign orders grew by 21% to DM 26.9bn.
The strongest increase in six month sales was at US Sub Osram, where they jumped 71% to DM 2.9bn from DM 1.7bn a year earlier. Sales at energy division KWU fell to DM 3.2bn from DM 3.3bn but new orders rose to DM 4.9bn from DM 3.6bn. In its communications activities, Co's sales related to public networks fell to DM 5.4bn from DM 6.2bn a year earlier, while private network sales saw a 2% drop to DM 2.9bn from DM 3.0bn. New orders for public networks fell to DM 6.2bn from DM 6.3bn, but private network order inflow was up 4% at DM 3.1bn. Automation technology sales fell 4% to DM 2.5bn from DM 2.6bn while order inflow falling to DM 2.7bn from DM 3.0bn. Sales at Siemens Nixdorf dropped to DM 5.2bn from DM 5.6bn, while new orders fell to DM 5.3bn from DM 5.7bn. Transport technology sales rose 11% to DM 1.6bn, while new orders were DM 2.7bn from DM 2.3bn a year earlier. Sales at the medical technology division rose 1% to DM 3.7bn and new orders rose to 4.0bn from DM 3.8bn. Investment to DM 2.4bn from DM 3.5bn a year earlier.

April 19, 1994

Trading Statement

Co expects new orders in its automation division to fall slightly to DM 5.5 bn in year to 30-09-94 (1993, DM 5.5bn) with sales up 10% to DM 5.9bn.

April 18, 1994

Contract

Co's KWU Power Generation division has been awarded a contract to equip the Hsinta gas and steam turbine power station by Taiwan Power Co.

April 12, 1994

Contract

Co has been awarded a contract jointly with GML Abfallwirtschaftsgesellschaft mbH to build an incineration plant in Ludwigshafen for DM 300m. Co's KWU Power Generation division will have a 49% stake in the operation.

April 8, 1994

Trading Statement

Co hopes to halve losses from its semi-conductor operations in year to 30-09-94 from DM 165m in 1993. Co expects sales to rise 25% to DM 2.7bn and reach DM 4.8bn in year to 30-09-98. Investment in semiconductors will total DM 500m over the next few years.

Activities

Co has formed a consortium with AEG AG and General Motors Corpn to bid for a tender to build high-speed trains for Amstrak's New York to Boston service.

March 8, 1994

Trading Statement

Co expects growth rates of 25% to 30% annually in sales of electronic components in the information technology and telecommunications sectors. Sales in year to 30-09-93 totalled DM 400m, which Co hopes to increase to DM 800m by 1997.

March 2, 1994

Trading Statement

Co increased sales in its Transportation Systems division by 17% in year to 30-09-93 to DM 4.2bn. Co expects this division to continue to grow more quickly than the rest of the Group. New orders in four months to 31-01-94 were up 3% year-on-year to DM 2.1bn. Co forecasts annual growth of 8% for its railway products to the year 2000.

February 19, 1994

Activities

Co intends to cut costs by DM 100m by reducing the number of computer centres it operates from current 80 to 11, of which five will be in Germany.

February 14, 1994

Activities

Co's rail Sub Siemens Schienenfahrzeug Gruppe GmbH (SFG) and SFG Sub Duewag AG plan to sign a control and profit transfer agreement, effective 01-10-93, to allow the 'better coordination' of SFG's activities. Siemens Schienenfahrzeug Gruppe holds 97.2% in Duewag, whose minority shareholders will receive an annual compensation payment of DM 22.05 of a one-time payment of DM 381.5 per nominal DM 50 share when the agreement is signed. Agreement is subject to Duewag shareholder approval at the AGM on 20-05-94. SFG comprises Duewag AG, Siemens Schienenfahrzeugtechnik GmbH, Krauss Maffei Verkehstechnik GmbH and SGP Verkehstechnik GmbH of Austria.

February 10, 1994

Contract

Co has been awarded a DM 230m contract to supply its EWSD digital connecting equipment to Philippine Long Distance Company as well as a DM 20m EWSD contract from Vietnam Post and Telecommunications.

February 9, 1994

Personnel

Co will cut 1,400 jobs in year to 30-09-94 in Power Generation division.

Trading Statement

New orders received by Co's Power Generation division were DM 8.7bn in year to 30-09-93 (1992, DM 8.6bn) with domestic new orders of DM 4.3bn (DM 3.2bn) and foreign new orders worth DM 4.4bn (DM 5.4bn). Sales were DM 8.7bn (DM 6.6bn) with domestic sales of DM 3.3bn (DM 2.8bn) and foreign sales of DM 5.4bn (DM 3.8bn). Nuclear sales totalled DM 2.6bn (DM 1.7bn) and fossils and regenerative sales were DM 6.16bn (DM 4.9bn). Orders in hand at 30-09-93 were DM 18.6bn (DM 18.8bn).

February 1, 1994

Dividend

Dividend of DM 13 per share for year to 31-12-93 (1992, DM 13), payable and xd 11-03-94.

January 20, 1994

AGM

Co's AGM will be held on 10-03-94.

Contract

Co has been awarded a contract to supply a power station 30km south-west of Budapest with capacity of 156MW. Contract is worth DM 75m.

Activities

With effect from 01-01-94 Co has merged Vertriebs- und Servicegesellschaft Siemens Kft and Villanyszereloipari Rt Hungarian Subs to form Siemens Rt (AG) with headquarters in Budapest.

January 18, 1994

Acquisition

Co has acquired ACT Cablestream Limited from ACT Group PLC through its UK Sub Siemens PLC. Consideration was £5m.

January 14, 1994

Quarterly Results

New orders by division in DM bn in three months to 31-12-93 were: Power generation (KWU) 2.5 (1992, 0.7); Power transmission and distributor 1.5 (1.6); Industrial and building systems 2.2 (2.1); Drives and standard products 1.7 (1.6); Automation 1.3 (1.5); Public communication networks 2.6 (2.9); Private communication systems 1.5 (1.4); Defence electronics 0.5 (0.3); Audio and video systems 0.06 (0.1); Siemens Nixdorf information systeme 2.4 (2.5); Transportation systems 1.4 (1.3); Automotive systems 0.7

———————————————————— **Exhibit 1.2** Analysts Report ————————————————————

Source: ALBERT E. SHARP & CO., Apr 27, 1993

Title: Tarmac — Company Report
Author: C. Porter

Abstract: The rapid resurgence of building materials stocks in the wake of the accelerating housing recovery and evidence of success in raising materials prices has brought Tarmac's shares along. This is understandable in that both factors are crucial to the group's well being and are the prime factors in more optimistic profits forecasts. The balance sheet remains stretched and may need refinancing at some stage while the government's need to address the PSBR deficit may lead to longer-term questions being raised on the road programme.

Price: 141 p Market Cap: 1.03 bn SEAQ: 52505

Hold/take profits into strength

The rapid renaissance of building materials stocks in the wake of the accelerating housing recovery and evidence of success in raising materials prices has swept Tarmac's shares along in its wake. This is understandable in that both factors are crucial to the group's well being and are the prime factors in our more optimistic profits forecasts. Enthusiasm for the new management team, particularly following the 'deck-clearing' provisions purge of 1992, is justified and could take the shares' recovery further. But enthusiasm needs to be tempered by thoughts that the balance sheet remains stretched and may need refinancing at some stage while the government's need to address the PSBR deficit may lead to longer-term questions being raised on the road programme. With the shares rapidly running out of yield, holders should consider taking profits into any further strength.

Forecasts

Year Dec	Pre-tax profit £m	EPS p	Actual tax %	Net Div p	Div Cover	Av Shares m	Yield %	P/E ratio
1992	(350)	(37.6)	(25)	5.5	—	729	4.9	—
1993e	45	2.7	30	5.5	0.6	729	4.9	52.2
1994e	95	7.5	30	5.5	1.5	729	4.9	18.8

Summary

Shares in Issue	729 m
Gearing	62% (inc AMPs)
Relative Performance:	1 mth +21.0% 12 mth −16.8%
Net Assets per Share	127 p
Final Div	2.5 p XD: 10 May '93 Paid 19 Jul '93
Next Declaration	September — Interims

●   Headline losses of £350 m ultimately came as no surprise. £372 m costs/provisions were taken on the sweeping restructuring programme with the £22 m pre-exceptionals profit £10 m above our expectations.

●   Despite the severity of the provisions, the cash implication was only £30 m with a further £30 m outflow in 1993. With £147 m from the divestment programme and a further £54 m received on acquiring PSA Projects, debt (inc. AMPs) fell by £40 m despite £106 m adverse currency movements on the group's substantial dollar debt.

●   £145 m of the provisions relate to the cost of withdrawal from properties, of which cash costs of circa £75 m will be borne in 1993. But, elsewhere, cash flow is expected to be positive with £250 m more coming from a combination of squeezing housing capital and completing the disposal programme. So, although dividend/cap ex will wipe out the operating cash, year end debt targets of circa £425 m suggest the debt/equity ratio falling from 62% to circa 50%.

● Prospects in at least two of the group's three core activities — Quarry Products, Housing and Construction — are now improving. Although unquantified, Housing has clearly shared in the national trend so far this year while last year's H2 recovery comfortably beat our expectations. Quarry Products will benefit from the industry-wide commitment to increased prices which should fully offset any further volume weakness. Only in Construction are profits likely to be lower, and cash generation negative, although the problems seem to be containable. For the rest, America's east coast exposure should support a return to profitability although recovery in Building Products will be delayed.

Final Results

Year to Dec % £m	*1991* Total	*I*	*II*	*1992* Total	Change
Sales	3225	1360	1575	2935	−9
Trading Profit	117	17	64	81	−31
Exceptional	(39)	—	(372)	(372)	
Interest (net)	(57)	(32)	(27)	(59)	4
Pre-tax Profit	21	(15)	(335)	(350)	—
Tax	(6)	5	83	88	—
Rate %	(29)	33		25	—
	15	(10)	(252)	(262)	—
Minorities	(2)	(1)	(1)	(2)	N/C
Dividends	(40)	(22)	(18)	(40)	N/C
Pref	(12)	(5)	(5)	(10)	−17
Retained Profit	(39)	(38)	276	(314)	—
EPS	0.2	(2.2)	(35.4)	(37.6)	—
DPS	5.5	3.0	2.5	5.5	N/C

Divisional Analysis and Forecasts

£m	1992	1993e	1994e
Quarry Products	29	30	40
Housing	38	45	60
Construction	23	18	20
Building Materials	(3)	—	5
Industrial Products	5	2	4
Tarmac America	(4)	3	7
Central Costs	(6)	(6)	(6)
Sold/Discontinued	2	—	—
Operating Profit	80	92	130
Interest Costs	(58)	(47)	(35)
PBT	22	45	95

Cash Flow

Year to Dec, £m	1991	1992	1993e	1994e
Operating Profit	129	80	92	130
Depreciation	68	84	68	70
Working Capital	119	92	75	(25)
Other	(37)	(95)	(75)	30
Op. Cash Flow	279	161	160	205
Interest	(56)	(59)	(47)	(35)
Div Paid	(90)	(48)	(48)	(48)
Taxation	(75)	13	—	(20)

Net Cash Flow	58	67	65	102
Cap Exp	(60)	(33)	(50)	(52)
Acquisitions	(35)	43	—	—
Disposals	27	95	150	—
Shares Issued	106	—	—	—
Currency Effects	(26)	(132)	—	—
Cash In/(Out Flow)	70	40	165	50
Net (Debt) Cash	(617)	(577)	(412)	(362)

Quarry Products: Given the persistent volume and pricing pressures in aggregates and ready-mixed, a profit of £30 m on turnover of £500 m was a creditable performance although the extent to which capacity reductions have been taken through the £40 m QPD/manufacturing restructuring provisions should be borne in mind. Some peripheral regional disposals are expected but the broad market-leading position in aggregates/blacktop and increasingly important ready-mixed exposure provides a strong strategic base for the future. Current year profits are likely to reflect the delayed disposal of Econowaste at some stage but this should be offset by increasingly positive benefits from the industry-wide move to raise prices. QPD, under new management, is more likely to lead than follow.

Housing: The lower contribution made in 1992 reflected not only the market's ongoing malaise, but the downsizing of the division, with £92 m being released from working capital as four of the twenty operating subsidiaries were closed and the landbank reduced by 3,000 units to 14,020. Average capital employed is forecast to reduce a further £100 m to £250 m in the current period, supporting 7,000–7,500 unit completions. An average selling price of 80,000 would imply turnover in the region of circa £600 m and an ambitious asset turn of 2.4×, although Tarmac's efficiency as a builder and ability to operate from a short landbank (20 months) make this an aggressive but not unrealistic target. The dilemma facing the group is the extent to which Tarmac will expose itself to the housing market's uplift. Much has been made of controlling the division's working capital requirements, which has the twofold benefit of reducing debt and producing a more balanced divisional contribution. However, whilst wishing to minimise financial exposure the temptation must be to participate as fully as possible in the housing recovery and allow starts to rise above the previously stated ceiling. Indeed, this is the nature of the industry and the sharply cyclical movements should be ridden, tempered wherever possible by prudence.

Construction: Profits suffered from competition intensifying, lower cash balances and lower interest rates. As a result operating margins fell from 3.4% to 2.3% despite the 10% reduction in overhead achieved in Autumn 1991, a process which was repeated in the Autumn of last year. Contracting activities, whilst not solely confined to this division, had provisions of £28.2 m taken against out turns and the debtor book and nagging doubts remain about further pain emanating from the longer-term fixed price contracts, as material prices and sub-contractor rates firm. The current order book indicates that turnover will be fully maintained, although we expect profits to show some slippage as heightened competition is not totally mitigated by lower overheads.

Balance Sheet: The £314 m deficit for 1992 reduced equity funds to £924 m. Total debt (including AMPs) fell by £40 m leaving the year end debt/equity at 62% (47% excluding AMPs). £500 m of the debt (inc. AMPs of £99 m) is dollar based with a further £100 m in Europe, offset by small UK cash deposits. The positive cash flow which housing/disposals is expected to provide this year should pull interest costs below £50 m although the group is unlikely to gain full benefit from current low US interest rates. But at least this should bring debt levels down sharply, into the £400–450 m range and although a maintained dividend will again have to be paid out of reserves, the debt/equity ratio should fall to around the 50% level.

Table 1.2 Sources of information relevant to financial analysis

1. Financial information	(a)	Annual report and accounts
	(b)	Interim accounting statements
	(c)	Official filings
	(d)	Prospectuses
	(e)	Aggregate financial data
	(f)	Share price performance
	(g)	Index price performance
	(h)	Financial analysts' forecasts
	(i)	Management forecasts
2. Quantified non-financial information	(a)	Production and consumption statistics
	(b)	Official industry statistics
3. Non-quantitied information	(a)	Audit reports and chair's and directors' statements
	(b)	Environmental and employees reports
	(c)	Management comment and news announcements
	(d)	Analysts' comment and recommendations
	(e)	Financial and trade press comment
	(f)	Credit assessments
	(g)	Independent valuations
	(h)	Personal contacts
	(i)	Previous dealings
4. Other analysts		

1. Financial information

(a) The annual report and accounts of a group or individual company are the basic sources of accounting data for financial analysts.[1] These normally comprise three basic statements which appear to measure in monetary terms (i) the income for the period, (ii) the assets and liabilities at the end of the period, and (iii) the cash flow during the period. These statements are supported by notes providing more detailed information. The requirement for a cash flow (or sometimes funds flow) statement varies and is not required in all countries. It can be seen that this accounting information, which starts on the second page of Exhibit 1.1a and extends to the fourth page is perhaps the category given the most weight by Extel Financial. Notice also that business and geographical anlyses are given considerable weight and that the important but brief note at the end of Exhibit 1.1a reports changes in accounting practice which would affect the accounting numbers reported.

The emphasis varies from country to country but the information content of the accounting statements presented may be controlled by corporate law, by taxation law, by the accounting profession's pronouncements , and by the listing agreement of the relevant stock exchange for those companies which are quoted. As such, the annual report and accounts are not a direct response to a demand for information by users, though the need for specific items of data may have filtered through to the regulatory process and on to the published statements.

As will become apparent, the attempt to produce meaningful sets of accounts is a remarkably difficult task and accounts have settled for a manageable method rather than an ideal one. Thus, an Institute of Chartered Accountants in Scotland discussion paper identified the basic shortcomings of financial accounts as

> the adherence to legal form rather than economic substance, the use of cost rather than value, the concentration on the past rather than the future and the interest in profit... rather than wealth.
>
> (ICAS, 1988)

Despite these difficulties numerous surveys (which are discussed in later chapters) have identified accounting statements as one of the most valuable sources of data for financial analysts of various persuasions. Typically, these investigations have been surveys of investment analysts or bank loan officers. Not only do the statements appear to be of value, but also they can be seen as the rock on which many other less reliable, though conceivably more relevant, items of data are founded. Thus, where forecasts concerned with wealth, economic substance and value are made available, they may be based on conventional accounting data and may be subject to later validation by accounting results. This may constrain any inherent optimism that the forecasters are tempted to exhibit. For example, in Chapter 4 it is apparent that the earnings forecasts of analysts tend to be rather extreme and often optimistic but as the date of the financial accounts release approaches these forecasts become more reasonable.

(b) Interim accounting statements are required in many countries from larger or publicly quoted firms. These may be quarterly, as in the US, or half-yearly as for most European countries. While the content of these releases is extremely modest — they may contain little more than turnover, profit, tax, dividends and earnings per share — their impact is invaluable. One of the major defects of financial statements is the delay in their publication, and the interim statements allow the analysts to adjust their expectations on a more regular basis. Interim reports covering the first nine months of the latest accounting year and the comparative numbers for the same portion of the previous year are included in Exhibit 1.1a on the second page and it can be seen that the quarterly accounting results are also contained in the announcements given in Exhibit 1.1c. In the case of quoted companies interim reports help to keep the share price closer to that price which would pertain if all data were made public and this can limit the severity of any market reaction when the annual statements are eventually published.

A further form of interim statement is the preliminary announcement which covers the full period of account but is as limited in content as the interim statement. It is produced shortly after the end of the period of account and some weeks before the publication of the formal reports.

(c) In some countries, detailed official filings are required by government or the security market regulators. For example, the Securities and Exchange Commission in the US requires quoted firms to submit reports which match the conventional accounts but are more detailed. These submissions, known as 10-K reports, are available to the public.

(d) Prospectuses, circulars and offer documents are issued by firms to their actual and potential shareholders under a number of circumstances and the actual content is regulated by a variety of sources depending on the specific case. These circumstances include: applications for admission to the stock exchange; other prospectuses involving the marketing of new securities including those issued as payment to the shareholders of the offeree company during a takeover; or circulars to inform the shareholders of listed firms when required to do so by the stock exchange. An example of the latter is when a substantial acquisition or disposal of assets is contemplated including the defence or supporting documents issued during a takeover.

The precise disclosures contained in the different documents vary but, for example, the prospectus is a crucial document in investment analysis and is an attempt by the directors of the issuing company to persuade its reader to purchase shares of a forthcoming issue. Thus the prospectus might include details of the issuing company and persons responsible, the securities offered, general information about the issuing company and its capital, the group's activities, financial information concerning the issuing company or group, the management, recent developments and prospects of the group, and additional information concerning debt securities. There may also be a quantified profit or dividend forecast, or more probably, a qualitative assessment of the firm's prospects.

(e) Aggregate financial data are available from government statistics, and from commercial firms that specialise in disseminating financial data. When this is published as hard copy, as with government statistics or the industry reports of the commercial firms, it is interpreted easily but it rapidly becomes dated and is not necessarily in the form required by the user. The advent of commercially available financial databases now allows the analyst to create aggregate datasets which apply to precisely the sample and information required and are based on the latest available information. Some caution is advisable when using such databases as they are prone to error, the aggregation process may be flawed and the sample on which the aggregation is made is likely to be restricted. In particular, financial data relevant to the large quoted firms which make up most databases might not be an appropriate point of comparison for smaller, privately controlled firms.

(f) Firm-specific stock market data are invaluable sources for the analyst. The capitalisation of a firm, the share price movements, the dividend yield on the share price, the sensitivity of the share price to movements in the market as a whole, and the ratio of the share price to the accounting earnings are all variables which may be of use to the analyst for a variety of purposes. Exhibit 1.1b graphs the share price performance of Siemens AG for five years ended 3/08/94 and contrasts this with the German market index (the dotted line). It would seem that Siemens mirrors, but exaggerates, market-wide movements and it would be interesting to investigate the reasons for the spectacular rises and falls which have occurred during the years.

Some, so-called, technical analysts or chartists base their work on an investigation of the past price performance looking for specific patterns or trends, but to non-aficionados this can look more like witchcraft than serious financial analysis. However, it should be acknowledged that considerable resources and attention are devoted to this practice and it is difficult to see why it survives if it has no merit. A great advantage of the capital market data is that there is no delay involved for wherever a newspaper is available there is no need to use a share price older than yesterday's. A second advantage is that there is an element of objectivity involved in that the share price is a consensus based on the unbiased estimate of a large number of investors. However, while the market-based estimate may be unbiased, it need not reflect the underlying worth of the share. Periodic crashes in share prices, most notably in October 1987, serve to emphasise the erratic nature of these prices. Finally, it should be noted that some analysts pay attention to the volume of shares traded and it can be shown that the market reacts to the volume of shares bought and sold.

(g) Generic stock market data, conveniently measured in various indexes, provide benchmarks against which an individual firm's market performance can be assessed, and an indication of the performance and prospects of a particular industry. Thus, if a firm's shares under-perform its competitors from the same industry sector, the stock market data indicate that the market sentiment is less sanguine regarding the individual firm's performance in comparison with its competitors than previously. That firm may still be out-performing the total market. Much the same can be said for an industrial group in relation to the total market, and for the total market index as an indicator of sentiment regarding the future performance of all quoted firms in the country.

(h) Financial analysts' forecasts are available on a private basis to clients of the broker and quite often to the public at large. These may be direct recommendations for trading in shares, or forecasts of future earnings or dividends. Again Exhibit 1.1a contains example earnings forecasts for the next two years earnings for Siemens AG. Large institutional investors receive a considerable number of forecasts from brokers hoping to encourage trade. They may use the collected forecasts of earnings to form expectations of sector and firm performance on which investment strategies may be formed. The collected forecasts of a sub-sample of analysts are available as consensus forecasts from which it is possible to derive more information regarding the number of analysts following a firm and the diversity of their expectations.

(i) Management forecasts are rarely issued in quantifiable form other than when required as part of a prospectus for a share issue, or when included in an offer document or its rebuttal during takeover disputes. However, management will often make comments 'correcting' the market's view when they feel that the market is getting out of line with their own expectations.

2. Quantified non-financial information

(a) Production, demand and employment statistics are all examples of quantified non-financial information which may be of use to the analyst. In particular, such information avoids the measurements and allocation problems of financial information and is usually available well in advance of financial data. In industries which have relatively homogeneous products non-financial data may convey considerable information regarding the performance of the firm. An example of where non-financial data is of recognised importance is the occupancy rate of hotel rooms. Where the firm has products which are disparate the non-financial information will be most useful if it is measured in some standard unit. Thus professional firms may use hours of chargeable time as a measure of output.

(b) Official economic statistics are available in various statistical office publications such as production monitors. Rarely will this be as timely as for 2(a) but it exhibits the same potential in relation to aggregate industrial performance assessment as does 2(a) to the financial analysis of the firm. The significance of general economic data can be seen in the anticipation with which the securities markets await their regular supply of government statistics and the subsequent market reaction.

3. Non-quantified information

(a) The audit report and the chair's and directors' statements are all required to be included in the annual report and are a rich source of data. The information content is open to dispute but there is evidence that these sections are amongst the most popular sections of the annual reports with investors and especially with those who lack financial training. The unqualified auditors' report is of no particular interest but a material qualification normally will have an impact on investors and creditors as well as other business contacts. In the case of Exhibit 1.1 no reference has been made to these but extracts from the chair's statement would often be included where available and the text of any audit qualification would also usually be included.

(b) Employee newsletters typically are an amalgam of the chair's statement and a cartoon version of the financial reports. Environmental reports are a more recent and less well-developed phenomenon and struggle effectively to measure the environmental costs and benefits of the firm's actions. Cynics might argue that these reports are probably more valuable as propaganda for the firm than as information to the employees or environmentalists. Indeed some research has suggested that the graphics employed in financial reports are often misleading representations of the underlying data. Where the employee newsletter is more timely, or more relevant (in that it refers to a sub-division of the firm) than other sources of data it may be of value to the analyst. Whether such documents are also of value to the employee to whom they are addressed or rather to the management who send them is a moot point. To date the environmental report has had little impact except where a firm, such as Body Shop, has positioned itself in the market as being particularly environmentally conscious.

(c) Management comment is both viewed with scepticism and carefully studied. Clearly management will make its thoughts known when it believes it is in its interests to do so and this is most noticeable during takeover activity. However, being self-interested, management comment is rarely taken at face value although it is reasonable to believe that management has access to information which is not yet public. Quite often a firm's management will address the financial world when it believes that its share price is inappropriate. When it appears over-valued, especially on the basis of optimistic expectations concerning earnings, management's protestations are likely to be effective. It is considerably more difficult to 'talk up' the shares.

Perhaps more credible are the news announcements the legal or stock exchange requirements demand of firms. Exhibit 1.1c contains a brief sample of such announcements from Siemens AG and it can be seen that these include information with regard to contracts, employment levels, accounting statements, investments, divestments etc. Another important group of announcements not represented here are changes in shareholdings by directors and/or substantial shareholders.

(d) Financial analysts' comments and the recommendations of tipsters have been seen to affect the price of shares. The weekly list of significant market movements provided by the *Financial Times* refers regularly to analysts' comments as being the cause of a notable movement in a firm's shares. One notable analyst, Abraham Briloff, has been able to exert a considerable influence on a number of firms' share prices in the US by his damning condemnations of the accounting reports of those firms. However, in general the tipster seems to provide data which have been pre-empted by share price movements and are difficult to profit from.

(e) Financial and trade press comment is a source of data and a flag which attracts the analyst's interest. It may be that the press report contains insufficient information on which to base action, but it may prompt more detailed investigation by the analyst. Monitoring press comment is becoming a simpler task with the improvement in information technology and in the cuttings services. The press may provide useful information in quite unexpected ways and some analysts even use the vacancies columns as a method of monitoring the activities of firms in which they are particularly interested.

(f) Independent credit assessments are available for firms who subscribe to the credit assessment agencies, or to the general public where the assessment is made available. In the second instance, the rated firm may pay the agency to provide an assessment though this is sometimes provided without charge where the agency is attempting to establish a position in the market.

(g) Independent valuations might be a rather dull example of information for the analyst, but they provide confidence in the security offered by borrowing firms and are an input to the annual reports of firms. Although most countries outlaw the practice, in the UK the financial reports of many firms often include revalued land and buildings, and the recent development of valuing brands and including them in the balance sheet has depended on independent valuations for whatever credence it possesses. These strategies are not necessarily available to firms that prepare their accounts under the regulations that apply outside the UK.

(h) Personal contacts provide what is arguably the most significant source of information on the prospects and performance of a firm. In most developed economies a companies securities law regulates the manner in which the information from personal contacts may, or may not, be exploited. The most visible example of this is the analysts meeting, where professional financial analysts are invited to attend a meeting and listen to presentations by the firm's senior management and to question the managers. It is interesting to note that recent research has shown that these meetings in both the UK and US are accompanied by high levels of trading and share price volatility suggesting that significant information is passed on in these meetings.

(i) The record of previous dealings is seen as especially important for business contacts and banks. A firm that has met its previous obligations is viewed as more likely to continue to do so. This intuitively appealing attitude has some empirical evidence to support it as financial failure is considerably more frequent among newly established firms than older ones.

4. Peer group assessment

Peer group assessment of a firm provides an invaluable source for the analyst. This is most apparent with financial analysts who carefully monitor their rivals' forecasts. If new forecasts are suddenly becoming available on a particular firm it would suggest that there is new information available and if the consensus of forecasts is considerably different from one analyst's assessment it would suggest that this forecast should be examined more carefully. It is either a poor interpretation of the available data or, if it correctly judges that data but disagrees with market sentiment, it is a case where the forecast might be successfully exploited.

1.2.3   *The firm*

The firm is, in general, the focus of financial analysis. As such it is helpful to have at least an overview of why firms exist in the form that they do, why they are managed as they are, and what the objectives of the owners and managers might be. This section will present a necessarily brief review of these matters.

In most capitalist countries the company is a legal entity separate from its members (shareholders) and the members have limited liability for the debts of the firm. This is known as an incorporated joint stock company. Thus the company can take, or be subject to, legal action in its own right and the shareholders are not normally liable for the debts of the firm other than to the extent that they still owe money to the firm for the shares that they own. Apart from limited liability and public shareholding, the modern limited company carries a number of other costs and benefits. The firm is able to issue debt instruments which carry a floating charge on the assets of the firm. But the firm is also subject to a great deal of formality and expense in complying with the legal and disclosure requirements of company law and, perhaps crucially, the limited company is subject to tax laws very different from those that apply to the partnership or sole-trader.

Incorporation

The firm is not the only form of economic grouping — partnerships and co-operatives can also trade as coherent organisations. Individuals may trade as sole-traders but the constraint on the financial resources of individuals means that such 'firms' are normally small. Most sizeable business entities are joint stock companies as there is a legal restriction on the numbers of members of a partnership; apart from professional partnerships such as accountancy and law firms. Even the distinctions between friendly societies, building societies and trustee savings banks and the normal limited companies have narrowed recently. Limited companies are divided typically into two different classes. Larger firms are usually a public limited company, where the ownership of shares is not restricted and may be on offer to the general public through a quoted market such as the various European stock exchanges. Smaller firms are typically a private limited company, where the shares are not traded generally. Although the restriction on share trading is an important dimension, the legal requirements which differentiate between the two classes of limited company may well depend on other criteria. In the UK the capitalisation of the company is a crucial factor while, for example, in Germany the legal structure under which the firm operates is fundamental to the distinction.

Thus joint stock companies can be differentiated on public/private and quoted/unquoted dimensions. There is also clearly a range from small to large. Typically the largest businesses are quoted public companies, often made up of many subsidiaries which are private limited companies. A few large firms are privately owned, either by wealthy individuals or families, such as the Netherlands-based C&A, though most of the largest private companies in Europe are the subsidiaries of foreign holding companies. Foreign-owned firms are often encouraged to establish themselves in host countries and there can be considerable competition to attract such inward investment. However, the legal and political control of such firms is awkward, most notably in less developed countries.

In practice, the smaller private limited company has many of the characteristics of a sole-trader or partnership. In order to gain access to finance, the proprietors may have had to give personal guarantees for the liabilities of the firm, thereby exposing themselves to the risk of personal bankruptcy. The existence of the firm is also likely to be inextricably bound up with its management/owners and on their departure the firm may cease to exist.

The reason why large businesses are joint stock companies is quite clear. As the size of a firm increases it becomes more difficult for the original owners to meet the requirement for finance. However, the public would be unwilling to invest in a firm where there is no direct means of monitoring its investment if it were to be liable for the debts of the company. Hence limited liability public companies arose.

Although the benefit of limited liability appears to operate only to the advantage of the shareholders in that the down-side potential of their investment is constrained, there are less obvious costs to be borne. The business contacts of the firm, and in particular the creditors and financing firms, will have to suffer losses occasionally. Due to the limited liability they cannot have undisputed access to the personal property of the shareholders in the case of the firm's failure. Under such circumstances it would seem reasonable to expect these firms to compensate themselves for the increased risk by demanding higher prices or sufficient information to assure themselves that failure is an unlikely prospect.

Firms and contracting

There are other benefits and costs of incorporation. While a case can be made for the joint stock form of incorporation for large firms, it is not so clear why these firms have grown to such an extent that such convoluted forms of finance and management are necessary. This is not to question economic growth, the personal accumulation of wealth or the existence of economies of scale, but the particular form of the economic unit. Growth, wealth and size of operation units could all be achieved by structures other than the monolithic firm. It may be presumed that there are some advantages with large firms as opposed to individuals, or more realistically to a collection of smaller business units, competing in an open market. With a large number of small firms there will be a need for inter-firm trading and contractual arrangements between the firms at the boundaries. When these contracts are complex, contractual arrangements are expensive, if at all possible, whereas one firm covering the whole group of business activities has no need to indulge in formal contracting.

The analysis is developed from Coase (1937) and Ball and Smith (1992, p. 1) summarise it thus:

> In the absence of contracting costs, firms would be irrelevant: consumers could contract directly with the owners of factors of production; there would be no demand for firms to intermediate between them; and all decisions would be based on a complete set of costlessly observable

market prices. This proposition is no less than a general institutional irrelevance theorem, in a hypothetical world without costs of contracting.

Obviously contracting costs do exist. The observed organisational form of firms, markets, accounting regulations and so on, which would all be irrelevant in the absence of contracting costs, can be assumed to be caused by these costs. The resultant structure would be contracting-cost-efficient in an economy without regulatory interference, and is contract-cost-efficient within the bounds of the contracting-cost-environment imposed in an economy which imposes regulations. Of course a contract-cost-efficient structure is not necessarily a socially desirable one. Government regulation may impose costs on the economy which could be avoided if unregulated but the society could prefer the less efficient regulated option: regulation can impose both costs and benefits.

The influence of this theory for accounting institutions and practices is demonstrated by another quote from Ball and Smith (1992, p. 3) who note that:

> The economics of costly contracting, modified to allow for economic regulation, can be used to explain the existence of accounting, the form taken by the profession, the existence of GAAP (generally accepted accounting principles), the process that determines GAAP, the content of GAAP, the selection from GAAP by corporations, and the most detailed institutional facts in accounting.

Similar conclusions would hold for financial institutions and practices - including the regulation of the stock markets, the activities of various information intermediaries such as bond raters, credit analysts, investment analysts and fund managers, and the availability of financial information other than accounting data.

Ownership, control and objectives of firms

The other crucial characteristic that differs between types of firms is the separation between ownership and control. The managers of small independent private limited companies, together with their families, are often the only shareholders in such firms. Thus the owners and managers are the same and there is no difficulty with ensuring that the firm is managed in the interests of the shareholders. As the size of firms increases there is more chance that there will be shareholders who take no part in management. They will either have to trust the managers (who will often be the principal shareholders) to manage in their interests, or set up systems to control and monitor the managers. In the case of the medium-sized subsidiary the problem is extreme in the sense that the managers are likely to be divorced from the eventual owners, the shareholders of the holding company, and also separate from the owner's agents, the management of the holding company. However, it is in the public quoted company where the separation between the ownership and control of the firm is most apparent. While many of the managers of a public limited company will have shares in the firm, most shareholders will not have any direct involvement in management and, given that the shareholdings are dispersed, it is difficult for shareholders to unite to form a pressure group which can effectively challenge the management. Thus the typical firm has owners who have contributed capital and managers who contribute their skill. The aims of these managers and owners will not always coincide.

Traditional investment theory assumes that the shareholder's sole objective is the maximisation of the value of the firm, and that the value of the firm is dependent on the future net cash flows and the risks attached to those cash flows. Any decision which increases the net present value of future cash flows will be in the shareholder's interest. For firms whose shares are quoted on a capital market, this is the same as saying that the objectives of the firm should be to maximise share price, if it is assumed that the capital market is able to evaluate the future cash flows and relevant risk and ensure that the share price reflects these factors.

However, it is not always going to be easy, or possible, for managers operating in an uncertain world to assess accurately the impact of their decisions on a firm's value. Nor will the effect on share price be of equal utility to all shareholders who have different tax positions. Perhaps the most fundamental difficulty with value maximisation is that managers may have their own goals which differ from value maximisation. Any number of individual goals for managers could be suggested but four distinct categories are often put forward, as follows.

1. Profit maximisation is the popular assumption for the objectives of the firm and, despite the vagaries of the accounting system which measures profit, it is difficult to think of a realistic case where increasing profit in one particular year will not increase the value of the firm, all other things being equal. However, more likely dilemmas are whether management should depress profits in one year in order to earn more in subsequent years, or should it pursue profitable opportunities even though this would increase the riskiness of the firm. It would appear that the management should do so if the action has a positive effect on the value of the firm. However, when contrasted with general European practice UK firms have been accused of stinting on their investment in marketing, research or new plant in order to protect their current profits, and the UK securities market has been accused of being unduly impressed by current rather than future profits. Thus the objective of profit maximisation fails to take account of the impact of the time and risk dimensions on the shareholders and other participants in the firm.

2. Maximising the size of the firm is also an objective which might guide management thinking. If managers' remuneration is linked to the size of the firm they work for, or if non-pecuniary rewards such as self- or peer-group esteem or even the splendour of their office, are determined by size, then there is an incentive to pursue this target. To a degree, the objectives of size and value maximisation may be related, but at some point striving for size must start to damage value. As with profit maximisation, sales maximisation ignores the impact that the pursuit of growth may have on subsequent periods or on risk.

3. The prudent investor will hold a diversified portfolio and basic finance confirms that this is more valuable than an undiversified portfolio. However, it is considerably cheaper for an investor to diversify by buying a selection of shares and unit trusts, than for the firm to diversify by buying other firms. Chapter 8 investigates takeover activity and confirms that the record of takeovers is poor, at least as regards the aggressor. However, managers are unable to diversify their commitment to the firm as easily as shareholders and having a great deal of human capital invested in the firm, they may be tempted to pursue diversification to reduce the risk attached to their own investment.

4. The idea that managers' goals are as easily described as profit, size or security maximisation is clearly a simplification. It may be that there is a combination of all three but a more sophisticated approach is to view the firm as a collection of socio-economic groups which participate in the firm because it is seen as being in their interest to do so. If any of these groups (investors, the workforce, middle management and so on) withdraw from the firm it will cease to function. Therefore, the prime task of the management is to ensure that each of these groups are persuaded in one way or another to maintain a commitment to the firm. This will involve meeting, or 'satisfying', their minimum needs. Thus each group must be satisfied and this imposes a series of constraints which curtail management discretion. Management can pursue its own interests only within these constraints.

Constraints on management objectives

While management may have its own objectives, the scope for discretionary activity may be circumscribed by a number of factors additional to the need to satisfy minimally the various interest groups involved. These factors are detailed as follows.

1. The management is the agent of the shareholders and may be appointed or dismissed by the shareholders at the annual general meeting if its performance is seen to be sub-standard. However, the directors are a coherent group of professionals with experience of management in general and the firm specifically, and with advantageous access to resources, particularly the information controlled by the firm. In contrast, the shareholders are usually a disparate group with few means of communication and are excluded from the resources of the firm. Those shareholders with professional expertise are fund managers but this group appears reluctant to become involved in the management of the firm. Under these circumstances it is not surprising that successful shareholder revolts are few and far between. Furthermore, to monitor the performance of the management the shareholders must be provided with information with which to make their assessment. To do so the information would have to be meaningful, but it has already been suggested that the financial reports are less than perfect representations of what has happened and they are poorly understood by many shareholders. The reports also focus on what has happened within the firm and fail to take account of what will happen, or what might have happened if alternative action had been taken.

2. Although shareholders have great difficulty unseating the incumbent directors and managers, they have a simple alternative when the firm's shares are marketable and can vote with their feet. If the performance of a firm is seen to be below par the share price will suffer. If the share price is less than the value of the assets of the firm, or of the constituent subsidiaries of the firm, or less than it would be under efficient value-maximising management, then there is an incentive for a takeover. The threat of takeover may work in the interest of the shareholders in two ways. Firstly, a takeover, especially if it is hostile, will often result in management redundancies and hence incumbent management will be encouraged to pursue value-maximising policies to discourage the attentions of unwanted predators. Secondly, if this fails and a takeover occurs, the shareholders will receive a payment in excess of the value of the firm

under the previous managers. Part or all of this payment may be in shares of the aggressor firm which may be managed as a value-maximising organisation. Clearly this is a convoluted route to ensure that management operates in the shareholders' interest. There are also problems with the theory that the threat of takeover is a constraint on management discretion. The empirical evidence is discussed in Chapter 8.

3. Where the market for the firm's products and its inputs are competitive, there will be limited scope for discretionary action. The market will only buy the firm's goods if they are of competitive quality and price, and suppliers will demand prices similar to those paid by the firm's competitors. In such a scenario, the management will have little option but to ensure that the firm is run as efficiently as possible. However, a competitive market is a theoretical model not a description of reality, and while some markets may approach this model many others will be somewhat removed.

4. The managerial labour market also has the potential to act as a constraint on the discretion of managers to pursue activities which are not in the best interests of the shareholders. The performance of managers is monitored by several groups, by their supervisors who are ultimately the directors, by their subordinates who may hope to out-perform and hence surpass them, and by other firms who will seek to employ managers who appear to be achieving the desired results. To the extent that these three groups are able to observe and respond effectively to poor performance, there is little incentive for managers to do other than strive for the goals that are seen as their targets. However, where those targets are not directly related to value maximisation, or where there is limited or inaccurate data concerning the managers' performance, the managerial labour market will not ensure that the managers' goals are congruent with the shareholders'. In practice, it might be assumed that managers are judged on the appearance rather than the substance of their efforts and, given job mobility, on short-term, rather than long-term, results.

1.3   Theoretical developments

1.3.1   *The role of theory*

In understanding the world of accounting and finance, there is a role for descriptions of current practice. There is also a need for informed prescriptions as to how to improve that practice. Both of these will be encountered in this text, but neither constitute genuine theory. Theoretical development requires a postulated model which either describes why things work as they do rather than simply how, or what reaction can be expected from a given set of circumstances. Put simply, it either explains or predicts. This model will often be based on simplified assumptions but in the first instance such simplifications may be required to construct a testable hypothesis. The researcher then collects information with which to confirm or refute the hypothesis. Subsequent researchers will further develop the hypothesis and the testing of it.

This should not be read as a call for large sample econometric research to the exclusion of other branches of financial research. The case study's approach to seeking information is no less valid than that adopted by market-based accounting researchers: they have just chosen to trade off the scope of the analysis for greater depth. These may well become more important in future research and one important journal is currently encouraging the development of so-called 'clinical papers' which have many of the characteristics of case studies. Even the increasingly important strands of research, based on political and philosophical sciences, often produce research which fits the model described. Such papers frequently outline an analytical approach and use an example drawn from the finance or accounting world to illustrate the benefits of this method. If the method fails to illuminate the example it is analogous to an empirical model failing to demonstrate statistical significance.

The advocates of scientific research assert that the model should pre-date and guide the empirical testing but, despite the convention in which many research reports are written, this is to some extent unrealistic. An interesting problem will often be first identified by the evidence, and researchers would be negligent if they failed to pursue evidence upon which they stumbled in the pursuit of quite separate problems. For example, the interest in calendar-based regularities in stock market returns came not from a theory that they should exist, indeed the prior presumption was that they should not, but from market practitioners' assertions that calendar regularities do occur.

Once a theory has been put forward and tested it will be imitated and adapted. Improved methodology may allow some of the simplifications in the basic assumptions to be relaxed and more realistic models tested. This procedure may lead to refinement and extension of the original proposal, the original results may be refuted subsequently, or more refined models fail to show a significant improvement on the simple and robust early specification. Many students are uneasy with models which contain clearly unrealistic assumptions. It is to be hoped that these will be replaced later but in the meantime, the assessment of a model's worth lies not in the face validity of its assumptions but in its descriptive power.

1.3.2   *Empirical research and financial databases*

Empirical research has been a fruitful seam for the academic to mine. Early evidence suggested that share prices follow a random walk and cannot be predicted from their past history, that professional fund managers struggle to out-perform the market, that annual reports supply information to capital markets, and that earnings behaviour is robustly described by a random walk, whereas accounting returns exhibit certain characteristics of a mean reverting process, and financial analysts are better predictors of earnings than mechanistic models. These are all valuable findings which have contributed greatly to an understanding of how capital markets and accounting numbers behave and on the relationship between the two. The ongoing development of the methodologies and databases available will no doubt ensure that a continuing stream of such studies provide further insights.

This methodology is not free from criticism. Its popularity with academics has been partly supply- rather than demand-driven. The emergence of easily accessible databases and the computer power to analyse large samples has provided a route for academic publications without the inconvenience of leaving the college and dealing with institutional and individual complications. The principal charge has been of data mining or brute empiricism. Given enough data, a statistically significant relationship within the data can be found and a theory derived to match the results. This is certainly a danger and later chapters will deal with a number of examples where respected researchers have conducted empirical investigations where the link between the theories and the tested variables is tenuous. However, theory is a guide to empirical research, not a requirement. Scientific mythology asserts that Fleming had no prior theory for penicillin and, even if Newton's apple is apocryphal, had his insight been jogged in the manner described we may still admire and use his results.

Practitioners appear to have a healthy disregard for the academic's squeamish approach to brute empiricism. For example, the ability of statistical failure prediction models to discriminate between potential bankruptcies and other firms has found considerable support, whereas the attractive theory of the capital asset pricing model is generally treated with tolerant disregard. Jacobs and Levy (1988, p. 57) approvingly cite Paul Samuelson who commented:

> I prefer paradigms that combine plausible Newtonian theories with observed Baconian facts. But never would I refuse houseroom to a sturdy fact just because it is a bastard without a name and a parental model.

1.3.3 *Efficient market research*

One of the most pervasive results of empirical research is the efficient market theory (EMT) or hypothesis (EMH). The evidence for the EMH has already been mentioned in the preceding section, and will be reviewed throughout this text. EMH is fundamental in its implications for the uses to which financial analysis can reasonably be put and the information that can be culled from capital market data. The basic case for the theory is that the actions of the many competing analysts who make up the market ensure that it is an efficient processor of information, and that the share price incorporates instantaneously, and in an unbiased manner, all available information. Some attention needs to be given to the appropriate definition of 'available'. It can be construed as meaning all known information whether public or not (strong form efficiency), all public information (semi-strong form efficiency), or a sub-set of public information such as the record of past price movements (weak form efficiency).

The ramifications of EMH are crucial. If EMH holds there is no point in analysing data to identify mis-priced shares, as the market price of shares can be assumed to be the best available estimate of the shares' worth. Furthermore, there is little point in worrying about the best method of presenting accounting data to the market, as an efficient market will decipher information regardless of its form.

However, empirical research in the 1980s and 1990s has identified a number of instances where the capital markets of the world appear to exhibit inefficiencies, or anomalies as they have become known. There may be rational explanations which are as yet unknown and the bulk of the basic EMH research has supported the case for an efficient market. The efficient market theory is a sound working assumption where the analyst has no reason to believe otherwise. But there is sufficient scope for doubt and evidence or circumstances which seem to suggest that the market is less than efficient should not be dismissed out of hand.

1.3.4 *Positive accounting theory*

Normative propositions have a long and distinguished history in the accounting profession and in academia. The world of business and finance has a need for accounting information, financial regulation and institutional structures. Given that there is no objectively correct model for any of these, individuals are entitled to assert their preferred solutions. Thus, when someone advocates the use of inflation adjusted accounting reports, or more open political access to the accounting regulatory framework, they are stating a viewpoint but not a theory. This person may ensure that the prescription is testable by importing an objective which may or may not be achieved, but the objective is personal. In questions of social choice, there are no absolute standards by which prescriptions can be judged or which ensure that the decision operates in the interest of all sections of society. The particular prescription adopted becomes a political issue.

However, when a positive theory is put forward it makes no claims regarding the desirability of its subject, but presents a model of how the world works or what will be the impact of a certain set of conditions on other unknown circumstances. Many of the following chapters deal with positive research of the former type where the financial numbers are explained by a simple model. Much of the remainder describes the financial world in the absence of stated theory, where the theory is implicit or trivial.

One of the strongest lines of positive research concerns the agency relationship between the firm's participants. The diversity of interests involved in a firm has been alluded to already, and it is clear that there is a potential conflict between the shareholders, as principals, and their managers, as agents. This conflict may lead to less than perfect allocation or management of resources within the organisation, at least when viewed from the investors' viewpoint. These agency problems can be controlled where there exists efficient capital and managerial labour markets, or where complex contacts enable the principal and agent to align their divergent interests. Many other agency problems are not resolved, either because it is impractical to do so, or because the problem has not been identified. These residual problems are one of the costs of operating a financial system which separates ownership from control and may be set against the benefits of doing so.

Thus, the study of the agency relationship can help to explain the behaviour of investors, managers and firms. Why do firms adopt the financial structures and dividend distribution policies that they do? Why do shareholders, other investors, and managers arrange the sort of contractual deals that exist? Why do the observed monitoring and bonding activities occur?

There are difficulties with positive accounting theory. Watts and Zimmerman (1986) highlight the problems of:

1. Developing proxy variables that actually represent contracting and political costs.
2. Specifying the cross-sectional model.
3. Collinearity among the contracting variables.

There may be a more fundamental difficulty if the insights gained by the theory are trivial. For example, Watts and Zimmerman state that positive models of accounting practice will assist the external analyst's interpretation of reported results as the analyst will be able to incorporate an evaluation of the impact of managerial action on the reported numbers (Watts and Zimmerman, 1986, p. 357). But the analyst will only be interested in this insofar as the managers' influence is material in relationship to the unbiased estimates of the underlying variables.

1.3.5 *Social and political considerations*

It is often easy to forget that accounting and finance are not mechanical activities. The annual reports of firms are prepared by individuals, using accounting practices developed by others, regarding the economic activities of the socio-economic grouping of people that is a firm. The securities markets are not unbiased measures of the value of the firm's shares, but the result of the interaction and bargaining of many fallible individuals with differing motivations, expectations and skills. To some extent, the viewpoint of positive accounting theory and the sub-set of agency analysis accept that people get in the way, but that they do so for self-motivated economic reasons. To the extent that behaviour which is not motivated by the maximisation of an individual's welfare cannot be accounted for, it is treated as a random variable which will cancel out over a large sample. Thus people's individuality is seen as noise in the system. This is a useful simplification and the student of finance and accounting can only be expected to use those analytical tools that are available. However, certain directions of research in accounting and finance are developing useful models of human behaviour concerning accounting and finance.

The final chapter of this text examines the regulation of accounting, and the social and political processes which influence this are starting to be identified. Considerations of organisational behaviour and individual motivation are pertinent to the merger phenomenon and its influence on management behaviour, to the practice of employee reporting, and to the impact on industrial relations. Human information processing examines the ability of analysts in various decision contexts to evaluate information, and the methods by which decision-makers reconcile an extensive supply of information with a bounded ability to assess it rationally.

1.4   The structure of the text

As with all texts, a neat division into separate compartments is impossible. Some topics appear to be mentioned in every chapter and each area seems to need skills mentioned in later chapters as essential prerequisites. Consequently basic introductions are used in many instances and other chapters have a brief recap of areas covered previously.

A further difficulty is the question of the skills of the reader. Most users of this text will have taken prior courses in accounting and most instructors consider this to be an essential prerequisite. However, it should be remembered that many professional analysts only have a cursory knowledge of accounting and accounting statements can be understood without detailed knowledge. The more thorough the reader's understanding of accounting the better. Conversely advanced students of accounting and finance may well find Chapters 2 and 5 a rather basic introduction to the limitations of accounting techniques and the implications of capital market theories, though they will appreciate the opportunity to review and synthesise areas studied previously. Throughout the text a basic facility with statistical techniques is assumed, though nowhere are techniques more sophisticated than those included in the commonly used MINITAB data analysis software. However, much of the research evidence alluded to uses complex research methodology and statistical techniques. The student studying this discipline in depth will find considerable scope for demanding analysis in these references. It is hoped that the student looking for a more intuitive understanding will not find the outlines presented too confusing.

The book may be considered as comprising four sections. This chapter is the first of these and has attempted to define the scope of the text and the work of financial analysis and analysts. The significance of various disciplines and advances in understanding have also been brought out. The second section comprises Chapters 2 to 5 and deals with the basic skills required to interpret financial information. Chapter 2 describes the accounting process and the information content of financial statements. No attempt is made to address accounting techniques in any detail, but instead it provides an appreciation of the strengths and weaknesses of accounting information and of the scope for alternative accounting practices. Chapter 3 illustrates the basic techniques of ratio analysis and considers the methodological implications of the statistical characteristics of accounting ratios. Chapter 4 examines models of the time-series behaviour of accounting data and the empirical evidence of accounting time-series observed, before conducting a review of forecasting techniques and in particular of the observed accuracy of financial analysts' forecasts. Chapter 5 presents the basics of theoretical models of risk, return and value in capital markets, and the crucial issue regarding the efficiency of the capital market and thus the scope for expecting abnormal returns.

The third section (Chapters 6 to 10) applies the skills covered in the second section to a variety of decision scenarios that analysts may face. Chapter 6 reviews the relationship between accounting information and capital markets, and addresses the possibility of using accounting information as an input to the valuation of firms or securities. Chapter 7 considers the rather tenuous scope for assessing the economic return and risk of the firm from financial data. There has been a considerable advance in the theoretical analysis of the link between accounting numbers and value over the last few years and this chapter introduces these developments. Chapter 8 considers the topical and fascinating area of merger activity with a view to evaluating the economic efficiency of this process. It identifies the characteristic of firms likely to participate, and the possibility of investing successfully in firms that are the targets of takeovers. Chapter 9 is concerned with the less glamorous, but possibly more practical, area of credit evaluation and failure prediction. Chapter 10 involves a switch in viewpoint in that the economic decision-making of preceding chapters is de-emphasised and greater consideration is given to social reporting requirements, though this chapter concentrates on reporting to employees, and environmental issues.

The final section (Chapter 11) considers the regulation of accounting practices. This area is divorced from the practice of analysis and could be put aside. However, financial analysts would do well to appreciate the potential for alternatives in accounting requirements and the scope to influence these. Indeed, a number of colleagues have advocated giving this section considerably more emphasis possibly dealing with it after Chapter 1. This seems to be a perfectly viable alternative.

Note

1. There is no substitute for detailed examination of the content of actual financial statements, and it is strongly recommended that the student of financial analysis collects a small library of examples, including foreign versions. Questions set at the end of each chapter will often refer to these examples.

---------------------------- QUESTIONS ----------------------------

Note that most of these questions require considerable research by the students. The best approach may be to require different students to investigate different questions and report back to the group.

1. Review one week's non-financial pages of a quality daily paper. How many times are financial considerations alluded to, how many other times are financial matters a consideration but ignored in the reporting, and is the analysis of the financial factors naive or sophisticated?

2. Review one week's financial pages of a quality daily paper. How many different sources of information are referred to by the reporters? For whose benefit is the information originally made available, and who else benefits? Who bears the cost of producing the information and why? If the information source is subject to regulation or prescription, who manages the regulation and why?

3. Carefully review the content of Exhibit 1.1 which contains the Extel card containing information from various sources. What data sources have been used by Extel in the preparation of their report? What other information might be valuable for their purposes?

4. Carefully review the content of Exhibit 1.2 which gives an example of professional analysis of a firm's performance and prospects. What data sources have been used by the analysts in the preparation of their report? What other information might be valuable for their purposes? To what extent do the analysts act as intermediaries merely collecting information from other sources? Do they introduce additional information, and, if so, what?

5. Read through the transcript of a meeting between analysts and the management of a firm. What is the focus of the presentation made by the managers and to what extent does this give genuine insights into the firm's prospects? To what extent are the analysts' questions challenging and to what extent do they depart from the agenda set by the managers? How important is financial information in the discussions and what other considerations seem to be influential?

The best source of such transcripts (or tapes) is the New York Society of Investment Analysts who go to some lengths to ensure that the information presented at their meetings is made public. Transcripts of these meetings are often available from electronic media; InfoTrac is one example source.

6. Obtain a graph of a firm's share price performance relative to the market over one year. Consider substantial changes in the share price and try and relate these to information that came to the market on or about that date. Are there other significant news events which did not seem to affect the market? Why do you think this is so?

7.   Provide definitions of the following terms or concepts as used in this chapter:
        (a) Fundamental analysis.
        (b) Financial statements.
        (c) Financial information users.
        (d) Ownership vs control.
        (e) Management objectives.
        (f) Profit maximisation.
        (g) Wealth maximisation.
        (h) Brute empiricism.
        (i) Positive accounting theory.
        (j) Efficient market hypothesis.
        (k) Contracting costs.
        Note that this may entail some research on your part.

References

Ball, R. and Smith, C. (1992) *The Economics of Accounting Policy Choice*, McGraw Hill.

Beaver, W. (1991) Ten commandments of financial statement analysis, *Financial Analysts' Journal*, January–February, **47**, no. 1, 7–9.

Coase, R. (1937) The nature of the firm, *Economica*, November.

ICAS (1988) *Making Accounting Reports Valuable*, Kogan Page, London.

Jacobs, B. and Levy, K. (1988) Disentangling equity return regularities: new insights and investment opportunities, *Financial Analysts' Journal*, May–June, **44**, no. 3, 18–43.

Watts, R. and Zimmerman, J. (1986) *Positive Accounting Theory*, Prentice Hall, Englewood Cliffs.

CHAPTER 2

Financial Statements and Creativity

――――――――――― CHAPTER OBJECTIVES ―――――――――――

This chapter will:

1   Remind the reader of the basic techniques and output of the financial reporting process.

2   Review the objectives of financial reporting and the methods used to try and achieve these objectives.

3   Present the limitations of financial reports and also review some of the methods used by firms to adjust their accounting statements.

This chapter will not discuss basic accounting procedures. However, an understanding of accounting practices is necessary. It is advisable to refer to a conventional accounting text and to relevant official pronouncements regarding Generally Accepted Accounting Practices (GAAP), such as the International Accounting Standards Committee's (IASC) recommendations and domestic regulations. The reader will also find it useful to refer to examples of financial reports for domestic and foreign firms.

2.1   Introduction

Some insight into the relative importance of the different sources of information can be derived from the surveys of investment analysts conducted by Arnold *et al.* (1984), Pike *et al.* (1993) and Vergossen (1993) (see Table 2.1). Some scepticism is required when interpreting survey data as respondents to surveys have a tendency to reply as they think they should rather than give unbiased responses, see Table 2.1.

Some of these results are 10 years old and changes might be expected as information technology makes some sources more accessible, changes in accounting procedures improve or impair the information content of different sources, or changes in law discourage the

Table 2.1 Influences of various information sources

	US '84	UK '84	UK '93	FRG '93
Company's annual report			3	2
Chair's statement	13	6		
Directors' report	9	8		
Balance sheet	2	2		
Income statement	1	1		
Cash flow statement	3	5		
Current cost data	11 =	10		
Unqualified audit report	14	15		
Qualified audit report	4	7		
Quarterly results	5	3		
Government statistics	15	13		
Statistical information	8	11		
Financial press	10	9	5	5
Industry/Trade journals	7	14		
Company personnel	6	4	1	3
Other financial analysts	11 =	12	6	6
Analysts meetings in company			2	1
General meeting			7	7
Preliminary announcement			4	4

Source: Arnold *et al.* 1984, and Pike *et al.* 1993.

use of certain sources, as with the influence of insider trading rules. Indeed, some difference can be observed between the two sets of UK data and Pike *et al.*'s (1993) data suggest a greater influence of company personnel than the earlier study does. In general the evidence tends to support the thesis that accounting information is of considerable importance, but is not uniquely important.

There are many examples of financial statement data throughout this text; for example in Exhibit 1.1 regarding Siemens AG, Exhibit 2.1 for DMS NV, and Exhibit 3.3 regarding Carrefour SA. However, two other interesting elements of the financial reports are discussions of performance or prospects by management, usually a statement by the chair of the board, and audit reports. The first is thought to be widely read (Hines, 1982) even if the surveys cited above downplay its importance. A full example is too long to be included here but extracts from the Chair's and Chief Executive's statements from Tarmac's (UK construction conglomerate) most recent accounts demonstrate why analysts might find these interesting.

CHAIR'S STATEMENT

A combination of divestments, careful cash management and a successful rights issue have reduced net debt from £577 m at December 1992 to £194 m at December 1993. Our progress is demonstrated by the improvement in profits from continuing businesses, which at the pre-tax level increased fourfold this year on a normalised basis. Exceptional non-operating items and the trading results of businesses now no longer part of the group have, however, given rise to a loss before tax in the year.

──────────────── **Exhibit 2.1** Extracts from the accounts of DSM NV ────────────────

These extracts are comprehensive with regards to the financial numbers and include consolidated income statement, balance sheet, cash flow and segmental analysis statements. In most cases analysts work with information from financial databases of which this is an example. However, in doing so a lot of information is lost including some detailed financial numbers, explanation of the accounting policies and discussions by the chair or other directors regarding the company's performance and prospects. Therefore readers are strongly advised to collect example financial reports from different countries and industries and to examine these in order to (a) learn to find their way around financial statements, (b) examine financial statements for additional information not apparent from financial databases, and (c) see the differences inherent in financial reports which derive from GAAP and industrial differences. Full example financial statements are too long to include in the text and can be understood by readers to represent a standard example when there is no such thing, despite progress with harmonisation within Europe.

DSM NV was originally active in the administration of publicly-owned collieries in the south of the Netherlands. However, today the Group is principally active in chemicals. Activities are concentrated in the following divisions: Hydrocarbons; Polymers; Elastomers; Chemicals and Fertilisers; Fine Chemicals; Resins; Plastic Products; Engineering Plastic Products and Energy.

DSM NV
CONSOLIDATED PROFIT AND LOSS ACCOUNT

	Dec 31 1991 Fl m	Dec 31 1992 Fl m	Dec 31 1993 Fl m
NET SALES	9,347	8,907	8,040
Other gross income	230	231	187
Change in stocks etc	(105)	26	(139)
Raw materials etc	(4,356)	(4,285)	(3,829)
Work subcontracted &c	(1,955)	(2,025)	(1,857)
Own work capitalised	48	36	24
Staff expenses	(1,944)	(1,935)	(1,803)
Other trading expenses	(635)	(673)	(714)
TRADING PROFIT (LOSS)	630	282	(91)
Interest/investment income	87	55	45
Interest payable	(198)	(177)	(179)
PROFIT (LOSS) BEFORE TAX	519	160	(225)
Tax	(89)	49	126
PROFIT (LOSS) AFT TAX	430	209	(99)
Net equity associated company income	73	48	43
Minority interests	(7)	(11)	(4)
Extraordinary (losses) gains	20	(22)	(58)
NET INCOME (LOSS)	516	224	(118)
Ordinary dividends	(281)	(144)	(54)
RETAINED PROFITS (LOSSES)	235	80	(172)

DSM NV
NOTES TO CONSOLIDATED PROFIT AND LOSS ACCOUNT

	Dec 31 1991 Fl m	Dec 31 1992 Fl m	Dec 31 1993 Fl m
STAFF EXPENSES BY TYPE			
Wages & salaries	(1,544)	(1,521)	(1,447)
Staff pensions	(65)	(78)	(47)
Other social charges	(335)	(336)	(309)
	(1,944)	(1,935)	(1,803)
OTHER TRADING EXPENSES			
Depreciation	(658)	(690)	(727)
Amortisation of intangibles	(16)	(16)	(17)
Misc. other trading expenses	39	33	30
	(635)	(673)	(714)
INTEREST/INVESTMENT INCOME			
Investment income	-	4	6
Interest income	87	51	39
	87	55	45
INTEREST PAYABLE			
Misc. interest payable	(205)	(202)	(214)
Interest capitalised	7	25	35
	(198)	(177)	(179)
EXTRAORDINARY (LOSSES) GAINS			
Tax on extraordinary items	54	38	4
Misc. extraordinary losses	(34)	(60)	(62)
	20	(22)	(58)
ORDINARY DIVIDENDS			
Interim ordinary dividends	(93)	(95)	-
Final ordinary dividends	(188)	(49)	(54)
	(281)	(144)	(54)
PROFIT BEFORE TAX is after (charging) crediting			
Research & development	(425)	(425)	-
No of staff at y/e	24,764	22,364	20,592

DSM NV
BUSINESS ANALYSIS (Fl m)

SALES

	Dec 31 1991	Dec 31 1992	Dec 31 1993
Hydrocarbons & Polymers	3,426	3,561	3,499
Base & Fine Chemicals	3,220	2,897	2,292
Resin & Plastic Products	2,887	2,660	2,409
Energy & Other	135	203	176
Internal Sales	(321)	(414)	(336)
	9,347	8,907	8,040

PROFIT (LOSS) BEFORE TAX

	Dec 31 1991	Dec 31 1992	Dec 31 1993
Hydrocarbons & Polymers	68	(53)	(183)
Base & Fine Chemicals	267	80	(105)
Resins & Plastic Products	111	71	14
Energy & Other	184	184	183
Financial Income (Expenses)	(111)	(122)	(134)
	519	160	(225)

GEOGRAPHICAL ANALYSIS - Turnover by Source

	Dec 31 1991 Fl m	Dec 31 1992 Fl m	Dec 31 1993 Fl m
Netherlands	5,783	5,551	4,960
Rest of EC	2,296	2,026	1,715
Rest of Europe (Non EC)	50	39	87
North America	1,200	1,273	1,243
Rest of world	18	18	35
	9,347	8,907	8,040

GEOGRAPHICAL ANALYSIS - Turnover by Market

	Dec 31 1991 Fl m	Dec 31 1992 Fl m	Dec 31 1993 Fl m
Netherlands	1,579	1,453	1,107
Rest of EC	5,273	4,964	4,491
Rest of Europe (Non EC)	428	414	447
North America	1,083	1,189	1,231
Rest of world	984	887	764
	9,347	8,907	8,040

DSM NV
CONSOLIDATED STATEMENT OF CASH FLOWS

	Dec 31 1991 Fl m	Dec 31 1992 Fl m	Dec 31 1993 Fl m
OPERATIONS	874	725	784
INVESTING ACTIVITIES			
Investments net	193	27	40
Subsidiaries acquired	-	(8)	(56)
Tangibles acquired	(1,326)	(1,040)	(672)
Subsidiaries sold	-	56	91
Tangibles sold	22	35	28
Intangibles acquired	(430)	(12)	(16)
	(1,541)	(942)	(585)
FINANCING ACTIVITIES			
Long-term debt raised	954	683	295
Long-term debt repaid	(297)	(253)	(858)
Share capital acquired	-	3	39
	657	433	(524)
CASH INCREASE (DECREASE)	(10)	216	(325)
Other adjustments (increase)	(19)	-	-
BALANCE SHEET CASH INCREASE (DECREASE)	(29)	216	(325)

NOTES TO CONSOLIDATED STATEMENT OF CASH FLOWS

	Dec 31 1991 Fl m	Dec 31 1992 Fl m	Dec 31 1993 Fl m
OPERATIONS			
Net income	516	224	(118)
Depreciation & amortisation increase	674	706	744
Provision increases	(45)	(59)	(55)
Other trading adjustment increase	(297)	(154)	(87)
Asset disposal	(84)	(16)	(37)
Decrease in stocks	133	66	233
Decrease in debtors	276	(22)	52
Other working capital decrease	(299)	(20)	52
	874	725	784

DSM NV
CONSOLIDATED BALANCE SHEETS

	Dec 31 1991 Fl m	Dec 31 1992 Fl m	Dec 31 1993 Fl m
FIXED ASSETS			
Intangible assets	58	54	53
Tangible assets	5,010	5,315	5,210
Financial assets	756	678	637
	5,824	6,047	5,900
CURRENT ASSETS			
Stocks	1,518	1,445	1,230
Receivable-equity associated companies	61	69	57
Trade accounts receivable	1,452	1,407	1,327
Deferred items	38	59	56
Misc. debtors	432	544	706
Cash & equivalents	901	1,116	791
	4,402	4,640	4,167
CREDITORS due within 1 yr			
Debt due within 1 yr	1,129	1,166	542
Payble-equity associated companies	25	34	44
Suppliers & trade credit	712	745	693
Deferred items	125	159	180
Prepayments	7	6	3
Tax & social security	105	94	103
Dividends	188	49	54
Misc. creditors	497	381	442
	2,788	2,634	2,061
NET CURRENT ASSETS	1,614	2,006	2,106
TOTAL ASSETS LESS CURRENT LIABILITIES	7,438	8,053	8,006
CREDITORS due after 1 yr			
Long-term debt	1,588	2,031	2,152
Other liabilities	25	17	9
	1,613	2,048	2,161
PROVISIONS	1,649	1,684	1,684
NET ASSETS	4,176	4,321	4,161
SHARE CAPITAL	702	720	720
Share premium	210	199	199
Misc. reserves	3,201	3,333	3,170
SHAREHOLDERS' FUNDS	4,113	4,252	4,089
Minority interests	63	69	72
NET ASSETS	4,176	4,321	4,161

DSM NV
NOTES TO CONSOLIDATED BALANCE SHEETS

	Dec 31 1991 Fl m	Dec 31 1992 Fl m	Dec 31 1993 Fl m
INTANGIBLE ASSETS			
Brands, patents etc	23	16	12
Start-up expenses &c	35	38	41
	58	54	53
TANGIBLE ASSETS			
Property - cost	1,846	2,071	2,137
Property depreciation	(756)	(812)	(875)
Property NBV	1,090	1,259	1,262
Other tangible FA-cost	9,967	10,411	11,235
Other tangible FA-depreciation	(6,932)	(7,350)	(7,748)
Other tangible FA-NBV	3,035	3,061	3,487
Capital WIP gross c/f	937	1,038	502
Capital WIP written off	(52)	(43)	(41)
Capital WIP NBV c/f	885	995	461
Tangible assets	5,010	5,315	5,210
FINANCIAL ASSETS			
Investments	41	3	15
Associated company loans	2	4	14
Investments in associated companies	582	576	526
Trade investments	584	580	540
Long-term receivables	131	95	82
	756	678	637
STOCKS			
Raw materials etc	425	357	305
Work in progress	81	77	72
Finished products	1,012	1,011	853
	1,518	1,445	1,230

DSM NV
NOTES TO CONSOLIDATED BALANCE SHEETS CONT.

	Dec 31 1991 Fl m	Dec 31 1992 Fl m	Dec 31 1993 Fl m
DEBT BY TYPE			
Debt & Private loans	1,809	2,095	2,328
Credit institutions	879	1,078	333
Notes & cheques due	29	24	33
	2,717	3,197	2,694
DEBT BY MATURITY			
Debt due within 1 yr	1,129	1,166	542
Due within 2 to 5 yrs	1,055	1,212	1,224
Due after 5 years	533	819	928
	2,717	3,197	2,694
PROVISIONS			
Deferred taxation	139	184	256
Pension provisions	33	34	42
Misc. provisions	1,477	1,466	1,386
	1,649	1,684	1,684
SHARE CAPITAL			
Ordinary shares	702	720	720
Priority shares	a	a	a
	702	720	720

a)Fl 100

CHIEF EXECUTIVE'S STATEMENT

Prospects. Although fortunes remain mixed from a geographical standpoint, our trading performance in the year to date is satisfactory. In Quarry Products, we anticipate better results, although a key factor will be the achievement of higher prices by the industry. Housing has started well and should achieve further margin improvements, principally as a result of firmer selling prices. Construction continues to show resilience in its performance and is pushing ahead selectively, both in the UK and abroad, capitalising upon its total offering from design, through construction to facilities management.

Building Materials has entered 1994 enjoying the benefits of plant rationalisation, cost reductions and a strengthening of prices; an improved result is expected. After a first quarter adversely affected by weather, the outlook for Tarmac America's principal markets is improving, particularly in Florida.

We are now seeing firmer indications of recovery in the UK led by housebuilding. In the US, market improvements are more advanced. With mainland Europe having entered recession later, we anticipate that these economies will remain sluggish in the current year.

Having concluded our remedial strategy, we have now embarked on the next phase of our corporate development. We plan to build on progress already made.

Whilst these may be interesting it is difficult for the analyst to disentangle informed comment from wishful thinking.

As regards audit reports these seem to be of interest only when qualified (see Table 2.1). The reason for their importance can be understood from the following example for Queensmoat, the UK hotel operators. The 1993 Auditors' Report states that:

> ... The accounts have been prepared on a going concern basis and the validity of this depends on the Group's bankers and other lenders continuing their support by providing adequate facilities pending the successful completion of a financial restructuring, on the successful completion of such a restructuring, and on the Company's first mortgage debenture stockholders not seeking to enforce their security. The accounts do not include any adjustments that would result should the group be unable to continue in operational existence. Our opinion is not qualified in this respect. We have also considered the adequacy of the disclosures made in the accounts concerning certain dividend payments made by the company during the year and prior year which were in breach of the Companies Act 1985 as the company did not have sufficient distributable reserves at the time of payment. Our opinion is not qualified in this respect.
>
> In our opinion the accounts give a true and fair view ....

From this example it is quite easy to see why analysts will be interested in unusual audit reports.

2.2 The role of accounting information in financial analysis

The annual audited and published accounts of a limited company are seen as a critical input to the financial analyst's work. The cited surveys show that analysts ranked the accounting statements first, or first after direct contact with company personnel. Yet despite this apparent reliance on formal financial statements even the most naive analyst will be aware that accounting reports are fallible.

The previous chapter has listed a number of different types of financial analysts all of whom may use accounting information. It is evident that these groups have distinct interests and may often be in conflict over the allocation of resources. In so far as accounting information is held to affect resource allocations, disputes can arise between these groups over the desirability of alternative disclosure policies. It is crucial to an understanding of the problems encountered by accountants to appreciate that financial statements try to satisfy the differing informational needs of a varied readership and that there is no objective definition of profit, equity or other accounting values that can be used to guide accounting practices. Given these difficulties it is not surprising that some measure of failure is experienced by the accounting reporting system. This happens periodically when a substantial firm fails even though its latest accounts show an apparently healthy situation. In the UK BCCI, British and Commonwealth, Coloroll, Maxwell Communications and Mirror Group Newspapers and Poly Peck are all examples where accounting information has not provided the prior warning that the users hoped for. It seems that much of the reliance put on accounting information is naive.

It should also be noted that conflict is possible within the user groups identified in Chapter 1. There is no guarantee that each group will have homogeneous informational needs and it will be seen that different sectors of one category may well dispute the desirability of certain disclosures. For example, conflicting enthusiasm for increased disclosure between investment advisers and portfolio managers is in part due to the preferential contacts that investment analysts may have with corporate management. Public disclosure of information, previously only available to the analysts, may be of use to the fund manager but could eliminate a valuable advantage enjoyed by the investment analyst. Furthermore, investors may have differing levels of interpretation skills, contract out varying proportions of the investment selection process to advisers and agents, adopt alternative strategies to risk diversification, and differ on their approach to passive or active investment management. For each of these sub-groups the 'ideal' level of information disclosure may differ.

The reporting firm's management is very much involved in the selection and implementation of accounting policies. The need for external funds is an incentive to management to disseminate sufficient data to allow the investor confidently to select alternatives and to monitor progress. Set against this need to disclose is a reluctance to inform competitors who may exploit the information, or shareholders, regulators, and others, who may constrain management's freedom of action.

Managers are also crucially concerned with accounting disclosures as it impinges on their remuneration and job security. If it is argued that share prices are influenced by the level, growth and variability of accounting earnings, and that managerial remuneration and security are in part dependent on the share price, there are incentives to management to manipulate the reported earnings figures. Even where the share price performance is not a determinant of managers' earnings they may well be paid according to some sort of profit related bonus. As management may well have considerable influence, at least over the variability of earnings, it is apparent that where disclosure is discretionary they will have a significant influence on the reporting practices of the firm. As the management also exercises considerable authority within the formal accounting standard setting process, it would be unwise to neglect management's role when considering the desirability of, or motivation for, changes in disclosure practice.

To try to meet the needs of shareholders and other interested groups, a number of different sections are presented in financial statements. In Europe this would usually include a statement by the company's chair of the board or other directors, an auditor's report and the accounting statements of the company, along with a considerable amount of promotional material. The accounting statements would normally comprise a balance sheet, a profit and loss account, a cash flow statement (in some countries a funds flow statement is required instead or, indeed, there may be no need to present a flow statement at all), together with extensive notes and explanations. Occasionally inflation-adjusted versions of the main statements are presented, either voluntarily or when required by the appropriate regulators. Taken together these reports are not an ideal solution to the informational needs of various users but it may well be doubted that an ideal solution exists. However, a number of bodies have come up with suggested definitions of the preferred method of producing financial statements.

2.3   A definition of 'ideal' financial statements

The form and content of financial statements differ considerably throughout the world but there are continuing moves towards harmonisation. The International Accounting Standards Committee has published a 'Framework for the Preparation and Presentation of Financial Statements' which is derived from US publications and has almost completely been adopted in the UK as a working framework. A number of definitions and objectives, as outlined by that statement, are presented below. It should be understood that these objectives are strongly influenced by the 'Anglo/American' tradition. Some continental European and Far Eastern economies use accounting practices which depart significantly from the approach outlined below. Important examples of divergent practices are France, Germany and Japan whereas other countries such as the Netherlands and Australia have accounting practices quite similar to the Anglo/American model. Even where GAAP is substantially different from Anglo/American, and it must be conceded that Anglo is rather different from American, individual firms are starting to move either towards international GAAP or produce supplementary reports based on international GAAP.

The extracts from the Framework cited here set out the scope of financial statements, their basic objectives, and brief definitions of the two most accepted formats for presenting financial results — the balance sheet and profit and loss (or income) statement. Even though cash flow or fund flow statements are required or common in many countries, the method of computation and the rules regarding disclosure show sufficient diversity to preclude a reliable definition.

Financial statements might be defined as follows:

7. Financial statements form part of the process of financial reporting. A complete set of financial statements normally includes a balance sheet, an income statement, a statement of changes in financial position (which may be presented in a variety of ways, for example, as a statement of cash flows or a statement of funds flow), and those notes and other statements and explanatory material that are an integral part of the financial statements. They may also include supplementary schedules and information based on, or derived from, and expected to be read with, such statements. Such schedules and supplementary information may deal, for example, with financial information about industrial and geographical segments and disclosures about the effects of changing prices. Financial statements do not, however, include such items as reports by directors' statements by the chairman, discussion and analysis by management and similar items that may be included in a financial or annual report.

Financial analysts seeking to make economic decisions are thought to require information regarding the financial position, performance and changes in financial position of an enterprise. As the IASC note:

15. The economic decisions that are taken by users of financial statements require an evaluation of the ability of an enterprise to generate cash and cash equivalents and of timing and certainty of their generation. This ability ultimately determines, for example, the capacity of an enterprise to pay its employees and suppliers, meet interest payments, repay loans and make distributions to its owners. Users are better able to evaluate this ability to generate cash and cash equivalents if they are provided with information that focuses on the financial position, performance and changes in financial position of an enterprise.

Financial position encompasses the following:

16. The financial position of an enterprise is affected by the economic resources it controls, its financial structure, its liquidity and solvency, and its capacity to adapt to changes in the environment in which it operates. Information about the economic resources controlled by the enterprise and its capacity in the past to modify these resources is useful in predicting

the ability of the enterprise to generate cash and cash equivalents in the future. Information about financial structure is useful in predicting future borrowing needs and how future profits and cash flows will be distributed among those with an interest in the enterprise; it is also useful in predicting how successful the enterprise is likely to be in raising further finance. Information about liquidity and solvency is useful in predicting the ability of the enterprise to meet its financial commitments as they fall due. Liquidity refers to the availability of cash in the near future after taking account of financial commitments over this period. Solvency refers to the availability of cash over the longer term to meet financial commitments as they fall due.

Similarly, information regarding the current performance of the firm is thought to be valuable in assessing future cash flows.

17.   Information about the performance of an enterprise, in particular its profitability, is required in order to assess potential changes in the economic resources that it is likely to control in the future. Information about variability of performance is important in this respect. Information about performance is useful in predicting the capacity of the enterprise to generate cash flows from its existing resource base. It is also useful in forming judgements about the effectiveness with which the enterprise might employ additional resources.

Finally, the changes in financial position shed light on managerial policies regarding the raising of finance and its investment and also the extent to which the apparent performance of the firm is translated into cash flows.

18.   Information concerning changes in the financial position of an enterprise is useful in order to assess its investing, financing and operating activities during the reporting period. This information is useful in providing the user with a basis to assess the ability of the enterprise to generate cash and cash equivalents and the needs of the enterprise to utilise those cash flows. In constructing a statement of changes in financial position, funds can be defined in various ways, such as all financial resources, working capital, liquid assets or cash. No attempt is made in this framework to specify a definition of funds.

These three dimensions are seen by the IASC as being most obviously reflected in the three main financial statements, but their interrelationship is stressed as is the need to utilise the full information set available, including notes to the accounts.

19.   Information about financial position is primarily provided in a balance sheet. Information about performance is primarily provided in an income statement, information about changes in financial position is provided in the financial statements by means of a separate statement.

20.   The component parts of the financial statements interrelate because they reflect different aspects of the same transactions or other events. Although each statement provides information that is different from the others, none is likely to serve only a single purpose or provide all the information necessary for particular needs of users. For example, an income statement provides an incomplete picture of performance unless it is used in conjunction with the balance sheet and the statement of changes in financial position.

21.   The financial statements also contain notes and supplementary schedules and other information. For example, they may contain additional information that is relevant to the needs of users about the items in the balance sheet and income statement. They may include disclosures about the risks and uncertainties affecting the enterprise and any resources and obligations not recognised in the balance sheet (such as mineral reserves). Information about geographical and industry segments and the effect on the enterprise of changing prices may also be provided in the form of supplementary information.

Whilst the IASC document contains a great deal more information regarding the essential elements of financial statements paragraph 49 defines the essential characteristics of the balance sheet, and paragraphs 69 and 70 do the same with regards to the income statement.

49. The elements directly related to the measurement of financial position are assets, liabilities and equity. These are defined as follows:
   (a) An asset is a resource controlled by the enterprise as a result of past events and from which future economic benefits are expected to flow to the enterprise.
   (b) A liability is a present obligation of the enterprise arising from past events, the settlement of which is expected to result in an outflow from the enterprise of resources embodying economic benefits.
   (c) Equity is the residual interest in the assets of the enterprise after deducting all its liabilities.
69. Profit is frequently used as a measure of performance or as the basis for other measures, such as return on investment or earnings per share. The elements directly related to the measurement of profit are income and expenses. The recognition and measurement of income and expenses, and hence profit, depend in part on the concepts of capital and capital maintenance used by the enterprise in preparing its financial statements. These concepts are discussed in paragraphs 102 to 110.
70. The elements of income and expenses are defined as follows:
   (a) Income is increases in economic benefits during the accounting period in the form of inflows or enhancements of assets or decreases of liabilities that result in increases in equity, other than those relating to contributions from equity participants.
   (b) Expenses are decreases in economic benefits during the accounting period in the form of outflows or depletions of assets or incurrences of liabilities that result in decreases in equity, other than those relating to distributions to equity participants.

To some extent these prescriptions of the IASC refer to ideals which are unlikely to be met and in some cases require trade-offs between various attributes of an ideal set of financial statements. The strengths and shortcomings of financial statements are discussed at some length later as are the meaning of specific elements of financial statements. This section and the previous chapter have made it clear that financial statements may be an important source of information for financial analysts but they are not the only source by a long way and many other types of financial information have been referred to and in some cases examples have been given.

2.4 Measurement problems and creativity in accounting

It is apparent from the previous discussion that the process of producing financial statements which are informative for analysts is difficult enough without any deliberate attempts to deceive and yet a series of accounting failures in the UK and elsewhere have convinced many observers that accounting statements are not to be relied upon. Whether or not the market is fooled by attempts to manipulate the numbers disclosed is an academic question which has not been resolved as yet. However, it is fairly certain that:

1. Some managers believe that firms can be shown in a better light by judicious choice of accounting policies and by applying bias to the necessary estimation procedures.
2. A number of firms have failed even though their financial statements gave no indication of the impending problems.

Possibly the most influential view regarding the problem of creative accounting was that presented by Smith and Hannah (1991) in the award-winning analysis entitled 'Accounting for Growth' published by UBS Phillips and Drew. It should perhaps be noted that a subsequent version of this work published as a text and written by Smith evoked considerable controversy which culminated in Smith and UBS parting company.

The report discussed a variety of methods of manipulating the accounting statements and gave specific examples where this appeared to have been done. They note that:

> It is fair to say that in many cases the use of such adjustments can be justified as the most appropriate accounting treatment and in virtually every case it has been approved by the group's auditors. Equally, however, there are times when the accounting policy seems wayward and generally in these cases, reported earnings are flattered at the expense of the balance sheet.

They also produce a classification of some of the commonest methods of accounting manipulation.

These were:

1. *Excessive provisions*. This involves the creation and use of significant balance sheet provisions. These may have been established when the firm acquired another firm in a takeover or acquisition. Where assets are reduced in value in this way the debit is not passed through the income statement but the asset value, and hence subsequent depreciation, is reduced. The net result is an increase in profits. This would not be such a problem were it necessary in the UK to write off goodwill on acquisition but unlike the US this is not required.

2. *Extraordinary items*. These are significant cash reorganisation/rationalisation costs which appear as extraordinary items (or just in the source and application of funds), but not against pre-tax profit.

3. *Off balance sheet finance*. Companies may have major off balance sheet debt. In most cases this is organised by raising capital in associate firms which are not fully consolidated. Often the parent group will guarantee the debt even though it does not appear on the balance sheet and the firm's gearing appears to be better than it is.

4. *Capitalised costs*. This involves significant capitalisation of interest and other costs. In most cases it may be uncontroversial that interest costs are a genuine expense involved with acquiring an asset and may be treated as a capital item. After all they will eventually appear as depreciation or losses on disposal. However, where this does not happen as with property companies a considerable expense may not appear as a cost on the income statement.

5. *Non-trading profits*. This occurs when significant non-trading profits are credited to pre-tax profits — asset disposals, sales and leasebacks etc. This applies to any profits which are transitory but it is understandable that firms will try and incorporate as much profit as possible in their normal earnings figure. However, it has been said that unusual losses will usually be classified below the line and unusual profits above the line.

6. *Brand accounting*. This involves companies which have significant brand accounting assets in their balance sheets. The late 1980s saw many firms realise that they had considerable assets in the reputation of their brands and some of them attempted to value these assets and include them on their balance sheets. Whilst this is legal in

the UK it would not be under most other regimes and it should be realised that (a) it is almost impossible to arrive at a reliable estimate of the brand's value and (b) the value is unstable and may be eliminated overnight.

7. *Depreciation rate changes*. Companies may make significant depreciation rate changes. The decision regarding the appropriate rate at which to depreciate assets is difficult and it is understandable that many firms will get it wrong and have to adjust the rate. However, some firms will reduce the rate without good reason and even where the adjustment is genuine it will give the impression of growth in profits where none existed.

8. *Pension fund holidays*. This involves companies whose pre-tax profits have benefited from a significant reduction in their pension fund contributions. The good performance of UK pension funds during the 1980s led to many firms reducing or cancelling their contribution or even reclaiming funds. These pension holidays give the impression of high and increasing profits but it is unlikely that such advantageous circumstances will be permanent.

9. *Earn-out commitments*. Companies may have significant earn-out commitments. Earn-outs are where a business has been acquired and important personnel are persuaded to remain with the business by generous profit-sharing schemes. However, it can be the case that meeting these terms becomes very demanding especially where the rest of the group is doing badly.

10. *Foreign exchange mismatch*. Companies may have a significant mismatch between their international debt and their deposits. Thus a firm can earn profits from speculation on the foreign exchange markets which may be genuine but are also unlikely to indicate continuing profits. The expected return from currency transactions is zero. It could also include firms which have borrowed in strong currencies or lent to weak ones. This will have a short-term beneficial effect on interest paid or received but the change in the value of the asset or liability, expressed in the firm's home currency will be expected eventually to offset the benefit.

11. *Low tax charge*. This occurs when companies have an unusually low tax charge. This category is different in kind from the others as it represents not an accounting manipulation but an indicator of possible accounting sleight of hand. Smith and Hannah (1991) argue that the tax authorities, having privileged access to the records of the firm are able more accurately to assess and tax the firm's profits. Where the tax charge is low in relation to the profit this may indicate that the profit is not as sound as it might be. An alternative interpretation is that a firm may be able temporarily to depress the tax charge but sooner or later it will return to normal levels reducing future post-tax profits.

Table 2.2 gives an indication of the frequency of these accounting problems and analyses their relationship with some stock market variables. It shows that the use of creative accounting procedures, as defined by Smith and Hannah (1991), are common among many of the largest UK quoted firms. What is more, a simple test which examines the relationship between the occurrence of such practices and three important security market variables (the price to earnings ratio, the annual abnormal return and beta) identify six cases where the ordinary least squares (OLS) regression coefficient is significant at a 5 per cent

Table 2.2 Frequency of creative accounting practices and their market impact

Accounting policy	% used	Rel. P/E	Ab. Ret.	Beta
Provisions	57.1	−	+(2)	+
Extraordinary costs	28.8	−(1)	−	+
Off B/S debt	12.0	−	−	+(2)
Capitalisation	27.2	+	+	−
Non-trading profits	34.2	−	−	−
Brand names	7.6	+(1)	−(2)	+
Depreciation	9.2	−	−	+
Pension fund	28.3	−	+(1)	−(2)
Earn-outs	4.9	−	−(1)	+(1)
Currency mismatch	8.1	−(1)	+	−
Low tax charge	12.5	+	−	+

The first column gives the title of the 'creative' accounting procedure and the second the percentage of companies that Smith and Hannah identify as using this approach. The third, fourth and fifth columns record the estimated coefficient between the accounting policies and the price/earnings ratio of the firm relative to the industry, the abnormal return on the firm's stock in the year prior to publication, and the beta of the firm. All variables are obtained from the LBS Risk Measurement Service. The accounting policies are measured as zero-one dummy variables. (1) indicates statistically significant at 5 per cent or better. (2) indicates some evidence of a significant relationship but collinearity renders the results tentative.

confidence level (or higher). Given that there are eleven categories times three dependent variables the expected number of significant relationships by chance alone would be 1.65 (33 × 0.5). Whilst this does not constitute formal research results it does seem to indicate that creative accounting practices are related to market variables though the direction of causality is not tested.

A more direct test of creative activity is to examine the number of times accounting practices are found to be unreliable. Feroz *et al.* (1992) analysed the source of accounting mis-statements according to the Securities and Exchange Commission's (SEC) investigations between April 1982 and April 1989. Even though these firms were all US companies it is quite likely that the sort of error or deceit found amongst US firms will be similar to those discovered in other developed economies.

Table 2.3 suggests that debtors are the main location of accounting mis-statements and that overall working capital is responsible for about two-thirds of the errors. It is also noticeable that these errors are not small. Indeed, about half of the errors account for 50 per cent or more of reported income.

2.5   Some specific examples of measurement problems in accounting

2.5.1 *Economics vs accounting*

There is no necessary link between accounting measures of income and wealth and the underlying economic values. The asset values in the balance sheet are neither an assessment of the realisable value nor the replacement cost of the asset. Even if they were, the value

Table 2.3 Accounts mis-stated according to SEC enforcement actions

Panel A: Accounts mis-stated	Market sample		Non-market sample	
	Number	Percentage	Number	Percentage
Receivables	29	50	71	55
Inventories	14	24	18	14
Investments	2	3	13	10
Long-term assets	6	10	23	18
Liabilities	3	5	30	23
Marketable securities	1	2	2	1
Miscellaneous assets	5	9	6	4
Reclassifications	3	5	10	8
	63		173	
Panel B: Income effects of mis-statements				
0 to 10%	8	14	10	21
10 to 50%	18	31	15	32
51 to 99%	11	19	10	21
100 or more	21	36	12	26
	58	100	47	100

These data are taken from table 2 of Feroz *et al.* (1992) and refer to SEC enforcement actions number 1 to number 224 (issued between April 1982 and April 1989).

of the firm based on its income-generating potential may well be very different from the value of its constituent parts.

Figure 2.1 plots the accounting assessment of the value of a firm to its shareholders — the sum of equity and reserves, against the market's estimate — the number of shares times their price. Again the link is obvious but it is approximate and erratic. A more specific example concerns DSM NV. The book value of equity for the last three years has been significantly more than the market value. Obviously the relationship is erratic for this firm and for the market as a whole. The latest market to book ratio for DSM is slightly less than 1 whereas the average for the Dutch market as a whole is 2.2, see Table 2.4.

Table 2.4 DSM NV Comparison of book and market value

	Dec 31 1991 (Fl m)	Dec 31 1992 (Fl m)	Dec 31 1993 (Fl m)
Book value of shareholders' equity	4,176	4,321	4,161
Market value of shareholders' equity	3,098	2,674	3,825
Market to book	0.74	0.61	0.92

Source: Extel Financial.

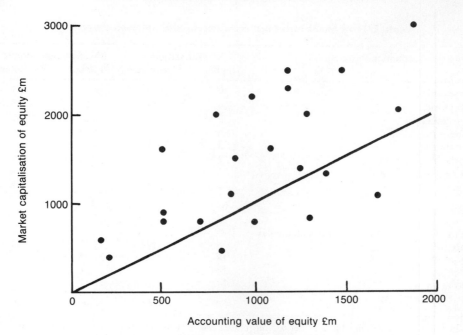

Figure 2.1 Accounting value of equity versus stock market capitalisation. The data refer to a cross-section of companies from the FT 100. Companies whose accounting value is equal to the market capitalisation would lie on the line shown.

2.5.2 *Profit vs cash flow*

There is no immediate relationship between profit and cash flow. Profit can be expected to generate cash flows, but the need for investment in working capital and fixed assets ensures that the link is indirect. There is no obvious relationship. The large degree of subjectivity and estimation required when computing a profit figure further distances the two concepts. A brief glance at the consolidated statement of cash flows for DSM NV reveals how substantially the measure of cash flow can depart from that of profit. The downturn in profit in 1993 has not significantly affected cash flows from operations, however, most of the adjustment is for depreciation as a non-cash expense. If we replace depreciation with the investment in tangibles which will have to be depreciated we see that only in 1993 does the cash flow provide sufficient funds for investment, see Table 2.5.

2.5.3 *Recognition and matching*

The income is taken to the profit and loss account not when the order is received, nor when cash payment is made, but (usually) when the product is delivered. Expenses are taken to the profit and loss account, either when incurred in the case of non-operating expenses, or when the revenue for the product they have created is accounted for. Thus an attempt is made to match expenses to relevant income. This is one of the primary

Table 2.5 DSM NV Comparison of profit and cash flows

	Dec 31 1991 (Fl m)	Dec 31 1992 (Fl m)	Dec 31 1993 (Fl m)
Net income after tax and extraordinary items	516	224	118
Cash from operations (actually after tax and extraordinary items)	874	725	784
Net investment in tangible assets	1,304	1,005	644

Source: Extel Financial.

problems of historic cost accounting, as the required valuation of expenses capitalised involves expectations about the future.

Four particularly troublesome problems concern the depreciation of fixed assets, the capitalisation of intangible assets, the recognition of income and expenses, ordinary or extraordinary, and the revaluation of property. These are expanded on below.

1. Depreciation

The problems of matching are especially significant in the case of the depreciation (or amortisation) charged for long-lived assets. This expense is accounted for gradually over the expected life of the asset. Thus the balance sheet item is not an assessment of the declining value of an ageing asset, but the residual value of an expense not yet written off.

As an illustration the case of Cable & Wireless Plc is interesting. In 1986 the depreciation charge was 10.4 per cent of net tangible assets. This rate of depreciation gradually declined to 5.9 per cent in 1989 then climbed back to 9.2 per cent in 1993. If the maximum rate had still been applied in 1986 a further £92 m would have been written off reducing after tax profit by 27 per cent. It should be pointed out that the depreciation charges made by Cable & Wireless could well be perfectly appropriate and there is no necessary reason why the expense should be proportional to net assets. The point is simply that a 'correct' computation of depreciation does not exist and that even within one firm year on year comparisons may be misleading, see Table 2.6.

Table 2.6 Cable & Wireless Plc — depreciation rates

Year	Net book value of tangible assets	Depreciation of tangible assets	Rate of depreciation	Profit after taxation
1986	840	88	10.4	215
1987	1104	89	8.1	267
1988	1312	99	7.5	292
1989	2029	119	5.9	345
1990	2667	196	7.3	432
1991	3082	239	7.7	493
1992	3535	300	8.4	509
1993	4227	392	9.2	743

Source: Extel Financial.

Table 2.7 Grand Metropolitan Plc — brand values, equity and debt

Year	Net book value of intangible assets (brands) (£m)	Shareholders' equity (£m)	Net assets less equity (£m)
1988	588	3407	1143
1989	2652	2810	4455
1990	2317	3401	3687
1991	2464	3422	3638
1992	2492	3759	3516
1993	2924	3715	3981

Source: Extel Financial.

2. Intangible assets

Apart from tangible assets the problem of amortisation is particularly acute with intangibles such as goodwill, advertising, or research and development expenditure. Due to uncertainty surrounding the duration of benefits from intangible expenditure, most UK firms write off their advertising, research and development, and often goodwill, immediately.

A further recent development with intangible assets concerns the valuation of brand names and the inclusion of these values as assets in the balance sheet. The considerable subjectivity of the process and the reluctance of the firms to attempt to attribute a full market value to each brand means that this is a problematical activity. Grand Metropolitan Plc were one of the first companies to use brand valuation starting in 1988 and building up in 1989. The figure for 1993 was £2,924 m which contrasts with shareholders' equity of £3,715 m and total debt of £3,981 m, see Table 2.7. The leverage of the firm looks quite high with the intangible assets on the balance sheet, it would look impossibly high if they were written off. Clearly intangible assets do have a value. The difficulty for the analysts is that the valuation is subjective and is included on the balance sheet by some firms and not by others.

Conversely a company will have tended to write off any goodwill on consolidation, indeed one of the incentives for valuing intangibles is thought to be the need for reserves against which to write off goodwill. Non-UK European firms usually don't write off goodwill immediately but depreciate it gradually thereby reporting higher equity and lower profits. For the last year Carrefour SA, dealt with in more detail in the following chapter, reported net intangible assets of FFr 5,714 m whilst total equity stood at FFr 14,544 m. Obviously gearing would have looked much worse without this asset on the balance sheet but the company had to write off depreciation on intangibles of FFr 341 m which has a considerable impact on profit after tax of FFr 1,878 m, see Table 2.8. It should be noted that the valuation and gradual depreciation of goodwill are the normal accounting practice in developed economies. In this the UK is something of an exception.

3. Extraordinary items

Firms will often categorise costs, or more rarely income, as extraordinary, meaning that they do not fall within the normal activities of the firm and are not expected to recur.

Table 2.8 Carrefour SA — valuation and depreciation of goodwill

	Dec 31 1990 (FFr m)	Dec 31 1991 (FFr m)	Dec 31 1992 (FFr m)	Dec 31 1993 (FFr m)
Valuation of goodwill	1,413	6,431	6,314	6,201
Shareholders' funds	6,852	8,193	9,416	11,922
Amortisation of intangibles	60	207	340	341
Profit after tax	1,504	1,335	1,484	1,878

Source: Extel Financial.

This can be a useful function as analysts want to estimate the long-run earning potential of firms and split out transitory elements which are not expected to recur. Unfortunately it also proves to be an area where firms take advantage of the permissive nature of UK regulation and try and pass off recurring costs as atypical. Since 1993 the UK regulations have been considerably tightened by FRS 2 'Reporting Financial Performance' which brings UK GAAP into line with US GAAP and makes extraordinary items much rarer. Table 2.9, an example from Associated British Foods Plc, is not intended to demonstrate inappropriate classification of extraordinary or exceptional costs but just the extent to which these costs, presumed to be occasional, can actually prove to be common.

It should be noted that FRS 2 became obligatory for accounting years ending after 21 June 1993 and was recommended practice prior to that. This would probably explain the shift from extraordinary for 1991 and before to exceptional items thereafter.

Table 2.9 Associated British Foods — extraordinary and exceptional costs

	Apr 01 1989 (£ m)	Mar 31 1990 (£ m)	Sep 14 1991 (£ m)	Sep 12 1992 (£ m)	Sep 18 1993 (£ m)
Exceptional (above the line) costs					
Property sale				2.0	2.0
Investment property				(8.0)	8.0
Short-term investments				(37.0)	—
Business disposal				(8.0)	1.0
Profit after tax	245.2	297.0	492.2	240.0	363.0
Extraordinary (below the line) costs					
Business disposal	52.1	90.3	(104.2)		
Discontinued costs	—	(14.0)	(9.0)		
Investments	(9.5)	—	—		
Tax on extraords	(6.8)	3.9	1.4		
Minority interest on extraords	(13.2)	(29.7)	41.8		

Source: Extel Financial.

4. Revalued assets

Under certain circumstances, long-lived items may be revalued to their current valuations even though all other items in the accounts are historically valued. Normally, this would only happen to property and introduces a considerable degree of subjectivity and a lack of consistency across firms within the UK. It is not accepted practice in most other Western economies.

2.5.4 *Definition of the firm*

A further definitional problem which plagues accounting is to decide which assets or liabilities form part of the firm and which should be treated as external. Should a firm in which the holding company has an investment become part of the group with its assets and liabilities fully disclosed on the balance sheet or should it remain an investment where the net asset only is recorded? To what extent are the pension fund assets or liabilities part of the assets of the firm and should any over- or under-investment in the pension fund in past years be allowed to affect the income and expenses of the group? To what extent should liabilities which may become due (contingent liabilities) be incorporated in the accounts of the group or disclosed as notes to the accounts?

2.5.5 *Inflationary distortion*

As there is a difference between the date at which inputs are purchased, notably fixed assets and stock, the date at which they are used in the production process, and the date at which the product is sold, the original measure of cost may no longer be meaningful. Typically during periods of high inflation industrial and commercial firms find that their costs are understated inflating profit and their assets are understated as they are valued at the price that was paid some years before when the cost was considerably lower. This dual bias of higher profits and lower assets has a multiplicitive effect on the reported return on equity or capital.

Few firms in Europe produce inflation-adjusted accounts but the magnitude of the impact on capital intensive firms can be seen in Table 2.10 which takes extracts from Scottish Hydro Plc's reports for recent years. Not only is the impact on the balance sheet extremely significant but more than doubling the value of the fixed assets would have the same effect on depreciation.

Table 2.10 Scottish Hydroelectric Plc — comparison of historic cost and CCA balance sheet

	31/3/91 (£ m)	31/3/92 (£ m)	31/3/93 (£ m)	31/3/94 (£ m)
Fixed assets	862.9	917.7	957.4	1,007.0
Shareholders' funds	526.6	581.3	639.4	712.8
Fixed assets — CCA	2,150.4	2,149.6	2,239.8	2,435.9
Shareholders' funds — CCA	1,510.8	1,813.8	1,922.4	2,142.2

2.5.6 *Number of transactions*

When accounts are prepared for any company, there will be a great many transactions in various stages of completion at the accounting date and many more that will have been completed during the period under review. The sheer magnitude of the task involved in collating and valuing these many transactions presents a serious practical measurement problem for the accountant, and the degree of subjectivity involved complicates the auditor's task of verification. Two clear examples are the valuation of inventory and debtors. US research (Feroz *et al.*, 1992) referred to earlier in the chapter specifically identifies debtors and inventory as the two categories of accounting 'mis-statement' most often discovered by the SEC's regulatory arm.

2.6   Example financial reports

It can be seen from the preceding discussion that accounting is not only an imprecise language, but it is not always sure what it is trying to say let alone how to say it. Under these circumstances, the significance of the accounting numbers comes not from their absolute value but from the comparison with others. The problem here is to find valid comparisons. The measurement difficulties and the instability of any inherent bias mean that the performance for one company in any one year cannot easily be compared with the results of a different company or year. To give some insight into the information that can be drawn from accounting statements this section will describe the accounts of DSM NV, the Dutch chemicals combine, reproduced in Exhibit 2.1 and consider the meaning of various items in the light of the IASC's definitions.

Some difficulties in the mass of data presented and the awkwardness involved in making comparisons between organisations of differing size can be countered by the use of ratio analysis. This concentrates the information contained in accounting statements into summary statistics and in doing so attempts to standardise the ratio for size. Analysts also often express balance sheet items as a percentage of total equity capital, income statement figures as a percentage of turnover, and funds flow items as a percentage of funds from operations. This technique is simply a particular form of ratio analysis and is usually known as 'common size statements' and can be seen to facilitate inter-firm or inter-year comparisons where the magnitude of the analysed firms varies. The use of any one statistic on the financial statement as the denominator is a subjective decision. However, the technique of ratio analysis is deferred until the following chapter and we will take the financial statement items at their face value.

2.6.1   *The accounting statements*

The following sections are not a detailed explanation of accounting requirements though reference is made to some of the more significant anomalies and issues.

The balance sheet

The balance sheet format shown is not that prescribed by the European Community's Fifth Directive but this is a common difficulty encountered when using electronic databases and the layout of the balance sheet is quite clear. Many items in the balance sheet are supported by notes giving details of the composition of the entries or their method of computation. For the sake of simplicity most of these have been ignored but readers are strongly recommended to familiarise themselves with actual annual reports and accounts including the considerable amount of information contained in the notes to the accounts.

As noted earlier the IASC gives a definition of the components of the balance sheet. However, the IASC document goes on to give a much fuller description of the various items on the balance sheet. These definitions are somewhat legalistic but if the accounts of a firm are reviewed carefully with these definitions in mind it helps to clarify what is, and what is not, understood by the entries therein.

> 50. The definitions of an asset and a liability identifying their essential features do not attempt to specify the criteria that need to be met before they are recognised in the balance sheet. Thus, the definitions embrace items that are not recognised as assets or liabilities in the balance sheet because they do not satisfy the criteria for recognition discussed in paragraphs 82 to 98. In particular, the expectation that future economic benefits will flow to or from an enterprise must be sufficiently certain to meet the probability criterion in paragraph 83 before an asset or liability is recognised.

This appears rather confusing but the main point here is the economic substance dominates legalistic form as illustrated with the example of finance leases.

> 51. In assessing whether an item meets the definition of an asset, liability or equity, attention needs to be given to its underlying substance and economic reality and not merely its legal form. Thus, for example, in the case of finance leases, the substance and economic reality are that the lessee acquires the economic benefits of the use of the leased asset for the major part of its useful life in return for entering into an obligation to pay for that right an amount approximating to the fair value of the asset and the related finance charge. Hence, the finance lease gives rise to items that satisfy the definition of an asset and a liability and are recognised as such in the lessee's balance sheet.

An examination of the balance sheets and notes to the balance sheets reveals how these definitions of assets and liabilities become translated into financial statements. The typical balance sheet includes fixed assets, current assets, current liabilities, long-term liabilities, and equity capital and reserves. In some instances these assets and liabilities may be readily valued using the historic cost of the transaction. However, even when there is a historic cost available it is often unlikely that the value of the asset or liabilities is close to the historic cost.

With regards to the fixed assets there are three categories: intangible, tangible and financial assets. Intangible assets which include brands, patents, goodwill and start-up expenses. In the UK some firms have recently started to place a balance sheet value on their brands even where no purchase price has been paid to assist with valuation. Thus a firm which owns a long-established and widely known brand may be able to exploit that brand name and it is indisputable that the brand has considerable value but the difficulty is firstly that any value placed on brands, and other such intangibles, is likely to be very subjective, and secondly that some firms may choose to value their brands whilst others don't, making inter-firm comparisons invidious. Another common type of intangible asset is goodwill on consolidation. This arises where a firm purchases a subsidiary and values the net assets at less than the cost of purchase. In most countries this premium is termed goodwill and is treated as an asset to be depreciated. In the UK the asset is normally, but not necessarily, written directly off the reserves of the company in the year in which the subsidiary is purchased. Both brands and goodwill can create substantial differences between the balance sheets of firms from the same country and more obviously between firms using accounting regulations of different countries. For most firms start-up expenses will be a trivial component of the balance sheet assets. They represent the costs, often legal, of forming the firm and they would normally be written off quite quickly.

Tangible assets include property and plant and machinery. In most cases the value placed on these assets is the original cost of the assets less that amount that has been written off as an expense via depreciation. The amount written off can be seen on the accounts and it is apparent that this is considerably more significant for non-property assets. For DSM NV some 41 per cent of the properties' original cost has been written off to expenses via depreciation whereas almost 70 per cent of the other tangible assets (probably plant and machinery) has been written off. Very few British firms depreciate their property to the extent that DSM NV does. With regards to property assets, particularly in the UK, these may actually have been revalued upwards to reflect something approaching their current market value. The valuation of fixed assets is troublesome because of the length of time the firms hold these assets. It is rarely difficult to establish what they cost but that original cost can be seen as becoming increasingly irrelevant and again when conducting an inter-firm comparison it is difficult when the tangible assets have been purchased at widely different dates.

The final category of fixed asset comprises financial assets and in the case of DSM NV this is largely accounted for by their investments in associated companies — firms where the group is a substantial but not a controlling shareholder. Definitions of precisely what constitutes an associate firm differ according to local GAAP as does the valuation. The UK and the Netherlands have used the equity method of valuation for some time, where associates are valued at original cost plus the group's share of any profits earned since acquisition which have not been paid over as dividends — unless the value of the shares dips below this. However, many other European countries, Spain for example, have only recently adopted this method and previously used to carry associates at cost.

With regards to current assets it is more difficult to establish what an appropriate figure is for the historic cost. These assets are rarely held long enough to make their original value meaningless although it should be noted that with regards to the assessment of profit a small error in the value measurement on a substantial element of the costs — such as the cost of sales, can make a considerable difference. The category of stocks is an area where there is considerable difference between the accounting policies employed by firms and between countries. For example, it is common in the US to use the 'Last In First Out' (LIFO) basis as it has tax advantages but it tends to increase the cost of goods sold and reduce the balance sheet asset. In the UK LIFO is not used and firms use the 'First In First Out' (FIFO) basis. Other areas of difficulty are the proportion of overheads which should be allocated to stocks and work in progress and what profits, if any, should be taken on long-term work in progress. It can be seen from these comments that the further the stocks are processed the more difficult is their valuation. It should also be remembered that it is in the area of current assets and liabilities that many of the accounting failures have been centred. Again the relationship between the different classifications of current assets is very different for the various industries. For example, debtors would be expected to be low for High Street retailers, whereas stocks would be low for firms offering services. As with DSM NV various other items may appear in current assets but stocks, debtors and cash would account for most current assets for most firms.

Current liabilities are almost wholly composed of creditors — amounts owing for goods, services, taxation, declared dividends and other incurred expenses. The classification will also include short-term debt but although a debt may be payable in the short term it is not clear that its payment will be required. In other words many firms hold continuing short-term debt. Thus many firms are largely financed by current liabilities whether it is interest-bearing debt or simply amounts outstanding to the suppliers of the firm. Difficulties in valuation here centre on the recognition of expenses. It may be that some claims for payment are in dispute but current liabilities are largely invoiced monetary amounts and the computation of a value is not difficult.

Long-term debt represents, in the main, fixed interest borrowings. However, the date of maturity and the currency in which repayment will have to be made are of interest to the analysts. More recently the development of financial instruments which combine many of the attributes of equity with those of debt have made the valuation of debt much more difficult. Without venturing into the details of this complex area it should be noted that some firms are able to comply with the reporting requirements of the regulatory system in which they operate and yet it is clear that their accounts do not conform to the economic substance of the transaction.

Provisions represent distant liabilities which are expected to fall due in the foreseeable future as a result of the current activities of the company, although there is no present legal obligation. The commonest and most significant provision is deferred taxation which is another item which occasions considerable diversity of treatment between individual firms and between the treatment required by different national jurisdictions. UK regulations require that 'tax deferred or accelerated by the effect of timing differences should be accounted for to the extent that it is probable that a liability or asset will crystallise'. Thus the diversity in observed practice may reflect diversity in the tax position of the firms. However, it is also to be expected that a standard which leaves the assessment of the proportion that will crystallise to the account's preparers, will experience considerable subjectivity in implementation.

The finance provided by the shareholders is divided into four sections. The nominal value of the shares sold is ordinary share capital, and any excess over the nominal value charged for those shares is the share premium. There is no general difference between these, as together they represent the funds input into the firm by shareholders. Many firms carry preference shares which usually represent fixed interest equity without voting rights. The reserves incorporate all reserves attributable to the shareholders, such as the other reserve which is the residual value of all profits earned on behalf of the shareholders which have not yet been distributed to them in the form of dividends and the revaluation reserves which represent the write up of fixed assets, usually property, to better approximate to their current value. However, as no profit has yet been realised, this adjustment is not taken through the income statement. Minority interests represent the proportion of subsidiaries' net assets not owned by the group due to a shareholding of less than 100 per cent.

The income statement

The IASC provides definitions of the income statement and its components.

69. Profit is frequently used as a measure of performance or as the basis for other measures, such as return on investment or earnings per share. The elements directly related to the measurement of profit are income and expenses. The recognition and measurement of income and expenses, and hence profit, depend in part on the concepts of capital and capital maintenance used by the enterprise in preparing its financial statements.

70. The elements of income and expenses are defined as follows:
    (a) Income is increases in economic benefits during the accounting period in the form of inflows or enhancements of assets or decreases of liabilities that result in increases in equity, other than those relating to contributions from equity participants.
    (b) Expenses are decreases in economic benefits during the accounting period in the form of outflows or depletions of assets or incurrences of liabilities that result in decreases in equity, other than those relating to distributions to equity participants.

These basic definitions fail to clarify in depth what can and cannot be treated as expenses and liabilities. However, the IASC expand their definition further:

72. Income and expenses may be presented in the income statement in different ways so as to provide information that is relevant for economic decision-making. For example, it is common practice to distinguish between those items of income and expenses that arise in the course of the ordinary activities of the enterprise and those that do not. This distinction is made on the basis that the source of an item is relevant in evaluating the ability of the enterprise to generate cash and cash equivalents in the future; for example, incidental activities such as the disposal of a long-term investment are unlikely to recur on a regular basis. When distinguishing between items in this way consideration needs to be given to the nature of the enterprise and its operations. Items that arise from the ordinary activities of one enterprise may be unusual in respect of another.

Recall, however, that the classification of expenses, and, less often, revenues as extraordinary is one of the persistent problems experienced when analysing performance.

73. Distinguishing between items of income and expense and combining them in different ways also permit several measures of enterprise performance to be displayed. These have differing degrees of inclusiveness. For example, the income statement could display gross margin, profit from ordinary activities before taxation, profit from ordinary activities after taxation, and net profit.

Income

74. The definition of income encompasses both revenue and gains. Revenue arises in the course of the ordinary activities of an enterprise and is referred to by a variety of different names including sales, fees, interest, dividends, royalties and rent.

75. Gains represent other items that meet the definition of income and may, or may not, arise in the course of the ordinary activities of an enterprise. Gains represent increases in economic benefits and as such are no different in nature from revenue. Hence, they are not regarded as constituting a separate element in this framework.

76. Gains include, for example, those arising on the disposal of non-current assets. The definition of income also includes unrealised gains; for example, those arising on the revaluation of marketable securities and those resulting from increases in the carrying amount of long-term assets. When gains are recognised in the income statements, they are usually displayed separately because knowledge of them is useful for the purpose of making economic decisions. Gains are often reported net of related expenses.

77. Various kinds of assets may be received or enhanced by income; examples include cash, receivables and goods and services received in exchange for goods and services supplied. Income may also result from the settlements of liabilities. For example, an enterprise may provide goods and services to a lender in settlement of an obligation to repay an outstanding loan.

As with assets the analyst's problem with income is usually to ensure that the figures displayed have not been overstated. With expense the problem is again to try and ensure items which should be recorded are correctly treated. Thus interest capitalised or hidden in the exchange rate fluctuations of loans is more difficult to assess simply because it is not brought to the analyst's attention in the first place.

Expenses

78. The definition of expenses encompasses losses as well as those expenses that arise in the course of the ordinary activities of the enterprise. Expenses that arise in the course of the ordinary activities of the enterprise include, for example, cost of sales, wages and depreciation. They usually take the form of an outflow or depletion of assets such as cash and cash equivalents, inventory, property, plant and equipment.

79. Losses represent other items that meet the definition of expenses and may, or may not, arise in the course of the ordinary activities of the enterprise. Losses represent decrease in economic benefits and as such they are no different in nature from other expenses.

80. Losses include, for example, those resulting from disasters such as fire and flood, as well as those arising on the disposal of non-current assets. The definition of expenses also includes unrealised losses, for example, those arising from the effects of increases in the rate of exchange for a foreign currency in respect of the borrowings of an enterprise in that currency. When losses are recognised in the income statement, they are usually displayed separately because knowledge of them is useful for the purpose of making economic decisions. Losses are often reported net of related income.

The income statement presented in Exhibit 2.1 is reasonably detailed. Accounting statements or notes to the accounts usually break operating expenses down into a few broad categories either by function — production, selling, administration, for example, or type and cost of goods sold, wages and salaries etc. From the summary profit and loss accounts and from the breakdown it is possible to see a number of interesting characteristics of the firm. For DSM NV costs are largely raw materials bought in, work contracted out, wages and salaries and depreciation. The last of these is, of course, a matter of considerable subjectivity and may, especially in inflationary times, have little to do with the economic cost of utilising these assets.

In certain industries the determination of revenue is simple — for example, the food retailing industry. In others it is complex and these problems particularly face the builders and engineers where it is often difficult to know when to take sales and profit on long-term contracts. It has already been pointed out that the charge to the income statement in these operational categories is largely determined by the inventory valuation and depreciation policies used by the firm, and that in some industries research and development costs will also be significant and subjective.

The subsequent adjustments to operating profit are even more contentious than its determinants and though covered by a battery of regulations, allow some scope for manipulation. The serious analyst will be well advised to develop an understanding of the various alternative accounting treatments and their impact. Possibly the most contentious topics, after deferred tax which is not substantial in the examples examined, are the definitions of extraordinary items. In most countries GAAP lays down the criteria by which an expense or revenue may be deemed not to be in the normal course of business and therefore suitably accounted for 'below the line', rather than an element of operating profit 'above the line'. Insofar as management believes that external analysts are misled by accounting manipulations, there is some scope for excluding unwanted costs from the computation of normal profit by their classification as extraordinary. The comment that debits are extraordinary items and credits are normal trading items is only partly made in jest.

Cash flow statement

The disclosure requirements of the UK cash flow regulation FRS2, which covers the cash flow statement, are undemanding and flexible, though much more tightly defined than the predecessor, SSAP10. There remains considerable international diversity between the disclosures for cash, or funds, flow statements. Even so the cash flow statement should include profit or loss for the period, adjustments for items not involving the movement of funds (usually depreciation but including profit or losses on disposal of assets) and extraordinary items. Whilst the format of DSM NV's cash flow statement takes a little getting used to, it displays the main categories that would be expected. Net income, as per the profit and loss account, is adjusted by those accounting items which did not involve cash flows, to give a cash flow from operations figure. The way cash flow has been spent or recouped from assets is then explained followed by the cash raised or expended in financing activities to leave the changes in the cash balances. In many ways the cash flow statement can be more informative than other statements. It is relatively free from subjective accounting and reveals managerial choices, such as investment and financing decisions, which are less apparent from the balance sheet or income statement.

2.6.2 *International accounting differences*

At this stage, it would be needlessly confusing to report in detail the differences between various national accounting requirements. However, the significance of these differences can be illustrated by the 1993 annual report for Hanson Plc. This company has substantially increased its investment in the US over recent years and is now quoted on the New York

Stock Exchange (NYSE) as well as the London ISE. On page 52 of its report a quantified assessment is given of the differences in the UK and US accounting requirements for the year ended 30 September 1993, as shown in Exhibit 2.2.

The return on equity ratio swung from 18.5 per cent (25.8 per cent) as reported under the UK regime to 7.7 per cent (12.1 per cent) as reported using US accounting policies. Many of the causes of the revision have already been discussed in this chapter. The two main adjustments to income are for goodwill amortisation, not required in the UK, and deferred taxation, which the UK only requires insofar as a liability is likely to arise in the foreseeable future, whereas the US required full provision. With regards to the book value of equity the inclusion of goodwill on the US balance sheet more than doubles equity whilst the full provision for deferred tax and the reversal of UK revaluations of property moderate this effect.

The causes of differences in accounting requirements have been subject to much speculation. Nobes and Parker suggest that these can be broken down into seven categories. These are the legal systems, financing and ownership arrangements, taxation rules, the development of professional accountancy, the typical rate of inflation, theoretical developments, and historical accident (Nobes and Parker, 1995). Of these, it might be argued that financing arrangements are fundamental, as the substantial reliance on equity finance in the UK, USA and Netherlands leaves shareholders depending on accounting information for a realistic assessment of the prospects and performance of the firms. Conversely, for the family-owned or bank-financed firms of most European countries,

---

Exhibit 2.2

HANSON plc — Reconciliation to US accounting principles
The following is a summary of the estimated material adjustments to profit and ordinary shareholders' equity which would be required if US Generally Accepted Accounting Principles (US GAAP) had been applied.

	1993	1992
Profit available for appropriation as reported in the consolidated profit and loss account	734	1,089
Estimated adjustments:	(94)	(95)
Goodwill amortisation	(7)	(11)
Foreign currency translation	34	52
Pensions	(32)	(36)
Timberlands depletion and reforestation	(22)	(96)
Taxation	(121)	(186)
Ordinary shareholders' equity as reported in the consolidated balance sheet	3,953	4,224
Estimated adjustments:		
Goodwill and other intangibles	4,379	3,340
Revaluation of land and buildings	(166)	(166)
Pensions	223	189
Timberlands depletion and reforestation	(105)	(60)
Taxation	(320)	(102)
Estimated ordinary shareholders' equity as adjusted to accord with US GAAP	7,967	7,425

there is less need for performance assessment by external investors and more attention to conservatism and creditor protection. This is not to suggest that the other reasons are insignificant and certainly the tax laws can distort financial accounts considerably where the tax assessment is based on the published accounts. Where there are significant differences in international accounting practices, this has been alluded to during discussion of that practice.

The differences between accounting reports from different countries could arise as follows:

1. *Structural differences*. Business practices differ markedly across national boundaries. Thus, although accounting measures of gearing are notoriously inaccurate it is clear that French and German firms rely on equity finance to a much lesser degree than their UK or US competitors.

2. *Measurement differences*. A wide variety of differences in the measurement of accounting numbers can bias the data presented. For example, the Hanson Plc adjustment to US generally accepted accounting principles (GAAP) reported above includes deferred taxation, foreign currency translation, and the valuation of assets as significant adjustments. The variety in consolidation practices is also often significant. Gray (1980) examined the reported earnings of French, West German and UK firms and the adjustments suggested by EFFAS (European Federation of Financial Analysts Societies) to the earnings figures to standardise different accounting practices. Whereas the reported earnings of 77 per cent of French firms were pessimistic and 15 per cent optimistic, and 75 per cent of West German firms pessimistic and 17 per cent optimistic, only 14 per cent of UK firms were pessimistic and 58 per cent were optimistic. These studies have since been replicated for the US versus the UK, Sweden and Finland and confirm that significant differences do exist. This evidence would suggest that there are significant biases between accounting measurement practices even within the EU.

3. *Disclosure practice*. Even where measurement practices are in broad agreement, the disclosure treatment may differ. This is particularly noticeable with the goodwill on acquisition which is written off immediately in most UK accounts, but is carried as an asset and amortised by US firms. This may well explain an element of apparently poor return on capital employed as reported by the US firms.

These various differences have lead some commentators to question the progress achieved in standardisation of accounting practices. Rudolph suggests that corporations in much of Europe often have considerable leeway in deciding what financial data they will disclose and how it will be presented. Even now, the professional investor or analyst who has followed a company over a period of time may find it very difficult to gauge true performance.

The main areas of contention as seen by this analyst are the lack of consolidated accounts in southern Europe and Germany, the lack of detailed classification of costs, the failure to provide segmented data, reporting delays and infrequent reporting (Rudolph, 1989, p. 2). Apart from the first of these (and the EC Seventh Directive will require member states to enact legislation requiring consolidated accounts for financial years commencing after 31 December 1989) the perceived failures are the main areas of criticism of financial reporting within the US and UK (Arnold, Moizer and Noreen, 1984).

2.7   The implications of the efficient market hypothesis (EMH)

Some of the most extensive and significant empirical evidence relevant to the accounting disclosure is the evidence of efficient markets. Analysts apparently invest a considerable amount of time and effort in fundamental analysis and much of this effort may be devoted to an evaluation of the companies' financial reports. However, considerable research has been conducted in the US and UK which appears, albeit not unanimously, to suggest that the EMH is a substantially correct description of the share valuation process. As Keane (1980, p. 3) summarises it:

> ... the Efficient Market Hypothesis which is already accepted as a fact by many market economists regards the stock market as incorporating a highly efficient pricing mechanism, where the resulting prices are not only good estimates of worth but possibly the best available.

This ability of capital markets to produce impressive value estimates from available information has been divided into three categories, as follows:

1. Weak form market efficiency contends that all information contained in the past movement of share prices is contained in the current assessment of share price. Thus, so-called 'technical analysis' of past share price movements and trends could not produce better than market returns and is therefore not a valuable activity.
2. Semi-strong form market efficiency contends that all information contained in publicly available data, including published financial statements, is incorporated efficiently in the current share price. Under these circumstances, 'fundamental analysis' of financial statements and other sources of publicly available information could not produce extra returns.
3. Strong form efficiency suggests that all public or privately held information is impounded in an unbiased manner in the valuation of shares. This implies that even 'inside information' cannot be exploited.

The evidence for weak and semi-strong form efficiency is convincing, but not conclusive, whereas strong form efficiency is both more awkward to evaluate and more contentious. Even so, if we temporarily accept weak and semi-strong form efficiency, this has startling implications for financial reporting and analysis. The apparent conclusion would be that once accounting information is published, there is no point in expending resources in its analysis in order to try and identify mis-priced shares. Annual reports are not only publicly available, but their content is pre-empted by previously released information and therefore stands twice condemned. Yet the study by Arnold et al. (1984) indicates that fundamental analysis is the main focus of the analyst's work and that this work is directed towards the identification of mis-priced shares. In addition, surveys of the activities of stockholders in general also confirm that a great deal of attention is given to financial statements. Hines (1982) has summarised eight surveys of stockholders as well as two surveys of specialists. She concludes that:

> The Chair(men)'s Report appears to be the most popular section of the annual report. The Profit and Loss Statement appears to be the most popularly used section of the annual report for decision

making. Annual reports are an important primary source of information to individual shareholders. If shareholders cannot hope to make an abnormal return by the fundamental analysis of publicly available information, why do they perform the analysis thereby keeping the market efficient?

There are a number of possible reasons why this anomaly might exist. It may be that the faith placed in the EMH is misplaced and there are a number of reports evidencing inefficient markets. For example, 'during the 1980s, finance researchers began to report an increasing (and increasingly bewildering) array of anomalies with respect to the joint hypothesis of the CAPM and the EMH' (Bowers and Dimson, 1988, p. 4). These include the 'small firm effect', the 'turn of the year effect', and the 'weekend effect' to name but a few. One investigation by Dimson and Marsh found a weak but not insignificant correlation between forecasted returns and actual returns of 0.08, which appears modest but enabled the investing institution to 'outperform the market by 2.2 per cent in the year following the deal, representing some £3 million' (Dimson and Marsh, 1984). Note, however, that in the cited work there is no suggestion that these fortunate individuals were necessarily basing their recommendations on the accounting statements. They may have had access to inside (strong form) information. It should also be pointed out that for the average investor, the evidence is as good as confirming an efficient market as the benefits are so negligible and ephemeral that most investors would be unable to exploit them.

Certain specialised users of financial statements may have the skills to profit from fundamental analysis of financial statements. It is unlikely that the sophisticated analyst will be unaware of the evidence concerning the EMH or ignorant of his or her own returns from trading in shares as compared to the market return. Unless evidence to the contrary is available, the assumption for these experts is that they either examine financial statements for different reasons or that their experience entitles them to expect abnormal returns. There is no reason to believe that investors are homogeneous in their ability to interpret accounting information or in their objectives. A situation may be envisaged where the market price of a share is at an equilibrium, maintained by the conflicting demands from investors who have marginally differing assessments of the worth of a share, who have different time horizons or who have differing requirements for shares with particular growth or tax characteristics. It is reasonable to suppose that some variation in ability enables the more competent analysts to exploit this diversity of opinion to earn themselves an abnormal return and thereby to encourage their continued participation in the analysis of investment opportunities. Were this extra return not available, some migration from this type of work might be envisaged reducing its overall efficiency and thereby increasing the potential return for participants.

There may be objectives in the analysis which do not conflict with the EMH. For example, the valuation of unquoted shares or the assessment of the creditworthiness of firms, may rationally involve the examination of financial statements. Financial statements are also often used as a variable in a contractual relationship, most notably in payment by results arrangements or possibly where the legal standing of individuals, such as debenture holders, is dependent on financial results. Even where the share is traded in an apparently efficient market, the estimation of certain parameters such as the risk of the investment or the likely split between income or capital growth may be assisted by financial analysis. The search for information relevant to portfolio management may be a valuable exercise even in efficient markets.

Although the information contained in financial statements is normally pre-empted by previous disclosures of one kind or another, the subsequently released accounts validate the prior information which may not be considered trustworthy without such validation. The most obvious example of this is the issue of a qualified audit report which will often induce a substantial drop in the value of that company's shares.

2.8   Conclusion

This chapter has tried to illustrate the manner in which financial statements are constructed. There can be no doubt that an understanding of the underlying concepts and techniques of accounting is important to analysts wishing to incorporate information derived from these statements in their decision models. This is particularly so where allowance has to be made for different accounting practices in different industries or different countries. Considerable diversity was discovered with regard to the implementation of deferred taxation, the capitalisation of leases, the revaluation of fixed assets, the definition and disclosure of funds flow statements, the classification of items as extraordinary, and the treatment of research and development expenses. In addition, novel problems have surfaced with the difficulties of off-balance-sheet financing and the valuation of brands.

Further, the crucial discussion of the choice of accounting practice made by society was addressed briefly. Alternatives are available, but the selection of any one option in preference to another will have implications for the well-being of different constituencies in the financial reporting environment and in society in general. Hence, it is the economic consequences of specific disclosure practices which are increasingly the focus of attention during considerations of accounting choice. This shift from traditional stewardship-economic income models of accounting practice, to an information-decision relevance basis has been characterised by Beaver (1981) as an 'accounting revolution'. It is this revolutionary approach which is addressed in the major part of this text, where specific economic decisions are examined and the techniques of incorporating financial information into those decisions are evaluated. The process of change in institutional and theoretical practices will continue to affect the quality and availability of financial statements available to analysts.

The contention that change is endemic to the financial reporting environment can be supported by the programme being pursued by the IASC, regulators in each country and the academic community. Academic research on matters directly relevant to disclosure practice include segmented information, interim financial reports, management forecasts of financial data, greater disaggregation of income statements, reporting to employees and to society. There is also a continuing contentious programme to move the accounting systems of EU countries closer together, which is supported, though less intrusively, by the IASC. Given this programme for development, the interaction between the analysts and the regulatory bodies, together with the scope for incorporating newly prescribed information into decision models, should ensure that the next few years will be challenging.

─────────────────── QUESTIONS ───────────────────

1. Obtain the most recent set of published accounts for two industrial companies quoted on a stock exchange. Examine the first firm's accounting policies for:
    (a) Depreciation.
    (b) Revaluation of property.
    (c) Deferred taxation.
    (d) Research and development.
    (e) Extraordinary items.
    (f) Other substantive items.
    To what extent do the directors of the firm have the option to adopt alternative accounting policies? Have there been any substantive changes in accounting policy? As far as possible quantify the impact on earnings and capital of adopting the second firm's policies to the first and vice versa.

2. Obtain the accounts of a firm which include both historic cost accounts and inflation-adjusted accounts. In most countries this is fairly rare but a number of Dutch companies have done this for some time as have some British firms — especially those providing utilities (power, water etc.) where the industry is regulated by government or quasi-government organisations.
    (a) Outline the main differences between historic cost and inflation-adjusted accounts and explain why these differences occur.
    (b) Discuss the implications of these differences for the financial analyst.
    (c) Outline the advantages and disadvantages to a company of providing supplementary inflation-adjusted accounts.

3. Obtain the accounts of a firm which is listed on your national exchange and in the US and examine the reconciliation of equity and profit measured under local GAAP to that under US GAAP. This may be included in the financial statements but if not will probably be provided by the firm on application.
    (a) Outline the differences in US and local GAAPs for each of the categories contained in the reconciliation.
    (b) Discuss the implications of these differences for the financial analyst.
    (c) Outline the advantages and disadvantages to a company of having its shares traded in another country.

4. Study a recent example of an historical cost five-year record for a company. You are required to:
    (a) Present a report on the overall financial performance of the company as revealed in the five-year record.
    (b) Discuss what further information would be useful in analysing the financial performance.
    (c) Explain, briefly, how 'minority interests' arise in a set of accounts.
    (Society of Investment Analysts, Interpretation of Accounts and Corporate Finance, June 1988.)

5. Select a number of the IASC's definitions of aspects of financial reports and critically evaluate these definitions. Is there scope for ambiguity? Are there alternative definitions which might be preferred by different user groups? Are there conflicts between the definitions?

6.   Obtain the financial statements, including cash flow (or funds flow) statements, for two firms. Contrast the apparent performance using only the income statement and balance sheet. Contrast the performance using the cash flow statement as well as the other statements. Are the additional insights available from the flow statement significant?

7.   Define the following:
      (a) Deferred tax.
      (b) Minority interests.
      (c) Associated companies.
      (d) Subsidiaries.
      (e) Long-term debt.
      (f) Long-term contracts.
      (g) Extraordinary items.
      (h) Cash from operations.
      (i) Revaluation reserve.
      (j) Amortisation of goodwill.

References

Arnold, J., Moizer, P. and Noreen, E. (1984) Investment appraisal methods of financial analysts: A comparative study of US and UK practices, *International Journal of Accounting*, **19**, no. 2, 1–18.

Beaver, W. (1981) *Financial Reporting — An Accounting Revolution*, Prentice Hall, Englewood Cliffs.

Bowers, J. and Dimson, E. (1988) Introduction, in Dimson, E. (Ed.) *Stock Market Anomalies*, Cambridge University Press.

Dimson, E. and Marsh, P. (1984) An analysis of brokers' and analysts' unpublished forecasts of UK stock returns, *Journal of Finance*, December, **39**, no. 5, 1257–1292.

Feroz, E., Park, K. and Pastena, V. (1992) The financial and market effects of the SEC's accounting and auditing enforcement releases, *Journal of Accounting Research*, Supplement, **29**, 107–148.

Gray, S. (1980) The impact of international accounting differences from a security-analysis perspective, *Journal of Accounting Research*, Spring, 64–79.

Hines, R. (1982) The usefulness of annual reports: the anomaly between the efficient market hypothesis and shareholder surveys, *Accounting and Business Research*, Autumn, 296–309.

IASC (1989) Framework for the preparation and presentation of financial statements, *International Accounting Standards Committee*, July.

Keane, S. (1980) *The Efficient Market Hypothesis and the Implications for Financial Reporting*, ICAS, Edinburgh.

Nobes, C. and Parker, R. (1995) *Comparative International Accounting*, Prentice Hall, Hemel Hempstead.

Pike, R., Meerjanssen, J. and Chadwick, L. (1993) The appraisal of ordinary shares by investment analysts in the UK and Germany, *Accounting and Business Research*, Autumn, 489–499.

Rudolph, S. (1989) *Understanding Financial Statements*, Phillips and Drew, London.

Smith, T. and Hannah, R. (1991) *Accounting for Growth*, UBS Phillips and Drew, January.

Vergossen, R. (1993) The use and perceived importance of annual reports by investment analysts in the Netherlands, *European Accounting Review*, September, 219–244.

CHAPTER 3

Ratio Analysis: Methods and Issues

—————————————— **CHAPTER OBJECTIVES** ——————————————

This chapter will:

1 Introduce the reader to the basic technique of ratio analysis.

2 Examine the statistical relationship between the numerator and denominator of a ratio.

3 Discuss the relationship between various ratios and the problem of selecting a sparse but comprehensive set of ratios.

4 Illustrate the cross-sectional distribution of ratios and describe how to deal with non-normal data sets.

The prominence of the technique of financial ratio analysis is primarily a response (a) to the quantity of information contained in a set of financial statements and (b) to the problem of comparability between firms of differing sizes. The most usual and least sophisticated use of ratio analysis is the substitution of a small set of ratios to replace the complexity of the detailed financial statements. Thus the MicroExstel data reproduced in Exhibits 3.1 and 3.2 contain a selection of ratios for four different UK industries to demonstrate inter-industry differences and four countries to illustrate international differences. Although these ratios exhibits include 20 to 30 ratios each they are still a selection from a more comprehensive set. However, this compares with an impossibly large set of financial numbers in the accounts of any one company.

The use of ratios to make comparisons between organisations of different scale is also crucial. In the year ended 31 December 1993 Carrefour SA's earnings, before extraordinary items, was FFr 1,665 m but how do we know whether that is good or bad? It is only when we compare the earnings with the shareholder's capital of FFr 11,922 m and compute a rate of return of 14 per cent that we can assess the firm's performance by comparison with competitors or prior years.

In some cases ratio analysis which relies on the skill of the analyst can be replaced

──────────── **Exhibit 3.1**　Average ratios for four UK industries ────────────

COMPANIES	Build 1993	Eng. Con 1993	Food. R 1993	Trans. 1993
PROFITABILITY RATIOS				
Return on equity	(9.8)	(3.8)	14.8	5.5
Return on net assets	(1.2)	2.0	17.4	7.7
Operating RoNA	(3.8)	(0.2)	17.1	6.3
Tax ratio	(15.4)	(93.3)	29.8	23.1
Investment return	9.7	15.5	19.0	12.2
Op profit margin	(1.5)	(0.1)	5.7	8.6
CoGS/Sales	71.3	67.3	73.7	61.6
Admin and dist/Sales	6.7	7.1	5.2	7.5
Staff cost/Sales	20.4	24.0	9.9	25.9
Sales per employee	107.71	81.21	86.61	74.22
Staff cost/Employees	21.97	19.48	8.57	19.24
ASSET UTILISATION				
Sales/Op net assets	2.61	2.06	3.01	0.73
Sales/Properties	16.67	9.39	3.22	3.19
Sales/OTFA	13.38	5.87	13.33	1.04
Stock days	101	68	18	25
Debtor days	59	67	7	71
Creditor days	99	81	41	90
Op NA per employee	41.27	39.43	28.73	101.21
FINANCIAL STRUCTURE				
LMS loan/NA (book)	33.8	26.9	22.4	46.8
LMS loan/NA (market)	0.0	0.0	0.0	0.0
Total debt/TA (book)	59.2	49.7	43.8	54.5
Short loans/Loans	43.3	37.0	24.4	30.3
Interest cover	(0.3)	0.6	6.7	1.6
Ave interest rate	0.0	0.0	0.0	0.0

by the explicit formulation of a statistical decision model. There are models which attempt to predict bankruptcy, merger activity, bond rating and changes in earnings which rely on ratios as the basic variables. The same considerations apply though. The ratios are used to encapsulate the firm's performance in a sparse manner and allow for contrast between firms of different size.

However, the use of financial ratios by both practitioners and researchers is often motivated by tradition and convenience rather than resulting from theoretical considerations or from careful statistical analysis. As Lev and Sunder (1979) comment in their comprehensive review:

> . . . it appears that the extensive use of financial ratios by both practitioners and researchers is often motivated by tradition and convenience rather than resulting from theoretical considerations or from careful statistical analysis.

It is for this reason that an analysis of the statistical properties of ratios is included in this chapter. It is dangerous to use ratios in an ad hoc manner without an understanding of (a) the relationship between the two components of the ratio, (b) the interrelationship between different ratios, and (c) the distributional characteristics of ratios.

———————————— **Exhibit 3.2** Average ratios for four countries————————————

	France 1992 Dec 31	Germany 1992 Dec 31	UK 1992 Dec 31	US 1992 Dec 31
Profitability				
Return on equity	6.4	2.4	8.7	2.2
Return on risk capital	6.1	2.3	8.6	1.4
PBIT/Cap employed	8.2	5.5	10.6	9.3
PAT/Capital employed	2.8	1.1	4.9	3.8
Tax ratio	32.7	66.2	38.1	37.7
PBIT/Sales	6.7	3.7	9.1	8.6
PAT/Sales	2.2	0.7	4.2	3.5
Gross profit/Sales	82.8	81.3	51.2	50.6
S,G&A/Sales	4.6	4.1	10.7	13.3
Mats and services/Sales	29.6	34.4	9.7	0.0
Staff costs/Sales	19.2	25.6	18.0	3.2
Number of employees	17,910	16,961	10,392	32,991
Asset utilisation				
Sales/Cap employed	1.23	1.50	1.16	1.08
Sales/Tangible FA	2.72	3.33	1.82	2.03
Stock days	65	45	45	35
Trade debtor days	58	42	46	12
Other debtor days	34	35	12	47
Trade creditor days	48	24	35	30
Gearing				
Gross debt/Equity	116.9	65.5	57.5	116.9
Gross debt/Risk capital	91.0	58.5	53.6	96.6
Net debt/Equity	83.8	21.3	31.6	95.8
Net debt/Risk capital	65.2	19.0	29.4	79.1
Liabilities/Risk capital	225.9	269.1	127.0	196.9
PBIT/Interest expense	2.0	2.1	3.5	2.8
PAT/Interest expenses	0.7	0.4	1.6	1.1
Ave interest rate	11.9	15.1	10.5	9.0
Dividend payout %	46.3	142.1	78.7	378.6
Liquidity				
Current ratio	1.62	2.99	1.78	1.43
Liquid ratio	1.03	2.11	1.13	0.89
Cash days	33	31	43	25

3.1 Introduction

The motivations for using ratio analysis might be classified into four overlapping categories, and these are detailed as follows.

To act as a summary statistic

Probably the most usual and least sophisticated use of ratio analysis is the substitution of a small set of ratios to replace the complexity of the detailed financial statements. This enables the analyst to screen the information rapidly and simplifies the assimilation of the crucial aspects of a firm's performance. The obvious limitations of this approach, the ad hoc selection of ratios and the loss of detail, are balanced by the simplicity and low cost entailed in its application. Detailed investigations of the techniques employed by investment analysts suggest that an approach using simplistic ratio analysis may be used to select companies as suitable for more detailed investigation, but once a company has passed through such screening a considerably more refined approach is adopted (Bouwman, Frishkoff and Frishkoff, 1987).

To identify industry benchmarks

It is suggested that corporations may use industry averages to identify areas of abnormal performance in their own organisation, in order to focus corrective action where necessary. Lev demonstrated the tendency for companies' financial ratios to drift towards industry averages over time (Lev, 1969).

The suitability of the industry average as an appropriate point of comparison is a matter of some interest. Attention needs to be paid to the distribution of the ratio. Figure 3.1 presents the return on capital employed (ROCE) for a cross-section of firms. Obviously, the distribution is not symmetrical. The mean (21.7 per cent) does not coincide with the mode (24 per cent), the most likely statistic, or the median (20.9 per cent), the middle reading. This is typical for accounting ratios and under these circumstances it is not obvious which measure of the centre of the distribution is to be preferred. Indeed, it may be that the weighted average ROCE, which measures the average profitability of the industry as a whole, is more useful. In this case, the weighted ROCE is 19.3 per cent.

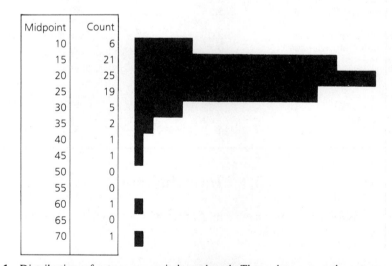

Midpoint	Count
10	6
15	21
20	25
25	19
30	5
35	2
40	1
45	1
50	0
55	0
60	1
65	0
70	1

Figure 3.1 Distribution of return on capital employed. These data report the return on capital employed for the industrial and commercial firms included in the FTSE 100 list as at November 1988. Return on capital is calculated here as pre-tax profit expressed as a percentage of equity plus debt.

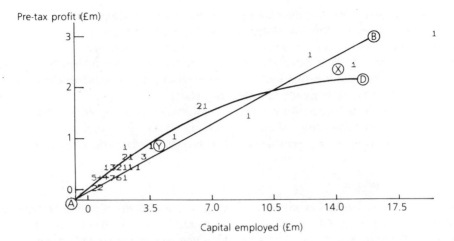

Figure 3.2 Pre-tax profit versus capital employed. + indicates more than nine readings at that co-ordinate.

If the relationship between the numerator and denominator is non-linear, for example there may be economies of scale which imply a higher rate of return in larger firms, or has a non-zero intercept, the distribution of the ratio is unlikely to be symmetrical. Thus, even where a measure of the central tendency is chosen, this may not be a suitable reference point for the whole industry.

Figure 3.2 displays the relationship between the measured pre-tax profit and the capital employed for the sample. In this instance, visual inspection suggests that the data are fairly well represented by a straight line passing through the intercept. However, for the sample examined, the weighted ROCE is 2.4 per cent below the mean ROCE which would suggest that larger firms tend to report lower ROCE than smaller ones. Cross-sectional regression analysis of the sample confirms a statistically significant positive intercept and a statistically significant departure from a linear relationship consistent with diseconomies of scale.

As an input to formal decision models

When interpreting ratios for decision-making purposes, the results depend on the individual decision-maker's experience of the industry, coupled with the information that can be drawn from time-series or cross-sectional trends. However, in some cases this intuitive analysis can be replaced by a statistical decision model. Many examples are available where such a modelling approach has become a generally accepted method of data analysis. These include share valuation or stock selection models, the identification of takeover targets, the estimation of investment risk, evaluating the investment rating of bonds and the use of 'Z-scores' to predict corporate failure.

Here again, the distributional characteristics of the ratio statistic are matters for consideration. Most statistical tests make assumptions regarding the probability distribution of the population; typically that the data are well described by the normal distribution. Some statistical techniques are sufficiently robust to deal with non-normal distributions of the variables, but even here this may have important practical implications, particularly for the diagnostic tests of the estimated relationship. Other procedures require that the variables exhibit normality, or at least a reasonable approximation thereof, or some other specified distribution. Still other (non-parametric) tests are able to handle data with unspecified distributions. Clearly attention should be paid to the distributional characteristics of ratios and the implications for statistical modelling.

Also problematical is the interrelationship between the variables. For example, a high correlation between supposedly independent variables could pose problems for statistical analysis as well as imply an element of redundancy in the data collection process.

To standardise for size

The use of ratios as deflators in order to make comparisons between organisations operating on different scales is implicit in all of the uses mentioned above. Indeed, in some cases this may be the prime reason for using ratios. If it is unreasonable to expect firms of differing sizes to perform in a comparable manner, some modification of the basic technique of ratio analysis may be required. In an economy where (dis)economies of scale are to be expected and market imperfections are likely, it is not apparent that a simplistic standardisation for size is desirable. It should also be noted that the removal of the size variable from the analysis may not be helpful. Size could well be an important explanatory variable for the decision in hand, in which case its elimination from the analysis will obviously be counter-productive. For example, it is clear that small firms bear considerably more risk of financial failure than do larger firms, yet some models of failure prediction carefully eliminate size from their analysis.

This chapter will proceed by informally reviewing the basic ratio analysis technique which may be familiar to many readers. A brief review of the problems inherent in this type of analysis is presented. Example financial statements from Carrefour SA, the French supermarket chain, will provide the illustrative material (see Exhibit 3.3). The following section will review the functional relationship between the numerator and the denominator of ratios to establish whether or not the basic ratio assumptions of linearity and a zero intercept are generally tenable. Attention is then turned to the distributional characteristics of selected ratios and the implications of any departure from normality. The last substantive problem addressed in this chapter is the selection of key ratios from the wide bank of alternatives.

3.2 Ratio analysis — techniques and problems

As with other examples of accounting, data ratios are only informative when related to a valid point of comparison. The ratio statistic in itself is uninformative and, despite their popularity, supposed benchmarks can be misleading, especially where applied to firms in different industries. Comparatives for financial analysis can be obtained, either through a time-series comparison with the examined companies' previous results, or from a cross-sectional perspective using competitors' performance or industry averages. Therefore a typical approach would be to set out the recent results for the ratio of interest for a firm,

———————— **Exhibit 3.3** Example accounts for ratio analysis ————————

CARREFOUR

CONSOLIDATED PROFIT AND LOSS ACCOUNT

	Dec 31 1989 FFr m	Dec 31 1990 FFr m	Dec 31 1991 FFr m	Dec 31 1992 FFr m	Dec 31 1993 FFr m
TURNOVER	73,866	75,848	100,377	117,139	123,204
Incr in stocks etc	686	427	456	791	483
Raw materials etc	(63,118)	(63,970)	(84,471)	(98,199)	(103,025)
Staff expenses	(5,366)	(5,969)	(8,451)	(10,167)	(10,171)
Misc provisions	(125)	(125)	(90)	(205)	(260)
Other trading exps	(4,775)	(4,921)	(6,961)	(8,345)	(8,764)
Rental income net	205	266	380	594	621
TRADING PROFIT	1,373	1,556	1,240	1,608	2,088
Interest/inv income	921	714	985	1,052	1,167
Interest payable	(458)	(279)	(805)	(1,297)	(1,191)
Other income net	174	230	389	725	684
PROFIT BEFORE TAX	2,010	2,221	1,809	2,088	2,748
Tax	(664)	(717)	(474)	(604)	(870)
PROFIT AFTER TAX	1,346	1,504	1,335	1,484	1,878
Net equity A/c inc	100	105	197	303	245
Minority interests	(265)	(257)	(325)	(448)	(458)
Net debits	(165)	(152)	(128)	(145)	(213)
Exord (losses) gains	–	–	–	(4)	1,345
NET INCOME	1,181	1,352	1,207	1,335	3,010
Ordinary dividends	(383)	(416)	(416)	(448)	(538)
RETAINED PROFITS	798	936	791	887	2,472

NOTES TO CONSOLIDATED PROFIT AND LOSS ACCOUNT

	Dec 31 1989 FFr m	Dec 31 1990 FFr m	Dec 31 1991 FFr m	Dec 31 1992 FFr m	Dec 31 1993 FFr m
OTHER TRADING EXPS					
Depreciation	(931)	(1,084)	(1,702)	(2,161)	(2,330)
Amortn of intangibles	(61)	(60)	(207)	(340)	(341)
Misc other tdg exps	(3,783)	(3,777)	(5,052)	(5,844)	(6,093)
	(4,775)	(4,921)	(6,961)	(8,345)	(8,764)
TAX BY TYPE					
Current taxation	(710)	(673)	(320)	(754)	(913)
Deferred taxation	46	(44)	(154)	150	43
	(664)	(717)	(474)	(604)	(870)
EXORD (LOSSES) GAINS					
Xord prof on disposal	–	–	–	287	1,605
Misc Xord losses	–	–	–	(291)	(260)
	–	–	–	(4)	1,345
Av no of staff	46,600	51,300	65,900	76,100	81,500
No of staff at y/e	–	–	76,200	79,500	85,200

CARREFOUR

CONSOLIDATED BALANCE SHEETS

	Dec 31 1989 FFr m	Dec 31 1990 FFr m	Dec 31 1991 FFr m	Dec 31 1992 FFr m	Dec 31 1993 FFr m
FIXED ASSETS					
Intangible assets	1,263	1,419	6,562	6,083	5,714
Tangible assets	9,822	11,859	18,189	19,837	20,674
Financial assets	2,076	1,906	2,981	3,628	3,863
	13,161	15,184	27,732	29,548	30,251
OWN EQUITY SHARES	-	-	348	425	757
MISC ASSETS	202	170	278	-	-
CURRENT ASSETS					
Stocks	4,465	4,804	7,689	8,420	8,631
Trade debtors	1,955	314	442	293	271
Tax recoverable	-	-	-	1,471	1,364
Misc debtors	6,373	6,139	9,693	9,237	9,545
Cash & equivalents	868	923	1,326	1,404	1,490
Notes, bills & invs	3,378	3,261	1,267	1,278	1,082
Misc current assets	152	152	149	-	-
	17,191	15,593	20,566	22,103	22,383
CREDS due within 1 yr					
Debt due within 1 yr	1,843	1,097	5,139	3,437	1,664
Trade creditors	13,469	14,831	22,197	23,286	23,586
Misc creditors	4,951	4,427	6,012	6,467	6,878
	20,263	20,355	33,348	33,190	32,128
NET CURRENT LIABS	(3,072)	(4,762)	(12,782)	(11,087)	(9,745)
TOTAL ASSETS LESS CURRENT LIABILITIES	10,291	10,592	15,576	18,886	21,263
CREDS due after 1 yr					
Long term debt	1,860	1,358	4,155	5,264	4,413
PROVISIONS	1,008	1,088	1,552	1,622	2,306
NET ASSETS	7,423	8,146	9,869	12,000	14,544
Ordinary shares	639	639	1,280	1,281	1,281
Share premium	890	896	266	274	274
Currency apprecn res	(87)	(386)	(77)	(283)	(370)
Misc reserves	4,740	5,703	6,724	8,144	10,737
SHAREHOLDERS' FUNDS	6,182	6,852	8,193	9,416	11,922
Minority interests	1,241	1,294	1,676	2,584	2,622
NET ASSETS	7,423	8,146	9,869	12,000	14,544

NOTES TO CONSOLIDATED BALANCE SHEETS

	Dec 31 1989 FFr m	Dec 31 1990 FFr m	Dec 31 1991 FFr m	Dec 31 1992 FFr m	Dec 31 1993 FFr m
TANGIBLE ASSETS					
Property cost/valn	7,769	9,423	15,378	16,514	17,926
Oth tang FA cost/valn	6,574	7,815	11,583	13,340	14,514
Cap w-i-p gross c/f	875	752	1,627	1,400	1,317
	15,218	17,990	28,588	31,254	33,757
Total depreciation	(5,396)	(6,131)	(10,399)	(11,417)	(13,083)
Tangible assets	9,822	11,859	18,189	19,837	20,674

CARREFOUR

FINANCIAL ASSETS

Invs in assoc cos	1,112	1,607	2,360	2,837	2,767
Other trade invs	964	299	621	388	579
Trade investments	2,076	1,906	2,981	3,225	3,346
Misc financial assets	-	-	-	403	517
	2,076	1,906	2,981	3,628	3,863

DEBT BY TYPE

Bonds	-	-	-	1,000	1,000
Bank loans	-	-	-	1,500	1,500
Bills & notes	-	-	-	2,674	1,260
Misc debt	-	-	-	3,527	2,317
	3,703	2,455	9,294	8,701	6,077

DEBT BY MATURITY

Debt due within 1 yr	1,843	1,097	5,139	3,437	1,664
Due within 1 to 2 yrs	-	-	-	1,462	699
Due within 2 to 5 yrs	-	-	-	1,400	1,368
Due after 5 years	-	-	-	2,283	2,105
Due after 1 year	1,860	1,358	4,155	-	-
Misc debt by maturity	-	-	-	119	241
	3,703	2,455	9,294	8,701	6,077

DEBT BY SECURITY

Secured	-	-	-	54	41
Unsecured	-	-	-	8,647	6,036
	3,703	2,455	9,294	8,701	6,077

PROVISIONS

Deferred taxation	558	680	709	620	697
Pension provisions	119	69	203	314	353
Misc provisions	331	339	640	688	1,256
	1,008	1,088	1,552	1,622	2,306

NET ASSETS include

Legal reserves	64	64	103	124	128

Additional notes to CONSOLIDATED BALANCE SHEETS

	Dec 31 1989 FFr m	Dec 31 1990 FFr m	Dec 31 1991 FFr m	Dec 31 1992 FFr m	Dec 31 1993 FFr m
INTANG FIXED ASSETS					
Goodwill	1,211	1,413	6,431	6,314	6,201
Other	440	489	1,276	1,060	1,069
Depreciation	(388)	(483)	(1,145)	(1,291)	(1,556)
	1,263	1,419	6,562	6,083	5,714

Table 3.1   Return on equity — time-series and cross-sectional comparison

	1988	1989	1990	1991	1992
Tarmac	30.8	16.4	7.7	0.9	(25.8)
Redland	20.6	23.0	18.5	9.2	8.5
Industry	19.5	22.1	19.2	12.6	6.1

together with those of the industry as a whole. As it is often difficult to find a homogenous industry with which to compare the firm it may well be useful to select one or more competitors who are of similar size and structure. It is quite usual to look at a series of about five years' results as the firm represented in the earlier years in a longer time-series has little to do with the firm at the end of the period. Here we use Tarmac, Redland and the industry average to illustrate the point.

It can be seen from Table 3.1 that Tarmac's return on equity has declined in recent years. This has been accompanied by a decline in the industry as a whole and for Redland but not to the same extent.

Some of the difficulties which beset the technique of ratio analysis are outlined in Sections 3.2.1 to 3.2.6.

3.2.1   *Ratio selection*

One problem that causes difficulties for the use of ratio analysis is the choice of ratios. Some attempt must be made to select those elements of corporate performance which are most revealing and to identify statistics which illuminate these factors effectively. The use of too many ratios often means that a sub-set of the ratios examined is redundant. For example, it is difficult to see what different conclusion an analyst would come to from examining Tarmac's return on capital rather than return on equity for the last five years. The use of too few may result in the analyst missing certain important considerations. Many analysts and texts suggest that analysts should examine the following dimensions of firm performance — return on capital, profitability, liquidity, gearing and asset turnover. The ratios presented in Exhibits 3.1 and 3.2 use similar classifications but put return and profitability measures into one group and liquidity and asset utilisation into another. A further group of ratios which might often be examined is the financial market ratios such as market-to-book and price-to-earnings measures. The next section examines this classification in more detail and investigates its source.

3.2.2   *Accounting estimation*

Ratios based on accounting numbers incorporate, and sometimes exaggerate, the limitations of accounting statements as discussed in the preceding chapter. The exaggeration comes when the two constituents of a ratio are biased in opposite directions and dividing one by the other expands the error. For example, during inflationary times accounting profits of industrial and commercial firms are often overstated whilst the balance sheet assets, and hence the equity, are often understated. A return on equity measure is therefore affected by two multiplicative errors and should be used with care. Hence it should be remembered that accounting-based ratios retain all the faults of accounting itself including subjectivity and bias. Occasionally analysts prefer to replace accounting-based measures with those derived from the market. This particularly applies to the capitalisation of equity and debt. Unfortunately in many cases accounting statements are the only source of estimates of financial variables. However, for Carrefour SA we are able to obtain an independent valuation of equity from the capital market as noted below.

Carrefour SA	Dec 31 1989 (FFr m)	Dec 31 1990 (FFr m)	Dec 31 1991 (FFr m)	Dec 31 1992 (FFr m)	Dec 31 1993 (FFr m)
Shareholders' funds					
Book value	6,182	6,852	8,193	9,416	11,922
Market value	22,890	20,5369	29,016	29,609	53,524

It is clear that substituting the market value for the book value would change most ratios and particularly the gearing and return to equity ratios.

3.2.3 Unavailable data

Unfortunately, the financial reports of private companies in particular are often severely delayed, and even quoted companies may require up to three months to prepare their annual report and accounts. Furthermore, the analyst will often be concerned with a subsidiary or division of the company publishing financial statements and these results may not be available. The improvements in the segmented data published by quoted firms help but do not entirely overcome this. Thus for Carrefour SA turnover and profit before taxation are provided each year for six geographical regions allowing analysts to compute growth rates and margins but many important considerations such as return on equity and gearing remain hidden.

3.2.4 Unsynchronised data

In the UK companies' accounting year-ends are varied which means that inter-company comparisons are often between accounting reports covering different periods. The reader only has to look at the results for Tarmac presented in Table 3.1 to see how much difference a change in year-end can make. If the year-end for Tarmac was shifted by six months the indicated performance of Tarmac could be very different. This problem must be especially severe for firms that deal in commodities for which the price is erratic. For example, the balance sheets of two petroleum firms might be very different if separated by six months which span one of the all too frequent substantial shifts in oil prices. Firms in many countries, France and Germany for example, tend to have December year-ends but even these are not uniform.

3.2.5 *Non-standardised accounting*

Accounting policies and practices can vary between companies with little to guide the analyst, save minimally informative policy statements, and the loose constraints imposed by the various elements of the regulatory system. The difficulties created are especially severe where the scope of the review crosses national boundaries, and accounting policies become susceptible to varying regulatory prescriptions and may be ineffectively monitored or enforced. Exhibits 3.1 and 3.2 demonstrate how much accounting results are subject to industry and/or country factors.

With regard to the example accounts for Carrefour the following information is available regarding the valuation of goodwill on consolidation. Whilst such valuation is common in most developed economies, UK firms would typically write the whole of goodwill off against reserves in the year of acquisition thereby reducing the value of equity but avoiding the need to charge depreciation against profits. It is quite clear that this adjustment would make a considerable difference to the financial statement and to ratios calculated from it.

Carrefour SA
Additional notes to consolidated balance sheets

	Dec 31 1989 (FFr m)	Dec 31 1990 (FFr m)	Dec 31 1991 (FFr m)	Dec 31 1992 (FFr m)	Dec 31 1993 (FFr m)
Intangible fixed assets					
Goodwill	1,211	1,413	6,431	6,314	6,201
Other	440	489	1,276	1,060	1,069
Depreciation	(388)	(483)	(1,145)	(1,291)	(1,556)
	1,263	1,419	6,562	6,083	5,714

3.2.6 *Negative numbers and small divisors*

Negative numbers can be problematical where a transformation of the original data is required, possibly to approximate better to a normal distribution or where a ratio is to be calculated by dividing through by a negative. It often happens that financial databases are rather stupid in their computation of ratios. Thus a loss of $10 m on a firm with a negative equity of $10 m (it does happen) will appear to be earning a return on equity of 100 per cent.

Equally difficult are the extreme ratio values that are calculated when dividing by a very small number. In academic studies the researchers often resort to eliminating outliers or rely on non-parametric statistics which are less susceptible to the influence of outliers but in many cases these odd results are quite genuine and would be more meaningful if they were more carefully specified. For example, earnings growth is problematical because earnings is an erratic variable and may in any one year be unusually small or negative. Thus in 1991 Carrefour's EPS declined from FFr 211 to 94, a fall of approximately 55 per cent. Over the next two years it recovered to FFr 130, a total increase of 38 per cent and yet the recovery of 38 per cent and FFr 30 accounts for nowhere near the decline of 55 per cent and FFr 117. If the analyst wishes to compare the increases in earnings between firms of different size, he or she may be better advised to divide the change in earnings by market value rather than by prior year earnings.

3.3 Examples of ratio computation and interpretation

This section is based on the accounting statements of Carrefour given in Exhibit 3.3. These accounts exclude certain details and notes to the accounts for the sake of simplicity but where relevant these are introduced in the text. It should be noted that ratios are not normally carefully defined. One analyst may choose to calculate them somewhat differently from another, or to adjust the accounting numbers before using them in a ratio.

The ratios are grouped under profitability, asset utilisation, liquidity and capital structure. This is fairly conventional but later in the chapter this is examined in more detail. The examples given are based on Carrefour's results for 1993 and are limited to some of the more commonly used ratios which allow the reader to practise calculating other years and ratios.

Profitability

The two most common measures of return are return on equity and return on capital. The first scales the profit earned for ordinary shareholders by the book value of the ordinary shareholders' investment. As dividends are a payment to the ordinary share-holders these are not deducted from profit, and because extraordinary items are supposedly rare these are also ignored. The reasoning is that analysts are interested in the ability of the firm to earn returns in the future and temporary costs and revenues should be ignored.

$$\text{Return on equity} = \frac{\text{Earnings before extraordinary items} \times 100}{\text{Shareholders equity}}$$

$$= \frac{1,665 \times 100}{11,922} = 13.96\% \tag{3.1}$$

From the equity investor's point of view this ratio is deemed to be the crucial measure as it is return on investment that is the motivation for investing in equity. In this case the adjustments for minority interest's share of the income ($-$FFr 458 m) and the associated companies' contribution ($+$FFr 245 m) are included in the computation of earnings whereas the extraordinary income ($+$FFr 1,345 m) is not. The return to minority shareholders is their reward for contributing capital in much the same way as interest is deducted before leaving the residual due to the shareholders, and the income from associates is the estimate of the profits earned by Carrefour's investment in these companies. Extraordinary items are usually excluded because we are interested in the future performance of the firm and current performance is a reasonable indicator of this but not for those elements known to be unlikely to re-occur. A fairly obvious example is available from the Carrefour case. Net profit after tax for 1993 was FFr 1,878 m to which an extraordinary gain of FFr 1,345 m was added which together with certain other adjustments left a total net income of FFr 3,010 m. As at July 1994 the consensus of the twelve analysts who had registered their forecasts with First Call International was FFr 2,050 m. They appear to have totally discounted the extraordinary item.

A direct comparison between the ROE of different firms may not always be meaningful. Apart from national or industrial differences in the accounting or business practices the risk of firms may well differ. For example, a firm with high gearing would be expected to earn a higher return on equity than would a firm with low gearing. This will be compensated for by higher risk but this is not incorporated in the ROE measure.

Return on capital

Although the ROE measures the return to shareholders it does not reflect the profitability of the firm as a whole. For example, a firm could report higher return on equity by increasing the proportion of the firm that is financed by fixed interest capital. Therefore the return on capital measure standardises total profit by total capital employed. Fixed interest capital is included in the denominator and interest in the numerator. Minority interests are also included in both and largely due to the structure of the income statement the profit figure is taken before taxation is deducted. A case can be made for excluding taxation in this manner as this measure investigates return irrespective of leverage and the leverage has a direct effect on the taxation levied on a firm as interest is tax deductible whereas dividends are not.

Return on capital employed (ROCE) is calculated as follows:

$$\text{Return on capital} = \frac{\text{Profit before interest} \times 100}{\text{Net assets}}$$

$$= \frac{2,088 \times 100}{(14,544+4,413+1,664)} = 10.12\% \qquad (3.2)$$

The computation of ROCE attempts to relate the net income to all sources of capital to the total value of capital contributions. Thus the income is taken before interest, minority interest etc., and the capital includes equity, minority interest and all sources of interest-bearing debt, be they short or long term. It may be difficult to identify all the debt on the balance sheet and some analysts treat some provisions as part of equity. However, if these provisions are genuine estimates of forthcoming tax and pension liabilities they should be excluded from equity. Traditionally, taxation charges are not deducted from profit. There seems to be little logic to this other than that they appear lower down the income statement and would therefore have to be added back but the example complies with this tradition.

There are, as always, possibilities for disputing this definition of return on capital. It could be argued that the income from associated companies (net equity a/c inc.) and other income should be included, and miscellaneous creditors and provisions may well include elements of capital. Some analysts insist on adding back provisions such as deferred tax as they view this as an accounting allocation of equity for which a liability is unlikely ever to appear. In the UK deferred tax should only be accrued for liabilities that have a reasonable likelihood of having to be paid but a strong case can be made for adding spurious provisions back to equity.

Return on sales (net profit margin)

The final profitability measure that we shall deal with here is profit to sales — often called the net profit 'margin'. Obviously this is a different dimension from the two 'return' measures discussed above. Some analysts differentiate between the two by using the term 'return' for the ratios of profit to capital, and 'margin' for ratios of profit to sales. Whereas, all other things being equal, higher margins are better than lower, for many firms there is a trade-off between profit margins and turnover. It is possible to achieve a high profit margin by charging high prices but the level of sales will fall. Consequently it may not be very informative to review a firm's profit margins without looking at its sales turnover. Whilst for most firms the definition of sales (turnover) is quite obvious it is less clear which profit figure to take. As the focus of attention is the price-to-costs ratio there is a case for looking at operating profit but if the analyst wishes to decompose the return ratio into margin and asset turnover then it is necessary to use the same definition of profit as for the return ratio.

$$\text{Net profit margin} = \frac{\text{Profit before interest} \times 100}{\text{Sales}}$$

$$= \frac{2,088 \times 100}{123,204} = 1.69\% \qquad (3.3)$$

The profit margin calculated appears to be very low, and, indeed, it is, but retail companies often operate on low margins and high turnover. As always the analysts should consider differences in accounting and business practices when comparing firms.

Asset utilisation

It is in the interest of the firm, all other things being equal, for it to maximise the output generated from a given level of investment. In ratio analysis this is usually measured as the turnover divided by the balance sheet value of assets or assets less liabilities. Probably the most frequently used is net asset turnover. This statistic could be decomposed into various elements such as fixed asset turnover or net current asset turnover. For many of the elements of current assets it is conventional to convert a measure of turnover into an equivalent number of days. Thus creditor turnover of 5.22 (123,204/23,586) is converted to 70 days (365/5.22) meaning that on average the firm takes 70 days to pay its debt. Note that a good case could be made for using 103,025 as the numerator as this is the expenditure on goods and it is this expense which will be the main component of creditors. In this case the turnover is used so that a standard unit can be used to compare all asset turnovers.

The asset utilisation ratio calculated here is net assets on the basis that it is all inclusive and has already been used in the return on capital computation.

$$\text{Net asset turnover} = \frac{\text{Sales}}{\text{Net assets}} = \frac{123,204}{14,544} = 8.47 \qquad (3.4)$$

As with all ratios investigated so far these results are sensitive to industrial differences. In this case 8.47 appears to be very high. As with profit margin the asset turnover is very sensitive to accounting and particularly business practices. A cross-industry comparison of asset turnover makes little sense.

Liquidity measures

It is clear that the liquidity of a firm is of interest to analysts whatever their reason for investigating the company. The equity investor may concentrate on the long-run cash-generating prospects of the firm but if short-run cash flow difficulties will put the firm into receivership the long run becomes rather irrelevant. However, liquidity is probably more important for short-term lenders, especially suppliers who provide goods and services on credit, and banks and others who provide short-term unsecured debt. As with all the other groupings of ratios a number of alternative measures may be used which either alter the focus of the analysis, marginally alter the definition, or concentrate on a larger or smaller element of the dimension under investigation. Thus the most common measure of liquidity is the current ratio which contrasts current assets with current liabilities on the rather rough approximation that assets may be used to pay off liabilities. Many analysts find it rather misleading to assume that stock (inventory) may be used to pay off liabilities and narrow the definition of current assets to exclude stock and work in progress. Still others focus on the ratio of debt to alternative definitions of cash generation, or on the number of days the firm could survive if cash generation ceased — the no credit interval.

$$\text{Current ratio} = \frac{\text{Current assets}}{\text{Current liabilities} + \text{Short-term loans}}$$

$$= \frac{22,383}{32,128} = 0.70 \qquad (3.5)$$

It can be seen from the elements that make up this particular definition of the liquidity ratio that a number of the assets and liabilities included could be usefully further investigated. Thus tax, dividends, and short-term loans will all have specified payment dates. An appreciation of the firm's liquidity would be better performed if these dates were investigated. The results for Carrefour suggest a value of 0.70 which is really quite low when taken in isolation. Indeed, 1.5 is sometimes thought to be a reasonable benchmark but in general the use of arbitrary benchmarks should be avoided.

Capital structure (gearing or leverage)

With regard to most ratios mentioned in this section there is a clear view that, all other things being equal, the firm is better off if the ratio moves in a particular direction. Thus more asset turnover, profit margin, or return on capital is better than less. However, with capital structure there is no obvious good or bad interpretation. Within most ranges a higher proportion of fixed interest capital is different from a lower proportion but not necessarily worse. The more fixed interest capital the firm has, the higher is the risk of its capital, both equity and debt. However, the return on capital is also expected to be higher. Fixed interest capital also has the advantage of being cheaper to raise than equity and interest payments are allowable against profits for tax purposes. Given these trade-offs it is not usually possible to say whether a firm's capital structure is good or bad. Even so the variable is important as it changes the risk of investment in the firm. There is a caveat to these comments and that is that if the gearing of the firm becomes unusually high the risk of financial failure is increased and the cost of failure (multiplied by the probability of failure) will affect the value of the firm. Thus excessive gearing is to be avoided.

The definition of gearing used here is the all inclusive one of long-, medium-, and short-term loans divided by net assets. Some analysts also include preferred stock as debt as it behaves as if it were debt and possibly overdrafts and other interest-bearing debt which may be classified as creditors but could be included. An alternative to using the balance sheet to calculate capital structure is to use the income statement and many analysts will examine the interest cover (profit after tax with interest added back divided by interest).

$$\text{Gearing} = \frac{\text{All debt}}{\text{Net assets}} = \frac{1,664 + 4,413}{14,544} = 0.42 \qquad (3.6)$$

It is interesting to note that the balance sheet value of debt is approximate but the balance sheet value of equity is grossly inaccurate. Consequently many analysts replace the book value of equity with the market value.

Earnings per share

The only ratio that has been subject to any attempt at formal definition is the earnings per share (EPS) ratio, due to its significance as the numerator of the widely used P/E ratio. In some ways EPS is not a full ratio. There is no attempt to standardise so that inter-firm comparisons can be made. Only to define the method of computation. SSAP3 requires the disclosure of EPS on the face of the income statement and has laid down certain rules which attempt to standardise the tax treatment of earnings and the adjustment for changes in capitalisation, in order to derive a more indicative EPS ratio.

The computation of EPS is essentially:

$$\text{EPS} = \frac{\text{profit after tax, minority interests and preference dividends}}{\text{nos of equity shares issued ranking for dividend}} \qquad (3.7)$$

However, there are complications with the treatment of taxation, and when there have been changes in capitalisation.

Taxation changes

Companies suffer tax which is either independent of the level of distribution that the firm makes in the form of dividends (such as corporation tax, tax on dividends received, and unrelieved tax on overseas earnings), or tax which is affected by the companies' distributions, such as irrecoverable advanced corporation tax (ACT) and overseas tax unrelieved due to the level of dividend payment. To enable comparison between the operating performance of the firm, EPS can be calculated ignoring the variable element of taxation. This is known as the 'nil basis' and disclosure is only required where it differs materially from the normal 'net basis' where EPS is calculated after the full tax charge.

Changes in equity

There are three circumstances where the impact changes in equity for the period under review are quite straightforward. Firstly, where equity is issued at full market price, the number of shares used in the denominator is simply the weighted average. Secondly, where a capitalisation (bonus) issue has been made, the number of shares used is the number after the issue and all comparative figures quoted are adjusted to bring them into line. Thirdly, where share or loan stock has been issued to acquire a subsidiary, the shares are deemed to have been issued from the date at which the subsidiary's profits are incorporated into the group accounts. However, where shares are issued at less than market price, as in the conventional rights issue, the transaction contains an element of the first two circumstances. In order to adjust the comparative figure for the bonus element, prior EPS are multiplied by the theoretical ex-rights price and dividend by the actual cum-rights price on the last day of cum-rights quotation. To adjust the current year's figures, the normal weighted average equity computation as for the first circumstance described above, is modified by uprating the pre-rights portion by the reciprocal of the previous computation, namely actual cum-rights price divided by the theoretical ex-rights price.

The final problem with EPS concerns the possible dilution of earnings in the future. Where the firm has equity issued that does not yet rank for dividend but will do so in the future, debentures or loan stock that is convertible to equity, or options or warrants to subscribe for equity, the future earnings of the firm may be dissipated over a greater number of shares. Where this would cause an appreciable drop in EPS, deemed to be more than 5 per cent, the diluted EPS must be calculated and disclosed as if the full number of shares had been issued for the whole of the reporting period.

The decomposition of ratios

A common approach to ratio analysis is ratio decomposition. In simple terms it is just an attempt to identify the cause of abnormal performance recorded in a ratio by splitting the ratio into elements. There is no single correct way to do this but a clear example is the decomposition of return on equity into asset turnover and profit margin.

$$\text{ROE} = \text{Margin} \times \text{turnover}$$

$$\frac{\text{Profit before extraordinary items}}{\text{Equity}} = \frac{\text{Profit before extraordinary items}}{\text{Sales}} \times \frac{\text{Sales}}{\text{Equity}}$$

$$\frac{1{,}665}{11{,}922} = \frac{1{,}665}{123{,}204} \times \frac{123{,}204}{11{,}922} = 0.1396 = 0.0135 \times 10.334 \tag{3.8}$$

Exactly the same sort of decomposition could be done with the return on capital although the asset turnover and profit margin would both be calculated differently.

Conclusion

This section has mentioned some of the difficulties of using ratio analysis and presented some simple ratio definitions with a brief comment on their meaning. It should be emphasised that many different ratios are in common usage and for each ratio there may be more than one acceptable specification. For example, gearing may be measured as debt (which may be restricted to long and medium, or all debt, or all interest-bearing liabilities) over the book value of equity, or equity plus debt, or market value of equity, or market value of equity plus debt. None of these are uniquely correct and analysts must be careful when using ratios. It is important to be clear as to the definition used and to be consistent when comparing firms. However, it is easy to calculate ratios in a manner that is clearly wrong or meaningless. For example, profit before interest expressed as a percentage of equity makes no sense as the profit and capital must be defined in a compatible manner. It is also apparent that calculating ratios is a fairly easy procedure and in many cases databases provide these ready calculated for the analyst. Yet the unthinking application of ratios is a dangerous business. It has already been emphasised in this part of the book that analysts must spend time investigating the accounting statements, and other sources of information, in some depth. It is also important that the analyst understands the behaviour of ratios and the next section examines the statistical characteristics of ratios thereby allowing the analyst to appreciate some of the pitfalls of using ratios.

3.4   The statistical properties of financial ratios[1]

It has been mentioned in earlier sections that the use of ratios is commonplace. This might be as part of a formal decision modelling exercise — such as an attempt to predict financial failure, or in an ad hoc manner as summary statistics. In most cases it is apparent that the analysts pay little attention to the properties of the ratios they use and this may well damage the effectiveness of the ratio analysis process. Particular considerations are the form of the ratio — the relationship between the numerator and denominator, the interrelationship between different ratios, and the distributional properties of the ratios.

In the first instance, if the relationship between numerator and denominator is not as simple as is implied by the ratio specification, analysts may draw incorrect conclusions from the analysis. In the second case the choice of ratios is affected as any two ratios may be collinear or independent. Collinear ratios provide little additional information given that the other is known and may affect the sensitivity of statistical tests. Finally the distribution of ratios may well differ from the regular, probably normal, distribution that is implied in much of the use of ratio analysis. If the relationship between the two components of the ratio is not linear or does not have a zero intercept (where a reading of zero for one component suggests a reading of zero for the other) a non-normal distribution is not surprising. Again the implications for analysts are that incorrect conclusions may be drawn, or unreliable statistical tests conducted where analysts do not adequately allow for the distributional properties of ratios.

3.4.1 *The form of ratios*

In a typical example of the use of ratios, the return on capital employed for the target company may be compared with that of the industry norm or of a competitor. The normal use of ratios implies that the ratios are proportional and possess no intercept, as demonstrated in Figure 3.2.

Hence, in Figure 3.2, the line *AB* would describe their expected values. Yet there is no reason why the relationship should be either linear, for economies/diseconomies of scale could imply an increasing/decreasing return on capital as size increases; or have a zero intercept, as an operating profit of zero is not necessarily implied by a capital employed of zero. The significance of the potential mis-specification of the relationship between profit and capital is that the position of a firm's indicator, relative to an industry standard or to another firm, may be interpreted incorrectly. Whereas point *X* on Figure 3.2 appears to be inferior to the standard ratio line *AB* and to point *Y*, it is in fact superior to the true relationship predicted by *CD*. This may be true where either an intercept exists, or the relationship is non-linear. Furthermore, under either of these circumstances, conventionally calculated ratios will probably exhibit non-normal distributions, the problems of which are examined in the last section of this chapter.

Further, the two variable proportional models may be mis-specified and omit relevant variables. The presumption is that *X* is a function of *Y* but in many instances the analyst might expect *X* to be related to *Z* as well. For example, the return on equity for the two hypothetical companies presumes that capitalisation of equity is the sole determinant of normal levels of profit. It has been pointed out already that size may be relevant and there is also reason to suppose that gearing will affect return on equity.

The basic ratio method implies that a specific fraction for a firm is compared to some standard deemed to be applicable. In the following approach the firm's performance is compared with the industry average.

$$\frac{Y_i}{X_i} = \left(\frac{Y}{X}\right)_I + DIFF_i \qquad (3.9)$$

where Y_i and X_i are the variables of interest for firm i, $(Y/X)_I$ is the average for the industry I, and $DIFF_i$ is difference from that average. As discussed above, this implies that the relationship between the two variables (a) has no intercept, and (b) is linear and given (a) and (b), the ratio is proportional.

Multiply through by X_i and the restated equation clearly represents the linear no intercept form:

$$Y_i = \left(\frac{X}{Y}\right)_I \cdot X_i + DIFF_i \cdot X_i \qquad (3.10)$$

Thus the expected value of Y_i is X_i multiplied by a constant, the industry average, plus an error term. The difference term is multiplied by X_i which means that it is heteroscedastic and this has implications for empirical estimation. The validity of this proportional model as a description of the relationship between the two variables can be tested empirically. A very simple test of non-linearity to identify mis-specification of this sort is the reset test where the predicted values from the model are used as the dependent variable with the original regressors plus the new dependent variable squared (Stewart, 1991, p. 73). Identification of the correct specification for the model could be attempted by estimating the relationship between the two variables possibly using a model as follows:

$$Y_i = \alpha + \beta (X_i)^{nl} + \epsilon_i \qquad (3.11)$$

Here, α and β are estimated coefficients, nl is a transformation of the variable X_i to allow for non-linearities and ϵ_i is a heteroscedastic error term. The transformation used could be based on some theoretical model of the expected relationship between the variables or it can be estimated by trial and error. If the relationship between the variables is as assumed in traditional ratio analysis, α should be insignificantly different from zero and nl insignificantly different from one. If we wish to test whether Y is dependent on X only, we can add other terms to the right-hand-side and the coefficients estimated on these variables will be insignificantly different from zero if the ratio form employed is appropriate.

The validity of this proportional model as a description of the relationship between the two variables can be tested empirically. In this section we deal with some very simple tests only. More complex and effective tests have been conducted in the various research papers (i.e. McDonald and Morris, 1985). The equations in Table 3.2 show the simple weighted least squares estimation for five selected ratios. The sample included all non-financial companies in the FTSE 100. It should perhaps be pointed out that although one of the variables is classified as dependent and the other independent, there is no contention that there is any causal relationship. The statistical test employed here is simply an attempt to elicit the form of any statistical connection between the variables and should be viewed as descriptive rather than explanatory.

Ordinary least squares (OLS) regression analysis calculates a linear relationship between the two variables in such a way that the squared error between the predicted and fitted values is minimised. In a simple two variable model like this the parameters α and β can be calculated as follows:

$$\beta = \frac{\Sigma (X_i - \bar{X})(Y_i - \bar{Y})}{\Sigma (X_i - \bar{X})^2} \qquad (3.12)$$

$$\alpha = \bar{Y} - \beta . \bar{X} \qquad (3.13)$$

These equations can be readily estimated using statistical packages but it is worthwhile doing it manually a couple of times with small data sets to ensure that you understand exactly what is happening.

Amongst other assumptions, it is assumed that the error terms (residuals) in the equations are normally distributed about the fitted line and are homoscedastic. But in the circumstances pertaining to the examples used heteroscedasticity is to be expected and

Table 3.2 Test for the existence of an intercept assuming linearity
(simple weighted least squares regression)

Profit	=	252	+	0.146	(capital)
		(54.3)		(0.004)	
Debt	=	44	+	0.248	(capital)
		(248.1)		(0.016)	
NCA	=	1010	−	0.767	(total assets)
		(185.5)		(0.017)	
Sales	=	− 3446	+	1.99	(total assets)
		(1207)		(0.092)	
Current assets	=	1016	+	0.826	(current liabilities)
		(162.1)		(0.034)	

Note: Figures in brackets refer to the estimated standard error.

the variance of the error term is of the form $\delta_i^2 = \delta^2 X_i^2$. In order to minimise the effect of heteroscedasticity simple weighted least squares estimations have been used though in each case the weights used to minimise heteroscedasticity are greater than X_i suggesting heteroscedasticity in the original ratio specification. This procedure has successfully eliminated heteroscedasticity in four equations in Table 3.2 but not in the second equation. The diagnostic statistics for that equation are therefore unreliable. This evidence seems to indicate support for the presumption of an intercept in four out of the five equations.

Further evidence is available from the logarithmic specification of the equations. The third equation in Table 3.2 includes negative numbers in the left-hand variable and logarithmic transformations are not available. The equation estimated is

$$\text{Log} X_i = \alpha + \beta \text{Log} Y_i + e_i \tag{3.14}$$

Such a model is equivalent to an equation without an intercept where α is the multiplier and Y_i is raised to the power of β. An estimate for β of 1 suggests a linear equation.

Table 3.3 restates the equations reported in Table 3.2 using a logarithmic formulation.

In the first equation the assumption of a linear relationship is convincingly rejected and in all four equations some support for non-linearity can be found. Again it should be emphasised that these models are indicative of empirical tests that could be undertaken but fall somewhat short of a comprehensive and reliable analysis. For that the reader should refer to the formal research papers.

A more comprehensive investigation of the form of accounting ratios is provided by McDonald and Morris who investigated the functional form of four common ratios across a homogeneous sample of firms operating utilities and a heterogeneous cross-industry sample (McDonald and Morris, 1985). This sample of slightly over one hundred US companies for each group covered asset turnover (current assets divided by sales), liquidity (current assets divided by current liabilities), profitability (cash flow divided by total debt) and debt (total debt divided by total assets) for accounting years ending in 1979.

As noted above, the normal use of financial ratios assumes a model where the specific firm's ratio is examined in comparison with a norm and the difference evaluated.

Table 3.3 Test for the existence of non-linearity assuming a zero intercept
(OLS regression)

Log(profit)	=	−0.516	+	0.849	Log(capital)
		(0.316)		(0.044)	
Log(debt)	=	−1.599	+	1.157	Log(capital)
		(0.656)		(0.091)	
Log(sales)	=	1.448	+	0.867	Log(total assets)
		(0.494)		(0.069)	
Log(current assets)	=	0.640	+	0.937	Log(current liabilities)
		(0.356)		(0.055)	

$$\frac{Y_i}{X_i} = \delta + \epsilon_i \qquad (3.15)$$

where δ represents the norm.

The researchers examined three alternative specifications of this basic relationship:

$$\text{PRO:} \ Y_i = \delta . X_i + \epsilon_i^* \qquad (3.16)$$

This is a direct estimation of the proportional ratio equation achieved by dividing through by X_i, therefore the variance of e_i^* is equivalent to $\sigma^2 X^2$ rather than σ^2. This is as tested in Section 3.1 above but with the intercept repressed.

$$\text{GFF:} \ Y_i^{(L)} = \alpha + \delta . X_i^{(L)} + \epsilon_i^* \qquad (3.17)$$

This is a generalised functional form of PRO which tests for the presence of a significant intercept $\alpha 3$ and non-linearity by applying a Box−Cox transformation (Box and Cox, 1964). The Box−Cox transformation is a relatively complex technique which is beyond the scope of this text, but the value recorded by (L) describes the form of any non-linearity in the relationships tested ranging through logarithmic, and square root to linear; e_i^* is specified as in the equation PRO above.

$$\text{REG:} \ Y_i = \alpha + \delta . X_i + \epsilon_i \qquad (3.18)$$

This is the straightforward bivariate regression format suggested by Barnes and Whittington (Barnes, 1982; Whittington, 1980). As such it is not an examination of a viable form of the ratio but an ad hoc estimation of the relationship between the two variables. In this instance, the variance of e_i is $\sigma 2$. It was estimated by a log-likelihood function rather than OLS techniques.

Interpreting the results requires some care and reference should be made to the original article. However, some generalisations can be made, as follows:

1. The bivariate regressions (REG) often appear to have a significant intercept but the distribution of the residuals is clearly non-normal. This suggests that the model is not a good specification of the relationship.

2. For the utilities sample, the slope of the bivariate model's equation is similar to that of the proportional model (PRO), but as the proportional model's residuals are closer to a normal distribution it may be thought to be a better specification.

3. This superior performance of the proportional model was not apparent with the cross-industry sample.
4. The generalised functional form (GFF) did not improve on the proportional model for the utilities sample.
5. In the case of the cross-industry sample the intercept of the generalised model was always significant and there was an improvement in the distributional characteristics of the residual.
6. While the Box—Cox transformation in the generalised model did not indicate that the relationship was linear, linearity is a closer approximation than either square root or logarithmic transformations.

McDonald and Morris summarise their results as showing that the ratio method proved to be consistently superior to alternative specifications in this series of tests only for the intra-industry sample. For a simple homogeneous industry, the simple ratio outperformed OLS alternatives with respect to residual variance and distributional tests. The extension of the proportionality model to include a Y intercept term was not statistically supported. When a heterogeneous group of firms was analysed, there was little consistency in the ability of any single model to provide an appropriate specification. These results cast some doubt on the usefulness of simple ratio analysis in cross-industry comparisons (McDonald and Morris, 1985, p. 96).

3.5 Distributional characteristics of accounting ratios

When dealing with a large group of statistics it is often convenient to generalise using statistical parameters, and the assumption of a normal distribution which can be described by the mean and standard deviation is the clearest case in point. It is convenient for statistical tests, measures of 'averages' are more reliable in that mean, median and mode should be similar, and the regular shape allows simple conclusions to be drawn. For example, if a firm's ratio is similar to the industry average there will be roughly as many outperforming as underperforming. However, this convenient state of affairs is rare, and perhaps this is to be expected.

The examinations of the distributional patterns of financial ratios discussed below strongly support the contention that these ratios are rarely normal in form. This is not surprising. Any ratio which is bounded is unlikely to be normal, and as many accounting ratios have a lower bound relatively close to the mean but no obvious upper bound, skewness is perhaps to be expected. For example, all the turnover ratios, the liquidity ratios and capital structure ratios have a minimum of zero but no theoretical constraint on the maximum reading. Even when there is no constraint, as with return or margin ratios, it is quite possible that the ratio will not be normally distributed. If the relationship between X and Y is non-linear or has a non-zero intercept, and we impose linearity and zero-intercept, the residuals — the deviation from industry average — will be normal only by chance.

Table 3.4 Example distribution of return on equity and gearing

Histogram of return on equity

Midpoint		Count
−40	1	*
−30	0	
−20	1	*
−10	0	
0	10	*********
10	48	**
20	39	**
30	10	**********
40	2	**

Histogram of debt ratio (Extel specification)

Midpoint		Count
20	8	********
40	24	************************
60	35	***********************************
80	19	*******************
100	8	********
120	4	****
140	6	******
160	4	****
180	2	**
200	0	
220	0	
240	0	
260	1	*

3.5.1 *Evidence on ratio and transformation distributions*

The histograms (Table 3.4) show the distributional patterns of two important ratios. The second of the two — the debt ratio — is bounded at zero and is clearly not normally distributed. The return on equity ratio is much closer to normal, although a statistical test still confirms that it is significantly different from a normal distribution. Even so a number of outliers were removed from both sets of ratios.

Table 3.5 shows the results of tests for goodness of fit with the normal distribution, and tests to establish the degree of skewness and kurtosis present. Skewness tests for a tendency for the data to extend further in one direction than the other, whereas kurtosis measures the extent to which there are more extreme readings than would be expected in a normal distribution; sometimes called 'fat tailed'.

As it is often suggested that transformations of the ratio statistic may well have 'better' distributional patterns, two of the most commonly suggested reincarnations of the raw data, the square root and the natural log, are also tested for normality.

The measure of standard deviation (the second moment) of a distribution is

$$\sigma = \left[\frac{1}{n-1} \sum_{i=1}^{n} (X_i - \bar{X})^2 \right]^{1/2} \tag{3.19}$$

FINANCIAL ANALYSIS

Table 3.5 Distributional tests on five ratios and transformations

	ROCE	Gear	NCA/TA	Sales/TA	WCR
Raw Data					
Skewness	2.66	0.17	0.06	1.74	1.03
Kurtosis	10.44	−0.59	0.14	4.85	1.90
Correlation	0.869	0.992	0.994	0.927	0.970
Square root					
Skewness	1.53	−0.53	N/A	0.59	**0.33**
Kurtosis	4.62	−0.07	N/A	1.38	**0.40**
Correlation	0.939	0.985	N/A	0.981	**0.994**
Natural log					
Skewness	0.57	−1.60	N/A	−0.59	**−0.36**
Kurtosis	1.45	3.18	N/A	1.32	**0.34**
Correlation	0.978	0.927	N/A	0.980	**0.992**

Notes: Those statistics in bold are held not to reject normality and skewness is suspected where Y_3 < −0/5 > + 0 ... 5, and kurtosis where Y_4 < −1.0 > + 1.0. The normal distribution can be rejected at 95% confidence levels if the correlation reported in < 0.9835 for a sample of this size. N/A = transformations are not available for this ratio as it contains negative readings.

the measure of skewness (the third moment) is computed as

$$\hat{Y}_3 = \frac{\sum\limits_{i=1}^{N} (X_i - \bar{X})^3 \div \sigma^{3x}}{N} \tag{3.20}$$

and the calculation of the kurtosis coefficient (the fourth moment)

$$\hat{Y}_4 = \frac{\sum\limits_{i=1}^{N} (X_i - \bar{X})^4 \div \sigma^{4x}}{N} - 3 \tag{3.21}$$

The correlations reported are the product moment correlation between the ratios or their transformations and 'normal scores' of that data. The correlation is calculated as

$$r = \frac{\sum\limits_{i=1}^{n} (X_i - \bar{X}) \cdot (Y_i - \bar{Y})}{\left[\sum\limits_{i=1}^{n} (X_i - \bar{X})^2 \sum\limits_{i=1}^{n} (Y_i - \bar{Y}) \right]^{1/2}} \tag{3.22}$$

As with regression analysis these statistics can be easily computed using statistical packages but it is worthwhile computing them manually, or using a spreadsheet at least, to see exactly how they are calculated.

Normal scores are computed by ranking the data and then allocating scores to the ranked data which will produce a distribution with a mean of zero and a standard deviation of one. Therefore, high correlations indicate a close fit with the normal distribution.

The statistical results confirm the visual impression. All ratios apart from gearing and NCA/TA appear closer to normality in a transformed version. The WCR is normally distributed in either transformation, and the sales/TA ratio is equally close to normality in either version. The ROCE statistic is still clearly not normally distributed whatever transformation is used, but is in its 'best' version when transformed to a logarithmic version.

If these rather limited results are confirmed by more substantial studies, the implications are encouraging in so far as a normal approximation can usually be achieved by transformation, but they offer no support for the habitual and comprehensive restatement of all ratios in natural log form for research purposes.

Evidence regarding the UK is presented by Ezzamel, Mar-Molinero and Beecher (1987) who used three industrially selected samples, supplemented by a random sample and examining five commonly used ratios used. They found that the Chi squared test does not reject the null hypothesis that the ratios are normally distributed (at 95 per cent confidence levels) for all five ratios (TD/TA, WC/TA, CA/CL, NI/TA, CA/sales) for retail foods, for three out of four ratios for the random sample (excluding TD/TA), for three out of five ratios for textiles, and for two out of five ratios for metals.

Given that non-normal ratios are common this leaves the problem of what to do with such data. One option is to transform it in some way to give a normal distribution. Many researchers have experimented with square root or log transformations. When Ezzamel *et al.* experimented with square root and natural log transformations they discovered that the square root improves eleven ratios but five deteriorate, and that natural log improves nine but eight deteriorate. 'Thus, although it is possible to change the shape of the histogram of a set of data — and hence approximate to normality — by applying transformations it is unclear which transformations to apply' (Ezzamel, Mar-Molinero and Beecher, 1987).

The problems caused in distributional analysis may be mainly due to a limited number of extreme readings known as 'outliers'. Thus one possibility is to remove outliers which may be the sole cause of non-normality. This is likely to be necessary in most samples anyway when some method of dealing with outliers will be required. Relatively recent approaches have attempted to avoid the rather frenetic search for the normal distribution described above, and have tried to find workable non-normal distributions with known statistical characteristics and which fit the observed data better than the normal. However, it may be that the most convenient route for handling non-normal data and which also works well with outliers is to use non-parametric statistics. The most common of these is to use ranks of the data rather than the data itself. The interpretation of the ranks is obvious unlike the more esoteric distributions or transformations of the data and there are many simple and effective statistical tests designed for dealing with non-parametrics.

3.6   Interrelationships between accounting variables

A basic problem for the analyst is to select a sample of financial statistics that is convenient and suitable for the investigation in hand. Chen and Shimerda comment that, 'there is one recurring question with the use of financial ratios: which ratios among the hundreds that can be computed easily from the available financial data, should be analysed to obtain information for the task at hand?' (Chen and Shimerda, 1981). This is not a trivial problem, for although a narrowly focused analysis may obviously require the use of a particular variable, the choice for more general analysis is unlimited. Two approaches have been adopted to deal with this problem. The first is to decide on the ratios to examine by using an analytical approach. The second is to determine the appropriate ratios on an empirical basis.

3.6.1   A priori *typologies*

The empirical approach to selection of accounting ratios is addressed later in this chapter, but advocates of various typologies of ratios originally adopted an *a priori* approach based on their experience and deductions. Most accounting texts contain a list of the different aspects of a firm's performance that an analyst will wish to examine, together with ratios appropriate to this task. To the extent that these lists are the distillation of prior experience, there is some rationale for the categories given, though the accompanying habit of suggesting benchmark statistics for each ratio is more dangerous as it often ignores national, industrial and temporal differences in business practices. The problems with *a priori* recommendations as described here are the lack of guidance regarding which ratio to select from those relating to a particular aspect of firm performance, and the subjective classification of ratios which is dependent on the personal experience of the researcher. There is no reason to suppose that any particular designation of ratio type is generally applicable to separate decisions or firms. Nevertheless the ratio trees are of some use and one based on the work of Courtis (1978) is shown in Figure 3.3.

3.6.2   *Statistical relationships*

Two approaches can be taken to extend and reinforce the approach just elaborated. Firstly, a further analysis of the relationship between various ratios to try to identify those which possibly contain unique information and those which are dominated by alternative formulations. Secondly, an examination of those predictive models which normally utilise financial information to determine which ratios are most consistently found to be useful in these studies.

Table 3.6 reports the correlation between five common variables intended to measure different aspects of financial performance for a sample of industrial and commercial firms taken from the constituents of the FTSE 100 index.

The second set of correlations are the correlations between the ranks of the variables. This non-parametric statistic is not so easily influenced by a few outliers.

The first of these two approaches often utilises the technique of factor analysis (sometimes termed principal component analysis) to identify independent patterns of financial ratios. Factor analysis produces linear combinations of the variables input, in this case accounting ratios, in such a way that the composite factors produced account for as much of the information content, or variability, as possible. Thus, it is normally possible for a limited number of factors to impound most of the information contained in a much larger set of variables; hence the term 'data reduction' which is also applied to factor analysis. The factor can then be viewed as one category of information that is obtainable from the original data. One further benefit is that the relationship between this

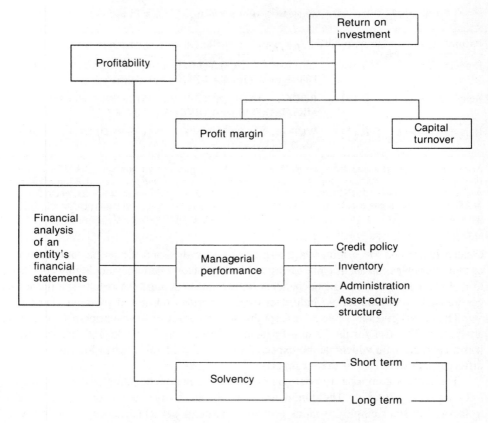

Figure 3.3 An example typology of ratios.
(*Source:* Courtis, 1978, p. 373.)

Table 3.6 Cross-correlation statistics

	ROCE	Gear	NCA/TA	TO/TA
Product moment correlations:				
Gear	−0.201			
NCA/TA	0.188	−0.173		
TO/TA	0.336	−0.014	−0.222	
WCR	0.142	−0.211	0.880	−0.234
Spearman rank correlations:				
Gear	−0.143			
NCA/TA	0.261	−0.136		
TO/TA	0.432	−0.017	0.008	
WCR	0.207	−0.151	0.939	−0.148

Notes: NCA = net current assets; TA = total assets; WCR = working capital ratio; ROCE = return on capital employed.

Table 3.7 Principal components of twenty financial ratios from the FTSE 100

Factor	Proportion	Closely correlated ratios
Productivity	0.246	OP/EMP (-0.866) TO/EMP (-0.824) CFM% (-0.822) PTP% (-0.756) CAP/EMP (-0.782)
Return/gearing	0.193	ROCE (-0.815) INCGRIG (0.745) ROSE (-0.655) MKTGRGIG (0.659) DIVCOV (-0.590)
Liquidity/turnover	0.124	WCR (0.682) QAR (0.598) EPS (0.569) DRSTO (-0.562) ASSTO (-0.433)

Notes: OP/EMP = operating profit per employee; TO/EMP = turnover per employee; CFM% = cash flow margin; PTP% = pre-tax profit percentage; CAP/EMP = capital employed per employee; ROCE = return on capital employed; INCGRG = income gearing; ROSE = return on shareholders' equity; MKTGRG = market-based gearing; DIVCOV = dividend cover; WCR = working capital ratio; QAR = quick assets ratio; EPS = earnings per share; DRSTO = debtors' turnover; ASSTO = asset turnover.

created factor and the original variables can be examined and it may be found that one or more variables can act as close surrogates for the factor where they are highly correlated to it. Factor analysis is totally dependent on the data input and the results should not be generalised to include ratios, industries or time periods not tested, without caution.

The results given in Table 3.7 are for the first three factors from a principal component analysis of 20 ratios for the 78 non-financial companies in the FTSE 100. Furthermore, it is a characteristic which can be expected to vary considerably when the sample spans different industries, as in this example.

The factors comprise a linear equation of the component ratios ($F_1 = f_1\text{Ratio}_1 + f_2\text{Ratio}_2 \ldots f_{20}\text{Ratio}_{20}$). The dominance of the productivity ratios is quite possibly due to the use of 3 per employee ratios in the original data set which correlate closely with the profit margin ratios, giving 5 out of 20 ratios relevant to this dimension.

Ezzamel, Brodie and Mar-Molinero (1987) used a large data set which was confined to manufacturing companies, and examined the cross-sectional evidence at 1973, 1977 and 1981. They considered 53 ratios. Using ten factors in each period, the researchers were able to account for 73, 66 and 76 per cent of the total variance in each period. More effective results have been achieved in earlier studies which had transformed the variables to achieve distributions that approximate to normality. As regards the stability of the data Ezzamel, Brodie and Mar-Molinero caution that, 'the reported long-term instability of financial patterns suggests that the extension of the results to different time periods or to different countries is not straightforward'.

3.6.3 *Conclusions for ratio choice*

The ideal result from the factor analysis tests cited above would be to establish a small group of factors, each closely represented by a surrogate ratio, which could be trusted to convey substantially the information contained in the full set of ratios, and for this group to be stable across time and across industries. The final position appears to be somewhat confused with a series of tests producing differing results. Chen and Shimerda attempted to bring some order to this confusion. They examined 26 studies which had incorporated financial ratios into predictive studies thereby establishing a comprehensive set of significant variables. The studies revealed 41 ratios that were tested, of which 34 were found to be significant. To reduce this set, it may be possible to identify certain ratios which are either alternative specifications of the same form, or, when taken together with other ratios, incorporate the form of a further statistic (for example, given capital turnover and profit margin, the return on capital can be derived).

Rather than get involved in a 'nit-picking' approach, Chen and Shimerda examined the success of principal component analysis-based studies of the type cited above to see if they offered a method of reducing the number of ratios utilised. Five studies were examined and the researchers concluded that, 'it seems that the results from principal component analysis are as diverse as the financial ratios themselves. Different sets of factors can be found in different studies with very little commonality among any of them.' However, closer examination by Chen and Shimerda seems to reconcile many of the differences. Further, when the 34 significant ratios from the failure prediction studies are compared with the factor analysis studies, 24 are found to be readily classifiable. The 10 remaining ratios were then included in a re-worked principal component analysis test, and it was found that the previously untested ratios fitted easily into the seven factor categorisation originally proposed by Pinches *et al.* (Pinches, Mingo and Carruthers, 1973). Therefore, Chen and Shimerda concluded that, 'financial ratios investigated previously in predictive studies of bankruptcy can be classified by a substantially reduced number of factors' (Chen and Shimerda, 1981).

3.7 Conclusion

This chapter has examined the properties of the basic material of financial analysis — accounting ratios. It is apparent that ratio analysis offers a useful and convenient method of financial statement interpretation. Indeed, it is difficult to conceive of financial analysis without the assistance of ratios.

Some reservations must be expressed with regard to the choice of ratios. In general, they incorporate the failings of the accounting system on which they are based though this problem can be minimised by careful selection of the ratios to be examined, and by care in the interpretation of the derived figures. In addition, attention needs to be paid to the problem of outliers as extreme observations can distort predictive models and summary statistics.

More specific considerations should also be borne in mind.

1. The choice of ratios for examination is not a trivial matter. Statistical techniques are available to separate ratios which contain similar information from those which contain dissimilar information. This reduces the information search costs and minimises any statistical problems of collinearity.
2. The ratio specification implicitly assumes a proportional relationship which would exhibit a zero intercept. The reality is somewhat different, and the resulting deviations in functional form and distribution require careful monitoring. In many cases, the use of fuller descriptions of ratio distributions, such as deciles, may be more meaningful

than summary statistics. The estimation of more sophisticated relationships may be derived and the form of this relationship may be informative.

The suggestion that care must be exercised in the use of ratios is not surprising and would possibly be countered by the suggestion that the costs of careful investigation may outweigh the benefits. For the casual user this may be true but the results of general research can be assumed to apply to the sample under analysis in the absence of evidence to the contrary, and the problems discussed would normally be readily apparent either as a skewed distribution of the sample or from high correlations between the ratios. Furthermore, apart from the casual user, detailed and in-depth studies are now conducted by commercial organisations to assist with problems such as investment selection and bankruptcy prediction. For these purposes, detailed analysis is likely to be cost-effective and necessary.

Note

1. In this chapter there are some basic statistics which might prove troublesome for readers not yet familiar with these techniques. However, most readers will find it a convenient opportunity to reinforce their statistical abilities.

─────────────── QUESTIONS ───────────────

1. Exhibit 3.3 presents extracts from the income statement and balance sheet for Carrefour SA. Calculate the five years' statistics for the following ratios and comment on their meaning:
    (a) Return on capital employed.
    (b) Return on shareholders' equity.
    (c) Profit margin (return on sales).
    (d) Gearing (leverage) ratio.
    (e) Income gearing (interest cover) ratio.
    (f) Dividend cover ratio.
    (g) Working capital ratio.
    (h) Quick assets ratio (acid test).
    (i) Debtor days ratio.
    (j) Creditor days ratio.
    (k) Stock days ratio.
    (l) Asset turn over ratio.

    Where helpful use the UK food retailing ratios as a comparison and note any terms in your computations which might be considered discretionary.

2. Select six important ratios from the above list that will be affected by (a) the replacement of the book value of shareholders' equity by market value, and (b) the write off of goodwill directly to reserves. Recalculate these ratios using the information given in the chapter (assuming that the change in depreciation of intangibles equals the charge to income which is approximately correct in this case) and comment on the change.

3.　　　Prepare a dataset containing the numerators and denominators of four commonly used ratios for (a) a sample (>30 firms) from one industry, and (b) a sample (>30 firms) from a cross-section of industries. Then answer the following:

　　(a)　To what extent would you expect the relationship $Y_i/X_i = \delta + e_i$ to be a full specification of the relationship between X and Y for each of your ratios? (δ = the norm for the sample.)

　　(b)　Can you find statistical evidence to support the use of the simple ratio format or would it appear that more complex specifications are required? Do the results differ for intra- and inter-industry samples?

　　Lecturers may well wish to alter the scope of questions 3a and 3b depending on the availability of computer facilities and financial databases.

4.　　　Prepare a dataset containing twelve commonly used but disparate financial ratios for (a) a sample (>30 firms) from one industry, and (b) a sample (>30 firms) from a cross-section of industries. Then:

　　(a)　Compute the mean, median and mode for each sample. What can you conclude from your results?

　　(b)　Compute the mean statistic for each quartile of firms ranked by size. Are you able to reach any conclusions regarding the proportionality of the ratios from your results? Do the results differ for intra- and inter-industry samples?

　　(c)　Examine the distributional charactistics of the ratios. For those ratios that do not conform to the normal distribution are you able to restate the data to better approximate a normal distribution? Do the results differ for intra- and inter-industry samples?

　　(d)　Calculate the cross-correlations between the ratios. What conclusions can you make concerning the information content of the relevant ratios?

5.　　　Chen and Shimerda (1981) comment that, 'there is one recurring question with the use of financial ratios: which ratios among the hundreds that can be computed easily from the available financial data, should be analysed to obtain information for the task at hand'. Discuss the problem and the methods which may be used to address the issues.

6.　　　'The extensive use of financial ratios by both practitioners and researchers is often motivated by tradition and convenience rather than by careful methodological analysis' (Lev and Sunder, 1979). Explain the significance of this statement and produce empirical evidence to illustrate the methodological problems.

7.　　　Using data on two firms other than Carrefour calculate the return on equity and the return on capital. Using ratio decomposition explain why these firms have different returns.

8.　　　Using a different firm from those used in any of the questions above obtain financial statements and ratios for the industry in which the firm operates. Using ratios where helpful write a short report discussing the recent performance of the firm and recommending action that could be taken to improve the performance.

9.　　　Provide definitions of the following terms as used in this chapter:

　　(a)　Return on capital.　　(e)　Profitability.　　　　　(i)　Normal distribution.
　　(b)　Gearing (leverage).　 (f)　Functional form.　　　(j)　Skewness.
　　(c)　Liquidity.　　　　　　 (g)　Heteroscedasticity.
　　(d)　Asset turn over.　　　 (h)　Proportionality.

References

Barnes, P. (1982) Methodological implications of non-normally distributed financial ratios, *Journal of Business, Finance and Accounting*, Spring, 51−62.

Bouwman, M., Frishkoff, P. and Frishkoff, P. (1987) How do analysts make decisions? A process model of the investment screening decision, *Accounting, Organisations and Society*, **12**, no. 1, 1−29.

Box, G. and Cox, D. (1964) An analysis of transformations, *Journal of the Royal Statistical Society*, 211−43.

Chen, K. and Shimerda, T. (1981) An empirical analysis of useful financial ratios, *Financial Management*, Spring, 51−60.

Courtis, J. (1978) Modelling a financial ratios categoric framework, *Journal of Business, Finance and Accounting*, Winter, **5**, no. 4, 371−386.

Ezzamel, M., Brodie, J. and Mar-Molinero, C. (1987) Financial patterns of UK manufacturing companies, *Journal of Business, Finance and Accounting*, Winter, 519−36.

Ezzamel, M., Mar-Molinero, C. and Beecher, A. (1987) On the distributional properties of financial ratios, *Journal of Business, Finance and Accounting*, Winter, 339−52.

Lev, B. (1969) Industry averages as targets for financial ratios, *Journal of Accounting Research*, Autumn, 209−99.

Lev, B. and Sunder, S. (1979) Methodological issues of financial ratios, *Journal of Accounting and Economics*, December, 187−210.

McDonald, B. and Morris, M. (1985) The functional specification of financial ratios; an empirical examination. *Accounting and Business Research*, Summer, **15**, no. 59, 223−8.

Pinches, G., Mingo, K. and Carruthers, J. (1973) The stability of financial patterns in industrial organisations, *Journal of Finance*, May, 389−96.

Stewart, J. (1991) *Econometrics*, Philip Allan, Hemel Hempstead.

Whittington, G. (1980) Some basic properties of accounting ratios, *Journal of Business, Finance and Accounting*, Summer, 219−23.

CHAPTER 4

Time-series Analysis and Forecasting[1]

─────────────── **CHAPTER OBJECTIVES** ───────────────

This chapter will:

1 Examine the behaviour of financial time-series and the difficulties of analysing such series.

2 Briefly review the techniques of financial forecasting.

3 Analyse the accuracy and rationality of analysts' forecasts of earnings.

4.1 Introduction

The focus of the preceding chapter was the inter-firm comparison and analysis of financial numbers on a cross-sectional basis. Given that the analysts' faith in the absolute value of accounting numbers may well be limited, reliance was placed on the relative values and on information derived from comparison of a firm with its competitors. This chapter takes an alternative approach and examines the time-series of financial numbers, assessing the relative value of any one number by comparison with the preceding stream of numbers.

Many of the problems discussed in the previous chapter will also occur here. It is necessary to select a particular series of financial figures to investigate. The economic relevance of accounting numbers is not always readily apparent and the method of calculating various accounting numbers can differ, making comparisons invidious.

However, time-series analysis also provides benefits. Where an accounting number is compared with its immediate predecessor, there is a presumption that no serious distortion results from size differences although in the medium or long term, growth and inflation will ensure that some standardisation for size is necessary. Furthermore, under normal circumstances, one can presume that a more consistent set of accounting policies has been employed in the preparation of the accounting statements than is the case with cross-sectional analysis. Where consistent policies are applied to a particular firm, any biases inherent in accounting measurement will tend to be replicated in each year, reducing the effect of the distortion in time-series comparison.

Perhaps the overriding benefit to be derived from the time-series analysis is its relevance to forecasting. As with any decision-making, the advantage of an investigation of historical data is its assistance in making predictions about the future. This is present in all financial analysis but is most obvious in the incorporation of time-series data into statistical forecasting models. Much of this chapter will examine the techniques of financial forecasting and the value to be gained from these techniques.

Analysts' forecasts of earnings have provided fertile ground for research for more than two decades, especially in the US where academics have had access to forecast data for a long time. Research which assesses the accuracy and other properties of analysts' forecasts of earnings is of interest both to academics and to practitioners. As Givoly and Lakonishok (1984, p. 143) comment:

> Given the important role that earnings should theoretically play in stock valuation, and the overwhelming empirical evidence that earnings do, indeed, possess an information content, it is clear why earnings forecasts have attracted much research effort.

Investment practitioners and advisors use earnings forecasts as an aid to the practical problems of security valuation and portfolio decisions. Arnold and Moizer (1984) found that the key factor in UK share appraisal methods was the price—earnings ratio, and this involved forecasts of future earnings per share. This result has recently been confirmed by Pike *et al.* (1993). Day (1986) also identified that analysts concentrate on P/E ratios and earnings forecasts. Benesh and Peterson (1986) identify similar behaviour in the US where analysts 'almost invariably employ valuation models that rely on earnings forecasts'. Circumstantial evidence of the value of analysts' earnings forecasts is the large number of analysts employed by brokers, investment funds and institutions to provide, *inter alia*, earnings forecasts.

Section 4.2 will examine the techniques of time-series analysis. This is followed by an explanation of the underlying reasons for variation and stability in time-series (Section 4.3). Section 4.4 will examine and evaluate the alternative techniques for deriving forecasts from a time-series. Section 4.5 assesses the accuracy of analysts' forecasts and Section 4.6 considers the forecast inherent in a firm's share price.

4.2   Accounting time-series

4.2.1   *Objectives of time-series analysis*

The analysis of a firm's performance by the examination of the historical sequence of accounting results is a basic technique employed by financial analysts. The principal reasons for this emphasis are twofold: one, the role that forecasts of future returns play in the company valuation process, and two, the assistance that a time-series analysis of past returns can give in arriving at that forecast. The systematic behaviour patterns of accounting variables established by analysis of time-series are essential both to the construction of forecasting models and for the subsequent verification and improvement of the model.

Other reasons for time-series analysis are:

1. Decomposition of the company's prior performance to separate out company-specific from industry/economy-wide influences may require time-series analysis. This is helpful where managerial performance or policies are to be assessed.
2. Analysis of what 'ought to have been' where some event such as a strike, restrictive practices, or accident has had a significant impact on the financial results. Thus, a time-series model of earnings might be compared with the actual results to measure the impact of the event. This estimation of the shortfall may be necessary for insurance or litigation purposes.
3. The time-series behaviour of accounting results is relevant to the regulation of private sector monopolies. The recent privatisation of certain natural or effective monopolies, and the proposals to extend this process require a regulatory system to ensure that the monopolistic firm does not abuse its position. Such a control or monitoring system is likely to include reviews of the time-series behaviour of the financial results. The US has a rich history of such work, but in the UK it is in its infancy, though the telecommunications, water and gas industry 'watch dogs' OFTEL, OFWAT and OFGAS are well-known examples of regulatory organisations.
4. Examination of the effect of accounting policies and practices on the characteristics of accounting numbers, and in particular the time-series behaviour of earnings. This may be as part of the process of the evaluation of accounting choices by standard-setting bodies, selection of alternative policies by management, or academic investigation of discretionary or illegitimate accounting practices.

4.2.2 *Expected behaviour of accounting numbers*

Some insights into the behaviour of accounting numbers can be gained from a simple analysis of what might be expected. Over time firms appear to grow. This is a function of (a) the retention and reinvestment of earnings, (b) the expansion of the firm by issuing new capital, possibly for takeovers or investment in new assets, and (c) the impact of inflation. Under such circumstances undeflated numbers such as earnings, sales, assets, etc. might be expected to grow; possibly exponentially. This can be illustrated by the following graph of earnings. Conversely where the time-series under review is deflated, for example where return on equity is calculated, it might be expected that the time-series will be more stable. After all the return on an investment will be governed, in part, by the characteristics of the industry. If returns are exceptionally high new competitors would be expected to enter the market driving down the rate of return, and the reverse might be expected where returns were low. Again this dispersion of the returns sequence about a mean can be clearly seen from the graphs in Figure 4.1.

It is also common practice to deal with the change in a financial series rather than the level. Again the graph illustrates these numbers for Glaxo Holdings Plc. As might be expected the returns series, which it was suggested might have some mean reversion characteristics, shows a tendency to reverse the sign — positive values being followed by negative. This is typical of mean reverting series. The basic earnings per share (EPS) series, however, is all positive — indicative of a positive growth term. Again this is to be expected and these results can be seen from Figure 4.2.

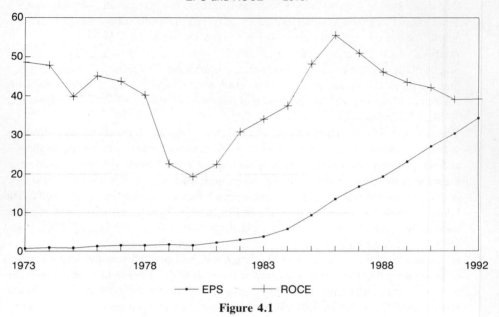

Figure 4.1

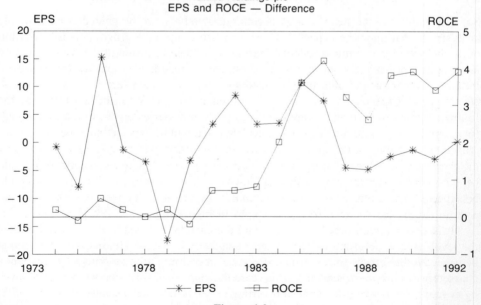

Figure 4.2

These observations do oversimplify the issue. For example, where a firm has made good investments the rate of return might be expected to remain above the industry average for some time, returning to the mean eventually but not immediately. Equally accounting practices, such as the write-up of land and buildings, might cause temporary or permanent differences in reported rates of return between different firms. Furthermore the accruals accounting procedure is known to smooth reported earnings and management are thought to have incentives to further encourage this tendency. Under such circumstances even if cash flows followed a 'random walk' and returns followed a 'mean reverting process' the observed accounting measures would be best described by a more complex time-series including some moving average elements.

Structural change in accounting time-series

One of the most troublesome difficulties when using accounting time-series is that of 'structural changes'. This instability in the series may be caused by changes within the firm or by external factors. For example:

1. The entity being measured has changed composition due to mergers or divestments. Tarmac Plc has been used as an example many times in this text and once more its history demonstrates that investment and/or divestment is a regular activity for larger firms.

Recent acquisition history — Tarmac Plc

1989	Nov	£26.4 m cash	Crown House Engineering Ltd
1990	Jan	FFr 35.7 m cash	51% of Sablieres de la Neste Group
	Mar	146,837 Ord plus cash and loan notes	Bothwell Park Brick Co Ltd
	May	FFr 125.0 m cash	Etablissement Barriaud SA
	Jun	FFr 30.0 m cash	90% of Etablissements Hecquet SA
1991	Jul	FFr 179.0 m (18.5 m) cash	Revillon group
	Oct	£5.6 m cash	The Expanded Piling Co Ltd
	Nov	FFr 80.0 m (£8.2 m) cash	50% of Entreprise Nicoletti SA
1992	Dec	£3.7 m cash	PSA Projects

2. The firm has not changed its legal composition but has experienced substantial change in its product mix.
3. The firm has changed its financing policy, which would not normally affect the operating profit but may alter the appropriation between equity earnings and interest, and hence the return on capital. Using Tarmac again this exhibit shows that even though dramatic changes in financing may be rare many firms are involved in an ongoing revision of capital structure.

Recent capital history — Tarmac Plc

1990	Mar	146,837 Ord	Part consideration for Bothwell Park Brick Co Ltd
	Jul	1,820,816 Ord	Scrip Dividend (xc 30-04-90)
	Oct	321,097 Ord	Scrip Dividend (xc 08-10-90)
	Oct	3,000 Pref	Placed at US$100,000 per share
		3,471,326 Ord	Options
1991		736,406 Ord	Options
	Jul	785,427 Ord	Scrip Dividend (xc 29-04-91)
1992		315 Ord	Options
	Mar	(750) Pref	Redeemed at US$100,000 per share
	Apr	(750) Pref	Redeemed at US$100,000 per share
	Dec	4,053,359 Ord	Scrip Dividend (xc 05-10-92)
1993		320,487 Ord	Options
	Jul	1,088,482 Ord	Scrip Dividend (xc 10-05-93)
	Sep	183,482,866 Ord	Rights — 1:4 at 120p (cum price 144p; (xr 23-09-93)
	Dec	840,239 Ord	Scrip Dividend (xc 04-10-93)
	Dec	(1,500) Pref	Redeemed at US$100,000 per share

4. The method of computing the accounting numbers has changed due to the adoption of different accounting policies, changes in the accounting techniques prescribed by the regulatory authorities, or a change in the presentation of the results. A brief examination of the record of new regulations issues in most countries shows that new regulations may be published at well over one a year. Perhaps the most fundamental change within the European Union (EU) over recent years has been the imposition of the requirement for groups to present fully consolidated accounts. Whilst this was common in some countries such as the UK and the Netherlands, in others such as Belgium, Germany and Spain, it has only been compulsory since 1991. The turnover, profit total asset and equity reported by Dragados y Construcciones SA reported in 1990 (unconsolidated), 1991 (consolidated) and what would have been the unconsolidated 1991 acounts shows that comparisons across accounting changes can be dangerous.

Dragados y Construcciones SA — extracts from 1990 and 1991 accounts

	1990 Company	1991 Company	1991 Group
Total assets	182,098	206,948	254,449
Equity	91,458	96,908	112,273
Revenue	276,182	302,013	354,307
Net income	7,503	9,613	12,719

5. Changes have occurred in external factors such as the level of competition, rates of inflation, economic growth, or technological developments.

6.   The time-series includes one or more readings which are clearly 'outliers'.

One or many of the above circumstances are likely to have occurred in any reasonable time span.

4.2.3   Dealing with structural change

When the assumptions necessary for valid comparisons are violated, as in the examples above, the analyst has to consider how to adapt the techniques employed. The first, and one suspects, most favoured response is to ignore the implications on the implicit justification that the effects are trivial. This may well be reasonable in some cases where, for example, a large holding company acquires a considerably smaller subsidiary.

The second and equally simple approach is to split the series of readings into segments that are comparable. Unfortunately, in many instances this will result in an inadequate number of readings to allow effective analysis.

The third option is to make the necessary adjustments to produce a homogeneous series. This could involve recalculation of returns to adjust for the effect of inflation, the reclassification of costs, for example research and development expenditure, between time periods or between categories such as extraordinary or ordinary expenditure, or the consolidation of the pre-merger results for companies that are subsequently amalgamated.

The fourth alternative is to attempt to allow for the structural change in the model. Thus, where structural change is suspected, the significance of this change can be tested by observing any change in the parameters before and after the adjustment. In cases where the model has undergone structural change, it may be possible to include variables to account for change in the coefficients.

The preceding analysis is primarily concerned with annual data. In many instances more precise and interesting data can be obtained from an analysis of interim information, either biannual or quarterly.

4.2.4   Modelling the data

Even the most basic analysis of time-series data will incorporate implicit model estimation. Comments such as 'sales growth has varied between 15 per cent and 20 per cent for the last five years and yet we have only managed 10 per cent this year' involve the construction of a model of expectations from which the latest reading has departed causing consternation.

Four simple examples serve to illustrate a formal modelling process where P is the profit figure.

1.   Random walk plus drift assumes that the variable will approximate to the previous reading after adjustment for some trend term. The trend term may be estimated as a long-term constant, a moving average, or simply last year's change in earnings. Over large samples of firms the random walk has proved to be a difficult model to beat. In this model a prediction error in period t influences the expectation regarding $t+1$ and subsequent readings.

$$P_t = P_{t-1} + D + \epsilon_t \qquad (4.1)$$

2. Deterministic time-series model the data as a function of time. Here C is a constant and X the multiplier times the number of years. There is no need for the relationship to be linear and the second term could be exponential. In this model errors in period t are ignored in $t+1$.

$$P_t = C + X(t) + \epsilon_t \qquad (4.2)$$

3. Auto-correlation functions examine the past values in the series to extract a persistent statistical relationship between variables in different time periods. Here the change in earnings is a function (F) of the previous year's change in earnings.

$$P_t = P_{t-1} + F(P_{t-1} - P_{t-2}) + \epsilon_t \qquad (4.3)$$

4. Causal models attempt to exploit some external variable which has a useful statistical relationship with the series under examination. Thus in the equation below V could be the change in the industry-wide profits, growth in GDP, or change in share price.

$$P_t = P_{t-1} + F(V_t) + \epsilon_t \qquad (4.4)$$

4.3   Evidence on the behaviour of accounting time-series

4.3.1   *Empirical evidence concerning earnings behaviour*

Early investigation of the earnings growth in the UK (Little 1962, and Little and Rayner 1966) was unable to find any persistent trends in the growth rates of UK companies which they characterised as 'higgledy-piggledy'. That is to say a random walk with no drift. A more precise examination of the underlying relationships in earnings figures was undertaken in an importrant article by Ball and Watts (1972). These researchers used earnings data available for 700 US firms covering the years 1947–66 and they subjected the data to a series of tests to identify 'runs', auto-correlation and predictive ability. They discovered that the runs, the series of changes in earnings which exhibit the same sign, were consistent with earnings following a random walk pattern. The serial correlation for lags of one to five years showed little evidence of any statistically significant relationship. The evidence so far is consistent with firms' earnings following a random walk.

While the basic findings that the earnings of firms in general follow a random walk have proved to be robust, some further investigations have produced refinements. Watts and Leftwich (1977), amongst others, showed that while the average firm's earnings might follow a random walk, some individual firms may differ. In these studies Box–Jenkins forecasting methodology was used to fit autoregressive or moving average models to the data. Even though more models could be succesfully fitted to individual firms than would have been expected by chance, these models have not been able consistently to out-perform random walk models when used in predictive tests.

More success has been achieved using autoregressive models of quarterly data (Foster, 1977). Here, the seasonal element can be represented effectively by a model which represents the next quarter's earnings as the last quarter's plus an autoregression coefficient times the change over the last four quarters.

$$Q_T = Q_{t-4} + \theta(Q_{t-1} - Q_{t-4}) + \epsilon_t \tag{4.5}$$

Beaver (1970) also produced some evidence that rates of return, as opposed to the level of earnings, do not necessarily follow a random process. He concludes that the rate of return on shares is 'well approximated by a pure mean reverting process', and that the accounting rate of return 'is consistent with these measurements coming from a moving average model, where the underlying process is mean reverting, but the reversion takes place over several years'. Mueller (1986) attempted to evaluate the persistence of the return on capital in a sample of 600 companies for the years 1950–72. He was able to model the cross-sectional variation in persistent rates of return for individual firms and the speed at which departures from that underlying rate adjusted back towards the long-term norm. Mueller regressed the excess rate of return (AR_{it}), expressed as a fraction of the cost of capital, on a constant and deterministic trend term ($1/t$).

$$AR_{it} = \alpha_i + \beta_i \frac{1}{t} + \epsilon_{it} \tag{4.6}$$

This equation was estimated across the sample and the mean α and β computed for six sub-samples. The sub-samples were categorised by average return over the first three years, see Table 4.1.

The estimated alphas are the long-run profitability relative to the sample mean and the betas the rate at which short-run rents decay towards the long-run profitability. Thus sub-sample 1 apparently exhibits a long-run return on capital 32 per cent higher than the overall mean, and while in the first year a short-term rent of a further 45.5 per cent was achieved this would decay to 27.75 per cent in year two, 15.16 per cent in year three and so on. Mueller (1986, p. 31) concludes that 'above- and below-average profits strongly tend to converge back towards the mean of the sample . . . but . . . also projected persistent differences in corporate profitability into the indefinite future'.

With regards to UK data O'Hanlon *et al.* (1992) attempted to fit various ARIMA models to 188 firms with EPS data from 1968 to 1988. The autoregressive integrated moving average (ARIMA) model is a generic term for a set of models, the precise form of which is identified by (p, d, q) where p identifies the order (number) of autoregressive terms, d identifies the number of times the series is differenced, and q the order of moving average terms. For example, ARIMA (1, 0, 0) would be the model

Table 4.1 Time-series reversion of return on capital

Sub-Sample	1	2	3	4	5	6
Alpha	0.321	0.093	−0.018	−0.054	−0.121	−0.288
Standard error	*0.061*	*0.037*	*0.033*	*0.033*	*0.031*	*0.028*
Beta	0.455	0.205	0.085	−0.094	−0.201	−0.488
Standard error	*0.099*	*0.054*	*0.052*	*0.050*	*0.042*	*0.051*

Source: Mueller, 1986, Table 2.2, p. 22.

$$P_t = \alpha + \theta P_{t-1} + \epsilon_t \qquad (4.7)$$

and ARIMA (0, 0, 1) would be the model

$$P_t = \alpha + \theta \epsilon_{t-1} + \epsilon_t \qquad (4.8)$$

For the data investigated only 24 out of 188 firms were better modelled using first differences than undifferenced, and 106 out of 188 were best modelled using ARIMA (1, 0, 0) a simple first order autoregressive model. A further 28 were best modelled using various slightly more complicated autoregressive models. Although O'Hanlon *et al.* (1992) do not report the parameter estimates should the autoregression coefficient be close to one the ARIMA (1, 0, 0) is in effect the random walk with drift model.

4.3.2 *The determinants of diversity in earnings behaviour*

The empirical research presented so far in this section has produced some interesting and useful conclusions. However, the work is based on ad hoc analysis of available data with little underlying theory to guide it. One attempt to set up hypotheses concerning the expected performance of accounting time-series is presented by Lev (1983). Although it is difficult to produce convincing evidence of consistent behaviour patterns in the typical firm, selected firms often display non-random characteristics. Lev suggested that there are various explanations for this diversity in time-series behaviour of firms such as product type, competition, firm size and capital intensity.

1. *Product type*

The demand for durable goods is thought to be more highly dependent on the level of discretionary income available to consumers than the demand for non-durables and services. As discretionary income is more variable than total income, results for durable goods companies may well be more erratic than for other firms. The argument that earnings behaviour is dependent on product type can obviously be extended to a more detailed analysis than a simple split between durables and non-durables.

2. *Competition*

Companies operating in a more competitive environment are likely to exhibit more random performance than those with the benefit of effective barriers to entry. Competitive firms will have to absorb shocks to their market, whereas protected firms can pass these on to the consumer. Serial correlation and stable earnings might be expected to be more obviously evident in companies trading with limited competition.

3. *Firm size*

Apart from any tendency for larger firms to benefit from a less than competitive environment, it is assumed that there is a greater chance of diversification in larger firms, and portfolio effects will tend to reduce random elements in company performance. This could lead to lower volatility and higher autocorrelation than would be the case for less diversified firms.

4. *Capital intensity*

It is readily apparent that firms in capital intensive industries will suffer more severely than less intensive firms as they are unable to shed variable cost as effectively. This may be expected to cause high earnings volatility and low autocorrelation.

Lev's (1983) examination of 385 US firms again confirmed low autocorrelations for the first difference series of net earnings, return on equity and sales. However, the spread of autocorrelations was sufficient to claim 'considerable heterogeneity' and 'the correlation coefficients for about 15–20 per cent of the firms were statistically significant at the 0.05 per cent level'. Obviously 5 per cent of firms are expected to be significant at 5 per cent confidence levels. In an attempt to explain this diversity surrogates for the hypothesised causal factors were regressed against the autocorrelations computed. While the explanatory power of the resulting equations was low, both product type and competition surrogates were usually statistically significant, whereas size and capital intensity surrogates were not.

Further interesting evidence emerged when the variability of the earnings series, net of the variability induced by the autocorrelation effect, was discovered to be positively correlated with product type and negatively with size. Thus the effect of economic determinants on time-series autocorrelation and variability would appear to be distinct.

One factor not dealt with above is the possibility that the behaviour of accounting variables will be in part dependent on the practices used to compute earnings. Beaver (1970) has shown that even where the underlying earnings stream is described accurately as a mean reverting process, the averaging effect of accounting computations will induce autocorrelation. This can be demonstrated by a simple simulation. The data in Table 4.2, simulated over 500 readings, are based on the profits for a firm obtaining an expected 10 projects per month, with an expected life span of two years and an expected profit of £1000 each. A stochastic (chance) element is built into each of the variables. The annual profit is computed in two ways. Firstly profits are accounted for when realised (profit on completion) and secondly profit is accounted for over the life span of the project (profit apportioned).

While the results are dependent on the model used and particularly on the assumptions concerning the underlying earnings-generating process, the results are very much as predicted by Beaver. A strong autocorrelation on the first order for the averaged series

Table 4.2 Impact of accounting policies on time-series

Lag	Profit on completion		Profit apportioned	
	Actual	1st diff	Actual	1st diff
T-1	−0.183	−0.572	0.516	−0.075
T-2	−0.013	−0.042	0.108	−0.371
T-3	0.059	−0.058	0.055	−0.026
T-4	0.007	−0.020	0.027	−0.033

Note: The results report the autocorrelation statistics for various time lags for the computed earnings and the first difference of the earnings series.

is observed, as is a strong negative first order on the first differenced series for the profit on completion. Such results would be expected where the underlying earnings are assumed to be mean reverting. The averaging in the accruals process also produced a considerably narrower dispersion of earnings, and the standard deviation of earnings fell from £9074 for the profit on completion figures to £4763 for the apportioned profit. A more detailed analysis of the effect of the earnings measurement process is given in Rees and Sutcliffe (1988).

Not only might the prescribed accounting technique alter the flow of reported earnings, but also managerial discretion (legitimate or otherwise) will also impact on the series. The most often hypothesised manipulation is that management smooth the earnings figures, possibly by over-accruing expenses in a poor year and charging them in later years. Conversely, there is the possibility that a bad year might well be a suitable occasion to get rid of costs. In this case, management live with the poor results for one year but subsequent years will appear to constitute a recovery.

4.4   Forecasting accounting numbers

Considerable resources have been devoted by practitioners and academics in an attempt to develop effective methods of forecasting accounting numbers, and earnings in particular. It is difficult to describe a generalised process of forecasting when it is subject to much variation due to forecasters' experience, technical ability and resources. However, a typical procedure might involve the following steps.

1. The industrial and geographical make-up of the company's operations are identified to enable the collection of statistical data which relate closely to those markets.
2. Potentially relevant data, such as industry specific costs, prices, orders and deliveries, would be collated and analysed in order to establish any useful statistical relationship between published data and the firm's profit figures.
3. The analysts are often required to forecast up to two years ahead. Consequently, predictions of the basic statistics will be required from which the earnings forecasts are derived.
4. The statistical relationship identified in 2 above, and the appropriate data collected or forecast in 3, can then be combined to produce an earnings prediction.
5. The firm's management may be contacted to confirm the assumptions and conclusions of the analysis as far as possible. The forecasted earnings will also be compared with forecasts prepared by other analysts.

The process described above is only one example of forecasting techniques, which could range from even more simplistic models to complex estimation of the cost and revenue functions of the various industrial or geographical segments of a firm. The different approaches can often be seen in the reports prepared by investment brokers. The following exhibit contains an explicit description of the forecasting approach employed by one firm looking to forecast earnings and cash flows for Tarmac Plc.

Academic forecasting models used in research tend to be somewhat sparse when compared with the practitioner's. This is in part due to the difficulty in obtaining usable

——— **Exhibit 4.1**   One approach to the forecasting of Tarmac Plc's earnings ———

To get to a value for each of Tarmac's division, there are three steps. The macro investigation of the industry's outlook, a micro analysis of Tarmac, and the application of a discount model.

The macro outlook
Given that we are assessing the long-term potential for the group, the starting point is the macro outlook. There are two components of this.

(i)   The construction economy's relationship to the macro economy. At the simplest level this is construction output as a percentage of GDP. On the basis of the long-term trend as illustrated in the following graph, we have assumed that construction remains at a constant 8 per cent of GDP.

[Graphical material omitted]

The graph above shows that since the late 1960s construction output has steadily fallen as a proportion of UK economic activity to an average of 8 per cent over 1980—91. In our model we have assumed that over the next 15 years (the time period we have chosen), construction remains at 8 per cent of GDP and that GDP rises 2.5 per cent annually on average.

(ii)   Change in the nature of construction. While the overall direction of UK construction activity is a relatively straightforward affair (essentially being a function of the macro economy), the various components of the construction economy are liable to relative changes in importance as a function of demographic changes, demand and supply of building stock and Government expenditure plans. In the model we class all types of construction into four categories; new housing (public + private), commercial (including industrial building), infrastructure (public + private) and housing RM&I. The table below illustrates how these sectors have moved since 1958.

[Graphical material omitted]

Our recent macro review of the sector (The UK Construction Economy, September 1992) we highlighted long-term trends in each area which we incorporate into the model as summarised in the following table:

UK construction activity by sub-sector, 1991—2006

	1991A	1996E	2001E	2006E
New housing	10	15	10	8
Commercial	33	20	20	20
Infrastructure	25	30	30	30
Refurbishment	32	35	40	42
Total	100	100	100	100

Hence we see that refurbishment is the largest single growth area of construction, although housing should see an improvement over the new few years as it corrects back to the normalised level of activity from 1985 onwards, but then declines as the demographic profile changes. Commercial and industrial will revert back to a more representative level of activity up to 1996, and thereafter we anticipate a stable market.

The micro approach
On the basis of our macro model, each material is broken down by end use between the sub-sectors to create a long-term demand profile. For example, for aggregates, with high exposure to infrastructure and low exposure to refurbishment, we envisage that the rate of growth will show a lower long-term demand profile than the average. From this starting point we estimate cashflow on the basis of the following calculations.

Turnover of, for example, Tarmac's aggregates operations is then estimated using market share (to give an estimate of Tarmac's volumes) and price of the commodity. Prices include an underlying level of inflation for the model (estimated at + 5 per cent throughout the whole model), plus any real increase for each material that we anticipate over the period. Real increases are possible, for example, where there is a low input of external raw materials so that the full effects of price increases can be passed on. Cement and aggregates fit well into this category.

Operating profit is based on what we believe is a realistic long-term margin based on the operational gearing as a result of fixed/variable cost relationship. Pre-tax profit is not included — net debt of the group is split equally for all divisions included in the discount rate (see below).

Cashflow is calculated in a similar way to the old source and application method, which is more systematic than the new cashflow statement when analysing individual divisions. The make-up of the divisional cashflow is as follows:

Sources
Profit
Depreciation (as % of volume consumed)

Applications
Capital expenditure (as percentage of depreciation)
Working capital
Taxation (NB not dividends)

Working capital here is the relationship between turnover and stock levels, using historic patterns to give some sensitivity. Long-term averages measured over the past 30 years have been used. Our cashflow is the residual of the sources minus the applications for each.

The discount model
The model we have chosen to use to calculate Tarmac's value is the discounted cashflow of each of the group's divisions to get an NPV for the group. For those interested in the mechanics of the model, our discount rate comprises two parts.

Debt funding is distributed across the group, so that each division has a certain percentage of its cashflow funded by debt equivalent to the group gearing figure. The remainder of the group is funded by equity. For Tarmac, we are assuming a debt/equity ratio of 30 per cent for reasons discussed in the 'Balance Sheet' section above. In our calculation of the discount rate, we have used what we assume is a realistic real interest rate for the debt financing (3.5 per cent here). Equity funding is more complex. Portfolio theory suggests that equity funding comprises the return needed to induce equity investment over and above the risk-free return. Risk-free return here is simply the real interest on a Gilt. For equity return, we have assumed an equity market premium, and multiplied this by a Beta factor to incorporate risk in a normal distribution risk/reward scenario. In the model 1 = zero risk, 1.1 = 10 per cent risk etc. For the most part we have assumed a low level of risk given that building materials follow a cyclical (and therefore predictable) long-term demand pattern, are asset backed and tend to be cash generative rather than negative. We subscribe a higher risk factor to Tarmac's housing (Beta = 1.5) and construction (Beta = 1.8) that do not fit as easily into these criteria. On this basis, the normal discount rate we use through the model is as follows:

Debt funding at 3.5% for 30% of funds (taken for group)   =   1.05%
Equity funding:
Equity market premium   =   7%
Beta (risk factor)   =   20%
Real risk-free return (i.e. Gilt)   =   5%
Equity rate = (7% × 1.2) + 5%   =   13.4%
Equity funding for 70% (taken for group)   =   9.38%
Discount rate   =   10.43%

On the higher risk profiles we have mentioned for housing and construction, the discount rate would be 12.5 and 13.37 per cent respectively.

forecasts of causal factors for the large samples used by academics. The complex models used by practitioners are sometimes difficult to defend theoretically and the naive models used by researchers have the advantage of an obviously impartial nature. It is possible to overfit a model. Given enough variables a model can be made to fit the observed behaviour of any variable being studied.

4.4.1 *Evaluation of forecast efficiency*

The normal method of assessing forecasting efficiency is to measure the error, that is the difference between the forecast and the subsequent observed value. However, it is quite conceivable that the decision-maker may view an accurate forecasting model as inferior to a less accurate and less costly version.

Some of the different measures of forecast accuracy, where A is actual, F forecast and X the deflator, are:

1. Mean absolute error:

$$MAE = \frac{\sum_{1}^{n} \left| \dfrac{A_i - F_i}{X_i} \right|}{N} \tag{4.9}$$

This measure simply takes the average of all the errors in the sample and gives equal weighting to each unit or error.

2. Mean square error:

$$MSE = \frac{\sum_{1}^{n} \left[\dfrac{A_i - F_i}{X_i} \right]^2}{N} \tag{4.10}$$

This measure averages the errors in the sample but gives higher weighting to extreme error values than to lower ones.

3. Average error:

$$AVE = \frac{\sum_{1}^{n} \dfrac{A_i - F_i}{X_i}}{N} \tag{4.11}$$

This measure allows over- and under-estimates to cancel out and therefore fails to provide a measure of the accuracy of the forecasts but it does measure any bias (persistent tendency to over- or under-estimate).

All of these measures are standardised by a deflator X which is often the outcome A, but could also be the forecast F, the standard deviation of previous actuals, or the price of the firm's share at the time of the forecast — assuming that the actual and forecast are earnings per share.

4.4.2 *Determinants of forecast error accuracy*

The evaluation of forecasting error is more complex than first appearances would suggest. The difficulty of selecting an appropriate measure which effectively captures the costs and benefits of forecasting is mentioned above. An equally complex issue is the assessment of appropriate reference points. In order to evaluate a forecast, or forecaster, some standard is required but it is apparent that a good estimate in certain circumstances may well be a poor one in others. Previous discussion of Lev's work has shown that we can expect certain determinants to affect the behaviour of earnings including their volatility. These factors can also be expected to impinge on the ease with which the earnings of different types of firms can be predicted.

Perhaps the most obvious variable that would affect forecast accuracy is the stability of the series being modelled. Certain industries are notoriously volatile, others produce a relatively stable sequence of earnings. A comparison of forecast accuracy is simplest for firms with a similar risk level. Alternatively, some method will have to be found to allow for the different level of errors expected for different firms.

The forecast horizon will also affect the expected accuracy of any estimates. As the date at which the actual earnings will be disclosed approaches, new information will become available and this may be relevant to the eventual outcome. The accounting results of competitors, interim results for the actual firm, data concerning the production and marketing success and problems of the firm, or more accurate predictions of economy-wide variables may become known, all expanding the relevant dataset available to the forecaster and allowing scope for improved forecasts.

It can be expected that any variable which might increase the level of relevant information about a firm's prospects would produce a reduction in the forecast error. The increasing amount and accuracy of data available through time have already been suggested. It is also reasonable to expect that the larger the firm the greater the amount of information generated. This may come through more frequent press references, more attention from other analysts, or greater resources being expended by the firm itself. Obviously, the interest expressed in a firm is not only a function of its size — other factors such as political or economic importance may well be relevant. Consequently, any assessment of forecast accuracy should attempt to allow for such factors. Others can certainly be posited. Ferris and Hayes consider those factors relevant to prospectus profit forecasts and additionally include issuing house, type of issue, year of forecast, growth rate of the firm, economic conditions and the scope for managerial profit manipulation (Ferris and Hayes, 1977). Research such as that of Bhaskar and Morris (1984), which is discussed later, attempts to evaluate the effect of these factors.

4.5   Management and security analysts' forecasts

The previous sections have examined the motivations for forecasting and the techniques available. This section will review some examples of forecasting in practice. While implicit or explicit forecasts are made in many circumstances, most noticeably as part of the management process, the external observer is only able to evaluate a limited number of these, such as:

1.   Non-quantified forecasts will often be made by management and the media. While their imprecise nature makes these difficult to evaluate, they may well have an important role in the external analyst's decision-making process.

2. Management will, under certain circumstances, publish quantified forecasts of company performance. These will usually be in the prospectus issued when raising capital, or during takeover battles. However, companies may issue unsolicited forecasts when it suits their purposes.
3. The forecasts of investment analysts are often made public and can be evaluated. However, this is only a sample of the forecasts actually made by brokers and may not be typical of all the forecasts made.

4.5.1 *Management forecasts*

In an attempt to come to some conclusion about the value of unquantified forecasts, Steele classified the forecasts made for an (admittedly) non-typical group of companies for the period 1969–78 (Steele, 1982). This is shown in Table 4.3. He classified the forecast outlook into improved 56 per cent (1), similar 27 per cent (2) and worse 17 per cent (3), and the outcomes where the subsequent change in profits was to within $\pm$ 10 per cent were treated as similar.

Steele finds a statistically significant relationship between the predictions and the outcome. However, only fairly crude analysis can be made of unquantified forecasts. If the researcher had concluded that in a period of high inflation 'similar' results would be the prior year plus some inflation allowance, a number of readings would have been displaced from the left-most column to the centre and from the centre to the right. Under such circumstances the statistical tests would be less convincing. Thus, the results of this test are largely dependent on the researcher's definition of no change. Nevertheless, the researcher felt able to conclude that despite 'their vagueness such (unquantified) forecasts are not meaningless, since to a small extent they reduce uncertainty about the future'.

While management forecasts may be published under a variety of circumstances, the most notable and readily accessible are those made available as part of a prospectus issued when a firm is raising capital or during takeover bids. While comparisons with other forecasts may be attractive, some reservations are necessary as there may be an incentive to produce a biased forecast and Dev and Webb (1972) suggest that prospectus forecasts may be understated deliberately. Further, the issuers of the forecasts are in a position to manage the company profits to ensure closer compliance with the forecast than would otherwise have been achieved.

Table 4.3 Predictive content of unquantified forecasts

		Realisation			
		1	**2**	**3**	**Total**
Prediction	1	0.383	0.119	0.057	0.560
	2	0.154	0.057	0.054	0.266
	3	0.060	0.030	0.085	0.174
	Total	0.597	0.206	0.197	1

Source: Steele, 1982.

4.5.2 *Investment analysts' published forecasts*

The forecasts produced by investment analysts are of central importance to this text. As an observable output of the financial analyst's work, an examination of the techniques and attributes of brokers' forecasts may well be instructive. Furthermore, they are available for direct input into valuation models and earnings, or EPS, and will be found to be a frequently exploited variable in such models. Analysts' forecasts of earnings demand much attention in the capital markets. Most of the analysts' forecasts which are publicly available are distributed in the form of consensus forecasts.

Consensus forecasts

Many of the tests reported in this chapter make use of data from consensus forecasts. These services collect the forecasts of a number of analysts and publicise the individual and consensus forecasts. The Estimate Directory provides this service for most UK companies and a considerable number of continental European and Far Eastern firms. Exhibit 4.2 gives an example of the collected forecasts for Rolls-Royce Plc. Obviously this does not include all forecasting organisations and not necessarily all or the most recent forecasts for the firms given. There are various problems related to using such data such as how the analyst should weight the forecasts in computing the consensus, and to what extent the forecasts included are genuinely independent. Nevertheless the output is valuable for a number of reasons, as follows.

1. It provides a benchmark against which the forecasting skill of analysts can be assessed, which obviously allows for the difficulties experienced when comparing forecasting accuracy across different firms.
2. The consensus forecast from a number of independent forecasters is normally found to be more accurate than the results for any individual. The errors are assumed to be independent and therefore will tend to cancel out (Coggin and Hunter, 1983).
3. Where the distribution of forecasts is a variable of importance, as in assessing the confidence to be attached to a forecast, or as an independent measure of the risk of a firm, the consensus database provides a useful cross-sectional sample.

Accuracy of analysts' forecasts

If the time and resources used in producing analysts' forecasts are to be justified, they must out-perform the more cost-effective naive models. The market appears to value forecasts as it allocates resources to their preparation and examination. Early research in the US, for example Cragg and Malkiel and Elton and Gruber, failed to find evidence of superior performance but both of these studies compared analysts' forecasts with a battery of naive models. It is not surprising that for the limited time span tested only one of these models out-performed the analysts (Cragg and Malkiel, 1968; Elton and Gruber, 1972).

Brown and Rozeff (1979), Collins and Hopwood (1980) and Fried and Givoly (1982) all discovered small but significant improvements in analysts' forecasts compared to mechanical models. The first two of these studies examined Value Line's forecasts. This is an interesting organisation which is often cited as an example of successful exploitation of an inefficient market. Its performance will be evaluated in Chapter 6.

———————————— **Exhibit 4.2** Example consensus forecast ————————————

ROLLS-ROYCE PLC   **Price 179**
Ordinary shares of 20p   Market Cap. 2,187

65 Buckingham Gate, London, SW1E 6AT   Tel: 071-222-9020

Activities Engineering, providing technology to aerospace and industrial power system markets worldwide with product fields such as aero, marine and industrial gas turbines, power generation, nuclear engineering and materials handling. The group operates through two main units; AEROSPACE: which specializes in gas turbines for civil and military aircraft. INDUSTRIAL: which designs, constructs and installs complete power generation, transmission and distribution systems and major equipment for marine propulsion, oil and gas pumping, offshore and defence markets.

Note: LIFFE Options available.

		Forecast Changed	12/94F Profit	EPS	DPS	12/95F Profit	EPS	DPS
Albert E Sharp	H	21/10/94	95.0	5.8	5.00	105.0	6.4	5.00
BZW	S	29/09/94	80.0	5.0	5.00	95.0	6.0	5.00
Charles Stanley	S	− 21/10/94	100.0	6.3	5.00	130.0	8.8	5.20
Charterhouse Tilney Secs.	STS	5/09/94	86.0	5.6	5.00	100.0	6.4	5.50
Credit Lyonnais Laing	H	6/09/94	95.0	6.0	5.00	135.0	9.0	5.50
Fleming Securities	B	20/09/94	110.0	7.4	5.00	175.0	12.2	5.50
Hoare Govett	**H**	**5/09/94**	**87.0**	**5.7**	**5.00**	**125.0**	**8.5**	**5.00**
James Capel	S	27/09/94	90.0	5.6	5.00	115.0	7.0	5.00
Kleinwort Benson	B	+ 22/11/94	100.0	6.4	5.00	160.0	9.0	5.00
Lehman Brothers	2H	+ 28/11/94	169.0	10.7	6.50	249.0	15.5	7.50
London Wall	H	28/10/94	95.0	6.1	5.00	125.0	7.7	5.50
Morgan Stanley	H	16/05/94	—	7.9	—	13.0	—	
NatWest Securities	ADD	31/08/94	90.0	6.0	5.00	136.0	9.0	5.20
Nikko	S	2/09/94	95.0	6.1	5.00	130.0	8.1	5.00
Nomura	H	24/11/94	100.0	6.1	5.00	120.0	7.1	5.00
Panmure Gordon	H	28/09/94	105.0	7.7	5.00	140.0	10.6	5.30
S.G.S.T. Securities	S	31/08/94	85.0	5.3	5.00	130.0	6.7	5.00
Smith New Court	B	22/09/94	100.0	6.8	5.00	140.0	9.9	5.30
UBS	B	20/09/94	108.0	7.2	5.00	149.0	10.2	5.30
Warburg	S	7/10/94	90.0	5.7	5.00	110.0	7.4	5.30
Williams de Broe	B	12/09/94	105.0	7.4	5.00	160.0	10.6	5.40
Yamaichi	H	1/09/94	89.0	5.8	5.00	150.0	9.5	5.00
Consensus	(quality YGU)		95.0	6.1	5.00	130.0	8.8	5.20
% Change on Previous Year			+ 25	+ 3	0	+ 37	+ 44	+ 4
Prospective P/E and DY on consensus				29.3	3.5		20.3	3.6

Year Ended 12/93   **Price Relative**

Profit	76.0	P/E	30.0	1m	+ 3%
EPS	6.0	Dividend Yield	3.5	3m	+ 0%
Tax Charge	24			12m	+ 6%
Dividend	5.00				

SEDOL 0747761   SEAQ 45386   EPIC RR. 240 220 200 180 160 140 120 100
FT77   DTSM RLRC   RIC RR   80 1990 1991 1992 1993 1994
Registrars   Nat West 0272 306600

Announcements
Interims   2/9/93
Finals   10/3/94
Report and Accounts   11/7/94
AGM   25/5/94

Table 4.4 Financial analysts' forecasts versus mechanical models

		Accuracy	Bias
All cases	FAF	16.4%	−5.3%
	Model (a)	19.3%	−1.2%
	Model (b)	20.3%	1.4%

Source: Fried and Givoly, 1982.

The following research evidence will concentrate on the work of Fried and Givoly (1982), as their findings usefully examine a number of different aspects of broker's forecasts and on that of Capstaff *et al.* (1995) for the insights into UK conditions. Although a number of researchers are currently investigating the performance of forecasters in continental European countries other than the UK no large-scale results are available as yet.

Fried and Givoly's study compared analysts' forecasts with two mechanical models, see Table 4.4.

$$\text{Model (a):} \quad E(P_t) = A_{t-1} + C \tag{4.12}$$

$$\text{Model (b):} \quad E(P_t) = A_{t-1} + f + k.E(\Delta A_{mt}) \tag{4.13}$$

Where A is the actual result, P the predicted, C the arithmetic past growth of EPS for the prior five years, f and k are regression coefficients and $(E\Delta A_{mt})$ is the expected change in the market earnings using a model similar to (a) to estimate this. The regression parameters were estimated from all available data which varied from 9 to 19 years. Fried and Givoly studied 1100 forecasts over 1969−79 and these out-performed the naive models.

Although financial analysts' forecasts are marginally more accurate than the naive models they appear to exhibit a tendency to optimism.

Accuracy of forecasts

Capstaff *et al.* (1995) present some large sample results from 1988 to 1991 for analysts' forecasts provided by I/B/E/S regarding UK firms. The mean forecast errors, deflated by actual EPS, both for analysts and the naive model are shown in Table 4.5 for the full sample, and in Figure 4.3 for horizons of up to 20 months. The tests on the data show that analysts' forecast errors are significantly smaller than naive (random walk) forecast errors for the full sample and for horizons of up to 17 months before the year-end.

The T-test is a paired test to examine the null hypothesis that the mean of the two sets of forecast errors are not significantly different. The W-test is the equivalent Wilcoxon non-parametric test that the medians of the matched pairs are not significantly different.

Table 4.5 Mean forecast errors for UK forecasters and a naive model

ANALYSTS' mean forecast error	NAIVE mean forecast error	Number of forecasts	T-TEST p-value	W-TEST p-value
0.166	0.243	52049	0.000	.000

Source: Capstaff *et al.,* 1995.

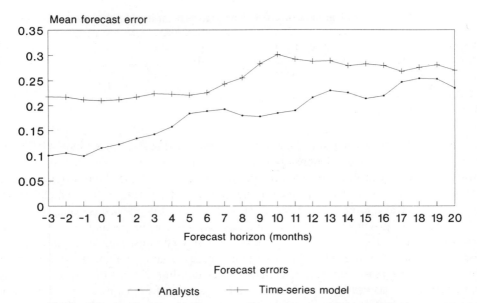

Figure 4.3 Analysts' and naive mean forecast errors and forecast horizon.

P-values less than 0.05 indicate that the null hypothesis has been rejected at confidence level of 5 per cent or better.

The time pattern of forecast errors and analysts' superiority is evident from Figure 4.3. Analysts' forecasts tend to become more accurate as the forecast horizon shortens. This is to be expected because more information becomes available as time progresses and, presumably, analysts make use of this timing advantage when producing forecasts. Temporary reversals in the downward trend of analysts' forecast errors occur at horizons of 14 and 13 months, and again at 7 months. A possible explanation in the latter case is the arrival of a significant news item, such as the earnings announcement, which marks the transition from one-year-ahead to two-year-ahead forecasts. For most companies this happens between the 8 and 6 month horizons as recorded by I/B/E/S. The blip in the trend at the 14 and 13 month horizons may to due to the arrival, approximately 6 months before the annual earnings figure, of news contained in the interim report. A worsening of forecast accuracy at this time implies over-reaction to the news.

Analysts' superiority over the naive model tends to diminish as the horizon lengthens, implying a lessening of the analysts' information advantages. The finding that the analysts' information advantage disappears beyond the 16 month horizon is perhaps surprising. The implication is that forecasts made earlier than 16 months prior to the earnings date have little economic value. Imhoff and Pare (1982), Conroy and Harris (1987), and Patz (1989) also report the disappearance of analyst superiority at longer forecast horizons.

Earnings increases and decreases

Analysts' inability to produce accurate forecasts of earnings may be constrained by agency relationships between forecasters and the forecasted firms. Some of the possible agency

Table 4.6 Mean absolute forecast errors split between earnings increase and decrease

Analysts' forecast error — earnings increased	Naive forecast error — earnings increased	Analysts' forecast error — earnings decreased	Naive forecast error — earnings decreased
0.094	0.209	0.329	0.320

Source: Capstaff *et al.*, 1995.

explanations for the inaccuracy of analysts' forecasts are discussed in Schipper (1991). In particular, broker—client relationships may encourage optimistic/favourable forecasts, for instance if the broker provides other fee-generating services to the client which might be threatened by adverse and unwelcome earnings forecasts. However, even in non-client relationships an adverse forecast could impair the analyst's access to the firm's management and other sources of privileged information and this may also encourage optimistic/favourable forecasts. Capstaff *et al.* (1995) hypothesise that if such constraints exist they will be especially evident in cases of declining earnings because analysts will be least comfortable forecasting a decrease, mindful of the agency relationship. To test this hypothesis they split the sample according to whether the earnings being forecast actually increased or decreased. Table 4.6 reports a selection of the forecast errors of analysts for earnings increases and decreases. It reports the average forecast error made by analysts and the naive model when earnings increased contrasted with earnings decreases.

It appears that forecasts are considerably more accurate when the outcome is an earnings increase. The average forecast error when earnings increase is less than 10 per cent whereas the average forecast error when earnings decrease is more than 30 per cent.

Figure 4.4 shows the relative accuracy of analysts' forecasts for earnings decreases and earnings increases. The accuracy of analysts' forecasts when earnings increase diminishes remarkably little as the horizon lengthens. In contrast, forecast errors associated with earnings decreases worsen considerably over time and become inordinately inaccurate at long horizons, so much so that average errors for all horizons beyond 12 months are close to or above 50 per cent. In fact the naive model predicts earnings decreases more accurately than analysts for all horizons longer than 4 months. This suggests an extreme reluctance of analysts to make pessimistic forecasts. A similar explanation is offered by Klein (1990). On the basis of her results she suggests that firms with unfavourable prospects put pressure on analysts to provide optimistic forecasts. Brown (1993) has anecdotal evidence that analysts tend to do this without any pressure being applied.

Bias in analyst's forecasts

Attributes other than accuracy are relevant to an assessment of analysts' forecasts and some investigation has been made into financial analysts' ability to incorporate all available information. Certainly, they should be able to assess any bias in their own estimates and adjust accordingly, hence rational forecasting should not produce consistent biases. Critchfield, Dyckman and Lakonishok (1978), and Malkiel and Cragg (1970), found no evidence suggesting that the forecasts reviewed were biased estimates. Critchfield, Dyckman and Lakonishok decomposed the mean square errors of predicted growth that they

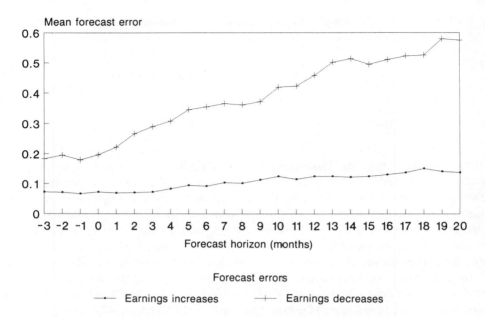

Figure 4.4 Analysts' mean forecast errors split by earnings outcome: increase and decrease.

discovered in their sample. Only 18 per cent of the error could be attributed to consistent bias.

Fried and Givoly (1982) were unable to improve analysts' forecasts by combining the naive model forecasts with the analysts' forecasts. However, the analysts' forecasts contained predictive information above that given in the naive forecasts. The implications are that analysts incorporate all information contained in the past earning figure, and further incorporate considerable data not available to the naive models.

However, newer research is less sanguine. Capstaff *et al.* (1995) estimated OLS models of actual change in earnings by forecasted change, where both changes are deflated by prior actual earnings, for a large sample of UK forecasts.

$$\left(\frac{A_{iT} - PA_{iT(h)}}{PA_{iT(h)}} \right) = \alpha + \beta \left(\frac{F_{iT(h)} - PA_{iT(h)}}{PA_{iT(h)}} \right) + e_{iT(h)} \tag{4.14}$$

$F_{iT(h)}$ is the analyst's forecast of firm i's period T earnings made at horizon h months prior to the year-end date, A_{iT} is firm i's earnings in period T, and $PA_{iT(h)}$ is firm i's most recently published annual earnings known at horizon h of year end T. The null hypothesis of rational behaviour requires that the intercept term should not be significantly different from zero and the slope coefficient should not be significantly different from one. Forecasts contain an optimistic bias (systematic over-estimation) if $\alpha < 0$, and a pessimistic bias (systematic under-estimation) if $\alpha > 0$. The interpretation of β is slightly different: $\beta > 1$ is taken as a sign of *under-reaction* to available information when the forecast is made because the absolute value of the forecast is too low; $\beta < 0$ is taken as a sign of *over-reaction* because the absolute value of the forecast is too high.

Table 4.7 Actual earnings change and forecasted earnings change

α (*t*-statistic)	β (*t*-statistic)	R^2	Number of forecasts
−0.085 (−62.47)[a]	0.815 (−39.89)	0.35	56,090

Source: Capstaff *et al.*, 1995.

Table 4.7 shows that for the whole sample α is significantly less than 0 and β is significantly less than 1. A qualitatively similar result was obtained for almost all of the individual horizons examined. These results strongly suggest that analysts are optimistic and over-estimate the change in earnings. This is consistent with over-reaction. These results are similar to De Bondt and Thaler (1990) for the US, but they conflict with O'Hanlon and Whiddett (1991) who used the regression technique on a small UK sample of consensus forecasts. De Bondt and Thaler interpret their results as a sign of optimism and over-reaction in the prior forecasts. They declare that, 'Forecasted changes are simply too extreme to be considered rational' (De Bondt and Thaler, 1990, p. 57). Abarbanell and Bernard (1992) provide a partial contradiction of De Bondt and Thaler's (1990) results by reporting evidence of under-reaction to recent earnings announcements. However, they also report evidence of over-reaction in forecasts made early in the accounting year which they interpret as a possible over-reaction to non-earnings information. Whilst there are a number of possible interpretations of the results they do not appear to be consistent with forecasts being formed in an efficient manner, nor are they consistent with under-estimation or under-reaction. One reservation applicable to all studies that have modelled actual change by forecast is that estimation problems will tend to bias the slope coefficient towards zero. A more robust model is to regress the error term on forecasted changes. In the case of Capstaff *et al.* (1995) the conclusions are unchanged.

A further test of the rationality of analysts' forecasts carried out by De Bondt and Thaler (1990) and Capstaff *et al.* (1995) is to examine the relationship between forecast revisions and prior forecasts. Rationality requires that forecast revisions cannot be predicted from previous forecasted changes. To test this hypothesis the revisions of forecasted change in earnings made at horizon h are regressed on the last forecasted change in earnings published by the same analyst prior to horizon h.

$$\left(\frac{F_{iT(h)} - PF_{iT(h)}}{PA_{iT(h)}} \right) = \alpha + \beta \left(\frac{PF_{iT(h)} - PA_{iT(h)}}{PA_{iT(h)}} \right) + e_{iT(h)} \qquad (4.15)$$

Here $PF_{iT(h)}$ is the most recent prior forecast by the same analyst which is available at horizon h when the new forecast $F_{iT(h)}$ is made. All other variables are as previously defined. The null hypothesis of unbiased forecasts is $\alpha = 0$ and $\beta = 0$. A systematic tendency to revise forecasts towards no change in earnings (negative slope coefficient) implies prior over-reaction, and a systematic tendency to revise forecasts away from no change (positive slope coefficients) implies prior under-reaction. The intercept can be interpreted as correcting prior optimism, if negative, or pessimism, if positive, see Table 4.8.

Table 4.8 The predictability of analysts' forecast revisions

α	β	R^2	Number of forecasts
-0.0209	-0.0469	0.01	45579
(-26.96)	(-16.51)		

Source: Capstaff *et al.*, 1995.

Capstaff *et al.* (1995) find that despite low R^2's for the full sample the results suggest a tendency to revise forecasts downwards, a sign of prior over-reaction. Of 45,579 matched pairs of revised forecasts and prior forecasts there were 27,715 (61 per cent) downward revisions in the absolute value of the prior forecast (suggesting prior over-reaction) whilst only 17,820 (39 per cent) were upward revisions (suggesting prior under-reaction). For certain horizons, centred on 7 and 19 months, the explanatory power of the model was much higher, approximately 10 per cent. Overall the results are in accord with De Bondt and Thaler (1990).

Surrogate for market expectations

Early work by Malkiel and Cragg (1970) attempted to explain diversity in price to earnings ratios by a regression model including growth, dividend yield and risk. The best explanatory historically-based predictor was used for the growth forecast, but nevertheless variables representing analysts' forecasts explained price earnings variability more effectively than did historically-based variables. This implies that investors alter their earnings capitalisation rate to take into account their expectations of earnings growth, and that earnings growth as measured by analysts' forecasts appears to be a more powerful description than other predictions of earnings growth.

Market expectations are normally modelled by use of time-series models of the type described in earlier sections of this chapter. In the absence of any accepted theory, a battery of models is used to show that the results are robust, as problems occur when the earnings process is not stationary and the 'best' predictive model alters.

In order to test financial analysts' forecasts as a surrogate for market expectations, Fried and Givoly (1982) analysed the market reaction to unexpected earnings measured as actual earnings less predicted earnings. The claim that the forecast mirrors market expectations is supported by the statistical relationship between the market reaction and the magnitude of unexpected earnings. Fried and Givoly's result assessed the earnings forecast error from the analysts' forecasts and from naive models (a) and (b) as described above. For the full sample correlation coefficients between prediction error and the cumulative abnormal return were 0.33 for the financial analysts' forecasts, 0.27 for both model (a) and model (b). Thus the analysts' errors were more strongly associated with abnormal returns, implying that they were closer to market expectations.

Forecast dispersion and risk measures

It is also possible that the information contained in the dispersion of forecasts made by analysts may be valuable in assessing the risk of companies. Normally, the assumption is made that prior distributions of accounting or stock market returns can be extrapolated to give a meaningful prediction of future risk. It will be seen from Chapter 5 that this does not necessarily hold, and it may be that the level of disagreement between analysts of the future is a better surrogate.

A number of different approaches have been tested in the research literature and detailed discussion of this matter will be left to Chapter 7. Note, however, that Comiskey, Mulford and Porter (1986) conclude that:

> . . . the theoretical expectation of a higher association of forecast difficulty with systematic risk is supported. In addition the expected higher association of systematic forecast-error (forecast-error beta) over systematic earnings variability (accounting beta) with systematic risk is found to hold.

4.6   Share prices, fundamentals and earnings forecasts

Early investigations of the relationship between accounting information and share price, discussed in Chapter 6, assumed that share values were in some way dependent on accounting earnings. However, while the information contained in changes in reported earnings and in share price movements reflect some of the same underlying factors, the delay inherent in preparing accounting earnings implies that share price movements will pre-empt accounting earnings. Under these circumstances, share prices act as a measure of, or surrogate for, that information processed by the market which is relevant to forthcoming earnings disclosures. It should also be expected that an accounting system that delays the recognition of profits until realisation will tend to be preceded by a share valuation system that recognises earnings as they become foreseeable. This additional information can be used to improve upon traditional earnings forecasts, which are based on trends in past earnings disclosures.

As Schipper (1991) made clear the test of analysts' forecast accuracy against the benchmark of a naive random walk model is hardly demanding. A number of routes are available to test whether analysts' forecasts take account of particular categories of information available at the time of the forecast. Capstaff et al. (1995) use share prices as a composite indicator of the future earnings potential of the firm. Share prices should capture all available information regarding future earnings although other information incorporated into share prices will add noise to the model. This noise may include information regarding the quality and riskiness of the earnings stream, as well as any long-term impact on earnings. However, the short-term predictive ability of share prices has been apparent since the seminal work of Ball and Brown (1968). The predictive content of price to earnings ratios has been demonstrated in a number of papers starting with Beaver and Morse (1978). More recently Ou and Penman (1989) have formally tested the predictive ability of E/P ratios. They show that an OLS model of percentage change in earnings with the E/P ratio as regressor is statistically significant. They contrast this with a model based on the accounting information contained in the prior set of accounts which is also highly significant but has marginally lower explanatory power. Ou and Penman (1989, p. 133) point out that the E/P ratio can be modelled using financial statement variables and conclude that, 'The information that is reflected in P/E ratios is also contained in financial statements.'

Whether the E/P ratio is viewed as an operational measure of the information available from financial statement analysis or simply as a repository of information, a sub-set of which is relevant to future earnings, is interesting but unimportant for the tests in hand. Whichever view is taken, it is apparent that the share price is readily available to analysts at the time they make their forecasts and that prior evidence seems to indicate that the ratio may have predictive ability. Capstaff *et al.* (1995) test the following equation:

$$
\left(\frac{A_{iT} - PA_{iT(h)}}{PA_{iT(h)}} \right) = \alpha + \beta \left(\frac{F_{iT(h)} - PA_{iT(h)}}{PA_{iT(h)}} \right)
$$
$$
+ \gamma \left(\frac{(E/P)_{mT(h)} \cdot SP_{iT(h)}}{PA_{iT(h)}} - 1 \right) + e_{iT(h)}
$$

(4.16)

Here the actual change and forecasted change terms are defined as in Equation 4.3. The second term on the right-hand-side represents a forecast derived from the market-wide average earnings to price ratio $(E/P)_{mT(h)}$ as published on the last day of the month preceding horizon h of year-end T. $SP_{iT(h)}$ is the firm's share price at horizon h and $PA_{iT(h)}$ is the latest publicly available annual earnings available at horizon h. This variable simply generates the change in published annual earnings that would be required for the firm's E/P ratio to equal the market average and the presumption is that the E/P ratio for the firm will move towards the E/P ratio for the market. Full adjustment would imply a coefficient of one in the absence of collinear analysts' forecasts. If the analysts' forecasts made at horizon h incorporate all information available in the earnings to price ratio γ will not be significantly different from zero.

The results of the analysis of the information content of price earnings ratios are presented in Table 4.9 for the full sample. The γ coefficient is positive and significantly different from zero, usually at very high confidence levels. These results suggest that price earnings ratios available at the time of the forecast contain information not utilised by analysts in making their forecasts. Over all horizons the γ coefficients are positive and significant. The E/P variable is calculated in such a way that the variable is interpretable as an independent forecast of earnings change directly comparable with the analysts' forecasts. Thus the accuracy of analysts' forecasts can be improved by weighting the forecast

Table 4.9 Incremental information content of price-earnings-based forecasts

α (t-statistic)	β (t-statistic)	γ (t-statistic)	R^2	Number of forecasts
−0.070 (−51.79)	0.795 (155.70)	0.226 (67.49)	0.50	51989

Source: Capstaff *et al.*, 1995.

submitted by the analysts with that derived from the share price and market E/P ratio. The conclusion is that valuable information is being neglected by analysts — assuming, of course, that their objective is to produce accurate forecasts.

Capstaff *et al.* (1995) comment that their results regarding the incremental content of E/P forecasts above those of analysts are stronger for smaller firms. This may be at odds with the findings of Freeman (1987) and Collins *et al.* (1987) who find that the information content of share prices with respect to earnings is weaker for small firms than for larger ones. This is consistent with intuition for if the incentives for private search are stronger for larger rather than for smaller firms, as is normally supposed to be the case, then 'if search activities are concentrated on large firms and are successful, security prices reflect more precise estimates of large firms' earnings than small firms' earnings' (Freeman, 1987, p. 199). However, the increased precision of the search will also be reflected in the explicit earnings forecasts published by analysts.

Some research in the US has shown that analysts appear to ignore information contained in share prices (e.g. Brown 1993). Abarbanell (1991) offers the explanation that analysts have incentives to revise forecasts only when they receive new private information, and ignore new information contained in share price changes. The reasoning is that investors can more easily discern the private information content of analysts' forecasts if this is not combined with information from other signals such as share prices on which they prefer to place their own interpretation. This is a possible explanation of Capstaff *et al.*'s (1995) results.

There is an alternative explanation. As noted earlier there is usually a delay between the date the forecast is originally produced by the analyst and the date it is submitted/logged by I/B/E/S. The delay means the share price at a particular horizon has a timing advantage over the I/B/E/S forecast logged for the same horizon, which might account for its incremental information content. Analysts do, of course, have access to share price data immediately prior to submitting the forecast to I/B/E/S and could, therefore, make an adjustment. However, they may choose not to do so. A delay is consistent with the view that analysts typically reveal their forecasts privately to favoured clients some time before making them public. For instance, Trueman and McNichols (1994) have developed a model whose predictions are consistent with the idea that security analysts' information activities are geared to providing private information to clients. Once analysts have provided a forecast privately it seems unlikely they will provide a *different* forecast for public consumption as this could damage client—broker relationships and cast doubt on the analysts' reliability. Trueman and McNichols' (1994) model implies that clients prefer 'perfect' private information about forthcoming public signals, rather than 'perfect' public signals at odds with previously acquired private information. However, Capstaff *et al.* (1995) investigate this possibility by using one and two month lagged E/P forecasts and find that the incremental content of the E/P forecast is only slightly lower and still significant.

Fundamentals

In the first of two related and seminal articles Ou and Penman (1989) investigated the information content of the financial statement fundamentals. They find that the share price changes, which a number of studies have demonstrated can be used to predict earnings changes, are a relatively poor basis for forecasting, but in common with the research referred to above they find that earnings to price ratios are quite good predictors. More importantly they also show that the information contained in the income statement and balance sheet can be used to predict earnings changes. In essence they build a statistical model which replicates the work of fundamental analysts. The paper is important in the insights it gives into fundamental analysis. In a related paper the authors go on to demonstrate that abnormal returns can be earned by using the earnings predictions as a basis for investment decisions but it must be conceded that the second paper is more controversial than the research which simply tries to predict earnings. Ou and Penman (1989, p. 112) summarise their work as follows:

> While accrual accounting rules produce an earnings number which reflects the information in stock prices with a lag, they also produce a large array of additional numbers presented in the income statement, balance sheet and changes in financial position. We demonstrate that certain of these numbers can be summarised into one measure that predicts future earnings and also filters out transitory components of current earnings.

The method used by Ou and Penman was to scan a set of 68 line items or ratios of line items derived from the financial statements of firms and estimate the relationship between these data items for a large sample of firms and the subsequent changes in earnings of these firms. They estimated the model twice using US data from 1965−72 and 1973−77 with more than 11,000 cases in each period. The model is estimated using logit techniques with the dependent variable indicating the direction of change in earnings not the magnitude. As the researchers simply load available ratios into the model it is to be expected that the significant variables switch from model to model and this is found to be the case. At this point the research has simply mined through a very large dataset for statistically significant relationships. The interesting results are obtained from using the model estimated in one period to predict changes in earnings in another period. Ou and Penman contrast the predictive ability of their model with last year's earnings changes, prior stock market returns, and the earnings to price ratio and these results are given in Table 4.10. The only two variables which have predictive power are the Ou and Penman model and the *E/P* ratio.

As reported earlier changes in earnings have little predictive power, and the price changes have modest predictive power with market-adjusted 12 months return performing best. The three models which help to forecast subsequent changes all have additional predictive ability given the other. In other words given the forecast derived from price changes or the proposed model or the *E/P* ratio either of the other two improve the accuracy of the forecast — although it should be noted that the new model has little to add to *E/P* ratios whilst *E/P* ratios add rather more to the model.

In a more recent but similar paper Lev and Thiagarajan (1993) also demonstrate the forecasting ability of fundamental analysis models. It is not the focus of their paper which concentrates on identifying the quality of earnings and is discussed in more detail in Chapter 6 but it adds some further insight to the Ou and Penman work discussed above. Firstly, the data is a more recent sample (1974−88) and rather than simply using all available line item data their model is based on an analysis of those indicators of high-quality earnings that are used by analysts. These include (a) increase in inventory at a higher rate than sales increase, (b) disproportionate increases in debtors, (c) cutback of capital expenditure,

Table 4.10 Results of regression of percentage change in earnings on lagged variables
1973−83

$$\Delta EPS_{it+1}/EPS_{it} = a + bX_{it} + \epsilon_t$$

Xit	Ave b	t(b)	#b>0	Ave R2	Min R2	Max R2	NOBS
DEPSit/EPSit-1	0.00	0.11	7	0.00	0.00	0.02	15,302
CR12it	0.20	4.74	11	0.02	0.00	0.06	15,022
CU12it	0.23	5.89	11	0.02	0.01	0.06	15,022
CU24it	0.07	2.60	9	0.01	0.00	0.05	14,754
(E/P)it	−1.06	−8.64	0	0.07	0.04	0.10	16,632
PRit	0.85	8.57	11	0.05	0.03	0.11	16,866
CU12it .4<PR<.6	0.31	6.31	11	0.06	0.01	0.14	7,029
CU12it PR>.6 and PR<.4	0.18	4.05	11	0.01	0.00	0.04	7,993

The cross-sectional regression equation is estimated for each of the 11 years. Ave b is the mean estimated slope coefficient over the 11 years and $t(b)$ is a t-statistic on the mean coefficient estimated from the time series of coefficient estimates. Ave R2 is the mean R" observed over the 11 years and min R2 and Max R2 the lowest and highest R2 observed respectively. NOBS is the number of observations pooled over all years.
CR12 is the cumulative monthly return for firm i for the 12 months from 9 months prior to the end of fiscal year t to 3 months after.
CU12 is the same calculation as CR12 using market-adjusted returns.
CU24 is the cumulative monthly market-adjusted return for 24 months prior to 3 months after the end of fiscal year t.
(E/P) is the earnings to price ratio three months after fiscal year end for year t.
PR is the estimated probability of an earnings increase in year $t+1$ given attributes reported for year t.

Source: Ou and Penman, 1989.

(d) cutback in R&D expenditure, (e) a disproportionate drop in the gross profit, (f) a disproportionate change in selling and administrative expenses, (g) a disproportionate change in doubtful debt provisions, (h) a change in the effective tax rate, (i) a disproportionate change in the order backlog, (j) changes in the workforce, (k) the use of LIFO accounting techniques, and (l) an audit qualification. The implications of these variables are considered later but it is sufficient to note that when modelling stock market returns over the accounting year most of these variable were statistically significant — especially when changes in the economic climate are taken into account.

With regards to the predictive power of the model the extracts given in Table 4.11 demonstrate that firms with high-quality earnings tend to have higher earnings growth than low-quality earnings. The researchers have split the sample into three groups of high, medium and low-quality earnings, and five groups ranging from a low change in the previous year's earnings to a high change. It is clear that for each group the high-quality earnings have higher growth in next year's earnings than the medium and the medium higher growth than the low. This is repeated for second and third year's earnings growth and the relationship gradually decays though is still statistically significant in the second year.

Taken together these two papers seem to indicate that fundamental analysis of financial statements can contribute to earnings forecasting. Of course, when we examined the forecasts of analysts these could well be based on fundamental analysis but at least we now have some evidence which gives an insight into how this process may work.

Table 4.11 Fundamental signals and subsequent earnings changes

	High quality	Medium quality	Low quality
Current year's earnings Change			
Low	2.08*	1.33	1.86
Medium 1	0.20*	−0.37	−0.46
Medium 2	−0.03*	−0.04	−0.26
Medium 3	0.12*	−0.09	−0.38
High	0.07*	−0.16	−0.26
All cases	0.49*	0.13	0.10

* = HQ significantly different from MQ+LQ at 0.05 levels. Earnings change is defined as the change in earnings divided by the prior year's absolute earnings level.
From Lev and Thiagarajan, 1993, Table 8.

4.7 Conclusion

The time-series behaviour of earnings and the forecasting of earnings have been areas of fundamental interest to the analyst primarily due to their importance in valuation models. While forecasting and analysis of other elements of the financial statement are of interest, most work by practitioners and academics has focused on the earnings or rate of return. In general, the results have been disappointing. It is difficult to specify a model that describes the earnings stream with any degree of accuracy and the working assumption often adopted is that earnings follow a random walk with drift. However, the general results do not hold for all firms and persistent statistical relationships can be used to forecast with some measure of skill for this limited sub-sample. Moreover, the work of Beaver (1970) and Mueller (1986) has shown that rates of return are more easily modelled than absolute earnings, and that these rates may often follow a mean reverting process, the mean being specific to the firm rather than the full sample.

The difficulty of modelling or predicting earnings is not uniform across all firms. Certain structural factors such as industry, competition, size, operating and financial gearing can all be seen to impact on the variability of earnings and consequently on the difficulty experienced in modelling them. Certain factors are also seen to impact on the difficulty in making the forecast, and these are based on the quantity of information available. Again, the size of the firm may be relevant, together with the time horizon of the forecast and the number of analysts following that stock. All these determinants of forecast accuracy have some measure of empirical evidence to back them, but in many cases this is not clear cut.

Two sources of information regarding forecasts of earnings appear to have some valuable information content.

1. The forecasts produced by financial analysts generally appear to out-perform any forecasts based on historical data and collectively are a good description of market expectations. Whether they contain any information that can be useful in investment strategies is another matter. Although analysts' forecasts are generally found to be more accurate than other forecasts there is some evidence that they are less than ideal

— if unbiased and accurate forecasts are thought to be ideal. These shortcomings appear to be especially severe when the earnings forecasted are declining. Indeed, Capstaff *et al.* (1995) conclude that 'Taken together these results cast considerable doubt on the rationality of earnings forecasts made by UK analysts during the period from 1988 to 1990. Researchers and practitioners should be wary when using analysts' forecasts, especially those made some months before the accounting year-end.'

2.　　The second effective predictor is the share price itself. It appears that part of the stream of earnings represents factors also measured in the share price, and the capital market's propensity to incorporate all available relevant information would suggest that forecasts built on share price movements will be difficult to out-perform. Research evidence suggests that financial analysts' forecasts have predictive ability beyond that incorporated into the share price, but also that the share price has predictive information beyond that of the analysts' forecast.

Note

1.　　This chapter draws heavily on the work of Capstaff, Paudyal and Rees (1995) and I am grateful to my colleagues for permission to use this evidence.

──────────────── QUESTIONS ────────────────

1.　　　(a)　Obtain as long a time-series of EPS for five companies as is possible (a minimum of 10 years might be required but a 30-year history should be available). Plot the time-series of EPS and the first differences of EPS. What conclusion can you draw from these plots?

　　　　(b)　Obtain, if possible, the book value of equity per share for the sample used in 1(a). Plot the time-series of return on equity and the first differences of return on equity. What conclusion can you draw from these plots?

　　　　(c)　Obtain, if possible, the market value of equity per share for the sample used in 1(a). Plot the time-series of the earnings yield and the first differences of earnings yield. What conclusion can you draw from these plots?

2.　　Using the data from Question 1 try and fit the four models given in Section 4.2.5 to each time-series. Which models best describe the series? Is it possible to combine the models to improve these results? Do the results you estimated conform with your expectations?

3.　　Two readily available sources of earnings predictions are available to investment analysts — concensus forecasts and share price-based forecasts. As Beaver, Lambert and Morse note (1980) 'Preliminary evidence indicates that price earnings-based forecasting models are more accurate than the random walk with drift model.' How might investment analysts utilise this information content of security prices? How might they be able to use it based on prices or price-earnings ratios?

4.　　Obtain the actual EPS subsequently disclosed, and the share price and concensus forecast at three consecutive year-ends for a small sample of firms (preferably more than 25 firms and it may be easier to use firms with the same year-end).

(a) Using the second year's EPS as a forecast for the last year's, and the second year plus drift estimated as the difference between the first and the second year, calculate the mean absolute, mean squared and average errors. Which forecast performed best?

(b) Using the consensus forecast and a forecast derived from the share price and the average price to earnings ratio, calculate the mean absolute, mean squared and average errors. Which forecast performed best?

(c) Is it possible to improve on the best of the four forecasts identified in (a) and (b) above by weighting and/or combining the forecasts?

5. Many valuation models require forecasts of earnings which may be based on a consensus of analysts' forecasts, on so-called 'naive models', or on share price movements. Consider the evidence concerning the accuracy of forecasts available from these three sources and discuss their value as an input to investment selection models.

6. (a) The following information gives some basic statistics concerning forecasts for three very different companies. Give your interpretation of the results given, and suggest some reasons why such disparities might have occurred with reference to research evidence where appropriate.

HANSON PLC			(a)Sep 1993	Sep 1994	Sep 1995
EPS	(Pence)	LATEST	14.81	14.77	18.03
		High		17.90	19.20
		Low		13.80	16.50
		Previous		14.86	18.15
		Std. Deviation		1.13	0.80
No. of brokers		LATEST		11	11
		Previous		12	12
LLOYDS BANK PLC			(a)Dec 1993	Dec 1994	Dec 1995
EPS	(Pence)	LATEST	47.33	62.11	70.20
		High		74.10	89.20
		Low		48.60	54.70
		Previous		62.17	69.79
		Std. Deviation		8.06	11.81
No. of brokers		LATEST		7	7
		Previous		0	0
MARKS & SPENCER PLC			(a)Mar 1994	Mar 1995	Mar 1996
EPS	(Pence)	LATEST	21.07	23.31	25.88
		High		23.80	26.70
		Low		22.80	25.10
		Previous		23.35	25.77
		Std. Deviation		0.33	0.49
No. of brokers		LATEST		10	10
		Previous		11	9

(a) Actual figures.
Consensus estimates and actuals provided by First Call International

(b) There is evidence that share price movements precede changes in accounting earnings. Discuss this evidence and its implications for financial forecasting.

7.   'Empirical tests have shown that there is a close correlation between analysts' forecasts of earnings and simple extrapolations of past earnings trends.' 'Earnings changes from year to year appear to follow a random walk.' What implications do you draw from these statements? (Society of Investment Analysts. Securities and Investment — sample paper.)

8.   Provide definitions for the following terms as used in this chapter:
      (a) Decomposition.
      (b) Structural change.
      (c) Mean reversion.
      (d) Random walk.
      (e) First difference.
      (f) Autocorrelation.
      (g) Forecast error.
      (h) Consensus forecast.

References

Abarbanell, J.S. (1991) Do analysts earnings forecasts incorporate information in prior stock price changes? *Journal of Accounting and Economics*, **14** 147–165.

Abarbanell, J.S. and Bernard, V.L. (1992) Tests of analysts' overreaction/underreaction to earnings information as an explanation for anomalous stock price behaviour, *Journal of Finance*, **47**, 1181–1207.

Arnold, J. and Moizer, P. (1984) A survey of the methods used by UK investment analysts to appraise investments in ordinary shares, *Accounting and Business Research*, Summer, 195–207.

Ball, R. and Brown, P. (1968) An empirical examination of accounting income numbers, *Journal of Accounting Research*, Autumn, 159–178 .

Ball, R. and Watts, R. (1972) Some time-series properties of accounting numbers, *Journal of Finance*, June, 663–82.

Beaver, W. (1970) The time-series behaviour of earnings, *Journal of Accounting Research, Empirical Research in Accounting: Selected Studies*, 62–107.

Beaver, W., Lambert, R. and Morse, D. (1980) The information content of security prices, *Journal of Accounting and Economics*, March, 3–28.

Beaver, W. and Morse, D. (1978) What determines price-earnings ratios, *Financial Analysts Journal*, July–August, 65–76.

Benesh, G. and Peterson, P. (1986) On the relationship between earnings changes, analysts' forecasts and stock price fluctuations, *Financial Analysts' Journal*, November–December, 29–39.

Bhaskar, K. and Morris, R. (1984) The accuracy of brokers' profit forecasts in the UK, *Accounting and Business Research*, Spring, 113–24.

Brown, L. (1993) Earnings forecasting research: its implications for capital market research, *International Journal of Forecasting*, **9**, 295–320.

Brown, L. and Rozeff, M. (1979) Adaptive expectations, time-series models and analysts' forecast revisions, *Journal of Accounting Research*, Autumn, 341–51.

Capstaff, J., Paudyal, K. and Rees, W. (1995) The accuracy and rationality of earnings forecasts by UK analysts, *Journal of Business, Finance and Accounting*, January, **22**, no. 1, 69–87.

Coggin, T. and Hunter, J. (1983) Analysts' EPS forecasts nearer actual than statistical models, *Journal of Business Forecasting*, Winter, 20–3.

Collins, D., Kothari, S. and Rayburn, J. (1987) Firm size and the information content of prices with respect to earnings, *Journal of Accountancy and Economics*, July, **9**, no. 2, 111–138.

Collins, W. and Hopwood, W. (1980) A multivariate analysis of annual earnings forecasts generated from quarterly forecasts of financial analysts' and univariate time-series models, *Journal of Accounting Research*, Autumn, 390–406.

Comiskey, E., Mulford, C. and Porter, T. (1986) Forecast error, earnings variability and systematic risk: additional evidence, *Journal of Business, Finance and Accounting*, Summer, 257–65.

Conroy, R. and Harris, R. (1987) Consensus forecasts of corporate earnings: analysts' forecasts and time series models, *Management Science*, 725–738.

Cragg, J. and Malkiel, B. (1968) The consensus and accuracy of some predictions of the growth of corporate earnings, *Journal of Finance*, March, 67–88.

Critchfield, T., Dyckman, T. and Lakonishok, J. (1978) An evaluation of security analysts' forecasts, *Accounting Review*, July, 651–68.

Day, J.F.S. (1986) The use of annual reports by UK investment analysts, *Accounting and Business Research*, Autumn, 295–309.

De Bondt, W.F.M. and Thaler, R.H. (1990) Do security analysts overreact?, *American Economic Review Papers and Proceedings*, **40**, 52–57.

Dev, S. and Webb, M. (1972) The accuracy of company profits forecasts, *Journal of Business Finance*, **4**, no. 3, 26–39.

Elton, E. and Gruber, M. (1972) Earnings expectations and the accuracy of expectational data, *Management Science*, April, 409–24.

Ferris, K. and Hayes, C. (1977) Some evidence on the determinants of profit forecast accuracy in the United Kingdom, *International Journal of Accounting, Education and Research*, Spring, 27–36.

Foster, G. (1977) Quarterly accounting data: time-series properties and predictability results, *Accounting Review*, January, 1–21.

Freeman, R. (1987) The association between accountancy earnings and security returns for large and small firms. *Journal of Accountancy and Economics*, July, **9**, no. 2, 196–228.

Fried, D. and Givoly, D. (1982) Financial analysts' forecasts of earnings: a better surrogate for market expectations, *Journal of Accounting and Economics*, October, 85–107.

Givoly, D. and Lakonishok, J. (1984) The quality of analysts' forecasts of earnings, *Financial Analysts' Journal*, September–October, 40–47.

Imhoff, E.A. Jr. and Pare, P.V. (1982) Analysis and comparison of earnings forecast agents, *Journal of Accounting Research*, 429–439.

Klein, A. (1990) A direct test of the cognitive bias theory of share price reversals, *Journal of Accounting and Economics*, **13**, 155–166.

Lev, B. (1983) Some economic determinants of the time-series properties of earnings, *Journal of Accounting and Economics*, April, 31–48.

Lev, B. and Thiagarajan, S. (1993) Fundamental information analysis, *Journal of Accounting Research*, Autumn, **31**, no. 2, 190–215.

Little, I. (1962) *Higgledy-Piggledy Growth*, Institute of Statistics, Oxford.

Little, I. and Rayner, A. (1966) *Higgledy-Piggledy Growth Again*, Kelley, New York.

Malkiel, B. and Cragg, J. (1970) Expectations and the structure of share prices, *American Economic Review*, **60**, 601–617.

Mueller, D. (1986) *Profits in the Long Run*, Cambridge University Press.

O'Hanlon, J., Poon, S. and Yaansah, A. (1992) Market recognition of differences in earnings persistence: UK evidence, *Journal of Business, Finance and Accounting*, June, **19**, no. 4, 625–640.

O'Hanlon, J. and Whiddett, R. (1991) Do UK security analysts over-react? *Accounting and Business Research*, Winter, **22**, no. 85, 63−74.

Ou, J.A. and Penman, S.H. (1989) Financial statement analysis and the prediction of stock returns, *Journal of Accounting and Economics*, **11**, 295−330.

Patz, D.H. (1989) UK analysts' earnings forecasts, *Accounting and Business Research*, Summer, 267−275.

Pike, R., Meerjanssen, J. and Chadwick, L. (1993) The appraisal of ordinary shares by investment analysts in the UK and Germany, *Accounting and Business Research*, Autumn, 489−499.

Rees, W. and Sutcliffe, C. (1988) Ex ante testing of accounting standards using stochastic models, *Accounting and Business Research*, Summer, 151−60.

Schipper, K. (1991) Commentary on analysts' forecasts, *Accounting Horizons*, December, 105−121.

Steele, A. (1982) The accuracy of chairmen's non-quantified forecasts: an exploratory study, *Accounting and Business Research*, Summer, 215−30.

Trueman, B. and McNichols, M. (1994) Public disclosure, private information collection and short-term trading, *Journal of Accountancy and Economics*, January, **17**, no. 1/2, 69−94.

Watts, R. and Leftwich, R. (1977) The time-series of annual accounting earnings, *Journal of Accounting Research*, Autumn, 253−71.

CHAPTER 5

Capital Markets and Asset Pricing

P. Draper[1] and W. Rees

This chapter will:

1 Provide a brief outline of the structure and importance of capital markets.
2 Outline the theoretical models which attempt to explain the links between returns, risk and value.
3 Review the efficiency with which capital markets incorporate information into prices and the opportunities for capturing excess returns.

5.1 Introduction

This chapter examines the capital market in which corporate securities are traded. Time is devoted to capital markets and finance theory because (a) a considerable amount of financial analysis is performed as part of the investment management process which cannot be understood without a basic understanding of capital market finance, and (b) financial analysis cannot simply be based on accounting numbers and the other single most important source of information is the prices derived from the capital market.

Two crucial theoretical issues are examined. Firstly, the 'asset pricing models', which academics and practitioners have used to make sense of the relationship between share values and their determinants, and secondly, the evidence concerning the 'efficient market hypothesis' which asserts that share prices instantaneously incorporate, on publication, all available information (such as company accounting information). Asset pricing models and efficient markets are singled out for three reasons, as follows.

1. Investing in shares is one of the principal motives for the analysis of financial information. The information that is considered by investors depends on the model or view of the determinants of value. Both asset pricing models and the efficient market hypothesis provide useful insights into the valuation process.

2. Much significant empirical research on accounting information has been both motivated by the investment opportunities presented by capital markets, and has relied heavily on asset pricing models and the efficient market hypothesis for its methodology. To understand the implications of the research results, the analyst requires an understanding of the basic techniques and methodology employed.

3. The objectives of the investment analyst when reviewing financial information are dependent on the analyst's perception of market efficiency. If the market is efficient a passive investment strategy is suggested since the analyst may find it difficult to identify under-valued shares. If, however, the market is not efficient then active investment management may be worthwhile. The choice between these strategies depends on the analyst's evaluation of the level of information efficiency that exists in the markets in which the analyst operates.

This chapter continues by describing briefly London's capital market (Section 5.2) and contrasting it with other significant markets. Section 5.3 examines the concepts of risk and return as they relate to ordinary shares and explains the theory behind portfolio investment. Section 5.4 uses these concepts to examine models that help us understand the pricing of investment assets. Section 5.5 reviews the efficient market hypothesis and Section 5.6 reports on evidence contrary to the efficient market and attempts to evaluate these 'anomalies'.

5.2   The capital markets

The London Stock Exchange is the dominant European equity market ranking third in the world behind the New York Stock Exchange (NYSE) and Tokyo (see Table 5.1). There are, of course, many other markets for finance besides the stock exchanges. The Eurobond and traditional corporate and government bond markets are important whilst many firms, especially continental European and Japanese, rely heavily on direct investment by the banking sector. Despite this, the focus of this chapter is on the equity markets since they represent both an important source of capital for firms, and, more importantly for this book, a major user of financial statement information.

There is no unique measure of market size. The market capitalisation values reported in Table 5.1 are erratic and may not reflect long-term relationships. They are also unlikely to correspond exactly to measures based on the turnover of stocks which is an alternative measure of market size. Furthermore, it can be difficult to define market capitalisation, since many countries have companies with interlocking shareholdings and more than one stock exchange. For example, at 31 December 1992 the NYSE and American Stock Exchange had 1969 and 740 domestic quoted companies respectively, while the National Association of Security Dealers Automated Quotation (NASDAQ) service provided quotations for 3850 domestic firms (*London Stock Exchange, Quality of Markets Review*, Spring 1993). Table 5.1 provides a variety of alternative measures. What is clear is the dominance of New York and the importance of London in Europe.

The principal categories of finance that affect the work of the financial analyst can be identified on the balance sheet of companies such as those reviewed in Chapter 2. They

Table 5.1 International stock market comparisons

	Fixed interest (MV) (£ m)	Equities domestic (MV) (£ m)	Equities overseas (MV) (£ m)	Number of Companies domestic	overseas	Fixed interest turnover (£ m)	Equities turnover (£ m)
Germany	918,362	217,935	n/a	425	240	639,299	258,718
Luxemburg	797,728*	7,865	131,595	59	162	544	192
Paris	310,814	216,947	n/a	515	217	507,100	75,048
UK (London)	402,195	624,393	1,552,750	1878	514	663,038	381,675
Nasdaq (US)	397	410,723	n/a	3850	261	284	588,575
New York	1,350,143	2,508,339	104,946	1969	120	7,681	1,152,881
Hong Kong	323	113,595	n/a	386	27	23.7	51,945
Osaka	822,302	1,583,463	416	1163	5	15,804	79,878
Tokyo	843,220	1,583,463	n/a	1651	117	78,224	315,043

* Predominantly overseas (£795,553).
Source: Quality of Markets Review, Spring 1993.

include equity, debentures, short-term loans and borrowing. The classifications can sometimes be difficult to define.

> Equity capital is generally issued without the presumption of any redemption, has a return which varies with the performance of the firm, and bears the residual risk of the firm which is not carried by other capital. If this risk is high then, on average, the return will be high. If this risk is low then, on average, the return will be low. Equity represents a share in the ownership of the firm.
>
> Debt can be short or long term, and the return varies primarily with the interest rates applying in the economy, rather than with firm-specific performance. In general, debt bears only limited risk and has only limited rights, if any, to influence management under normal business circumstances, though debt-holders may be able to assert their influence where management action would appear to damage the value of the security for the loan.

Table 5.2 highlights the trade-off between risky equities with high returns and safer debt such as gilts and treasury bills. In itself, the capital market for companies' shares is not the main source of finance for most firms as issues of new finance are often small in comparison to the value of retained profits or the inflow of investment from banks. However, two qualifications to this statement must be made.

1. The first is that the profits retained by companies are attributable to the shareholders and are in effect a further investment by the shareholder. Abstracting from tax and transaction costs, the company could be seen as paying out the full amount of any profits attributable to shareholders as dividends and issuing new capital to make up the difference. Thus, the capital market, by providing a forum for trading in existing shares, encourages investors to allow the firm to retain earnings, and to accumulate capital without going through the expensive process of issuing equity.
2. The second qualification is to realise that ordinary shares encompass the residual value and risk inherent in a firm after all other claims on the assets are satisfied. The ordinary shareholders are the owners of the company and stand to lose their capital if the firm does poorly. This risk-taking function facilitates the raising of fixed interest capital from other sources since it largely removes the risk and hence risk measurement and pricing problems from this category of investment.

Table 5.2 Historic returns (30 years)

	Return %
UK Treasury Bills	9.02
UK Equities	15.32
US Treasury Bills	7.72
US Equities	15.38
Japanese Treasury Bills	4.73
Japanese Equities	10.76

Equity figures exclude dividends and represent change in major security indices.

5.3 Risk and return

The essential requirement of an investment is that it should give an adequate return to compensate for the risks involved. Of course, other factors such as capital growth versus investment income, the tax efficiency of particular investments and even ethical considerations, may affect an investor's choice of investments but such influences either affect an investor's returns directly or have, at best, a small influence on the average investor's choices and can safely be ignored. This section addresses the measurement of return and risk for single assets, and establishes the requirement for a trade-off between the two. The annual returns on UK equities since 1962 have been very variable. The median return has been in the range 10−30 per cent (0.1 to 0.3 in decimal notation) with annual losses of as much as 60 per cent and annual gains of as much as 120 per cent. Both the mean return and the variation in returns on risk-free securities such as UK Government bonds have been very much less. This section also examines the possibility of reducing risk through diversification and the consequences of such possibilities for the relationship between risk and return.

5.3.1 *Return on investment*

The return on an investment is made up of a capital gain (or loss) and the dividends or coupons received. For convenience, it is assumed that the dividends and capital gains are equally valuable to the investor, though this may not always be the case as tax regimes sometimes favour capital growth over dividends.

   Writing the return as R_i (per cent) it may be expressed as:

$$R_i = 100 \times \frac{(D+P_1-P_0)}{P_0} \qquad (5.1)$$

where P_1 is the price of the share in period 1, P_0 is its price in period 0 and D is the dividend. R_i is the return on an investment over a period, where the period may be any convenient interval of time such as a day, week, month or year. Table 5.3 provides example calculations of the returns on securities A and B over the periods $t=0$ to $t=12$. Note in particular the addition of dividends in periods when they are paid. Thus for period 1 the return on A is $100 \times ((967-1065)+40)/1065 = -5.16$ per cent and in period 2 it is $100 \times (1079.5-967.0)/967 = 11.63$ per cent The average return recorded at the bottom of the table is the arithmetic average calculated by summing returns over the twelve periods and dividing by twelve.

5.3.2 *The risk of an investment*

Risk in finance generally refers to the chance that a cash flow or return does not occur as expected. If the investor expects a 10 per cent return but there is a possibility that they may receive only 5 per cent or even 0 per cent then the investor is assuming a risk since the return may be lower than the 10 per cent expected. To assess the risk attached to a financial asset ideally requires knowledge of the probability distribution of all the possible future return outcomes. In practice, it is usually assumed that the distribution of returns

Table 5.3 Example computation of rates of return

	Price	Firm A Dividend	Return	Price	Firm B Dividend	Return
T0	1065.0			200.0		
T1	967.0		−5.16	171.0		−14.50
T2	1079.5	40.0	11.63	183.0		7.02
T3	1072.0		−0.69	180.0		−1.64
T4	1089.0		1.63	176.0	7.0	1.67
T5	997.0		−10.32	174.0		−1.14
T6	983.0		0.61	179.0		2.87
T7	973.0		1.02	177.0		−1.12
T8	1094.0		12.44	174.0		−1.70
T9	1044.0		−4.57	173.0		−0.57
T10	995.0	60.0	1.05	150.5	12.0	−6.07
T11	1025.0		3.02	163.0		8.31
T12	1045.0		1.95	173.0		6.13
			Firm A			Firm B
Average rate of return			0.0857%			−0.061%

observed in the recent past is an appropriate guide to the form of the future distribution of returns. However, even if we are prepared to accept the validity of this assumption, the problem remains of how best to describe the information contained in the probability distribution.

One possibility is a direct comparison of the distribution of returns on one investment with the distribution of returns on another. Some progress has been made in this direction for well-behaved distributions but difficulties remain. In general, attempts are made to summarise the information contained in the distribution using well-known statistics such as the standard deviation. The standard deviation is particularly appropriate for certain classes of distributions such as the normal since such distributions can be completely described by knowledge of two statistics, the mean and the standard deviation of the distribution. For non-symmetric distributions the standard deviation may be very misleading and it can be shown that for investors who obey a reasonable set of rules in making investment choices, other measures, such as the semi-variance, are to be preferred. Despite this, the algebraic convenience of the standard deviation and the ease with which it may be calculated lead to a preference for its use and attempts to overcome some of the associated problems by transforming the distribution of returns. For example, the logarithm of return may be used to improve the symmetry of the distribution of returns rather than using alternative measures to summarise the distribution.

The standard deviation also has appeal as it can be given an intuitive interpretation. The standard deviation of a distribution measures the variability of the underlying variable, in this instance the returns on a share or portfolio. This variability in returns is taken to represent the risk of the investment to investors since the variability reflects the uncertainty attached to returns. Low variability (standard deviation) indicates that the actual outcomes will correspond reasonably closely with average or expected outcomes. High variability indicates that actual outcomes may correspond poorly with expected returns.

5.3.3 *Risk aversion*

A frequently used assumption in the analysis of investor behaviour is that of risk aversion. A precise definition need not detain us but in intuitive terms investors who are risk averse when faced with a choice between two investments having the same expected return but different risks will choose the investment which has the lowest risk. If we measure risk using the standard deviation of return then the investor would choose the investment with the lowest standard deviation.

Hence, Trust House Forte would be preferred to Lucas where the returns on both companies are as described in the probability distributions illustrated in Figure 5.1. This is explained by the 'diminishing marginal utility of wealth'. The additional benefit from a small extra unit of wealth diminishes as the investor becomes richer. Thus, in moving an investment from Trust House Forte to Lucas, the investor could be seen as swapping an area in the peak of the distribution of Trust House Forte's returns for the two tails of the distribution of returns for Lucas. The risk-averse investor does not, however, value receiving returns in the upper tail of the distribution of returns as highly as the cost of paying returns in the lower tail of the distribution. In short, the chance of a lower than average return by investing in Lucas is higher than for an investment in Forte. The choice between BMW and Allweiler is not so easy. BMW offers lower returns but also lower risk (standard deviation). The investor using standard deviation as a measure of risk would have to trade off the additional return against the additional risk.

The assumption of risk aversion may be stronger than the minimum assumptions required by the theory in some circumstances. Quite how a manager will feel about the risk involved in investing someone else's money is unclear, nor is it clear that all investors avoid risk. For many non-professional investors, share ownership may be another form of gambling providing a pay-off in the form of entertainment. However, what is apparent is that to some extent financial markets act as if investors are risk averse and risky investments are priced so as to offer a higher return and attract investors.

The difficulty in choosing between distributions is in deciding the additional return that an investor would require before accepting a riskier return. What is the trade-off between risk and return? It is clear that if an investment is preferable in both risk and return it will be chosen. Even if it is equal in one dimension and preferable in the other it will be chosen, but if the investment is better in one dimension and worse in another, what then?

5.3.4 *Portfolio theory*

The graph in Figure 5.2 shows the reduction in the standard deviation of a portfolio as it moves from containing only one share to gradually including all the 30 securities contained in the FT30 index is initially rapid but gradually moderating. There is still room for a reduction in the portfolio's risk as the standard deviation of the FT All Share Index, a much more comprehensive stock market index containing hundreds of different companies, was 0.0535 over the same period, but it is clear that a considerable amount of diversification will be required for this minor improvement.

Allied to the reduction in the standard deviation or diversification is an increasing

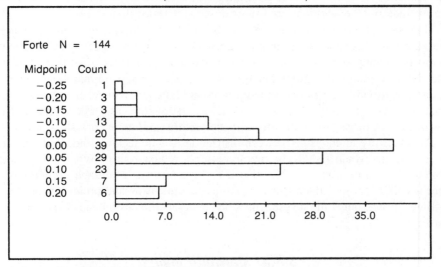

+ *Source*: Datastream January 1979–December 1991

Figure 5.1 Distribution of monthly returns.

correlation of the return on our portfolio with the market's return. For the sample used here, the correlation, on average, for a portfolio of one share with the FT All Share Index was 0.587. This rapidly improved to 0.903 for a portfolio of six shares, and more gradually thereafter to 0.968 for the full portfolio of 30 stocks. The final portfolio behaves in a similar fashion to the total equity market (as measured by the FT All Share Index) and

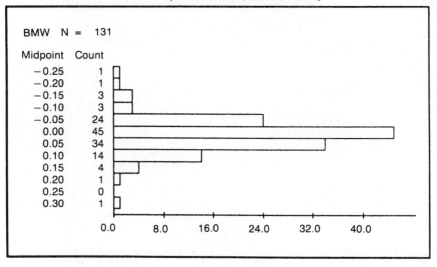

*BMW (mean 0.01345, stdev 0.07355)

BMW N = 131

Midpoint	Count
−0.25	1
−0.20	1
−0.15	3
−0.10	3
−0.05	24
0.00	45
0.05	34
0.10	14
0.15	4
0.20	1
0.25	0
0.30	1

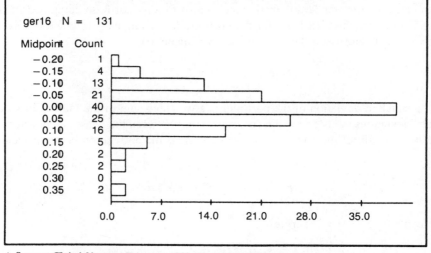

*Allweiler (mean 0.01381, stdev 0.09118)

ger16 N = 131

Midpoint	Count
−0.20	1
−0.15	4
−0.10	13
−0.05	21
0.00	40
0.05	25
0.10	16
0.15	5
0.20	2
0.25	2
0.30	0
0.35	2

* *Source*: Global Vantage February 1982−December 1992

the addition of further equities cannot substantially improve this relationship. Of course, if all equities were included in the portfolio in proportion to their market capitalisation, the portfolio would mimic the FT All Share Index and would be a 'market portfolio'. However, the FT30 portfolio used here is a good surrogate for that market portfolio, even though the equities involved have not been chosen for their diversifying properties. Given

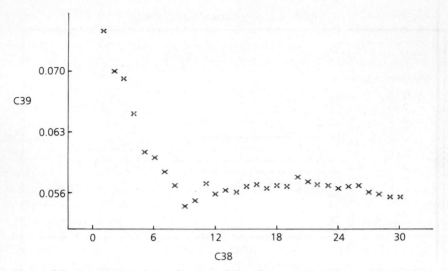

Figure 5.2   Standard deviation for a portfolio of one to thirty shares (30 = FT30).

the standard deviation, expected returns and covariance between a selection of investments we can calculate the standard deviation and return for any portfolio composed of those assets. The expected return $E(R)$ for the portfolio (p) is simply a weighted (w) average of the expected returns on the constituent investments (i).

$$E(R_p) = \sum_{i=1}^{n} w_i E(R_i) \tag{5.2}$$

The standard deviation of the portfolio is a weighted sum of the individual security standard deviations adjusted for the covariance (σ_{ij}) between the constituents where w is the relative weight of the constituent shares and ρ_{ij} is the correlation between security i and j.

$$\sigma^2(R_p) = \sum_{i=1}^{n} \sum_{j=1}^{n} w_i w_j \rho_{ij} \sigma_i \sigma_j \tag{5.3}$$

For the case of two securities,

$$\sigma^2(R_p) = w_1^2 \sigma_1^2 + w_2^2 \sigma_2^2 + 2 w_1 w_2 \rho_{12} \sigma_1 \sigma_2 \tag{5.4}$$

If the returns of the constituent shares are perfectly correlated $(\rho_{ij} = +1)$, no reduction in portfolio variance can be achieved, but if the correlation is less than perfect any pooling of assets will produce some reduction in variance. In an extreme case, when two securities are perfectly negatively correlated, $\sigma^2(R_p)$ may be zero for some values of w_1 and w_2.

Assuming that it is in the investors' interests to reduce the risk of their portfolio, what is the best mix of securities? It is not possible to dispose of all risk. Even the full FT30 portfolio has some risk associated with it. This risk arises from the fluctuations of the market as a whole and is known as the 'systematic or market risk' of a share or portfolio.

The quadratic nature of the relationship between the variances and covariances of individual securities within a portfolio gives rise to the curved leading edge or 'efficient frontier' of portfolio theory. Efficiency implies that portfolios cannot be dominated by alternative portfolios since efficient portfolios offer the highest return available for given risk, or the lowest risk for given return. The selection of any non-efficient portfolio would be foolhardy as there are portfolios located on the efficient frontier which are better by definition. The concept of efficiency does not, however, eliminate all choices. The choice between alternative portfolios on the efficient frontier requires a trade-off between risk and return, dependent on the investors' personal preferences. Choice of a particular portfolio of risky securities from along the frontier may be avoided by the imposition of an additional assumption which allows investors to lend and borrow at a specified risk-free rate of interest. This asset with its certain fixed return and correlation with the return on any risky portfolio of zero is known as the risk-free asset. The risk of a portfolio consisting of a risky asset (or portfolio) and the risk-free asset will be a simple, value weighted average of the risk of the two elements. Thus, if the portfolio is comprised of a 100 per cent risk-free asset, the standard deviation is zero, shown by X in Figure 5.3; if it consists of 100 per cent risky assets then its location in terms of risk and return will be given by point Y; and if it is comprised 50:50 risky to risk-free assets its location will be given by the point Z. The crucial proposition is that by mixing the tangent portfolio Y and the risk-free asset X, composite portfolios can be created that give a mix of risk and return that dominates that offered by almost all portfolios composed of risky assets only.

Additional assumptions allow us to secure further insights from the model. If, for example, we make assumptions that guarantee that Figure 5.3 is the situation that faces every investor — all investors can borrow or lend as much or as little as they like at the same risk-free rate, and all investors appraise investment in the same way as well as having the same portfolio opportunities and information available to them — then all investors, regardless of their personal risk—return preferences, will hold, as the risky part of their personal portfolios, identical risky portfolios indicated by Y. Investors will adjust for their

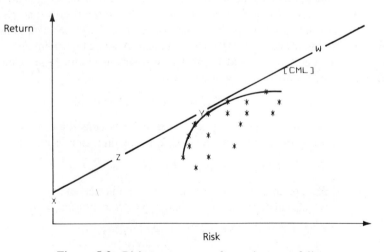

Figure 5.3 Risk versus return for various portfolios.

own risk—return preferences by borrowing and lending at the risk-free rate of return. Since all investors will purchase the same portfolio of risky assets (although in different proportions to the risk-free asset to enable them to secure their own particular risk—return trade-off preference), this portfolio must contain all assets in proportion to their market value. Such a portfolio is known as the market portfolio. A diversified portfolio very similar to the market would involve excessive transaction costs. It is, however, relatively easy to approximate the market and indeed, as we have seen, the mixture of investments comprising the FT30 comes close to behaving like the market portfolio (assuming of course that the market is defined as UK equities).

5.4 Asset pricing models

This section examines some techniques, particularly the capital asset pricing model (CAPM) and the arbitrage pricing theory (APT), which attempt to measure and price risk.

5.4.1 The capital asset pricing model

Presentations of the capital asset pricing model (CAPM) can be severely off-putting, but as Modigliani and Pogue explain in their admirably lucid exposition, CAPM is based on 'elementary logic and simple economic principles' (Modigliani and Pogue, 1974). The fundamental principle is that assets which bear the same level of risk must offer the same level of return. The relevant risk for capital market assets is assumed to be the systematic risk as all other risk may be diversified away by investors holding portfolios of assets. This systematic risk is measured as the extent to which an asset exaggerates or understates the movements of the market and is normally referred to as 'beta'. A beta of one implies that the asset is expected to replicate market-wide movements in returns and hence should expect to receive a return equal to that of the market. A beta of zero refers to assets whose returns have no correlation with the movements in market returns so that the expected return of the asset equals the risk-free rate of interest. Since the return (and risk) on the market portfolio and the risk-free asset are known we can derive a linear relationship, the Capital Asset Pricing Model (CAPM), between them. Assume that an investor combines the two assets (with betas $\beta_m = 1$ and $\beta_{Rf} = 0$) in proportion w and $1 - w$. The investor would then have a new portfolio p with a beta of:

$$\beta_p = w.\beta_m + (1-w).\beta_{Rf} = w.(1) + (1-w).(0) = w \tag{5.5}$$

since the beta of a portfolio is the weighted average of its constituent parts.

The expected return on this new portfolio $E(R_p)$ is again a simple weighted average:

$$E(R_p) = E(R_m).w + R_f(1-w) \tag{5.6}$$

Where $E(R_m)$ and R_f, are the expected returns on the market and the risk-free asset respectively. We have already shown above that $\beta_p = w$. Substituting β_p for w we have:

$$E(R_p) = E(R_m).\beta_p + R_f - R_f.\beta_p \tag{5.7}$$

Or as it is more commonly expressed:

Table 5.4 The fundamental assumptions of the CAPM

1. Investers are wealth maximisers behaving in an economically rational manner.
2. Investors are all risk averse and the expected standard deviation of returns is the appropriate measure of risk.
3. Investors have common time horizons.
4. Investors have the same expectations about future returns.
5. Information is costless and equally available to all investors.
6. There are no transaction costs or other market imperfections.
7. All investors can borrow or lend at the risk-free rate.

$$E(R_p) = R_f + \beta(E(R_m) - R_f) \tag{5.8}$$

This is the infamous CAPM which asserts that the expected return on an asset $E(R_p)$ is the return on the risk-free asset (R_f), plus the risk premium on the market $(E(R_m) - R_f)$, times the risk on the asset relative to the market (β_p).

The simplicity of this result hides both the power of the model and the assumptions on which it is based. The CAPM provides a simple, but plausible description of expected returns by relating them to risk (β) which, in turn, is easily shown to be a measure of the correlation (strictly the covariance) between the asset and the market. In short, it focuses attention on the marginal risk of an asset and shows that expected return is related not to the total risk of an asset (its variability) but to the asset's contribution to portfolio risk.

To achieve such powerful conclusions requires assumptions that abstract from reality. The assumptions are set out in Table 5.4. Considerable controversy has surrounded some of them. Suffice it to say that any theory requires abstraction from reality and the test of a model is in the accuracy of its predictions.

The validity of the listed assumptions is only of limited interest to the analyst whose essential question is: does the capital asset pricing model describe reality with sufficient precision, and can the analyst obtain estimates of the necessary variables to utilise the model?

Some of the assumptions have been noted as they were introduced in the analysis, but a brief review of their implications and techniques available to overcome these is worthwhile. The first five assumptions describe the stylised behaviour of investors. The effect of rejecting these assumptions would be that the single efficient portfolio, and the unique trade-off between risk and return for all investors would no longer hold. Individual investors, even if they used means and standard deviations to measure returns and risk, would have their own personal efficient frontiers and the lending–borrowing line would intercept the efficient frontier at different points.

The CAPM's other basic assumptions are also problematic. The risk-free asset is difficult to identify because uncertain inflation will have an effect on the real return from even the safest of government stocks, and it is clear that most investors cannot both borrow and lend at the risk-free asset. The introduction of higher rates of interest for borrowing than lending would imply different intercepts with the efficient frontier. Black suggested replacing the risk-free asset with a zero beta portfolio constructed by selling stocks short to balance precisely the assets held (Black, 1972). However, the conclusions of the CAPM model, particularly its basic linearity, are not substantially altered, whilst many investors are in practice constrained from the short selling that would be necessary. Inflation might have a further impact if it were to create an interdependence between the parameters of the model. A variety of researchers have established strategies to allow for the effect of uncertain inflation (see Hagerman and Kim, 1976, and Friend, Landskroner and Losq, 1976, for example), but these models lose the simplicity of the original CAPM. The existence of inflation does imply that the CAPM may be less accurate as a description of reality but the question at issue is 'Does it still approximate reality to a useful extent?'

A number of studies have examined the impact of market imperfections on the model. One particularly influential study has been an attempt to incorporate differential taxation which requires an allowance for dividend yield, and a coefficient to reflect the superiority of capital gains (Brennan, 1971). The CAPM user has to trade-off the benefits from a more accurate description of reality against the cost of using the more complex model.

5.4.2 *Predicting beta and other parameters*

Beta is the measure of risk specific to the investment under examination. To utilise the CAPM we also need forecasts of the risk-free rate and the expected return on the market.

The basic estimation technique used to arrive at a forecast of beta is to estimate the parameter β_i (the covariance (R_i, R_m) divided by the variance of the market σ_m^2) using OLS regression on a recent time-series of returns. The following plots of share returns against market returns for two very different companies show the fitted line (see Figure 5.4).

The equation estimated is the market model for the individual security. Although extensively used and calculated, the use of the market model is not grounded in finance theory but rather is a convenient assumption. It is a reflection of the observation that security returns tend to behave in a similar fashion to the market. Estimates of beta tend to be treated as reasonably precise but, in fact, are well known to vary substantially depending on the number of observations used in their calculation, the interval over which returns are calculated, the presence of outliers and a number of other factors. Figure 5.4 illustrates the variability of beta estimates and is calculated by means of a moving regression which uses a window of 200 observations to calculate beta. Thus the first value of beta reflects the previous 200 observations. The second value also reflects the previous 200 observations and is calculated by dropping out the very first observation in the sample of 200 and adding in the 201st observation. By repeating this procedure a picture is obtained of how beta changes over time. The difficulty, of course, is in isolating the effects of changing risk as a reflection of altered perceptions of the company and changes in its activities, from the statistical problems associated with estimating beta. Increasing the number of observations used in the estimation procedure can greatly reduce the variation in the beta estimates but as always there is a trade-off between the advantages of increased numbers of observations and the reduced probability that risk remains constant over a longer period. In short, the estimation of the market model is subject to a series of practical decisions which may affect the results. These are as follows:

1. Which period to use as the sample? Statistical techniques are more reliable with large datasets but structural change in the firm and its environment (for example, a change in the nature of its business and hence its risk) will tend to make older observations less relevant to the current reality of the firm.

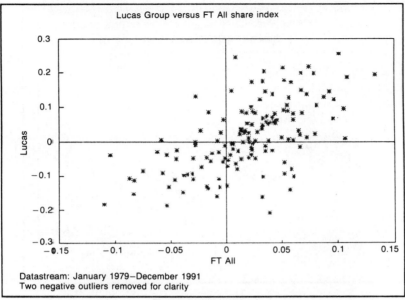

Datastream: January 1979–December 1991
Two negative outliers removed for clarity

The regression equation is
Lucas = −0.0103 + 1.31 FT All

R-sq = 35.6%   R-sq(adj) = 35.2%

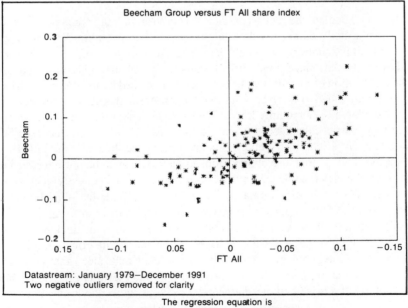

Datastream: January 1979–December 1991
Two negative outliers removed for clarity

The regression equation is
Beecham = 0.00641 + 0.824 FT All

R-sq = 31.5%   R-sq(adj) = 31.0%

Figure 5.4

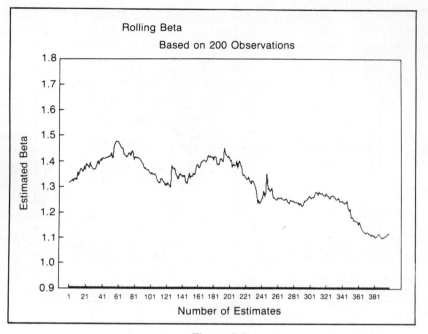

Figure 5.5

2. How often to calculate the returns on the security? Again more frequent observations (such as using daily data) provide a larger sample but are more difficult to collect than say monthly, quarterly or annual data. The calculation of returns over short time periods may also introduce some difficult statistical problems. It is common to assume that the distribution of returns may be adequately described by the normal distribution. Following Fama (1976) there appears to be a consensus that it is reasonable to treat returns calculated over monthly intervals as normal. There is, however, evidence to suggest that returns calculated over shorter periods may not be normal (see Section 5.3.2). The empirical distribution is sometimes described as 'fat tailed'. Such distributions have many more observations in their tails than the normal distribution. Large price changes (and hence returns) occur much more frequently than we would expect if returns followed a normal distribution. Some 'fat tailed' distributions have infinite variance. This implies, in practice, that samples of returns can have widely different variances. This occurs because the variance squares the deviations from the mean and in doing so large deviations have a disproportionate effect on the variance of the sample. The problem is far from academic. It may mean that conventional methods of estimating beta result in poor and unreliable estimates. The problem is often ignored but it is well known that in practice large observations may have a major impact on the beta of a security. As we noted earlier opinions vary on the correct treatment of very large 'outlier' observations.

3. Which index to use as a measure of the return on the market? It is relatively easy to use a comprehensive index for the investment opportunities in a particular capital

market, but attempts to measure the returns on a more realistic set of investments require investment opportunities such as bonds, foreign investments and property to be included.

Practice in calculating betas varies. For example, the LBS Risk Measurement Service uses five years of monthly data of returns whereas Datastream uses four years of weekly readings. Datastream uses its own total market index, and although LBS is not explicit, it probably uses its own Market Index. Furthermore, it is not clear that Datastream includes dividends as part of total return, and whilst this is unlikely to be significant for returns over short periods of time, it will seriously under-estimate returns over longer periods.

There are further problems which generate differences in treatment. Where there is infrequent trading, usually in small companies, the closing price quoted (from which return is calculated) may actually reflect the trading price of an earlier period. Thus in calculating monthly returns, the end of the month quoted price on, say, Savoy Hotels may actually be the price at which the last trade was done five days previously. LBS attempts to deal with this by using trade to trade returns in which the last traded price on a security is matched with the return on the index for the same date. Further adjustments may be made to the raw estimate of beta to allow for bias in the estimates (as discussed below) and may include adjustments derived from fundamental analysis (to be examined in Chapter 7). LBS incorporates the former of these adjustments but not the latter, whereas Datastream does not report that it uses either.

Once the estimation procedure is chosen, there remains a fundamental problem. The CAPM relates to investors' expectations whereas the market model estimates a beta based on historic data. Is the historic estimate a good forecast of actual beta in subsequent periods and is it closely related to the expectations of market participants? The stability of beta over time is relatively easy to evaluate. Whether or not the historic beta is a reasonable surrogate for investors' assessment of future risk is not easy to evaluate.

Decomposition of the beta estimate into two components, the correlation between the firm and the market, and the volatility of the firm's returns reveal that both estimates contribute to this instability. Indeed, an investigation by Elton, Gruber and Urich seemed to indicate that more accurate estimate of future betas could be derived using the average correlation for all firms in the sample, rather than the specific estimate for the individual firm's correlation (Elton, Gruber and Urich, 1978).

Fortunately the stability of betas is much improved for portfolios as opposed to individual firms. Blume has reported that correlations between betas in subsequent periods rise from approximately 0.60 to over 0.90 for portfolios of ten or more stocks and approach 0.99 for portfolios of fifty (Blume, 1971). For the UK, Dimson and Marsh (1984) report average correlations between two adjacent periods as varying from 0.47 for portfolios containing one security, to 0.82 for portfolios of ten securities and 0.96 for portfolios of fifty securities.

The instability in beta demonstrated by individual firms could be derived from a number of sources. Genuine changes in the systematic risk of the firm or estimation difficulties are two clear possibilities. A further possibility, not immediately apparent from the results of the FT30 sample, results from the movement of beta towards the mean of one. Again Blume discovered strong evidence of this mean reversion for portfolios of shares.

Obvious examples by which the beta of a firm can change over relatively short periods of time include adjustments to the capital gearing or to the assets managed by the firm, particularly as a result of mergers or divestments. For example, if a firm currently exhibits a high beta of 1.5, then there is a strong expectation that any acquisitions will have a lower beta than the firm's current assets, moving the firm's overall beta towards one (see Ball and Kothari, 1989 for empirical testing of this issue).

Blume (1975) also provided evidence of the estimation problems that can affect beta. If our estimation process results in a very high (low) risk of the firm this may reflect the high (low) risk of the firm, but it may also reflect a large sampling error increasing (decreasing) the value of beta. Very high or very low values of beta are likely to be systematically affected by such 'regression' bias. Dimson and Marsh (1983) showed that for the UK, raw beta estimates for the portfolios of the highest and the lowest beta stocks of 1.29 and 0.18 respectively became 1.10 and 0.60 when appropriately adjusted for bias.

The empirical finding, that betas tend to migrate towards one, has led a number of beta forecasting organisations to use a weighted forecast, in part dependent on an assumed beta of one and in part on the historical OLS estimate. Thus the equation that most accurately predicts $\beta 2$ for a sample of companies included in the FT30, given $\beta 1$ is:

$$\beta_2 = 0.446 + 0.542\beta_1 \quad R^2 = 29.9\% \tag{5.9}$$

β_1 was calculated from data available for seventy-two months starting January 1979 and β_2 from a consecutive seventy-two month sample. Five companies were excluded as a result of missing observations.

This equation would represent an extreme weighting. Research evidence in general suggests a more modest practice. Foster reports Merill Lynch using weights that approximate to one-third (prior expectation of one) and two-thirds (OLS estimated parameter) (Foster, 1986, p. 349).

While estimates of beta are problematic the remaining two variables used in the CAPM (risk-free and market rates) are not significantly less prone to difficulties in their estimation. The risk-free rate should represent the riskless return on an asset for the investment period under consideration. It should have no variability and consequently no covariance with the market return. Such assets are difficult to find since even short-term treasury bills are subject to uncertainty. It is true that the monetary return for the particular period over which the bond is issued is certain but the real rate of return after adjustment for inflation is not. It is also possible that the return to government stocks is priced to account for factors other than risk. It has been suggested that the liquidity of such assets persuades investors to accept a lower return than would be considered otherwise. Despite this, the return on government bonds, either treasury bills or index linked for longer periods, remains the usual source for estimates of the risk-free rate.

Although estimates of the market may be derived from a variety of share price indices, it is more usual to estimate the risk premium of the market as an entity in itself. In order to avoid the effects of temporary changes in the risk premium it is usually estimated using long periods of historic data so that short-run movements are smoothed out and one is left with a stable, reliable estimate of the risk premium on the market. Typically, for example, returns on equities and bonds are estimated since 1919 (with the de Zoete Index) and an arithmetic average used to calculate the risk premium. UK regulators and others have argued that such estimates of the risk premium are too high and attempted to argue in favour of a geometric method of averaging and/or in favour of limiting the risk premium to the long-run (real) growth in dividends. Although such arguments are often unconvincing much remains to be investigated in determining the risk premium in the UK. Merton (1980) for the US provides a range of estimates based on alternative reasonable approaches which reveal the very real difficulties in estimating the risk premium with any degree of precision.

An alternative approach, which has the advantage of complying with the expectational characteristics of the CAPM, is to derive a forecast of market returns from market analysts' predictions of individual share returns. Some of the larger firms input forecasts of many stocks into models to derive a forecast of the market as a whole. This requires a considerable investment in data collection and for that reason is rarely used.

5.4.3 *Evidence on the capital asset pricing model*

One common view is that the appropriate test of a theory is its predictive ability. If the predictions reflect reality then the theory may be considered to be useful. Such an approach to model building places the onus for accepting or rejecting the CAPM firmly on the results of empirical tests of the model. Unfortunately, it is rare for empirical tests in finance to provide results that are unambiguous. Differences in data, methodology and interpretation may result in very different conclusions and leave the analyst unable to choose between models except on rather vague and incomplete criteria. Testing of the CAPM has not been free of these difficulties and despite an extensive body of literature that has attempted to discover whether the CAPM is mis-specified (incorrectly defines the relationship between risk and return) or inadequate (is correct as far as it goes but omits significant elements), there continue to be unresolvable doubts and arguments. Severe problems exist with many of the tests apart from the usual straightforward difficulties of faulty or insensitive methodology. Two problems particularly worthy of note are:

1. The CAPM relates to investors' expectations about risk and return. Trying to model investors' expectations using historical information, or testing modelled expectations against realisations, is not a direct examination of the CAPM.
2. The CAPM depends on a trade-off between the risk-free asset and a portfolio that represents all risky investments. This portfolio of risky assets is unknown and unknowable and any ex-post test of the CAPM is as much a test of the validity of the index used to represent the market portfolio as it is of the CAPM. Roll (1977) demonstrated that a linear relationship exists between any index portfolio that is efficient, and the risk-free asset. By the same token, non-linearity is a consequence of the use of an inefficient index. Hence, empirical tests that discover non-linearity may be simply revealing that the proxy used for the market is inefficient whilst tests that reveal linearity may be simply showing that the proxy used for the market is efficient. Neither result necessarily reveals whether the CAPM holds or not.

Despite these difficulties the CAPM has been subjected to a considerable amount of empirical testing. Given the limitations of these tests it is sufficient to mention their overall conclusions here. In general, the tests are performed on portfolios rather than on individual securities. This has the advantage of minimising the measurement errors that are assumed to be random across individual securities. However, using portfolios may have the effect of disguising characteristics that are diversified away and which would be relevant when attempting to compute the required return for an individual firm.

The basic results of the tests performed have tended to be as follows:

1. Beta is a better explanatory variable for returns on the capital market than other characteristics, such as the standard deviation of the firm's returns.
2. The estimated intercept indicates that the return on the risk-free asset is higher than expected (though this could be an error in the definition of the risk-free asset rather than the CAPM), and that the slope of the risk—return trade-off is insufficiently steep.
3. When other parameters are introduced into the CAPM these may be found to be significant and 'improve the fit' of the tested model.

These conclusions have generally come to be accepted as received wisdom on the CAPM. However, a recent series of papers by Fama and French threatens to overturn these views. Fama and French (1992) after reviewing the more important empirical contradictions of the CAPM, notably the size effect (small firms offer higher returns for given beta than large firms), leverage (this should be captured by beta but inclusion of a separate leverage variable adds explanatory power), book value/market value of equity (there appears to be a positive relationship with returns) and the earnings/price ratios, demonstrate that size and book to market equity (book values of equity/market value of equity), 'provide a simple and powerful characterization of the cross-section of average stock returns for the 1963–1990 period.' They suggest that these two variables must proxy for risk. There does not appear to be any 'reliable relation between β and average return'. In short, according to Fama and French (1992) β seems to have no role in explaining the average returns on NYSE, AMEX and NASDAQ stocks for the period 1963–1990.

Fama and French (1993) extend their analysis to both stocks and bonds. They conclude that there are at least three stock market factors and two term structure factors in returns. For the stock portfolios a market factor and proxies for the risk factors related to size and book to market equity do a good job explaining the cross-section of average returns. The market factor is particularly important for explaining the difference between the average returns on stocks and one month bills. For bonds a term premium and a default premium explain most of the variation in returns.

The results of Fama and French have yet to be replicated and the methodology to be examined in exact detail. However, the results and methodology of Fama and French are currently the subject of intense debate the likely outcome of which is far from clear. It is possible that much of our current thinking on asset pricing may have to be revised and that much of the evidence on capital market efficiency may require reappraisal.

5.4.4 *Arbitrage pricing theory*

It is clear from the preceding part of this chapter that the CAPM is a sparse and illuminating model. However, a number of problems are apparent; its precise specification is dependent on the assumptions made; the empirical results lend it only modest support and are arguably not genuine tests; the model fails to explain some persistent anomalies in market returns; practitioners have great difficulty making reliable and stable estimates of the parameters and some intuitively doubt that return is dependent on only one characteristic of risk. There is obvious room for alternative models and the subsequent development of the arbitrage pricing theory (APT) proposed by Ross, has provided an alternative asset pricing model (Ross, 1976, 1977). The APT relates the expected returns to a variety of factors to which each security is more or less sensitive and is equally valid as a description of ex-post returns. Thus,

$$E(R_j) = R_f + B_{j1}[E(RF_1) - R_f] + \ldots + \beta_{jk}[E(RF_k) - R_f] \qquad (5.10)$$

where R_j refers to the return on asset j, R_f to the risk-free asset, β_{jk} to the sensitivity of that asset to factor k, and RF_k to the expected return on an asset with average sensitivity to factor k. The underlying rationale is that if an element of risk such as interest rate risk is particular to a sub-set of securities, then this element of risk will be incorporated in the pricing of the shares to ensure that an appropriate return compensates for the additional risk. If this were not so, in an efficient market arbitrageurs would be able to trade assets to eliminate risk and receive an excess return. (For a clear numeric illustration see Bower, Bower and Logue, 1984.)

An immediate difficulty of the APT model is that it provides no help with the identification of the relevant factors that affect returns. A series of tests (Dhrymes, 1984; Dhrymes, Friend and Gultekin, 1984; Fogler, 1982 and Roll and Ross, 1980) have used various forms of factor analysis to try to identify economic variables which appear to be priced in share valuation. The results are inconclusive both as to the number of factors and the identification of those factors. The theoretical assumption is that the number of factors which affect portfolio returns is small, though poorly diversified holdings or individual assets could be subject to many more factors. Roll and Ross, for instance, identify possible factors as industrial production, inflation, interest rate term structure, and risk premiums, and they point out the intuitive link between these factors and the traditional net present value (NPV) calculation of share values (Roll and Ross, 1984). Changes in industrial production and inflation are likely to affect future cash flows and term structures, and risk premiums can reasonably be expected to affect discount rates. As these factors can be expected to some extent to make an impact across the economy as a whole, it is not surprising that they cannot be diversified away. Unfortunately, whilst intuitively appealing the published studies report alternative factors for different datasets and periods. It is difficult to have a great deal of confidence in reported factors that reveal a considerable degree of instability.

The work of Roll and Ross found factors in stock returns and then attempted to identify these factors with macroeconomic variable. A subsequent paper, Chen, Roll and Ross (1986), used specific macroeconomic variables as proxies for the factors in the APT and reported that sources of risk from industrial production, changes in the risk premium on bonds, the term structure and in some circumstances unanticipated inflation and changes in expected inflation were significant and systematically priced in the stock market. Poon and Taylor (1991), however, applying and extending the Chen, Roll and Ross techniques did not find that similar variables affected share prices in the UK. They conclude that 'It could be that other macroeconomics factors are at work, or the methodology in Chen, Roll and Ross is inadequate for determining such pricing relationships, or possibly both explanations apply.'

A simple example of the difference between the APT and the CAPM is provided by the estimates of expected return produced by Bower, Bower and Logue (1984) for seventeen US companies. They find little agreement in this application of the contrasting theories, with the APT providing lower estimates on average (the APT mean is 18.8 per cent, and the CAPM mean, 23.0 per cent), but a higher dispersion (APT standard deviation is 6.1 per cent and CAPM standard deviation, 4.4 per cent).

5.5 Capital market efficiency

The concept of an efficient market has already been mentioned in earlier chapters. In this section the theory, evidence and implications are examined in greater detail. Considerable consequences hinge on the viability of the efficient market theory. The degree of efficiency in any particular market impinges on the effective use to which financial analysis can be put. Further, the most appropriate form of disclosure of accounting and financial data to investors operating in that market also depends on the level of market efficiency. In this section the concept of capital market efficiency will be discussed together with some relevant evidence.

5.5.1 *Definitions of market efficiency*

An efficient capital market may be described in terms of the constituent stocks being valued fairly in the light of all available information, or equally that the purchase or sale of securities will have an expected NPV of zero. While these expressions convey the essence of the concept, they are too broad in scope and ill-defined to bear examination or to serve as a basis for testing. It is perhaps simpler to define those circumstances that illustrate market inefficiency. A market would be inefficient if a participant in that market were able to expect positive abnormal returns. A market might also be described as inefficient with respect to a particular item of information if trading based on that information is capable of producing abnormal returns. Thus if a market is to be considered efficient with respect to a specified category of data, it must rapidly incorporate into share prices, in an unbiased manner, the value implications of information. If the market is unable to comply with these criteria, possibly through delayed or gradual incorporation of the impact of new information, participants would be able to trade during the period before the incorporation of the impact of the information and thereby out-perform the market.

Evidence of market efficiency for one category of data has no necessary implications for other markets, for other sets of data, or even for the same category of data at a different time. However, given the impossibility of testing every possible type of information it has become common to accept stock markets as efficient provided contrary evidence of inefficiency is limited. Examples of the difficulty of generalising about efficiency with respect to particular sets of information are readily constructed. Prior knowledge of a takeover bid, for example, might convey valuable information concerning a certain stock price and enable those who have access to such restricted information to trade profitably. Once the information becomes generally known, however, buyers and sellers are equally able to evaluate the information and the opportunity for abnormal gains may no longer exist. Thus, if the same data can be used to demonstrate inefficiency under one set of circumstances and not under another, it is obvious that care must be exercised when generalising and evaluating the results of market efficiency tests.

It is conventional to differentiate between different levels of capital market efficiency, as shown in Chapter 2, and the division between strong and semi-strong form efficiency is of some importance to this text. The essential distinction here is whether or not the market is efficient with regards to all relevant information (strong form) or only publicly available information (semi-strong form). The answer to this question decides the useful scope of the analyst's work, the significance of certain forms of financial disclosure and the regulatory authorities' attitudes towards specific aspects of disclosure policy. The alternative division between semi-strong and weak form efficiency is of convenience in classifying tests of market efficiency, but is of limited significance otherwise.

5.5.2 *The determinants of market efficiency*

The characteristics of a developed capital market might possibly encourage observers to expect an efficient market or some close approximation thereof. These characteristics include the following:

1. The number of traders. The stock exchange is made up of many thousands of individuals willing to buy or sell quoted shares. Under such circumstances no individual or cabal is likely to be able to influence prices consistently or effectively in a deliberate way.
2. Information availability. It is difficult to think of another market place where such a comprehensive or reliable set of data is available and rapidly disseminated at relatively low cost. It is not necessarily a full set of data, for not all relevant knowledge is made public, nor are the data of obvious economic validity or decision relevance, and yet the data availability appears unmatched.
3. Low transaction costs. While the expenses incurred through commission, stamp duties and the market spread may frustrate the transactor, it is difficult to think of many other markets where ownership can be routinely exchanged for less than a few percentage points of the total value.
4. Location independence. Though shares may be registered in a particular country or city, and the assets reflected in that value can be located elsewhere, this will often be no barrier to the traders who are able to obtain the benefits they seek for the expense of a telephone call without incurring transportation costs.
5. Homogeneity. The securities traded on stock markets represent claims on the future cash flows of the companies at an expected level of risk. Rarely do other considerations impinge on the investors' decisions. For a limited number of investors, political or emotional factors may be influential (as evidenced by the growth of 'ethical investments').
6. Competitive analysis. Many analysts operate in the capital markets and the majority are trying to identify mis-priced shares. While it is normal that errors in analysis are made, it is unlikely that such errors are for any given set of information, systematic. Available relevant information is unlikely to be missed by such a formidable set of searchers.

5.5.3 *Efficient and perfect capital markets*

The capital markets do not have the attributes of the perfect market set out in Table 5.5. We cannot assume that a security price reflects the 'true' value of a share but, if efficiency holds, then it reflects the best available estimate of underlying value.

Table 5.5 Attributes of a perfect market

1. There would be full, costless information simultaneously available to all participants.
2. There are no transaction costs and the tax system is neutral with respect to the market.
3. There are many buyers and sellers, so that participants are 'price takers'.
4. Participants are rational in that they make choices in such a way as to follow basic axioms such as seeking higher returns and lower risk.

5.5.4 *Testing capital market efficiency*

Two alternative approaches can be adopted when examining evidence of market efficiency. Firstly, the implications of a precisely defined item of information for the relevant share price can be examined. This direct test of efficiency, focusing on one element of the data set available to the market, is useful when interest centres specifically on that class of data rather than on market efficiency *per se*. Typically, a trading rule is defined utilising the appropriate information, and the returns from such trading are assessed for any evidence of abnormal returns (returns greater or less than those expected). While such a test can produce evidence of inefficiency, the converse only illustrates that the particular item of data utilised in the manner specified is ineffective.

The second method of testing market efficiency depends on identifying a group of participants in the capital market and analysing their performance to test for abnormal returns. This can be a more powerful tool for assessing general levels of market efficiency but many problems still exist. It will often be unclear which categories of data are available to the investors studied. The investment decisions analysed might be based primarily on fundamental analysis of publicly available accounting data, or conversely on private interviews with a firm's management.

The tests reviewed in this chapter concentrate on those that have general implications for an assessment of capital market efficiency. Those tests which pertain more precisely to aspects of financial analysis or accounting theory are examined in the chapters most relevant to those topics.

Weak form efficiency

Much of the work on weak form testing in Europe was conducted during the early 1970s and in some cases appears to show some evidence of market inefficiency. While the researchers often considered that the inefficiency was not exploitable, the types of inefficiencies found are instructive.

Solnik produced a useful review of tests of random walk behaviour in European stock markets and was able to compare his results with those of Fama in the US and examine the importance of the period examined (Solnik, 1973). Constructing a set of daily returns for 244 large companies quoted on eight European exchanges from 1966–71 Solnik found that:

1. Daily arithmetic returns did not conform to a normal distribution but moved towards this model as the time span increased and approximated a normal distribution for monthly returns.
2. European stocks exhibited greater serial dependence than US stocks, though this rapidly disappeared as the time span increased with 113 stocks displaying 95 per cent significant serial correlation coefficients for daily returns, 47 weekly, 21 bi-weekly, and 10 monthly.
3. In all countries, apart from the UK and to a lesser extent the Netherlands, serial correlation was maintained between two adjacent periods tested.
4. Patterns of correlation could not be generalised effectively within countries, and traders wishing to profit from these data would have to examine the correlation of particular stocks.

Brealey also confirmed that there was some degree of serial dependence in security returns as measured by indices between 1962–68 (Brealey, 1970). This appears to be exaggerated by the use of the FTA index which uses an average of closing prices in computation. However, a smaller but more carefully constructed index still evidenced some dependence though 'the regularity observed is almost certainly insufficient to be profitably exploited and does not seriously infringe the random walk hypothesis'.

This evidence does not overwhelmingly support the claim that 'the pattern of share price movements substantially follows a random walk and that price changes are independent of prior movements' (Keane, 1983, p. 35). However, all researchers referred to the difficulties of successfully exploiting inefficiencies given transaction costs and the autocorrelation (dependence in returns between sucessive periods) resulting from the use of indices in many of the tests may account for some of the apparent inefficiency. In addition, problems of non-trading are known to have affected some tests and resulted in higher serial correlation and hence apparent evidence of predictability than is the case after correction for such factors.

Semi-strong form tests

If information can be used to make excess returns we would expect investment professionals, analysts and fund managers, to make better informed and more profitable investment decisions than other investors. Early evidence on the recommendations available from professional analysts was provided by Firth who examined the returns of tipsters in national papers. While the publications were usually able to claim to beat the market, Firth suggests that this was in part due to the trading induced by the recommendations in firms with relatively small capitalisation and 'once an analyst has gained a reputation it becomes very difficult for investors following the recommendations to profit — the initial mark-ups usually leave the share price at the intrinsic value suggested' (Firth, 1972).

Dimson and Marsh studied 862 tips published during this period from 1975 to 1982. They found that the tipster recommended stocks that had out-performed the market in the prior year and that the tip generated abnormal returns of approximately 4 per cent in the month of publication, though again this gain could not be captured by the reader. However, the apparent performance of the shares subsequent to the release of the tip depended almost entirely on the benchmark used, and varied from $+3.2$ per cent to -3.8 per cent for a twelve-month period. The UK stock market typically provides excess returns for investors in small firms and the tips studied produced a portfolio biased towards smaller firms. When the tips are compared against a value weighted index 'far from displaying selection ability the analysts now appear to be exhibiting perverse forecasting skills' (Dimson and Marsh, 1988. p. 232).

A number of researchers, Firth, Ward and Saunders and others, examined the performance of unit trusts but, as with the seminal work of Jensen in the US, they were unable to provide evidence of abnormal performance and, indeed, in many cases the unit trusts notably under-performed the market. Thus funds managed by experienced portfolio managers backed by considerable resources appeared unable to beat passive buy and hold strategies (Firth, 1977; Jensen, 1968; Ward and Saunders, 1976). However, more recently a number of studies in the US, and Brown, Draper and McKenzie (1994) in the UK appear to find limited evidence that some fund managers are able to provide some consistency of performance. Although complicated by survivorship bias, Brown *et al.* find statistically significant evidence that pension fund managers who rank in the upper quartile of the pension fund performance league table in one period are more likely to remain in the upper quartile in the next period, than would be expected by chance. In particular, one fund manager revealed considerable persistence in achieving good performance.

Dimson and Marsh (1984) studied the value of unpublished analysts' forecasts of security returns and an investment institution's trades based on 4187 forecasts. They found that the analysts' forecasts were related to subsequent returns.

Though the forecasts were typically over a medium-term horizon, the predictive power was concentrated in the first few months after the forecast.

When trades were executed as a result of the forecasts available, Dimson and Marsh claim that 'this exercise indicates that the transaction-value weighted specific return achieved on the portfolio of all 2950 transactions over the twelve-month period following the trade was 2.2 per cent representing some £3 million'. While transaction costs and administration expenses need to be deducted there would still appear to be a convincing surplus (Dimson and Marsh, 1984).

5.6   Efficient market anomalies

While the history of the efficient market hypothesis (EMH) can be characterised as the gradual triumph of academic evidence over conventional practice, the increasing sophistication of the tests employed have identified a growing number of EMH anomalies. Often these are specialised cases, but the number of general instances are sufficient to at least cast doubt on the validity of the EMH as a working assumption. Some of these idiosyncrasies are sufficiently relevant to the practice of financial analysis to be left to more specialised chapters. Examples are the evidence on earnings drift, the Modigliani and Cohn (1979) accusations of misinterpretation of inflation-adjusted data, the performance of the Value Line investment model and the Briloff phenomenon. Others, such as the apparent excessive volatility of stock market returns, have been the subject of intense econometric debate and are essentially unresolved (Sheffrin, 1983). We concentrate here on two important sets of anomalies, the weekend and other calendar effects, and the firm size anomaly.

5.6.1 *The weekend and other calendar effects*

Evidence that stock market returns are not random and exhibit seasonal regularities has grown over recent years. In particular, early work found that the US market exhibited significantly lower returns from the Friday close (of the exchange) to the Monday close (Cross, 1973). This work has been imitated in many other studies and Condoyanni *et al.* replicated much of this work for 1969 to 1984 for the US, Canadian, UK, French, Australian (1980–84 only), Japanese and Singaporean stock markets (Condoyanni, O'Hanlon and Ward, 1988). Table 5.6 summarises their results.

A weekend effect is not universal but it is apparent that there is a general tendency for stock markets to exhibit significant day of the week effects. Although the day of the week effect is supported by the evidence, the results are far from overwhelming. Condoyanni *et al.* conclude that, 'on the basis of this study, we would tentatively suggest that persistent weekend effects do appear to be the norm rather than the exception in a range of capital markets around the world' (Condoyanni, O'Hanlon and Ward, 1988, p. 62). Choy and O'Hanlon (1989) on the basis of two separate datasets conclude that there appears to be a strong underlying day of the week effect in UK share returns which is stronger in large frequently traded issues than in small ones. This finding is 'almost diametrically opposite to the US studies' but the reasons for this contrast await investigation.

Table 5.6 reveals that while the stock markets in North America and the UK exhibit significant negative returns on Monday, the Far Eastern markets typically have negative returns on Tuesday. This neat geographical symmetry is only marred by the French negative return on Tuesday, but this may be explained by the French index being compiled at 1.30 pm, before trading on the NYSE is well under way. One explanation could be that the US market has a worldwide effect and while Canadian and European markets are able to react in the same day as the US market, Far Eastern markets must wait until the next day.

Table 5.6 Test for weekend effect — national markets 1969–84

Country	Monday	Tuesday	Wednesday	Thursday	Friday	F
US	−1.34*	0.13	0.57	0.21	0.58	4.16*
Canada	−1.57*	−0.03	0.73*	0.75*	0.94*	9.97*
UK	−0.95*	1.06*	0.90*	0.11	0.44	3.75*
France	−0.50	−1.57*	1.00*	1.52*	0.87*	7.68*
Australia	−0.49	−2.00*	0.40	0.17	1.63*	3.25*
Japan	0.90*	−0.95*	1.39*	0.25	0.39	10.72*
Singapore	−0.36	−1.07*	0.79*	1.21*	1.00*	5.47*

Notes: This table reports the coefficients (times 10) from a regression of logarithmic daily returns. Dummy variables for each day of the week were used as explanatory variables, * indicates statistically significant at < 95 per cent confidence levels.
Source: From Condoyanni *et al.*, 1988, Table 1, p. 54.

5.6.2 *Firm size anomaly*

One area where a growing stream of evidence has arisen to suggest an apparent inefficiency is the 'firm size effect'. It would appear that in many markets small firms often out-perform larger companies, in some cases by apparently substantial margins. Dimson and Marsh have constructed an index of share prices for smaller companies in collaboration with Hoare Govett (Dimson and Marsh, 1987). During the period 1956–1986, the HGSC index had an annual arithmetic mean return of 24.5 per cent and a standard deviation 27.5 per cent, which compares to the 18.3 per cent return and 27.2 per cent standard deviation for the FT All Share Index. While the standard deviation of returns for both indices from 1956–86 are similar, there is some evidence that the HGSC index shares are less risky. The HGSC index monthly returns for 1982–86 had a beta of 0.69 relative to the FT All Share Index.

Factors which might explain the premium on small firms are:

1. Liquidity. Smaller companies tend to be traded less often; delay may be experienced when shareholders wish to realise their investment or effect a trade based on market information.

2. Bankruptcy. A further element of risk not accounted for in the CAPM is the possibility of bankruptcy and Keane notes that, 'evidence indicates, however, that small firms may have a greater likelihood of becoming bankrupt and are subject to significantly higher costs of bankruptcy' (Keane, 1983). Not only will this suggest a case for higher returns than the CAPM predicts to compensate for the effects of bankruptcy, but also there is the possibility that estimates of small firm returns are overstated where they ignore the (presumably) severely negative return on extinct firms which may have been omitted from the sample (survivorship bias).

3. Information availability. Less information reaches the market concerning small firms and fewer analysts track small company stocks. It may be that small firms are exposed to additional risk which cannot be measured using traditional measures of systematic risk.

The firm size effect is intertwined with other anomalies. By definition, the investigation of the size effect involves a sector which is earning abnormal returns. The returns are high when compared to price, and insofar as returns are linked to accounting earnings this would suggest that small firms may be low price earnings stocks. Indeed, the 'small firm effect' has rather taken over from the P/E ratio as a focus for anomalies investigations as much of the P/E effect may be explained by small firm influences. A further complication arises from seasonalities and related effects. A number of studies have suggested that the bulk of the small firm effect is concentrated into certain months of the year.

A number of attempts have been made to disentangle the impact of various equity return regularities. Jacobs and Levy have used multiple regression to attempt to isolate the impact of particular anomalies once the impact of other variables has been allowed for (Jacobs and Levy, 1988). This should allow the researchers to investigate whether various apparent anomalies are in fact proxies for other effects or genuinely independent. However, as Jacobs and Levy used monthly data, they were unable to examine the impact of short-term regularities such as day of the week, or week of the month effects.

The researchers studied the monthly returns for 1500 shares for the period from January 1978 to December 1986 and investigated 18 categories of possible anomalies for which they derived 25 independent variables. Some of the sources of apparent inefficiency are discussed in later chapters, but in general:

> The strength and persistence of returns to some of the anomaly measures, such as trends in analysis' earnings estimates, represent evidence against semi-strong market efficiency. Furthermore, the significant payoffs to other measures, such as the residual reversal, suggest that past prices alone do matter — that is, the market is not weak form efficient (Jacobs and Levy, 1988, p. 18).

Conclusions regarding efficient market anomalies

There is considerable evidence suggesting that capital markets exhibit persistent regularities which appear to be in contravention of the efficient market hypothesis. Some of these studies are referred to above. While these are interesting in that they offer hope for the active investment manager, and research possibilities for the academic, there is reason to be cautious regarding their exploitation. If genuine inefficiencies exist it is to be expected that they will be exploited until they are arbitraged away. In some cases this does not appear to happen.

Firstly, it could be that the costs involved in pursuing the inefficiencies are in excess of the gains to be made. In the study cited above the largest abnormal return identified was 0.59 per cent per month for low P/E stocks. To the extent that the costs of the investor are variable, it is unclear that this return would provide adequate compensation.

Secondly, the measure of what is the normal rate of return is equivocal. Just as astronomers might speculate as to the presence of an invisible body in space due to the observed behaviour of observable characteristics, such as the bending of light from an identified star, the advocates of the EMH insist that unexplained returns are due payment for some factor of asset pricing which is as yet elusive.

Finally, the market prices are affected by the activities of professional practitioners who invest the wealth of others. The impact of the incentives for fund managers, and for information intermediaries, may or may not motivate the pursuit of market inefficiencies. This aspect of principal and agent problems is not well researched.

5.7 Conclusion

The work of the financial analyst is frequently connected to the capital market. The analyst may be actively involved in investment strategy or advising others, but equally the returns on the capital market may be seen as useful indicators for other decisions. In either case, an understanding of the relationship between risk and return and of the efficiency or otherwise of the market is necessary. Simple methods of portfolio and asset pricing models have been presented, and while these are sparse and illuminating, they do not seem to be reliable or clearly operational descriptions of share price behaviour. However, until more developed models are available the CAPM and the APT remain informative if incomplete.

The evidence regarding the efficient market theory is considerably more compelling. As a working hypothesis, the presumption that the shares' current price incorporates all publicly available information relevant to that price, and quite possibly reflects some element of privileged information, is convincing. However, certain instances are apparent where empirical research supports the contention that there are market inefficiencies. It is not unequivocal, for it is possible that these market anomalies are the result of imperfections in the research methodology. Are they either exploitable market inefficiencies or a reward for some element of asset pricing which is not as yet incorporated into theory? Whichever is the case, an understanding of these empirical regularities is important.

Finally, the institutional aspects of the stock markets have recently undergone a considerable amount of change and there is reason to suppose that this has not yet stabilised. These changes are altering the opportunities and challenges faced by market participants and the analyst is advised to remain in touch with developments.

Note

1. Paul Draper is Professor of Finance in the Department of Accounting and Finance at the University of Strathclyde.

QUESTIONS

The following data reports the monthly return $(P_t + D_t)/(P_{t-1})$ for four shares and for the FT All Share Index.

A	B	C	D	FT
0.946	1.031	0.954	0.936	0.972
1.161	1.023	1.097	1.087	1.051
1.027	1.045	1.004	1.052	1.046
1.108	0.997	1.012	1.026	1.004
0.932	0.935	0.948	1.000	0.980
1.058	1.128	0.989	1.095	1.035
0.965	0.890	1.002	1.007	1.004
1.017	1.042	1.084	1.042	1.033
1.056	0.986	1.050	0.996	1.006
0.901	0.940	0.923	0.939	0.926
1.019	1.005	0.991	1.022	1.040
1.126	1.010	1.065	1.054	1.035

You are required to:
(a) Calculate the arithmetic average monthly return and the standard deviation for all four shares.
(b) Calculate the parameters α and β for the OLS regression of $R_i = \alpha_i + \beta_i(R_m) + e$.
(c) Calculate the correlation between four equally weighted portfolios comprising, A, $A+B$, $A+B+C$, and $A+B+C+D$ and the FT All Share Index and the standard deviation for all four portfolios.
(d) Comment on your results for (a)−(c) above.

2.   Obtain monthly readings for the FT All Share Index and market indices for at least two other European exchanges for recent years. From each exchange select one stock and obtain estimates of monthly returns for the same period that you have obtained index returns for. Compute monthly returns and the correlation between the index returns and the stock returns for all pairs. Compute the first order autocorrelation for each series. What conclusions can be drawn from these results?

3.   Assume that a member of your family has explained to you that they intend to provide for their retirement by building up a small group of houses and flats which they will let, renovate or sell as required. They are impressed with their entrepreneurial activity. Provide a one-page document which is both rigorous and simple which explains why this might not be a good idea.

4.   You new boss is sceptical regarding the relevance of your finance education. Produce a one-page document which provides a simple but rigorous (as far as possible) explanation of the CAPM and its relevance for financial managers of firms and fund managers of investment institutions.

5.   Your next boss is the proud owner of a new MBA and convinced of the importance of the CAPM for financial and investment management. Provide a brief review of the assumptions that underlie the CAPM and point out the impact of relaxing such assumptions. Conclude by contrasting the CAPM with the APT, after which you can start looking for a new job.

6.   Select one firm for which you can readily get stock market data. Estimate the beta of the stock using various time periods and intervals. Contrast this estimate of the beta with estimates from risk measurement services for other similar firms. Recalculate beta using these beta for other stocks adjusted for different gearing (leverage) of the firms. Using CAPM assumptions calculate a cost of equity for the firm.

7.   As of one year ago you were required to form a portfolio of 30 stocks which must out-perform the market. Assume that your life depends on it. Explain your strategy for picking these stocks. Now select 30 stocks as of one year ago and test your strategy. Did your portfolio beat the market index, and did it beat it when adjusted for risk?

8.   Provide definitions for the following terms as used in Chapter 5:
   (a) Risk aversion.
   (b) Diversification.
   (c) Unsystematic risk.
   (d) Capital market line.
   (e) Arbitrage.
   (f) Security market line.
   (g) Stock market regularities.
   (h) Insider dealing.
   (i) Beta stability.

References

Ball, R. and Kothari, S. (1989) Risk shifts and serial correlation in returns, *Journal of Financial Economics*, **25**, 51–74.

Black, F. (1972) Capital market equilibrium with restricted borrowing, *Journal of Business*, July, 444–55.

Blume, M. (1971) On the assessment of risk, *Journal of Finance*, March, 1–10.

Blume, M. (1975) Betas and their regression tendencies, *Journal of Finance*, **30**, no. 3, June, 785–795.

Bower, D., Bower, R. and Logue, D. (1984) A primer on arbitrage pricing theory, *Midland Corporate Finance Journal*, Fall, 31–9.

Brealey, R. (1970) The distribution and independence of successive rates of return from the British equity market, *Journal of Business Finance and Accounting*, Summer, 29–40.

Brennan, M. (1971) Capital market equilibrium with divergent borrowing and lending rates, *Journal of Finance and Quantitative Analysis*, December, 1197–1205.

Brown, G., Draper, P. and McKenzie, E. (1994) Consistency of UK pension fund investment performance, Discussion Paper, University of Strathclyde.

Chen, N.F., Roll, R. and Ross, S. (1986) Economic forces and the stock market, *Journal of Business*, **59**, 383–403.

Choy, A.Y.F. and O'Hanlon, J. (1989) Day of the week effects in the UK equity market: a cross-sectional analysis, *Journal of Business Finance and Accounting*, **16**(1), Spring, 89–104.

Condoyanni, L., O'Hanlon, J. and Ward, C. (1988) Weekend effects in stock market returns: international evidence, in Dimson, E. (Ed.), *Stock Market Anomalies*, Cambridge University Press.

Cross, F. (1973) The behaviour of stock prices on Fridays and Mondays, *Financial Analysts' Journal*, November–December, 67–9.

Dimson, E. and Marsh, P. (1983) The stability of UK risk measures and the problem of thin trading, *Journal of Finance*, **38**, 3, June, 753–783.

Dimson, E. and Marsh, P. (1984) An analysis of brokers' and analysts' unpublished forecasts of the UK stock returns, *Journal of Finance*, December, 1257–92.

Dimson, E. and Marsh, P. (1987) *The Hoarse Govett smaller companies index for the U.K.*, Hoarse Govett, London.

Dimson, E. and Marsh, P. (1988) The impact of the small firm effect on event studies, in Dimson, E. (Ed.), *Stock Market Anomalies*, Cambridge University Press.

Dhrymes, P. (1984) The empirical relevance of arbitrage pricing models, *Journal of Portfolio Management*, Summer, **10**, no. 4, 35–44.

Dhrymes, P., Friend, I. and Gultekin, N. (1984) A critical reexamination of the empirical evidence on arbitrage pricing theory, *Journal of Finance*, June, 323–50.

Elton, E., Gruber, M. and Urich, T. (1978) Are betas best?, *Journal of Finance*, December, 1375–84.

Fama, E. (1976) *Foundations of Finance*, Blackwells, Oxford.

Fama, E. and Blume, M. (1966) Filter rules and stock market trading profits, *Journal of Business*, January, 226–41.

Fama, E.F. and French, K.R. (1992) The cross-section of expected stock returns, *Journal of Finance*, June, **47**, no. 2, 427–465.

Fama, E.F. and French, K.R. (1993) Common risk factors in the returns on stocks and bonds', *Journal of Financial Economics*, **33**, no. 1, February.

Firth, M. (1972) The performance of share recommendations made by investment analysts and the effect on market efficiency, *Journal of Business Finance*, Summer, 58–67.

Firth, M. (1977) The investment performance of unit trusts in the period 1965—75, *Journal of Money, Credit and Banking*, 597—604.

Fogler, R. (1982) Common sense on CAPM, APT and correlated residuals, *Journal of Portfolio Management*, Summer, 20—8.

Foster, G. (1986) *Financial Statement Analysis*, Prentice Hall, Englewood Cliffs.

Friend, I., Landskroner, Y. and Losq, E. (1976) The demand for risky assets under inflation, *Journal of Finance*, December, 1287—98.

Hagerman, R. and Kim, E. (1976) Capital asset pricing with price level changes, *Journal of Financial and Quantitative Analysis*, September, 381—92.

Jacobs, B. and Levy, K. (1988) Disentangling equity return regularities: new insights and investment opportunities, *Financial Analysts' Journal*, May—June, 18—43.

Jensen, M. (1968) The performance of mutual funds in the period 1945—64, *Journal of Finance*, May, 389—416.

Keane, S.(1983) *Stock Market Efficiency*, Philip Allan, Oxford.

London Stock Exchange (1993) *Quality of Markets Review*, Spring, London Stock Exchange, London.

Merton, R. (1980) On estimating the expected return on the market: an exploratory investigation, *Journal of Financial Economics*, December, **8**, no. 4, 323—361.

Modigliani, F. and Cohn, C. (1979) Inflation, rational valuation and the market, *Financial Analysts' Journal*, March—April, 24—44.

Modigliani, F. and Pogue, G. (1974) An introduction to risk and return: concepts and evidence. Parts 1 and 2, *Financial Analysts' Journal*, March—April, 68—80 and May—June, 69—86.

Poon, S. and Taylor, S.J. (1991) Macroeconomics factors and the UK stock market, *Journal of Business Finance and Accounting*, **18**(5), September.

Roll, R. (1977) A critique of the asset pricing theory's tests, *Journal of Financial Economics*, March, 126—176.

Roll, R. and Ross, S. (1980) An empirical investigation of the arbitrage pricing theory, *Journal of Finance*, December, 1073—104.

Roll, R. and Ross, S. (1984) The arbitrage pricing theory approach to strategic portfolio planning, *Financial Analysts' Journal*, May—June, 14—26.

Ross, S. (1976) The arbitrage theory of capital asset pricing, *Journal of Economic Theory*, December, 341—60.

Ross, S. (1977) Risk return and arbitrage, in Bicksle, J. and Friend, I. (Eds), *Risk Return in Finance*, Ballinger, Cambridge.

Sheffrin, S.M. (1983) *Rational Expectations*, Cambridge Surveys of Economic Literature, Cambridge University Press, 141—146.

Solnik, B. (1973) Note on the validity of random walk for European stock prices, *Journal of Finance*, December, 1151—9.

Ward, C. and Saunders, A. (1976) UK unit trust performance 1964—74, *Journal of Business Finance and Accounting*, Winter, 83—99.

CHAPTER 6

Accounting, Value and the Capital Market

—————————————— CHAPTER OBJECTIVES ——————————————

This chapter will:

1 Review the link between security price movements and accounting disclosures.

2 Consider the evidence regarding the use of accounting information to exploit stock market inefficiencies.

3 Examine the practice of share valuation models and the importance of accounting variables in those models.

6.1 Introduction

The subject of this chapter, the relationship between accounting information and share prices, is a crucial part of this text. Accounting information is one of the most significant sources of financial information for analysts, and valuing companies is one of the most important applications to which they address themselves. Active investment management requires the identification of discrepancies between 'value' and price, and the financial press at least is convinced that accounting earnings and share prices are closely connected. However, there are some reasons to believe that exploiting accounting information to identify incorrectly valued shares will be difficult, as follows:

1. It has been shown that accounting information is a poor indicator of the economic transactions and values which affect share prices. A balanced assessment might be that while the absolute measures of accounting data are not informative, as relative indicators there may be some worth in accounting information. The cross-sectional and time-series behaviour of accounting numbers has been examined in Chapters 3 and 4 to clarify these relative relationships.

2. It has also been made apparent that, to be valuable, accounting data must be of use

for making decisions. This requires that accounting information must have some predictive value, for any decision will require information inputs regarding the future. The predictive value of accounting information was also assessed in Chapter 4, and while it is apparent that some evidence of predictive skill can be shown in the ability of analysts, naive presumptions of predictability need to be treated with great care.

3.   The previous chapter addressed the scope for exploiting market inefficiency in general and concluded that a reasonable assessment of the evidence is that there is a strong argument for presuming semi-strong efficiency, though sufficient indicators that marginal inefficiencies exist to suggest that the search for abnormal returns is not pointless. Indeed, one of the most renowned examples of abnormal performance in investment selection, the Value Line system, ranked shares almost exclusively on published accounting information. Their performance was examined by Black, a self-confessed sceptic, who concluded that, 'according to the analysis that Value Line did with my help, its ranking system appears to be one of the few exceptions to the rule that attempts to separate good stocks from bad stocks are futile' (Black, 1973). It is the task of the investment analyst who advocates active portfolio management to find and exploit further exceptions to that rule. This chapter will examine some of the techniques and possibilities for doing so.

The following section (6.2) examines the relationship between accounting information and stock market reactions. Insofar as accounting profits and share returns attempt to measure the same characteristic, the change in wealth of the firm, and accounting information is presumed to be a crucial input into share valuations, it would be surprising if no reaction or relationship could be measured. Section 6.3 examines the evidence on market efficiency and accounting data, with particular regard to any anomalies which seem to indicate scope for using fundamental analysis to achieve abnormal returns. Section 6.4 reviews theoretical valuation models and the evidence on the valuation techniques employed by financial analysts.

6.2   Market reaction to accounting announcements

Accounting disclosures are only one example of the information which can affect capital market prices. The results of various surveys strongly suggest that accounting information is significant, though not exclusively so.

There are a number of characteristics that can be looked for in the relationship between accounting information and share prices. Firstly, perhaps, is the issue of measurement. Accounting purports to measure the value (capital), and changes in value (profit), of the firm. The price of a share and the returns on holding shares in a firm should also reflect these same factors. It can, therefore, be expected that there will be some association between accounting information and share prices. This is investigated in a seminal article by Ball and Brown (1968).

Secondly, not only is the existence of the relationship important, but also the timing. Accounting information is delayed by the need to complete reporting periods and by the accounting process, yet accounting information is thought to be one of the inputs to the valuation process. Therefore, it is not clear whether the market or the accounts will first report changes in value. This is again addressed by Ball and Brown. However, the ability to exploit any time lags between earnings disclosure and market reaction to achieve abnormal returns is an intricate problem which requires more detailed examination. This is left to Section 6.3.

Finally, if accounting data is of significance to the capital market, it might be expected that some reaction to the publication of accounting data will be displayed. This is the simplest characteristic of the relationship between capital markets and accounting data and is dealt with next.

6.2.1 *Market response to accounting disclosures*

The analysis performed by Firth is interesting as this examines the relationship between share prices and accounting information in the UK stock market, and researches four different categories of accounting information releases. His research confirms the findings of Beaver relating to the US evidence (Beaver, 1968; Firth, 1981).

In the UK, accounting information for quoted companies is presented partway through the year as interim reports (IR), shortly after the year-end in the form of a preliminary announcement (PA), followed by the formal annual report and accounts (ARA), and lastly by the annual general meeting (AGM). Firth quite simply examined the return on a firm's ordinary shares, after adjustment for the return expected by the CAPM, in each week of a year spanning six months either side of the PA. Thus, the market performance in weeks in which accounting information was released can be compared with the other weeks of the year. The sample examined covered 120 randomly selected firms releasing accounting data during 1976, 1977 and 1978, with year-ends spread throughout the calendar year. As the CAPM requires estimates of beta, and there are difficulties involved in computing this statistic for small firms, due to thin trading, no firms capitalised at under £10 million were included in the sample. Weekly returns data for 48 weeks were used for the beta estimation for the firms in the sample.

Table 6.1 ranks the absolute abnormal returns for the four weeks in which information was discussed, and for all the other weeks of the year, averaged over the 120 firms.

Table 6.1　Ranking of average abnormal weekly residuals

	1976		1977		1978	
Rank	Week	AAWR	Week	AAWR	Week	AAWR
1	PA	0.0683	PA	0.0642	PA	0.0641
2	IR	0.0510	ARA	0.0486	IR	0.0562
3	ARA	0.0476	IR	0.0486	ARA	0.0501
4	6	0.0381	37	0.0402	26	0.0401
...						
55	24	0.0273	21	0.0287	44	0.0286

Note: AAWR = absolute abnormal weekly return
Source: Abridged extract of Table 1, Firth, 1981, p. 524.

While the AGM appears unimportant, weeks in which IR, PA, or ARA information was released tended to have considerably higher absolute abnormal returns than normal weeks. This suggests that significant information was imparted to the market by these disclosures and the resulting interest in the shares produced higher than normal fluctuations in the price. There is no evidence from the reported results indicating that weeks adjacent to disclosure weeks had any abnormal levels of fluctuations.

Firth also shows that the PA, ARA and IR all generate unusually high levels of share trading when measured as either the number of shares sold or the number of transactions conducted. Two further points of interest were disclosed by Firth's work. Firstly, in common with a number of other studies, it is apparent that the price and trading volatility induced by accounting disclosures are more extreme in smaller firms. The hypothesis put forward to explain this factor suggests that smaller firms will receive less attention from analysts, and have less information conveyed to the market by media reports and other sources, than would larger firms. Thus, any accounting disclosures are more likely to contain significant unanticipated elements than for better researched firms, occasioning greater market reaction. Secondly, there was a statistically significant relationship between the size of the informational effects in the IR, PA and ARA weeks. Whether this second effect is divorced from the size variable mentioned above, or whether this constitutes information valuable in predicting abnormal returns, is unclear from this research.

Firth concludes that, 'although earnings announcements are anticipated to a large extent by the stock market, the actual release of the figures still results in substantial additional information being given' (Firth, 1981, p. 528).

6.2.2 *Abnormal returns and unexpected earnings*

While the work of Firth is useful in assessing whether there is any market reaction to accounting data, earlier evidence gives a more complete picture of the relationship between accounting and market returns. The seminal work by Ball and Brown is important and relevant for three main reasons.

Firstly, it illustrates the now widely used 'event study' methodology where some specific event is deemed to have an effect on security returns and the cumulative abnormal return (CAR) is plotted for a period of time both prior to, and after, the event. By aggregating over a number of examples of the particular event, a typical picture is established of the effect of this occurrence and of its expectation. As an early example of this methodology, the Ball and Brown study reveals some differences from the typical event study. In particular, they compute an abnormal price index which is based on a simple market model, rather than the more usual CAR which is founded on the CAPM.

Secondly, this work was a crucial departure from traditional normative theoretical studies where accounting usefulness was judged by its compliance with some ideal. In the research cited, the participants attempted to evaluate the usefulness of accounting numbers, in this case income computations, by evaluating their effect on investment returns. Thus the research is claimed to be 'positive in that it investigates why accounting earnings and stock prices are related and why earnings convey information to the stock market' (Watts and Zimmerman, 1986).

The third justification for examining this research in detail is that its objectives impinge directly on the focus of this chapter, namely the relationship between accounting information and share price.

The work was founded in the implications of EMH research which concludes that, if information is a useful input to determining asset prices, the market will respond quickly to the release of that information and will incorporate the effect fully. In order to examine this the researchers had to establish two parameters, the first being an assessment of the unexpected earnings disclosed. The market can be deemed to have a prior expectation of the firm's earnings and it is only the departure from that expectation that is new information. As earnings can be shown to be affected significantly by economic trends, an OLS regression is used to evaluate the impact of economy-wide influences on the specific firm's earnings. This equation is then available to compute expected earnings. It is the difference from this prediction that is recognised as new information. As Ball and Brown encountered some statistical difficulties, a naive estimation model was also used where the actual change in earnings in the previous year is the expected change in the year under review. The model is as follows.

Step 1   Estimate the sensitivity of the firm's earnings to changes in all firms' earnings:

$$\Delta I_{j,t-\tau} = \hat{a}_{1jt} + \hat{a}_{2jt}\Delta M_{j,t-\tau} + \hat{u}_{j,t-\tau} \tag{6.1}$$

Step 2   Use the estimated equation to forecast the change in the firm's earnings given knowledge of the change in all firms' earnings.

$$\Delta I_{jt} = \hat{a}_{1jt} + \hat{a}_{2jt}\Delta M_{j,t-\tau} \tag{6.2}$$

Step 3   Compare estimated change with actual to give a value to 'unexpected earnings'.

$$\hat{u}_{jt} = \Delta I_{jt} - \Delta \hat{I}_{jt} \tag{6.3}$$

The symbols used by Ball and Brown are ΔI_{jt}, the change in firm j's income at time t; ΔM_{jt}, the change in all other firms' income for the same period; $u_{j,t-\tau}$, the residual for period t; and $\tau = 1,2, t-1$. u_{jt} in step three represents the estimated unexpected earnings; $\hat{}$ denotes estimates.

Remember that the alternative test, where the change in earnings in one year is contrasted with the change in the previous year, is also used as a parallel experiment.

The second parameter established by the researchers was that the reaction to the disclosure of earnings and the unexpected element therein must also have industry-wide influences removed. Despite its superficial similarity to the conventional CAPM, this was estimated as a specification of the market model as discussed in Chapter 5, and is as follows:

$$[PR_{jm} - 1] = \hat{b}_{1j} + \hat{b}_{2j}[L_m - 1] + \hat{v}_{jm} \tag{6.4}$$

$[PR_{jm} - 1]$ is the monthly 'price relative' which measures the return for the individual share and $[L_m - 1]$ the equivalent for the market. The residual v_{jm} estimates market reaction to the disclosure of new information in the appropriate period. m refers to all months since January 1946 for which information was available.

The study included firms with available earnings data for 1946–66, with 31 December year-ends, having at least 100 months of share price data available, and for which earnings announcement dates were available from the *Wall Street Journal*. The analysis examined the years 1957−65, the previous years being required for forecasting purposes.

The results were analysed by comparing the abnormal performance index (API) for six overlapping portfolios. Two are based on the regression model using net income and earnings per share, plus a further portfolio based on the naive prediction model, where the unexpected earnings were positive and therefore represented 'good news', and three where the equivalent unexpected earnings were negative and were assumed to show 'bad news'. A seventh portfolio represents all the firms in the sample.

The API at month M was calculated as follows:

$$APINM = \frac{1}{N} \sum_{n}^{N} \prod_{m-11}^{M} (1 + V_{nm}) \tag{6.5}$$

Thus it represents the average return on an equal investment in all N securities in the portfolio from a time twelve months prior to the accounting disclosure date up to M.

Ball and Brown conclude that the results 'demonstrate that the information contained in the annual income number is useful in that if income differs from expected income the market typically has reacted in the same direction'. Indeed, Ball and Brown compute that earnings figures capture about half the net effects of all information available throughout the twelve months before their release. More detailed analysis of the results contained in the cited article conform with the overall picture presented by Figure 6.1.

Apart from the general conclusion that there is a link between accounting earnings and security prices, the most startling result is that the performance of the good news and bad news portfolios start to diverge from the moment, twelve months prior to disclosure, when the researchers commenced testing. Indeed, very little abnormal return is perceivable after the announcement and Ball and Brown suggest that 85−90 per cent is incorporated into the share price prior to disclosure. Apparently, from this evidence there is only limited scope for using accounting earnings for investment analysis purposes (Ball and Brown, 1968).

Since the Ball and Brown study of 1968, a number of researchers have extended and refined the initial work. One of the more significant is the analysis of the magnitude of the forecast error rather than the more basic examination of the sign of the error. Intuitively, one would expect that if stock prices tend to exhibit abnormal reactions in the same direction as any unexpected earnings disclosure, as shown by Ball and Brown, then the size of the unexpected earnings would also be reflected in the magnitude of the stock price reaction.

This research (Beaver, Clarke and Wright, 1979) investigated the presence of any ordinal relationship, using Spearman rank correlation, between the abnormal returns on a company's stock returns and the unexpected component in earnings. The tests were conducted on NYSE firms for the period 1965−74, though these firms required earnings datasets back to 1956 and security return data from 1960−75.

The abnormal returns were estimated using the market model to estimate the parameters a and b for the months -71 to -12. The estimated model is then used to find the residual abnormal return over the period -11 to 0 where 0 corresponds to 3 months after the year-end and is assumed to approximate to the earnings announcement date which would conclude the gradual public dissemination of the earnings signals.

Beaver *et al.* used two models to forecast expected earnings. Model A computes the

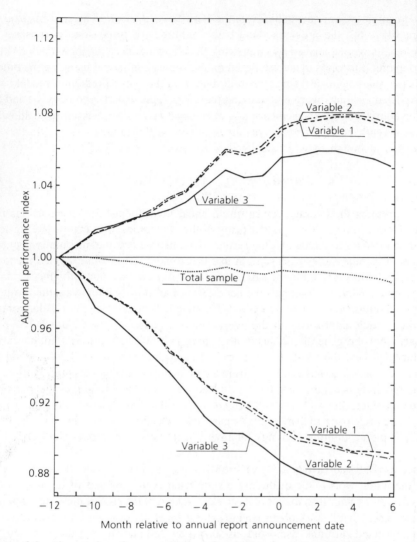

Figure 6.1 Abnormal performance indexes for various portfolios. Variable 1 — portfolio based on net income for regression model; variable 2 — portfolio based on EPS for regression model; variable 3 — portfolio based on EPS for naive model.
(*Source*: Ball and Brown, 1968, Figure 1, p. 169.)

expected change in earnings per share (EPS) as the average of the prior available changes and the error between this forecast and the actual results is the unexpected earnings. This mirrors the Ball and Brown naive model, except that Ball and Brown took only one year for their estimation of the trend term, while Beaver *et al.* use from nine to eighteen years depending on the date of the reading in the sample. Model A is as follows.

$$f(\Delta EPS_{it}) = \frac{1}{K} \sum_{k=1}^{K} \Delta EPS_{i,t-k} \qquad (6.6)$$

Thus the forecast change in EPS ($f(\Delta EPS_{it})$) for firm i in time period t is the average of all preceding changes in EPS for that firm from $t-k$ where $k=1$ to $t-K$ where K is the number of years in the sample prior to time t.

Model B equates to Ball and Brown's forecasting model for EPS where the sensitivity of a specific firm's change in EPS to changes in the market's EPS is estimated by an OLS regression of the previously available data. The parameters y_1 and y_2 are estimated by regressing changes in EPS for firm i against the change in average EPS across all firms for the same time period. The number of readings change from nine to eighteen years depending on where t occurs in the sample. Model B is as follows.

$$f(\Delta EPS_{it}) = y_{1i,t-1} + y_{2i,t-1}\Delta EPS_{mt} \tag{6.7}$$

Thus the forecast change in EPS ($f(\Delta EPS_{it})$) using model B is equal to a constant y_1 plus the current change in EPS across all firms adjusted by a sensitivity factor y_2. y_1 and y_2 are estimated at time $t-1$ using all available readings up to and including $t-1$.

The forecast errors ($\Delta EPS_{it} - f(\Delta EPS_{it})$) for each of these models is then standardised by the standard deviation on the prior nine years' forecast errors, and alternatively by the forecast earnings per share. The performance of forecasting techniques such as those employed in models A and B has been evaluated in Chapter 4, as follows:

$$e_{sit} = \frac{\Delta EPS_{it} - F(\Delta EPS_{it})}{\theta[\Delta EPS - F(\Delta EPS_{it})]} \tag{6.8}$$

$$E_{pit} = \frac{\Delta EPS_{it} - f(\Delta EPS_{it})}{f(EPS_{it})} \tag{6.9}$$

where e_{sit} and e_{pit} are the standardised and percentage errors for firm at time period t.

The work described above produced four sets of results where the companies were grouped into 25 portfolios of increasing forecast errors for percentage and standardised errors for the two forecasting models. All four groupings revealed similar results with a strong relationship between unexpected earnings and abnormal share returns.

The robustness of these results is illustrated by the Spearman correlation statistic between the median percentage forecast errors and the unsystematic returns at the portfolio level, as set out in Table 6.2.

Table 6.2 Spearman correlations between median percentage forecasts error and unsystematic returns (portfolio level)

Model A Percentage	$- 0.74$ ($t = 10.35$)
Model A Standardised	$- 0.66$ ($t = 12.93$)
Model B Percentage	$- 0.69$ ($t = 11.81$)
Model B Standardised	$- 0.69$ ($t = 13.90$)

Notes: All correlations are significant at any reasonable level of confidence statistics were observed at the individual firm level, all are still significant at 99 per cent confidence levels.
Source: From Table 7, Beaver, Clarke and Wright, 1979, p. 331.

One concern which is partially answered by further evidence included in this study, is the explanation for the difference between firms' performance. Firms with high levels of unexpected earnings, as defined by the forecasting models used, also experience high levels of abnormal returns, but is there any explanation or pattern explaining why these firms do suffer such forecast errors? Beaver *et al.* (1979 p. 334) show that:

> for the percentage form of the forecast error, there appears to be a positive relationship between the (absolute value of the) forecast error and systematic risk. The rank correlation was computed between the $|ep|$ and β_p; for model A the correlation was 0.96 and for model B it was 0.81.

One explanation for this phenomenon is that if all other parameters are constant, beta is a function of the dispersion in share returns. The dispersion of beta will be related to the dispersion in earnings and consequently in the difficulty of forecasting earnings. Hence it is feasible that firms with higher betas will experience higher forecast errors.

6.2.3 *Other characteristics of accounting disclosure*

The preceding research studies are convincing evidence that market movement largely pre-empts the information content of accounting reports, but share prices react to accounting information when disclosure takes place, suggesting that accounting reports do convey some information to the market. Further evidence on the direction and magnitude suggests that share prices and accounting earnings contain substantially similar information. Further extensive research has been conducted on this relationship and in particular on the link between interim reports and share prices, the importance of differing levels of accounting and other information, and the relative importance of earnings and cash flow disclosures. These are summarised briefly below.

Interim earnings and share price reaction

Interim earnings and share price returns are examined by Foster as they could be expected to influence the apparently small reaction to accounting earnings in the month of annual earnings disclosure. Reaction during the year to the release of interim earnings would minimise subsequent movement implying that accounting information is less important than it is. A further benefit from Foster's study is the computation of abnormal returns using daily data, hence reaction can be judged more finely than with other studies which were constrained to examining the month of disclosure. Foster's work is illustrated in Figure 6.2.

Figure 6.2 reveals a cumulative average residual (CAR) of 0.8 per cent during day -1 and 0. Foster also reports 2.53 per cent reaction over the full 60 days implying a disclosure date reaction of 32 per cent of the information contained in the interim report (Foster, 1977).

Another hypothesis that follows from Foster's research is that if interim earnings reports convey information to the market that would otherwise be left to the annual report, then firms publishing interim information should experience less market reaction than others. McNichols and Manegold found that for a small sample (34 US firms), these firms

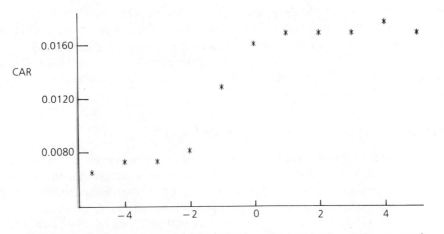

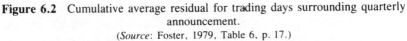

Figure 6.2 Cumulative average residual for trading days surrounding quarterly announcement.
(*Source*: Foster, 1979, Table 6, p. 17.)

experienced less volatility in share prices in the days (-5 to $+2$) surrounding the disclosure of annual earnings than the same firms did before quarterly disclosure was required in 1962. They 'observed (1) a statistically significant decrease in the variance of returns of the annual report announcement date and (2) no statistically significant change in the risk of the portfolio of sample firms' (McNichols and Manegold, 1983, p. 70).

Small firms and the market reaction to accounting disclosure

It has already been noted that Firth found greater reaction to earnings disclosure in small firms. Grant found similar results for 'smaller' firms traded on the over-the-counter (OTC) market than for senior stock exchange firms. He explained that, 'the annual earnings announcements of OTC firms appear to possess more information content than those of the NYSE firms'. The argument to support this observation suggests that between earnings disclosures the analysts of OTC firms have relatively little information available during the intervening period. 'Therefore, when the annual earnings announcement is made, the market reaction to the information contained in the report may be significant' (Grant, 1980, p. 267).

Market reaction to delayed accounting disclosure

Despite the fact that accounting information induces stock market reaction, there is ample evidence that much of the information reflected in accounting reports is conveyed to the market before accounting disclosure by other sources. Therefore, it is feasible that if accounting reports are delayed, the search activities of the analysts will further denude the value of the accounting information. Chambers and Penman addressed this problem but concluded that their results were 'consistent with the notion that accounting reports contain some information about specific firms which is not provided by other sources regardless of the time lag'. However, they did discover that when report disclosure dates are compared with the expected date, early reports tended to occasion positive abnormal returns and late reports negative abnormal returns (Chambers and Penman, 1984). This is consistent with a firm's management delaying the publication of bad news. Perhaps in response to this, the market tends to suffer a negative abnormal return when reports are not published when expected.

Market reaction to earnings or cash flow disclosure

The change in share values and the resultant abnormal returns are dependent on the change in expected cash flows to the shareholders, or the risk attached to those cash flows. Insofar as earnings changes are a reliable indicator of alterations to the characteristics of future cash flows, a relationship between earnings and returns is expected. However, it could be presumed that changes in future cash flows are best predicted by changes in current cash flows rather than current earnings. However, Beaver and Dukes found a stronger relationship between earnings and abnormal returns than with operating cash flows. This study utilised funds from operations rather than cash flows, the former being closely tied to reported earnings, and might therefore be expected to report little difference (Beaver and Dukes, 1972). However, perhaps the essential reason for profits' superior performance is that cash flows exhibit a greater dispersion than earnings. Much of the change in cash flows in any one year will be random, whereas the averaging process in accruals-based earnings removes much of this random element, possibly leaving the underlying trends as more effective indicators of subsequent permanent change.

6.2.4 *Conclusions regarding market reaction to accounting disclosures*

Certain conclusions might be drawn from the research evidence examined above. It seems clear that capital markets are not strong form efficient with regards to accounting disclosures. The accounting numbers are known to a firm's management prior to release, but this information is not fully incorporated into the share price as shown by the conclusive reaction found on disclosure. However, there is no result yet examined which leads to any conclusion that the capital market is not semi-strong form efficient. While earnings, in part, measure the same aspects of performance as does the share price, the capital market is able to incorporate this information into the share price well before earnings are released.

Accounting information's impact on the capital market appears to be influenced by a number of factors which will impinge on the quality and quantity of relevant information held by market participants, as follows:

1. The level of uncertainty surrounding the announcement. Where the information disclosed is significantly different from expectations, a substantial response may be expected and this is more likely to occur where the level of other relevant information is low and/or the firm is subject to a high degree of risk.
2. The reliability of the information available. The impact of dubious data is likely to be heavily discounted by the market. Thus even where superior earnings are expected,

but with a high degree of uncertainty, their eventual occurrence may well be greeted by share price reaction.

3. The impact of the information on future cash flows from the firm. Thus, it would appear that changes in earnings are deemed to be superior indicators of changes in future cash flows than changes in the actual cash flows, due to the high degree of transitory change in cash-based figures.

6.3   Accounting information and market efficiency

The previous section has demonstrated convincingly that accounting information measures, at least in part, the same factors which are apparent in the returns on shares. To the extent that the accounting information precedes market returns, or is capable of prediction, there is the opportunity for exploitation of accounting information. In this section, the possibilities of exploiting post-earnings drift, creative accounting and the forecast revision of analysts are examined. These are followed by discussion of potential inefficiencies induced by the claim that the capital market is myopic and/or mechanistic.

6.3.1   *Post-earnings drift*

That there are post-earnings announcement drifts was first hinted at by Ball and Brown (1968). Returns on the good news and bad news portfolios continue the pre-earnings trends for a couple of months after the earnings announcements. Later, more precisely focused research tended to confirm that suggestion. That security prices adjust to unexpected earnings announcements gradually rather than instantaneously is both surprising and, if valid, significant. Whereas a capital market inefficiency is feasible where the relevant information is either restricted in availability or not readily exploited, there seems to be no difficulty inherent in observing earnings' surprise effects when accounting information is disclosed and traded therein. The doubt that such an inefficiency might exist lies in the assumption that if it is so readily observable, market participants would commence trading on that basis. The potential gains would be rapidly incorporated into the share prices, thereby dispersing the potential for long-term gains. The significance lies not only in the implications for the efficient market hypothesis, but also in the appealing possibility of making abnormal returns on stock market investments.

In 1984 Foster, Ohlsen and Shevlin published research which attempted to establish the existence, or otherwise, of this anomaly and to establish the causes. They suggested that the previous results indicating inefficiency could be consistent with six different explanations. These reservations would apply equally well to most other empirical studies of market efficiency; they are detailed as follows:

1. Capital market inefficiency. It is quite clear that the earnings drift could be a result of the capital market failing to react promptly to available information, but as previously mentioned this does not sit easily with an intuitive assessment.
2. Alternatively, it is possible that the tests which suggested an apparent inefficiency place undue faith in the two parameter CAPM, as there could be further relevant factors

which remain unaccounted for. Chapter 4 discussed the possibility of further explanatory characteristics to explain expected earnings.

3. It is also possible that even if the CAPM is an accurate description of the stock market's pricing process, the difficulty of accurately estimating the elements of the CAPM may render the tests inaccurate.

4. The capital market might also appear to be inefficient if information assumed to be available to the market in the research design had not yet been made public. Foster *et al.* cite examples of earnings announcements occurring after the assumed date, subsequent data being used to estimate the expected earnings model, and unavailable data being used to rank companies into portfolios.

5. The apparent inefficiencies could be sample-specific, possibly as a result of bias in the sample selection, due to survivorship characteristics of the sample, or from using too brief a period for review. It is possible that a sample might cover a period where the market was in the process of observing an apparent inefficiency before incorporating that information into improved trading strategies.

6. Lastly, it may be that the market is inefficient in that it appears to mis-price stocks, but there are unobservable costs, such as information processing costs, which are a rational explanation for this behaviour.

Foster *et al.* examined data on 1495–2053 US companies during the period 1974–81 and estimated the unexpected earnings for each quarter using four models. Models 1 and 2 used a univariate time-series forecast as follows:

$$E(Q_{i,t}) = Q_{i,t-4} + \theta_i(Q_{i,t-1} - Q_{i,t-5}) + \delta_i \tag{6.10}$$

where the θ and δ parameters are estimated using the last 20 quarters (Q), and the forecast errors are standardised by the absolute value of the actual earnings, or by the standard deviation of the forecast error on preceding periods.

$$FE_i^1 = \frac{Q_{it} - E(Q_{it})}{|Q_{it}|} \tag{6.11}$$

$$FE_i^2 = \frac{Q_{it} - E(Q_{it})}{\theta[Q_{it} - E(Q_{it})]} \tag{6.12}$$

Models 3 and 4 estimate the earnings surprise by observing the market's reaction directly and using the abnormal return ($u_{i,t}$) for the 2-day and 61-day trading periods, up to and including the earnings announcement date, standardised by the deviation of the abnormal returns for the preceding 250 trading days.

$$FE_i^3 = \frac{\sum\limits_{t=-1}^{0} u_{i,t}}{\theta(u_{i,t})} \tag{6.13}$$

$$FE_i^4 = \frac{\sum\limits_{t=-60}^{0} u_{i,t}/61}{\theta(u_{i,t})} \tag{6.14}$$

Each model was used to rank the firms into portfolios representing deciles of ascending forecast error. When tested for the persistence of classification of firms into certain portfolios, it was found that models 1 and 2 displayed a persistent tendency to classify firms into particular portfolios, thereby displaying possible 'proxy bias'.

The abnormal return calculation for each period takes an unusual approach of computing the firm's return standardised by the returns for the appropriate firm size decile for the market. This may be interpreted as a rejection of the CAPM or alternatively an assumption that companies within firm size deciles have homogeneous betas.

For both models 1 and 2, significant pre- and post-earnings drifts were found. Neither model 3 nor 4 showed evidence of post-earnings drift. Examination of the results for sub-periods showed no evidence of any notable instability in these results. When examined for firm size effects, the stock returns models, 3 and 4, still showed no post-earnings drift of any significance, yet the earnings forecast models showed significant drift for all five capitalisation size categories (see Figure 6.3).

Foster *et al.* conclude that post-earnings announcement drift occurs only with those portfolios classified using earnings forecasting models, and that 'the earnings magnitude effect and the firm size effect were collinear; together they explained 85% of the variation across portfolios in their post-announcement security return behaviour'. Why no post-earnings drift was identified when using price effect models of earnings surprise is interesting. Foster *et al.* found that these models had less of a tendency to perform as proxy variables, for the earnings-based models tended to repeat classification over time (Foster, Ohlsen and Shevlin, 1984).

6.3.2 Creative accounting

The evidence reviewed so far appears conclusive that accounting information not only reflects information impounded in the capital market, but also conveys information to the market. It is therefore possible that managers in a position to influence either the form or substance of accounting reports can affect share prices. This does not necessarily imply illicit action, as accounting regulations leave considerable scope for subjectivity. Again conventional wisdom does hold that scope for manipulation exists. Press commentary on the growth of off-balance-sheet financing illustrates this.

> If the purpose of a balance sheet is to display a company's true assets and liabilities — what else could it be? — it must follow that arranging for assets (or liabilities) not to appear on the balance sheet will tend to diminish its usefulness. And that does seem to be the main point of the various off-balance sheet devices. (*The Financial Times*, 1987b)

However, the weight of evidence to date suggests that the market is able to see through accounting sleight of hand, and values companies according to the underlying basics. Beaver and Dukes examined two groups of companies with differing P/E ratios that were similar in all respects except their choice of depreciation policies. When the different effect on earnings of the various depreciation policies was cancelled out the P/E ratios became comparable (Beaver and Dukes, 1973). Kaplan and Roll examined changes in accounting policies occasioned when firms adjusted their depreciation policies, and their accounting for investment tax credits, and in both cases the accounting manipulation appeared to have

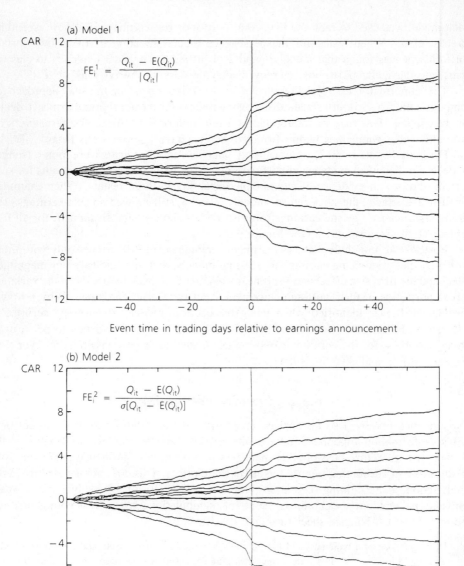

(a) Model 1

CAR

$$FE_i^1 = \frac{Q_{it} - E(Q_{it})}{|Q_{it}|}$$

Event time in trading days relative to earnings announcement

(b) Model 2

CAR

$$FE_i^2 = \frac{Q_{it} - E(Q_{it})}{\sigma[Q_{it} - E(Q_{it})]}$$

Event time in trading days relative to earnings announcement

Figure 6.3 Behaviour of CARS over $(-60, +60)$ trading day period using $R_I - R_F$.
(*Source*: Foster, Ohlsen and Shevlin, 1984, Figure 1. pp. 588–91.)

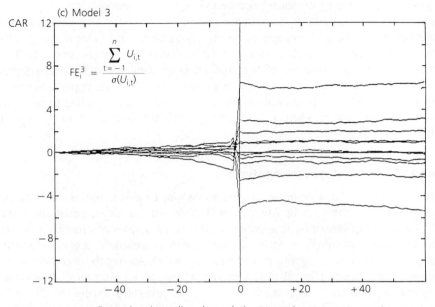

(c) Model 3

$$FE_i^3 = \frac{\sum\limits_{t=-1}^{n} U_{i,t}}{\sigma(U_{i,t})}$$

Event time in trading days relative to earnings announcement

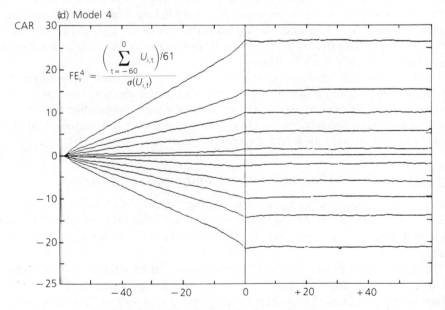

(d) Model 4

$$FE_i^4 = \frac{\left(\sum\limits_{t=-60}^{0} U_{i,t}\right)/61}{\sigma(U_{i,t})}$$

Event time in trading days relative to earnings announcement day

negligible effect on the firms' share price behaviour (Kaplan and Roll, 1972). More recent evidence has not been so sanguine, and the analysis is complicated where the accounting changes result in subsequent changes in cash flows, and hence the value of the companies. The most thoroughly researched area is the adoption of last in/first out (LIFO) stock valuation by US firms, which will often reduce future tax liabilities but also has a depressing effect on reported profits. Ricks and Biddle's work, cited in Foster, appears to imply that analysts are, at least in part, misled by the adjusted profit figure leading to unwarranted negative abnormal returns when the accounting reports are disclosed (Foster, 1986; Ricks and Biddle, 1985).

Abraham Briloff and market reactions

A further indication that accounting manipulations may be able to fool some of the people some of the time is the work of Abraham Briloff. Briloff, an experienced and respected critic of accounting practices, is apparently able to affect the stock market's perception of a firm's value by detailed and critical dissection of that company's reports and accounting practices. Foster investigated this phenomenon and concludes that those companies whose accounts were criticised by Briloff suffered a loss in capitalisation on average of approximately 8 per cent, and that this loss was not reinstated during the 30 days after publication. It does not appear from the research that this reaction is due to the publication of previously private information, that the publication itself will impact on the cash flows of the firm (possibly through government or regulatory intervention), nor did the publications coincide with other damaging information releases. This leaves the possibility that the market is simply inefficient or that Briloff is able to generate new information from especially skilled analysis (Foster, 1979).

These last two possibilities are extremely difficult to disentangle but Keane agrees that this phenomenon may be a result of the analyst's superior ability to synthesise available data more effectively than others, thereby creating privileged information (Keane, 1983). This does not negate the apparent conclusion that the market has been fooled by creative accounting, at least until unfortunate enough to be selected for 'review'.

6.3.3 *Abnormal returns and analysts' forecasts*

Chapter 4 mentioned briefly that the stock market appeared to take notice of analysts' forecasts, and consequently there is an apparent case that forecasts have value. This section will consider more closely the possibility of exploiting analysts' forecasts in investment strategies.

Neiderhoffer and Regan examined the relationship of stock returns to earnings changes, and analyst's forecasts for those 50 stocks which performed best in 1970–71. Unsurprisingly, earnings changes had a strong relationship with stock returns, but so did the error between forecast earnings and actual.

> The common characteristic of the companies registering the best price changes included a forecast of moderately increased earnings and a realised gain far in excess of analysts' expectations. The worst performing stocks were characterised by severe earnings declines combined with unusually optimistic forecasts.   (Neiderhoffer and Regan, 1972)

Table 6.3 Forecast error and earnings change as determinants of annual return

Year	Forecast error			Earnings change		
	a_1	b_1	R^2	a_2	b_2	R^2
1980	0.293	4.274	0.205	0.263	3.511	0.145
	(19.05)	(9.87)		(16.75)	(8.00)	
1981	0.066	2.637	0.174	0.023	2.766	0.194
	(4.54)	(8.97)		(2.00)	(9.57)	

Source: Table VIII, Benesh and Peterson, 1986, p. 35.

Jacobs and Levy refer to these effects as the 'earnings torpedo' (Jacobs and Levy, 1988a). More recent work by Benesh and Peterson supports Neiderhoffer and Regan's 1972 findings. These researchers examined 380 and 384 US firms' results for 1980 and 1981, dividing these into portfolios of the best and worst 50 share returns and the remainders. Preliminary results are unsurprising. Typically the best firms achieved higher growth in earnings than the worst and the disparity in actual and expected is accentuated by the worst performing companies having higher forecast earnings. These conclusions are supported by regression analysis of returns as the independent variable explained by earnings change and forecast error (see Table 6.3). No attempt appears to be made to combine the predictive variables (Benesh and Peterson, 1986).

However, these results are further confirmation that forecasts potentially hold value. The ability to produce quality forecasts which can identify erroneous expectations in others appears to be exploitable. A difficulty lies in establishing those individuals, organisations or techniques that demonstrate this superiority. In an attempt to identify more tractable methods of exploiting the predictive power of analysts' forecasts, a number of researchers have examined the market reaction to the publication of forecast revisions and the efficiency of that reaction. If forecasts have value, then their revision should induce stock market adjustments, and if the market is efficient this should have an immediate and unbiased effect. Givoly and Lakonishok (1979) use the familiar market model to separate abnormal from normal returns on a monthly basis and examine the share price reaction in the months $t-1$ to $t+2$ relative to the revision. They examined the revisions of the most active forecaster of 49 US companies over the period 1967–74 and discovered that the market reaction was apparent and that it persisted for two months after the revision date, as shown in Table 6.4 (Givoly and Lakonishok, 1979).

It would appear that forecasts do have valuable information content and what is more the market allows considerable scope for its exploitation. Freid and Givoly report that Givoly and Lakonishok further tested this evidence for operational possibilities and deduced that abnormal returns could be earned by exploiting information on forecast revisions, as shown in Table 6.5 (Fried and Givoly, 1982). Even given 2 per cent trading costs a strategy-based on purchase at the end of a month of revision, followed by a sale at the next downward revision, would have produced an abnormal return of nearly 15 per cent.

Support for this conclusion again comes from Benesh and Peterson, who computed the holding gain or loss on shares experiencing forecast revisions greater than 5 per cent and 2 per cent from the month of revision to the year-end. This is contrasted with the monthly return on a value weighted index. Although there appears to be no adjustment

Table 6.4 Average abnormal returns per holding period by direction of financial analysts'
earnings forecast revisions, for revisions over 5 per cent

Abnormal returns	%	Month relative to revision			
		-1	0	1	2
All revisions	Up	1.1	0.9	1.7	1.0
	Down	-1.6	-1.2	-0.4	-0.6
No earnings	Up	1.4	0.7	2.5	0.9
Announcement	Down	-1.1	-0.9	-0.9	-0.5

Note: All values are different from zero for a two-tailed test at the 5 per cent significance level.
Source: Givoly and Lakonishok, 1979, Table 4, p. 176.

Table 6.5 Mean annual abnormal returns from a strategy based on analysts'
forecast revisions

Revision size %	(a)%	Trading rule (1)%	(2)%
0	0	12.94	15.20
	1	5.79	7.34
	2	1.36*	1.22*
5	0	22.11	26.21
	1	17.51	18.93
	2	9.55	12.20
10	0	25.62	29.45
	1	18.60	21.80
	2	12.29	14.92

Notes: Column (a) represents level of round trip transaction costs; column (1) represents
buy at end of revision month, sell at end of following month; column (2) represents buy
at end of revision month, sell at end of first month with a downward revision, * = not
significant at 99 per cent.
Source: Givoly and Lakonishok, 1984, Table III, p. 44.

made for the systematic risk of the shares, appropriate buying or selling on the basis of
the forecast revisions produces an average additional return per month of 1.45 per cent
and 1.365 per cent for the two trading rules (Benesh and Peterson, 1986).

Of course, there is no clear evidence that it is the analysts' forecasts which have induced
the trading. The forecasts may be revised in response to some other factor which is causing
the extra returns on the shares, but this does not prevent the revision's usefulness as an
indicator. It is an interesting reflection that chartists and fundamental analysts attempt to
predict good investment decisions by examination of past share price movement on the
one hand, and accounting and other fundamentals on the other. Yet here, preliminary
evidence suggests that investment decisions can be made on the basis of observing changing
expectations in those analysts.

6.3.4 *Inflation and market values*

Modigliani and Cohn levelled a startling accusation at the valuation of companies on capital markets. They claim that shares are systematically undervalued in inflationary times as investors capitalise current earnings at nominal rather than real rates of return, and fail to allow for the gain to shareholders resulting from the decline in value of monetary liabilities. This has deflated the ratio of the market value of the firm and the replacement cost of its assets — Tobin's Q. (Tobin's Q is defined as the ratio of the market value of the firm to the replacement cost of the assets less liabilities.) With some courage Modigliani and Cohn claim that 'rationally valued, the level of the S&P 500 at the end of 1977 should have been 200. Its actual value at the time was 100. Because of inflation-induced errors, investors have systematically undervalued the stock market by 50 per cent (Modigliani and Cohn, 1979).

Evidence for the UK shows that in common with the sample investigated by Modigliani and Cohn the ratio of the market value to the replacement cost of capital has declined since the early 1970s, while adjusted profits after taxes plus interest have maintained a broadly stable relationship to the replacement cost of capital. This measure of after-tax returns on the total capital attempts to assess the real profitability of the assets of the company, and Modigliani and Cohn concluded that it was unchanged and therefore did not explain the decline in market values. Some decline in profitability may occur, especially for measures of shareholder returns not adjusted for the element of capital repayment included in interest during inflationary times. Only where real interest rates rise would a decline in stockholder profitability be experienced.

Modligliani and Cohn claim that further to this understatement of profit, investors compound the problem by using a nominal rather than a real capitalisation rate. Needless to say, the accusation of a substantial inefficiency in the capital market attracted some attention, but despite adverse response and further data, Modigliani and Cohn have maintained their basic hypothesis (Modigliani and Cohn, 1985).

If Modigliani and Cohn are correct in their assertion of aggregate mis-valuation of stock markets at least one element, the misinterpretation of interest payments, should be ascertainable in the case of individual shares. However, in Chapter 2 the inability of researchers to evidence market reaction to CCA disclosures was discussed. Companies could be graded into portfolios which predict the susceptibility of accounting earnings to CCA adjustments. This should not be an onerous task. In the subsequent period of high inflation and CCA disclosures, those firms predicted to suffer higher negative adjustments under-performed those with relatively minor adjustments. However, Keane points out that the abnormal return can be seen as accruing from the ability to predict the level of inflation. In the period examined here, inflation is thought to have exceeded expectations and it is hardly surprising that those firms especially susceptible to inflation under-performed (Keane, 1983).

6.3.5 *Myopia in capital markets*

It is an often cited criticism of stock markets, including the LSE, that investors are obsessed by short-term returns and concentrate excessively on the current profits of the firms in which they invest, to the exclusion of future returns. This complaint comes most forcefully from the managers of the industrial and commercial firms and is heard regularly at the annual Confederation of British Industry (CBI) conference. If the market is indeed mechanistic, in that it concentrates overmuch on reported profits, or myopic, focusing on current rather than future results, it is a powerful rejection of the efficient market hypothesis and an indictment of the financial system. Short-termism will allocate finance inappropriately and provide a disincentive to management to invest in the future through training, research or capital investment, if this will temporarily depress profits. The percentage of gross domestic product devoted to gross fixed capital formation has been lower in the UK than in West Germany, Japan and the OECD generally throughout 1960–85, and although higher than the US in percentage terms it is lower per capita (CBI, 1987, p. 17).

Some casual evidence is available as follows:

1. The market can be seen to attach very different multiples to the current earnings as shown by the dispersion of price earnings ratios. Such variety is visible both within and between industry groups and is normally thought to be a reflection of the firm's growth potential. However, it is also a reflection of accounting policy differences and transient departures from normal levels of profitability. It is comforting that the market is not fooled by these factors, but the extent to which the variety in P/E ratios is explained by these considerations detracts from any claim that the spread of P/E ratios is in itself an indication of long-term outlook by investors.

2. Analysts provide forecasts of next year's profit. Brown, Foster and Noreen provide evidence that forecasts of profit two years ahead are valued by the market (Brown, Foster and Noreen, 1985).

3. Fund managers are rewarded for short-term performance of the investments they control, but the assessment of their portfolio is made on the market returns not the accounting profitability. For the short-term performance assessment to be significant requires that the market neglects the future profits. This might arise where the market is unable to predict future profits effectively, which is quite conceivable, or where future profits are predictable but are not valued by the market. This seems unlikely

Table 6.6 Constraints on long-term investment

Percentage respondents mentioning:	Of major significance	Significant	Not significant
Shortage of capital	5	10	85
Cost of capital and/or fears of inadequate rate of return	24	53	23
Exchange rate uncertainties	2	26	72
A lack of confidence in market prospects	9	39	52
Weakness in your share price or rating	7	34	59
Fear of takeover	0	12	88
Pressure from financial institutions/analysts	4	19	77

as it would present arbitrage possibilities, the exploitation of which would tend to remove the inefficiency.

A survey by the CBI suggests that firms' managers do not see short-termism as a problem with regards to long-term investment (see Table 6.6).

The evidence of academic studies is not all benign. In particular, recent evidence in the UK has suggested that dividends are more highly valued than capital gains, providing an incentive to divert funds from growth to payout (Nickell and Wadhani, 1987). However, this conclusion is not generally supported and there is limited clear evidence that the market is myopic.

6.4 Accounting and valuation models

All financial analysts who attempt to monitor or select firms as investments utilise a valuation model. This may be explicit or implicit. Even the investment in an index fund which mimics the market portfolio assumes that the CAPM is appropriate. Others attempt to incorporate their assumptions about the factors that affect value into a formal model. The formal model is used as a black box into which forecasts are input, valuations computed and investment action initiated. Even where analysts accept the EMH as a sound description of the capital markets, the use of a valuation model may still be beneficial. The careful definition of the relevant parameters, the systematic collection of data, and the opportunity present for feedback and control, are all possible sources of improvement in the management of investment analysis.

Despite the presumption of an efficient market a vast, some would claim disproportionate, amount of time has been spent on the development of valuation models. Some variables that affect value are readily identifiable as earnings, dividends, risk, cost of borrowing and growth rates. However, difficulties of estimating these parameters have lead to a great diversity of alternative models which try and identify determinants of value or practical surrogates thereof. In order to assess these models, the basic valuation model will be presented, commencing with the relatively simple risk of valuing fixed interest securities, and then moving on to ordinary shares. The actual valuation practices of analysts are then contrasted with the sparse theoretical models.

6.4.1 *Valuation of fixed interest securities*

The UK market for fixed interest securities denominated in sterling is dominated by government issues which are principally classified by their due date for redemption as 'shorts' (within five years), 'mediums' (five to fifteen years), 'longs' (over fifteen years), and 'undated' (which have no redemption date). A further classification of government issues are the 'index-linked' bonds which have redemption dates spanning 1990 to 2024. Other bonds are issued by local government corporations, building societies, foreign banks and governments, and by commercial firms. Tables 6.7 and 6.8 give some basic data regarding yields on UK and international bonds.

Theoretical valuation models are normally based on discounted cash flow techniques.

Table 6.7 Yields on UK government fixed interest securities

Coupons	Low	Medium	High
5 years	9.5	10.6	10.9
15 years	9.1	9.7	9.8
25 years	9.0	9.3	9.3
Irredeemable	9.0		
Index-linked	2.6–3.9		
Yields on other bonds			
Debentures and loans	10.9-11.7		
Preference shares	10.4		

Source: Financial Times, 4 January 1989, p. 23.

This is relatively non-contentious when dealing with certain cash flows and interest rates. The cash flows may be discounted from their due date to their present value using the risk-free rate of interest. However, even the simplest of situations fails to comply with this ideal. While investors might be prepared to treat commitments by borrowers, such as the Bank of England, as effectively without risk, even the rate of interest relevant to risk-free investments is still uncertain. Interest rates can be disaggregated into two elements. Firstly, a charge for the borrowing of the sum involved, and secondly, an element to compensate for inflation. Clearly, future inflation carries a level of uncertainty. Despite this difficulty, the valuation of fixed interest securities is clearly founded on discounted cash flows. Thus, the present value of a bond may be defined by the standard formulae:

$$PV_0 = Co_1/(1+R_{s1}) + Co_2/(1+R_{s2})^2 + \ldots Co_t/(1+R_{ST})^t + Red_t/(1+R_{s1})$$

$$(6.15)$$

Where Co_t refers to the coupon at time t and Red_t to the redemption amount at time t, and the annualised discount (or spot) rate R_{ST} is the appropriate discount for a certain income t periods into the future. This discount (R_{ST}) rate may be computed as $(t + r_1)$ $\times (1 + r_2) \times \ldots (1 + r_t)$ where r_t is the one period interest rate. However, it can be seen that the term structure of the various spot rates is not necessarily level. In general, as t increases, the spot interest rate also increases, probably as compensation for lost liquidity. However, expectations regarding future inflation and interest rates will also have an effect and where the term structure is not stable the scheduling of the repayments is also of significance. Where the bonds have a high coupon rate, a greater proportion of their return is paid in the early days. This diversity can be seen in Table 6.8.

This basic structure of the NPV model of bonds allows the analyst to compute some useful variables, as follows:

1. Where coupons and redemption amounts and dates are known and the bond is traded on an efficient market, thereby giving a reliable price, the yield to maturity may be computed. This is the single interest rate, or internal rate of return, which discounts

Table 6.8 Benchmark government bonds

		Coupon	Red date	Price	Day's change	Yield	Week ago	Month ago
Australia		6.500	09/04	91.9500	−0.800	10.33	10.00	10.17
Belgium		7.750	10/04	94.8000	−0.410	8.55	8.41	8.24
Canada*		9.000	12/04	98.5500	−0.150	9.22	9.10	9.01
Denmark		7.000	12/04	86.6200	−0.080	9.10	9.12	8.65
France	BTAN	8.000	05/98	100.2500	−0.130	7.89	7.69	7.27
	OAT	7.500	04/05	93.5600	−0.340	8.45	8.24	7.94
Germany Bund		7.500	11/04	98.2500	−0.540	7.76	7.55	7.40
Italy		8.500	08/04	79.7200	−0.530	12.14†	11.98	11.70
Japan	No 119	4.800	06/99	103.6400	—	3.94	3.83	3.91
	No 164	4.100	12/03	96.1280	−0.030	4.72	3.83	3.91
Netherlands		7.250	10/04	95.8400	−0.420	7.87	7.80	7.52
Spain		10.000	02/05	87.8200	−0.870	11.75	11.88	11.19
UK Gilts		6.000	08/99	90−05	−1/32	8.63	8.70	8.49
		6.750	11/04	87−02	−2/32	8.73	8.75	8.57
		9.000	10/08	102−15	−3/32	8.69	8.70	8.51
US Treasury*		7.875	11/04	100−03	−3/32	7.86	7.81	7.80
		7.500	11/24	95−15	−4/32	7.90	7.84	7.90
ECU (French Govt)		6.000	04/04	82.6400	−0.230	8.81	8.60	8.33

London closing, *New York mid-day   Yields: Local market standard.
†Gross (including withholding tax at 12.5 per cent payable by nonresidents).
Prices: US, UK in 32nds, other in decimal.
Source: MMS International, *Financial Times*, 6 January 1995, p. 18.

the present value of the income stream from a bond to zero. There is an implicit assumption that the term structure of the interest rate is level (namely, that $r = r$ for all t).

Example 1: A 10 per cent bond 'A' is trading at £98 having just paid a six-monthly coupon and is due for redemption in two years' time and has a yield to maturity as follows:

$$98 = \frac{5}{(1 + r)} + \frac{5}{(1 + r)^2} + \frac{5}{(1 + r)^3} + \frac{5}{(1 + r)^4} + \frac{100}{(1 + r)^4}$$

This may be solved by an iterative process if no suitable calculator is to hand.

(Coupon × Annuity factor) + (Redemption × Discount factor) = Present value

(5 × 3.546) + (100 × 0.823) = 100.0 at 5 per cent
(5 × 3.465) + (100 × 0.792) = 96.5 at 6 per cent

Taking a straight line interpolation between the two points gives 98 as 57 per cent of the distance from 100 to 96.5 and the appropriate rate per six months is therefore 5.57 per cent. This is annualised to 11.45 per cent.

2. Where coupons and redemption amounts and dates are known for a selection of bonds and those bonds are prices on an efficient market, it may be possible to compute the appropriate spot rates by using simultaneous equations.

    Example 2: In addition to the bond 'A' in Example 1, a further bond 'B' is trading for £88.50 and offers a £2.50 coupon every six months and matures on the same date. If two of these 'B' bonds are held, the coupons received on the 'A' and 'B' bonds are equal, but an additional £100 is received on maturity of the 'B' bond and a further investment of £79 is required. The cash flows involved in bond 'A' may then be deducted from those in the two 'B' bonds as the present values of the cash flows in the former must have an NPV of zero. This leaves only the opening and closing differential investment and maturity which must also have a zero NPV when discounted at the spot rate.

    $$79 = \frac{100}{(1 + S)^2}$$

    where s, the spot rate from t_0 to t_2, is 12.5 per cent per annum.

3. Where coupon and redemption amounts and dates are known and the various relevant spot rates are also known, the present value of the bond may be computed.

    Example 3: Bond 'C' delivers a half-yearly coupon of £7.50 and matures in two years' time. The annualised spot rates for the six-month periods are 10.25 per cent, and 10.5, 10.75 and 11.0 per cent thereafter. These convert to half-yearly rates of 5.0, 5.1, 5.2 and 5.4 per cent to one decimal place.

    $$PV(BOND\ C) = \frac{7.5}{(1 + 0.05)} + \frac{7.5}{(1 + 0.051)^2} + \frac{7.5}{(1 + 0.052)^3} + \frac{7.5}{(1 + 0.054)^4}$$

    $$PV(BOND\ C) = 7.5(0.952) + 7.5(0.905) + 7.5(0.859) + 107.5(0.810)$$

    $$PV(BOND\ C) = 107.44$$

4. The final parameter which is of fundamental interest to the analyst is the duration of the security. This measures the bond's sensitivity to changes in the interest rate. Clearly, a short-term asset will not be as severely affected by interest rates as a long-term asset. However, with bonds that pay coupons throughout, there is no obvious measure of the life and a weighted average of the present value of the cash flows is computed as follows:

    $$DUR = [PV(CO_1) + PV(CO_2)2 + \ldots PV(CO_t)t + PV(RED)_t]/PV$$

    Clearly, wherever bonds make a portion of their total distribution prior to their final maturity, the duration will be less than the maturity but a pure discount bond that pays no coupons will have a maturity equal to its duration. The concept of duration may be of importance where managers of investment need to know the susceptibility of their investment and liabilities to changes in interest rates. As an approximation portfolios with similar durations will be equally susceptible to interest rate changes.

Example 4: The duration of bond 'C' is computed as follows:

Duration bond 'C' (in half years) = [7.5(0.952)1 + 7.5(0.905)2 + 7.5(0.859)3
+ 107.5(0.810)4]/107.77 = 3.6

The duration of bond 'C' is therefore 1.8 years or 1 year 9.6 months.

6.4.2 *The valuation of ordinary shares*

During the discussion of the valuation of bonds, the issue of uncertainty was sidestepped. Typically, it is not a factor of great importance, for the timing and magnitude of the cash flows are known and the possibility of default insignificant when dealing with government securities. Only the appropriate discount rate is problematical, and the presence of a market which can be deemed to be competent in pricing the spot rate for borrowing funds to specific future dates allows the analyst to incorporate a reliable expected interest rate given the information set available to the market. Unfortunately, the degree of uncertainty endemic when valuating ordinary shares poses serious problems for NPV models of share valuation. Such models would expect that all future dividends from a share would be discounted by a required rate of return to compute the present value of the share. Firstly, this demands viable estimates of the expected dividends. Secondly, an estimate of the required rate of return is necessary and where this estimate is derived from an application of the CAPM this requires some formidable estimating. Finally, the presumed dividends need to be treated correctly for the tax regime applicable to the shareholder.

While net present value models are awkward when dealing with risky securities, the basic model still illustrates those factors which are crucial in determining share value. Where an investor holds a share for a limited time period, the value of the share to that investor is determined by the present value (PV_0) of the dividends (DIV_t) expected and the capital receipt on disposal (VAL_T), discounted at an appropriate cost of capital (r_t):

$$PV_0 = \frac{DIV_1}{(1 + r_1)} + \frac{DIV_2}{(1 + r_2)^2} + \cdots \frac{DIV_t}{(1 + r_t)^t} + \frac{VAL_T}{(1 + r_T)^T} \qquad (6.16)$$

However, the receipt on disposal is a function of the present value that the second investor will derive from dividends received and eventual disposal value. Thus:

$$VAL_T = \frac{DIV_{1*}}{(1 + r_{1*})} + \frac{DIV_{2*}}{(1 + r_{2*})^2} + \cdots \frac{VAL_{T*}}{(1 + r_{T*})^{T*}} \qquad (6.17)$$

where * indicates time after the first disposal date T. By replacing VAL_T of equation 6.16 with 6.17, and subsequent shareholders' valuation equations to replace the disposal element of the valuation equation, it is apparent that PV_0 is wholly dependent on dividends received.

$$PV_0 = \sum_{t=1}^{\infty} \frac{DIV_t}{\prod_{t=1}^{t}(1 + r_t)} \qquad (6.18)$$

Assuming that r, the discount rate, is constant then:

$$PV_0 = \sum_{t=1}^{\infty} \frac{DIV_t}{(1 + r)^t} \tag{6.19}$$

For constant growth, this equation collapses conveniently if we further assume that dividends grow by a constant rate:

$$P_0 = \sum_{\tau=1}^{\infty} DIV_0 \frac{(1 + g)^t}{(1 + r)^t} \tag{6.20}$$

which simplifies further to:

$$P_0 = DIV_1/(r - g) \tag{6.21}$$

This relationship, often known as the Gordon growth model, is probably too much of a simplification to use as a complete valuation model but it clearly illustrates the variables which affect share value. These are the level of dividends, the expected growth in dividends, and the appropriate discount rate for the dividends.

Where growth is not expected to be constant the equations may be combined, for example, by estimating the dividends for the next few years when special circumstances might apply, such as unsustainably high growth rates, and then including the constant growth model as a valuation of all future dividends, as follows.

$$P_0 = \frac{DIV_1}{(1 + r)} + \frac{DIV_2}{(1 + r)^2} + \cdots \frac{DIV_t}{(1 + r)^t} + \frac{DIV_{t+1}}{(r - g)(1 + r)^t} \tag{6.22}$$

Clearly the use of a constant growth model from period t onwards will be in part an approximation, but the discounting effect minimises the implications of any unrealistic assumptions incorporated in the constant growth model.

The appropriate discount rate

The assumption of a constant discount rate is unconvincing. The asset pricing models described in Chapter 5 provide a means of computing an appropriate discount rate. The CAPM, the sparser of the two models explained, suggests that $r_i = r_f + \beta_i(r_m - r_f)$ where r_f is the risk-free rate, r_m the return on the market and β_i the firm-specific measure of systematic risk. Thus, even if all other parameters are stable, as r_f varies, possibly resulting from inflation or as a result of government policy, then r_i will fluctuate. It is also generally thought that if r_f rises, then so will r_m to maintain the risk premium, though the spread is not necessarily expected to be a constant.

If it is accepted that r_i will fluctuate this can be readily built into the general valuation model, though the constant growth simplifications are no longer practical, as follows.

$$P_0 = \frac{DIV_1}{(1 + r_1)} + \frac{DIV_2}{(1 + r_1)(1 + r_2)} + \cdots \frac{DIV_t}{(1 + r_1)(1 + r_2)\ldots(1 + r_t)} \tag{6.23}$$

However, the need for further estimates of the parameters of the CAPM or the APT complicate an already uncertain process. It was pointed out in Chapter 5 that while the asset pricing models appear to be reasonably effective descriptions of the trade-off between risk and return for portfolios, they are considerably less successful at the single asset level necessary for the valuation of an individual company's shares. One possible method to resolve this latter problem is to use discount rates computed for a relevant group of companies such as at the industry level. This is discussed in more depth in Chapter 7.

6.4.3 *Valuation practices*

It is perhaps unsurprising that the discounted cash flow models described above have little support amongst practical analysts. The presumptions required, and the estimation problems involved, require a level of precision that would daunt most valuers. It is apparent from discussion with brokers and other analysts that less rigorous but more tractable techniques are employed.

The analysts' approach to valuation

Chugh and Meador (1984) have presented the analysts' approach graphically. This work is not based on observation of the actual working practices of analysts but is a rationalisation of the response received to a conventional survey (see Figure 6.4).

However, survey responses together with cautious descriptions of an individual's valuation methodology make an unreliable indicator of the actual methods employed. Attempts to conduct laboratory experiments have started to produce insights. Biggs identified that his subjects (eleven financial analysts) exhibit strikingly similar patterns in their 'information search in the assessment of corporate earnings power'. This similarity of decision behaviour is one conventionally accepted indicator of expert judgement. However, two distinct strategies were also identified. The analysts either attempted to assess the company's earning power 'without any attempt to make quantified predictions' or they produced a 'quantified prediction of the company's future earnings power' (Biggs, 1984).

Bouwman, Frishkoff and Frishkoff further examined the initial screening process for investment selection by twelve financial analysts. It is interesting that although survey responses have tended to indicate the dominance of accounting data in the investment process, when the actual use of data in the analysis is examined the perception of usage is somewhat different. Standard accounting statement data is the first source of information for many analysts but its use is largely constrained to the initial stages of an analysis to provide a general awareness of the standing of the firm.

> Financial information in general is used primarily as a screen for early rejection of unacceptable investment candidates. The development of a 'positive case' for the company, however, appears to be based largely on (qualitative) information about segments, products and markets. (Bouwman *et al.*, 1987, p. 24)

They also found that the segment information relating to geographical or industrial splits of the firm's activities was an important source of information for the analyst and this data figured prominently in the conclusive stages of the analyst's work.

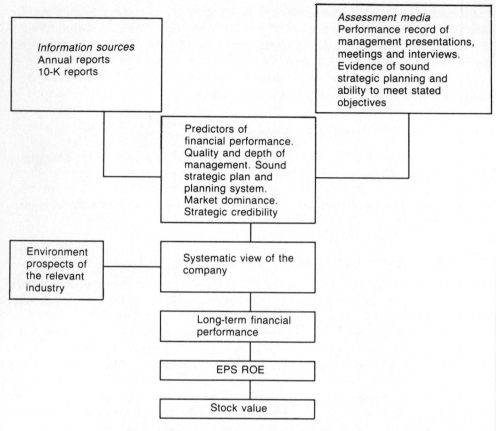

Figure 6.4 Stock valuation: a process model.
(*Source*: Chugh and Meador, 1984.)

Price/earnings based valuations

Arnold and Moizer report that investment choice would normally involve the use of price earnings ratios. Dividend yield and asset-based valuation techniques are used 70–80 per cent of the time whereas discounted cash flow (DCF) techniques would only be used in 30 per cent of the cases (Arnold and Moizer, 1984). In general, a forecast of the earnings of a company for a period into the future, normally somewhat less than two years, is conducted using a variety of techniques incorporating forecasting models and the disaggregation of accounting statements. This is combined with an assessment of an appropriate price earnings ratio, based on the analyst's experience, to compute a future share price. The return on the investment implied by the calculation is compared with that available from other investments and the relative attractiveness assessed. This combination of intuition, statistical analysis and relative rather than absolute pricing, is typical of models used by professional analysts.

Analysts may be required to submit forecasts of profits, earnings, dividends and dividend cover for a sample of the largest companies. These are then processed to produce estimates of various statistics, but most crucially for the price/earnings relative. It is the analysts' interpretation of the company's forecast price/earnings ratio in the light of predicted and historic trends that is crucial to the assessment of the potential return from an investment in that firm.

Dividend discount models (DDM) of relative value

Many of the larger US investment houses have developed models to assess the attractiveness of alternative investments. Value Line, in particular, operated a famous model which is still credited with having persistently achieved returns above normal (Black, 1973). Sharpe and Foster respectively describe in some detail the workings of the Merril Lynch and Wells Fargo models (Foster, 1986; Sharpe, 1985). Donnelly describes the degree to which these models became accepted in normal practice in the US (Donnelly, 1985).

Dividend discount models typically compute an implied rate of return from analysts' forecasts of dividends and the current share price, and compare this with the required rate of return for the firm in question. In this forecast, dividends may be predicted directly or determined from predicted earnings and pay-out ratios. The disaggregation of dividends into earnings and pay-out may be helpful for the analyst, as it allows for the return based on the firm's market position to be examined separately from the pay-out ratio which may be a function of the demands placed on internal finance by the rate of growth.

The difficulty of forecasting forward into infinity may be managed by subdividing the forecast into the following three stages.

1. Short term

This period may be one where the firm's performance is expected to differ from the average firm, or simply where the analyst has more information regarding likely earnings or dividends. If this period is seen to be one of unusual growth or decline, it may be assumed that the pay-out ratios will also be unusual. This period using explicit forecasts of dividends is unlikely to extend over more than five years.

2. Medium term/transitional

At some stage competitive pressure is expected to drive the firm's performance from the individually forecast results towards a mean which may be industry- or economy-specific. Chapter 4 discussed the mean reversion tendencies of accounting rates of return. Mueller provided strong evidence that reversion is to be expected though it appeared that an individual firm's long-run average might differ from an economy-wide mean (Mueller, 1986). Nevertheless, the tendency to revert towards a mean is stronger than the residual differences between firms. The analyst will have to forecast the rate of decay towards the steady state for the parameters included in the model and the period over which this change will take place.

3. *Steady state*

After the transitional period is complete, the firm is assumed to enter a steady state where growth and return are typical of the appropriate industry or economy. A simple model of value such as the Gordon growth model may well be used to collapse all subsequent dividends to a single point estimate at the start of this period.

Example: Firm 'A' is expected to report high levels of profitability for the next two years which will jump in year three on the introduction of new products. Competitive pressures are expected to drive profitability down to 25 per cent in year 5 and by an average 2 per cent thereafter, until the industry average of 15 per cent is reached in year 10. Internally funded investments are expected to pressure already low pay-out ratios especially in years 3 and 4, whereafter they will gradually improve to industry averages in year 10. The current market capitalisation of equity is £92 million. The implied return on equity for all stocks is 16 per cent, the risk-free rate of return on a zero-beta portfolio is 7 per cent, and the estimated beta for firm 'A' is 1.1 (see Table 6.9).

The implied return on the stock market from the above forecasts is 19 per cent per annum. The required rate of return on firm 'A' using the CAPM estimates is 16.9 per cent. This would indicate that the shares are an attractive investment, but the strength of the analyst's recommendation would depend on the relative attractiveness of other investments examined.

In this example and using the implied rate of return to discount future dividends, 24.5 per cent of the present value of firm 'A' is derived from the short-term estimates, 25.7 per cent from the transitional stage and 48.8 per cent from the steady state from year 10 onwards. However, it should be remembered that this example is hypothetical and rather unusual in that dividends are delayed from the immediate years to the transitional stage by the demands of the investment programme. More typically the first five years might contain one-third of the present value.

Table 6.9 DMM example forecasts

Short-term forecasts					
	Year 1	Year 2	Year 3	Year 4	Year 5
Equity	100 m	120 m	144 m	180 m	224 m
ROE	25%	25%	30%	30%	25%
Earnings	25 m	30 m	43 m	54 m	56 m
Pay-out	0.20	0.20	0.165	0.185	0.215
Dividends	5 m	6 m	7 m	10 m	12 m
Transitional period forecasts					
	Year 6	Year 7	Year 8	Year 9	Year 10
Equity	268 m	314 m	362 m	410 m	459 m
ROE	23%	21%	19%	17%	15%
Earnings	62 m	66 m	69 m	70 m	69 m
Pay-out	0.24	0.27	0.30	0.30	0.33
Dividends	16 m	18 m	21 m	21 m	23 m

Steady state: Dividends are expected to grow at 10 per cent per annum thereafter

Clearly forecasts become less reliable the longer the horizon. However, the discounting effect reduces the impact of any error in distant forecasts.

Empirical evidence on DDM

Jacobs and Levy note that 'while previous evidence thus suggests that DDM is a useful construct, it appears to be far from the complete answer to modelling returns'. They proceed to examine two aspects of dividend discount models. Firstly, they investigate the relationship between the expected ex ante returns as forecast by a DDM and other attributes of equities to establish which characteristics are favoured, or incorporated, into value by the DDM used. Secondly, they examine the relationship between actual ex post security returns and the forecasts of DDM and other equity returns to establish the benefit derived from modelling value using DDM or by examining other equity attributes (Jacobs and Levy, 1988b).

Ex ante returns forecast by DDM and equity attributes

The researchers gathered returns forecasts based on consensus earnings forecasts incorporated into a commercially available DDM model for 1,183 of the largest capitalisation stocks for the 20 quarters to June 1987. These returns were the dependent variables in univariate and multivariate cross-sectional regressions using 18 equity attributes. They discovered that many of the attributes tested were significantly related to the DDM ex ante return. In some cases, such relationships were to be expected if simplifying assumptions held even as approximations. 'For example, if value is a constant multiple of dividends, and if the pay-out ratio is also assumed constant, then value is just a fixed multiple of earnings. In this case, low-P/E stocks would be undervalued' (Jacobs and Levy, 1988b, p. 48). Thus the attributes are discovered to be feasible proxies for value as measured by DDM. Whether the share value as measured by DDM, or as proxied by the attributes, has any worth is tested by examining ex post returns, DDM forecasts, and the forecasts implied in the individual attributes. Table 6.10 reports the explanatory ability of these various attributes. In univariate and multivariate regressions, DDM exhibited a positive but statistically insignificant relationship to actual returns. Other variables were able to out-perform DDM but in the full test, including all variables, sales/price, sigma (dispersion of the beta equation's error term), neglect (reflection of the number of analysts following a stock), relative strength (intercept of the beta regression), residual reversal (most recent

Table 6.10 Explanatory power of regression equations

		Average adjusted R^2
Panel A:	DDM	0.37%
Panel B:	DDM and P/E	3.38%
Panel C:	DDM and simple financial ratios	8.94%
Panel D:	DDM and all equity attributes	43.93%

Source: Jacobs and Levy, 1988b, Table IV, p. 56.

errors from beta regression), short-term tax loss (derived from propriety models of tax loss selling pressure), trend in analysts' earnings estimates and earnings surprise (latest quarter's actual earnings against consensus) were all statistically significant.

This work should not be interpreted as a conclusive test of market efficiency. There is insufficient evidence presented concerning the construction of the variables used, and the work primarily addresses the predictive power of the DDM actually used. It should be noted that the forecast of earnings used was based on a consensus and it might be expected that some difficulty would be experienced in out-performing the market when using market consensus data.

6.4.4 *Price earnings ratios and valuation*

Day, using the protocol analysis technique described above, confirmed Arnold and Moizer's survey results that 'the analysts seen were aiming to forecast earnings so that, via an appropriate price/earnings (P/E) ratio, they could form an opinion as to whether the shares were currently under- or over-valued'. Given this apparent significance of the P/E ratio, it will be useful to clarify the inherent assumptions involved in the analysts' valuation model (Arnold and Moizer, 1984; Day, 1986).

To relate DCF to P/E valuation models, a number of restrictive assumptions are required, as follows.

1. The firm does not alter the proportion of earnings retained within the business for expansion $(1 - b)$.
2. The retained earnings are reinvested in projects which produce a constant internal rate of return (R).
3. The internal rate of return earned is the same as the required rate for the specific share to be valued $(r=R)$.

This will ensure that earnings in any future time period are:

$$E_{t+n} = E_t(1 + bR)^n \tag{6.24}$$

and the growth rate in earnings bR will be identical to the growth rate in dividends g. Under these conditions the constant growth model can be adapted to reflect earnings and earnings growth, as follows.

$$P_0 = DIV_1/(r - g) = (1 - bR)/(r - bR) \tag{6.25}$$

and as $r = R$:

$$P_0 = \frac{E}{r} \tag{6.26}$$

or:

$$r = \frac{E}{P_0} \tag{6.27}$$

Thus, under three very restrictive assumptions the price/earnings ratio does have a conceptual base and it reflects the reciprocal of the required rate of return for a share of a given risk. If analysts are prepared to use the price/earnings ratio in share valuation, they should therefore be aware of the constraints. In normal usage the analyst will have a norm to apply to shares of a certain industry, which will go some way to standardising for the appropriate level of risk while adjustment to this base ratio will have to be made to allow for violation of the other constraints. Most notably, the appropriate growth characteristics of the firm and any deviation of reported earnings from the permanent earnings of the firm.

An alternative specification of the price to earnings ratio clarifies the role of growth. The value of a firm's share can be thought of as two separate elements. One element being the present value of a perpetuity where earnings are deemed to remain constant (a no-growth model), and the other element being the present value of growth expected to be achieved by the firm, stated:

$$P_0 = \frac{EPS_1}{r} + PVGO \qquad (6.28)$$

PVGO is the present value of the growth opportunities which is the discounted cash flow relating to changes in the business (Brealey and Myers, 1988). Note that this is the change in cash flow rather than the change in earnings. The price earnings ratio will therefore be:

$$\frac{EPS_1}{P_0} = r(1 - PVGO/P_0) \qquad (6.29)$$

However, the practicality of the valuation techniques outlined is crucially affected by the predictability of the various elements in the models. Chapter 4 examined the scope for forecasting earnings and reviewed the lack of success experienced by formal forecasting models, but evidence that analysts were able to out-perform such models was encouraging.

Diversity in P/E ratios

Given the importance of the P/E ratio in the valuation process adopted by analysts, some investigation of its characteristics is in order. It might be thought that the market will mark up shares where there are expectations of above average growth and yet it has been shown that earnings growth is difficult to predict. An alternative explanation is that the earnings figure contains transitory elements which would be disregarded by the market when assessing permanent earnings. The extent that they are not separated out as extraordinary items would affect the accounting measure of earnings. It has already been suggested that risk will influence the P/E ratio though the direction of influence needs careful consideration. Finally, differences in accounting policies or systematic biases in accounting figures would, if perceived by capital markets, result in variance in P/E ratios.

Beaver and Morse (1978) examined the behaviour of NYSE P/E ratios from 1956–74. Figures 6.5 to 6.8 graphically present some of their more significant findings. The first (Figure 6.5) tracks the rank correlation of the P/E ratios of portfolios formed by their P/E ranking with subsequent years' P/E ratios, and the second (Figure 6.6) the relative price earnings ratio of the highest and lowest P/E portfolios. The third (Figure 6.7) tracks the rank correlation of the earnings growth of those portfolios, and the last (Figure 6.8) the relative earnings growth of portfolios 1 and 25. These graphs are based on summary

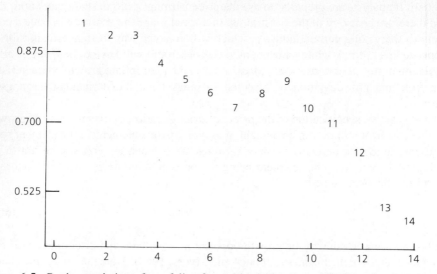

Figure 6.5 Rank correlation of portfolios formed by P/E ratios with P/E ratios in subsequent years.

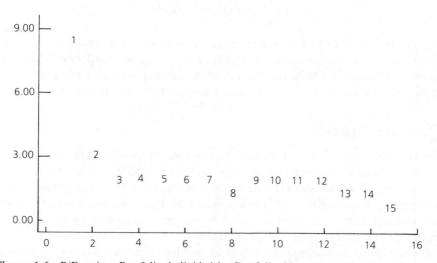

Figure 6.6 P/E ratios. Portfolio 1 divided by Portfolio 25, *t* years after formation.

statistics which Beaver and Morse quote with some reservations, though the conclusions that can be drawn are supported by more detailed evidence contained in the cited article.

The first conclusion of importance is the persistence of P/E ratios which still exhibit meaningful correlations ten years after portfolio formation. However, this is not supported by evidence of persistent growth, the first year negative result suggesting transitory elements in earnings. The failure of other posited reasons to explain fully the persistence of P/E

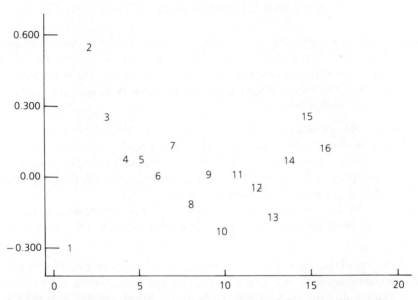

Figure 6.7 Rank correlations of portfolios formed by P/E ratios with earnings growth in subsequent years.

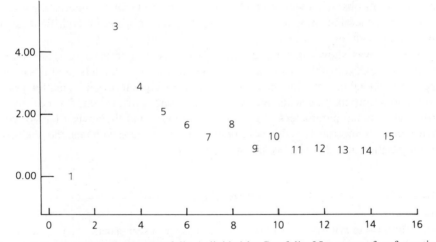

Figure 6.8 Earnings growth. Portfolio 1 divided by Portfolio 25 t years after formation.

ratio differences, led the researchers to conclude that accounting differences must be the remaining factor. There is independent evidence from Beaver and Dukes (1973) that different depreciation policies explain diversity in the price earnings ratios of otherwise similar portfolios.

6.5 Conclusion

The relationship between accounting information and security market prices is fundamental to the work of the analyst. It draws its significance both from the importance of using financial information in share valuations and in the information that can be derived about financial performance from share prices. The evidence reported in the early part of this chapter convincingly shows that:

1. Share prices and accounting earnings both measure some elements of the same characteristic and while the capital market is not omniscient, and the accounting measure of earnings is severely flawed, there is a considerable degree of agreement.
2. Although share prices and accounting earnings are strongly related, the capital market is largely able to pre-empt the delayed accounting disclosure.
3. Despite this, the accounting disclosure contains valuable information as shown by the reaction to the disclosure, implying that new information is being brought to the market.

Closer examination of the market reaction produced inconclusive evidence regarding exploitable post-earnings drift, but there is evidence which indicates that the forecasts of financial analysts may contain valuable information. More general information on accounting-related market anomalies suggested that the commentary of a reputed analyst is sufficient to change market perceptions, that the market as a whole might have been mistaken in its evaluation of the impact of inflation, and that the market is possibly shortsighted in its obsession with current earnings. These claims are interesting and offer scope for a considerable amount of further research, but at present it is difficult to come to conclusions with any confidence.

Finally, it was shown that the evidence, such as it is, regarding share valuation practices, indicates a healthy disregard of academic valuation models, and possibly less reliance on financial information than was first indicated by surveys of valuation practice. This does not imply that the academic models are wrong or irrelevant, for they may well describe the essential parameters of the valuation model, but the analyst has to work in an environment of uncertainty and in developing practices to cope with this, the link between valuation practice and theory may become disguised.

QUESTIONS

1.   The yield to maturity for a 10 per cent bond paying a semi-annual coupon due to mature in two years is 12 per cent. The spot rate of interest for the first three six-month periods are 7, 6.5 and 6.5 per cent.
     (a) What is the market value of the bond?
     (b) What is the spot rate to the end of year 2?
     (c) What is the bond's duration?

2.   The market value of an 8 per cent bond paying an annual coupon due to mature in three years is £90 and the spot rate of interest for years 1 and 2 is 10 per cent per annum.
     (a) What is the spot rate of interest to year 3?

(b)   What is the equation to compute the yield to maturity?

(c)   What is the bond's duration?

3.   Gamma Plc has a forecast beta of 0.9 and the forecast return on the market is 18 per cent per annum. Thirty-day treasury bills are currently yielding 12.5 per cent per annum. The annual dividend forecast for next year is £1.00 and is expected to grow at 8 per cent per annum for four more years and at 5 per cent per annum thereafter. At what price would you expect the shares to trade if they had just become ex dividend?

4.   What parameters would you expect to affect the magnitude of any market reaction to earnings disclosure and to what extent are such reactions susceptible to exploitation by informed investors?

5.   Nostradamus, an analyst, selects stock by predicting the future price from forecasts of earnings per share and the P/E ratios and ranking shares according to the implied return given their current price. Nostradamus' reputation implies that this system repeatedly out-performs the market. How would you test the performance of this investment selection process and how might you identify what element of the system produces any abnormal returns?

6.   Alpha Plc has a forecast beta of 1.1 and the forecast return on the market is 18 per cent per annum.

(a)   Thirty-day treasury bills are currently yielding $12.5 per annum. What is the required rate of return on Alpha Plc?

(b)   If the dividend at 31/12/T4 is forecast as £1.00 and expected to grow at 5 per cent thereafter, what price is expected for Alpha Plc shares at 31/12/T4?

(c)   Dividends of 50p, 65p and 80p are forecast for 31/12/T1, 31/12/T2 and 31/12/T3 respectively. What price will the ex dividend shares of Alpha Plc trade at on 31/12/T0?

7.   Many texts advocate the use of dividend discount models for share valuation. Describe the requirements of such models, the practical difficulties of using DDM for share selection, and the evidence regarding the procedures used by analysts in the UK.

8.   'Although earnings announcements are anticipated to a large extent by the stock market, the actual release of the figures still results in substantial additional information' (Firth, 1981). Discuss the evidence concerning the relationship between accounting disclosures and the resulting stock market reactions. What are the implications for financial analysts?

9.   Many valuation models require forecasts of earnings which may be based on a consensus of analysts' forecasts, on so-called 'naive models', or on share price movements. Consider the evidence concerning the accuracy of forecasts available from these three sources and discuss their value as an input to investment selection models.

10.   Provide definitions for the following terms as used in the chapter:

(a)   Cumulative abnormal return.   (e)   Tobin's Q.

(b)   Unexpected earnings.   (f)   Term structure.

(c)   Post-earnings drift.   (g)   Dividend discount models.

(d)   Forecast revisions.   (h)   Present value of growth opportunities.

References

Arnold, J. and Moizer, P. (1984) A survey of the methods used by investment analysts to appraise investments in ordinary shares, *Accounting and Business Research*, Autumn, 195–208.

Ball, R. and Brown, P. (1968) An empirical evaluation of accounting numbers, *Journal of Accounting Research*, Autumn, 159–78.

Beaver, W. (1968) The information content of annual earnings announcements, Empirical research in accounting: Selected studies, *Supplement to Journal of Accounting Research*, **6**, 67–92.

Beaver, W., Clarke, R. and Wright, W. (1979) The association between unsystematic security returns and the magnitude of earnings forecast errors, *Journal of Accounting Research*, Autumn, 316–40.

Beaver, W. and Dukes, R. (1973) Interperiod tax allocation, earnings expectations, and the behaviour of stock prices, *The Accounting Review*, April, 320–33.

Beaver, W. and Morse, D. (1978) What determines price–earnings ratios? *Financial Analysts' Journal*, July/August, 65–76.

Benesh, G. and Peterson, P. (1986) On the relation between earnings changes, analysts' forecasts and stock price fluctuations, *Financial Analysts' Journal*, November–December, 29–39.

Biggs, S. (1984) Financial analysts' information search in the assessment of corporate earnings power, *Accounting, Organisations and Society*, 3/4, 313–23.

Black, F. (1973) Yes, Virginia, there is hope: Tests of the Value Line ranking system, *Financial Analysts' Journal*, September–October, 10–14.

Bouwman, M., Frishkoff, P. and Frishkoff, P. (1987) How do analysts make decisions? A process model of the investment screening decision, *Accounting, Organisations and Society*, **12**, 1–29.

Brealey, R. and Myers, S. (1988) *Principles of Corporate Finance*, McGraw-Hill, New York.

Brown, P., Foster, G. and Noreen, E. (1985) *Security Analyst Multi Year Earnings Forecasts and the Capital Market*, American Accounting Association, Saratosa, Florida

CBI (1987) *Investing for Britain's Future*, CBI, London.

Chambers, A. and Penman, S. (1984) Timeliness of reporting and the stock price reaction to earnings announcements, *Journal of Accounting Research*, Spring, 21–47.

Chugh, L. and Meador, J. (1984) The stock valuation process: the analyst's view, *Financial Analysts' Journal*, November–December, 41–48.

Day, J. (1986) The use of annual reports by UK investment analysts, *Accounting and Business Research*, Autumn, 295–307.

Donnelly, B. (1985) The dividend model comes into its own, *Institutional Investor*, March, 77–88.

The Economist (1987) Why is Wall Street booming while the reported profits of corporate America are not?, 31 January, 61.

Firth, M. (1981) The relative information content of the release of financial results data by firms, *Journal of Accounting Research*, Autumn, 521–9.

Foster, G. (1977) Quarterly accounting data: time-series properties and predictability results, *Accounting Review*, January, 1–21.

Foster, G. (1979) Briloff and the capital market, *Journal of Accounting Research*, Spring, 262–74.

Foster, G. (1986) *Financial Statement Analysis*, Prentice Hall, Englewood Cliffs.

Foster, G., Ohlsen, C. and Shevlin, T. (1984) Earnings releases, anomalies, and the behaviour of security returns, *The Accounting Review*, October, 574–603.

Fried, D. and Givoly, D. (1982) Financial analysts' forecasts of earnings: a better surrogate for market expectations, *Journal of Accounting and Economics*, **4**, 85–107.

Givoly, D. and Lakonishok, J. (1979) The information content of financial analysts' forecasts of earnings, *Journal of Accounting and Economics*, Winter, 1–21.

Givoly, D. and Lakonishok, J. (1984) The quality of analysts' forecasts of earnings, *Financial Analysts' Journal*, September–October, **40**, no. 5, 40–48.

Grant, E. (1980) Market implications of differential amounts of interim information, *Journal of Accounting Research*, Spring, 255–68.

Jacobs, B. and Levy, K. (1988a) Disentangling equity returns, *Financial Analysts' Journal*, May–June, 47–62.

Jacobs, B. and Levy, K. (1988b) On the value of value, *Financial Analysts' Journal*, July–August, 47–62.

Kaplan, R. and Roll, R. (1972) Investor evaluation of accounting information: some empirical evidence, *Journal of Business*, April, 225–57.

Keane, S. (1983) *Stock Market Efficiency: Theory, Evidence, Implications*, Philip Allan, Oxford.

McNichols, M. and Manegold, J. (1983) The effect of the information environment on the relationship between financial disclosure and security price variability, *Journal of Accounting and Economics*, 5, 49–74.

Modigliani, F. and Cohn, R. (1979) Inflation, rational valuation and the market, *Financial Analysts' Journal*, March–April, 24–44.

Modigliani, F. and Cohn, R. (1985) Inflation and corporate financial management, in Altman, E. and Subrahmanyan, M. (Eds), *Recent Advances in Corporate Finance*, Irwin, Homewood.

Mueller, D. (1986) *Profits in the Long Run*, Cambridge University Press, Cambridge.

Neiderhoffer, V. and Regan, P. (1972) Earnings changes, analysts' forecasts and stock prices, *Financial Analysts' Journal*, May–June, 65–71.

Nickell, S. and Wadhani, S. (1987) Myopia, the dividend puzzle and share prices, Discussion paper No 272. London School of Economics.

Ricks, W. and Biddle, G. (1985) LIFO adoptions and stock price reactions: a comparison of methods and results, Working paper. Duke University.

Sharpe, W. (1985) *Investments*, Prentice Hall, Englewood Cliffs.

Watts, R. and Zimmerman, J. (1986) *Positive Accounting Theory*, Prentice Hall, Englewood Cliffs.

CHAPTER 7

Links between Accounting Numbers and Economic Fundamentals

J. O'Hanlon[1] and W. Rees

CHAPTER OBJECTIVES

This chapter will:

1 Describe a model of the links between the earnings and book value of equity numbers derived from accrual accounting and share price as proposed by Ohlson (1991).

2 Describe links between the accounting rate of return calculated from accrual accounting statements and the internal rate of return highlighted by Peasnell (1982).

3 Summarise the Edwards, Kay and Mayer (1987) analysis of the usefulness of accounting rate of return for economic decision-making purposes when the 'value to the owner' convention is used to arrive at the book value of equity capital.

4 Suggest ways in which accounting information may be useful for the purpose of estimating a company's risk premium.

7.1 Introduction

A company's financial statements contain a balance sheet, in which the equity and certain of the assets and liabilities of the company are valued in accordance with accounting valuation rules, and an income statement (profit and loss account) in which the company's income is reported, as computed in accordance with accounting recognition criteria. For a given period the accounting income number can be divided by the opening accounting value number to give an accounting rate of return. Note however that, although measures of income, value and return are obtainable from financial statements, these are not measures of economic income, economic value and economic return which, for many users of financial statements, are the fundamental objects of interest. For quoted companies it is

226

possible to use stock market data to make estimates of these variables, although this does not stop analysts from using the information disclosed in financial statements to help them to identify mis-priced shares. For unquoted companies accounting information may be all that there is to go on, even with all of its shortcomings, as a source of information on economic fundamentals.

The purpose of this chapter is to highlight the theoretical links between the outputs of accrual accounting and the underlying economic fundamentals of the firm. It will not seek to provide a complete answer to the question of how one draws inferences about economic fundamentals from accounting information but it will seek to show that, under certain simplifying assumptions, formal links exist between the outputs of accrual accounting and economic fundamentals. Highlighting these links will assist the financial statement analyst in the task of building a framework within which inferences about economic fundamentals can be drawn from financial statements.

Section 7.2 describes the links outlined by Ohlson (1991) between the outputs of accrual accounting and the value of a firm's equity capital. Section 7.3 considers the links highlighted by Peasnell (1982) between accounting rate of return (ARR) and internal rate of return (IRR). Section 7.4 summarises parts of the Edwards, Kay and Mayer (1987) analysis of the usefulness of ARR for economic decision-making purposes when the 'value to the owner' convention is used to arrive at the book value of equity capital. Section 7.5 discusses the usefulness of accounting information for the purposes of estimating a company's risk premium.

At first sight this chapter may appear rather daunting to the reader. It is packed with equations from beginning to end, but these equations are simply a shorthand which precisely defines the relationships being studied and allows the theoretical developments that we discuss to be explained concisely. Nowhere in the chapter are there mathematical operations any more complex than simple algebraic manipulation. The chapter can be read by simply taking these manipulations on trust but we do advise the reader to go through them in detail.

7.2 Links between the outputs of accrual accounting and the value of equity capital

7.2.1 *Introduction*

In recent years there has been much debate in academic accounting circles motivated by the view that accountants have not yet developed a generally accepted model of the links between the accrual accounting numbers such as earnings and equity and the market value of equity capital. Brennan (1991 p. 74) points to the problems that this has created for academics seeking to observe the empirical association between share prices and accounting numbers, noting that:

> . . . a significant weakness of much of the literature attempting to relate accounting earnings to stock prices is the lack of an adequate theoretical framework for relating stock prices to accounting earnings.

Penman (1991a) suggests that the failure to develop such a model has limited the ability of accounting educators to provide practical assistance to finance and accounting practitioners and comments that:

> The success of a research field — particularly one so close to professional experience as accounting — is the ability to deliver innovations that are useful in practice. Finance academics refer to them as 'products', by which they mean they meet the market test. The question of the value relevance of accounting surely is an important, practical one. Every day thousands of investors ask themselves what price they should pay for firms or shares of firms. Presumably they attempt to know how to utilize the information in firm's financial statements in making these pricing decisions. An understanding of how one might bring the large array of information in financial statements to the assessment of how much a firm is worth would clearly be an important contribution.

It could also be argued that much of the controversy surrounding the creative accounting activities reviewed in Smith and Hannah (1991), and discussed in Chapter 2, is caused by the preparers of financial statements taking advantage of the users' tendency to treat accounting profits, incorrectly, as though they were cash flows or other measures of direct economic relevance.

In this section, we seek to provide some insights into recent work which has sought to define the links between the value of equity capital, as computed from the dividend capitalisation model, and the outputs of accrual accounting. The section draws heavily upon work by Ohlson (1991) which is increasingly being used in support of research aimed at observing the links between accounting earnings and share prices. Before commencing the formal analysis it may be useful to recall Beaver's (1989, p. 90) statement of the links between earnings and share (stock) prices since the analysis in this section is specifically concerned with the links which Beaver refers to:

> A conceptual relationship can be developed between accounting earnings and the price of common stocks by introducing three critical links: (1) a link between security price and future dividends, (2) a link between future dividends and future earnings, and (3) a link between future earnings and current earnings.

7.2.2 *The value of equity capital as the sum of book value and discounted residual income expectations*

As discussed in earlier chapters the theory of finance suggests that the market value of a company's share capital at year-end t (P_t) is equal to the present value, using an appropriate risk-adjusted required rate of return, of the dividends that are expected to accrue to that share capital in periods subsequent to year-end t (in the analysis which follows it is assumed that dividends are paid at year-end dates):

$$P_t = \sum_{\tau=1}^{\infty} R^{-\tau} E_t[d_{t+\tau}] \tag{7.1}$$

where $d_{t+\tau}$ is the dividend expected to be paid at year-end $t+\tau$, $E_t[.]$ indicates expectations at year-end t and R is 1 plus the required rate of return on equity capital (or 'cost of equity'). This is a slightly different method of writing the equation than that adopted in earlier chapters but it is exactly equivalent and it is used here as it is the style adopted by Ohlson (1991).

In order to use the outputs of the accounting model within a valuation procedure that is consistent with this dividend capitalisation model it is convenient to use the clean surplus definition of accounting earnings. According to this definition of earnings all items, apart from injections and distributions of capital, which give rise to changes in the book value of equity capital are reported as part of earnings. Clean surplus earnings thus include earnings as conventionally defined plus items which affect the value of equity capital but which are charged/credited directly to reserves without passing through the income statement.

In the US earnings are defined in such a way that they are quite close to clean surplus earnings with only a few minor reserve accounting transactions. However, UK GAAP allows a great deal of reserve accounting and probably more than in any other major Western economy. In the UK reserve accounting currently includes goodwill write-offs, foreign exchange translation differences and revaluation surpluses. Most other European countries have GAAP which comes some way between these extremes. Remember that creating sizable hidden reserves, as is common practice in some European countries, does not in itself dirty the earnings. As long as the transaction reduces earnings when it reduces reserves and vice versa then it is not dirty accounting whatever its other advantages or disadvantages. It should also be noted that the clean or dirty terminology should not be considered judgmental. UK GAAP is usually considered to be dirtier than most and yet we saw in an earlier chapter that of all the GAAP earnings examined by Alford et al. (1993) the UK earnings appeared to have the highest association with share returns which could be interpreted as meaning the highest association with at least one economically meaningful variable.

The clean surplus relation can be expressed as follows:

$$x_t = y_t - y_{t-1} + d_t \qquad (7.2)$$

where x_t is earnings in the year ended at year-end t (hereafter the year ended at year-end t will be described as year t) and y_t is the book value of equity capital at year-end t. Residual income for year t (x_t^a) is defined as earnings for year t less a capital charge based on the opening book value of equity:

$$x_t^a = x_t - (R-1)y_{t-1} \qquad (7.3)$$

Substituting (7.2) into (7.3) gives

$$x_t^a = y_t + d_t - Ry_{t-1}$$

which can be re-arranged to give

$$d_t = Ry_{t-1} + x_t^a - y_t \qquad (7.4)$$

and which is true by definition and asserts that the year's dividend is equal to the opening equity times 1 plus the required rate of return on capital, plus residual income for the year, less the closing equity.

In what follows, it will be shown, via substitution of the right-hand side of (7.4) for d_t in the dividend capitalisation model (equation (7.1)), that the market value of the equity capital of the firm is equal to book value of equity capital plus the present value of future expected clean surplus residual income. In expression (7.5) below (which is simply an expanded version of equation (7.1)), the company is expected to pay annual dividends from year-end $t + 1$ to year-end T and to pay a liquidating dividend at year T at which time its book value, y_T, will be represented by a positive cash balance to be paid as the liquidating dividend. This is identical to the normal net present value computation where its price, P_t, can be stated as the discounted value of the dividends (including the liquidating dividend, y_T) that are expected to be paid during the period from year-end $t + 1$ to year-end T inclusive:

$$P_t = E_t[d_{t+1}]R^{-1} + E_t[d_{t+2}]R^{-2} + \ldots$$
$$\ldots + E_t[d_T]R^{-(T-t)} + E_t[y_T]R^{-(T-t)} \tag{7.5}$$

Substituting (7.4) into (7.5):

$$P_t = E_t[y_t R + x^a_{t+1} - y_{t+1}]R^{-1} + E_t[y_{t+1}R + x^a_{t+2} - y_{t+2}]R^{-2} + \ldots$$
$$\ldots + E_t[y_{T-1}R + x^a_T - y_T]R^{-(T-t)} + E_t[y_T]R^{-(t-t)} \tag{7.6}$$

Rearranging and cancelling terms, this collapses to the following:

$$P_t = y_t + E_t[x^a_{t+1}]R^{-1} + E_t[x^a_{t+2}]R^{-2} + \ldots + E_t[x^a_T]R^{-(T-t)} \tag{7.7}$$

The price of the company's equity capital is equal to the book value of the company's equity capital plus the discounted present value of its expected future clean surplus residual income. If the company is expected to have an infinite life, (7.7) becomes (7.8):

$$P_t = y_t + \sum_{\tau=1}^{\infty} E_t[x^a_{t+\tau}]R^{-\tau} \tag{7.8}$$

Equation (7.8) expresses the value of the equity capital as the sum of (a) the book value of equity capital and (b) the present value of future expected clean surplus residual income, this second term representing unrecorded goodwill. It is a general expression of the relationship between the value of equity capital and the outputs of accrual accounting. It holds for any set of accounting valuation rules which abide by the clean surplus convention. This result forms one of the bases of the Ohlson (1991) analysis, which has recently attracted much attention. However, it is not a new result. It has been lying around, somewhat neglected, in the literature for decades having appeared in Edwards and Bell (1961), Edey (1962) and Peasnell (1982). Expression (7.8) is a formal statement of the relationship which underlies the intuition that goodwill is a measure of 'super-profits' expected to be earned in the future.

The general nature of expression (7.8) can be illustrated by the following example. A company is incorporated at year-end 0 at which time it raises £1 m in cash by way of an equity issue with the result that $y_0 = £1$ m. The company immediately communicates to the market the expectation that this £1 m will all be used to buy inventory during year 1. Of this inventory half will be sold during year 1 for £0.6 m and half will be sold during year 2 for £0.6 m. No other income will be earned, no costs other than the cost of the inventory will be incurred and no tax will be payable. At year-end 1 the company's entire cash balance of £0.6 m will be paid as a dividend. At year-end 2 the company's entire

Table 7.1 Example of application of equation (7.8)

	Basis (1)	Basis (2)	Basis (3)
y_0	1.0	1.0	1.0
Add: $E_0[x_1]$ (*)	0.1	−0.4	1.6
Less: $E_0[d_1]$	0.6	0.6	0.6
$E_0[y_1]$	0.5	0.0	2.0
Add: $E_0[x_2]$ (*)	0.1	0.6	−1.4
Less: $E_0[d_2]$	0.6	0.6	0.6
$E_0[y_2]$	0.0	0.0	0.0

(*) = Arrived at from the clean surplus relation in equation (7.2).

cash balance of £0.6 m will be paid as a liquidating dividend. The company's net assets at year-end 1 are expected to consist entirely of the unsold half of the inventory which will have cost £0.5 m. Table 7.1 gives the book value and earnings expectations of a company under three different accounting valuation bases.

1. The historic cost basis under which the inventory at year-end 1 will be valued at £0.5 m.
2. A decelerated income recognition basis under which the inventory at year-end 1 will be valued at zero.
3. An accelerated income recognition basis under which the inventory at year-end 1 will be valued at £2.0 m.

Assuming a cost of equity of 10 per cent, P_0 according to the dividend capitalisation model (expression (7.1)) is:

$$\frac{0.6}{1.1} + \frac{0.6}{1.1^2} = \text{£1.0413 m}$$

The application of expression (7.8) to each of the three sets of expected accounting numbers gives £1.0413 m as the sum of book value and the present value of expected future clean surplus residual income:

Basis 1

$$1 + \frac{(0.1 - (0.1 \times 1.0))}{1.1} + \frac{(0.1 - (0.1 \times 0.5))}{1.1^2} = \text{£1.0413 m}$$

Basis 2

$$1 + \frac{(0.4 - (0.1 \times 1.0))}{1.1} + \frac{(0.6 - (0.1 \times 0.0))}{1.1^2} = \text{£1.0413 m}$$

Basis 3

$$1 + \frac{(1.6 - (0.1 \times 1.0))}{1.1} + \frac{(-1.4 - (0.1 \times 2.0))}{1.1^2} = \text{£1.0413 m}$$

The above analysis is very simple but has a number of interesting implications. It suggests that discounted accounting earnings expectations can be used to value the equity capital of a company provided that earnings are transformed to a residual income basis and are considered in conjunction with book value. As well as being of interest as a statement of the relationship between the outputs of accrual accounting and the value of equity capital, this relationship does convey a message that is of practical importance to analysts. Value can only be inferred from earnings expectations if earnings expectations are considered in conjunction with book value and can only be inferred from book value if book value is considered in conjunction with earnings expectations.

In earlier chapters the tendency to inflate earnings at the expense of the balance sheet was discussed and reinforced by the quote from Smith and Hannah (1991). In such circumstances a creative accountant might seek to 'undervalue' y_0 by making unnecessary fixed asset and inventory write-downs in the hope that the consequent low future depreciation and cost of sales charges would increase expected future earnings. The use of an earnings-based valuation model such as expression (7.8) would prevent the analyst from using the increase in earnings expectations to increase the estimate of the value of the company since the effect of the increased earnings expectations in the second term would be exactly counterbalanced by the reduction in book value in the first term. Awareness of such a model might also prevent euphoric reaction to spectacular earnings growth in years immediately following large asset write-downs. It also puts into context the discussions which can sometimes be heard between standard setters, regulators, managers of regulated firms, investment analysts, and financial managers regarding the relative importance of the income statement and balance sheet. In general neither is more important than the other and both should be equally considered by users of accounting statements although a particular firm might choose accounting policies which affect the weight that should be put on one or other of the financial statements.

7.2.3 *An example of the use of a residual income forecasting model*

The previous section suggested that the use of the outputs of accrual accounting to form an estimate of the value of the firm requires that we add to book value, however it has been arrived at, the present value of expected future clean surplus residual income. This requires that forecasts of the amount and timing of expected future residual income be made and that these be appropriately capitalised. A detailed consideration of earnings forecasting models is beyond the scope of this chapter. Nevertheless it is interesting to evaluate how one particular forecasting model of residual income might be superimposed on equation (7.8) to provide an earnings-based valuation model. This particular model was proposed by Ohlson (1991) and is convenient but it is not the only possible model of how residual income might behave, nor, indeed, is it the most likely one. In a world where the book value of equity is normally conservative the average of the residual income is likely to be greater than zero. The model can be adapted to deal with alternative models although they may not be quite so convenient.

Ohlson imposes particular assumptions concerning the time-series process generating residual income on the model of share price as the sum of the book value of equity and present value of residual income. He assumes that residual income is generated by the following process:

$$x_{t+1}^{a} = \omega x_t^{a} + v_t + \epsilon_{1t+1} \tag{7.9}$$

Here ω is constrained to be non-negative and to be less than 1 and reflects the extent to which the current level of residual income is likely to persist into the future. ϵ_1 is a zero mean random disturbance term. In other words if ω is 0.5 and the residual income in year t is £100 it is expected to be £50 in year $t+1$, if we ignore the effect of v. v_t represents the effect of information, other than that contained in the current level of residual income and the coefficient, ω, of the generating process, which influences the prediction of expected future residual income. It is assumed to come from a zero mean series and is generated as follows:

$$v_{t+1} = \gamma v_t + \epsilon_{2t+1} \tag{7.10}$$

where γ is an autoregressive coefficient constrained to be non-negative and less than 1 and ϵ_2 is a zero mean random disturbance term.

Note that, according to (7.9) and (7.10), x^a will always be expected to converge towards zero from its current level and has an unconditional mean of zero. It is quite possible that the assumptions about the time-series properties of residual income made in Ohlson's analysis are sometimes violated in practice but similar pricing models to that discussed here can be developed to cope with different assumptions about the residual income-generating process (see, for example, Ramakrishnan and Thomas (1992) and Feltham and Ohlson (1992)).

Ohlson derives a multiplier, α_1, which, when applied to the residual income of year t, will give the present value of future expected residual income for year $t+1$ to infinity. Ignoring for the moment the 'other information' variable, v, equation (7.9) says that, given a unit of current residual income in year 0, residual income in year 1 is expected to be ω, residual income in year 2 is expected to be ω^2, etc. . . . The present value (denoted by PV) of this series for use in equation (7.1) will be (continuing in perpetuity):

$$PV = \left(\frac{\omega}{R}\right) + \left(\frac{\omega}{R}\right)^2 + \left(\frac{\omega}{R}\right)^3 \cdots \tag{7.11}$$

Multiplying both sides of (7.11) by $(R)/\omega$:

$$PV\left(\frac{R}{\omega}\right) = 1 + \left(\frac{\omega}{R}\right) + \left(\frac{\omega}{R}\right)^2 \cdots \tag{7.12}$$

Since $R > 1$ and $0 \leq \omega \leq 1$, distant terms on the right-hand side of (7.12) become vanishingly small. Thus subtraction of (7.11) from (7.12) gives the following which is Ohlson's residual income multiplier, α_1:

$$PV\left(\frac{R}{\omega}\right) - PV = PV\left(\frac{R-\omega}{\omega}\right) = 1$$

$$PV = \frac{\omega}{(R-\omega)} = \alpha_1 \tag{7.13}$$

Ohlson's residual income multiplier, α_1, converts knowledge of current residual income into the present value of expected future residual income. Each unit of current residual income generating the expectation of future residual income with a present value of α_1.

Ohlson's model also incorporates the term, v_t, which captures information other than that contained in the history of earnings which is relevant to the formation of expectations concerning x_{t+1}^a and which 'naive' univariate earnings forecasting models ignore. Although in Ohlson's analysis 'other information' is modelled as a single series, with a simple generating process and a straightforward link to residual income, it is likely in practice to consist of a large number of information sets with generating processes and links to residual income which are difficult to model. In practice, of course, much of the financial analyst's effort is aimed at acquiring information about future earnings from this 'other information' set which will include items such as macroeconomic activities and their relationship to the company's activities, breakdowns of the company's activities by industrial and geographical segment, knowledge of the company's relative strength in the markets in which it operates, knowledge of patent protections and so on. Some of this information will be available in notes to the financial statements but some will not.

As mentioned above, Ohlson assumes the following autoregressive generating process for v:

$$v_{t+1} = \gamma v_t + \epsilon_{2t+1} \tag{7.10}$$

where γ is an autoregressive coefficient constrained to be non-negative and less than 1 and ϵ_2 is a zero mean random disturbance term. Remember that v, which follows an autoregressive process feeds into x^a which itself follows the process described by expression (7.9):

$$x_{t+1}^a = \omega x_t^a + v_t + \epsilon_{1t+1} \tag{7.9}$$

Thus v_t will have the effect of raising $E(x_{t+1}^a)$ by v_t. However, because of the process generating x^a the effect will be felt beyond year-end $t+1$ (this secondary effect having a present value at year-end $t+1$ of $\omega/(R-\omega)$). This change to $E(x_{t+1}^a)$ will change the value at year-end t of the company's equity by:

$$\frac{1}{R}\left[1 + \frac{\omega}{(R - \omega)} \right] \tag{7.14}$$

However, v itself follows an autoregressive process which means that $E_t[v_{t+1}] = \gamma v_t$, $E_t[v_{t+2}] = \gamma^2 v_t$ etc. Each of these effects will set off an effect on x^a which will produce a 'knock on' effect over subsequent years via the process generating x^a. This means that the total effect on the value of the company's equity of v_t will be as follows (the terms in the first bracket continuing to infinity):

$$\left[\frac{1}{R} + \frac{\gamma}{R^2} + \frac{\gamma^2}{R^3} \cdots \right]\left[1 + \frac{\omega}{(R - \omega)} \right] \tag{7.15}$$

This can be rearranged as follows:

$$\left[\frac{\gamma}{R} + \frac{\gamma^2}{R^2} + \frac{\gamma^3}{R^3} \cdots \right]\left[\frac{R}{\gamma(R - \omega)} \right] \tag{7.16}$$

Since the terms in the first bracket continue to infinity, the first bracket collapses to the following (using the same logic as that used in the derivation of (7.13):

$$\frac{\gamma}{(R - \gamma)} \tag{7.17}$$

The present value of the effect of v_t on future expected residual income is therefore as follows, this being Ohlson's α_2 which is the multiplier applied to the 'other information' variable, v_t:

$$\frac{R}{\gamma(R - \omega)} \cdot \frac{\gamma}{(R - \gamma)} = \alpha_2$$

$$\frac{R}{(R-\omega)(R-\gamma)} = \alpha_2 \tag{7.18}$$

The price of the company can now be expressed as the sum of (a) book value, (b) the expectation of the present value of future residual income generated by knowledge of the current level of residual income and (c) the expectation of the present value of future residual income generated by knowledge of the current level of 'other information' that has not yet impacted on residual income:

$$P_t = y_t + \alpha_1 x_t^a + \alpha_2 v_t \tag{7.19}$$

where, as described above:

$$\alpha_1 = \omega/(R-\omega)$$

$$\alpha_2 = R/((R-\omega)(R-\gamma))$$

It is appropriate at this stage to reflect briefly upon the connections between the relationship described by expression (7.19) and practical problems of concern to financial analysts and accounting regulators. Expression (7.19) suggests that the value relevance of the earnings variable used in the model is positively related to:

$$\alpha_1 = \frac{\omega}{R-\omega}$$

which reflects the extent to which the current residual income level is likely to persist into the future. This issue of earnings persistence is of great concern to financial analysts whose reports on companies are usually heavily devoted to the identification of permanent and 'one-off' sources of earnings. Thus a practical operationalisation of (7.19) would probably require that the x^a term be replaced by a series of terms each representing an earnings source. Here, some sources of clean surplus earnings (for example, 'operating profit') might be expected to have an ω value close to 1 whilst others (for example, 'profits and losses on termination of a operation') might be expected to have an ω value close to zero. Also the desire to help users to identify different earnings streams with differing levels of persistence underlies many of the requirements of Financial Reporting Standard No. 3 published by the UK's Accounting Standards Board (1992).

7.2.4 *Ohlson's example of weighted book value and earnings pricing model*

Ohlson develops (7.19) further and arrives at a model which expresses price as a weighted average of book value and (total) earnings. It must be stressed that the ability to arrive at a model of share price as a weighted average of book value and earnings does not exist for all possible classes of residual income-generating process. The model is presented here, however, because it represents an interesting example of how book value and total earnings can be combined into a pricing model if particular assumptions are made about the behaviour of residual income. Also, the model has been used to justify the research designs of a number of recent capital market-based accounting studies.

The derivation of the weighted average model requires that residual income be expressed as the difference between (a) earnings and (b) a capital charge based on opening book value (n.b. opening book value $(y_{t-1}) = y_t - x_t + d_t$):

$$x_t^a = x_t - (R-1)(y_t - x_t + d_t) \tag{7.20}$$

Equation (7.19) can thus be re-expressed as follows:

$$
\begin{aligned}
P_t &= y_t + \alpha_1 x_t \\
&\quad - \alpha_1 (R-1)(y_t - x_t + d_t) + \alpha_2 \nu_t
\end{aligned}
\tag{7.21}
$$

This can be re-arranged to give:

$$
\begin{aligned}
P_t &= y_t - \alpha_1 (R-1) y_t \\
&\quad + \alpha_1 (x_t - (R-1)(d_t - x_t)) + \alpha_2 \nu_t
\end{aligned}
$$

and

$$
\begin{aligned}
P_t &= y_t (1 - \alpha_1 (R-1)) \\
&\quad + \alpha_1 x_t - \alpha_1 (R-1)(d_t - x_t) + \alpha_2 \nu_t
\end{aligned}
\tag{7.22}
$$

This can be further re-arranged to give:

$$
\begin{aligned}
P_t &= y_t (1 - \alpha_1 (R-1)) \\
&\quad + x_t R \alpha_1 - d_t (\alpha_1 (R-1)) + \alpha_2 \nu_t
\end{aligned}
$$

$$
\begin{aligned}
P_t &= y_t (1 - \alpha_1 (R-1)) \\
&\quad + \alpha_1 (R-1) \left[\frac{x_t R}{(R-1)} - d_t \right] + \alpha_2 \nu_t
\end{aligned}
\tag{7.23}
$$

Ohlson thus arrives at an expression which states that price is determined partly by the present value of the effect of shocks which have not yet impacted on earnings and partly by a weighted average of (a) book value and (b) a current earnings multiple minus current dividends where the weights on (a) and (b) are $(1 - (\alpha_1 (R-1)))$ and $(\alpha_1 (R-1))$ respectively. Expression (7.23) is increasingly being used to justify the use of research designs which model share price in terms of book values and earnings and which model share price changes in terms of the level of earnings and changes in earnings. See, for example, Easton and Harris (1991), Penman (1991b) and Strong and Walker (1993).

Expression (7.23) states that, given the time-series process that is assumed to generate residual income, both book value and earnings have a role in the valuation of equity capital. Note that since

$$\alpha_1 = \frac{\omega}{R - \omega}$$

the relative value relevance of the book value and earnings variables depends crucially upon the magnitude of the ω term which captures the extent to which the current level of residual income is likely to persist into the future. Ignoring for the moment the last term on the right-hand side, consider what happens to (7.23) in the two cases in which the persistence coefficient, ω, takes its extreme values of 0 and 1. When $\omega = 0$, $\alpha_1 (R - 1) = 0$. Here P_t is equal to y_t. Thus if residual income is always expected to revert immediately to zero, regardless of its current level, market value will track book value. When $\omega = 1$, $\alpha_1 (R - 1) = 1$. Here, the current level of residual income is expected to continue in perpetuity and earnings become the key basis for valuation. In fact when $\omega = 1$ (7.23) collapses such that the cum-div value of equity capital can be stated as a multiple of total earnings:

$$P_t + d_t = x_t \left(\frac{R}{R - 1} \right)$$

So a persistence coefficient of 0 gives an expression for price totally in terms of book value and a persistence coefficient of 1 gives an expression for (cum-div) price totally in terms of an earnings multiple.

Section 7.2 has presented an example of a model that links the value of equity capital and the outputs of accrual accounting taking account of each of the three links in the chain referred to by Beaver in the quotation reproduced at the end of Section 7.2.1. It deals with the dividend/price link because it is based on the dividend capitalisation model, it deals with the future dividends/future earnings link by rewriting dividends in terms of a capitalisable transform of accounting earnings and it deals with the current earnings/future earnings link by incorporating a forecasting model for the capitalisable transform of earnings. It provides a theoretical framework within which to situate the roles of book value, current earnings, earnings persistence and the cost of equity in the task of financial analysis.

7.3 The link between accounting rate of return (ARR) and internal rate of return (IRR)

Examples of where measures of return might be required are in assessing the relative performance of different industrial sectors, perhaps with a view to commenting on the existence of monopoly profits, or more generally on the incentive to invest in those sectors, or the analysis of performance before and after corporate takeovers to identify any resultant efficiencies. The measure of return which is conventionally deemed to be pertinent to such analyses is internal rate of return (IRR). Assuming that cash flows arise at annual intervals,

IRR is computed by estimating the cash flows (CF) arising at each date from year-end 0 to year-end T, where T is the date of the last cash flow, and solving the following for IRR[2]:

$$0 = \sum_{t=0}^{T} \left(\frac{CF_t}{IRR^t} \right)$$

The desire to use accounting measures of the return earned by an enterprise is founded on the difficulty of obtaining better estimates. The absence of information on the necessary cash flows has driven many researchers to rely on the more accessible accounting information and to use the ARR as a surrogate for the IRR. But, 'the traditional methods used by accountants to calculate ARR are quite different from the method implied in economic investment theory, it is highly probable that the indiscriminate use of ARR as a proxy for IRR is a dangerous exercise' (Luckett, 1984, pp. 213–14). Therefore, there is some interest in examining those circumstances where the ARR is an acceptable surrogate for the IRR or whether one can be calculated from the other.

The early work on the relevance of the ARR is characterised by Harcourt's (1965, p. 80) somewhat depressed conclusions that:

> It seems safe to add to the already well-known defects of accounting data on profits and capital that as an indication of the realized rate of return the accountant's rate of profit is greatly influenced by irrelevant factors, even under ideal conditions. Any 'man of words' (or 'deeds' for that matter) who compares rates of profit of different industries, or of the same industry in different countries, and draws inferences from their magnitudes as to the relative profitability of investments in different uses or countries, does so at his own peril.

A variety of reviews in the following decade came to no effective advance on the earlier pessimism. Idealistic accounting policies or restrictive assumptions were shown to move ARR towards IRR but as these circumstances do not, or rarely, pertain they are of little help.

The argument that the ARR can be converted to IRR only under certain restrictions has been advocated by a number of academics in a variety of sources. To some extent this may contribute to the conventional wisdom that, 'it is widely presumed in the accounting and economic literature that, for the most part in practice, ARRs are artifacts without economic significance' (Peasnell, 1982, p. 368). These difficulties have led various academics, from Beaver and Demski (1979) to Solomons (1961), to despair of economic income as either a model for, or an estimate available from, accounting profit. Consequently, it is accepted that accounting information is valuable as an input to the valuation process of individuals who wish to value firms or estimate returns, but not as a measure of these factors.

Whether the IRR is the only measure of the 'true' rate of return is contentious. Firstly, Whittington (1979) cautions that under certain circumstances the accounting rate of return (ARR) with all its measurement errors may still be the valid focus of attention for

> If the object of an empirical study is positive (i.e. explaining actual behaviour) rather than normative (i.e. defining optimal behaviour) ARR may be superior to IRR or other measures merely because, in a world of uncertainty and imperfect information, it is the rule of thumb to which decision-makers cling.

Secondly, it may be claimed that the ARR is an adequate focus of research interest where the error in the ARR, as an indicator of the IRR, is unsystematic . The substitution of the ARR for the IRR will be misleading only if the difference between the ARR and the IRR is systematically correlated with the explanatory variable. Finally, known sources of bias in the ARR can be incorporated as a variable. Whittington cites the example of recent growth depressing the ARR in inflationary times and suggests incorporating growth as an independent variable. Similar conclusions would hold where the ARR does not equal the IRR, but variations in one are reflected by variations in the other. This would preferably be reflected in the magnitude of the variation, but for some investigations it may be adequate for the ranking or direction of change to be unbiased indicators.

Despite the conventional wisdom, many researchers or analysts have been compelled to use accounting measures of return in their work for want of a more reliable estimate. The argument that this unsatisfactory state of affairs was avoidable has been developing since Kay's (1976) demonstration of the formal links between ARR and IRR. This paper and many other developments employed integral calculus in order to incorporate the 'continuous time' element inherent in cash flows occurring throughout accounting periods (Fisher and McGowan (1983), Kay and Mayer (1986), Stark (1982), Wright (1978)). This does render the analysis less accessible. However, Peasnell (1982) has shown that the conventional simplification of year-end cash flows aids the presentation without significant loss of generality and it is on his analysis that the remainder of the material presented in this section is mainly based.

The relationship between the market value of equity share capital (P) and book value (y) at the start (year-end 0) and end (year-end T) of the investment period is as follows:

$$P_0 = y_0 + e_0$$

$$P_T = y_{T-1} + x_T + e_T$$

where x denotes clean surplus total earnings (N.B. not residual income) as previously defined and e denotes a valuation error being the excess of the market value of equity capital over book value of equity capital. P_0 represents the initial investment and P_T represents the proceeds when the investment is disposed of. As earnings are expressed in clean surplus terms, the dividends received between year-end 0 and year-end T can be expressed as follows:

$$d_t = y_{t-1} + x_t - y_t$$

The IRR earned between year-ends 0 and T can thus be computed by solving the following for IRR:

$$0 = -y_0 - e_0 + (y_0 + x_1 - y_1)(1 + IRR)^{-1} + (y_1 + x_2 - y_2)(1 + IRR)^{-2} + \ldots$$

$$\ldots + (y_{T-1} + x_T)(1 + IRR)^{-T} + e_T(1 + IRR)^{-T}$$

Rearrangement of this gives:

$$\sum_{\tau=1}^{T} y_{\tau-1}(1 + IRR)^{-(\tau-1)} = (e_T(1 + IRR)^{-T} - e_0) + \sum_{\tau=1}^{T} (y_{\tau-1} + x_\tau)(1 + IRR)^{-\tau}$$

$$(1+IRR) = \frac{\sum_{\tau=1}^{T}(y_{\tau-1}+x_{\tau})(1+IRR)^{-\tau}+(e_T(1+IRR)^{-T}-e_0)}{\sum_{\tau=1}^{T}y_{\tau-1}(1+IRR)^{-\tau}}$$

$$IRR = \frac{\sum_{\tau=1}^{T}x_{\tau}(1+IRR)^{-\tau}+(e_T(1+IRR)^{-T}-e_0)}{\sum_{\tau=1}^{T}y_{\tau-1}(1+IRR)^{-\tau}}$$

Defining ARR, denoted by $(A-1)$, as follows:

$$(A_t-1) = \frac{x_t}{y_{t-1}}$$

the expression for IRR becomes:

$$IRR = \frac{\sum_{\tau=1}^{T}(A_{\tau}-1)y_{\tau-1}(1+IRR)^{-\tau}}{\sum_{\tau=1}^{T}y_{\tau-1}(1+IRR)^{-\tau}} + \frac{e_T(1+IRR)^{-T}-e_0}{\sum_{\tau=1}^{T}y_{\tau-1}(1+IRR)^{-\tau}} \qquad (7.24)$$

Peasnell's analysis thus shows that the IRR earned between year-ends 0 and T is the sum of:

1. A weighted average of the annual ARRs reported during the period where the weight applied to each year's ARR is the opening book value of equity discounted at the IRR, and
2. A term reflecting the opening and closing differences between the market value of equity and the book value of equity.

Note that this is a general expression which will hold for any set of asset/liability valuation criteria provided that earnings are expressed in clean surplus form.

A simple numerical example is provided to demonstrate the relationship derived above (see Table 7.2). The IRR on the capital market transactions approximates to 15.5 per cent. Using the weighted ARR information from Table 7.2 and assuming that the market value of equity is an appropriate benchmark measure for the valuation error, we arrive at this value:

$$IRR = \frac{94.06}{501.50} + \frac{((280-220)*1.15^{-4})-(200-150)}{501.50}$$
$$= 0.188 + (-0.033)$$
$$= 0.155$$

Whilst this statement of the relationship between economic returns and accounting returns is interesting, it could be argued that its practical usefulness is limited since it suggests that computation of the IRR requires the use of weights which are themselves partly derived from the IRR. However, ignoring for the moment the valuation error term, if the book

Table 7.2 Example ITT computation

	t_0	t_1	t_2	t_3	t_4	Total
Accounting results						
Book value of equity	150.0	190.0	180.0	200.0	220.0	
Movements in year:						
Equity raised		10.0			20.0	
Dividends		20.0	20.0	25.0	25.0	
Clean surplus earnings		50.0	10.0	45.0	25.0	
Clean surplus ARR		0.333	0.053	0.250	0.125	
Present value (at IRR of 15.5%) of opening book value of equity		129.9	142.4	116.8	112.4	501.5
Weighted clean surplus ARR (= product of previous 2 rows)		43.26	7.55	29.20	14.05	94.06
Capital market data						
Market value of equity	200.0			280.0		
Dividends less equity raised		10.0	20.0	25.0	5.0	
Cash flow (calculated from previous 2 rows)	−200.0	10.0	20.0	25.0	285.0	
Present value (at IRR of 15.5%) of cash flow	−200.0	8.7	15.0	16.2	160.1	0

value weights applied to the annual ARRs are all positive as they normally would be, the IRR must fall within the range delimited by the highest ARR and the lowest ARR. Also, Steele (1986) reports the results of the application of an iterative algorithm designed to estimate IRR from ARRs using Peasnell's result under the assumption that the term capturing the opening and closing valuation errors can be ignored. Using data for the period from the late 1960s to the early 1980s, Steele reports that, for 99 out of the 100 companies to which the algorithm was applied, convergence to an IRR estimate was achieved. However, he also reported that in his sample these 'pseudo IRRs' deviated significantly from economic IRRs computed on the basis of error-free market value information. Notwithstanding Steele's evidence concerning the importance of the valuation error term, it is useful to consider that the valuation error term is likely to be of little importance where:

1. The valuation error at both the opening or closing dates tends to zero. This could be the case for those few firms most of whose assets and liabilities are accounted for at market values.
2. The discounted value of the closing error approaches the value of the opening error. This could occur where the proportional error on the net assets is approximately constant and the assets are growing at a rate close to the cost of capital.
3. The discounted value of the change in the valuation error tends towards an insignificant proportion of the sum of the discounted net book values due to either the length of the measurement period, or the relative size of the net book values.

Relying again on the statement of earnings in clean surplus form, this section showed that there is a relationship between ARR and IRR. The IRR of a segment of a company's life span can be derived from accounting information where the opening and closing book values encapsulate the cash flow expectations at that time or, in other words, where the opening and closing book values are respectively the opening and closing NPV of the firm. This will generally not be the case and the analyst seeking to estimate IRRs from accounting data will inevitably be faced with the problem of making a judgement as to the magnitude of the error induced by valuation error.

7.4   The Edwards, Kay and Mayer (EKM) analysis

Edwards, Kay and Mayer (1987) present an exposition of how the relationship between expected ARR over a limited segment of a business's life and required rate of return could be used to guide an investor in deciding whether to enter or stay out of a business and in deciding whether to remain in or exit from a business. Unfortunately, this absorbing demonstration of the potential practical usefulness of accounting information is built around an asset valuation convention, 'value to the owner', which differs from the asset valuation convention generally used in financial statements. One might therefore argue that the main value of the EKM analysis is as an argument in favour of the adoption of the 'value to the owner' asset valuation convention and that there are severe practical limits to its usefulness as a guide to the use of accounting information, as currently provided, for economic decision-making purposes. A more positive attitude is to view the EKM analysis, in conjunction with the analyst's judgement regarding the extent to which asset valuation conventions depart from 'value to the owner', as a useful guide to the use of expected ARR in economic decision-making.

That part of EKM's analysis presented here is based on a single period model in which the difference between (a) opening economic value less opening book value and (b) closing economic value less closing book value is expressed in terms of the relationship between the required rate of return and the ARR expected in the period. An expression similar in form to that used by EKM can be obtained by re-arrangement of equation (7.8) from Section 7.2. In the following analysis R denotes 1 plus the required rate of expected return, as before, and A denotes 1 plus the ARR. First expand (7.8) as follows:

$$P_0 = y_0 + \sum_{\tau=1}^{\infty} E_0[x_\tau^a]R^{-\tau}$$

$$= y_0 + E_0[x_1^a]R^{-1} + \sum_{\tau=2}^{\infty} E_0[x_\tau^a]R^{-\tau} \tag{7.25}$$

Then express the second term of (7.25) in terms of expected year 1 book value and price:

$$E_0[P_1] = E_0[y_1] + \sum_{\tau=2}^{\infty} E_0[x_\tau^a]R^{-(\tau-1)}$$

$$\sum_{\tau=2}^{\infty} E_0[x_\tau^a]R^{-(\tau)} = \frac{E_0[P_1] - E_0[y_1]}{R} \tag{7.26}$$

Substituting (7.26) into (7.25) gives:

$$P_0 - y_0 = \frac{E_0[x_1^a]}{R} + \frac{E_0[P_1] - E_0[y_1]}{R}$$

Thus $P_0 - y_0$, the unrecorded goodwill at year-end 0, can be expressed as the present value of the residual income that is expected to be earned in year 1 plus the present value of the expected (at year-end 0) unrecorded goodwill at year-end 1. Note that, since residual income is accounting profit less a capital charge based on opening book value, the first term on the right-hand side of this expression can be expressed in terms of the difference between the expected ARR and the required rate of return.

$$P_0 - y_0 = \frac{y_0(E_0[A_1] - R)}{R} + \frac{E_0[P_1] - E_0(y_1)}{R} \tag{7.27}$$

The question which EKM address is that of the extent to which investment decisions can be based on the relative magnitudes of the single period ARR (A_1) and R. The general expression (7.27) is of no use for this purpose because it says nothing about how equity is valued in the financial statements at year-ends 0 and 1. For example, if a company's asset valuation policies at year-end 0 were highly conservative one could have $(A_1 - 1)$ greater than $(R - 1)$ even though the realised rate of economic return were less than $(R - 1)$. Similarly, accounting policies which caused the book value of equity at year-end 0 to be substantially higher than its market value could result in $(A_1 - 1)$ less than $(R - 1)$ even though the realised rate of economic return were greater than $(R - 1)$. EKM, however, show that the relationship between A_1 and R can be used to support economic decisions if a particular asset valuation convention, 'value to the owner', is used.

The value to the owner (sometimes termed 'deprival value') asset valuation convention requires that assets be valued at the loss that would be suffered by the firm if it were deprived of the asset. A firm which is deprived of an asset will either:

1. Replace the asset (which it will do if the replacement cost (RC) is less than the economic value (EV) of the asset) in which case the loss is RC, or
2. Not replace the asset (which it will do if RC is greater than EV) in which case the loss is EV.

EV will be the greater of

1. The present value (PV) of a decision to continue operating the asset, and
2. The net realisable value (NRV) of the asset if it were to be disposed of.

Stated formally, book value (y_t) under the value to the owner asset valuation convention is

$$\min\{RC_t, EV_t\} \quad \text{where } EV_t = \max\{PV_t, NRV_t\}$$

The possible combinations of ranking between PV, RC and NRV and the book values to which they give rise are given in Table 7.3.

EKM note that the three situations in which $NRV > RC$ are unlikely to persist since, under these conditions, firms could profit simply by selling and replacing their assets. This leaves the three possibilities given in Table 7.4.

Table 7.3 Value to the owner rules

If	PV	>	RC	>	NRV	then	y	=	RC
If	PV	>	NRV	>	RC	then	y	=	RC
If	RC	>	PV	>	NRV	then	y	=	PV
If	RC	>	NRV	>	PV	then	y	=	NRV
If	NRV	>	PV	>	RC	then	y	=	RC
If	NRV	>	RC	>	PV	then	y	=	RC

Table 7.4 Value to the owner rules excluding cases in
which $NRV > RC$

If	PV	>	RC	>	NRV	then	y	=	RC
If	RC	>	PV	>	NRV	then	y	=	PV
If	RC	>	NRV	>	PV	then	y	=	NRV

EKM show that economic decisions can be based on the relative magnitude of the expected accounting rate of return and the required economic rate of return where book value is arrived at in accordance with value to the owner rules. They demonstrate in an appendix to their work that their results can be generalised to a multi-period setting but the analysis in the main body of their text is based upon a single period model.

The analysis discussed in the main body of the text of this chapter is based on the analysis of expected future ARRs. In the Appendix to this chapter we consider the use of realised ARRs. The model on which the analysis of the usefulness for decision-making purposes of ex-ante ARRs is based is of a similar form to (7.27), differing from it in that P_0 is replaced by PV_0 and in that $E_0(P_1)$ is replaced by $E_0[EV_1]$:

$$PV_0 - y_0 = y_0 \left(\frac{E_0[A_1] - R}{R} \right) + \frac{E_0[EV_1] - E_0[y_1]}{R} \tag{7.28}$$

The three possible relative rankings of expected accounting rate of return and required economic rate of return are each considered in turn.

Expected ARR greater than required rate of return $(E_0[A_1] > R)$

Since the book value of capital employed is determined by the value to the owner convention, $E_0[EV_1] - E_0[y_1] \geq 0$. Therefore, provided that y_0 is positive, $E_0[A_1] > R$ implies that $PV_0 > y_0$. It can be seen from Table 7.4 that PV_0 will only exceed y_0 when $y_0 = RC_0$. Since $E_0[A_1] > R$ implies $PV_0 > y_0$ which implies $PV_0 > RC_0$, $E_0[A_1] > R$ suggests that it would be profitable to enter the line of business. Since $NRV < RC$, if one is already in the business one should remain in it.

Expected ARR less than required rate of return $(E_0[A_1] < R)$

This implies, provided that y_0 is positive:

$$PV_0 - y_0 < \frac{E_0[EV_1] - E_0[y_1]}{R} \qquad (7.29)$$

If $E_0[EV_1] = E_0[y_1]$, $PV_0 < y_0$ which from Table 7.4 can only occur when $PV_0 < NRV_0 < RC_0$ (and therefore $y_0 < NRV_0$). Thus, if one is in this business, one should exit from it and if one is not currently in the business one should not enter it.

If $E_0[EV_1] > E_0[y_1]$, EKM note that it is not possible to draw conclusions about the relationship between PV_0, RC_0 and NRV_0 from the fact that $E_0[A_1] < R$. However, they do point out that, even if $PV_0 > y_0$ (and therefore $PV_0 > RC_0$), the present value of entering the business at year-end 0 is less than that of deferring entry until year-end 1.

Expected ARR equal to required rate of return ($E_0[A_1] = R$)

From (7.28) this implies

$$PV_0 - y_0 = \frac{E_0[EV_1] - E_0[y_1]}{R} \qquad (7.30)$$

If $E_0[EV_1] = E_0[y_1]$, $PV_0 = y_0$. Referring to Table 7.4, this implies that

$$NRV_0 < PV_0 < RC_0$$

which suggests that an existing activity should be continued but that a new one should not be entered.

If $E_0[EV_1]$ is greater than $E_0[y_1]$ then PV_0 is greater than y_0 which implies that PV_0 is greater than RC_0 which is assumed to be greater than NRV_0. Thus, since PV_0 is greater than NRV_0, an existing activity should be continued. As far as a potential new activity is concerned, Table 7.4 suggests that, since $E_0[EV_1]$ is greater than $E_0[y_1]$, the right-hand side of (7.30) can be written as

$$\frac{E_0[PV_1] - E_0[RC_1]}{R}$$

Since $PV_0 > y_0$, the left-hand side of (7.30) can be written as

$$PV_0 - RC_0$$

Therefore

$$PV_0 - RC_0 = \frac{E_0[PV_1] - E_0[RC_1]}{R}$$

The present value of a decision to enter the new business at year-end 0 is exactly the same as the present value of a decision to defer entry until year-end 1. One is thus indifferent between immediate entry and deferred entry. The foregoing analysis is summarised in Table 7.5.

EKM also present a similar analysis, summarised in the Appendix to this chapter, of the inferences that can be drawn from realised ARRs over a limited segment of a business's life.

Table 7.5   Summary of decision rules in ex-ante EKM analysis

Relationship between expected single period ARR $(E_0(A_1))$ and required rate of return (R)	Current status (in/out of the business)	Decision at year-end 0
$E_0(A_1) > R$	In	Stay in
	Out	Enter
$E_0(A_1) < R$	In	Exit (if $y_0 = NRV_0$)
	Out	Stay out
$E_0(A_1) = R$	In	Stay in
	Out	Stay out (or, possibly, indifference between entry at year-end 0 and deferral of entry until year-end 1)

As mentioned earlier, the practical usefulness of the EKM analysis is tempered by the fact that it is based on a valuation convention that does not currently form the basis of published financial statements. It does, however, suggest that a combination of ARR forecasts and analyst judgement about the extent to which valuation conventions depart from 'value to the owner' can form a useful basis for investment decisions.

7.5   Accounting information and risk assessment

The value of a company's equity share capital derives from:

1. The cash flows that are expected to accrue in the future to the holders of that share capital.
2. The discount rate, being the required rate of expected return or 'the cost of equity', to be applied to those cash flow expectations.

In Sections 7.2, 7.3 and 7.4 it was shown that there exist formal links between accounting numbers and information required for economic decision-making purposes. Since the analysis in those sections took the cost of equity as given, it was effectively concerned only with the first of the two items listed above. We now consider the extent to which accounting data might assist the analyst in arriving at an estimate of the appropriate risk premium to use in arriving at an estimate of a company's required rate of expected return on equity capital.

CAPM and the prediction of beta using security market variables have been discussed more fully in Chapter 5. However, we will briefly review the issues here. The standard theoretical models of the required rate of expected return on a risky investment are the

Capital Asset Pricing Model (CAPM) and the Arbitrage Pricing Theory (APT). The discussion in this section will centre on the CAPM. This model suggests that the required rate of expected return on equity capital will be determined partly by interest rates and partly by a risk premium. This risk premium will not be generated by the total variability of the return on the equity capital; it will be generated by that part of the variability which cannot be diversified away because it is due to the share's sensitivity to market movements. Algebraically, the required rate of return for the equity capital of company i $(R_i - 1)$ is equal to the risk-free rate of interest $(R_f - 1)$, the required rate of expected return on the optimal diversified portfolio (hereafter termed 'the market portfolio') $(R_m - 1)$ and the beta of company i (β_i):

$$(R_i - 1) = (R_f - 1) + (R_m - R_f)\beta_i$$

where β_i, which is the only right-hand side variable specific to firm i, is given by:

$$\beta_i = \frac{\sigma_{im}}{\sigma_m^2} = \frac{\rho_{im}\sigma_i\sigma_m}{\sigma_m^2}$$

Here σ_m^2 is the variance of expected return on the market portfolio and σ_{im} is the covariance between the expected return on share i and the expected return on the market portfolio. Beta is a measure of the sensitivity of the return on share i to change in the return on the market portfolio and it is a measure of that part of the equity capital's risk which derives from sensitivity to market movements. Its algebraic form is similar to that of the slope coefficient in a univariate regression which is a measure of the sensitivity of the dependent variable to changes in the independent variable. Indeed, the slope coefficient from a regression of a time-series of realised company share returns on a matching time-series of realised returns on a suitable proxy for the market portfolio is often used as the forecast of beta, although more complex models are sometimes used in order to deal with problems caused by thin trading and the tendency of beta to move towards 1. Conventional practice uses four or five years of monthly return data in the regression model.

There are a number of difficulties with this process. Apart from technical problems, such as the thin trading problem referred to above, there may be problems of data availability and beta stability. There may not be a sufficiently long history of company share returns to enable beta to be estimated from historical data. Even where there is a sufficient history there may be reason to suppose that the risk characteristics of the firm have changed if, for example, the firm's gearing has been changed or the firm has acquired or disposed of substantial assets or liabilities. There may also be external changes such as energy shocks or changes in inflation which will impact on the firm's riskiness. If the analysts understand the implications of these changes with regards to beta risk then they are more likely to be able to incorporate the changes into their decision-making, and if financial analysis techniques are able to help them measure the impact of the changes they are even better off. Even where there is no reason to suppose a change in beta and where historic share price data are available it may simply be the case that the historic market sensitivity of the return on a share is not the best available guide to its future market sensitivity. Information available from financial statements may help to improve estimates.

Beaver, Kettler and Scholes (1970) suggested that a beta forecasting model using the dividend payout ratio, the asset growth rate and the variability of earnings gives more accurate forecasts of beta than do historic market data. Eskew (1979) reported similar results for a forecasting model using asset size, asset growth rate and earnings variability. Eskew's results are, however, disputed by Elgers (1980) who asserts that 'accounting-based predictions of beta do not improve over naive (market data only) forecasts'.

More obvious practical applications of accounting information in beta estimation are suggested by an expression proposed by Mohr (1985), following Hamada (1972) and Rubinstein (1973). This expression enables estimates of a company's beta to be generated from knowledge of:

1. The lines of business in which the company is engaged.
2. The typical beta for a company devoted exclusively to each of those lines of business.
3. The company's gearing ratio.

It combines two well-known properties of beta. Firstly, just as the beta of a portfolio of investments is a value-weighted average of the betas of the constituents of the portfolio, so the beta of a company's total operations is a value-weighted average of the betas of the lines of business that make up the company. Secondly, the inclusion of riskless borrowing in the capital structure drives up the beta of equity, this being so because the existence of riskless debt in the capital structure of a company causes 100 per cent of the risk of the company's operations to be borne by the equity holders who will represent less than 100 per cent of the providers of capital. Mohr's expression for the beta of the equity capital of a geared company is as follows (the company subscripts are suppressed):

$$\beta_i = \left(\frac{P + D}{P} \right) \sum_{c=1}^{A} s_c \beta_{Uc} \qquad (7.31)$$

where P is the market value of equity of the company, D is the market value of the company's debt (assumed riskless), A is the number of lines of business in which the company is engaged, s_c is the proportion of the market value of the company devoted to line of business c and β_{Uc} is the ungeared beta appropriate to line of business c. The ungeared beta is the equity beta that one would expect to observe in an entirely equity-financed company operating in line of business c.

We consider first the line of business information. Estimates of beta for different lines of business are readily available from such sources as the London Business School's Risk Measurement Service (RMS). The diversity in betas for different lines of business can be seen from the extract from the April–June 1993 edition of RMS presented in Table 7.6. This gives estimates of both equity beta and standard deviation of return for selected industrial sector indices.

It must be noted here that these are geared betas and that the diversity of these may well be less than that of ungeared betas. It is possible that companies which operate relatively risky businesses tend to choose safer (i.e less highly geared) capital structures, thus causing the diversity of asset betas to be mitigated when the betas are stated in geared form. Thus, the variety exhibited in Table 7.6 is possibly an understatement of the variety of the ungeared betas.

Once estimates of ungeared beta have been obtained for each line of business in which the company operates, the theory suggests that they should be weighted by the market

Table 7.6 Industrial variation in investment risk

	Equity beta	Standard deviation of return
Contracting, construction	1.39	29%
Textiles	1.15	24%
Chemicals	0.99	19%
Food manufacturing	0.84	16%
Water	0.76	21%

value of the net assets invested in each line of business. It is extremely improbable that these market values can be observed so a proxy must be found. The most likely source of such a proxy is the segmental data found in the notes to the financial statements. In the UK, large companies are required by SSAP 25 to disclose sales, profit and book value of assets by geographical and line of business sector.

There is no easy answer to the question of which of the three sets of segmental data provides the best proxies for the weights in (7.31). A flavour of the difficulties can be obtained from Section 7.2.3 which describes a model according to which, at the extremes, market price can be determined entirely by book value of net assets or (in cum-div form) by a multiple of earnings. An empirical study by Mohr (1985), which required estimates of ungeared betas, used two weighting methods: one based on sales and one based on book value of assets. The inferences drawn from the tests did not seem to be sensitive to the weighting scheme used.

In adjusting for the effects of gearing, similar problems arise. Although the market value of equity capital is relatively easy to observe, at least for quoted companies, the market value of debt may not be observable. The information provided in the financial statements provides two possible proxies:

$$\frac{P_B + D_B}{P_B}$$

and

$$\frac{P_M + D_B}{P_M}$$

where P and D are as defined earlier and the subscripts B and M denote book value and market value respectively. Empirical results reported by Bowman (1980) suggest that the use of book value of debt to market value of equity gives the preferable of the two proxies. This proxy was used in the empirical work by Mohr (1985) referred to above.

We have not attempted here to demonstrate that formal links exist between accounting variables and risk. What we have tried to do is to highlight the availability in financial statements of data from which can be constructed useful proxies for the gearing and line of business information required to convert a set of ungeared line of business betas into a geared equity beta. Even if one feels uncomfortable with the Capital Asset Pricing Model because it is 'too theoretical', it is difficult to imagine that information on gearing and line of business is irrelevant to the purpose of estimating the risk premium for a company.

For all their faults, the financial statements will usually be the most accessible source of this information.

7.6   Conclusion

It has been shown in Sections 7.2 and 7.3 of this chapter that formal links exist between the value of equity capital and the outputs of accrual accounting and between internal rate of return and accounting rate of return. It has also been shown in Section 7.4 that, if a particular accounting valuation convention ('value to the owner') is used, economic decisions can be based upon the relationship between the accounting rate of return and the required economic rate of return. Section 7.5 showed how accounting information could be of use in determining the risk premium to be applied in arriving at the value of equity capital. It should be clear from the analysis presented here that frameworks exist which can help to deal with the problems of linking accounting to value referred to in the quote from Penman reproduced in Section 7.2.1. The relationships highlighted in this chapter are very much in the realm of theory rather than practice and are far from providing a complete practical guide to the task of inferring economic fundamentals from accounting information. However, they do provide a framework to guide the analyst in the task of inferring economic fundamentals from accounting information.

Appendix 7.1   The EKM analysis of the usefulness of ex-post ARRs

EKM also consider the inferences that can be drawn from the relationship between realised ARRs and required rate of return. This sort of ex-post analysis is likely to be of particular interest to regulators seeking evidence of barriers to entry which might facilitate the exercise of monopoly power. As with the ex-ante analysis, the three possible relative rankings of realised accounting rate of return and required economic rate of return are each considered in turn. The equation upon which this analysis is based is the following adaptation of (7.28) in the main text, in which expectations are replaced by realisations.

$$RPV_0 - y_0 = y_0\left(\frac{A_1 - R}{R}\right) + \frac{EV_1 - y_1}{R} \qquad (A.1)$$

Here,

$$RPV_0 = PV_0 + ERR_0$$

where RPV_0 denotes the 'realised' PV_0 being the PV_0 that would have been calculated at year-end 0 if the year-end 1 outcomes had been known and ERR_0 denotes the difference between the expected and realised present values.

Realised ARR greater than required rate of return ($A_1 > R$)

Since $(EV_1 - y_1) \geq 0$, a value of A_1 greater than R (with y_0 positive) implies that RPV_0

is greater than y_0. Therefore,

$$PV_0 + ERR_0 > y_0$$

Thus one or both of two things must have happened in the period under review. Either ERR_0 was greater than 0, in which case expectations were exceeded, and/or PV_0 was greater than y_0. Under the value to the owner convention, the latter implies that PV_0 was greater than RC_0 which suggests the existence at year-end 0 of barriers to entry enabling the firm to earn returns in excess of the required rate of return.

Realised ARR less than required rate of return ($A_1 < R$)

If y_1 is equal to EV_1, (A.1) suggests that a value of A_1 less than R implies that:

$$PV_0 + ERR_0 < y_0$$

Thus one or both of two things must have happened in the period under review. Either ERR_0 was less than 0, in which case expectations were not met, and/or PV_0 was less than y_0. Under the value to the owner convention, the latter implies that PV_0 was less than NRV_0 which suggests that the business should not have been continued beyond year-end 0. EKM observe that if EV_1 is greater than y_1 (i.e. if y_1 equals RC_1) it is not possible to draw any conclusions.

Realised ARR equal to required rate of return ($A_1 = R$)

Here, if EV_1 equals y_1, $RPV_0 = y_0$, from which little can be deduced. If, however, EV_1 is greater than y_1, a value of A_1 greater than R implies that RPV_0 was greater than y_0 which implies

$$PV_0 + ERR_0 > y_0$$

Again, one or both of two things must have happened in the period under review. Either ERR_0 was greater than 0, in which case expectations were exceeded, and/or PV_0 was greater than y_0 which suggests that PV_0 was greater than RC_0 which suggests the existence of barriers to entry enabling the firm to earn returns in excess of the required rate of return.

Notes

1. John O'Hanlon is Senior Lecturer in the Department of Accounting and Finance at the University of Lancaster and an ICAEW Academic Fellow.
2. The solution to this equation normally requires the use of an iterative algorithm. Financial calculators and spreadsheets will normally calculate IRR using such an algorithm. IRR can be estimated manually by trial and error. There are a number of problems with the use of IRR. For example, if the time-series of cash flows is such that the sign of the cash flows changes more than once, there will be more than one solution to the IRR equation. Also IRR is not a sound basis for comparing two projects. See Brealey and Myers (1991) for a discussion of these issues.

——————————————— QUESTIONS ———————————————

1.   Ohlson's model provides a theoretical link between clean surplus earnings and value.
       (a)   To what extent does this provide an incentive to regulate for accounting policies which produce clean surplus earnings?
       (b)   To what extent do the earnings disclosed in your domestic market comply with the clean surplus definition, and how difficult would it be to estimate clean surplus earnings?
       (c)   Take one firm's recent (five year) history of earnings and attempt to re-estimate clean surplus earnings for this period.

2.   Many researchers assume that the models:

$$P_t = \alpha_0 + \alpha_1 y_t + \alpha_2 x_t$$

$$R_t = \beta_0 + \beta_1 x_t + \beta_2 \Delta x_t$$

where P is price, R is return, x is earnings and y book value, are consistent with Ohlson's framework.
       (a)   To what extent do they depart from the Ohlson model?
       (b)   Is there a strong case for imposing a more rigorous version of Ohlson's results?

3.   For a sample of firms estimate either the return or price version of the model given in Question 2 above. Critically evaluate the results.

4.   Obtain a sample of five quoted companies. Using their accounting statements and market capitalisations over a 5-year period:
       (a)   Calculate the IRR by applying Peasnell's result to the ARRs. Assume that there are no valuation errors at the opening and closing dates, and that dividends and any other capital transactions are carried out on the year-end date.
       (b)   Recalculate (a) above using a valuation error term computed using the market capitalisation as the value of equity and compare the answers to (a) and (b).
       (c)   What conclusions can you draw regarding the use of accounting-based IRR?

5.   You have been asked to provide an analysis of the relative rates of return for three industries, electrical engineering, brewing, and retailing.
       (a)   Compute the conventional accounting-based rate of return.
       (b)   Provide a criticism of the usefulness of the numbers presented in (a).
       (c)   Indicate how you would in principle be able to derive information regarding the relative rates of return which you believe to be more reliable than (a)?

6.   The chapter highlights a number of financial statement-based variables which might be used to model a firm's beta. For a sample of firms estimate the multivariate relationship between either (a) the beta published by a commercial risk measurement service, or (b) the beta calculated using the market model. Discuss and evaluate the results of your model.

References

Accounting Standards Board (1992) Financial reporting standard No.3: Reporting financial performance.

Alford, A., Jones, J., Leftwick, R. and Zmijewski, M. (1993) The relative informativeness of accounting disclosures in different countries, *Journal of Accounting Research*, **31**, Supp., 183–229.

Beaver, W. (1989) *Financial Reporting: An Accounting Revolution*, 2nd edition, Prentice Hall, Englewood Cliffs.

Beaver, W. and Demski, J. (1979) The nature of income measurement, *Accounting Review*, January, 38–46.

Beaver, W., Kettler, P. and Scholes, M. (1970) The association between market determined and accounting determined risk measures, *Accounting Review*, October, 654–82.

Brealey, R. and Myers, S. (1991) *Principles of Corporate Finance*, 4th edition, McGraw Hill, New York.

Brennan, M. (1991) A perspective on accounting and stock prices, *Accounting Review*, 67–79.

Bowman, R. (1979) The theoretical relationship between systematic risk and financial [accounting] variables, *Journal of Finance*, June, 617–30.

Bowman, R. (1980) The importance of a market-value measurement of debt in assessing leverage, *Journal of Accounting Research*, Spring, 242–54.

Easton, P. and Harris, T. (1991) Earnings as an explanatory variable for returns, *Journal of Accounting Research*, **29**, no. 1, 19–36.

Edey, H. (1962) Business valuation, goodwill and the super-profit method, in Baxter, W. and Davidson, S. (Eds) *Studies in Accounting Theory*, Sweet and Maxwell, London.

Edwards, E. and Bell, P. (1961) *The Theory and Measurement of Business Income*, University of California Press.

Edwards, J., Kay, J. and Mayer, C. (1987) *The Economic Analysis of Accounting Profitability*, Oxford University Press, Oxford.

Elgers, P. (1980) Accounting-based risk prediction: a re-examination, *Accounting Review*, July, 389–408.

Eskew, R. (1979) The forecasting ability of accounting risk measures: some additional evidence, *Accounting Review*, January, 107–18.

Feltham, G. and Ohlson, J. (1992) Valuation and clean surplus accounting for operating and financial activities, Working paper, University of British Columbia and Columbia University.

Fisher, F. and McGowan, J. (1983) On the misuse of accounting rates of return to infer monopoly profits, *American Economic Review*, **73**, no. 1, 82–97.

Hamada, R. (1972) The effect of the firm's capital structure on the systematic risk of common stocks, *Journal of Finance*, May, 435–52.

Harcourt, G. (1965) The accountant in a golden age, *Oxford Economic Papers* 17, March, 66–80.

Kay J. (1976) Accountants, too, could be happy in a golden age: the accountants' rate of profit and the internal rate of return, *Oxford Economic Papers*, November, 447–460.

Kay, J. and Mayer, C. (1986) On the application of accounting rates of return, *Economic Journal*, March, 199–207.

Luckett, P. (1984) ARR vs IRR: a review and an analysis, *Journal of Business Finance and Accounting*, Summer, 213–23.

Mohr, R. (1985) The operating beta of a US multi-activity firm: an empirical investigation, *Journal of Business Finance and Accounting*, Winter, 575–93.

Ohlson, J. (1991) Earnings, book values and dividends in security valuation, Working paper, Columbia University.

Peasnell, K. (1982) Some formal corrections between economic values and yields and accounting numbers, *Journal of Business Finance and Accounting*, Autumn, 361−81.

Penman, S. (1991a) Return to fundamentals, Working paper, University of California at Berkeley.

Penman, S. (1991b) An evaluation of accounting rate of return, *Journal of Accounting Auditing and Finance*, **6**, no. 2, 233−255.

Ramakrishnan, R. and Thomas, J. (1992) What matters from the past: market value, book value or earnings? Earnings valuation and sufficient statistics for prior information, *Journal of Accounting Auditing and Finance*, **7**, no. 4, 423−464.

Rubinstein, M. (1973) A mean-variance synthesis of corporate financial theory, *Journal of Finance*, March, 167−81.

Smith, T. and Hannah, R. (1991) *Accounting for Growth*, UBS Phillips and Drew, January.

Solomons, D. (1991) Economic and accounting concepts of income, *Accounting Review*, July, 374−83.

Stark, A. (1982) Estimating the internal rate of return from accounting data — a note, *Oxford Economic Papers*, November, 520−25.

Steele, A. (1986) A note on estimating the internal rate of return from published financial statements, *Journal of Business Finance and Accounting*, Spring, 1−13.

Strong, N. and Walker, M. (1993) The explanatory power of earnings for stock returns, *Accounting Review*, April, 385−399.

Whittington, G. (1979) On the use of accounting rate of return in empirical research, *Accounting and Business Research*, Summer, 201−8.

Wright, F. (1978) Accounting rate of profit and internal rate of return, *Oxford Economic Papers*, November, 464−8.

CHAPTER 8

Corporate Takeovers and Allied Activity

CHAPTER OBJECTIVES

This chapter will:

1 Explain the recent developments in merger activity and review the reasons behind mergers.

2 Examine the characteristics of merging firms and the potential for predicting and exploiting mergers.

3 Review the basic techniques for accounting for mergers and the difficulties encountered.

8.1 Introduction

Mergers, acquisitions and takeovers are a fascinating area of study for the financial analyst and accountant. Vast resources are shunted around the globe in an overt display of corporate and personal acquisitiveness which stands comparison with the more glamorous American soap operas. The motivations of the participants are unclear, the performance record of such activity is dubious, the accounting problems inherent in reporting the acquisition and the subsequent group's performance are problematical, and the legal and fiscal implications are complex. Further, the process of a takeover can transfer wealth between different interest groups within the firm, and the gains to be made on the capital markets from anticipating takeover bids are substantial. These factors ensure that takeover activity is an area of some interest and controversy.

The merger activity of firms is also of some importance when analysts attempt to understand the incentives that influence a firm's management. In most public companies the distribution of share ownership is such that shareholders are unable to exert strong influence over management. Even those institutions which maintain sizeable shareholdings seem reluctant or unable to participate in managerial supervision. This contrasts starkly with the practice in many continental European or Japanese firms where there is a much closer involvement between the firm and the commercial banks which provide the majority of the firm's finance. It would appear that where ownership is divorced from control as in the US and the UK, there are incentives for management to pursue objectives other than the maximisation of the shareholders' wealth. Yet under these circumstances it is argued that the share price will suffer, opening the way for a takeover with the predator company seeking a return through boosting the share price by introducing wealth-maximising management. Thus the threat of takeover may act as an incentive to management to maximise share price both in the shareholders' interest and to defend the management's own careers. However, it should be pointed out that there are further constraints on managerial activity which have the potential to achieve the same effect. Not least of these is the requirement to contest effectively with the firm's competition.

Although takeover activity is the most visible and newsworthy aspect of corporate restructuring, it is by no means exclusively significant when measured by the resources that are transferred. Voluntary transactions negotiated by management represent a significant part of restructuring, whether this takes the form of the transfer of divisions between holding companies, management buy-outs and spin-offs, or changes in the ownership structure through going public/private or privatised/nationalised. These aspects are related to takeovers not only as they have a similar restructuring impact on the productive assets employed, albeit through a very different procedure for implementation, but also the incentive for voluntary transfer is partially founded in takeover activity. If inefficiently utilised assets are retained, the firm's share price will suffer making it an attractive target to predators. Thus takeovers may be a powerful incentive to other forms of corporate restructuring.

All these aspects of reorganisation are potentially 'creating benefits for the economy as a whole by loosening control over vast resources and enabling them to move more quickly to their highest-valued use' (Jensen, 1988, p. 23). Whether they actually benefit the economy as a whole, or simply sub-sections (possibly to the detriment of others), is a moot point. Indeed, some would argue that the overall costs of merger activity outweight any marginal, and possibly illusory, benefits and such activity should therefore be discouraged (Scherer, 1988).

This chapter will firstly examine the history and motivations for merger activity, examining the gains to be made from mergers, the effect on industrial performance, and the significance of this type of corporate activity. The insights to be gained from this activity are then allied to empirical research which attempts to identify those firms susceptible to merger activity and crucially whether any capital market gains can be made from this information. The technique for analysing the costs and benefits of a merger are then reviewed. Finally, a brief examination of the accounting techniques applied to mergers and to the resulting groups is presented, for it is very difficult to evaluate corporate restructuring without an understanding of the system that reports the results of that activity.

8.2   Background and motives for mergers

In this section, the recent history and trends in corporate takeovers are presented and the methods and types of restructuring illustrated. Some alternative hypotheses regarding the motivation for takeover activity are then presented.

8.2.1 *Categories of corporate restructuring techniques*

Merger, acquisition or takeover

While the accounting techniques applied to takeovers distinguish between a merger or acquisition, in common business parlance these two terms are practically synonymous with takeover. In the UK the procedure is normally conducted by the aggressor firm making a public bid for the shares of the target after establishing a significant holding through normal buying. This bid may be opposed but is normally approved by the acquiree's management, though not necessarily at the start of negotiations. On successful completion the target company will become a subsidiary of the aggressor. This procedure is known as a tender offer in the US. Another US version of the change in corporate control is the proxy contest where the aspirant managers attempt to convince sufficient shareholders to back them and overthrow the incumbent management.

The theoretical discussions on mergers began by looking at the underlying motives. Various economic arguments in favour or against mergers have been put forward especially in relation to both the shareholders' interest and the public interest. Policies imposing restrictions on mergers that are anti-competitive have been implemented in the UK and the EU in general. Conversely, the effects of restructuring and growth inherent in merger activity have often been seen as beneficial. Also certain types of merger activity which promote efficiency, or are 'national champions', have been encouraged by the authorities. With regard to the shareholders' interests, a dominant concern in corporate finance, the arguments against managerialism and for the existence of market for managerial control became important. Since then the emphasis in the studies of mergers has shifted towards the intangible economic benefits that could only be gained through an internal rather an external market. Arguments of such nature include consideration of economies of scope, such as sharing research, development and technology, and removing incompetent management.

Management buy-outs

Often called leveraged buy-outs, due to the unusually high proportion of fixed interest capital employed to allow management to obtain a significant stockholding. This is a rapidly growing procedure for divesting a holding company of a subsidiary or division. A spin-off refers to a buy-out where the holding company maintains a significant, though not controlling, interest.

Joint ventures

As will be seen takeovers are an expensive method of restructuring the firm. It may be that many of the benefits from a takeover can be achieved by other means which are less costly or risky. One such approach which is becoming common is the joint venture. Here two or more firms combine their different skills or competitive advantages with a view to exploiting a particular opportunity. Many of the most visible joint ventures are transnational where one firm that wishes to enter a new market collaborates with a local firm with experience of the market but without the resources to exploit it. Another group of well-known examples are the combinations between vehicle or aircraft manufacturers where they need to pool resources and/or skills to develop new products. The Rover—Honda alliance was a sucessful example of the former and the Airbus consortium an example of the latter.

Transfers of assets

As pointed out above, corporate restructuring can take place without any changes in share ownership. The sale of a subsidiary/division from one corporation to another is a common occurrence, and it is quite conceivable that the whole or main part of the assets of a firm could be disposed of by management in a transaction that would have the restructuring substance of a takeover without any change in ownership of the legal entities. Throughout 1984—88 the acquisition of subsidiaries accounted for approximately one-quarter of the value of assets transferred by takeover of independent companies.

Going private/public

The other reorganisation which is often considered at this point, but which does not affect the composition of the group or firm in question, is the change in ownership, and possibly management, when the organisation moves across the public—private company barrier. The two main motivations for going public would be to access the stock market to raise additional funds, or to provide a convenient method for the present owners to realise some portion of their holding. The creation of the unlisted securities market has been a successful development which has attracted many firms to quoted status without incurring the full cost of compliance with normal market quotation. A less common move is going private, the reverse of the above. In this case, the would-be private owners buy up the stock on the open market and if successful the company is de-listed.

A substantial amount of research, much of it reviewed in Byrne and Rees (1994), has investigated the initial public offer (IPO) which is the process by which a firm goes public. It is of interest because the IPO is an investment opportunity which typically produces abnormally high returns during the first week in which the firm is listed on the market. Worldwide the returns available on IPOs in the first week of trading have been estimated to range from 4 to 80 per cent with most developed stock markets falling in a narrower band of around 7 to 16 per cent. This has been taken by some commentators to be an example of market inefficiency but convincing arguments can be put forward that the underpricing is deliberate and a necessary part of the new issue process. In general evidence also suggests that the pattern of initial returns on IPOs through time is not random and there have been sustained 'hot issue' periods when the number of IPOs and the initial returns are substantially greater than at other times. More recently new evidence has been made available which casts doubt on the notion of deliberate underpricing. This evidence shows that in the UK, US and many other markets new issues under-perform the index, or equivalent established stocks, for a number of years after the issue of the shares suggesting that the high initial returns are due to over-valuation in the initial market. This evidence is surprising as it suggests long-run market inefficiency but, although few of these studies have been published at the time of writing, evidence of long-run under-pricing has been found in many countries.

Privatisation/nationalisation

A further change in ownership which may be accompanied by a change in structure is the move between national and private ownership. The proponents of nationalised control consider that for social or strategic reasons, or because the industry is naturally monopolistic, the resources in question are best managed through national ownership. The advocates of privatisation believe that competitive forces improve performance and that in the long run government interference is damaging. It is clear that, in common with but more extreme than non-privatisation IPOs, the privatisation process is very expensive. It order to ensure wide share ownership and to avoid the political embarrassment of a failed issue the Government has had to under-price the issues by a rather greater margin than is normal.

8.2.2 *Recent history of mergers and allied activity*

Mergers

Recently, the value of merger activity has reached unprecedented levels and the explanation for this trend is not well established. To analyse these trends effectively it is helpful to split the data into the number and value of merger activity. What is then apparent is that the number of firms acquired stabilised after falling from the heights of the late 1960s/early 1970s, and has only recently increased significantly. Conversely, the resources expended on mergers is currently running at an all-time high and, 'taken together the years 1984, 1985, and 1986 have produced by far the largest and most sustained boom in merger expenditure in British history at a time when merger activity (that is the number of mergers) was not particularly high' (Scouller, 1987, p. 16). This reference would apply equally as well to 1987 and 1988.

Figure 8.1 shows the number and value of mergers and acquisitions in the UK. Table 8.1 shows the scope of recent UK takeover activity emphasising the importance of US targets and the growing importance of targets in other European countries.

Table 8.1 Takeover activity by UK based firms

	1987	1988	1989	1990	1991	Total
Number						
UK	1 463	1 633	1 402	912	747	6 157
US	256	389	262	167	97	1 171
Euro	145	258	410	298	194	1 305
Total	1 864	2 280	2 074	1 377	1 038	8 633
Sterling (millions)						
UK	20 297	24 369	36 416	17 457	12 180	110 719
US	18 130	21 149	11 176	5 604	1 381	57 440
Euro	1 342	2 788	2 724	4 699	1 634	13 187
Total	39 769	48 306	50 316	27 760	15 195	181 346

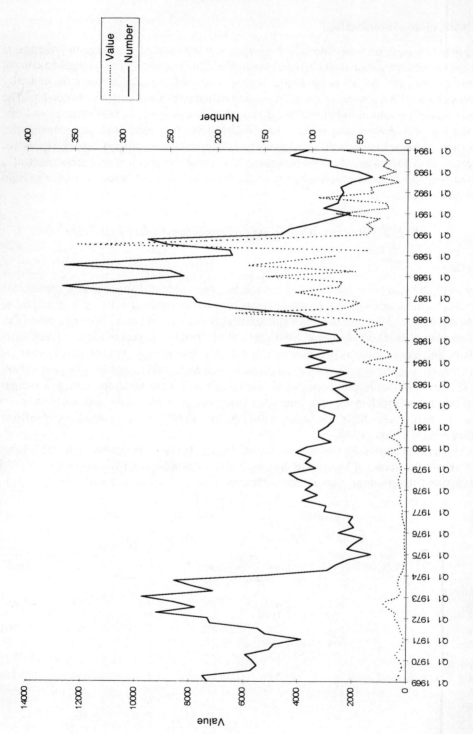

Figure 8.1 Number and value of mergers and acquisitions.

Drawing conclusions from trends is awkward when they are distorted by a few very large cases. Thus, the 1986 boom includes two takeovers (Hanson Trust of Imperial Group and Guinness of Distillers) which are reported at £2.6 billion and £2.5 billion respectively, which would together exceed the total expenditure at 1986 prices for nine years out of ten since 1960. Extrapolating a trend which includes extraordinary instances such as these might be misleading, but there is some evidence that these are merely precursors of a more general move to mega-mergers of this type.

The recent activity in the UK has been mirrored elsewhere, particularly in the USA, and has been accompanied by a commensurate rise in the number of transnational takeovers, with UK companies generally making considerably more investment in foreign companies than the reverse. The vast majority of this outward trade, if measured by value, has been with North America, though the number of outward transactions and the number and value of inward acquisitions are more widely distributed.

In the average year, the financing of takeover activity tends to approximate cash:equity:loan capital in the ratio of 5:4:1. In previous boom periods equity and loans tended to play a considerably greater role, but there is little evidence of unusual financing in the current wave. To some extent the dominance of cash may be overstated. There is evidence that issues of equities by UK firms are often followed by acquisitions which may on average disperse as much as half of the sum raised.

The fluctuations in merger activity have often been described as following waves and some effort has been expended in trying to explain such cyclical activity. Conventional wisdom would assert that merger activity is higher when the stock market is high but, 'the most recent merger wave of the 70s and early 80s is inconsistent with the earlier popular theory of mergers because it came with the economy in recession and a very depressed stock market' (Lev, 1983). Furthermore, Lev concludes that, 'not only am I forced to doubt the theories of merger waves, I am also inclined to doubt the existence of the waves themselves'. What seems more striking from the evidence is that the number of mergers has stabilised at a substantially reduced level since the economic crisis of 1974, but the value of the firms acquired has consistently and dramatically increased. Further generalisations can be made that the premium paid by acquiring firms over and above the pre-bid share price has risen from 15–20 per cent to 30–35 per cent, though some research suggests that the premium is nearer to 50 per cent, and that the type of takeover, particularly in the USA, where anti-trust laws are severe, has shifted towards conglomerate and vertical mergers.

While it is difficult to explain 'wave' effects, the growth in merger activity (and in the size of the target company), has a number of viable explanations. Firstly, the presumption that a merger is anti-competitive seems to have declined and even in the US horizontal mergers now seem almost as acceptable as vertical or conglomerate activity. Indeed, national interests are often seen as being best served where corporations are sufficiently large to stand comparison with foreign competition, and governments tend to take a relatively benign attitude to takeovers which appear to promote international competitiveness of home-based firms. In the UK, references to the Monopolies and Mergers Commission since 1984 have been made primarily on competitive grounds, thereby permitting mergers which might previously have been referred on considerations of national interest.

Secondly, the deregulation of many industries has also facilitated takeover activity permitting restructuring in industries which previously were ossified by government or self-imposed restrictions.

Thirdly, the development of more imaginative financing systems has provided additional funds with which to seek targets. In particular, there has been a noticeable growth in the number of occasions where smaller companies are able to make realistic bids for larger targets.

Fourthly, continued growth in international trade and flow of funds may help account for some of the growth in transnational takeovers. In particular, the pressure that effective foreign competition puts on domestic industries may promote an attempt by home firms to exit from these markets. A takeover is one technique which is sometimes used to facilitate such exits.

Finally, the financial position of the acquiring firms has been exceptionally strong. Benzie (1988, p. 83) notes that firms have:

> since 1984, been in a financial position of exceptional strength. They appear to have been in substantial financial surplus throughout the period, their holdings of liquid assets have reached unprecedented levels and, until the recent rise in short term interest rates, income gearing figures suggested substantial scope for increased use of debt finance.

These suggestions primarily relate to the easing of constraints on takeover activity rather than to any change in the fundamental benefits to be obtained from the takeover. The motives for takeovers are reviewed later and it is interesting to speculate as to the existence of any fundamental change in these.

Complementary activity

The takeover where an acquiring company bids for the shares of its target might be the most visible aspect of corporate restructuring, but it would be misleading to concentrate exclusively on this attribute. Considerable resources are devoted to the agreed transfer of subsidiaries or divisions between firms and to the divestiture of subsidiaries through management buy-outs or spin-offs (see Figure 8.2).

Despite the considerable difference in the formal process of takeovers, buy-outs, or transfers of divisions, the basic economic considerations are similar. Control over the assets is transferred to restructured groups so as to form organisations which are more effective in meeting the objectives of the interested parties. This might be achieved through improved management, freedom of action or through synergies and economies including considerations of scope or scale. However, the expected benefits may not be distributed generally. The interests of national economic performance, the shareholders, the workforce, and management, are not necessarily in accord, and as it would seem to be management which has the most obvious influence over merger activity, its motives might be expected to be dominant, subject to the constraints mentioned earlier.

One complementary activity directly related to mergers is the growing occurrence of divestments subsequent to takeovers. This could result from a need to reduce high gearing occasioned by the merger, failure of all or part of the merger, or evidence of a case of asset stripping. Scherer reports that one-third of US acquired divisions were divested within

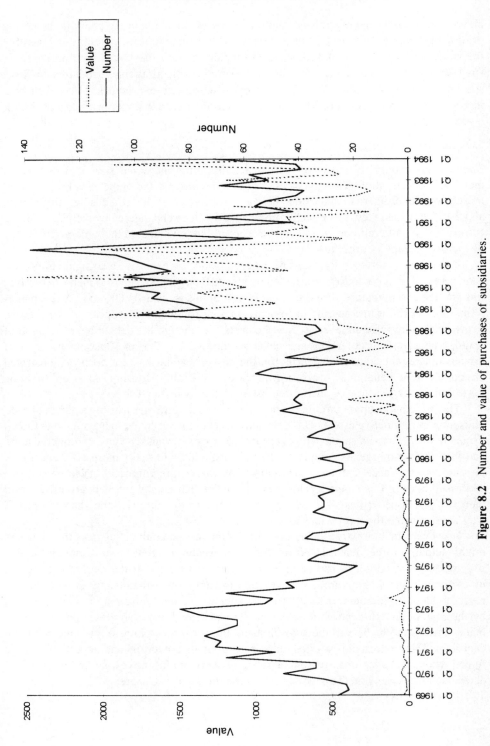

Figure 8.2 Number and value of purchases of subsidiaries.

eleven years and the average divested unit reported negative operating profit in the period prior to divestment. Scherer postulates that the cause of failure is the complex and possibly the irrelevant organisational structures into which the divisions were incorporated. He suggests that the divestment was usually to simpler organisational structures in firms specialising in allied industries. This element of corporate restructuring may well be a more successful reorganisation of productive assets than the initial merger (Scherer, 1988).

Economy-wide effects

The obvious economic impact of merger activity is the increased size of firms and of industrial concentration. The advocates of economies of scale and of the need for industrial muscle to counter international competition are ranged against the 'small is beautiful' lobby and the widely held view that effective competition will be endangered by the giant holding companies. No overall conclusion can be reached but evidence on the general efficiency of merged groups is presented later.

More recent merger activity has been accompanied by extensive gearing up to finance takeovers and, less obviously, gearing up by potential target companies to make themselves less attractive to predators. The economic impact of this is unclear. UK and US companies traditionally exhibit low gearing in comparison with continental European or Far Eastern firms, and an increase in leverage may be desirable, though the debate over the issue of optimal capital structures remains undecided. As discussed in Chapter 3, despite the apparent tax advantages the impact of gearing on the cost of capital has not been demonstrated effectively to be beneficial. A case for increased vulnerability during recession might be made but in the absence of such circumstances this is difficult to evaluate.

The principal claim regarding the beneficial impact of merger activity is the improved utilisation of productive assets. This comes from two sources in that management is forced to pursue wealth-maximisation policies or face the risk of unwanted attention from predators, and that when a merger is completed the new grouping will make more efficient use of the assets of the target company. These two hypotheses are empirical questions and are addressed later in this chapter. This view presumes that capital markets are efficient in their pricing of securities so as to recognise inefficiency and price the share in such a way as to reward the aggressor firm.

However, an alternative view, and perhaps the most damning, suggests that mergers might actually force departure from long-run wealth maximisation. Implicit in this suggestion is the failure of capital markets to react efficiently. If the market is obsessed by earnings figures or myopic in its reaction to capital investments, firms indulging in research and development or long-term investments for the future may be under-valued by the market and susceptible to takeover. The penalty that this imposes on incumbent managements might be sufficient to dissuade them from economically sound long-run decisions. There is certainly a widely held perception that investors and in particular large funds, whose managers may be remunerated by short-run incentives, act myopically and deter capital investment. This issue has been addressed in Chapter 6.

8.2.3 *Alternative industrial structures of mergers*

Reference above to conglomerate mergers is part of the typology of merger activity which attempts to differentiate by examining the relationship between the relevant firms. This is expanded as follows:

1. A horizontal merger occurs where the merged firms would otherwise be competing in the same industry and has implications for the market power of the firms. While figures for horizontal takeovers compared to other categories are not available, the Office of Fair Trading suggests that in excess of two-thirds of the proposed acquisitions it considered involve the acquirer increasing its share of the output in its existing markets.

2. A vertical merger is where one of the firm's products is potentially part of the supplies demanded by the other, which may enable the merged organisation to exercise greater control over its inputs or outputs. Examples of vertical mergers are not as readily provided as for the other categories.

3. A concentric merger (a less common classification) applies where the firms are linked by related aspects of their operations such as research, technology or distribution.

4. The alternative category is the conglomerate merger where there is no operating reason for the merger and the benefits, if any, come from diversification, the benefits from improved management, or the sharing of overheads and allied costs.

With the first three categories suggested above arguments for operating synergy can be moderately persuasive, though the lengths that executives will go to to argue that there is a logical reason for particular mergers is an amusing pastime available in the financial media.

Typologies of the sort given above are not always helpful as most takeovers will not fit neatly into any one category. Nevertheless, it can be instructive to analyse the impact of a corporate acquisition across these various dimensions to try to elicit the benefits which might be sought from a particular reconstruction.

8.2.4 *Motives for merger activity*

There is no single clear rationale for mergers which is either dominant theoretically or unequivocally evidenced empirically, and the significance of various explanations may vary with the category of merger to be considered. Lev neatly summarises the hypothesised motives into three distinct categories, as set out in Table 8.2 (Lev, 1983). The classification given by Lev is only one of a number of possible typologies. The potential number of possible rationales for merger activity is almost boundless.

Synergistic reasons

Synergistic reasons are those which claim that the combined firms are in some way more efficient agents by virtue of their ability to minimise taxation, diversify risk, improve financing ability, reduce agency contracting costs, or achieve operating or marketing economies. Not all the synergy arguments are necessarily convincing. For example, the financing argument is based on a presumption of an inefficient market for finance. But a further weakness with many of the synergy-based arguments is that even where the benefits are real there may be simpler and less costly methods to capture them. Thus tax losses

Table 8.2 A classification of motives for mergers and takeovers

---

Synergy (neoclassical motives):
    Short-term financial synergy
    EPS or PE effects
    Improved liquidity
    Tax effects
Long-term financial synergy:
    Increased debt capacity
    Improved capital redeployment
    Reduction in debt, bankruptcy costs
    Stabilising earnings
Operating synergy:
    Economies of scale
    No-growth in own industry
    Limit competition
    Acquiring technological or managerial knowledge
    Product or market extension
    Reduction in risk and uncertainty
Target undervaluation:
    Market inefficiency (economic disturbances)
    Inside information
    Superior analysis
    Displacing inefficient managers
Managerial motives:
    Power needs, size, growth
    Executive compensation
    Insider trading
    Human capital risk diversification

Source: Lev, 1983, Exhibit 3.

can be shifted between firms by means of leasing arrangements. The 1970s was a boom period for this sort of arrangement, where profitable financial institutions were able to utilise the tax losses of industrial and shipping concerns by acquiring assets on their behalf and leasing them out. Shareholders can diversify cheaply and effectively by adjusting their personal portfolio, and contractual arrangements between firms to capture operating synergies incur contracting costs but avoid the often excessive merger costs. Formal arrangement to acquire the benefits of vertical integration without actual restructuring has also been a growth area and the symbiotic relationship between retailers such as Marks and Spencer and its suppliers, and motor manufacturers such as Jaguar and component producers, are cases in point.

It needs to be emphasised that while real synergies may exist, some scepticism is appropriate when these are put forward as reasons for corporate restructuring . However, economies of scale can be achieved, especially where production of similar goods can be consolidated or more effective marketing or distribution are made available. The existence of an internal market for finance might be useful where the market for finance is poor (in developing countries) or has legal/fiscal barriers (across national boundaries). In the UK, the presence of tax losses in an acquired firm are difficult to exploit as they may normally only be set against subsequent profits of the same firm. No doubt the acquiring firm can devise means to exploit these losses, but they may not be immediately accessible. However, it may be possible that there are less direct tax benefits. A significant proportion of the expenditure on acquisitions is in a form which is a disbursement from the corporate sector. While this will normally be subject to capital gains tax, it will be a tax-effective way for the corporate sector as a whole to make disbursements to shareholders.

Agency theory — debt and free cash flow

An interesting theoretical justification for mergers, which illustrates the insights that can be drawn from agency theory, suggests that there may be previously unexpected gains from diversification. The firm may be seen as a coalition of conflicting interests most readily illustrated as equity versus debt-holders. Where the firm's prospects are unstable, the contractual and monitoring arrangements are expensive, but if a diversified firm results in more stable returns to the firm these costs would be reduced increasing the value of the firm. Equally, where a firm generates 'free cash flow' (namely, funds from operations exceed available positive present value investment opportunities), management may be loath to lose control over these resources by returning them to the shareholder, but the monitoring of these discretionary funds is an unnecessary cost.

Accounting distortions (bootstrapping)

Synergistic benefits could also appear to be evidenced in subsequent financial statements but this may well be misleading. It has been suggested that firms with high P/E ratios acquired other firms with lower ratios, thereby inflating their reported EPS. If the market applied the holding company's old P/E ratio to the new EPS, a rise in the share valuation would occur. If the market extrapolated the one-off rise in EPS into longer-term growth, a further increase in capitalisation would also be observed.

In the example given in Table 8.3, firm A acquires firm B at the end of 1990 by the issue of 2,277 ordinary shares in A for 5,000 ordinary shares in B. A and B are presumed to be valued at P/E ratios of 20 and 10 respectively. The synergistic gains in this example are nil, hence the efficient market value of AB is simply the total of A plus B. The acquisition at the end of 1990 is assumed to be financed by 2,277 shares at £2.42. However if the market were to use A's old P/E ratio of 20, a new value of £35,220 (20 + 1761) would imply a rise in value of £5,510.

Table 8.3 An example of artificial boosting of EPS

	1988	1989	1990	1991
Earnings A	1 000	1 100	1 210	1 331
Earnings B	500	525	551	579
Shares A (10 000)	20 000	22 000	24 200	
Shares B (5000)	5 000	5 250	5 510	
Shares AB (12 277)				29 710
EPS A	0.100	0.110	0.121	
EPS B	0.100	0.105	0.110	
EPS AB				0.143

If the valuation of these shares is modelled using the simple constant growth model and assuming earnings are an unbiased estimate of cash generation, it is apparent what has happened:

$$P_0 = \frac{E_1}{r-g} \qquad (8.1)$$

P_0 is the current price, E_1 is the next period earnings, r is the cost of capital, and g is the growth in earnings.

Prior to the takeover, $r_{A \text{ and } B}$ was 15.5 per cent, g_A was 10.0 per cent and g_B was 5.0 per cent; after the takeover, growth for AB will no longer be constant, being a mix of two different but constant rates, but with the value given and the required return remaining constant, a growth rate equivalent to a constant growth of 9.0 per cent can be calculated. However, the valuation using a P/E ratio of 20 assumes an implicit constant growth rate of 10.0 per cent.

An alternative source of error would be to re-estimate the growth rate for A which appears to change from a historic 10 per cent per annum to 29 per cent ($(156 - 121) + 100/121$). Any weight given to this spurious growth would further distort the market valuation, and this illustrates the care that must be given to estimating growth rates for firms which have bought growth through takeovers. The existence of either of these sources of error would, of course, evidence a fundamental rejection of the efficient market theory.

Target under-valuation

Target under-valuation is where the market price of the firm is seen to understate the true value which the acquiring firm will be able to realise. This presumes either that the market is inefficient, participants have access to inside information or exceptional analytical skills, or that the firm is not realising its full potential due to poor management.

In the first two instances, an alternative and cheaper strategy than takeover is available by conducting normal investment in the stock of the company either by the shareholders or the firm. Obviously, a limited investment only can be made by other corporations or issues of control would arise, but if one assumes that this particular target is not the only available under-valuation excess, funds can be invested fully in suitable targets without the actual takeover of control.

Possibly the most pertinent form of mis-valuation relevant to takeover activity is the debate over market myopia. While it is clear that capital markets are not exclusively obsessed by accounting earnings (or the observable diversity in P/E ratios would disappear), it is less easy to prove that markets efficiently value growth prospects. The popular case is that demand for short-term returns by powerful institutional investors discourages research and development or capital investment, which will depress short-term accounting earnings. The annual CBI conference in the UK is a forum in which this claim is aired repeatedly.

Managerial motives

Managerial motives which assert that the motive for the aggressor's action is not for the benefit of the shareholders of that firm but for that of its management, is a further rationale for merger activity. Managers' remuneration and status are related to the size of the firm they control, and it is argued, at least until recently, that one of the best defences against an unwanted takeover, and the possible loss of employment, is also size/complexity. Thus taking over other companies may be seen to enhance managers' career expectations considerably and safeguard their personal human capital. One further newsworthy, but poorly evidenced possibility, is the opportunity for massive returns from insider dealing prior to the announcement of takeovers by the instigating management or co-conspirators.

8.2.5 *Motives for joint ventures*

Joint ventures are formed to capture benefits that flow from the potential of co-operation between firms. These include the joint use of complementary technology or research techniques, spreading of risks when establishing an enterprise in a new product or geographical market, achieving economies of scale, overcoming entry barriers to domestic and international markets, creation of new competitors, greater flexibility through internal coordination and the acquisition of market power. These motives differ in different economic situations. In US/non-US, JVs the motives could be attributed to multinational enterprises that felt constrained due to the increasingly competitive world economy, combined with the growing protectionist sentiment against wholly owned operations in many host countries (Hladik, 1985). In Europe, however, economic integration with the removal of non-tariff and fiscal barriers has encouraged factor mobility as well as the formation of JVs. Thus the motives for joint ventures in Europe would relate to the potential economic benefits of the integration.

Kogut (1990) analysed the organisational properties of JVs which are different from other forms of FDI such as mergers and greenfield investments. Using the transaction cost approach he focused on the firm's boundaries and explained how the institutional design reflects efforts to minimise the sum of production and transaction costs. Due to the sharing of ownership of assets, and associated monitoring and control, JVs create incentives for parties to co-operate but are subject to constant negotiation. According to this approach the choice between full and partial ownership (joint ventures relative to wholly owned subsidiaries) depends on the costs and benefits of sharing ownership (Hennart, 1991).

The use of JVs could be due to four factors. Firstly, joint ventures could be the most efficient form of geographical diversification if it is difficult to acquire by contract (or costly to replicate it) an access to distribution held by another firm. In the second instance a firm that enters a foreign country for the first time is more likely to undertake JVs due to lack of knowledge of local conditions. Thirdly, the need to access resources which are controlled by local firms may encourage firms to engage in JV, especially in natural resource industries. This was confirmed by Gomes-Casseres (1989) who studied the ownership policies of US MNEs. Finally, JVs are used to combine complementary inputs held by two separate firms, when the markets for both of these inputs are subject to high transaction costs. A full takeover is also less efficient than a JV when the assets sought cannot be separated from unwanted ones or resistance is faced from the target's management team.

The limitations of joint ventures include goal distortion due to the hierarchy in organisational structure, opportunities for partners to resort to guile, risk of leakage of proprietary knowledge and the high cost of ignorance of local politics and culture. Since the claims on residual wealth vary amongst the partners, the efficiency of a JV hinges on the convergence of the partners' goals, or, failing this, on the degree to which opportunism by the partners can be controlled by other means, such as contracts or hostages. Anti-trust problems arise for JVs as with mergers unless the partners can point to efficiency gains and the need for promoting economic growth or international trade. When local laws prohibit foreign ownership sovereignty conflicts occur. JVs may also face conflicting objectives between host nations and home partners with a possible risk of expropriation. Conflict may also arise when foreign JVs export to the parent's home market or to third countries in competition with the home partner.

Due to the nature of European economic integration where corporate expansion focuses on entry into new markets JVs are a suggested method of dealing with transaction costs. Various other costs to cross-border integration such as (a) differences in business culture and language, (b) differences in legal institutions and accounting conventions, (c) distance and travel time, and (d) differences in ownership pattern of firms in other member states, particularly the importance of family-controlled firms, further support the need for partial integration through joint ventures.

8.3   Performance record of merger activity

The performance of mergers and allied activity is of fundamental interest. Investors in the capital market are interested in the potential for abnormal returns, management may be concerned about the impact on shareholder wealth, and there is a public policy issue regarding the impact on national economic efficiency. We are also concerned to establish the discipline effect of the threat of corporate takeover, though the interpretation of the available empirical evidence is not simple. In this section the securities market impact of takeover activity will be examined and the support (if any) from accounting measures will be assessed. In addition, a brief look at the impact of defensive strategies will be included.

8.3.1   *Capital market evidence of merger performance*

By now the reader will probably place greater faith in the market's assessment of the economic performance of the firm than in the information available from accounting data which would be incorporated into the share price as far as is relevant. Indeed, if the focus of attention for the respective shareholders is the gains from merger, the share price is the variable of interest and not potentially flawed accounting measures. The methodology employed to assess the market reaction to merger activity is the event study which analyses the cumulative average residual for a sample cross-section. This methodology was described in Chapter 6 and it should be recalled that its validity crucially rests on assumptions of stock market efficiency in evaluating the impact of the event, and the applicability of the CAPM to determine abnormal returns. Jensen and Ruback (1983) report averaged results over 14 different studies of the stock market reaction to merger or tender activity. While these averages are for different time periods in each test, and the detail of the methodology may differ and the samples overlap, the conclusions are clear enough (see Table 8.4).

Jensen and Ruback conclude that 'the evidence seems to indicate that corporate

Table 8.4 Average abnormal returns to offerors and offerees

	Bidding firms		Targets firms	
	Successful	Not successful	Successful	Not successful
Tender offers:				
Announcement effects	+3.81	−1.11	+29.09	+35.17
	(478)	(236)	(653)	(283)
Mergers:				
Two-day announcement effects	−0.05	+0.15	+7.72	+9.76
	(358)	(212)	(339)	(200)
One-month announcement effects	+1.37	+2.45	+15.90	+17.24
	(784)	(251)	(457)	(219)
Total abnormal returns from offer	−1.77	−4.82	+20.15	−2.88
announcement through to outcome	(256)	(171)	(282)	(188)

Note: Figures in brackets refer to total number of firms examined in each category.
Source: Jensen and Ruback, 1983.

takeovers generate positive gains, that target firm shareholders benefit, and that bidding firm shareholders do not lose' (Jensen and Ruback, 1983, p. 47). These results are confirmed for 1980−85 by Jarrel, Brickley and Netter who also report that premiums to target companies in the 1980s declined to 30 per cent (from 35 per cent in the 1970s), and premiums to bidders were marginally negative, though the net effect was still positive (Jarrel, Brickley and Netter, 1988).

Despite the convincing evidence summarised above, the conclusions from one particular environment and market are persuasive but not conclusive for other circumstances, and it is as well to review the evidence for the UK.

Firth examined 486 target companies and 563 aggressors in the period 1969−75. There were 434 successful bids, though 79 after revised offers, and 52 failed. Table 8.5 gives some summary statistics of Firth's results (Firth, 1980).

Table 8.5 Significance tests for average monthly portfolio residuals

Period	Targets taken over	Targets not taken over	Acquirers complete	Acquirers incomplete
1. m−48	−0.014	−0.018	0.018	0.028
to m−13	(−0.083)	(−0.251)	(0.197)	(0.316)
2. m−12	0.021	0.029	−0.003	−0.009
to m−2	(0.910)	(0.726)	(−0.082)	(−0.092)
3. m−1	0.065	0.084	−0.001	−0.004
	(5.423)	(6.171)	(−0.041)	(−0.037)
4. m 0	0.281	0.312	−0.063	−0.060
	(31.070)	(31.866)	(−5.971)	(−5.545)
5. m+1	0.010*	0.040	0.005	0.043
to m+12	(0.011)	(1.015)	(0.051)	(2.128)
6. m+13	N/A	−0.015	−0.004	−0.008
to m+36		(−0.344)	(−0.069)	(−0.051)

Notes: The first figures give the cumulative average residual for the portfolio holding period; figures in brackets relate to the portfolio *t* statistic; * = months +1, +2, +3 only.
Source: Firth, 1980, Table V, p. 248.

From Table 8.5 it can be seen that none of the portfolios experienced significantly abnormal share price performance in the four years prior to the month in which the bid is announced, except for the positive returns in m − 1 enjoyed by both groups of target firms. This implies some element of expectation of the planned takeover, or the impact of pre-bid buying by the acquirer. The month of the bid announcement shows the expected substantial positive return to the target company, and a smaller, though still highly significant, negative return to the aggressor firm, which perhaps indicates the UK market's jaundiced view of merger activity. Subsequent clear results are confined to a recovery in the share price of those firms whose bid failed. Those results which are statistically significant regarding the target companies are consistent with US research. The clear adverse reaction to making bids is particularly apparent with the UK market but has been more equivocal in the US. The US evidence of the positive pre-bid return on acquiring companies and the negative pre-bid for the acquiree has not been confirmed.

However, Firth also provides evidence that for his sample the gains of the acquired are cancelled out by the loss suffered by the acquiring shareholders and, on balance, there is a minor negative net response to completed mergers. His evidence 'shows that there is virtually a no-gain-no-loss position attached to takeovers in the United Kingdom in the period 1969−75' (Firth, 1989, p. 252). Similar results were documented by Limmack (1991).

If this research is taken as a valid description of the capital market's reaction to mergers, it can be rationalised by the assumption that the market does not expect synergistic gains from the mergers. As such, gains could be taken to include replacement of inefficient management and there is no market evidence of under-performance in the acquired firms as compared to the acquiring, there is little comfort here to the advocates of a 'market for managerial control'.

However, Franks, Broyles and Hecht examined the distribution of stock market gains between the acquirer and acquiree for the breweries and distilleries section of the London ISE. They confirm a net gain to the shareholders and again suggest that 'most if not all these gains seem to accrue to the acquiree's shareholders' (p. 1525) and that the market begins to anticipate mergers at least three months prior to the merger announcement. They point out that this is consistent with the perfectly competitive acquisitions market hypothesis, which asserts that the competition between aggressors will ensure that the target company is able to capture any gains and further, that the anticipation noted is consistent with the efficient market hypothesis (Franks, Broyles and Hecht, 1977). Of course this is only valid if no adequate information was available to predict the merger more than three months in advance. The efficiency of the capital market with regard to anticipating mergers is examined later.

A further set of investigations concentrate on the returns to transnational mergers. As a form of FDI transnational mergers may be beneficial to the acquiring firm in terms of increased flexibility in the transfer of resources across borders through a globally maximising network. In this respect, Doukas and Travlos (1988) postulated the 'positive multinational-network hypothesis' which states that an expansion of the firm's operation on a global scale tends to accomplish the investor's international diversification objectives while enhancing the firm's ability to benefit from the systemic advantages inherent in a multinational network. They used the impact on market value of the firm to investigate whether FDI through acquisition is a wealth-increasing decision and discovered that the positive wealth effects arose when MNCs entered new product or geographical markets or less developed economies.

Later studies, including Conn and Connell (1990), showed share prices in post-announcement periods remain unchanged or declined for both US and UK acquisitions in UK and US respectively. Harris and Ravenscraft (1991) studied the role of acquisitions in FDI in the US and examined abnormal returns of target shareholders. The abnormal returns that arose from foreign acquisitions were higher than those from domestic acquisitions even after controlling for factors such as all-cash bids and multiple bids. Cakici *et al.* (1991) also found the abnormal returns of 245 foreign acquisitions to be higher than domestic acquisitions. Abnormal returns to the target shareholders of foreign acquisitions were greater than for domestic acquisitions, and it could be concluded that benefits gained from foreign acquisitions were not only greater than domestic acquisitions but were largely captured by the target shareholders. Cebenoyan *et al.*'s (1992) study of foreign takeover activity in the US and wealth effects for target firm shareholders found that the wealth gains realised from 73 foreign bids relative to those realised from 134 domestic bids, increase with foreign takeover activity in the respective industry of the target. This finding is consistent with the competitive acquisitions market paradigm, that is, if cross-border expansion via corporate acquisitions produces superior (relative to domestic acquisitions) gains, foreign bidders pass them to target firm shareholders only when the demand of foreign firms for US firms in a particular industry is relatively strong. Some more recent evidence regarding the impact on UK acquirers' share price of acquisitions in Europe suggests that the market reaction tends be negative. Alhabshi and Rees (1994) report a gradual negative reaction to a sample of 447 acquisitions during 1989–91 as shown in Figure 8.3.

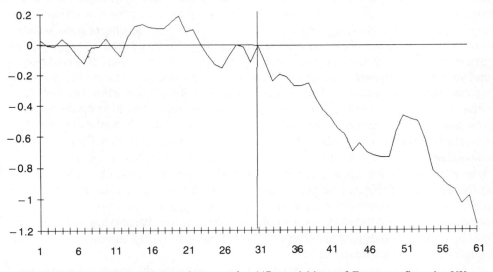

Figure 8.3 Cumulative abnormal returns for 447 acquisitions of European firms by UK companies during 1989–1991.

Some reservations are in order for this stream of event studies. While net short-term gains are generally evidenced, the limited amount of long-term data suggests that acquiring firms subsequently under-perform (Jensen and Ruback, 1983). Scherer points out that short-term gains were evidenced for the conglomerate mergers of the 1960s and 1970s, but subsequent experience has largely revealed this euphoria to be misplaced (Scherer, 1988). This cynicism regarding the results of the event study methodology rejects the efficient market hypothesis. Considerable evidence exists that the capital markets will exhibit inefficiency to strong form information at least, and Chapters 5 and 6 discussed some evidence that even semi-strong form efficiency is contentious. These reservations suggest that some support from non-share price-based research would be helpful.

Evidence on the wealth effect of joint ventures

In a study on the effects of international JVs on shareholders' wealth Lee and Wyatt (1990) analysed the stock valuation effects of international joint ventures on US firms' shareholders and determined whether these valuation effects are related to the economic status of the partners' home country. The results suggested that overall investor reaction to international JVs showed significant negative abnormal return on the day of announcement and significantly negative cumulative abnormal return. In less developed countries it appeared that JVs do not significantly reduce shareholders' wealth as much as JVs in developed countries.

In Lummer and McConnell's (1990) study of the stock valuation effects of international JVs it was assumed that corporations undertook international joint ventures when they provided a positive net present value which implied that unanticipated announcements of international joint ventures should be associated with increases in the market price of the common stock of companies announcing them. It was found that, on average, the announcements of international JVs by US firms are associated with an increase in the company's market value and the magnitude of the stock price reaction was related to the amount invested by the firm. The valuation effects were also dependent upon whether it had a private or government partner. The JVs involving a foreign private company yielded greater value when compared to those with a foreign government partner. This could imply that foreign governments can and do exploit a certain degree of monopoly power in international joint ventures. There was no evidence that US firms enjoy any particular value premium as a result of participating in joint ventures in less developed countries. The study also showed that increases in value are not the result of diversification benefits.

The differing nature of the relationship between the parties and the selective resource combination could indicate that the wealth effects of joint ventures may be different from those predicted by the whole-unit combination. However, Finnerty, Owers and Rogers (1986) found no significant evidence of abnormal returns being associated with joint venture formation and the wealth effect for stockholders of participating firms was similar to those of acquirer firms' stockholders in a whole-unit combination. Partitioning of the sample into domestic and international ventures also did not give rise to significantly different patterns of abnormal returns.

In evaluating the shareholders' wealth gains in mergers, the sources of gains could be due to synergy or management displacement. An investigation of wealth gains in US domestic joint ventures had been used to isolate the management displacement hypothesis from the synergy hypothesis as the source of gains in corporate combinations (McConnell and Nantell, 1985). It was found that there are significant wealth gains from joint ventures, the smaller partner earns a larger excess rate of return while the dollar gains are more equally divided, and the gains, scaled by resources committed, yield premiums similar to those in mergers. Previous studies of US JVs have shown mixed results on the wealth effects of JV announcements and these are attributed to different factors. Preliminary evidence on the wealth effect of UK JVs with European firms (Alhabshi and Rees, 1994) indicates that there may be positive returns but this work is based on a small sample and the results should be viewed as tentative.

Evidence regarding motives for mergers

The evidence presented above may provide a justification for merger activity but has little to say about the importance of various motives. By linking cumulative average residuals (CARs) to evidence of particular circumstances some tentative evidence is available. This research is summarised in Jarrel, Brickley and Netter, as follows:

1. The myopia argument states that institutions in particular disregard long-term invest-ments and research and development, but there appears to be little link between institutional shareholdings, research and development and merger activity. McConnel and Muscarella show the market responding positively to increased capital expenditure (McConnel and Muscarella, 1985).
2. The reversion of the targets' share price to pre-bid offers in the case of a successful defence suggests that the firm was not initially under-valued.
3. That tax benefits are significant in certain takeovers and that the price paid is in part dependent on the tax losses available seems apparent, 'however the evidence suggests that much of the takeover activity in the last twenty years was not tax motivated' (Jarrel, Brickley and Netter, 1988, p. 56).
4. There is no consistent evidence that the gains to the target's shareholders come from redistribution from other investors such as debenture holders or from imposed renegotiation of implicit long-term contracts between the workforce and incumbent management.

8.3.2   Other evidence on merger performance

The basic premise of the advocates of the market for corporate control is that commercial competition may be unable to ensure that firms utilise their assets economically, and that shareholders are unable to discipline management to ensure compliance with value-maximising activity. Thus, takeover activity is beneficial for shareholders and generic economic performance. Yet Scherer points out that some economies such as Japan, West Germany and the pre-takeover boom US and UK, have all performed admirably despite self-evident separation of ownership and control (Scherer, 1988). An effective market for corporate control is obviously not a necessary condition for economic efficiency. A recent attempt to evaluate the impact of tender offers is reported in Scherer, and the wider impact of all categories of acquisitions in Ravenscraft and Scherer (Ravenscraft and Scherer, 1987; Scherer, 1988). Scherer's work, based on a small sample of 95 takeovers during 1950−76, reveals that the profitability of acquired companies prior to the transfer of ownership was on average 8 per cent less than the industry norms. Post-acquisition profitability of acquired units was also considerably down (23 per cent) on assets not acquired, but this could be largely the effect of accounting adjustments (writing up assets on takeover coupled with the increased resulting depreciation). An alternative efficiency measure of cash flow to sales avoids the accounting problems and revealed an under-performance of 11 per cent which was statistically insignificant. This style of analysis lacks the clear-cut results of event studies but Scherer concludes that, 'the hypothesis that takeovers improve performance is not supported' (Scherer, 1988, p. 76).

8.3.3 *Economic performance of defensive strategies*

If the conclusion based on research evidence is that merger activity promotes economic efficiency, there must be some prior expectation that defensive strategies are undesirable. To the extent that defensive strategies promote an auction, which on average can increase the returns to the target shareholders, they can be seen to be operating in the shareholders' interests. However, a number of takeovers will be deterred and will have an economy-wide disadvantage if takeovers are thought to be wealth-creating. Obviously an auction for the target firm will tend to bid up the final price, but occasionally the aggressor will be dissuaded from continuing and the general increase in the cost of takeovers must deter some potential aggressors from instigating or pursuing takeovers.

Table 8.6 gives Jarrel *et al.*'s list of US defensive strategies in their review of the market effects (Jarrel, Brickley and Netter, 1988). The dilemma apparent here is that shareholders benefit when subject to takeover bids and yet they are prepared to vote in amendments to the firm's constitution which might deter such bids. Possibly, the potential for higher premiums on those bids that go through compensate for the number that fail or are not instigated, but it is also feasible that the decisions are irrational. Some element of influence by management must be expected as management surely gains from deterring takeovers. The evidence is surveyed by Jarrel *et al.* who conclude that 'the general finding, although it is far from conclusive, is that defensive measures that require shareholder voting approval are less likely to be harmful to shareholder wealth than are defensive measures not subject to shareholder approval' (Jarrel, Brickley and Netter, 1988, p. 66). However, it should be noted that (4) and (5) in Table 8.6 appear to be exceptions to this rule.

Conclusion

The management team of the acquiring company which instigates the takeovers is in the market for the right to manage the assets of the acquiree company. While these managers may be driven by selfish motives, the right of shareholders to accept the best offer available and the threat to incumbent management if the share price drifts too low, will act as an inducement to management to act in a wealth-maximising manner.

In this perspective, competition among managerial teams for the right to manage

Table 8.6 Defensive strategies open to US firms

1.	Supermajority amendments *
2.	Fair price amendments *
3.	Dual class capitalisation *
4.	Changes in the state of incorporation *
5.	Reduction in cumulative voting rights *
6.	Litigation by target management
7.	Targeted block share re-purchase (Greenmail)
8.	Poison pills
9.	State anti-takeover amendments

Note: * denotes measures requiring shareholder approval in the US where the research has been conducted.
Source: Jarrel *et al.*, 1988.

resources limits the divergence from shareholder wealth-maximisation by managers and provides the mechanism through which economies of scale or other synergies available from combining or reorganising control and management of corporate resources are realised (Jensen and Ruback, 1983, p. 7).

The evidence on the impact of takeover activity is mixed. In general US results suggest that an overall gain results from the average merger, though most of this gain accrues to the target shareholders. If the efficient market theory is accepted, this would be interpreted as evidence of gain to the shareholders, though there is insufficient evidence to conclude that these gains are not, at least in part, a redistribution of value from other participants in the firm or from society generally. Furthermore, the existence of gains can be interpreted as evidence that the threat of takeovers is only a poor disciplining device, for if managements were pursuing wealth-maximising management, such gains would only accrue from synergistic reasons.

As regards the UK, the evidence is less convincing as the shareholders of the aggressor company seem to do less well than in the US and there is some evidence that there is an overall loss of shareholders.

8.4 Characteristics of acquired firms

The characteristics of acquired firms are of particular interest, as the identification of the dominant reasons might assist the analyst in identifying firms likely to become takeover targets or to help in identifying desirable candidates for acquisition. Some generalisations can be made from the considerable evidence available and these are listed in Table 8.7. However, the little evidence from the traditional accounting-based measures of efficiency shows that on average more than trivial improvements in efficiency have been achieved. This result could imply either that most mergers do not result in synergistic benefits, or that accounting techniques are unable to measure them.

Some of the most recent evidence on the distinguishing characteristics comes from Benzie whose snapshot survey of 1552 companies in 1985−86 contained 273 firms making acquisitions, contrasted with 135 firms which were acquired during 1985−87 (Benzie, 1988).

Table 8.7 Differences between acquiring and acquired companies

Size	Few acquired firms were large, in comparison with the total sample. A relatively large number of acquiring firms were large, in comparison with the total sample.
Profitability	Relatively few acquiring companies made losses. Acquiring companies appear to be slightly more profitable than on average. The profitability of acquired companies was similar to that of companies in the total sample.
Income gearing	Acquired companies tended to have lower than average income gearing. A relatively small proportion of both acquired and acquiring companies had high income gearing.
Liquidity	Little difference between acquired firms and the total sample. Acquiring companies less likely than on average to be ill-liquid.

Notes: The estimates for the characteristics examined were: size = gross fixed assets; profitability = trading profits as a proportion of gross fixed assets; income gearing = total interest charges as a proportion of post-tax profit; liquidity = total cash and equivalent as a proportion of gross fixed assets. *Source:* From Table C, Benzie, 1988, p. 81.

Singh in his extensive, though now dated, study of merger activity in the UK, sought to investigate the 'nature of the selection process on the stock market, as represented by the take-over mechanism, and the nature and degree of stock market discipline implied by this process' (Singh, 1975, p. 45). The sample was examined on ten criteria as set out in Table 8.8.

The first four variables measure the performance of the firm and the fifth and sixth the structure of the firm. The retention ratio is a measure of the dividend policy, while size and growth are self-explanatory. The valuation ratio, which is market value of equity divided by the book value, is based on the work of Marris and it is argued that this will subsume the other variables capturing the value of the assets, albeit imperfectly, and the market's expectations of the use to which the assets will be put (Marris, 1963). When assessing the importance of these variables it will be necessary to recall that they capture both the causal factors of takeover and the ease with which the stock market can effect the takeover.

The results are difficult to summarise given that they cover ten variables, five industries and two time periods. In general, Singh notes (pp. 58−9) that 60−65 per cent of target firms have lower rates of return, growth rates and valuation ratios; that 60 per cent of target firms were smaller than on average; that retention ratios were higher in target firms though liquidity and gearing ratios were indistinguishable; and whereas these factors were statistically significant, 'there is, however, a very large degree of overlap between the two groups, so that the ability of these variables to usefully discriminate between them on a univariate basis is very small' (Singh, 1975, p. 80).

Singh accepts that the univariate nature of the tests implies that no reliable conclusions can be drawn about the market's ability to discipline management, though he refers to the expectation that Marris' valuation ratio has been postulated as an all-in measure of the inefficient management of a firm's assets. This measure, together with the other variables, exhibits considerable overlap and is only a weak indicator. It may be a mistake to read too much into this as the denominator of the ratio, the historic cost value of equity, is a notoriously unreliable indicator of the replacement value of the assets employed.

Table 8.8 Possible determinants of takeover activity

Pre-tax rate of return on net assets
Post-tax rate of return on equity assets
Dividend return (gross of tax) on equity assets
Pre-tax 'productive' rate of return
Liquidity ratio (stock measure)
Gearing (stock measure)
Retention ratio
Size
Growth of net assets
Valuation ratio

Source: Singh, 1975.

The limited but apparent difference between taken-over and other firms encourages development of multivariate models. It must be admitted that the univariate results are not as encouraging as with other uses of financial discrimination such as bankruptcy. However, the possibility of ratios which are ineffectual when considered independently but effective in combination, suggests that multivariate examinations should be investigated.

Singh uses discriminant analysis on all companies in his sample for each industry sector, but is unable to present discriminant functions which are statistically significant. However, the valuation ratio was omitted from the test, and no pooling of the data was performed to enable general conclusions. By producing a restricted sample for which both valuation ratios and matched acquired and other firms are available, it is possible to pool the data enabling some generalisation and the use of the valuation ratio which was *a priori* credited with the greatest explanatory power. Some improvement was found, but in general the discriminant functions were still unable to reject the null hypothesis that the two groups of companies were from the same population for most sub-samples. However, 'it is important to note that for data appropriately pooled across industries and time periods, the null hypothesis is rejected at the 5 per cent level for firms' short-term records and at the 10 per cent level for their long-term records' (Singh, 1975, p. 121). While this offers some encouragement for later work, possibly using more sensitive statistical tests, the discriminant ability is only about 65 per cent. This is similar to univariate discrimination using pre-tax profitability and only a marginal improvement over a random allocation which would achieve 50 per cent.

It is also of interest to examine the determinants of the propensity to acquire other firms through merger activity. Chappell and Cheng examined how the impact of managerial discretion, financial structure and performance, and Tobin's Q affect merger activity. The focal issue of this study is the impact of Tobin's Q, the ratio of the market value of the firm to the replacement cost of the assets. The specification of the variable tested was Q at the preceding year-end expressed as a fraction of average Q over the simple period. Some 260 manufacturing firms were examined for the years 1971−78, and the dependent variable was the assets acquired standardised by the book value of the acquiring firm's assets in the preceding year. The researchers conclude that, 'our results are consistent with the hypothesis that q is a determinant of merger activity' (p. 38), and that 'q affects growth of assets by merger more strongly than by internal growth' (p. 41). Additional evidence available from other independent variables suggested that profitability and growth have positive effects on merger activity while larger firms show a less than proportional increase in acquisitions.

Chappell and Cheng consider a number of explanations for this link between Tobin's Q and merger activity, as follows:

1. It could be the result of market anticipation of the merger inflating the acquiring firm's stock price, hence it is not a causal variable.
2. It is possibly an indicator of the acquiring firm's ability to invest in assets, producing higher returns than the cost of capital. While this should relate to marginal Q, the average Q is thought to perform as an effective indicator.
3. Short-run fluctuations in Q may be seen to indicate temporary over-valuations of the firm's stock which, if management awareness of this state is assumed, would imply that the firm's shares are an economical currency for acquiring firms (Chappell and Cheng, 1984).

It is difficult to disentangle the alternative explanations, but the impact of (2) would seem to apply more appropriately to investments in the firm's own line of business and to be measured by the level of Q rather than the relative level. The tenor of the researchers' conclusion that, 'Tobin's Q ratio signals profitable opportunities for mergers', would seem to favour (3) above (1), but they also note that the statistical results are not conclusive and further work is needed.

8.5   Predicting and exploiting mergers

The ability of researchers to identify merger profiles is potentially valuable if these determinants can be put to effective predictive use. Many studies such as Mandelker, Firth, and Franks, Broyles and Hecht, have demonstrated that there are considerable abnormal returns available to the shareholders of the target firm (Firth, 1980; Franks, Broyles and Hecht, 1977; Mandelker, 1974). Thus, if investors are able to develop a reliable merger prediction model, there may be potential for improving investment performance. However, this must be tested specifically, for the implicit contention is that a semi-strong form of market inefficiency exists. It is conceivable that the market has allowed for the anticipated takeover bid in the price of the shares and the premium experienced when the bid occurs is balanced by the additional price paid for other potential targets which fail to attract a bidder. Therefore, there is no *a priori* case that an inefficiency exists simply because abnormal returns are evidenced in takeovers and takeovers may be predictable.

Results of empirical studies attempting to predict the occurrence of merger activity have been mixed but Dietrich and Sorensen were able to construct a model which appeared to work with some success on the samples examined. They treat the acquisition decision as similar to conventional capital investment decisions, where the size of the expected net present value (NPV) determines the attractiveness of the investment. This, of course, neglects some possible motives for merger, such as management career incentives, and since the indicators of the NPV are determined from the financial attributes of the target firm, other factors will be left unmeasured (for example, synergistic characteristics) or are unquantifiable. Thus, the 'model postulates that the probability that a firm will become a merger target is a function of observable firm characteristics and a random element resulting from unobserved or unmeasurable firm characteristics' (Dietrich and Sorensen, 1984).

The results, estimated on a sample of 24 and 43 non-merged firms for the period 1969–73 were reasonably encouraging, and the estimated equation using only those variables found to be significant was as follows where * indicates that the estimated coefficient is significantly different from zero.

$$\text{Prob.} = -10.84^* - 0.74^* \text{ (PAY) } 11.64^* \text{ (TURN)}$$
$$- 5.74^* \text{ (SIZE) } - 1.33 \text{ (LEV) } + 2.55 \text{ (VOL)} \tag{8.2}$$

The likelihood ratio statistic is 63.83 which is significant at 95 per cent and 89.55 per cent of the sample is correctly classified. The variables are the pay-out ratio, asset turnover, size measured as equity market value, leverage measured as long-term debt divided by total assets, volume of trading in equity stock. Discarded variables were P/E ratio, profit margin, times interest earned, capital expenditure/total assets, and the current ratio. The estimated equation was then tested on a 'holdout' sample of 22 cases, including 6 merged firms, and 20 cases were classified correctly, with 1 merged and 1 unmerged firm wrongly identified. The sample is small and the theoretical link between the NPV of the investment decision and the variables used is not clear cut, but the results are sufficiently encouraging to suggest that the methodology could be developed further. The researchers put their relative success down to the use of logic analysis, rather than the previously conventional discriminant analysis, and the standardising of the ratios for each firm against the industry average, thereby making some allowance for normal inter-industry diversity.

Rege and Belkaoui both investigated the possibility of predicting Canadian takeovers (Belkaoui, 1978; Rege, 1984). Again the researchers found considerable variety in their results, the former noting that, 'the results in summary, suggest that it is not possible to locate take-over targets, either domestic or foreign by using characteristics of taken-over firms based on published accounting information as suggested by some writers' (Rege, 1984, p. 310).

Stevens, and Simkowitz and Monroe, were able to achieve some success in predicting mergers from financial profiles of the target firms (Simkowitz and Monroe, 1971; Stevens, 1973). Wansley, Roenfeldt and Cooley examined the potential for abnormal investment returns from merger prediction. They took a sample of 101 firms that merged during 1973–77 and isolated the abnormal returns for the 30 months prior to the merger using the conventional event study methodology based on the CAPM. The cumulative abnormal returns are similar to those discovered by Mandelker and show a 29.1 per cent abnormal return for the 7 months prior to merger on the 101 firms (Mandelker, 1974; Wansley, Roenfeldt and Cooley, 1983).

Wansley *et al.* then estimated a discriminant analysis profile using 44 merged firms from 1975–76, and an equal random sample from matching years. Their profiles were based on P/E ratios, long-term debt to assets, the natural log of sales, compound growth in sales, and the market value of equity to total assets. They achieved an explanatory power of 75 per cent using the Lachenbruch test, and 69.2 per cent on a subsequent validation sample of 39 merged and non-merged firms for 1977. Another 15 variables were discarded

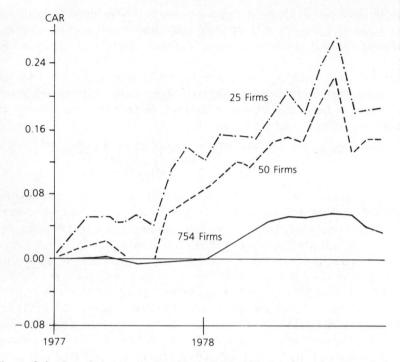

Figure 8.4 Cumulative average residuals for top 25, top 50 and top 754 firms.
(*Source*: Wansley, Roenfeldt and Cooley, 1983, Figure 2.)

and potential users of these techniques may find that, as with bankruptcy prediction, the data-mining approach to estimating these equations fails to produce any agreement on significant variables. Using the original equation based on pre-1977 data, the probability of takeover was computed for all 754 firms with December 1977 year-ends. Allowing a 3-month lag for the dissemination of financial results, the performance of the 25 most likely and the 50 most likely target firms were assessed. Figure 8.4 shows the impressive performance of these portfolios giving a maximum CAR of 28 per cent. These abnormal returns are found to be statistically significant, though only marginally so in the case of the top 50 portfolio.

The results reported above appear to identify a market inefficiency which can be exploited by investors with sufficient resources to perform the necessary research. However, some reservations are in order. Transaction costs would be incurred where the investment requires purchases or sales that would not otherwise occur. The result is as yet unconfirmed by further tests and other apparent market inefficiencies have often seemed less convincing on further examination. The methodology leaves room for doubt especially since P/E ratios and size are included in the discriminant technique, and both these ratios are identified with abnormal returns in other studies. Wansley *et al.* report that the merged firms in the sample have mean P/E ratios of about half that of the non-merged firms and are approximately one-third the size where measured by turnover. The possibility remains that these, or other variables utilised, represent factors incorporated in the market's pricing mechanism and the failure of the CAPM to account for these elements is the root cause of the apparent inefficiency.

8.6 Identifying, valuing and costing mergers

A merger will create a surplus where the two firms are worth more together than apart, but it is only of benefit to the aggressor's shareholders where they can capture some portion of that surplus, as follows:

$$\text{SURPLUS} = \text{VALUE}_{AB} - \text{VALUE}_A \ \text{VALUE}_B$$

$$\text{GAIN}_A \quad = \text{SURPLUS} - \text{GAIN}_B \tag{8.3}$$

$$\text{GAIN}_A \quad = (\text{VALUE}_{AB} - \text{VALUE}_A - \text{VALUE}_B) - (\text{COST} - \text{VALUE}_B)$$

Thus, if firm A has a pre-merger value of £1 million and firm B a pre-merger value of £100,000, and firm A is to pay £200,000 in cash for firm B's shares, the shareholders will only gain to the extent that the post-merger value of AB is greater than £1,200,000. Assuming a post-merger value of £1,250,000 the gain to firm A is as follows:

$$\text{GAIN}_A = 1.25 - 1.0 - 0.1 - 0.2 + 0.1 = \text{£0.05 m} \tag{8.4}$$

There are a few difficulties with this simplistic analysis, namely:

1. Where is the estimate of the post-merger value of AB to come from when the analyst is trying to pre-judge the gains from a merger? An attempt to discount the future cash flows encounters all the normal difficulties of share valuation. Estimates of cash flows and discount rates are required.
2. It is tempting to use current equity market valuations for the pre-merger value of firms A and B, but these market values may already be tainted by expectations of this merger, or more generally by the likelihood of some bid for the target, and also by the expectations of takeover activity by the aggressor.

In general, when assessing the gains from a merger it may be as well to focus on the marginal changes in firm value expected to be captured from the synergies envisaged. Myers explains the rationale for this by suggesting three benefits that might be available from a merger. These are as follows:

1. The ability to utilise otherwise unavailable tax losses which are assumed to have the risk of a debt equivalent.
2. Operating cash flows with normal business risk.
3. Some strategic opportunity, such as growth possibilities, which theoretically might be evaluated as an option.

These three benefits all have associated difficulties in valuing, which range from the manageable in the first instance, through to difficult to guess. However, the valuation of the individual benefits is recommended as preferable to attempting to value the complete post-merger group, as follows:

$$\text{SURPLUS} = \sum_{s=1}^{S} \sum_{t=1}^{T} \frac{\Delta CF_{ts}}{(1+r_s)} \tag{8.5}$$

Where ΔCF_{ts} refers to the incremental cash flow of type s resulting from the merger in time t, and r_s the appropriate discount rate for income stream s (Myers, 1983).

Other possible benefits not explictly mentioned by Myers which should perhaps be brought into the computation are:

1. Unused debt capacity, where debt is presumed to have tax advantages which will affect security prices. The combined unit may be able to increase the level of debt held due to lower risk through diversification.
2. Change in the value of the firm following the lower risk of bankruptcy following the diversification.
3. Changes in the allocation of the firm's value to the various participants.

This computation of the surplus can be converted to an estimate of the gain to the acquiring company by deducting the gain accruing to the target shareholders and the costs of implementing the takeover. Recall though that the pre-merger share price of the acquiree may already incorporate an element of gain, and therefore cost minus target share value will understate the target's gain and consequently overstate the acquiring company's return.

If the takeover is to be financed in part by share exchange, the calculation is not quite as simple as if cash only were used. The temptation is to value the price paid as the number of shares differed at their pre-merger price. The relevant cost is actually the shares at their post-merger price. Using the same example as before it is assumed that firm A has 1,000,000 shares in existence, and offers a further 200,000 in payment, the gain to firm A is then:

$$\text{GAIN}_A = 1.25 - 1.0 - 0.1 - (2/12 \times 1.25) + 0.1 = \pounds 0.4 \text{ m} \tag{8.6}$$

This computation still assumes that the values of both companies prior to the merger are their values as independent organisations and have not been corrupted by expectations concerning the merger.

There is little evidence available regarding the search techniques of potential aggressors when seeking targets. The suspicion is that it is an ad hoc process, and in economies with a limited number of quoted companies this may be sufficiently thorough. However, this would display the normal failings of human search procedures of bounded rationality, limited search and information reduction techniques. No doubt, computer-based search techniques are available and allied with the available data on typical merger targets and the aggressor's desired characteristics, database lists could be produced.

8.7 Accounting for merger activity and holding companies

Accounting for inter-company relationships is a complex area which has to incorporate investments in other companies, which range from trivial trade investments which confer no noticeable level of control, through substantial investments in associated companies which imply substantial influence, through to controlling shareholdings in subsidiaries. It is also one area where there is considerable diversity between national requirements which can hamper any attempt to make transnational comparisons.

8.7.1 *Associated companies and trade investments*

Where an investment in a company confers no effective control and is held as a trade investment for either the short term (current assets) or the long term (fixed assets), there is little problem. The asset is valued at the lower of cost or market value and dividends are taken to the profit and loss account as income. Substantial holdings of this type may require certain additional disclosures. However, where the arrangement is 'effectively that of a partner in a joint venture', or 'having regard to the disposition of other shareholdings', and as such 'the investing group or company is in a position to exercise a significant influence over the company', SSAP1 then calls the equity method into play. In this process no operating details are shown on the investing company's accounts regarding the operating performance of the associated company, but the appropriate share of pre-tax profits and all subsequent adjustments (taxation, extraordinary items and minority interests) will be added to the investing company's income statement. The share of profits (losses) is accounted for by adjustment to the asset value in the balance sheet and dividends received will also adjust the asset value (SSAP1).

8.7.2 *Subsidiaries and group accounts*

When the investment in a subsidiary is sufficiently significant to confer control which is deemed to occur where the holding company:

● is a member of it and controls the composition of its board of directors;
● or holds more than half the nominal value of its equity share capital;
● or the first mentioned company is a subsidiary of any company which is that other's subsidiary (SSAP14).

The accounting requirements of SSAP14 would require the aggregation of all assets, liabilities, revenues and expenses on the rationale that the share ownership may only indicate that the holding company is entitled to a portion of the subsidiary's operations but it has control over the whole. The intra-group transactions such as sales, dividends, loans, investments etc. are cancelled out. The minority's shareholding is valued as the share of the net assets of the subsidiary and disclosed on the balance sheet of the holding company as a liability. A goodwill amount will usually appear to record the surplus paid for the subsidiary over and above the fair value of the net assets. Such goodwill is amortised over some appropriate period as laid down by SSAP22.

Note that the use of control as a decision rule implies that anomalies can be observed. For example, three investments of identical value and return could be disclosed (and aggregated) on the balance sheet at cost, cost plus share of retained profit, and as individual assets, and in the income statement as dividend received, share of profit, and total profit less minority interest.

8.7.3 *Accounting for acquisitions and mergers*

The accounting techniques differentiate between an acquisition where one company purchases another (and this is deemed to occur when more than '10 per cent of the fair value given for equity may be in a form other than equity, such as cash or loan stock'), and a merger where the consideration is basically an exchange of equities.

In acquisition accounting, 'fair values' are to be attributed to the 'separable net assets including identifiable intangibles' and any surplus paid is identified as goodwill and dealt with as per SSAP22. The fair value is the consideration paid for the target on acquisition less the element thought to be for goodwill. This is readily determined where the consideration is cash, but less straightforward where shares or loan capital are involved. This revaluation may occasion additional expenses in the form of amortisation of goodwill and additional depreciation resulting from the revaluing of the asset base. However, the fair value exercise can also be used to set up provisions which, when released, will reduce expenses in later years. In the year of acquisition the revenue results of the acquired company are incorporated only from the date of acquisition, the pre-acquisition reserves are frozen as capital and are not available for distribution.

In the case of a merger where there is only trivial reduction in the fair value of the equity, the new grouping is treated as a simple amalgamation. The assets are not revalued, goodwill (as defined by SSAP22) does not arise, and the results for the year and disclosures regarding prior years are reported as if the two companies or groups had always been merged. Some adjustments to values may occur as the group is required to standardise accounting policies.

Some difficulties arise for the analyst from the availability of alternative techniques, namely:

1. The revaluation of assets under acquisition accounting ensures a structural change in the reported earnings series.
2. The scope for different practices requires the analyst to determine the method and impact of the accounting technique used.

As to whether or not there is any advantage to a firm to choose merger rather than acquisition accounting when it has the option is a moot point. Certainly an effect will be observed on the reported earnings and this can be either positive or negative, but no economic impact should be observable. Tax assessments are unlikely to be affected in either the UK or the US. It is conceivable that management remuneration contracts may be manipulated, but the economic impact of this is unclear. The more recent reservations concerning the accounting for merger activity centre not on the choice of alternatives, but on the failure of either system to define permissible procedures adequately, or to ensure that the impact of the discretion allowed is reported.

8.8   Conclusion

This chapter has reviewed merger activity and allied corporate restructuring behaviour from a number of points of view. What is clear is that while a number of tenable hypotheses emerge which might explain the motives for these activities, little definitive information is available regarding the relative importance of the motives. Certainly the event studies appear to suggest that in general there is an overall gain from mergers, though this is less convincing for the UK. It requires a strong faith in the efficient market to interpret this as unequivocal confirmation that mergers increase wealth, and the dubious returns to acquiring companies provide no clue as to the motives of management. It is also misleading to interpret the benign stock market reaction as an indicator of more widespread social desirability. An increase in shareholders' wealth could be a result of better utilisation of productive assets, but it could also be a reallocation of wealth from other parties. Examples are the workforce members who have their implicit contracts with incumbent management broken, or customers who may face a less competitive market for the products or services they desire. While the event studies present a favourable picture, the direct analysis of changes in efficiency have been much less encouraging. There are difficulties involved with this, not least of which is the problem of disentangling the accounting requirements and opportunities that are available to merging companies.

In the light of the apparent uncertainty about the efficiency of mergers or the rationale for pursuing them, Rappaport (1983, p. 64) suggests that researchers concentrate on the incentives of the individuals who instigate and conduct corporate restructuring.

> I believe that the most promising approach to understanding merger activity is to begin with a model based on the assumption that managers behave as rational actors, pursuing their own economic self-interest, and then link that model to changes in the environmental forces affecting the firm.

For example, he points out that after the stock market decline of the 1970s, managerial incentive plans tended to switch from security price-based plans, to incorporate a greater reliance on accounting numbers, which it has just been pointed out are fundamentally susceptible to manipulation during restructuring.

While little confidence can be drawn from the analysis of economic benefits or the relative importance of variable motives, the empirical evidence enables the analyst to create a viable picture of the characteristics of the average merger. Considerable evidence is available regarding the pattern of share price movement of both the target and the aggressor, and the market reaction of US stocks to defensive manoeuvres is also becoming available. Furthermore, the typical characteristics of the acquiring and acquired are sufficiently well established to allow analysts to construct reasonably descriptive models and even to indulge in prediction. In one instance, researchers found evidence that effective investment strategies might be based on merger prediction models.

--------------------------------- QUESTIONS ---------------------------------

1. Firm A, with 250 million shares in issue and a market capitalisation of £500 million, takes over firm B with a pre-takeover capitalisation of £200 million. The shareholders of firm B received £50 million in cash and 100 million new shares in firm A. The merger is expected to create synergy worth £10 million in year one growing at 8 per cent per annum thereafter. The cost of capital attributable to all income streams is 15 per cent per annum.
    (a) What market capitalisation of firm A would you expect after the merger?
    (b) How much did firm A pay for firm B?

2.   Alpha Plc, with 500 million shares in issue and a market capitalisation of £750 million, is considering Beta Plc as a target for takeover. Beta Plc's present capitalisation is £250 million. The members of the management of Alpha believe that they have identified synergies worth £20 million per year for five years. An appropriate discount rate for the synergistic cash flows is thought to be 15 per cent per annum. If consideration of £300 million is to be paid to Beta's shareholders, how many Alpha shares will have to be issued in full settlement?

3.   It has been suggested that a fund manager's selection of securities is largely a compromise between the need to balance the portfolio and the desire to select prospective takeover targets. Discuss the potential for investment strategies based on merger profiles for funds operating in the EU.

4.   Takeover activity in the UK has been running at unprecedented levels for the last few years. To what extent might this be of benefit to the following?:
    (a) A passive investor.
    (b) An active investor.
    (c) What prospects are there for increased takeover activity in the EU.

5.   (a) Discuss how companies can account for the goodwill arising on acquisitions. Your discussion should include the various alternatives that may be or have been adopted by companies which do not have large reserves.
    (b) Discuss the consequences of the October 1987 stock market crash on mergers and takeovers in the UK (Society of Investment Analysts, *Interpretation of Accounts and Corporate Finance*, June 1988)

6.   Examine the circumstances of a recently completed takeover and schedule the significant dates and share price movements.
    (a) What were the stated reasons behind the takeover initiative and do these seem to be valid motivations?
    (b) Did the market react to any significant events during the takeover and what was the market sentiment regarding the prospects for the target firm's shareholders and the aggressor firm's shareholders?
    (c) How much did the acquiring firm pay for the acquired and does the market value the combined firm at a higher capitalisation than the individual firm?
    (d) What significant accounting transactions were made to incorporate the acquired firm into the group and what alternatives were available?

7.   Provide definitions for the following terms as used in this chapter:
    (a) Horizontal merger.
    (b) Associated companies.
    (c) Merger accounting.
    (d) Defensive strategies.
    (e) Bootstrapping.
    (f) Conglomerate.
    (g) Synergy.

References

Alhabshi, S.M. and Rees, W. (1994) The share price reaction to the announcement of European acquisitions and joint ventures by UK firms. Working Paper, University of Strathclyde.

Belkaoui, A. (1978) Financial ratios as predictors of Canadian takeovers, *Journal of Business Finance and Accounting*, Spring, 93–107.

Benzie, R. (1988) Takeover activity in the 1980s, *Bank of England Quarterly Review*, 78–85.

Byrne, A. and Rees, W. (1994) Initial public offers in the United Kingdom. Chartered Association of Certified Accountants, Research Report no. 36, April.

Cakici, N., Hessel, C. and Tandon, K. (1991) Foreign acquisitions in the United States and the effect on shareholder wealth, *Journal of International Financial Management and Accounting*, 3(1), 39–60.

Cebenoyan, A.S., Papaioannou, G.J. and Travlos, N.G. (1992) Foreign takeover activity in the US and wealth effects for target firm shareholders, *Journal of the Financial Management Association*, 21, no.3, Autumn.

Chappell, H. and Cheng, D. (1984) Firms' acquisition decisions and Tobin's q ratio', *Journal of Economics and Business*, February, 29–42.

Conn, R.L. and Connell, F. (1990) International mergers: returns to US and British firms, *Journal of Business Finance and Accounting*, Winter, 689–711.

Dietrich, J. and Sorensen, E. (1984) An application of Logit analysis to prediction of merger targets, *Journal of Business Research*, September, 393–402.

Doukas, J. and Travlos, N.G. (1988) The effect of corporate multinationalism on shareholders' wealth: evidence from international acquisitions, *Journal of Finance*, December, 1161–1175.

Finnerty, J., Owers, J. and Rogers, R. (1986) The valuation impact of joint ventures, *Management International Review*, 26.

Firth, M. (1980) Takeovers, shareholders' returns and the theory of the firm, *Quarterly Journal of Economics*, 235–60.

Franks, J., Broyles, J. and Hecht, M. (1977) An industry study of the profitability of mergers in the United Kingdom, *Journal of Finance*, December, 1513–25.

Gomes-Casseres, B. (1989) Ownership structures of foreign subsidiaries: theory and evidence, *Journal of Economic Behaviour and Organisation*, 11, 1–25.

Harris, R. and Ravenscraft, D. (1991) The role of acquisitions in foreign direct investment: evidence from the US stock market, *Journal of Finance*, Vol XLVI, no.3, July, 825–844.

Hennart, J.F. (1991) The transaction costs theory of joint ventures: an empirical study of Japanese subsidiaries in the United States, *Management Science*, 37, no.4, April, 483–491.

Hladik, K. (1985) *International Joint-Ventures: An Economic Analysis of US Foreign Business Partnerships*, Lexington Books, Lexington, Mass.

Jarrel, G., Brickley, J., and Netter, J. (1988) The market for corporate control: the empirical evidence since 1980, *Journal of Economic Perspectives*, Winter, 49–68.

Jensen, M. (1988) Takeovers: their causes and consequences, *Journal of Economic Perspectives*, Winter, 21–48.

Jensen, M. and Ruback, R. (1983) The market for corporate control: the scientific evidence, *Journal of Financial Economics*, April, 5–50.

Kogut, B. (1990) A study of the life cycle of joint ventures, in Casson, M. (Ed.), *Multinational Corporations*, Edward Elgar, Aldershot.

Lee, I. and Wyatt, S.B. (1990) The effects of international joint ventures on shareholder wealth, *The Financial Review*, 25, no.2, November, 641–649.

Lev, B. (1983) Observations on the merger phenomenon and a review of the evidence, *Midland Corporate Finance Journal*, Winter, 6–28.

Limmack, R.J. (1991) Corporate mergers and shareholder wealth effects: 1977–1986, *Accounting and Business Research*, **21**, no. 83, 239–251.

Lummer, S. and McConnell, J. (1990) Stock valuation effects of international joint ventures, in *Pacific-Basin Capital Markets Research*, (Ed.) S.G. Rhee and R.P. Chang, North Holland, Amsterdam.

Mandelker, G. (1974) Risk and return: the case of merging firms, *Journal of Financial Economics*, December, 303–36.

Marris, R. (1963) A model of the 'managerial' enterprise, *Quarterly Journal of Economics*, May, 185–209.

McConnell, J. and Muscarella, C. (1985) Capital expenditure decisions and market value of the firm, *Journal of Financial Economics*, **14**, 399–422.

McConnell, J. and Nantell, T. (1985) Corporate combinations and common stock returns: the case of joint ventures, *The Journal of Finance*, **40**, no. 2, June, 519–536.

Myers, S. (1983) The evaluation of an acquisition target, *Midland Corporate Finance Journal*, Winter, 39–46.

Rappaport, A. (1983) Programme overview: what we know and don't know about mergers, *Midland Corporate Finance Journal*, Winter, 63–67.

Ravenscraft, D. and Scherer, R. (1987) *Mergers, Sell-offs, and Economic Efficiency*, Brookings Institution, Washington.

Rege, U. (1984) Accounting ratios to locate take-over targets, *Journal of Business Finance and Accounting*, Autumn, 301–11.

Scherer, R. (1988) Corporate takeovers: the efficiency arguments, *Journal of Economic Perspectives*, Winter, 69–82.

Scouller, J. (1987) The United Kingdom merger boom in perspective, *National Westminster Bank Quarterly Review*, May, 14–30.

Simkowitz, M. and Monroe, R. (1971) A discriminant analysis function for conglomerate targets, *Southern Journal of Business*, November, 1–16.

Singh, A. (1975) Takeovers, economic natural selection, and the theory of the firm: evidence from the post-war United Kingdom experience, *Economic Journal*, September, 497–515.

Stevens, D. (1973) Financial characteristics of merged firms: a multivariate analysis, *Journal of Financial and Quantitative Analysis*, March, 149–58.

Wansley, J., Roenfeldt, R. and Cooley, P. (1983) Abnormal returns from merger profiles, *Journal of Financial and Quantitative Analysis*, June, 149–162.

CHAPTER 9

Corporate Failure Prediction and Credit Evaluation

CHAPTER OBJECTIVES

This chapter will:

1   Review the recent history of financial failure in the UK and the development of failure prediction models.

2   Critically assess the usefulness of failure prediction models and the recent developments in this technique.

3   Use the failure prediction decision to illustrate the insights available from the analysis of human information processing.

9.1   Introduction

So far, this text has examined a number of applications of financial analysis and previous chapters have concentrated on the decision needs of investors. However, throughout this text the variety of users of financial information and the diversity of applications of financial analysis have been stressed. In this chapter the focus shifts to the evaluation of the credit-worthiness of borrowers. This is probably the most important function of financial analysis besides equity investment analysis. Avoiding the costs of loan default is of immense significance to banks which provide a considerable proportion of the finance for industry, to those who provide fixed interest finance to business, and to suppliers whose terms of payment commit them to considerable investment in their customers. Apart from these 'investors', the financial stability of firms is of concern to the governmental and quasi-governmental organisations which maintain a watching brief over the activities of businesses with regards to merger activity, industrial policy and liquidity (of the finance sector in particular). The auditors of firms are also interested in the ability of their clients to function as a going concern. Any company which is unlikely to remain a going concern for the foreseeable future and fails to reflect this in the financial statements should be subject to a qualification of the audit report, and auditors failing to ensure this might well be liable to negligence claims.

The actual decision environment, and in particular the information available to the decision-makers, will differ greatly for the various users listed above. However, the basic decision remains the same, namely, will the firm be able to meet its commitments as and when they fall due? This basic similarity in the task provides a justification for the analysis in one chapter of such disparate decision contexts as the corporate lending decision of the clearing banker and the assessment of creditworthiness by industrial suppliers. Despite this similarity it should be remembered throughout that the decision-makers will differ in motivation, training and access to information. Research results which apply to the banker do not necessarily apply to the auditor.

The argument that reliable evaluation of a firm's credit rating is an important function of financial analysis seems self-evident in the light of the preceding comments. Yet, as evidence presented later will show, the 1980s and early 1990s have been a particularly bad period for company liquidations. High interest rates and recession combined to induce a crisis which has only recently begun to abate. During the early 1980s certain sectors of the UK economy, such as small industrial businesses in depressed areas, experienced failure rates as high as 50 per cent over a five-year period. The need for reliable credit evaluation and failure prediction techniques was especially important under these circumstances. However, according to Zavgren (1983, p. 2),

> considerable progress has yet to be made both in understanding the causes of financial distress and in acquiring the ability to predict it.

While this chapter is concerned with the prediction of firms that will experience financial failure, and, in particular, will fail to meet their debts in full, it is not always easy to identify such firms. Many firms that are obviously 'failing' do not become insolvent as they might remain liquid by severe retrenchment. They may also be rescued by other firms or by government intervention. Even when a firm does become insolvent there are various procedures for dealing with this, some of which will be difficult for the outsider to observe and in many cases, particularly with the small firm, they may simply cease trading.

This chapter will concentrate on the techniques for predicting imminent failure. In particular, the scope of utilising financial statements as raw material in distress prediction is examined and the alternatives of univariate and multivariate models are discussed in Sections 9.3 and 9.4. In addition to the basic ratio models, three developments incorporating capital market data, non-financial indicators, and inflation-adjusted accounting information, are examined in Section 9.5. Much of the research available has concentrated on quoted companies, due to the availability of relevant data. However, the increased risk of financial failure amongst smaller firms means that close attention should be paid to the limited amount of evidence available on the predictive ability of models estimated with small firms. This is also examined in Section 9.5. It is perhaps inappropriate to spend much time in examining empirical evidence concerning failure prediction without some consideration of the practice of credit evaluation. The terminology and background of financial failures are discussed in the next section (9.2) and some evidence is presented concerning the credit assessment practices of the clearing banks.

9.2   Financial failure in the UK

Despite the prevalence of 'bankruptcy prediction' studies in the US, in the UK the term bankruptcy applies to individuals and not firms. Insolvency is usually considered to apply to a company if it cannot pay its debts as they fall due, and it is the threat or occurrence of insolvency which is normally the precursor of formal restructuring arrangements. Insolvency could arise from any number of causes and there are numerous classifications of these. Table 9.1 presents one such listing.

Where a firm is displaying some of the characteristics which might lead to insolvency, it may be possible for interested parties to ensure that action is taken to avoid the crisis of insolvency. In particular the firm's bankers, who may well find it difficult to otherwise extricate themselves from involvement, will often attempt to assist the firm's management with the problems faced. Although formal reconstruction of the firm's financing through rescheduling or the conversion of debt to equity is rare because of the bureaucratic difficulties involved, an influential creditor may agree to support the firm while an agreed programme of reorganisation is undertaken under close supervision. The 1985 Insolvency Act introduced formal procedures whereby administration orders could be used to manage this process of reconstruction.

9.2.1   *Historical evidence of financial failure*

The available figures, plotted in Figure 9.1, confirm a considerable increase in liquidations throughout the 1980s when compared with the preceding decade. The year 1987 appears to show a distinct improvement but a reduction of approximately 500 liquidations per quarter may be due to a break in the continuity of the statistics following the introduction of the 1986 Insolvency Act (*British Business*, 1989, p. 26). However, 1988 figures reveal a further drop in the number of insolvencies. The ratio between compulsory and voluntary liquidations over the period 1975–87 averages approximately 3:5.

Table 9.1   Possible causes of insolvency

Low and declining real profitability.
Inappropriate diversification — into unfamiliar industries or not away from declining ones.
Import penetration into the firm's home markets.
Deteriorating financial structures.
Difficulties controlling new or geographically dispersed operations.
Over-trading in relation to the capital base.
Inadequate financial control over contracts.
Inadequate control over working capital.
Failure to eliminate actual or potential loss-making activities.
Adverse changes in contractual arrangements

Source: Based on Bank of England, 1980, p. 430.

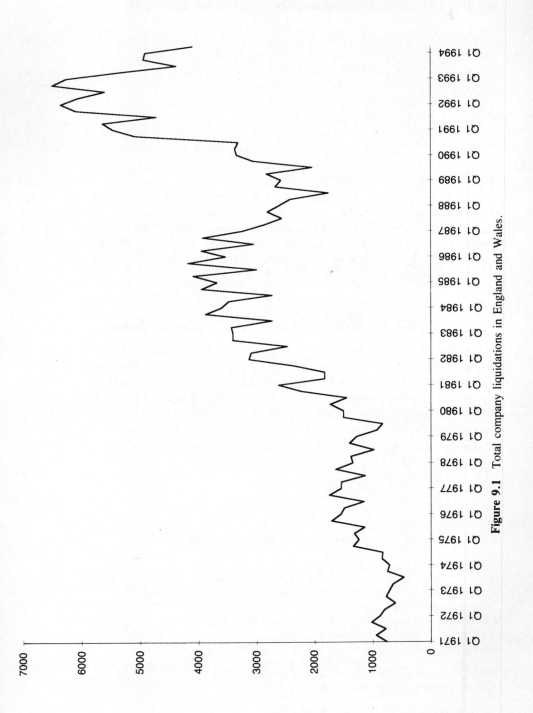

Figure 9.1 Total company liquidations in England and Wales.

Age characteristics of liquidating firms

Based on a sample of firms liquidated during 1978—81, a period just prior to the depression-induced peak of the mid-1980s, Hudson (1987) is able to show that quite clear age structures are apparent. Firms that are wound up through a creditor's voluntary liquidation or a compulsory liquidation are typically two to four years old and fully three-quarters of these firms are less than ten years old. However, firms which are liquidated through a member's voluntary liquidation are considerably older and the age distribution is more even with a modest peak in the late teens. Unfortunately this information could not be linked to the age distribution of the population of firms and no clear-cut conclusions can be derived concerning the propensity of firms of different ages to go into liquidation. Similar generalisations can be made regarding the frequency of financial failure of firms in different industrial sectors.

9.2.2   Information used in credit analysis

When assessing the credit rating of a potential client/customer organisation, there are a variety of information sources available to the decision-maker. Clearly, any evidence of the client/customer's previous record of meeting its obligations would be valuable. This might come from previous dealings between the lender and borrower, information from credit agencies, or from other business contacts who have dealt with the potential client/customer. It is also common practice for firms considering extending trade credit to new customers to seek a bank reference.

The information available on the firm may be informative regarding the ability of the firm to service debts of a given amount, but the probability of failure should also be adjusted for the position of the proposed debt in the borrowing firm's financial structure. If the debt is secured before any other claims on valuable assets, there is less cause to worry than if other debts have prior calls on the assets of the firm. If the debt in question is subordinated to a significant amount by superior claims, a more comprehensive investigation of the credit rating of the firm may be required. Apart from those debts secured by a fixed or floating charge on the assets of the firm, certain debts are specified as preferential by the 1986 Insolvency Act.

The decision-maker may also attempt to analyse publicly available financial information. Ratio analysis of the latest available accounts would be normal practice. Yet the period between the date of the latest set of accounts and the credit decision is a serious problem.

The financial markets may be a valuable source of further information. Share prices are dependent on the market's assessment of the growth and investment risk attached to future dividends, but this clearly includes the possibility of bankruptcy. Thus although the share price is influenced by other factors, it may still be valuable as a predictor of failure, and a sharp fall in the share price or unusual market-based ratios might be viewed as a warning. More directly relevant to the loan decision is the credit rating of fixed interest securities, and in particular corporate debentures. For a long time US firms have been able to look up ratings of corporate bonds issued by half a dozen organisations such as

Moodys or Standard and Poor. In general, such a comprehensive service is not available to firms operating outside the US but the coverage of firms outside the US is expanding rapidly. Foster (1986) reports that Canadian, Australian, Japanese and British investors all have access to at least one service, and the development of the Eurobond market has encouraged the development of such services. Even without the direct assessment of credit risk available from a commercial organisation, it would still be possible to compute the yield to redemption implicit in current prices of bonds and to compare these with other bonds in the same currency of similar coupon and duration. If a bond A exhibits a higher yield to redemption than bond B, despite being similar in all other aspects it is a reasonable presumption that firm A is considered a worse credit risk than firm B. The prime difficulty here is the absence of a liquid market for most corporate debentures. For large issues or for Eurobonds a reasonably reliable price should be readily available.

The industrial, geographical and size characteristics of the client/customer may also be referred to for the credit analysis. Financial failure is not evenly spread throughout an economy and tends to occur more often in small, provincial firms in declining industries. In the UK the most recent recession also hit the capital and surrounding areas. It is clear that a credit analyst cannot turn down a firm simply because it falls into a group of unfavoured categories. It would be wise to look more carefully at such firms than would otherwise be the case. Unfortunately, such a luxury would not be available to another small firm, trading in the provinces and supplying a declining industry.

Survey results from Berry, Citron and Jarvis (1987) provide interesting information about the information requirements of bankers. Although the survey was designed to elicit the differences in information requirements between large and small borrowers to assess the impact of reduced disclosure rules on smaller companies, it provides an insight into the usefulness of financial data which can be compared to the Arnold and Moizer's (1984) and other surveys of investment analysts. The 254 respondents to the survey were branch managers or their equivalent and the principal results can be assessed from Table 9.2.

As always with survey results some scepticism is advisable. In this case, the response rates do not present a sample selection bias but there is always a tendency for participants to respond as they feel is expected, rather than accurately. It can be recalled that similar dependence on accounting data was expressed by investment analysts, yet more detailed studies have tended to put more weight on subject considerations. However 83 per cent of respondents claim always to utilise financial statements and further claim to read the main statements 'thoroughly'. A prima facie case that financial statements are a significant input to the lending decision has been made.

The relevance of these results to more general instances of credit evaluation is also contentious. The bank loan officer has access to information sources within the firm which are not available to less influential business contacts, and these groups, possibly suppliers, may well seek other sources of expert help such as bank references or reports from outside credit agencies. The information available from the stock market may be of considerable interest when examining quoted companies or to evaluate the capital market's sentiment concerning a particular industrial sector.

When the credit analyst has compiled the available information on the client/customer, the decision may often be awkward. There are a number of possibly conflicting indicators, and possibly only limited time to investigate each case. Under these circumstances many

Table 9.2 Sources of information for bank loan decisions

Actual frequency of use:	Always	Often	Rarely or never
Banker's records of prior loans	84	12	4
Audited accounts	83	16	1
Interviews with company personnel*	79	18	3
Interim reports	59	23	18
Memorandum Articles of Association	57	13	30
Register of charges	41	17	42
Visit to company premises*	28	53	19
Information in financial press	19	41	40
Management accounts*	16	55	29
Financial forecasts by borrowers*	15	58	27
Independent valuations*	14	48	38

Notes: Other sources that were always referred to less than 10 per cent of the time were information published by banks' own intelligence units, reports on companies from outside agencies, comparisons with other companies in like industries, minutes of directors' meetings and published government statistics.
* denotes items which were classified as information not available to the public, and others as information available to the lender without recourse to the borrower.
Source: From Tables 1 and 3, Berry, Citron and Jarvis, 1987, p. 24 and p. 26.

firms have developed credit scoring schemes which attempt to weight the different factors and combine them into a single measure of the credit risk of the firm under review. Typically, these schemes have only limited empirical backing, though the experience of the manager designing the scheme may be valuable, and the simple additive schemes normally employed fail to allow for any interrelationship between the variables included. A more sophisticated version of the credit scoring scheme is the empirically-based discriminant analysis, reviewed later in this chapter.

9.3   Distress prediction and financial variables

It is unsurprising that accounting information is valuable for the prediction of corporate failure. A company exhibiting liquidity problems, the inability to earn adequate profits

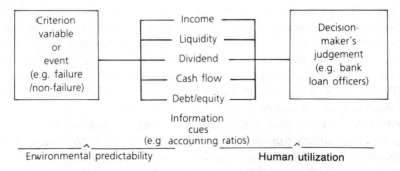

Figure 9.2   Illustration of simple lens model based on banker prediction of failure.
(*Source*: Houghton and Woodliff, 1987, p. 538.)

or to turn those profits into cash flows, or with capital or financing commitments beyond its means, is readily identified as potentially insolvent. Where the Tobin's Q of a firm is less than unity, at least one group would have an incentive to liquidate and that short-term liquidity problems might enable one of those groups, such as the creditors, to insist on insolvency.

Most of the empirical studies described below are wide-ranging searches for any statistically reliable relationship between failure and accounting variables without the benefit of theoretical backing. As such they have been occasionally characterised as 'brute empiricism', but nevertheless have been widely accepted by the commercial world as useful decision tools. Beaver, in one of the earliest empirical studies of the determinants of failure, developed a simple cash flow model of the probability of failure.

The firm is viewed as a reservoir of liquid assets, which is supplied by inflows and drained by outflows. The reservoir serves as a cushion or buffer against variations in the flows. The solvency of the firm can be defined in terms of the probability that the reservoir will be exhausted, at which point the firm will be unable to pay its obligations as they mature (i.e., failure) (Beaver, 1966, p. 80).

The probability of failure is therefore seen as being influenced by the size of the reservoir, the inflows from operations, the magnitude of the expenditures for operations and the burden of debt borne.

9.3.1 *Univariate analysis of corporate failure*

Early and convincing evidence of the usefulness of accounting variables was provided by Beaver, who analysed the trends of seven financial ratios for five years prior to the failure of 79 firms. This was compared with 79 firms matched for industry and size. The plots shown in Figure 9.3 are the equally weighted means for those samples and the distinct differences and clear trends apparent in the ratios suggest that they are potentially useful.

To examine the predictive ability of the ratios more effectively, the sample was divided into two sub-samples and an appropriate cut-off point was selected from the first sample and tested against the second sample for predictive ability. The technique can be illustrated with evidence from Beaver's research. The data given in Table 9.3 show the frequency of net income to total assets in the year before failure for the full sample. A cut-off point can then be chosen for testing against a new 'validation' sample.

An immediate problem is the absence of a clear distinction between the groups. The alternative cut-off points will all involve some element of error. These are known as 'type 1' errors where failed firms are classified as non-failed, and 'type 2' errors where non-failed are classified as failed. The cut-off which minimises the total number of mis-classifications in the estimation sample is 0.00, which suggests 0.177 per cent type 1 errors and 0.038 per cent type 2 errors. However, this may not be the best cut-off point if the costs of making type 1 and type 2 errors are not the same.

The total mis-classification percentage is calculated as follows. If, for example, it is presumed that a validation sample of 50 failed and 50 non-failed firms have 45 readings below the cut-off, two of which have not failed, and seven above the mark have failed, the 'confusion matrix' shown in Table 9.4 can be constructed. This suggests a 9 per cent mis-classifications rate. The actual results achieved by Beaver are shown in Table 9.5.

Table 9.3 Frequency distributions class intervals for net income to total assets

	Failed	Non-failed	Errors %*
Below −0.25	0.227		38.6
−0.25 to −0.20	0.089		34.2
−0.20 to −0.15	0.127		27.8
−0.15 to −0.10	0.076		24.0
−0.10 to −0.05	0.102		18.9
−0.05 to 0.00	0.202	0.038	10.7
0.00 to 0.05	0.152	0.367	21.4
0.05 to 0.10	0.025	0.418	41.1
0.10 to 0.15		0.140	48.1
0.15 to 0.20		0.025	49.4
0.20 to 0.215		0.013	50.0

Note: * denotes that the percentage error is calculated assuming an equal number of failed and survived companies and that the cut-off point is at the higher end of the frequency band.
Source: From Beaver, 1966, Table A-7, p. 110.

These results are impressive but a series of problems arise nevertheless, as follows:

1. The loss function to a decision-maker of a type 1 and a type 2 error is unlikely to be the same. The identification of a safe company as a potential failure will presumably lose the decision-maker's company the profits it would have made in dealings with the client firm. However, the identification of a failing company as safe could lose the decision-maker the full value of any trade or loan. There is some evidence to suggest that type 1 errors in bank loan decisions are approximately 35 times more costly than

Table 9.4 Hypothetical mis-classifications (confusion) matrix

Actual	Failed	Non-failed
Prediction		
Failed	43	2
Non-failed	7	48

Table 9.5 Percentage of firms mis-classified by univariate analysis

Ratio	Years before failure				
	1	2	3	4	5
Cashflow/total debt	13	21	23	24	22
Net income/total assets	13	20	23	29	28
Total debt/total assets	19	25	34	27	28
Working capital/total assets	24	34	33	45	41
Current ratio	20	32	36	38	45
No-credit interval	23	38	43	38	37
Total assets	38	42	45	49	47

Source: From Beaver, 1966.

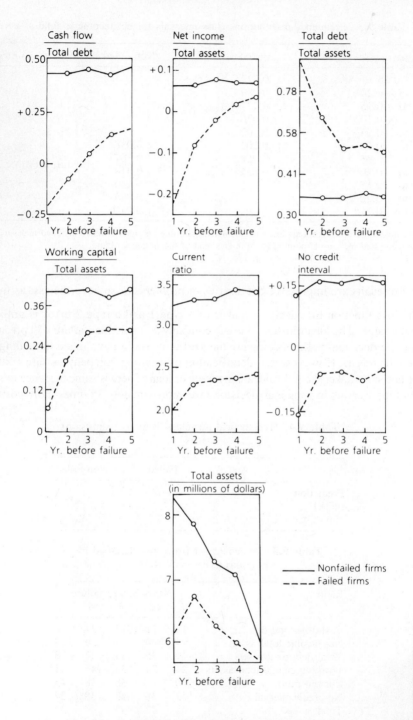

Figure 9.3 Profile analysis, comparison of mean values.

Table 9.6 Hypothetical mis-classifications matrix using realistic probabilities of failure

Actual	Failed	Non-failed
Prediction		
Failed	43	2
Non-failed	70	480

type 2 errors (Altman, Haldeman, and Narayanan, 1977). Returning to the example from Beaver's research in Table 9.3, the decision-maker may therefore prefer to select 0.10 as the cut-off point. Although this greatly increases the chance of mis-classifications it is less likely that these will be type 1.

2. Further difficulties arise where, as would be expected, there are many more secure than failing companies. Thus if the results for the example validation sample were 45 failure predictions of which two did not fail, and 550 non-failure predictions of which 70 failed, the confusion matrix suggests a total mis-classification of 12.1 per cent and a rather different and more worrying profile of the relative frequency of type 1 and type 2 errors (see Table 9.6). Thus, the accuracy of reported results is only applicable to the circumstances in which a decision-maker would wish to use the model if the proportion of failed to survived companies in the sample is realistic.

3. Any such analysis of failure prediction encounters a problem in identifying failed firms. While in some circumstances companies will undergo clear cases of insolvency, especially smaller organisations, in many other instances a firm heading for failure will, either by severe rationalisation, government intervention or takeover by a more successful company, avoid such an indignity. In these latter cases it may be difficult to identify failing or surviving firms. The researcher's discretion will then have to be used which may impact on the reliability of the results. This is further complicated by the time span during which failure may occur. For example, a prediction technique might identify a firm as a failure but it may be able to 'hang on' beyond the completion date of the research study and thereby would be classified as surviving.

4. The selection of ratios incorporated into the test is also problematic. A ratio may be widely used but not necessarily useful for the particular problem. As noted, Beaver discussed briefly a theoretical framework for failure prediction, but the ratios used were also influenced by their popularity in the literature and they are not obviously determined by the postulated theory. Furthermore, Zavgren (1983) suggests that it is the popular ratios which may be most susceptible to window dressing by the management of a troubled firm.

5. Finally, the test used by Beaver is univariate. Failure could come from a number of causes measured by separate ratios, so it is possible that a multivariate model will out-perform this simpler specification. Indeed, it is probable that some ratios will be meaningless without the information contained in others.

Despite these problems, the work of Beaver is encouraging. Not only do all the ratios tested exhibit some degree of predictive ability, but also the more successful ones appear to be able to discriminate well in advance of the failure date. This is important as it is of little help for the last set of financial statements to identify a failing company when those statements are issued after or only shortly before the crash.

The evidence cited above refers to US companies during the period 1954−64 and has little relevance to current events, yet the vast numbers of subsequent studies appear to confirm that ratios can usually be used to predict bankruptcy successfully. This does not apply to all ratios, and no doubt the appropriate cut-off points vary considerably over time, industries and countries. Some generalisations regarding the ratios used are of interest. Strangely, the liquidity position ratios are often ineffective as are asset turnover measures, leaving rates of return and gearing measures as more usually reliable. In addition, analysis of the variability of earnings and stock market returns, or trends of earnings or stock market returns, have proved valuable.

9.4 Multivariate models of distress prediction

If financial ratios can discriminate individually between successful and failing firms, then there may well be scope for more accurate predictions by combining these ratios. Financial distress could arise for a number of different reasons and these may be measured by different variables. For example, the presence of a respectable financial leverage statistic does not imply that inadequate profitability will not strike down a firm. Conversely, it may well be possible for a firm to survive on a narrow margin due to its ability to achieve a high level of turnover on its assets.

Most of the early work on multivariate modelling of distress prediction utilised the statistical technique of 'discriminant analysis'. In this procedure a linear equation is estimated which produces an individual 'Z-score'. This is simply a composite ratio with the most effective weights such that the dispersion of Z is minimised for each category (failed and survived), and the distance between the mean Z for each group is maximised thereby reducing the chance of any overlap. Thus, the resulting equation combines and weights the included variables in such a way as to maximise its ability to discriminate between groups. This technique can categorise a sample into two or more groups and can use many independent variables. However, classification into more than two groups or using more than two variables uses an iterative process which requires computer facilities. A simple calculation is available when two categories are required and two variables used.

9.4.1 *Example discriminant procedure*

An example of the estimation of a simple two variables and two groups model is given below. This example uses the quick ratio and profitability to attempt to classify correctly ten failed and ten surviving firms. If the firms are plotted on these two dimensions, it can be seen that there is no clear distinction between the two groups (see Figure 9.4 and Table 9.7).

The discriminant score is calculated using equation (9.1) and the coefficients for equation (9.1) are derived from equations (9.2) and (9.3):

$$Z_i = X_1 a_i + X_2 b_i \tag{9.1}$$

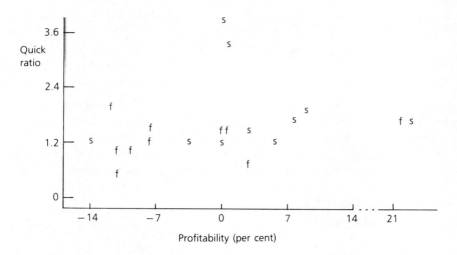

Figure 9.4 Bivariate distribution of failed (f) and surviving (s) firms.

Table 9.7 Example discriminant analysis using the quick ratio and profitability to describe failed and surviving firms

| | Failed companies | | | Surviving companies | |
Quick	Profit %	Z-score	Quick	Profit %	Z-score
1.81	−12%	1.25	3.33	1%	3.40
1.58	22%	2.63	1.65	8%	2.04
0.95	−10%	0.48	1.30	6%	1.59
0.48	−11%	−0.03	1.86	9%	2.30
0.86	−11%	0.34	1.17	−3%	1.04
1.33	1%	1.37	3.75	0%	3.77
1.34	0%	1.35	1.30	1%	1.36
1.17	−7%	0.85	1.57	23%	2.67
0.81	3%	0.96	1.43	3%	1.58
1.33	8%	0.96	1.19	−13%	0.59
Means					
1.17	3.3%	1.02	1.85	3.5%	2.13

Variance $s2q = 0.599\ s2p = 104.83$
Covariance $sqp = 1.815$
Difference $dq = 0.689\ dp = 6.8$

$$X_q = \frac{(104.83 \times 9.689) - (1.815 \times 6.8)}{(0.559 \times 104.83) - (1.815^2)} = 1.006$$

$$X_p = \frac{(0.599 \times 6.8) - (1.815 \times 0.689)}{(0.599 \times 104.83) - (1.815^2)} = 0.047$$

$$Z = (1.006 \times Xq) + (0.047 X_p)$$

Note: This information is taken from the dataset at the end of this chapter. I am grateful to Keasey and Watson for permission to use the examples from their research (Keasey and Watson, 1986).

$$X_1 = \frac{\sigma_b^2 \cdot d_a - \sigma_{ab} \cdot d_b}{\sigma_a^2 \cdot \sigma_b^2 - \sigma_{ab} \cdot \sigma_{ab}} \qquad (9.2)$$

$$X_2 = \frac{\sigma_a^2 \cdot d_b - \sigma_{ab} \cdot d_a}{\sigma_a^2 \cdot \sigma_b^2 - \sigma_{ab} \cdot \sigma_{ab}} \qquad (9.3)$$

where d is the distance between the mean value for the subscript variable for each of the groups in question, σ^2 is the variance of the subscript variable for the full sample, and σ_{ab} is the covariance between the variables for the full sample.

As with univariate analysis the selection of the cut-off point is subjective, and the estimation of the discriminant function should be tested on a validation sample. For example, if the estimation sample used a cut off Z-score of 1.45, this would result in four mis-classifications (see Figure 9.5).

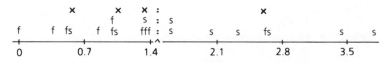

Figure 9.5 Distribution of sample on Z-score axis. X = mis-classified cases.

In this example, the univariate measures appear to be able to classify correctly 15 readings at best. An alternative technique sometimes employed is to select two values for Z where all readings below the lower value are classified into one group and all those above the higher into the other. Intervening readings fall into a 'zone of ignorance'. Table 9.8 gives a computer-based analysis of the same data using a slightly different methodology.

Most early examples of discriminant analysis, such as Altman (1968), estimated an equation of the form below:

$$Z = 0.012X_1 + 0.014X_2 + 0.33X_3 + 0.006X_4 = 0.999X_5 \qquad (9.4)$$

where: X_1 = working capital/total assets
$\quad\quad X_2$ = retained earnings/total assets
$\quad\quad X_3$ = earnings before interest and taxes/total assets
$\quad\quad X_4$ = market value equity/book value of total debt
$\quad\quad X_5$ = sales/total assets
$\quad\quad Z$ = overall index.

This equation was estimated using data from 1946−65 on 33 pairs of failed and surviving firms matched for industry and size. The set of variables remaining in the discriminant equation comprises the sub-set of 22 tested ratios which give the most efficient discriminant function. Some of the variables excluded were individually better predictors than some included ratios. The resulting confusion matrix is shown in Table 9.9. The overall error rate for the validation sample is 16.5 per cent which generally out-performs Beaver's univariate analysis, although the predictive ability of Altman's equation decayed rapidly when the prediction horizon was extended beyond one year. Altman was unable to discriminate as accurately when the horizon was greater than two years (28 per cent mis-

Table 9.8 Computer-based discriminant analysis of failed and survived groups

A computer-based analysis of the same problem produces results which achieve the same number of mis-classifications but provide additional information.

The summary classification reports the confusion matrix and predictive ability. Group 1 are failures and group 2 survivors.

Put into group	True group 1	2
1	9	3
2	1	7
Total N	10	10
N correct	9	7
Proportion correct	0.900	0.700

$N = 20$ Number correct $= 16$ Proportion correct $= 0.800$

Rather than produce a single Z-score function this procedure estimates an equation for each group. The classification into each category then depends on the closeness of the score to the typical score for that group.

Linear discriminant functions for the groups

Group 1: $= -1.4741 + 2.3904[QR] - 0.0488[P\%]$
Group 2: $= -3.4464 + 3.6921[QR] + 0.0126[P\%t]$

The summary of mis-classified observations produces a useful probability estimate of the likelihood of each reading fitting into either of the groups. Thus it can be seen that for observation 17 of the classification into group 1 [failed] was equivocal with an almost equal chance of classification into group 2.

	True group	Predicted group		Distance	Probability
2	1	2	1	6.675	0.193
			2	3.808	0.807
15	2	1	1	0.00093	0.653
			2	1.26765	0.347
17	2	1	1	0.2121	0.554
			2	0.6497	0.446
20	2	1	1	0.9765	0.772
			2	3.4179	0.228

classifications) prior to bankruptcy, whereas Beaver was able to show some predictive power up to five years before (Altman, 1968; Beaver, 1966).

Some remaining problems with Altman's study are as follows:

1.   The variables were chosen for their impact on the efficiency of the discriminant equation, rather than from any underlying theory, and they exhibit a considerable sample dependence. Highly correlated variables which were excluded were able to produce a discriminant equation which was equally as effective as the equation employed. Whereas Altman has reduced the deficiency of Beaver's univariate study,

Table 9.9 Classificatory accuracy for Altman's 1966
study

Actual	Failed	Survived
Predicted		
Failed	24 [31]	1 [1]
Survived	14 [2]	52 [32]

Notes: The figures in brackets are from the estimation sample
and the remaining results are from the validation sample. In the
case of the surviving validation sample the firms are all ones
that were experiencing financial difficulties.
Source: Altman, 1966.

there is no assurance available that all significance variables have been included in
this analysis, nor that they have been weighted in appropriate ways. Subsequent
research attempted quadratic rather than linear formulations (Altman *et al.*, 1977)
and allowed for the trend of the variable rather than simply measuring the value
(Edminster, 1972).

2. The samples used were not random but were matched for industry and size which
    is a useful method of controlling for these variables. However, this contravenes the
    basic assumptions of discriminant analysis which specifies random samples from
    independent populations. The matching procedure should require more complex
    statistical procedures than those utilised. The statistical tests also assume that the
    samples are multivariate normal but no evidence of this is presented, and Chapter
    3 suggested that even univariate normality would be unusual.

3. The prior probabilities of failure and survival are assumed to be equal for failed and
    surviving firms, and the different costs of type 1 and type 2 errors are not allowed
    for when assessing the performance of the model.

4. The definition of a failed firm is difficult and Altman used firms filing under 'Chapter
    10'. It is not clear that failed firms might not have proceeded through 'Chapter 11'
    procedures or undergone any other of a number of reconstructions.

5. The variables incorporated in the classification equation are based on accounting values.
    They are therefore imperfect estimates of the underlying characteristic they purport
    to measure. Where the sample studied crosses industrial, national or even size
    boundaries, it may be that the error in the measured variables is systematic, producing
    a bias in the results.

Despite these reservations the innovative approach introduced by Altman was imitated
widely, and has led to a series of empirical work. Although having detractors this has
led to further developments in the practice of credit evaluation.

Despite its theoretical problems, the basic technique has proved quite robust. While
improvements in the dataset and statistical techniques used in subsequent research refined
the techniques, they did not alter significantly the conclusions reached (Altman, Haldeman
and Narayanan, 1977; Deakin, 1972; Diamond, 1976; and Ohlson, 1980). For example,

Deakin reverted to the original ratios tested by Beaver and incorporated a random, rather than matched, sample of surviving firms. The resulting discriminant equation out-performed the classificatory accuracy Altman had achieved and was able to discriminate effectively up to three years in advance of failure. However, when tested against a validation sample, the results showed some inconsistency suggesting that there was considerable instability in the estimated model. This would be expected where the results are sample specific. Altman, Haldeman and Narayanan developed Altman's earlier work by refining the accounting data carefully to standards for some of the discretionary reporting practices and alternative financial strategies. This included capitalising leases, consolidating subsidiaries, transferring deferred expenditure to expenses and contingency reserves to equity. In addition a more appropriate 'quadratic classifier' was substituted for the linear relationship previously used. While these improvements were theoretically sound, though still leaving room for development, the results were no more impressive than the earlier work. Indeed, the linear classifier achieved lower error rates than its quadratic competitor.

Zavgren notes that amongst the many examples she reviewed, Diamond's (1976) study represents the most advanced of those using discriminant analysis. Yet, such refinements in technique and meticulous adherence to statistical assumptions have failed to produce a significant improvement in predictive accuracy (Zavgren, 1983, p. 23). This might be interpreted as suggesting that this technique has reached the practical limit of its development.

9.4.2 UK evidence of failure prediction

Perhaps the UK's most active advocate of the Z-score style of failure prediction models is Taffler. His research includes a sample of firms selected as being at risk using the conventional methodology, the accuracy of which was retrospectively reviewed (Taffler, 1983). This model was estimated on 46 quoted companies that failed between 1969 and 1976, and a matched and edited non-failed group of quoted companies. The resulting discriminant equation was:

$$Z = C_0 + C_1 \text{ return} + C_2 \text{ working capital} + C_3 \text{ financial risk} + C_4 \text{ liquidity}$$

Taffler (1983) assessed the contribution of the variables to the model as 53, 13, 18 and 16 per cent respectively. The equation then classified 115 out of the 825 quoted industrial companies available on the database as at risk. Over the next four years '35 per cent had gone bankrupt or experienced events that approximate economically to insolvency and a further 27 per cent were still at risk'. The researcher concludes that the model exhibits 'true predictive ability in a statistical sense because the probability of an at risk firm subsequently failing within a year was about six times as great as for a firm selected at random'. It is clear that the model did exhibit some predictive ability. It is less obvious whether the model is valuable or not. Some estimate of the loss function of type 1 and type 2 errors would be required, but as well as 44 of the original 115 at risk companies surviving the four years, and one not at risk company failing, there is the practical problem for a lending institution when between 11 and 21 per cent of its potential customers are classified as at risk over the years 1973–80.

9.4.3 *Conditional probability models*

The primary development in prediction techniques since the late 1970s is the use of conditional probability models to replace the discriminant analysis technique. The logit or probit techniques estimate the probability of occurrence of a result, rather than producing a dichotomous analysis of fail/survive as is the norm with basic discriminant techniques. This is thought to fit more appropriately with the needs of the decision-maker who will often have to contend with firms that are less than healthy but not certain failures. The discriminant technique can produce probability results, as shown in Table 9.8 but these are less convenient or reliable than the conditional probability models.

Ohlson, using conditional probability methods, illustrated the fragility of the results when he used a sample with a prior probability of failure that approximated to reality. The estimated equation achieved a mis-classification of 3.88 per cent, whereas a naive model assuming no failures would have only been wrong in 4.95 per cent of the cases. Furthermore, the overall results for this conditional probability model were no apparent improvement on discriminant techniques despite the reasons for supposing logit techniques to be a superior specification (Ohlson, 1980). Zavgren reports in summary an attempt to improve on Ohlsen's results and to determine the relative importance of various financial indicators. The results again showed no noticeable improvement over earlier research (Zavgren, 1983).

9.4.4 *Difficulties of failure prediction models*

While considerable success has been claimed for many failure prediction models, Foster (1986, pp. 556−60) notes that: 'the absence of an economic underpinning to modelling

Table 9.10 Summarised results concerning empirical prediction models

	One year predictive ability	Sample details	Ratios included	Estimation technique
Beaver	[13] 10	79 —	6	MDA
Altman	[27] 5	33 [46−65]	5	MDA
Deakin	[22] 3	32 [64−70]	14	MDA
Edminster	— 7	42 [58−65]	6	MDA
Diamond	[9] —	75 [70−75]	23	MDA
Wilcox	— 6	— —	—	MDA
Blum	[5] 7	115 [54−68]	8	MDA
Altman	[7] 9			MDA
Ohlsen	15	105 [70−76]	7	CPM
Zavgren	18	45 [72−78]	7	CPM

Notes: CPM = conditional probability model; MDA = multiple discriminant analysis; results in brackets are percentage mis-classifications from a holdout sample and other results are mis-classifications on the estimation sample; the sample refers to the number of cases used for estimation; and the years over which the sample was extracted are in brackets.
Source: From Zavgren, 1983, Table 1 [pp. 4−5] and Table 2 [pp. 6−7].

in this area has led to trenchant criticism of research on financial distress', but concludes that 'the major contribution of this research to date is documenting empirical regularities. This documentation is important both for decision-making by creditors and management and to researchers wishing to model economic aspects of financial distress.' Nevertheless, certain caveats must be borne in mind, as follows:

1. Typically this research has been conducted on matched samples for industry and size, even though the failure rate for companies differs markedly over both of the variables which have been excluded from the analysis. Thus, while the models may perform better than chance, do they out-perform a simple analysis extrapolating sector and size characteristics from past performance, and would statistically significant variables remain important if these two characteristics were included in the model?

2. The value, rather than the accuracy, of the models used is extremely difficult to assess. Realistic costings of type 1 and type 2 errors have to be assessed, together with the frequency of these errors, compared with their frequency under alternative credit management systems. In the discussion of the research evidence given above, predictive power has normally been assessed in comparison with a naive model. In fact, the alternative to discriminant analysis is more probably a traditional credit management system, based on the experience and intuition of the managers involved. Finally, the cost of setting up and administering the system is relevant.

3. The precise specification of the model will be sample-specific, dependent on the particular characteristics of the sample chosen, the other variables entered into the model, and the prediction horizon. Given that the typical research methodology is to seek an effective discriminating model from a large set of variables, with potential for editing the sample, it is unsurprising that some predictive power is observed. Unfortunately, the portability of the estimated model is unknown to the decision-maker. A great deal of care must be exercised by decision-makers when trying to utilise previously estimated failure prediction models or assess the accuracy of such models on validation samples.

The examples cited above either use a validation sub-sample from the sample collected and test the equation on a subsequent sample which will also examine the instability in

Table 9.11 Results from re-estimation of Table 9.10 using cross-validation

	Put into	True group
Group	1	2
1	9	4
2	1	6
Total N	10	10
Number correct	9	6
Proportion correct	0.90	0.60

Notes: $N = 20$; number correct = 15; proportion correct = 0.750; one further reading has now been mis-classified.

the model, or use the Lachenbruch jack-knife method to re-estimate N times for a sample of N with one case missing each time (see Table 9.11).

This is a useful test of the data to discriminate between classifications when the case is independent of the estimation sample. However, it is unconvincing evidence of the predictive power of the procedure. This will require estimation and validation samples that are independent in time as well as in cases (Lachenbruch, 1975).

9.5   Developments of the prediction models

The straightforward development of the empirical base and statistical sophistication of failure prediction models has proved a sterile branch of research. Typically, the model has retained discriminant ability whatever the methodology used, but has exhibited little improvement to reward the efforts of the researchers. In this section some alternative developments are examined. Firstly, the information content of the securities market is reviewed. This is followed by an examination of non-financial indicators of insolvency. The benefits from the refinement of the accounting information using inflation-adjusted figures are assessed, and the relevance of models estimated using large firm data for smaller more failure-prone businesses is reviewed.

9.5.1   *Capital markets and the prediction of failure*

Some of the underlying difficulties of failure prediction models are the lack of relevance, reliability, timeliness and consistency in accounting variables. Accounting numbers are computed by means of a set of rules which are not designed to measure economic characteristics. They are prone to estimation errors, may well be delayed beyond the crucial date and allow considerable scope for alternative specification. When evaluating failure prediction models based on accounting ratios, considerable care can be taken by the researcher to exclude data that would be unavailable to the decision-maker and to standardise accounting techniques. However, an alternative approach ignores the troublesome accounting data and substitutes capital market-based variables. While this precludes the analysis of unquoted companies, the analysis of an industry based on a sample of quoted firms operating in that industry might provide valuable information when generalised to include all firms in an industry.

The underlying assumption implicit in the use of equity market data is that while share prices reflect a wide variety of information relevant to the future cash flows to be expected from a share, a sub-set of that information will be relevant to the likelihood of liquidation and the cash flow impact. Although the share performance will include reactions which are irrelevant to insolvency, if these are random, or not so great as to swamp data relevant to credit analysis, the price movement may still have predictive ability. Early research by Beaver confirmed that small share price movements could be detected as far as five years prior to bankruptcy, but the bulk of the price reaction was in the year before failure (Beaver, 1968b).

Queen and Roll (1987) adopt market-based variables and, in the cavalier spirit of earlier failure prediction results, accept any of the usual market-based variables as potential

Table 9.12 Twenty-three year unfavourable mortality

	1	2	3	4	5	6	7	8	9	10
Size	30.5	26.2	15.2	13.1	13.8	9.0	6.2	6.2	0.7	0.7
Price	43.8	39.5	30.2	24.9	19.0	12.7	10.7	8.3	8.3	6.8
Return	44.9	30.7	21.5	21.0	11.7	13.7	12.2	13.2	16.1	19.5
Variance	11.6	11.7	11.2	11.7	17.1	16.1	21.0	24.4	33.2	46.8
Beta	31.6	21.7	16.3	19.7	15.8	13.8	19.7	18.2	17.2	29.6

Source: Queen and Roll, 1987.

predictors, specifically capitalisation, price, return, variance and beta. In this research the focus was on firm mortality which was sub-divided into favourable (acquired by merger) or unfavourable (bankrupt, suspended from trading or delisted). The evidence reported below will concentrate on the unfavourable aspect. Queen and Roll ranked all CRSP (Center for Research in Share Prices) firms into deciles according to the relevant variable in each year and assessed the cumulative mortality in subsequent years from 1963 to 1985, shown in Table 9.12.

The first four variables in Table 9.12 all display clear predictive ability with the first two showing a monotonic ranking of size and price to unfavourable mortality. In general, the bigger the size, the higher the price and return and the lower the volatility the less likelihood there is of unfavourable mortality. The ability to predict imminent bankruptcy and to combine the variables into multivariate prediction is of interest but Queen and Roll's results suggest that in a multivariate framework beta and price seem to be poor indicators and even return and variance are unconvincing. While this research has not presented its results in a way which is immediately comparable with other cited evidence, it does suggest that there may well be predictive power in market-based variables, and size is such an obviously significant variable that any model excluding this parameter is probably mis-specified.

Earlier work on the value of market-based predictions by Aharony, Jones and Swary (1980) confirmed that market expectations for failing firms indicate such failure well in advance of the event. In general, it is unsurprising that market-based statistics are useful in predicting bankruptcy. Considerable evidence is available, and has been discussed earlier, which suggests that the market is an efficient processor of publicly available information. While market prices reflect a consensus judgement of future earnings, such earnings are likely to be affected by bankruptcy. Thus, the market movements and future failure should be closely related. Insofar as the market can access multiple information sources, process the data in complex manner and pre-empt accounting data, it would be surprising if market indicators could not out-perform accounting-based variables where available. That the market is not omniscient is confirmed by Clark and Weinstein (1983) where the market reaction on the day of bankruptcy filing was an average daily return of −28.5 per cent.

Debt rating

The credit standing of corporate debt quoted on capital markets is also relevant to the credit analysis decision. This could be significant for current investors in that issue, those

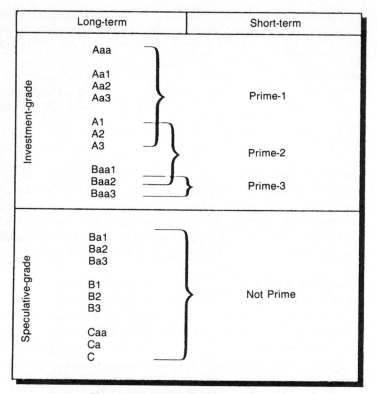

Figure 9.6 Moody's rating system.

considering investment, and other firms which are attempting to assess the general credit rating of the debt-issuing firm. It has already been noted that the cost of debt capital implicit in the bond's current price might be considered a reflection on the riskiness of that debt. Although the debt examined may have advantageous security, it may still provide useful information concerning the credit rating of the firm as a whole.

However, it is simpler for analysts to utilise available credit rating services rather than to perform their own analyses of the risks attached to particular debt issues. While these are not as widely accepted in Europe as in North America, they are gradually developing and in part are stimulated by the lively market for Eurobonds which has attracted the attention of the bond rating agencies. In January 1989 Moody's Investors Service (1989) announced that 'it will now expand its rating activities to encompass long-term fixed-income Eurosecurities of international companies considered important by investors' (*Moody's Credit Opinions*, p. 11). However, at the time of writing the service only covers some 60 UK firms, about half as many French firms, some 20 German and a dozen or so from most other European countries. A description of the rating system is given in Figure 9.6 and an example rating in Figure 9.7.

The advantages of subscribing to such a service are much the same as using a conventional credit rating agency such as Dunn and Bradstreet, rather than performing in-house credit analysis. The advantages are as follows:

Ratings

Category	Moody's Rating
MEPC plc	
Eurobonds	A3
MEPC Finance Inc.	
Gtd. Commercial Paper	P-2
Metropolitan Estate and Property Intl. NV	
Gtd. Euroyen Notes	A3
Gtd. Commercial Paper	P-2

Contacts

Analyst	Phone
Niel Bisset/London	(071) 621-9068
Robert H. Ray/London	
Angela Jameson/New York	(212) 553-1653

Rating History

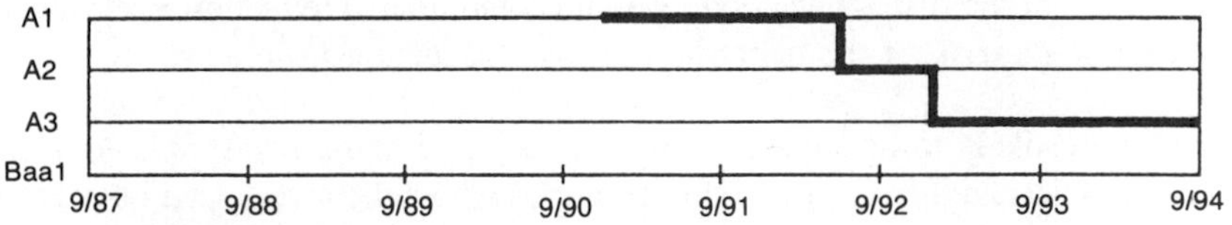

Operating Statistics

MEPC Plc	[1]1993	1992	1991	1990	[2]5-Yr.Avg.
Int. cov (X)	1.6	1.5	1.6	1.8	1.7
RCF % TD	−2.5	8.8	0.6	5.3	3.3
Op. margin (%)	71.6	73.0	74.5	74.9	73.4
ROS (%)	18.9	28.4	37.5	43.7	34.3
ROC (pretax) (%)	7.2	7.2	6.8	5.8	6.4

[1] For the 12 months ended September 30, 1993.   [2] 5-year average 1993–1989

Balance Sheet Statistics

MEPC Plc	[1]1993	1992	1991	1990	[2]5-Yr.Avg.
TD % cap.	33.2	43.9	41.2	32.9	35.6
DIT & min. int. (%)	12.1	5.9	5.1	4.4	6.5
Pfd. stk. (%)	0.1	0.1	0.1	0.1	0.1
Common (%)	54.7	50.1	53.7	62.6	57.9
Tot. cap. (£ bil.)	3.0	3.0	3.7	4.1	[3] −3.1

[1] As of September 30, 1993.   [2] 5-year average 1993–1989.   [3] 5-year compound annual growth rate.

Opinion

Rating Rationale

Moody's rates the long-term debt of MEPC Plc and its wholly owned and fully guaranteed subsidiaries, Metropolitan Estate and Property International N.V., and MEPC Finance Inc. at A3. In addition, we rate the companies at Prime-2 for commercial paper. The ratings are based on our expectation for continued pressure on the group's debt-protection measurements due to expected delays in the recovery of the U.K. property market and the uncertain outlook for the overseas markets in which the group operates. MEPC's recent one-for-five rights issue reinforced its financial strength, helped offset declines in group asset valuations, and eased pressure on the group's asset disposal program.

There are indications that valuations in certain segments of the U.K. property market may have stabilized. However, we remain concerned about the outlook for the market overall and the London office market in particular, which remains characterized by falling rental levels and significant over-supply and where MEPC has a substantial exposure.

MEPC's strategy to increase the proportion of retail properties held will improve its portfolio mix in the longer term, but will have little immediate impact. Our ratings also reflect the high quality of MEPC's properties and the company's strong market position as the second-largest property company in the United Kingdom. In addition, a large proportion of MEPC's U.K. income is secured by leases that expire after the end of the decade, have no break clauses, and have upwards-only rent reviews.

Rating Outlook

The rating outlook is stable. Any strengthening of the markets in which the group operates may have a positive impact on the rating.

Figure 9.7   Example rating.

(*Source:* Moody's Investors Service, Euromarket, Credit Opinions, October 1994.)

1. The commercial service will specialise in debt rating and may have privileged access to relevant information.
2. The collection of data by the rating agency for all bonds analysed is likely to be more cost-effective than occasional information searches by credit analysis.
3. Investment in bonds with good professionally accredited ratings will strengthen the investment managers' case against charges of inappropriate investments by their principals.
4. The investigation by the debt rating agency of the activities of the firm will tend to act as an audit of the firm's behaviour, possibly leading to a reduction in the market's perception of the risk of the debt and thus to a reduction in its cost.

These benefits are likely to be significant particularly where the investor is considering new business contacts with firms from other countries where the investor will have limited experience of the credit environment.

As with conventional credit analysis, the rating attached to a debt may be based upon fundamental analysis of the firm, or a quantitative discriminant model, or a combination of both. Despite the cost of setting up a discriminant model, most debt rating agencies will place some reliance on statistical models. The results of such a model might be used as a first estimate by the rating analyst, to identify ratings which are inconsistent with the underlying dataset and should be double-checked to ensure that analysts attach realistic weights to the data analysed.

The process can also be reversed. Rather than use the quantitative analysis to produce the rating, ratings produced independently might be explained by this model. This might be useful for extending the model to other debt issues not rated by the service, for discovering the information set and relative weights attached used by the expert analysts, also for assessing the relative importance of information sources and possibly for regulating or improving financial disclosure.

The analysis of debt rating lends itself readily to academic analysis and a host of studies have been spawned. (For example, see Belkaoui, 1983; Horrigan, 1966; Kaplan and Urwitz, 1979; and Pinches and Mingo, 1973.) Where the task is to describe the ability of a set of data to explain the ratings awarded to a sample of bonds, the task is somewhat easier than failure prediction. There is little difficulty in defining the groups into which the bonds fall and there is no obvious problem with the distribution of each group, whereas most failure prediction models used unrealistic matched samples. However, the other difficulties of failure prediction remain. These include problems with the choice of variables to include in the study, difficulties with choosing cut-off points between the groups, and inadequate information regarding the weights to attach to errors between different classes.

9.5.2 *Inflation accounting and failure prediction*

It is argued elsewhere in this text that one constructive approach to the problematic choice between alternative accounting measurement systems and accounting policies is to evaluate the predictive ability of the alternatives. In failure prediction we have a clear example where the ability of inflation-adjusted accounting or cash flow measures can be assessed and contrasted with conventional historic cost accounting. To some extent it might be expected that the more economically relevant current cost approach and the liquidity focus of funds or cash flows would produce improved predictions. This could occur where the unconventional measures are added to historic cost variables, but there is also interest in the performance of the new measures where they replace conventional variables. However, available evidence suggests that current cost accounting (CCA) measures are close substitutes for historic cost measures. The income measures from the one system can be estimated from the other with considerable reliability, and when inflation-adjusted accounting ratios are added to a dataset previously containing only historic cost variables no new dimensions are revealed from factor analysis. Much the same can be claimed for funds from operations, but when this is further adapted for changes in working capital to give cash flows from operations some evidence is available to suggest that new information is produced.

Keasey and Watson (1986) examined the predictive power of discriminant analysis techniques on a sample of small UK companies both before and after CCA adjustments. Little evidence could be deduced for any change in the predictive ability of CCA or historic cost accounting numbers. The researchers conclude that 'there is little evidence to suggest that an outside decision-maker, interested in the prediction of failure in small companies, would achieve superior predictions by adjusting the financial statements in line with the recommendations in SSAP 16' (Keasey and Watson, 1968, p. 68). However, they also point out that the user would not be disadvantaged as the two datasets are close substitutes for each other, the inflation adjustments being largely proportional across the sample.

Earlier American research by Norton and Smith into general price level-adjusted accounts and Mensah using specific price level-adjusted data achieved similar results to Keasey and Watson, concluding that there is little difference in using inflation-adjusted accounting data or historic cost data when attempting to predict bankruptcy (Mensah, 1983; Norton and Smith, 1979).

Funds flow information as a predictor of failure has been assessed by Gentry et al. (1987, p. 587) who attempt 'to determine if the pattern of a firm's cash inflows and outflows can differentiate between financially successful and financially failing firms'. Further advantages claimed by the researchers include the circumvention of the ratio choice problem and its associated charge of brute empiricism, by categorising total net funds flows into twelve categories and dividing all by total net flows. Further total net flows were included as a ratio to total assets 'because previous studies have found size to be significant'. However, it appears that a similar total flows approach could be utilised with accrual-based accounting information and a more straightforward size measure might be appropriate. The researchers compare the predictive power of funds flow information with that of seven traditional accounting ratios plus the log of total assets as a size measure.

Using probit analysis, the researchers are able to show that the equation with nine financial ratios and the equation with twelve funds flow ratios both contribute information which significantly improves the classification of failed and non-failed companies. Furthermore, combining the financial and funds flow data significantly improves the discriminating power. While the test is not powerful enough to choose clearly between the alternative measurement methods, the researchers feel able to conclude that, 'financial and credit analysts should benefit from a continuous monitoring of cash based funds flow components over time' (Gentry et al., 1987, p. 605).

Non-standard accounting

Apart from the alternatives of different systems of accounting, there is also scope for choice in the accounting policies adopted. At one level it might be expected that firms experienceing difficulty might feel under pressure to adopt less stringent accounting policies. Hence changes in accounting policies or optimistic accounting policies may be in themselves indicators of impending difficulties. Equally problematically, the differing policies adopted by firms to account for or implement decisions can impinge on the predictive ability of models. Altman, Haldeman and Narayanan (1977) took considerable pains to standardise reporting practices in the samples examined, but failed to improve significantly on the predictive ability experienced by less comprehensive analysis.

9.5.3   *Predicting the failure of small firms, and the use of non-financial indicators*

The basic financial failure procedures described above are less suitable for small companies where financial indicators are less readily available or reliable. The use of equal samples in most of the tests examined above makes it difficult to assess their suitability for failure prediction decisions where the actual performance can be expected to differ greatly from a 50 per cent failure rate. Perhaps the clearest example is the case of firm size. Simply by classifying large firms as non-failed, a decision-maker will quite possibly out-perform a decision model which excludes this variable from its analysis. Thus, the available benefits from classifying large firms are limited as the failure rate is low, whereas in the small-firm sector approximately 50 per cent of firms can be expected to fail in a five-year period (Storey, Keasey, Watson and Wynarczyk, 1987).

No doubt due to the difficulties of data collection, little research has been done with small firms until recently, but Keasey and Watson suggest that the lack of adequate internal control procedures, the lateness of filed accounts at Companies House and the generous scope for abridged accounts in the Companies Act 1981, will ensure collectively that accounting information is either unavailable or unreliable for small companies (Keasey and Watson, 1987). It is this group of companies which are very much more likely to fail than their larger competitors for which a comparatively rich information set is available. In an attempt to circumvent this problem Keasey and Watson drew on the theories of corporate collapse expounded by Argenti which included consideration of many qualitative variables such as the management structure, inadequate financial information, manipulated accounting information and high levels of gearing (Argenti, 1976). To operationalise these factors, a battery of 18 non-financial variables addressing such indicators as presence of secured loans, departing directors or submission lags for the annual accounts were tested against 28 conventional financial ratios. The estimation sample was 146 small firms (typical total assets were between £25,000 and £50,000) from the north-east of England and the validation sample a similar 20 firms.

The researchers used logit analysis, rather than discriminant analysis. This is necessary when some independent variables are dichotomous as discriminant analysis assumes multivariate normality. They discovered that the qualitative variables predicted failure in the estimation sample as well as the financial variables did (75.3 per cent correct to 76.6

per cent) and out-performed for the validation sample (65 to 55 per cent). Average submission lag (positive), the number of directors (negative), bank floating charge (positive), prior year qualification (negative) and current year qualification (positive) were the explanatory variables. While the dominance of non-financial variables is not proven, the fact that failing companies exhibited submission lags of 14 months will suggest that in practice financial data will be of little utility. This study actually incorporates submission lags whereas most investigations omit firms with missing data from their samples.

Other work which attempted to incorporate qualitative variables evidenced that changes in directors' equity shareholdings, resignation of directors and delay in submitting accounts were all statistically significant predictors (Peel, Peel and Pope, 1986). Schwartz and Menon showed that failing firms have a greater tendency to switch auditors than successful companies, and Whittred and Zimmer investigated the reporting delays of Australian companies and confirmed a statistical relationship but were unable to evidence any predictive power (Schwartz and Menon, 1985; Whittred and Zimmer, 1984). While the last three studies confirm that non-financial characteristics are potentially useful, they basically provide a further set of seams for the data-miner, for they are mainly free of theory and performed with larger companies. This type of information is likely to be especially useful in the small-firm sector where financial results are unavailable or unreliable.

9.6   Conclusion

This chapter has reviewed the ability of financial information to predict financial failure in firms and the methods by which decision-makers review the creditworthiness of the borrowers or customers. Financial failure has been noted as difficult to define. The statistical evidence from the myriad empirical studies is generally impressive with consid￰￰able predictive power often displayed. However, this approach has been accused of displaying characteristics of data-mining and close examination suggests that practitioners will have considerable problems using the techniques. It is a tribute to th￰ ￰ortance and difficulty of the failure prediction decision that despite these problems Z-scores have been one of the successful exports from academia to practice.

Exhibit 9.1

An example of the application of discriminant analysis to failure prediction

This section provides an example of how a discriminant model might be estimated. It is not supposed to be an exhaustive or ideal model but simply an indicator of some of the steps that a modeller might go through. The full procedure involved in producing a reliable and comprehensive model is more time consuming and difficult than can be illustrated in this module. The data used represent two groups of firms:

1. A list of those 75 companies identified as in receivership by MicroExstat in December 1993.
2. A random sample of 196 firms that are identified as live by MicroExstat at the same time.

Nine ratios were also collected for each firm. They represent a sample of commonly used ratios but are not selected using any particular theory but simply represent a number of different dimensions of corporate performance. They are return on equity (roe), return on capital (roc), return on sales (ros), sales over assets (soa), stock days (std), debtor days (drd), creditor days (crd), debt ratio (dbr), and interest cover (icv). As always with discriminant models one of the difficulties is correctly classifying the firms on which the model is estimated. Firms can be in receivership without failing and firms can fail without going into receivership. They might be liquidated or even taken over by other firms.

Table 9E.1 displays a panel of results showing the distributional characteristics of the data for both samples combined using the MINITAB describe command. It is immediately apparent that the distribution of the ratios is strange. Many are truncated at zero and others have extreme outliers. This can be seen from the low mean of the return ratios, the difference

Table 9E.1 Descriptive statistics for relevant variables

	N	N*	Mean	Median	Stdev	Min	Max
roe	271	2	−17.2	7.6	255.0	−3954.3	442.4
roc	271	2	8.17	11.10	33.17	−252.60	119.50
ros	266	7	−4.48	4.60	108.95	−1690.00	146.60
soa	271	2	453	191	3109	−4144	47441
std	266	7	99.7	45.0	303.6	0.0	4179.0
drd	266	7	98.8	70.5	196.8	0.0	2512.0
crd	266	7	92.06	64.00	154.35	0.00	1671.00
dbr	271	2	42.41	38.30	50.98	−487.60	327.50
icv	265	8	12.27	2.10	58.10	−48.20	507.20

Table 9E.2 Histograms of return on capital before and after transformation

```
Histogram of roc   N = 271   N* = 2
Each * represents 5 obs.
Midpoint          Count
−240                2          *
−200                0
−160                0
−120                1          *
 −80                4          *
 −40               14          ***
   0              195          ******************************************
  40               47          **********
  80                5          *
 120                3          *
```

```
Histogram of roc   N = 271   N* = 2
Each * represents 2 obs.
Midpoint          Count
−3.0                1          *
−2.5                2          *
−2.0                8          ****
−1.5               18          *********
−1.0               32          ****************
−0.5               48          ************************
 0.0               53          ***************************
 0.5               48          ************************
 1.0               32          ****************
 1.5               18          *********
 2.0                8          ****
 2.5                2          *
 3.0                1          *
```

between the mean and median for most of the ratios and the extreme values. With almost all empirical methods of analysis such erratic variables would cause problems and this is particularly true of discriminant analysis which requires variable approximating to normality. There are a number of approaches which might be adopted.

1. Cases with outliers could be removed from the sample.
2. Outliers could be 'truncated' with the extreme value being changed to some more acceptable reading.
3. Estimation procedures could be used which are robust to the impact of outliers. Non-parametric approaches often make use of ranks of the variables rather than the variables themselves.
4. The data could be transformed by taking the log or root of the variable. This can be effective but is not always so.
5. The data could be changed to give a more tractable distribution whilst maintaining the ordering of the variables.

It is the last of these three approaches which is used here with each variable being converted to a distribution with a mean of zero and a standard deviation of 1 using the MINITAB nscore function. The two histograms of return on capital show the data before and after transformation.

Following transformation the data is examined for interrelationships between the ratios collected. The correlation matrix shown in Table 9E.3 reveals that the three return variables are all correlated and are also related to the interest cover variable. The debtor days and creditor days are also quite highly correlated. This implies that there is some redundancy in the data and that statistical models will have difficulty correctly weighting the different ratios. In turn, this implies that the analyst will want to exclude some of the ratios from the final model to achieve a sparser and, hopefully, robust model.

Table 9E.3 Cross-correlation between relevant variables

	roe	roc	ros	soa	std	drd	crd	dbr
roc	0.732							
ros	0.605	0.650						
soa	0.076	0.099	−0.084					
std	−0.096	−0.081	0.078	−0.147				
drd	0.026	−0.019	0.177	−0.126	0.136			
crd	−0.107	−0.111	−0.029	−0.108	0.115	0.544		
dbr	−0.068	−0.137	−0.101	0.105	0.148	0.032	0.179	
icv	0.635	0.704	0.671	0.064	−0.026	−0.005	−0.163	−0.324

Table 9E.4 Univariate analysis of individual ratios and failure/survival

Analysis of variance on roe

Source	DF	SS	MS	F	p
code	1	2.513	2.513	2.56	0.111
Error	269	264.439	0.983		
Total	270	266.952			

Individual 95 PCT CI'S for mean based on pooled stdev

Level	N	Mean	Stdev	--- + --------- + --------- + --------- + ---
2	75	0.1557	1.1381	(-------------*--------------)
4	196	−0.0596	0.9298	(-------*--------)

--- + --------- + --------- + --------- + ---

Pooled Stdev = 0.9915   −0.16   0.00   0.16   0.32

For the sake of brevity only the univariate results for return on equity are included. The two groups were found to be significantly different at 5 per cent confidence levels for return on sales, stock debtors and creditors turnover, and debt ratio.

Table 9E.5   Results of comprehensive discriminate analysis

Linear Discriminant Analysis for code
Group   2   4
Count   74   188
  262 cases used   11 cases contain missing values

Summary of classification
Put into   ...True group...
Group   2   4
2   55   46
4   19   142
Total *N*   74   188
N Correct   55   142
Proport.   0.743   0.755
N = 262   *N* Correct = 197   Proportion Correct = 0.752

Table 9E.6   Results of selective discriminant analysis

Linear discriminant analysis for code
Group   2   4
Count   75   191
  266 cases used   7 cases contain missing values

Summary of classification

Put into   .....True   group.....
group   2   4
2   58   51
4   17   140
Total *N*   75   191
N correct 58   140
Proport.   0.773   0.733
N = 266   *N* Correct = 198   Proportion Correct = 0.744

Squared distance between groups
              2   4
2   0.00000   1.47802
4   1.47802   0.00000

                 Linear discriminant function for group
                  2   4
Constant   −0.38915   −0.05564
ros   0.24955   −0.09664
std   0.32375   −0.11764
drd   0.35104   −0.13771
dbr   0.79180   −0.29863

Summary of mis-classified observations

Observation	True Group	Predicted Group	Group	Squared distance	Probability
2 **	2	4	2	18.04	0.018
			4	10.09	0.982
10 **	2	4	2	2.561	0.453
			4	2.185	0.547

To aid the choice the difference between the means of each ratio for both groups is examined. To do this an analysis of variance is used. The programme calculates the mean and standard deviation of both groups and calculates a *p*-value indicating the probability the two samples are drawn from the same population. A diagram is also presented which shows the degree of overlap. Table 9E.4 shows the results for return on sales, stock days, debtor days, creditor days, and the debt ratio and all reveal statistically significant differences between the two groups at 95 per cent confidence levels.

Before estimating the reduced model the full ratio set is used to discriminate between the receivership and live groups. The results in Table 9E.5 show that with 262 cases 197 were correctly classified by the model giving 75.2 per cent correct. Whilst almost 72 per cent could have been correctly classified by assuming all firms were live it can be seen that for the crucial decision — the classification of failure — only 19 out of 74 were wrongly allocated.

The model is now re-estimated using only four variables — return on sales, stock days, debtor days, and the debt ratio. Additional results are collected from the output including the estimates of the equations which are used to classify the firms and the details of cases which are wrongly classified - only two of which are reported here. It can be seen from Table 9E.6 that the model is almost as accurate with four predictors as with nine as the per centage of firms correctly classified has dropped from 75.2 to 74.4 per cent and the model is actually marginally better at classifying the failed firms.

It can be seen that of the two wrongly classified firms reported here number ten was quite a marginal case whereas number two was very clearly predicted to be a live firm when it actually was in receivership. It might be worth pursuing as the firm may not have failed financially but may have been put into receivership for some other reason.

The model is a long way from complete. The essential next step is to test the model using a different 'validation' sample. Only if the estimated model is proven to work with data other than the estimation sample should analysts place any reliance on it. It is one thing for a model to be able to correctly classify observed cases. It is another for it to be able to predict results.

QUESTIONS

1.   Using the following dataset, estimate a two variable discriminant model based on the gearing and profitability ratios. What is the classification accuracy achieved? Does the model display any classificatory ability using data from T-2?

Failing firms

Dataset		F1	F2	F3	F4	F5	F6	F7	F8	F9	F10
Current	T-1	1.81	1.58	0.95	0.48	0.86	1.33	1.34	1.17	0.81	1.33
ratio	T-2	3.13	0.55	1.09	0.48	1.24	1.28	1.51	3.00	0.70	0.90
	T-3	2.59	0.71	2.90	0.70	1.38	1.10	1.34	1.52	0.21	1.05
Retained	T-1	− 12	22	− 10	− 11	− 11	1	0	− 7	3	− 8
profit/	T-2	8	13	− 14	2	3	4	− 1	8	− 20	8
assets	T-3	− 3	4	11	4	11	23	12	47	1	7
All debt/	T-1	2	117	313	389	509	222	328	141	1300	15
equity	T-2	8	104	118	291	318	211	156	0	575	524
	T-3	10	28	30	271	227	405	122	11	310	381
Net	T-1	30	21	− 3	− 48	− 10	25	19	8	− 20	1
current/	T-2	50	− 29	5	− 45	14	21	26	39	− 32	− 7
assets	T-3	46	− 11	47	− 21	17	8	22	18	− 47	3
Fixed/	T-1	33	43	*	56	38	2	19	47	16	38
total	T-2	26	64	*	59	26	2	16	41	23	29
assets	T-3	25	72	*	50	38	2	14	47	87	45

Surviving firms

Dataset		S1	S2	S3	S4	S5	S6	S7	S8	S9	S10
Current	T-1	3.33	1.65	1.30	1.86	1.17	3.75	1.30	1.57	1.43	1.19
ratio	T-2	2.81	1.32	1.67	1.01	1.23	2.27	2.07	1.33	1.81	1.37
	T-3	2.41	2.14	2.52	1.49	1.08	1.79	1.24	1.02	1.27	1.45
Retained	T-1	1	8	6	9	− 3	0	1	23	− 3	− 13
profit/	T-2	11	6	− 1	− 39	9	7	− 1	13	1	8
assets	T-3	18	23	− 1	− 3	− 7	− 4	12	17	3	7
All debt/	T-1	15	0	266	23	120	15	219	87	35	765
equity	T-2	20	0	192	110	61	16	203	203	37	212
	T-3	13	0	76	60	470	30	145	150	146	265
Net	T-1	55	37	18	16	13	66	14	28	23	6
current/	T-2	49	19	29	1	16	51	26	17	33	17
assets	T-3	40	48	41	19	7	40	13	1	19	23
Fixed	T-1	21	5	22	65	9	11	41	22	25	61
total	T-2	23	21	28	55	12	9	49	33	25	38
assets	T-3	31	9	32	42	9	10	32	41	14	25

This data is taken from the examples used in Keasey and Watson (1986) and refers to accounting data from 1975—80 for independently-owned engineering companies from the north-east of England with total assets between £10,000 and £100,000.

2.   Discuss how accounting data may be used to identify companies which are likely to become insolvent. (Society of Investment Analysts, Interpretation of Accounts and Corporate Finance, sample paper.)

3.   Taffler (1983) estimated a discriminant model which exhibited predictive ability. What further considerations need to be examined before it can be concluded that the model is valuable?

4.   Information from historic cost, current cost and cash flow accounting, and capital market statistics and qualitative variables have all been used in failure prediction models. What are the advantages and disadvantages of using these different sources?

5.   Examine the ratios tested in two different models of failure prediction. How many ratios are common to the sets tested and how many are included in the final model? Does the lack of standardisation present difficulties for failure prediction in practice?

6.   (a) What are the advantages and disadvantages of utilising external credit or bond rating agencies as opposed to in-house assessment of credit risk?
        (b) If credit assessment is performed in-house, what are the advantages and disadvantages of using a formal discriminant model as opposed to relying on the experience of credit managers?

7.   A new graduate has recently joined the industrial firm of which you are the financial manager. He has estimated a model using linear discriminant analysis which correctly classified 80 per cent of his sample of 50 randomly selected quoted industrial and commercial companies (ICCs) and 50 previously quoted ICCs which have ceased independent trading. The model most accurately classifies the sample when using gearing, return on equity, dividend yield and the current ratio as the independent variables. All 45 ratios available on the financial database were tested for predictive power. The graduate has recommended to the managing director, his aunt, that his model is used to assess the creditworthiness of your firm's customers. Advise the managing director as to what further development is required before the model can be employed for credit assessment.

8.   Provide definitions of the following terms as they relate to this chapter:
        (a) Human information processing.
        (b) Financial failure.
        (c) Discriminant analysis.
        (d) Bond rating.
        (e) Insolvency practitioner.
        (f) Administration order.
        (g) Voluntary liquidation.
        (h) Environmental predictability.
        (i) Confusion matrix.

References

Aharony, J., Jones, C. and Swary, I. (1980) An analysis of risk and return characteristics of corporate bankruptcy using capital market data, *Journal of Finance*, September, 1001—16.

Altman, E. (1968) Financial ratios, discriminant analysis and the prediction of corporate bankruptcy, *Journal of Finance*, September, 589—609.

Altman, E. (1984) A further empirical examination of the bankruptcy cost question, *Journal of Finance*, September, 1067—89.

Altman, E., Haldeman, R. and Narayanan, P. (1977) ZETA analysis: a new model to identify bankruptcy risk of corporations, *Journal of Banking and Finance*, June, 29—54.

Argenti, J. (1976) *Corporate Collapse: The Causes and Symptoms*, McGraw Hill, Maidenhead.

Arnold, J. and Moizer, P. (1984) A survey of the methods used by UK investment analysts to appraise investments in ordinary shares, *Accounting and Business Research*, Summer, 195—207.

Bank of England (1980) Corporate insolvency, *Bank of England Quarterly Bulletin*, December, **20**, no. 4, 430—436.

Bank of England (1982) Techniques for assessing corporate financial strength, *Bank of England Quarterly Bulletin*, June, 221—3.

Beaver, W. (1966) Financial ratios as predictors of failure, *Journal of Accounting Research Supplement*, **4**, 71—111.

Beaver, W. (1968a) Alternative financial ratios as predictors of failure, *Accounting Review*, January, 113—22.

Beaver, W. (1968b) Market prices, financial ratios, and the prediction of failure, *Journal of Accounting Research*, Autumn, 179—92.

Belkaoui, A. (1983) *Industrial Bonds and the Rating Process*, Quorum, Westport.

Berry, A., Citron, D. and Jarvis, R. (1987) *The information needs of bankers dealing with large and small companies*, Research Report 7, ACCA, London.

Clark, T. and Weinstein, M. (1983) The behaviour of the common stock of bankrupt firms, *Journal of Finance*, May, 489—504.

Deakin, E. (1972) A discriminant analysis of predictors of business failure, *Journal of Accounting Research*, Spring, 167—179.

Diamond, H. (1976) Pattern recognition and the detection of corporate failure, Ph.D dissertation, New York University, cited in Zavgren, 1983.

Edminster, R. (1972) An empirical test of financial ratio analysis for small business failure prediction, *Journal of Financial and Quantitative Analysis*, March, 1477—93.

Foster, G. (1986) *Financial Statement Analysis*, Prentice Hall, Englewood Cliffs.

Gentry, J., Newbold, P. and Whitford, D. (1987) Funds flow components, financial ratios and bankruptcy, *Journal of Business Finance and Accounting*, Winter, 595—606.

Horrigan, J. (1966) The determination of long-term credit standing with financial ratios, in Empirical research in accounting selected studies, *Journal of Accounting Research*, **4**, 44—66.

Houghton, K. and Woodliff, D. (1987) Financial ratios: the prediction of corporate '%success' and failure, *Journal of Business Finance and Accounting*, Winter, 537—54.

Hudson, J. (1987) The age, regional and industrial structure of company liquidations, *Journal of Business Finance and Accounting*, Summer, 199—213.

Kaplan, R. and Urwitz, G. (1979) Statistical models of bond ratings: a methodological inquiry, *Journal of Business*, April, 231—61.

Keasey, K. and Watson, R. (1986) Current cost accounting and the prediction of small company performance, *Journal of Business Finance and Accounting*, Spring, 51—70.

Keasey, K. and Watson, R. (1987) Non-financial information and the prediction of small company failure: a test of the Argenti hypothesis, *Journal of Business Finance and Accounting*, Autumn, 335–54.

Lachenbruch, P. (1975) *Discriminant Analysis*, Hafner, New York.

Mensah, Y. (1983) The differential bankruptcy predictive ability of specific price level adjustments: some empirical evidence, *Accounting Review*, April, 228–46.

Moody's Investors Service (1989) *Moody's Credit Opinions*, February, New York.

Norton, C. and Smith, R. (1979) A comparison of general price level and historical cost financial statements in the prediction of bankruptcy, *Accounting Review*, January, 72–87.

Ohlson, J. (1980) Financial ratios and the probabilistic prediction of bankruptcy, *Journal of Accounting Research*, Spring, 109–31.

Peel, M., Peel, D. and Pope, P. (1986) Predicting corporate failure: some results for the UK, *Omega*, **14**, no. 1, 5–12.

Pinches, G. and Mingo, K. (1973) A multivariate analysis of industrial bond ratings, *Journal of Finance*, March, 1–18.

Queen, M. and Roll, R. (1987) Firm mortality: using market indicators to predict survival, *Financial Analysts' Journal*, May–June, 9–26.

Schwartz, K. and Menon, K. (1985) Auditor switches by failing firms, *Accounting Review*, April, 248–61.

Storey, D., Keasey, K., Watson, R. and Wynarczyk, P. (1987) *The Performance of Small Firms*, Croom-Helm, London.

Taffler, R. (1983) The assessment of company solvency and performance using a statistical model: a comparative UK-based study, *Accounting and Business Research*, Autumn, 295–307.

Whittred, G. and Zimmer, I. (1984) Timeliness of financial reporting and financial distress, *Accounting Review*, April, 287–95.

Zavgren, C. (1983) The prediction of corporate failure: the state of the art, *Journal of Accounting Literature*, **2**, 1–38.

CHAPTER 10

Social, Environmental and Employee Reporting

C. Cooper[1] and W. Rees

CHAPTER OBJECTIVES

This chapter will:

1 Review the case for social reporting.

2 Review the case for environmental reporting including an analysis of one well-known example.

3 Review the role of accounting information in employee reports and collective bargaining.

10.1 Introduction

This chapter will be rather different from the others in the sense that it will reconsider some of the unstated assumptions which underlie most of this book. Indeed, the whole underlying theoretical basis of this book must be that it is possible to analyse financial statements, and that there is some point in so doing. The book is based on the assumption that traditional financial accounts are useful for decision-making purposes. This chapter reviews these assumptions and presents an alternative perspective on accounting. You will probably have already given some of these issues some thought but perhaps without the theoretical framework which underpins some of the alternative views contained in this chapter. The main focus of this chapter is accounting's significant but under-estimated impact on our overall quality of life and the possibility of producing other types of more socially-oriented accounts. As Tinker (1985) points out, accounting impinges on much more of our lives than the narrow focus of the traditional annual reports suggests.

> Members of society are interconnected through their economic and social interdependencies: employees to investors to consumers to taxpayers to mothers to welfare recipients to students to insomniacs. Accounting information is not merely a manifestation of this myriad of interdependencies; it is a social scheme for adjudicating these relationships. We are all costs

and revenues to each other; everyone is potentially a benefactor and a victim in the accounting nexus of social decisions.

Parker (1986, p. 70) attributes the impetus for the consideration of a wider focus for annual reports as coming from:

> the student activism of the 1960s, increasing social criticism of capitalism and 'big business', the increasingly pervasive liberal outlook of social planners and reformers, the growth in publications concerned with the ecological impact of industrial production processes, and the broadening of union concerns beyond mere wages to include health and safety issues.

This chapter will concentrate on the possibility of widening traditional annual reports in order that they may reflect the wider social issues which many believe accounting itself affects. The chapter will consider three possible supplements to traditional accounts:

1. Social reports — which focus on assessing and reporting the impact of the firm's activities on society as a whole.
2. Environmental reports — which try to measure and disclose the specific impact of a firm's activities on the environment defined narrowly or broadly.
3. Employee reports — which review the employees' relationship with the firm and consider the total remuneration, general conditions of employment and the firm's prospects.

At first sight, given that accounting and business in general play an important role in our society, it might seem fair to add such supplements to annual reports. However, it should also be pointed out that the opportunities for companies to use such supplementary reports for public relations purposes are substantial. For various reasons calls for the production of supplements is a fiercely contested academic area. The debate is an important one for students, practitioners and society in general since it encourages a wider understanding of the important social issues surrounding accounting. Most accounting education is technically oriented, especially the training given by the accounting profession. This makes it very difficult for practitioners to develop a critical awareness of the social impact of accounting. As Tinker (1985) puts it, 'students are trained to become greyhounds in bookkeeping and ignoramuses in social analysis'. However, there are increasing calls for changes in accounting education to prepare students to evaluate alternatives in the face of inevitable changes in the social, economic and political environment (Kinney, 1989). An example of the need for accountants to be aware of social, economic and political issues is highlighted by Gray (1989) who considers CIMA members' concerns over exactly how to implement the European Commission's harmonisation programme for the 1992 single market. The programme contains four elements: 1 — political, 2 — economic, 3 — social and 4 — cultural. Gray (1989) details the problems which CIMA members face in dealing with the harmonisation programme. Had CIMA, and other accountancy group members' training included a critical awareness of political, economic, social and cultural choices they may have been more able to cope with change.

There is no agreed framework in the UK for producing social, employee or environmental reports. Certain other countries, notably the Netherlands, do have social and environmental accounting regulations. However, since there is no agreed framework for social, environmental or employee reporting, this chapter will be unable to present a methodology for analysing such reports. Instead it will present the debates surrounding the production of supplementary reports so that readers can make up their own minds as to how to analyse such reports. The chapter will proceed as follows. Firstly, the very broad topic of social reports including the possibility of setting an accounting standard on social accounting will be covered. The second section will deal with environmental accounting and will include environmental reporting practices in the Netherlands. The final section will look at reporting to employees.

10.2   Social reporting

Despite the accounting profession's protestation that its regulation system's objectives are to operate in the 'public interest', no recommendations have been issued that specifically address reporting to society on the social impact of organisations. The basis of accounting regulation and the current system of corporate reporting are founded on the assumptions that (a) the shareholders as owners of the invested capital are entitled to any surplus from a firm's activities, and (b) it is primarily to these shareholders that the management must report giving information which mainly relates to the amount of such surpluses. As yet there is little requirement on organisations to report on their general impact on society (but see Chapin (1992) who notes that the US judicial, congressional and regulatory viewpoint is that accountants have a broad responsibility to the general public rather than specifically to the management and shareholders of an organisation; also Carey (1992) points out that in order to fulfil its duty to serve the public interest the accountancy profession must at all times be ready to address the main questions facing society). Moreover, such phrases as 'an organisation's general impact on society' are problematic since society is not a cohesive unit but rather an assortment of various groups who each have their own interests and needs. It is extremely unlikely that it would be possible to produce a report that would meet the interests of all groups in society, especially where the needs of different groups are in conflict with each other. However, advocates of social reporting believe that it would be of overall benefit. Despite the myriad of problems surrounding the production of reports which reflect the social impact of organisations the serious academic work in this area makes it worthy of consideration.

There are different characteristics of social reports cited in the literature. Some writers wish narrowly to focus on (supposedly) more easily auditable numerical information and suggest that social reports should include financial information on amounts spent by an organisation on crèche facilities, donations to local charities, staff welfare, health education programmes and so on. Other numerical information could include statistics on staff turnover, promotion of women and minority groups. Other writers would like to see more non-quantifiable information presented in a narrative report. Narrative reports could perhaps overcome some of the complex measurement problems involved in the provision of numerical information. For example, while it might be possible to report the amount of money a mining organisation has spent on safety, it is not possible to measure in financial terms (or probably in any other terms) the value of the lives of workers killed in mining accidents, even though insurance companies may attach a figure to the life lost. Furthermore, it is impossible to measure the social costs of closing the mine.

Parker (1986, p. 72) found four major characteristics commonly cited in social accounting definitions:

1. Assessing social impact of corporate activities.
2. Measuring effectiveness of corporate social programmes.
3. Reporting upon the corporation's discharging of its social responsibilities.
4. External and internal information systems allowing comprehensive assessment of all corporate resources and impacts (social and economic).

While most advocates of social accounting recognise the problems of trying to produce genuinely unbiased information regarding the above four areas, they believe that the advantages outweigh the disadvantages.

At this point it is worth making a general comment about the different names given to social accounting. Parker (1986) found seven different names for such reporting in the literature: 'social responsibility accounting', 'social accounting', 'social audit', 'societal accounting', 'socioeconomic accounting', 'social reporting', and 'social responsibility disclosure'. The most common term used is 'social accounting' and this will be used throughout this chapter. In the UK there is a further commonly used term, 'corporate social reporting' (Grey, Owen and Maunders, 1987, 1991).

Grey, Owen and Maunders also usefully summarise the spectrum of views within society regarding social accounting as follows:

1. Social accounting interferes with the profit-seeking and is thus inimical (e.g. Friedman, 1962; Benston, 1982). Directors have no right to spend shareholders' money on socially responsible activities. Indeed, companies make a unique contribution to society by their concern with profit maximisation. Failure to attempt to maximise profits would lead to the organisation concerned suffering a cost disadvantage. Companies have historically provided society with the products it wanted, and any pollution, safety or other social problems caused by meeting the demands of society are part of the price which society is willing to pay.
2. Organisations (and the society of which they are a part) are fundamentally benign. Social accounting is a mechanism for demonstrating this (Parker, 1986). Social accounting developed as a response to a combination of public opinion, investor assessments, and changes in the corporate self-concept. It is ultimately in the long-term interests of organisations to be concerned with their social responsibilities.
3. Organisations and society co-exist in some sort of social-contractual relationship in which the agents (organisations) are accountable to the principals (society at large) (Grey, Owen and Maunders, 1987; Shocker and Sethi, 1973).
4. Organisations (and the society of which they are a part) are fundamentally inimical and thus social accounting is an activity of controlled legitimation (Puxty, 1986).

Most writers on social accounting fall into the second and third groups and there is much common ground between them.

10.2.1 *Accountability*

Many of the proponents of social accounting justify their calls for the promotion of social accounting on the grounds of a narrowly defined concept of accountability. Their viewpoint broadens the traditionally held belief that accounting should provide information to shareholders. These proponents typically hold views about both accounting and society in general which would place them in the third group in the above spectrum. They believe that organisations would not exist without 'society at large' and thus owe society a duty of accountability, although what exactly is meant by society at large is rather difficult to define. Grey, Owen and Maunders (1991, p. 2) propose a 'simple' model of accountability. They define accountability as:

> the onus, requirement or responsibility to provide an account (by no means a financial account) or reckoning of the actions for which one is held responsible.

Such a model would appear as shown in Figure 10.1.

However, Grey, Owen and Maunders (1989) see two problems with this simple model. It fails to determine (a) the responsibilities of the contract, and (b) when a contract can be said to exist. They therefore argue for a more legalistic *compliance with standards* approach to social accounting. To them, the setting of social accounting standards would both define the responsibilities under a social contract between organisations and (as they describe it) society at large, and state when such a contract can be deemed to exist. 'Society at large' would be the principal legally entitled to accountability (information) by organisations (the agents).

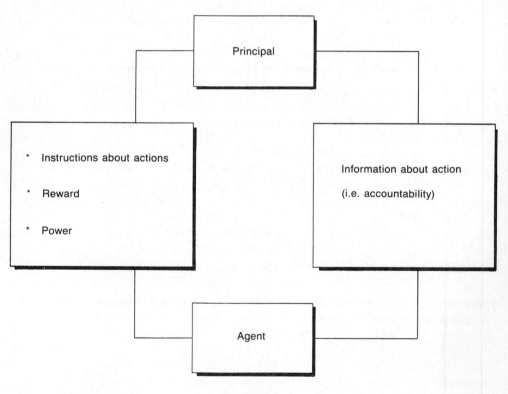

Figure 10.1

10.2.2 *Social accounting standards*

Parker (1986, 1991) also proposes the use of social accounting standards. He believes that the simple process of setting a social accounting standard,may promote the widespread discussion and analysis of basic social accounting concepts to be employed, users to be served, available versus desired databases, types of information susceptible to uniform accounting and reporting methods, and basic disclosures already practicable. Parker (1991, p. 72) further states that:

> in the longer term, such standards, however elementary, would assist in bringing all corporations subject to them to a common baseline of disclosure which would then serve as a springboard for future advances.

While Parker pays attention to some of the criticisms levelled at social accounting he believes the setting of social accounting standards may steer a path between social accounting critics and proponents by:

1. Seeking limited forms of social performance disclosure that are both practicable and achievable at reasonable cost to the corporation.
2. Demonstrably assisting continued progress by encouraging focused discussion of both theoretical and applied dimensions of social accounting.
3. Establishing the primacy of social accounting purposes other than corporate 'image making'.

10.2.3 *The case against social accounting*

One of the major arguments against social accounting is that its proponents seem to assume either explicitly or implicitly that the need for social accounting has been expressed through the pluralist medium of a democratic society. Or in other words, that interest groups such as trade unions, local community and so on seek social accounting information and that organisations begin to provide that information, either willingly or because the interest groups have managed to win certain legal changes.

Those writers who are cynical about the benefits of social accounting do not believe that our society is a pluralistic one in which the needs of various groups will be met in a democratic fashion. They see society as being dominated by one or more groups with their own ideology and systems designed to retain their dominance. Accounting reflects these ruling ideas and helps to reproduce the current social system. In short accounting serves to promote the interests of the dominant power group within society. It does not come about in a democratic manner in order to meet the needs of different interest groups within society. They would further contend that accounting's claims to provide neutral information to certain user groups hides the true nature of accounting as a mystifier of social relations and as a legitimator of the status quo. There are many ways in which accounting mystifies social relations and of particular importance for social accounting is the one-sided picture which an annual report presents. There are many aspects of an organisation which are totally excluded from traditional accounts.

A possible solution to these problems would be to encourage accounting which would present a wider view of society. However, there is a problem with this simple solution if it is not necessarily accepted that we live in a pluralist society. If not, calls for wider social accounting may be used by the dominant groups in society to maintain their privileged positions. Indeed, because of its supposed progressive character, social accounting may be deemed to be more insidious that conventional accounting. As Puxty (1986, p. 99) puts it,

> insofar as conventional accounting is infused with the problematic characteristics of the social context within which it operates, social accounting in fact is only a truer reflection of that context . . . to the extent that it legitimates and reproduces class relations, social accounting is only a more effective way of doing so.

However, it may be wrong to suggest that social accounting is solely determined by the interests of the ruling class. Social accounting may well have been stimulated by the political conflict of the 1960s and 1970s, as Parker suggests. Even so the dominant forces in society have the power to turn seemingly radical positions and changes to suit their own ends. Some see this as the fate of social accounting.

To those who believe that it is not possible to have true democratic social accounting, there is little point in issuing social accounting standards. Puxty (1986, p. 104), in response to Parker's (1986) claim for social accounting standards that they would promote widespread discussion of basic concepts responded that:

> The kind of discussion that necessarily is undertaken in a society in which there is domination of some by others is a discussion in which the agenda is fixed by powerful interests, the terms of the debate are distorted by the ideology implicit in the language of communication that is employed, and the possibilities of true discourse leading to a freely arrived-at result that is genuinely the outcome of the discussion is rendered impossible by the domination of one party by another that is immanent in the debate.

There is a further problem noted by those who oppose social accounting. There is as yet no evidence for believing that social accounting would bring about greater social responsibility on the part of organisations. In fact the production of social reports might have the opposite effect. For example, if employers were forced to disclose details on the percentage of women staff promoted, this may lead investors to suppose that organisations which do treat women fairly are poor investments in terms of narrow corporate interests rather than wider societal ones. The cost to the employer for maternity leave is quite high and some companies may attract disproportionately high members of women staff thus increasing their expenses. This could be damaging to the firm if it were true that women employees were more expensive than male or if investors wrongly believed that to be the case. Some more radical writers suggest that social accounting is insignificant, likening it to rearranging the deck-chairs on the *Titanic*.

10.3   Environmental reporting

Environmental accounting can be viewed as a sub-class of social accounting. It has received increasing attention over the past few years along with rising public concern over green issues and the future of the planet. The problem for accounting is that many natural resources are at present, in accounting terms at least, considered to be free (MacCalman, 1993).

According to Henderson (1991, p. 75):

> At present most economic activity takes little account of the costs it imposes on the surroundings. Factories pollute rivers as if the rinsing waters flowed past them for free, power stations burn coal without charging customers for the effects of carbon dioxide belched into the atmosphere, loggers destroy forests without a care for the impact on wildlife or climate. These bills are left for others to pick up — neighbours, citizens of other generations and future generations.

The state of our environment has been disregarded by traditional economics-derived accounts which have to date treated the environment as a free good or as an externality. This means that the Earth has been commonly regarded as a free reservoir and bottomless rubbish dump (Cottrell, 1978). Accounting has never tried to calculate the cost of using up non-renewable resources. Even potentially renewable resources are being tragically depleted since there is a seeming refusal to acknowledge renewable time. Cottrell (1978, p. 39) suggests that pollution should be seen as the consumption of environmental quality — 'The release into a shared environment and against the common interest, of

Table 10.1 Environmental information which is practical within the current financial reporting framework

Category 1 Information which is currently deliverable	*Category 2* Information which is deliverable given some developments in accounting practices
Provisions for clean up costs (P&L, balance sheet)	Historical annual spend on cleaning up, capital expenditure driven by purely environmental needs
Subsequent movements on established provisions	Prospective future capital expenditure driven by purely environmental needs
Disclosure of the basis for computing the provisions	Disaggregated historical environmental performance summary against established lead indicators for each industry/activity segment
Contingent liability data	
Corporate environmental policy statement	
A statement of intent with regard to environmental audit	Value for money data focusing on VFM derived from environmental compliance or other voluntary environmentally beneficial corporate activity
A summary of the results of environmental audits together with copies of the external verifier's reports	A statement similar to the OFR in which management summarises its belief in the environmental positioning of the company vis à vis expected developments in environmental legislation in the foreseeable future
A management statement covering their belief that the company has complied in full with all external standards (à la Cadbury)	
A bad news statement	
A reference to the location of detailed environmental disclosures	

an offensive by-product or waste'. Furthermore by viewing pollution as a by-product, we would regard environmental quality as an input to economic activity on the same basis as other inputs such as capital and raw materials. In this way environmental quality would be seen as having *value* and thus resources such as air, water, space and protection from the sun through the ozone layer may no longer be ruthlessly exploited. This brings the first major impediment to environmental accounting. Value is a subjective concept. As was pointed out in the section on social accounting above, it is impossible to value a human life, human happiness and so on although, as we noted, it is possible to put a *price* on these. It is also impossible to measure the value of the ozone layer, a cubic metre of clean air or a mile of unpolluted beach.

Until recently the accounting literature has not given much attention to attempts to classify, record and measure externalities, such as the effects of pollution or the inappropriate use of non-renewable resources (Mathews, 1991). But as in social accounting there are mounting calls that financial statements should be expanded to include social and environmental information; indeed, increasing numbers of companies now produce environmental accounts.

In a recent review following the Chartered Association of Corporate Accountants' annual competition for environmental statements Adams (1994) concluded that two categories of information are relevant and practical for environmental reporting as shown in Table 10.1. Adams also considered a third category of financial information, that which might be sought by analysts but seemed unlikely to be forthcoming in the foreseeable future. This included the impact of environmentally related expenditure on performance and information relating to sustainability.

10.3.1 *Sustainability*

The issue of environmental accounting is much more complex than simply a concern with environmental pollution. The previous section gestured towards a need to be concerned with our failure to sustain the world's natural resources. Buck (1992) contends that the natural resources consumed in the production of economic wealth during the twentieth century are unsustainable into the next century. The concern with sustainability is not a new one. During the late 1970s and 1980s there was a recognition that squandering our resources could not continue (Laughlin and Varangu, 1991). The problem with the use of the sustainability is that it means very different things to different people. Pearce *et al.* (1989) suggest that the level of activity which is sustainable is that which leaves future generations no worse off than the present generation. Gray (1992) sees a sustainable action as one which does not disturb the 'essential ecology'. The difficulty with this definition is that all actions could be regarded as disturbing the essential ecology. It is always a political problem as to what constitutes acceptable ecological behaviour.

Sustainable development has been described as something that:

1. Uses renewable resources in preference to non-renewable.
2. Uses technologies that are environmentally harmonious, ecologically stable and skill-enhancing.
3. Designs complete systems in order to minimise waste.

4. Reduces as much as possible the consumption of scarce resources by designing long-life products that are easily repairable and can be recycled.
5. Maximises the use of all the services that are not energy — or material-intensive, but which contribute to quality of life (Davis, 1991, p. 38).

Again there are certain difficulties with such descriptions. Given the above, should the ecologically friendly parent choose disposable or cotton nappies (diapers)? Both probably use renewable resources. But which uses a technology which is environmentally harmonious? Perhaps the minimum waste could be achieved by cotton nappies and certainly, cotton nappies have longer lives and are more easily repairable than disposable ones. However, it could be argued that disposable nappies contribute towards many parents' quality of life. Since the majority of child-care burdens in Western society fall on women, this issue could be considered to be a political one.

Again we return to some of the same debates we encountered in social accounting. If we lived in a pluralist society, it might be possible for environmental groups to join forces to bring about some kind of change. Accounting could be used in part to promote change. However, if we live in a society which is dominated by one group then change may be slow and difficult.

However, some companies have been quick to use environmental accounting and adopt environmental advertising, promoting environmental awareness. The public relation possibilities of appearing to be 'green' are important (Cooper, 1988). For example, in a 'green' issue of *Accountancy*, Maxwell (1990, p. 70) quotes, and does not disagree with David Smith, a director of Environment Services, speaking about environmental audit,

> It is, of course, possible merely to measure the effect of your activities, how much pollution you are causing, and whether you are within the law . . . But in the context of a highly-competitive market, compliance in itself is unlikely to be sufficient. There are two further factors for consideration — the chance to enhance your corporate image, and the *opportunity to create business advantage and maximise profitability* [emphasis added].

Within the business community, support for environmental initiatives is seemingly often accompanied by a profound reluctance to release detailed information into the public domain (Harte and Owen, 1992). Environmental campaigns that are designed to elevate the corporate image make it extremely difficult to assess whether companies adopting these marketing strategies are, in fact, helping the environment (Kagan, 1991). Accounting report users may selectively fail to communicate information when they perceive such action to be against their self-interest (Guthrie and Parker, 1990).

Those who think that environmental accounting *can* change things would argue that if accounting information included the environment then organisations would alter their behaviour. For example, it may be that under traditional accounting conventions, renewable energy appears to be much more expensive than the alternative; however, if the social costs of using up the Earth's precious resources were to be included in the non-renewable energy costing then renewable energy might become more attractive economically (Hoymeyer, 1992). Apart from subject valuation problems there are other problems concerning the provision of environmental reports which promote sustainability. Accountants are preoccupied with very short time horizons so that a project, for example, harnessing the sun's energy, with a time scale of 120 years would be totally beyond an accountant's conceptual reach (Bhattacharya, 1990). There are therefore enormous changes required in accountants' thinking before sustainable accounting could become accepted.

10.3.2 *Opponents of environmental accounting*

There are a growing number of critics of environmental accounting who feel that to account for the environment may be neither feasible nor desirable. These critics are most likely to be placed at either end of the political spectrum. The right wing perspective here is similar to that under social accounting, i.e. that such reports hinder profit maximisation and are malevolent. Accordingly, expenditure on socially beneficial causes may be seen as detrimental to the interests of the owners of organisations (Cooper, 1988). Faithful disciples of neo-classical economic theories, believing that markets react appropriately before annual reports are issued might also believe that for this reason annual reports are totally unnecessary. Those on the left who feel that environmental accounting is undesirable believe that accounting's historical alignment with, and support for, the capitalist system means that, however much work environmentally concerned individuals and groups put into designing fair and decent environmental accounts, these accounts will only be used to help maintain the capitalist system which has caused much environmental destruction in the past and which (partly because of the profit motive) will do so in the future.

There are other opponents of environmental accounting who feel that environmental accounting simply is not feasible. Tinker (1985) coherently contests that any social accounting system should always include externalities. But the degree of subjectivity and reductionism involved in putting monetary values on these externalities causes insurmountable problems (Cooper *et al.*, 1993). The issues have been regarded as too soft for a proper form of external public reporting (Harte and Owen, 1992). Schumacher (see Owen, 1992, p. 23) asserts that undertaking to measure the immeasurable is absurd but 'what is worse is the pretence that everything has a price, or in other words, that money is the highest of all values'. Hines (1991) asserts that:

> to reduce a friend to a number, or worse, a money equivalent is likely to have even worse consequences than excluding them from accounts altogether.

A further concern expressed by those opposed to environmental accounting is that it may lead to a greater concern for nature than for humankind. Power (1992) notes the difficulties which exist for the concept of sustainability in deciding which state is to be maintained. Owen (1992) makes the important political point that in pursuing the ideal of sustainability which entails shifting resources from current to future production, care needs to be taken to ensure that people in real need today are not forgotten. It is frequently argued that contemporary environmental or population control initiatives are simply set up to serve the interests of the West at the expense of the rest of the world. Cooper *et al.* (1992) criticise a proposal by Gray (1992) that it is possible to separate capital into critical, natural and *man*-made capital. If people are regarded as man-made capital and trees natural capital, disastrous results could occur if our concern is for the sustainability of natural capital. We may become more concerned with the destruction of the Brazilian rain forest than with the nightly murders of Brazilian children.

10.3.3 *Current environmental disclosure practice*

Adams (1994) comments that in 1994:

> There are now 30 or 40 UK companies that are making extensive environmental disclosures in stand-alone reports, and many hundreds more disclosing environmental policies through their annual statements. But the amount of financial data revealed at present is minimal.

Some companies appear on the surface at least to take environmental reporting seriously (Motyl, 1992). However, a closer analysis of environmental reports seems to support those who believe that environmental reports will be used solely for public relations purposes. There is a reluctance on the part of business to release detailed information into the public domain (Harte and Owen, 1991). Discussion of green issues in annual reports appears to be very general (Motyl, 1992; Harte and Owen, 1991), the majority in narrative form (Harte and Owen, 1992) and they are highly selective and public relations-driven (Owen *et al.*, 1992).

Some illustrations of current best practice in the UK include Norsk Hydro (UK), who issued the first environmental report, Body Shop, Thorn EMI, British Gas, British Petroleum, Caird Group and British Airways (Owen *et al.*, 1992; Harte and Owen, 1992). The Chartered Association of Certified Accountants (ACCA) awarded an annual Environmental Reporting Award, assessments being made on the usefulness and adequacy of environmental disclosures and whether an unbiased and complete picture of the corporation's environmental performance was presented (Owen *et al.*, 1992). Those companies regarded as reporting in the best manner were praised for providing specific quantified information that is auditable, disclosure of compliance with regulations and the employment of the services of authoritative independent consultants (Owen *et al.*, 1992). Most of the reports, including the 1992 joint winners, British Airways and Norsk Hydro (UK) and the 1993 and 1994 winners, British Telecom, produce reports dedicated to environmental issues which are not necessarily distributed to shareholders. The ACCA has been highly criticised for not considering this issue in their assessment (Motyl, 1992). Motyl reports that in future environmental reports may follow recommendations which have been issued by the ICAEW including:

> that company annual reports should contain details of the company's environmental policies and objectives, its impact on the environment, compliance (or otherwise) with regulations and guidelines, and should identify the directors responsible for dealing with green issues.

10.3.4 *British Petroleum health, safety and environmental report*

In 1993 British Petroleum (BP), amongst others, produced a publicly available environmental report. The document looks rather like a traditional annual report in terms of page size, and includes a mix of glossy photographs, narrative, statistical information and a report by Ernst and Young, the company's auditors. On its opening page the report reproduces a quotation from Jack Doyle, (Senior Analyst, Technology and Corporate Policy, Friends of the Earth):

> We are certainly no friends of the oil industry, and BP still has a long way to go despite recent improvements. The need for better disclosure to citizens, for example, remains paramount.

Whether or not this report would qualify as 'better disclosure' is extremely difficult to determine. There are six glossy pages full of narrative covering such topics as 'Preventing oil spills', 'Protecting the environment', and 'Ensuring health and safety'. There are a further five pages containing glossy photographs of people who may be considered to be concerned with environmental issues and their comments. For example, there is a photograph of John Chen (Chairman, Government Parliamentary Committee for the Environment, Singapore); superimposed on the photograph is the following quotation

> As concern for the environment gathers momentum in the coming years, being green also means good business.

This is followed by a twelve-page data section which contains statistical information frequently presented in the form of pie or bar charts covering four areas, chemicals (worldwide summary emissions), oil refining (worldwide summary emissions), group safety performance and exploration and production (worldwide summary emissions and Clyde case study). Perhaps this report confirms Owen's concern that organisations are unwilling to give detailed information regarding environmental matters. The statistical section contains a two-page glossary of such terms as *sulphides* (compounds of sulphur which can be toxic to aquatic life and are generally regulated in aqueous discharges) and *total emission* (total estimated, calculated and measured emissions excluding CO_2).

There are a further two pages of narrative, one containing a list of awards which were won by BP in 1992, the other containing BP policy and focused programmes. There is a further page containing a report by Ernst and Young who list four procedures which were carried out in reviewing this report.

They state that (p. 28):

> Our review this year has been less in scope than a full attestation of the HSE (Health Safety and Environmental) report, the objective of which would be the expression of an independent opinion on the statement of environmental policy objective, procedures and Focused Programmes. Accordingly we do not express such an opinion this year.

It seems that BP have taken care with the visual aspects of the report employing excellent photographers and designers. The report paper is made from recycled fibre that include post-consumer waste; the printing inks are vegetable-based; the gloss finish on the cover is obtained from a water-based coating; and the glue used in the binding process has been recycled. It will be interesting to see if BP pay this much attention to the environmental aspects of this year's traditional financial statement.

10.3.5　*Environmental reporting in the Netherlands*

Environmental reporting in the Netherlands is in a more advanced state than in other European countries. This is probably largely due to a combination of practical, political, economic and cultural factors (Buckley, 1993):[2]

1. *Practical*: the Netherlands are extremely flat with much land reclaimed from the sea. Many inland areas lie at or beneath sea level. A vast network of dams keeps water levels under control but there is always a real threat from rising sea levels. Furthermore,

the combination of a large chemical industry and a heavily populated country means that chemical waste and pollution present immediate and profound problems to the Dutch people.

2. *Political*: the proportional representation system of election means that the Green party (Groen Links) holds 5 of the 150 available seats which ensures that they often hold the deciding vote on certain issues. Environmental matters are a primary concern to the Dutch electorate and are firmly on the political agenda.
3. *Economic*: the stability and affluence of the Dutch economy may mean that there is more money available for environmental matters.
4. *Cultural*: there seems to be a higher level of environmental awareness in the Netherlands than in the UK. Children are taught about environmental issues at primary school.

In August 1989 the Dutch government issued a general policy statement to encourage companies voluntarily to introduce 'internal management systems' (Buckley, 1993). Furthermore, the statement means that companies should:

> start looking for solutions to limit and if possible, to prevent environmental impact with a view to sustainable development.

The statement recommends that such a system should contain (a) an environmental policy statement, (b) an environmental programme, (c) the integration of environmental management in business operations as well as an environmental coordinator, (d) measurements and registrations, (e) internal monitoring, (f) internal information and training, (g) internal and external reporting/environmental reporting, (h) the examination of total environmental management system/environmental audit.

It appears that the government wanted such systems available in all 10,000 to 12,000 companies considered to have medium to large environmental risk or impact by 1995. A further 250,0000 companies with limited environmental impact should have partial environmental management systems in progress. As well as encouraging internal audits of such systems, the government would also require external reporting to themselves of measurement and registration data necessary under environmental legislation and permits. The government leaves open the possibility of auditing by outside experts 'on the basis of financial accountancy auditing methods' (p. 2). The Dutch government sees no need to introduce a standardised environmental management system, perhaps because of the lack of experience with such systems and the need to conduct trial projects.

Dekker and Huizing (1992) trace the development of environmental issues in the Netherlands. They outline the interests of the main stakeholder groups in the Netherlands and the conflicts that exist between them. The interests of environmental and employee organisations are aligned against employers' confederations. The government is put in the middle.

At the heart of the Netherland's policy on the environment is the 'Polluter Pays Principle' (PPP). Companies found guilty of pollution could be made to pay the full cost of rectifying any damage caused. The amounts involved are not insubstantial, up to 1992 the government had filed claims amounting to £185 m. Dekker and Huizing (1992) outline the existing and possible future roles for accountants in the environmental arena. Whilst

--- Exhibit 10.1 ---

oil refining

Worldwide Summary Emissions[1] (Tonnes)

Air Emissions	1990	1991	1992	1995 Target
VOCs	84,650	83,330	n/a[2]	61,280
Nitrogen Oxides (NOx)	30,830	29,430	31,660	
Sulphur Oxides (SOx)	94,780	84,600	81,880	
Carbon Monoxide (CO)	19,100	27,800	10,650	
Particulates	5,780	5,990	6,670	
Total	235,140	231,150	n/a	
TRI Substances (U.S. data only)	1,670	1,500	n/a	600

Aqueous Discharges	1990	1991	1992	1995 Target
Oils and Greases	472	478	502	
Sulphides	150	149	150	
Ammonia	889	959	905	
Phenols	203	213	173	
Suspended Solids	1,227	1,041	1,093	
Total	2,941	2,840	2,823	1,405
Chemical Oxygen Demand (COD)	7,386	8,383	7,008	3,782

Offsite Disposal	1990	1991	1992	1993 Target
Solid Waste	211,360	60,860	122,040	63,950

[1] Data are for 14 major operated production facilities. Emissions from joint venture facilities have been pro-rated based on BP equity share.
[2] n/a= not available at time this report went to print.

exploration
and production

Worldwide Summary Emissions[1] (Tonnes)

Aqueous Discharges	1989	1990	1991	1992	1993 Target
Oil in Produced Water	487	588	616	869	
Oil on Muds/Cuttings	4,835	4,827	2,988	867	
Total	5,322	5,415	3,604	1,736	2,400

Oil Spills[2]	1989	1990	1991	1992
Number of Spills	278	349	370	229
Quantity	153	257	287	61

[1] Data are for major exploration and production sites operated by BP.
[2] Oil spills are as defined by local law, which varies across locations in which BP operates.

worldwide summary of emissions

The tables show the quantities of BP's worldwide emissions and depict the company's targets for reduction. The expenditures necessary to achieve these targets are already built into the BP Group plan.

The tables show best current estimates. BP is working to improve the quality and comparability of this data. Improvements in measuring techniques and methods of estimating could revise some figures in future reports. For example, BP has participated in developing a sophisticated monitoring technique known as DIAL, which may alter estimates of certain emissions compared with current methods.

Prior year data are provided for the purpose of comparison. Changes from prior year data result from actual changes in operation and, in some cases, changes in methods of measurement or estimation.

CO_2 is excluded from the tables and all totals. Likewise, water is excluded from air and aqueous emissions.

chemicals

Worldwide Summary Emissions[1] (Tonnes)

Air Emissions	1990	1991	1997 Target
Hydrocarbon Emissions	36,100	27,290	18,050
Other Chemicals[2]	2,520	2,060	
Nitrogen Oxides (NOx)	12,070	12,720	
Sulphur Oxides (SOx)	22,530	25,000	
Carbon Monoxide (CO)	20,780	19,090	
Particulates	860	810	
Total	94,860	86,970	
TRI Substances[3]	18,050	11,400	

Aqueous Discharges	1990	1991	1997 Target
TRI Substances	8,880	8,580	
Other Chemicals[4]	14,180	14,450	
Total	23,060	23,030	7,690

Offsite Disposal	1990	1991
TRI Substances	5,250	2,070
Other Chemicals[4]	23,720	21,850
Total	28,970	23,920

Deepwell Disposal	1990	1991
TRI Substances	24,080	24,350

[1] Data are for 10 major chemical production facilities.
[2] Non-hydrocarbon air emissions not individually reported.
[3] A subset of compounds included in the hydrocarbon and other chemical categories. Also see glossary.
[4] Hydrocarbon and other chemical emissions such as ethane, propane, not included on the TRI list.

accountants would obviously record/audit the clean-up costs of pollution, they will have problems dealing with contingencies. Would the government make polluters pay for pollution caused before relevant legislation was enacted? What would be the contingent amount for sustainability? There are four possible roles that accountants could play in company-wide environmental control (CWEC).

1. Auditing the financial statements.
2. Auditing the green report and material registrations.
3. Conducting internal and external audits.
4. Acting as external consultants.

Whether accountants would require special training in this area is obviously a serious concern. Most medium to large-sized audit firms in the Netherlands have already established working relationships with environmental auditors (Dekker and Huizing, 1992). Such companies conduct both internal and external audits, testing control techniques, measuring emissions, and advising on how to implement CWEC systems. Those accountants who are involved in these joint ventures tend to have an education grounded in the natural sciences and generally have a better understanding of ecological matters than the average British accountant.

However, it seems that economic imperatives have started to take effect; since the economic recession has begun to take hold, environmental concerns have begun to seem more like luxuries rather than necessities. The environmental audit departments, enthusiastically set up by the large accountancy firms, have had very little substantive work, and their funding is being scaled down (Buckley, 1993).

10.4   Employee reporting

Employee reporting has been a growth area in most Western economies over the last two decades. In the UK it has been suggested that intended legislation in the 1971 Industrial Relations Act which required an annual statement to be presented to employees was a catalyst (Maunders, 1981), but the scope of development both before and after that occasion implies that other factors are also at work. Given that there are costs involved in the production of employee reports which fall on management and the shareholders, and that their production appears to be at the instigation of management, it might be expected that some benefits to management are perceived.

If an analogy were to be sought with conventional financial reporting, it might be assumed that the users of these statements saw some benefits through improved decision-making and were therefore prepared to pay for access to the information. This payment could take many forms including supplying labour at preferential rates, reducing employee turnover or absenteeism, or persuading employees to refrain from industrial action. However, there is little evidence of such pressure for disclosure from the recipients of the reports, and the most consistent advocation of employee reporting has come from associations representing management or industry, such as the CBI or the British Institute of Managers (BIM), periodically abetted by political parties of various colours. It is difficult to analyse the influence of such exhortations, but UK firms have shown themselves remarkably impervious to other encouragement to do good works, and the suspicion must persist that the motivation for employee reporting lies in the benefits accruing to management, either directly, or through management's ability to further the cause of the shareholders.

10.4.1 *The case for the disclosure of financial information*

It is possible to make a strong normative case for the disclosure of financial information to employees or trade unions, though the impact of these incentives is limited by a number of real or apparent constraints. Corina and Rees (1981) argue that the motives for disclosure might be separated into six categories. Two of these, accountability and the development of collective bargaining, are dealt with elsewhere in this chapter. The remaining four categories are human relations, industrial democracy, the management of change and political motivations, and are dealt with in more detail below.

Human relations

A recurrent aspiration of management is to improve productivity and reduce industrial conflict through the application of low-cost human relations techniques. Ever since the famous experiments at the Hawthorne Works in the 1920s, and the later popularisation of human relations theory, the importance of effective channels of communication between management and employees has been one of the aspects of human relations theory that has received continuing attention. Much of this earlier work has been challenged, yet its influence particularly on managerial thinking is still strong. However, despite the commitment to improved communications, there is a continued reluctance to divulge the information of importance that would give the communication process any meaning. Unless there is the necessary factual information presented for discussion, it is difficult to see how employers and employees can have meaningful communications with each other.

It is not the purpose of this text to debate the weakness of the human relations school and this task has been thoroughly performed elsewhere (Fox, 1974). While the more obviously unitary aspects of 'human relations' models of industrial relations may be difficult to justify, the benefits to management of open planning processes and open information in the conveying of instructions to employees are more plausible. It is feasible that employees may be more sympathetic to organisational change, and equally there may be more commitment to tasks where the reasons for performing those tasks are understood. However, the implicit assumptions that conflict between employees and employers is abnormal is dubious, and if the converse is true, greater openness may well make the causes of conflict all the more apparent.

Industrial democracy

It is a well-established tenet that for worker participation to be successful it is essential that a high standard of relevant information is made available to the participants in order that they can take part in effective and meaningful discussion. It can be envisaged that information will fulfil two roles within systems of industrial democracy.

First, those persons within the system who are involved with decision-making, be they worker directors concerned with corporate planning or members of the workforce determining conditions, must have available the necessary data for efficient and informed decisions, together with the relevant feedback to correct and improve decisions already made.

Second, where the democratic arrangements in operation require the election of representatives, there will be a need for a continuous system of accountability which will provide the members of the electorate with the means of monitoring their representatives and of choosing between candidates. It can be argued that a corollary of this is that if information is made available outside of a participative arrangement, this will tend to promote discussion which may lead towards participation. As the Commission on Industrial Relations (CIR, 1972) noted, 'it could be argued that a dramatic increase in participation would result by adopting European information provisions up to the current German or Belgium standards'.

Since that suggestion, there has been little clear evidence of any increase in information disclosure or participative management practices in the UK. Indeed, the decade of high unemployment and a government committed to defending 'managements' right to manage' have encouraged a step back from earlier presumptions that industrial democracy was a natural route for the development of industrial relations in the UK.

However, there is the prospect of a substantial change in the relationship between management and employee, with the proposals from the EU for a social charter (ratified in 1993 by all member countries except the UK) which will attempt to impose more liberal working practices. The UK Conservative government is convinced that the costs of implementing the social charter outweigh the benefits — although, as with all accounting regulations, the costs and benefits tend to fall on different groups. However, there is an unambiguous trend in many OECD countries to require enterprises to provide increasingly detailed information on their holdings and operations, the stringency of such requirements varying from country to country. The provision of more information to unions may be a consequence of the trend towards their greater participation in the management of the enterprises.

The management of change

The need for information disclosure with reference to ever increasing rate of change, especially technological change, has been treated here as a separate case, though it is clearly caught up in considerations of democracy, bargaining, and human relations. The manner in which technological change can affect the working lives of employees and their security of tenure is apparent with regards to industrial concerns, and most clearly where the modern factory is operated using computer-integrated manufacturing. However, the impact can be no less dramatic for the white-collar or service worker.

Thus, it can be seen that the introduction of new technology can have devastating effects on the workforce. Not only can it mean loss of jobs or lower growth in job opportunities with its implications for the unemployed and union strength, but also individuals can experience de-skilling, the worsening of working conditions and disruption of career paths.

Obviously members of the workforce will be concerned to ensure that management has taken sufficient account of their needs and expectations, and for that reason will insist on accountability. In addition they are unlikely to leave such investment decisions as an uncontested area of management prerogatives and will attempt to bring them within the bargaining circumference. The impact of 'microchip technology' upon industry, and its accelerated consequences for employment and industrial relations, emphasise the new pressures placed upon unions for information.

Political motivations

The call for greater disclosure has been articulated by most political parties in Europe. While disclosure may well mean different things to groups of varying political persuasions, it seems that nearly all feel compelled to pay at least lip service to the concept since, 'it is scarcely possible to deny the virtues and likely advantages of being well informed; such a denial may all too easily appear to signify approval of ignorance and who in a democracy can credibly do that' (Marsh and Rosewell, 1976). Thus, political mandates for disclosure may be only passing facades in electoral campaigns, and in practice the demands of economic efficiency and the influence of commerce and industry, especially transnational organisations, could severely constrain political initiatives.

The more moderate political parties are perhaps likely to promote disclosure as a method of providing accountability, or as a method of reducing industrial conflict and 'improving' collective bargaining. In addition, labour-orientated parties may wish to rationalise the bargaining position of trade unions to achieve a more equitable balance of industrial power. All or any of these aims may coincide with other reasons for promoting disclosure as discussed elsewhere but more militant groups are interested for self-perceived strategic reasons. While such groups may have as a final aim the establishment of 'proletariat control' over the means of production and distribution, in the short run they also hope to exercise some control over the current 'anti-social aspects' of business. For instance the Institute for Workers Control claims that, 'the trade union and labour movement needs information in order to make a social audit of the consequences of capitalist decision-making, and to prepare alternative plans based on the social needs of communities' (Coates and Topham, 1972). While such advocates may deem the possibility of a stronger bargaining position a consistent goal, their principal objective is to expose the shortcomings of transnational corporations and to reduce, and eventually control, ostensible excesses. Consequently, obtaining the necessary information to achieve transnational countervailing power is often perceived as a strategic objective.

10.4.2 *The practice of employee reporting*

Traditional communications procedures and methods are undoubtedly ill-equipped to cope with many of the information aspects of the complex pressures of the 1980s and 90s arising from growth in unemployment and the dislocation of technological change. Where companies and industries are seriously affected by the environmental pressures of industrial conversion, new stresses are put on the bargaining and arbitration processes. It is one thing to bargain about terms and conditions of employment, and quite another to bargain about the conditions on which workers are to yield their jobs to machines. Information and efficient communication channels are essential to reduce the fear that exists among employees concerning their fate in the face of change.

The absence of meaningful two-way communications between management and employees is thus a justifiable lament, mainly heard from management, especially those still fondly envisaging 'human relations techniques' as a central method of curing their industrial relations problems. A different view of the world might lead one to see that the problem is not one of communication, both sides mostly understand all too well what the other is trying to communicate, but is rather a problem in the sense that the groups have such different interests that they are rarely (if ever) likely to agree on anything. One attempt to fill the communications gap has been the rapidly increasing practice of issuing employee reports. While these documents are obviously an imperfect method of communication, since they are only a one-way system for imparting of information, it is commonly argued that the disclosure of information by this method will provide employees with the means to improve their decision-making and conduct their relationship with their employers on a more informed basis. The problem with this is that the 'information' with which employees are armed is solely provided from the viewpoint of their employers.

To examine disclosure practice as represented in the form of employee reports, it is essential to project some model of the information needs of employees, or their representatives, since the disclosure is aimed at these groups. However, it is no simple matter to establish these informational needs, for it is inadequate to enthrone user-sovereignty as user perceptions may be moulded directly by what information is currently available. Conversely, the observer cannot presume to know what information employees actually utilise or what information employees should require.

Various attempts to derive the minimal information needs that might be required from employee reports show little obvious similarity in their checklists, but sufficient congruence in the conclusions to suggest that the research is not overly sensitive to the specified requirements. Thus Lyall (1982) sought information regarding profitability, product development, sales development, financial resources, budgets and long-range plans, order levels, exports, divisional information, manpower information, cash flows both experienced and expected, research and development and finally capital investment levels, to allow the employee to assess job security. He also suggested that production costs and profitability, selling and distribution costs including divisional allocations, and administrative and management costs would help assess company performance, and lastly that value added statements disclose the wealth sharing by the firm. Typically Lyall found that most reports he examined (60 randomly selected examples) failed to provide more than a few categories of information. Corina and Rees (1981) examined a sample of award-winning Australian employee reports. They examined the reports for evidence that:

1. Demonstrates management concern for the job security and human values of enterprise. Employees would require information on: manpower planning, manpower forecasting, planned changes in working practices, technology, current liquidity, inventories, sales, mergers, market prospects and net worth. Such information clearly cuts across categories, but it may be grouped loosely under the heading of 'performance of the firm and personnel matters'.

2. Demonstrates management commitment to creative negotiation. This would require data on wage and salary earnings, reserves, productivity, profit margins, cost components, product markets, and gross profit forecasts. Such data could be classified as information related to 'negotiating activity'.

3. Demonstrates management encouragement of 'human relations' and 'good industrial relations'. This would require information for the feedback of financial performance indicators alongside explanations of organisational structure and goals.

The list does not purport to represent a comprehensive list of requirements, but only a minimal test for compliance with aims which may be considered legitimate by employees. In general, it would be required that the information would relate to the workplace rather than the legal unit of the firm and favour forecast information over ex post data. The survey concluded that:

> in general reports do not satisfy any of the fundamental needs of employees as earlier hypothesised. Nor would it appear that they are intended to, since most of the information requirements would appear to be readily available to management and could easily be inserted into employee reports.

10.5   Disclosure of information for collective bargaining

It can be argued that collective bargaining, whatever the national context, is undergoing continued change under the influence of differing determinants. The growth of the firm, the intervention of government, and changes in economic circumstances are believed to be three influences which have produced recent developments. The scope and depth of the negotiating process fluctuate as does the relative power of the employees' bargaining position and their share of the value added by the firm. While it can be shown that the underlying proportion of gross national product commanded by employees changes only slowly, unions are not only concerned with redistributing income but also with extending the influence of the workforce over its working environment and with exercising some measure of control over non-wage issues. However, union power has often been over-estimated and unemployment, new technology and new work patterns are showing a capacity to drain union strength. Unions now appear more vulnerable than powerful and hope that information will enable them to bargain as equals, and to bargain over issues of vital concern apart from the conventional wage issue.

10.5.1   *Information disclosure in collective bargaining*

Much of the work reviewing the development of financial disclosure to employees has been conducted from the managerial viewpoint. The control of financial information is seen to rest with management and the analysis of motivations and consequences are reviewed from a managerial or perhaps pluralist perspective. This is possibly a narrow or even prejudiced analysis but it may partly explain the developments as the decision to disclose rests with management. However, an explanation based on managerial rationality will omit considerations of union motivations and ability, as well as the economic and institutional environment. The evaluation of developments in information disclosure in the light of the effect of 'efficiency and rational economic decision-making', or in the promotion of industrial relations free from 'the underlying antagonism and conflictual relationship between capital and labour', are heavily value-laden. In particular, successful development of information disclosure, from a management point of view, will most likely require union enthusiasm (perhaps by buying-off union leaders) rather than mere compliance. A rejection of, or indifference to, economic decision-making on managerial terms negates much of the rationale for information disclosure.

While disclosures prescribed by external bodies and in particular the requirements of law are not explicitly managerial, the enacting bodies will act to maintain the status quo. Insofar as management interests are coupled to the performance of the firm, government action will rarely deliberately affect managerial interests adversely, as the government will rarely tolerate damage to the performance of the corporate sector. The British government's refusal to accept the EU social charter provides some evidence of this.

10.5.2 *Constraints on information disclosure*

Previous sections have argued a case for the use of financial information in collective bargaining and as incentives for the use of employee reports. These factors will produce pressures for greater disclosure, but there are a series of constraints which will dissuade the relevant parties from pursuing the disclosure of financial information. This contingency model has been employed by Corina and Rees (1981), Craft (1981), and Moore and Levie (1981). Examples of these constraints are bargaining power, relevance to bargaining, union competence, confidentiality and technical issues.

Bargaining power

The ability of management to achieve its objective without resorting to information disclosure will depend in part on the relative strengths of the participants. The stronger the position of the union, the greater will be the firm's incentive to introduce information that management feels is helpful to its case and the more successful will be the union's demands for information.

Relevance to bargaining

A further crucial characteristic might be the relevance of firm-specific or issue-specific data to the bargaining issues. If bargaining is conducted at the national or industrial level there will be little incentive for either side to seek data relevant to the firm. It can also be argued that in some industries, and more obviously in some countries, union negotiations concentrate on terms and conditions of work, whilst in other circumstances wider issues are accepted by both parties as appropriate issues for negotiation.

Union competence

Union-specific characteristics include the union's ability to handle significant amounts of financial data, and their possession of the necessary skills to analyse it. Not only will management be reluctant to provide information which it feels may be misinterpreted, but the union pressure for disclosure might be expected to be a function of its ability to process the information.

Confidentiality

A conventional response to a request for the disclosure of information is to claim that such information is confidential, and that disclosure would be damaging to the commercial interests of the company. Management's claims for privacy may be valid, unthinking, a strategic move to avoid disclosure, or a means of influencing legislators drafting disclosure requirements. The problem of confidentiality is not trivial, and it is one which the regulators of financial reporting have had to deal with. Where management is hoping to improve the industrial relation's climate within a firm, the maintenance of confidentiality may have a cost in the impact on those aspirations.

Technical issues

Even given an environment in which information disclosure is encouraged by both parties, there are technical difficulties which increase the cost of disclosure and reduce the benefits. Many of these factors are experienced by conventional reporting. They include the concentration on past rather than future results, the preparation of reliable rather than relevant information, the focus on legal reporting units rather than the workplace, the difficulties of presenting complex information to non-specialists, and the problem of attestation of financial statements to the satisfaction of the parties involved.

10.5.3   *The impact of information disclosure*

Whereas considerable normative claims are made for increased disclosure, it is difficult to provide obvious evidence of all-round benefits. Even if a specifically managerial viewpoint is taken, the costs and benefits are difficult to assess. If increased disclosure is to be advocated 'for the public interest' in the same manner as SSAPs the problem becomes increasingly complex. In an adversarial bargaining situation a benefit to one party may well result in disadvantage to the other and a normative case for disclosure disappears. The actual impact will be dependent on the relative power of the interested participants, their perception of the benefits involved and the political process which will attempt to resolve the conflict.

Where management control the disclosure of information, items of data favourable to management's case can be expected to be more likely to have been introduced into the bargaining context than those with an adverse consequence for management. Under this hypothesis, newly regulated disclosure might have beneficial implications for union negotiators. However, the opposite case has also been put. Foley and Maunders (1977) have suggested that it would be in the interests of union negotiators to be over-optimistic, and whether this is deliberate or subconscious information disclosure will tend to moderate union expectations.

Ogden and Bougen (1985) reject the presumption that accounting information is objective, neutral and a sound basis for rational economic decision-making. Not only do they perceive accounting information as a 'malleable resource', which can be used to legitimise decisions by diverting attention from non-economic or capricious rationales, but management can use apparently scientific accounting numbers to validate their role.

Empirical studies (Bougen *et al.*, 1990; Cooper and Hopper, 1988; Knights and Collinson, 1987) which have considered the acceptance or rejection of accounting 'information' in industrial disputes seem to show that accounting information is sometimes accepted almost fatalistically (Knights and Collinson, 1987) but at other times is rejected (Bougen *et al.*, 1990; Cooper and Hopper, 1988). Knights and Collinson analyse strategies of management control and their impact on the shopfloor of a heavy motor vehicle manufacturer. They found that managements attempt to communicate with, and be more available to, the shopfloor served only to reinforce worker suspicion and distrust. By contrast, the financial accounts presented in a redundancy audit went unchallenged.

Cooper and Hopper (1988) consider the use of accounting during the 1980s' coal dispute during which the National Coal Board justified the 'need' for coal pit closures by pointing to uneconomic pits. Several people pointed out, both during and after the strike, that the figures were based on a misleading use of accounting. The figures given for pits' operating losses included costs, such as pensions to retired miners and payments by the NCB in respect of subsidence which were not part of the actual cost of producing coal. Such commentaries threw doubt on uninformed use of accounting figures put forward by the management and in doing so presented a real challenge to the NCB. However, the NUM refused to take on board accounting arguments and publicly insisted on the importance of community and the effects of job losses on communities only.

The use of financial information in collective bargaining

It has been argued that bargaining is based largely on the power relationships and influenced by the general economic environment, with the attention to information confined to the cost of living, changes in productivity and reference to comparable groups. Given that plant level bargaining is highly developed in the UK, even firm-specific data may be seen as irrelevant. This apparent irrelevance is supported largely by the evidence on attitudes and use of data. While both management and unionists (Cooper and Essex, 1977) appear to be aware of the potential of information to plant level bargaining, the actual pressure from unionists for information has been shown to be low (Jackson-Cox *et al.*, 1984; Mitchell, 1980), and management are reluctant to make information available as a matter of course. Explanations for this low rate of take-up are unclear. A series of constraints has already been suggested, but Owen and Lloyd (1985) consider that the unquestioned importance of information for traditional collective bargaining and the extension of the role of bargaining are not proved. Nor are the domestic circumstances of the union negotiators irrelevant. The union shop steward may be inexperienced in financial data analysis, lack trust in management and hence in management-provided information, and be unable to obtain members' backing when using financial data-based arguments in negotiations (Owen and Lloyd, 1985).

The assumption that information is important can be challenged on a number of grounds. Firstly, for financial information to play a role in collective bargaining there 'must obviously be a large measure of specific and shared calculative rationality in union-management negotiations' (Owen and Lloyd, 1985, p. 337). Secondly, the union negotiators may feel that without access to management information systems in an active manner, rather than as passive receivers of financial data, they are unable to question the underlying assumptions in the data. Thirdly, accounting information can be used to justify dubious decisions and to perpetuate a managerial view of the world. 'Thus in an environment of uncertainty characterising the collective bargaining context, accounting information can function as an ideological mechanism for propagating and re-enforcing managerial values and purposes rather than as an objective and neutral input into the bargaining process' (Owen and Lloyd, 1985, p. 338). Thus where union objectives are to ensure that the members do not lose out in comparison with reference groups, where integrative bargaining may be seen as illusory, where union negotiators lack the skill to use financial arguments, and information is a relatively weak power resource in the hands of the union, it is questionable whether financial information is of use to unions.

10.5.4   *International comparison of the role of information in collective bargaining*

Generally in continental Western Europe disclosure practice seems to be well in advance of that of the United Kingdom and the United States, and just as the Commission on Industrial Relations (CIR) (1972) suggests 'that a developed policy on disclosure is often a feature of a situation where industrial relations are generally good' it can be claimed, arguably, that the high standard of disclosure is a product of 'good' industrial relations, although how the 'goodness' of the industrial relations system is measured rather depends on what is looked for from the system.

A review of disclosure practice provides a rough continuum, from the more developed examples of Germany and Belgium, through the spasmodically evolving system in the UK to the limited interpretation of disclosure within the US. Some tentative generalisations can be drawn from the manner in which the disclosure requirements have developed to accommodate the position of the 'frontier of control' found in these countries. In the US, bargaining remains essentially a distributive mechanism and the disclosure requirements are typically constructed to facilitate this process. While it would be a gross exaggeration to claim that American unions offer no challenge to managerial prerogatives, there is sometimes less adversarial disputation of prerogatives than in the other countries reviewed, and the apolitical characterisation of American unions suggests that changes in this may well be slow. Consequently, disclosure practice in the US remains essentially limited to the distributive process.

In the UK, legislation has also been enacted to assist with the bilateral determination of labour's share of the product. However, while the distributive bargaining system may be less developed than the American model, paralleled in the less developed use of information in this process, examples of integrative bargaining and the more political nature of British trade unionism have presented a challenge to traditional managerial prerogatives and create the demand for information on which to base such a challenge. Therefore, in the UK there has been a move towards providing certain types of information not normally divulged in the US. However, the erosion of the legal, political and economic position of British unions in the 1980 and 90s has effectively put a stop to further development and any advance of information disclosure is likely to come from the influence of the EU rather than from within.

Continental Europe, or at least its principal economies, has long experience of works councils and worker directors, and it can be argued that in those enterprises where such arrangements are found, the frontier of control has moved further than the British model and management fundamentally accepts more dilution of prerogatives. In these circumstances, the extent of disclosure is more developed and discloses regularly, for example, details of forward planning seldom displayed in either the American or British systems.

A review of international experience also shows the difficulty of relying on legal enactment to encourage the development of information disclosure. In all the systems cited there is evidence, to a greater or lesser extent, of the failure of the unions to make full use of the opportunities available to them. Nevertheless, these countries have steadily progressed through the enactment of laws enabling the representatives of the workforce to obtain otherwise confidential information. This tendency to legal facilitation of the rights of the workforce is presumably based on the social belief that workforce and management should primarily negotiate, and that if negotiation is to be meaningful both sides must have access to any significant information. However, the reliance on legalistic provisions has not only shown the participants to be preoccupied with other priorities, but where contentious issues arise the legal system frequently exhibits a bias towards protecting static managerial prerogatives. It would seem, therefore, that any widespread development of disclosure practice will be best served where at least some significant worker groups within the union movement are committed to obtaining access to information, and are prepared not only to use the established procedures of industrial and labour law but also to bargain more intensively and directly with managements.

10.5.5 *Empirical evidence regarding information disclosure*

The normative case for information disclosure to employees can be quite strong. However, there is little evidence that financial information has any predictive value for variables of interest to employees. This section reviews the limited evidence available which seems to indicate weak predictive power if any. This does not imply that the information is not of value to participants in the bargaining process.

Changes in remuneration

Early work by Horwitz and Shabahang (1971) and by Foley and Maunders (1977) suggest that there is some limited information contained in the financial dataset with regards to the prediction of wage changes. Horwitz and Shabahang investigated the predictive content of seven ratios measuring the productivity, liquidity and profitability of 15 American companies over the period 1945−65. The only variables that proved to be statistically significant were the profit margin which improved remuneration and dividends per share which depressed them. Foley and Maunders performed a similar examination for 117 UK companies for the year 1971—72. They were rather conservative regarding the interpretation of their results, in part due to collinearity in the independent variables, but the explanatory power of 10 per cent and weakly significant variables of sales/net worth, the working capital ratio, and earnings per share suggest that there may be value in the financial ratios.

Peel and Pope (1984) confirmed the poor predictive power of financial ratios in the format tested. Peel and Pope utilised seven accounting variables plus the abnormal return on the capital market for 97 Plcs taken from the years 1977—80. The innovation of using capital market data was allied to tests of the change in the variables as well as the level. The only formulation in which the explanatory variables exhibited a statistically significant relationship with the rate of change of the average remuneration was where the capital market return was concurrently regressed against wage changes.

Employment change

This author has conducted an informal study of employment change for 140 cases in the mechanical engineering industry during the years 1979—82 and found modest explanatory power for prior changes in employment, capital market returns, changes in profit per employee, and investment in fixed assets. All variables were statistically significant but the predictive power of this relationship is only 19 per cent for the full sample although 50 per cent when one outlier is removed. Some reservations are in order for this result, but if confirmed by more extensive research it suggests that financial data may convey considerable information regarding the employment prospects within firms in an industry.

The poverty of the relationships tested does not necessarily imply that financial information is of little use for the prediction of remuneration or employment. Only a limited amount of work is available regarding this topic, and in most cases some reservation regarding the specification of the equations tested is in order. In part this is difficult to avoid. Much of the data used relates to Plcs and these will rarely conform to a bargaining unit or even a coherent firm, being amalgamations of many disparate operating units. Furthermore, the failure of the measured variables employed to capture the underlying parameter is well known when dealing with accounting data and this failing is exacerbated when cross-sectional studies are performed with a sample which spans different industrial sectors.

10.6   Conclusion

Of the three supplementary reports considered in this chapter the one with the best prospects of survival is the Environmental Report. In the 1990s employers do not have to be overly concerned about union power and so have little incentive to try to set an information agenda in their own favour. The notion of stakeholders groups and accountability to society seems an obsolete one in the 1990s. However, there does still appear to be a genuine concern for the future of our planet. Whether or not the production of environmental reports will aid the struggle to save the planet is a question which we cannot answer.

Notes

1. Christine Cooper is a Lecturer in Accounting in the Department of Accounting and Finance, at the University of Strathclyde.
2. This section follows Buckley (1993).

---------------------------------- QUESTIONS ----------------------------------

1.   Obtain a sample annual report and employee report for a firm, and review the financial press for commentary regarding that firm since the date of publication of the employee report.

      (a) Prepare a schedule of information that you as an employee would be interested to know regarding your employer. How much of this information is contained in the employee report? Is any of the missing information contained in the annual report?

      (b) Compare the content of the annual report and the employee report. Does the information in the two reports correspond? Are there significant disclosures absent from the employee report? Is there any information contained in the employee report which is not meaningful without further information contained in the annual report?

      (c) Review the firm's performance and any significant developments since the date of the employee report. Were these mentioned in the employee report and does the commentary in the employee report coincide with subsequent happenings?

2.   Obtain a sample annual report and environmental report for a firm, and review the financial press for commentary regarding that firm since the date of publication of the environmental report.

      (a) Prepare a schedule of information that you as a concerned environmentalist would be interested to know regarding the firm. How much of this information is contained in the environmental report? Is any of the missing information contained in the annual report?

      (b) Compare the content of the annual report and the environmental report. Does the information in the two reports correspond? Are there significant disclosures absent from the environmental report? Is there any information contained in the environmental report which is not meaningful without further information contained in the annual report?

      (c) Review the firm's performance and any significant developments since the date of the environmental report. Were these mentioned in the environmental report and does the commentary in the environmental report coincide with subsequent happenings?

3.   Using the annual reports and other publicly available data for an example firm attempt to evaluate the full social costs and benefits available from the operations of the firm.

      (a) What would be the costs of closing down the firm?

      (b) What further information would you require to improve your estimate of (a)?

4.   Using the annual report together with any other available information you deem to be relevant:

      (a) Prepare a wage claim for the workforce of the firm; or

(b) Prepare a defence against a wage claim representing the expected inflation rate plus 4 per cent; and

(c) What further information do you require to improve on (a) or (b)?

5.   What are the major similarities and differences between the three 'supplements' to annual reports outlined in the chapter?

6.   Design a corporate social report for an organisation of your choice. Would you mostly use quantitative or qualitative information? Give reasons for your choice of issues covered in the corporate social report.

7.   To what extent do you think that 'supplementary' reports of the types mentioned in this chapter would represent the interests of employers? Give specific examples.

8.   Would the setting of accounting standards help to alleviate the problems of companies using social or environmental reports for PR purposes?

9.   Provide definitions of the following terms as used in this chapter:
   (a) Corporate social reporting.
   (b) Employee reporting.
   (c) Environmental reporting.
   (d) Stakeholders.
   (e) Industrial democracy.
   (f) Human relations.
   (g) Collective bargaining.
   (h) Accountability.

References

Adams, R. (1994) Ready for greening, *Accountancy Age*, May, 16.

Benston, G.J. (1982) Accounting and corporate accountability, *Accounting, Organisations and Society*, **7**, 87–105.

Bhattacharya, K, (1990) Tomorrow's world, *Management Accounting*, September, 32–33.

Bougen, P.D., Ogden, S.G. and Outram, Q. (1990) The appearance and disappearance of accounting: wage determination in the UK coal industry, *Accounting, Organisations and Society*, **15**, 149–170.

Buck, J. (1992) Green awareness: an opportunity for business, in Owen, D. (Ed.) *Green Reporting — Accounting and the Challenge of the Nineties*, Chapman and Hall, London.

Buckley, A.D. (1993) Accounting for the environment: a pragmatic appraisal, University of Strathclyde Dissertation.

Carey, A. (1992) A questioning approach to the environment, in Owen, D. (Ed.) *Green Reporting — Accounting and the Challenge of the Nineties*, Chapman and Hall, London.

Chapin, D.H. (1992) Changing the image of the CPA, *Certified Public Accountant*, **62**, 16–25.

CIR (1972) *Disclosure of Information*, Commission on Industrial Relations, HMSO.

Coates, K. and Topham, T. (1972) *The New Unionism*, Owen, London.

Cooper, C., Dunn, J. and Puxty, A. (1992) Anxious murderers? — Death drives in accounting, University of Strathclyde Working Paper.

Cooper, C., Pheby, D., Pheby, K. and Puxty, A.G. (1993) Accounting truth and beauty, University of Strathclyde Working Paper.

Cooper, D. and Essex, S. (1977) Accounting information and employee decision making, *Accounting, Organisations and Society,* **2**, 57–74.

Cooper, D.J. (1988) A social analysis of corporate pollution disclosures, *Advances in Public Interest Accounting,* **2**, 179–186.

Cooper, D.J, and Hopper, T. (Eds) (1988) *Debating Coal Closures: Economic Calculation in the Coal Dispute* Cambridge University Press, Cambridge and New York.

Corina, J. and Rees, W. (1981) *The Disclosure of Company Information to Trade Unions and Employees: Australian Problems and Perspectives.* Occasional Paper No. 2., University of Sydney.

Cottrell, A. (1978) *Environmental Economics,* Edward Arnold, London.

Craft, J. (1981) Information disclosure and the role of the accountant in collective bargaining, *Accounting, Organisations and Society,* **6**, 97–107.

Davis, J. (1991) *Greening Business: Managing for Sustainable Development,* Basil Blackwell, Oxford.

Dekker, H.C., and Huizing, A. (1992) The environmental issue on the Dutch political market, *Accounting Organisations and Society,* **17**, 427–448.

Foley, B. and Maunders, K. (1977) *Accounting Information Disclosure and Collective Bargaining,* Macmillan, London.

Fox, A. (1974) *Man Mismanagent,* Hutchinson, London.

Friedman, M. (1962) *Capitalism and Freedom,* University of Chicago Press, Chicago.

Gray, R.H. (1989) Accounting and democracy, *Accounting, Auditing and Accountability Journal,* **2**(3), 52–56.

Gray, R.H. (1992) Accounting and environmentalism: an exploration of the challenge of gently accounting for accountability, transparency and sustainability, *Accounting, Organisations and Society,* **17**, 399–426.

Grey, R.H., Owen, D. and Maunders, K. (1987) *Corporate Social Reporting — Accounting and Accountability,* Prentice Hall, Hemel Hempstead.

Grey, R.H., Owen, D. and Maunders, K. (1991) Accountability, corporate social reporting and the external social audits, *Advances in Public Interest Accounting,* **4**, 1–22.

Guthrie, J. and Parker, L. (1990) Corporate social disclosure practice — A comparative international analysis, *Advances in Public Interest Accounting,* **3**, 159–175.

Harte, G. and Owen, D. (1991) Environmental disclosure in the annual reports of British companies: a research Note, *Accounting, Auditing and Accountability,* **4**, 51–61.

Harte, G. and Owen, D. (1992) Current trends in the reporting of green issues in the annual reports of UK companies, in Owen, D. (Ed.) *Green Reporting — Accounting and the Challenge of the Nineties,* Chapman and Hall, London.

Henderson, H. (1991) *Paradigms in Progress — Life Beyond Economics,* Knowledge Systems Inc., Indianapolis.

Hines, R. (1991) On valuing nature, *Accounting, Auditing and Accountability Journal,* **4**, 27–29.

Horwitz, B. and Shabahang, R. (1971) Published accounting data and general wage increases of the firm, *Accounting Review,* April, 243–252.

Hoymeyer, O. (1992) Renewables and the full costs of energy, *Energy Policy,* **20**, 365–375.

Jackson-Cox J., McQueeny J. and Thirkell, J. (1984) The disclosure of company information to trade unions — the relevance of the ACAS Code of Practice on Disclosure, *Accounting, Organisations and Society,* **9**, 253–273.

Kagan, D. (1991) The greening on environmental P. R., *Insight,* **7**, 38.

Kinney, W. (1989) The return of accountancy research to teaching and practice: a positive view,

Accountancy Horizons, **3**, no. 1, March, 119–124.

Knights, D. and Collinson, D. (1987) Disciplining the shopfloor: a comparison of the disciplinary effects of managerial psychology and financial accounting, *Accounting, Organisations and Society,* **12**, no. 5, 457–477.

Laughlin, B. and Varangu, L.K. (1991) Accounting for waste or garbage accounting: some thoughts from non-accountants, *Accounting, Auditing and Accountability Journal,* **4**, 43–50.

Lyall, D. (1982) Opening the books to the workers, *Accountants Magazine,* July, 246–248.

MacCalman, J.M. (1993) A critique of environmental accounting — The green dimension of social reporting, University of Strathclyde Dissertation.

Marsh, A. and Rosewell, R. (1976) A question of disclosure, *Industrial Relations Journal,* **7**, 4–16.

Mathews, M.R. (1991) A limited review of the green accounting literature, *Accounting, Auditing and Accountability Journal,* **4**, 110–111.

Maunders, K. (1981) *Financial Information and Industrial Relations,* Barmarick, Hull.

Maxwell, S. (1990) The rise of the environmental audit, *Accountancy,* June, 70–72.

Mitchell, F., Sams, K., Tweedie, D. and White, P. (1980) Disclosure of information: some evidence from case studies, *Industrial Relations Journal,* **11**, 55–63.

Moore, R. and Levie, H. (1981) *Constraints upon the Acquisition and Use of Company Information by Trade Unions,* Occasional Paper, 67, Trade Union Research Unit, Oxford.

Motyl, K. (1992) Fog hides green reporting flaws, *Accountancy Age,* 17 September, 10.

Ogden, S. and Bougen, P. (1985) A radical perspective on the disclosure of accounting information to trade unions, *Accounting, Organisations and Society,* 211–224.

Owen, D. (1992) The implications of current trends in green awareness for the accounting function: an introductory analysis, in Owen, D. (Ed.) *Green Reporting — Accounting and the Challenge of the Nineties,* Chapman and Hall, London.

Owen, D. Gray, R. and Adams, R. (1992) A green and fair view, *Certified Accountant,* April, 12–15.

Owen, D. and Lloyd, A. (1985) The use of financial information by trade union negotiations at plant level collective bargaining, *Accounting, Organisations and Society,* **10**, 329–352.

Parker, L. (1986) Polemical themes in social accounting — A scenario for standard setting, *Advances in Public Interest Accounting,* **1**, 67–93.

Parker, L. (1991) External social accountability: adventures in a maleficent world, *Advances in Public Interest Accounting,* **4**, 23–34.

Pearce, D., Markandya, A. and Barbier, E.B. (1989) *Blueprint for a Green Economy,* Earthscan, London.

Peel, D. and Pope, P. (1984) Corporate accounting data, capital market information and wage increases of the firm, *Journal of Business Finance and Accountancy,* Summer, 177–188.

Power, M. (1992) After calculation? Reflections on critique of economic reason by Andre Gorz, *Accounting, Organisations and Society,* **17**, 477–500.

Puxty, A.G. (1986) Social accounting as immanent legitimation: a critique of a technicist ideology, *Advances in Public Interest Accounting,* **1**, 95–111.

Shocker, A.D. and Sethi, S.P. (1973) An approach to incorporating societal preferences in developing corporate social action, *California Management Review,* Summer, 97–105.

Siebert, H., Antal, A. and Ingo, W. (1994) The political economy of environmental protection, in Altman, I. *Contemporary Studies in Economic and Financial Analysis,* Volume 24, JAI Press Ltd.

Tinker, T. (1985) *Paper Prophets: A Social Critique of Accounting,* Holt, Rinehart and Winston, London, New York.

Tricker, R.I. (1983) Corporate responsibility, institutional governance and the roles of accounting standards, in M. Bromwich and A.G. Hopwood (Eds) *Accounting Standards Setting: An International Perspective,* Pitman, London.

CHAPTER 11

Regulation of Accounting

C. Cooper[1] and W. Rees

CHAPTER OBJECTIVES

This chapter will:

1 Describe and give a brief history of the accounting regulation system in the UK, and contrast this with the system in other countries.

2 Review the rationale for regulation of accounting disclosure when economic incentives to disclose exist.

3 Consider the difficulties of setting out definitive criteria regarding good accounting practice and the political process which develops to resolve the debate.

We emphasise the UK system largely because of the recent changes experienced in the UK which highlight some of the more important issues relevant to accounting regulation systems in general.

11.1 Introduction

This text is mainly concerned with understanding how financial information can be utilised in economic decision-making by financial analysts using publicly available information. This chapter will address the problem of how accounting is regulated. This is worthy of consideration because of the close relationship between the use of financial information and its regulation. The value of financial analysis is, at least to some extent, dependent on the quantity and quality of available financial data. This is partly determined by the prescriptions of the regulatory framework. Analysts are therefore interested in regulation insofar as it determines the standard and quantity of their raw material and, due to the political processes for determining standards, the opportunities to influence forthcoming regulations.

It will be seen that the regulatory system adopted in the UK is idiosyncratic in many respects, and differs considerably from the continental European and North American approaches. Despite the diversity of regulatory systems it is difficult to identify any one national system which is obviously 'successful', partly because it is difficult to identify the criteria by which success is to be measured.

There are a number of questions to address in this chapter.

1. Is there a need for a regulatory system? It is frequently argued that in the absence of regulation the interests of the many parties involved will ensure that some level of disclosure exists and that, to the extent that individuals can both pay and be charged for the costs of the disclosure that they require, an 'effective' market may develop. However, many circumstances exist where it can be expected that the level of accounting disclosure derived from market forces will be less than ideal, and it is on this premise that the argument for regulation rests.

2. While some attention can be paid to the hope of designing an optimal regulatory system, the current system will be judged by the casual observer on its perceived success in producing effective standards. Yet 'many of the tasks expected to be fulfilled by accounting policy makers are unlikely to be amenable to solution by logical thought alone' (Bromwich, 1985, p. 3). Furthermore, the standards issued are compromises between legislators and vested interests resulting in standards which are dependent on political processes. Thus, attention must be paid to the decision criteria employed by the policy makers and to the political processes involving those who attempt to influence such decisions.

3. There is also a difficulty in that the accounting standards are the pronouncements of a body set up in a particular political, economic and social system, as a result of a partisan contest. As a result it can only have a limited mandate. Given this imperfect mandate and the lack of any clearly correct criteria for choosing regulations, any failure of the accounting system is likely to be blamed on the standard-setting process and its self-regulatory aspects.

4. The case for public regulation can be contrasted with the private alternatives. Public systems have a greater apparent legitimacy and should find enforcement less troublesome enabling more radical development. Yet it is argued that private systems of regulation can be more informed and responsive, and may be able to encourage compliance with the substance of the rules enacted rather than with mere legal form. The difficulties of the accounting standard-setting process are emphasised by the comment from Hope and Gray (1982, p. 531) that:

> The lack of any clear policy guidelines in the form of an agreed conceptual framework and the potential economic consequences (either real or assumed) emanating from policy decisions have combined to make it impossible for policy makers to select a single non-controversial accounting treatment on any of the major issues they have faced.

Before we move onto a discussion of regulation it may be that some justification for an examination of accounting regulation in a financial analysis text is called for. Perhaps the easiest way to do this is to look at a research study which investigated the impact on two variables of interest to analysts — forecasts and prices. Swaminathan (1991) investigated an old example of regulatory imposed changes in disclosure, the 1970 requirement by the SEC for US firms to report their revenue and income by segment. Earlier studies had shown that segmented data improve the accuracy of earnings predictions, and cause a downward shift in firms beta, but no security price reaction has been discovered. These results are inconsistent and Swaminathan's paper re-examined the evidence.

Four hypotheses were put forward:

H1 Price variability around the date of release of 10-Ks (the official SEC required annual filing) that contain SEC-mandated segment data is greater than price variability around the date of 10-Ks that do not contain SEC-mandated segment data.

H2 The release of SEC-mandated segment data in 10-K reports decreased divergence of beliefs regarding future earnings among market participants.

H3 The magnitude of any increase in price variability as a result of SEC-mandated segment disclosure is positively correlated with the number of segments of a firm.

H4 The magnitude of any decrease in divergence of expectations regarding earnings as a result of SEC-mandated segment disclosure is positively correlated with the number of segments of a firm.

The sample consists of a control group of 101 firms which made prior segmental disclosure and an experimental group of 160 firms which made no (or incomplete) segmental disclosure prior to 1970.

Swaminathan found that: (a) the average price variability is higher in the year after enforced segmental disclosure for the experimental group, and significantly so for the two days before and the day of filing; (b) measures of the divergence of analysts' beliefs regarding future earnings show that the divergence of beliefs for the experimental group has declined significantly whereas the control group has not; (c) the analysis demonstrated that price volatility was higher for those firms that had segmental disclosure forced on them than for those firms that had previously adopted it voluntarily; and (d) the reduced dispersion of analyst's beliefs about future earnings was higher for those firms that had segmental disclosure forced on them than for those firms that had previously adopted it voluntarily.

There do not seem to be any obvious alternative hypotheses to explain the results other than the disclosure requirement impacted on prices and forecasts. Taken together with other results presented in this chapter it can be viewed as evidence that analysts should be concerned about accounting regulation.

11.2   History of accounting standards setting in the UK[2]

The UK accounting regulatory system is dominated by the standard setting process, which means that in the UK the accounting standards governing the form and content of annual reports are set by a body other than the national government. Other influences on accounting practice do exist, principally the requirements of the Stock Exchange Listing Agreement and of Company Law. This mix of reliance on the accounting profession, the stock exchange requirements and law is common to most developed economies but the relative importance of each source of authority varies widely. In the UK the additional prescriptions of the London Stock Exchange enforce specific disclosures but have no substantial impact on the basic accounting measurement system. Company law rarely disputes the professional requirements. The dominant requirement of UK Company Law is that the accounts of a company should show a 'true and fair view' of the financial position of an organisation which *can* be viewed as compliance with generally accepted accounting principles.

The first British accounting standard was set in 1970, much later than in the US. Twenty-six SSAPs were issued before the UK standard setting process was changed in 1990. An Exposure Draft (ED) would be issued on a given topic. After public and professional debate, either a new ED would be issued or a fully fledged SSAP would be released. Since 1990 UK accounting standards have been called *Financial Reporting Standards* (FRS). FRSs will gradually replace SSAPs, but at present, most SSAPs are still in force. In order to understand the UK system of accounting standard setting it is useful to consider certain social, political and economic factors that surrounded the introduction of accounting standard setting in the UK.

11.2.1 *Political, social and economic influences of the 1960s*

It is argued that the regulatory system in the UK evolved as a result of a number of accounting scandals. The GEC/AEI case evolved at the time of a hostile takeover bid for AEI by GEC. AEI had produced a profit forecast in the tenth month of its financial year stating that the annual pre-tax profit would be £10 million for 1967. Following the takeover, the accounts of AEI showed a loss of £4.5 million. A report on the difference of £14.5 million attributed £5 million to 'matters substantially of fact' whilst the remaining £9.5 million was said to be due to 'adjustments which remain matters substantially of judgement', arising from variations in accounting policies. So more than 60 per cent of the difference could be blamed on different accounting treatments used by AEI and GEC accountants. The accounting profession urgently needed to reduce the amount of subjective judgement involved in financial reporting and it is argued that this problem led to the introduction of accounting standards in the UK.

The GEC-AEI case was followed by the equally troubling Pergamon–Leasco affair and Professor Stamp claimed that such examples cast serious doubts on the usefulness of accounts, and highlighted the fact that accountants found it extremely difficult to agree upon and to apply principles. He suggested that it was principles as well as practice that were the source of conflict and suggested that the profession's principles were:

> merely descriptions of current or past practice, rules which were drawn up on an ad hoc basis to deal with expediencies of a passing moment.

Stamp claimed that the second problem the profession faced related to the functions of the independent auditor. Auditors were not always independent as they often provided additional services for their client.

Leach, then President of the Institute of Chartered Accountants in England and Wales, published a reply to Professor Stamp of Edinburgh University. Stamp had suggested that accountants were confused by the numerous accounting principles and that a set of logical, consistent accounting principles should be set up which were simple, unambiguous and generally applicable. Leach replied that ideally every accountant would wish for this, but that in the ever-changing and volatile world of business it was an objective that was almost impossible to achieve in the short run. He also expressed concern over Stamp's idea of referring auditors to judges. The accounting profession has always been unwilling to give up any autonomy and come under a quasi-legal umbrella. On the question of auditors' independence and objectivity Leach admitted that there may be a few instances where the auditor was deceived or less vigilant.

There were therefore several forces at work promoting changes within the accounting profession. Accountants were to a large extent being used as scapegoats for many of the financial scandals of the late 60s despite the fact that the problems were typically caused by illegal activities far beyond the scope of audit involvement. However, the accounting profession felt the need to do *something*. All the better for accountants if that *something* would also enhance their professional standing.

11.2.2　*The Accounting Standards (Steering) Committee*

In January 1970, the Council of the ICAEW issued its Statement of Intent on Accounting Standards in the 1970s. This took the form of a five point plan.

1. Narrowing the areas of difference and variety in accounting practice.
2. Disclosure of accounting bases.
3. Disclosure of departures from established definitive accounting standards.
4. Wider exposure for major new proposals on accounting standards.
5. Continuing programme for encouraging approved accounting standards in legal and regulatory measures.

The profession avoided addressing the contentious issue of auditor independence. This remains a serious problem today.

As a result of the Statement of Intent, and in spite of criticism, the Accounting Standards Steering Committee (ASSC) was set up in January 1970 by the Council of the ICAEW and was later re-named the Accounting Standards Committee (ASC). Following this, in June 1970, the Consultative Committee of Accounting Bodies (CCAB) was established to enable the profession to co-ordinate activities in certain areas. The Committee's objectives were to propose definitive standards of financial accounting and reporting for the approval of the Councils of the governing bodies. Its objects encompassed:

1. The fundamentals of financial accounting.
2. The definition of terms used.
3. The application of fundamentals to specific classes of business.
4. The form and content of financial statements including presentation and disclosure.

From February 1976, the ASC was reconstituted as a joint committee of the six governing bodies of the CCAB, and then consisted of 23 committee members nominated by the professional bodies. All 23 members were part-time and unpaid and there was extensive reliance upon the voluntary efforts of numerous firms and organisations. This seemed to work especially in favour of the large accountancy firms who had the resources to allow technical personnel to attend ASC meetings. With hindsight this could be seen as a significant problem for the ASC since its overdependency on certain organisations could lead to accusations of undue influence by vested interests.

11.2.3 *Problems confronting the ASC*

The ASC's early work was very much a case of codifying practice on non-contentious issues; most organisations were either already carrying out the practices contained in the standards or they found some way around the standards which they did not wish to follow. It was not until the second decade of its existence that the ASC began taking on more contentious issues. The issues were contentious because they threatened companies' 'bottom line' distributable profit figure. One such issue was the inflation accounting problem. The ASSC issued provisional (P)SSAP 7 but the government ignored the accounting profession's solution and appointed its own inquiry into inflation accounting. (P)SSAP 7 was not liked by the government because it recommended that accounts be adjusted according to a 'general price index'. The government was concerned that inflation would become institutionalised and so wanted to avoid the use of general indices.

The government's own investigation (The Sandilands Report) whose conclusions were opposed to those of the ASC, recommended the use of specific rather than general price indices. Leaders of the accountancy profession backed down and accepted the report's conclusions and it became the ASC's responsibility to implement them. The ASC, in an attempt to comply with the report, published an extremely complex and technically difficult exposure draft (ED 18) in 1976. This was soon engulfed in a surge of criticism which came to a head in July 1977 when at a special general meeting, the members of the ICAEW voted to reject ED 18. The ASC began to restrict the new system solely to large and listed companies. The result of this was SSAP 16, *Current Cost Accounting*, which was issued in March 1980. Initially it managed to secure a fairly high degree of compliance but this rapidly faded with inflation accounting soon becoming defunct.

The onslaught on the accounting profession by government was not the only one which the profession had to endure. Ebling (1990) wrote that:

> this probably started with the debacle over inflation accounting, and then snowballed as the Committee twisted and turned in search of solutions to problems such as goodwill, merger accounting, deferred taxation and pension cost accounting . . . As respect was lost, preparers felt able to stand up to the committee, even when they knew that its arguments were strong and virtuous.

The first example of this concerned a proposed standard on research and development expenditure. In the first ED the ASC proposed that all such expenditure should be written off in the year that it was incurred reducing both profit and net worth on the balance sheet. A number of powerful companies in the electronics and aerospace industries objected. The industry lobby won and the draft was revised allowing the capitalisation of development expenditure under certain circumstances.

A further battle ensued over the accounting standard concerning deferred taxation. A number of influential companies threatened to ignore the standard because of their fear that the Labour Government might, on seeing the large deferred tax credits in companies' balance sheets, use them as a pretext to obtain a further share of British industry. Thus a new standard was developed allowing companies much greater flexibility in their accounting for deferred tax.

The next challenge arose over the standard for depreciation. The original standard provided that all freehold buildings should be written off over their useful lives. However, property investment companies objected to this and even went as far as to lobby the Council of the ICAEW, arguing that their buildings did not depreciate and moreover, that it was impossible to separate the value of land from buildings. The Council directed the ASC to reconsider its position. The ASC reacted by making property investment companies exempt from the standard.

The beginning of the end appeared to come for the ASC in December 1984 when it issued SSAP 22, *Accounting for Goodwill*. The basic choice that the standard setters had to make was between a standard that affected the balance sheet, or one that affected the profit and loss account. The ASC allowed companies to adopt whichever course they preferred. This 'liberal' trend continued in relation to SSAP 23, *Accounting for Acquisitions and Mergers* in April 1985, which allowed companies to structure acquisitions in such a way that would permit them to be accounted for as mergers. Other issues also began to come to light; there were problems with accounting for pension costs and off-balance sheet financing. The same lack of standardisation predominant at the end of the 1960s was again becoming visible in the 1980s. The atmosphere at that time is reflected by Griffiths (1986).

> Every company in the country is fiddling its profits. Every set of published accounts is based on books which have been gently cooked or completely roasted. The figures which are fed twice a year to the investing public have all been changed in order to protect the guilty. It is the biggest con trick since the Trojan horse.

Again accountants were being accused of an inability to produce 'standardised' accounting.

In 1987 the Guinness scandal broke. Guinness had taken over Distillers for £2.7 billion in what was a bitterly fought contest with the Argyll Group. Guinness had not offered the shareholders of Distillers cash, instead, as was common practice at the time, an offer of Guinness shares was made. This meant that if the share price went up, so then would Guinness's offer to the shareholders of Distillers above that of Argyll's bid. It was later alleged that a Wall Street speculator, along with various other brokers, had agreed with Guinness to buy substantial quantities of their shares in order artificially to improve the share price. Guinness offered to indemnify the brokers against any losses they made and also paid direct incentives. Such share price support was illegal in the UK under the Companies Act 1985.

A further financial scandal came to light in 1988 when the Barlow Clowes affair broke. In this case at least 2,000 British investors, mainly retired people, placed savings with Barlow Clowes International based in Gibraltar believing that it carried out investment management. A further 7,000 investors had placed £51 million in the London-based operation, Barlow Clowes Gilt Managers. Barlow Clowes specialised in gilt bond washing, i.e. buying and selling gilts at particular times to convert income into capital. They offered investors a gilt-edged fund that could yield a return above that on gilt-edged stocks.

It was discovered that £130 m of the Gibraltar funds did not exist. Indeed, some of the funds supposedly held in cash were in fact invested in private property. It was alleged that Barlow Clowes had doctored clients' records, made unauthorised removal of clients' records and money, and had also made inaccurate returns to the Department of Trade and Industry (DTI). On 7 June 1988, *The Times* reported that steps had been taken to close down Barlow Clowes International and that a liquidator or receiver was to be appointed. The blame to some extent was laid at the feet of the government and more specifically the DTI. The city watchdog, the National Association of Security Dealers and Investment Managers (NASDIM), had detected that Barlow Clowes had been operating illegally four years before the incident had come to light and, indeed, they had warned the DTI of the situation. Following this there was an independent inquiry into the affairs at the DTI. Their report was held as a vindication of the government's role in the whole affair. However, this was not such good news for the profession as the role of the auditors had become one of increasing public importance following evidence in the report that emphasised the extent to which reliance had been placed by the DTI on the clean bills of health given by Barlow Clowes's auditors.

The accounting profession perceived one further problem in the 1980s. This was the threat from the European Community. Accountants did not want to lose control of their profession to EC bureaucrats. They especially wanted to resist any possibility of a European-wide imposition of the French system under which accounting is regulated by government and accountants have less autonomy and professional standing than in Britain.

11.2.4 *Social, political and economic events leading to the creation of the Accounting Standards Board*

In 1987 the profession agreed to an independent review of the standard setting process. The report summarised certain fundamental weaknesses in the existing standard setting process.

1. That the process lacked an agreed conceptual framework. This led to difficulties in achieving consistency of approach towards standard setting, and ultimately to a lessening of the authority that standards commanded.
2. That several standards lacked precision and therefore left themselves open to a variety of interpretations. It found that there were unacceptable delays in the time taken in some instances to develop standards.
3. That there was no formal mechanism whereby newly emerging issues could be dealt with quickly and effectively, and as a result the profession tended to treat items on an ad hoc basis with little consistency.
4. There were inadequate resources to carry out the tasks required.
5. That the process demanded more than a largely voluntary, part-time and unpaid body supported by a secretariat.
6. That, from time to time, there was strong pressure on auditors to accept interpretations of accounting standards that conformed with the interests of preparers rather than the spirit of the standards themselves.
7. That financial statements did not state whether they had in fact been prepared in conformity with all national and international accounting standards.

Several structural changes were proposed. Firstly, the ASC should be replaced by the

Accounting Standards Board (ASB), under the guidance of a Financial Reporting Council (FRC) and supported by a Review Panel. The body charged with the broad oversight of the new system would be the FRC, the other two bodies would act as subsidiaries but would remain very much independent entities. The FRC was to secure finance to facilitate these new arrangements and fund the other two bodies and ensure that work was carried out efficiently and effectively. It would also be responsible for guiding the ASB on its programme of work and on broad matters of policy and it would further provide a support for the actual accounting standards themselves. Membership of the FRC would consist of about 25 members covering a wide constituency at a senior level in order to give a voice to all concerned in the process. There would be representation from both users and preparers drawn from the accountancy profession, the financial community and the world of business and administration at large. The chair would be appointed jointly by the Secretary of State for Trade and Industry and the Governor of the Bank of England, and it was proposed that the council would meet around three times a year. The key characteristic of the new FRC was that it would radically widen the field of those involved in the standard setting process.

The ASB was proposed as being a much smaller body than the ASC with only nine members and both a full-time chair and a full-time technical director. An offshoot to the ASB, an Urgent Issues Task Force (UITF), was also proposed whose responsibility it would be to deal with urgent matters. The proposed ASB, unlike the ASC, would be able to issue standards on its own authority, a majority of two-thirds of the board would suffice. This meant that the CCAB would be freed of responsibility for approving standards.

The Review Panel was to be created under the aegis of the FRC to examine and question departures from accounting standards by large companies. This panel would have around 15 members from which smaller panels would normally be formed to tackle individual cases as they arose. The new legislation would require large companies to state whether their accounts had been prepared in accordance with accounting standards and to give mention to any particular departures and reasons for them. This mechanism, it was hoped, would bring possible cases to the attention of the Review Panel. The structure is shown in Table 11.1

For the first time the law was introduced into the standard setting process. If the Review Panel concluded that revision to a company's accounts was required in order for them to comply with the Companies Act to show a true and fair view, and the company concerned was unwilling to take action, then in extreme cases the Panel or the Secretary of State could initiate civil actions. The court in such an instance may order the company concerned to prepare revised accounts and circulate these to all persons likely to have relied on the previous accounts.

Accounting standard setting was effectively no longer the sole province of the accounting profession. The accounting profession may have been willing to accept this partly because of their fear of a threat from European Community changes. In 1991 the EC proposed a Directive that would make auditors more independent by preventing them from selling additional services to clients that would result in a conflict of interest, and by suggesting a cyclical rotation of auditors. These proposals met with very spirited resistance in the UK from the profession. The profession feared becoming akin to civil servants, simply following strict rules and thereby losing their autonomy.

Table 11.1 The new structure

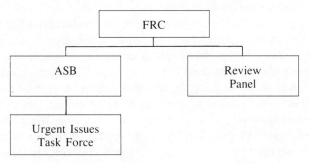

This section has highlighted the events and pressures that influenced changes in the accounting regulation system in the UK. Many of these problems and influences apply to regulatory systems in other countries and it is interesting to contrast the systems that exist in these countries and the reasons for their particular structures.

11.3   International comparison of accounting regulation

Most advanced capitalist economies pour significant resources into accounting practice, education and regulation. However, due to cultural, economic and political differences, each country has its own system of regulation. It is within the context of these differences that the various systems of regulation should be considered. It is impossible to suggest that one system is better than any other system. It is also probably impossible effectively to impose any one country's regulatory system of accounts onto another country.

The diversity of practices within free market economies will be illustrated by a brief description of the regulatory framework in the US, France, Germany and Japan.

11.3.1   *United States*

While US accounting practices are closer to those in the UK than to most other regimes, there is greater emphasis on the needs of the investor and creditor and a list of requirements which is considerably more detailed than in the UK. In the US, companies which do not offer securities to the public are not necessarily subject to audit or accounting prescriptions. However, those that do are required to register with the Securities and Exchange Commission (SEC) which monitors and prescribes the information disclosure requirements of those companies. The SEC is presidentially appointed and while it has made mandatory demands for accounting disclosures, these are not generally concerned with the measurement of accounting numbers. The actual practices and policies of US accounting statements are ruled by a private sector body, the Financial Accounting Standards Board (FASB), which issues 'Statements of Financial Accounting Standards'. The SEC has only rarely interfered with the FASB's pronouncements, though it ensures compliance with these requirements. The FASB differs from the ASB in that it receives strong support for enforcement from the SEC, its procedures are specified in a detailed constitution which requires that its deliberations are open to the public, and it has devoted a considerable amount of its resources to the development of a conceptual framework.

One of the few academic studies of enforcement was conducted by Feroz *et al.* (1992). This paper is unusual in that it examines the activities undertaken by the SEC to enforce regulation, and in particular it documents the problems investigated, the consequences, and the market impact. They investigated 188 cases, 58 of which form a sub-sample having a clear event date and available stock prices. The main source of complaint is overstatement of receivables (50 per cent) followed by overstatement of inventory, and the typical impact of reversing the mis-statement is to lower income by 50 per cent. Many of the firms were in the electronics or financial sector. The investigation of audit failure indicated a tendency amongst auditors to neglect to collect sufficient information. The paper also discusses the sanctions available to the SEC and it is notable that censure of auditors is much more common when the auditor is a small firm.

Feroz *et al.* (1992) also investigated the earnings forecast and share price impact of the investigations. Only a small sample of the companies were covered by Value Line's earnings prediction service. Of these 22 firms 15 earnings increases and 17 decreases were predicted before disclosure of the results of the investigation, whereas afterwards there were only 5 increases and 17 decreases. The authors also report negative performance for the year prior to the initiation (-6 per cent) of the investigation, and the year prior to the disclosure of the results (-24 per cent). The announcement effects are also significantly negative at, and just prior to, the first disclosure date and the disclosure of SEC investigations.

These results suggest that an enforcement system can be influential and it is a feature of the regulation system in most other countries that enforcement is weak.

11.3.2 *France*

In France the accounting practices are quite rigid insofar as they apply to unconsolidated accounts and are determined by the state through the taxation system and the Plan Comptable Général (national accounting plan). The influence of the equity investor on the accounting practices has been small since in France accounts are legally viewed more as documents of proof and verification than as sources of information for decision-making. Having said this, it should be pointed out that French accounts are detailed and sophisticated. As with many European countries, the profit which serves as a base for taxation is basically the same as the profit reported in the financial statements. This ensures that any developments which would occasion an increase in taxation are unlikely to receive support from the business community and that there is little discretion available to the accountant.

The national accounting plan which applies to public and private firms is a detailed description of how sets of accounts are to be produced. Its rigidity should not be overstated as there are many aspects of financial accounting which require expert estimation, and the plan is subject to revision and to explanation through accounting standards issued by its management body. There are four major organisations involved in accounting standard setting in France (Choi and Mueller, 1992). These are:

1. Conseil National de la Comptabilité, or CNC (National Accounting Board).
2. Commission des Operations de Bourse (COB).

3. Ordre des Experts-Comptables et des Comptables Agrées (OECCA).
4. Compagnie Nationale des Commissaires aux Comptes (CNCC).

The CNC is charged with keeping the Plan up to date and for approving exemptions for certain industries. CNC is a prestigious body but does not actually have any power since its recommendations need to become law before they become effective.

COB is a little like the SEC. It is caught in a dilemma in that it would like large publicly listed French companies to comply with Anglo/American-style accounting standards but has to recognise the importance of the Plan.

The OECCA has twelve thousand members who practise public accounting but not auditing. Auditing is carried out by CNCC members. There is a large overlap in the membership of both bodies. CNCC issues a member's handbook which contains comprehensive technical standards.

As with the US and the UK the French system can be seen as a mix of governmental, professional and securities market-based regulation.

11.3.3 *Germany*

In common with the French system, German accounting practice is derived largely from government action, but there is no detailed equivalent to the national plan. Choi and Mueller (1992, p. 96) note that:

> The Fourth, Seventh and Eighth EC directives all entered German law through the Comprehensive Accounting Act of December 19, 1985. This legislation is remarkable because (1) it integrates all existing German accounting, financial reporting, disclosure and auditing requirements into a single law; (2) this single law is specified as the 'third book' of the German Commercial Code, thereby achieving applicability to all business entities from limited partnerships to private as well as publicly held corporations; and (3) the legislation is anchored in predominantly European concepts and practices.

Of particular influence is the requirement that accounting statements should agree with taxation laws, which are, of course, subject to change. The influence of the accountancy profession in Germany is modest and exercised through the release of non-mandatory recommendations, though the representations to law-making bodies are possibly more influential. In fact the only things that have any authoritative status are statutes and court decisions. The consequence of the importance of law and taxation is a noticeable tendency towards conservatism in German accounting statements.

Unlike previous analysed countries it could be argued that the German system of regulation is not particularly pluralistic.

11.3.4 *Japan*

Japanese regulation of accounting practice comes from three government-based sources. A commercial code requires a legalistically precise, though not necessarily economically informative, set of accounts which are apparently designed for creditor protection and do not require group accounts. For those firms that are traded on stock exchanges, the Securities and Exchanges Law requires more detailed disclosure of benefit to investors.

Finally, Japanese tax law requires that the financial accounts, as detailed by commercial law, match the taxation computations, thereby imparting a bias and rigidity to the accounting system.

The decisions regarding accounting legislation are controlled by the government, though there is an advisory body including accountants and business representatives. The direct influence of the accounting profession is limited to making recommendations.

For the countries reviewed there are many dimensions which affect accounting regulation. Of these, the existence of a private or public sector body, the influence of the tax regime, and the relative importance of equity versus fixed interest capital, seem to be the more important characteristics.

11.3.5 *European Union*

In late 1989 the ICAEW, ICAS and ICAI bowed to what they described as the 'inevitable', in considering the plan to establish such a European Accounting Standards Body. However, as an Institute Council member put it in *Accountancy* (May, 1988, p. 8):

> the UK profession does not support the idea of European standards as such, but would welcome greater harmonisation in Europe, as this is where international standards are furthest apart.

It was clear that although the British profession said that they saw a need for some sort of harmonisation they were not prepared to have standards dictated to them. As Dearing put it:

> the profession must act in order to give credibility back to accounting standards or face the threat of a legal approach to standard setting.

Dearing warned that unless the British approach to standard setting could demonstrate its superiority as the pressures of the international market place grew, the UK was likely to find itself moving into line with the legalistic approach of Europe and the US. He further stated that the legalistic approach was gaining ground and, indeed, countries such as Australia and Canada, who in the past had adopted the British approach, had now changed over to a more legalistic style of setting standards. It seems that at least for the present the British accounting profession has managed to retain at least partial control of the accounting standard setting process.

11.4 The case for the regulation of accounting practices

The case for accounting regulation can be divided into the scope for repairing imperfections in the market mechanism, and other rationales which incorporate considerations of equity and social objectives.

11.4.1 *Disclosure and market failure*

In the absence of regulation, the vested interests of the many parties involved will ensure that some level of accounting disclosure exists, and to the extent that individuals can both pay and be charged for the costs of any disclosure, a market for financial information might develop. Insofar as that market is effective it could be argued that an optimal level of disclosure will be achieved. However, many circumstances exist where it might be expected that the level of accounting disclosure will be less than ideal.

Traditionally market failure is characterised as occurring when:

1. The supplier of information is unable to charge effectively all the potential users of the information, and in the absence of this compensation the supplier will underproduce. The demand for financial information by prospective shareholders, or by competitors, is an example of this 'public good' aspect of accounting disclosures, where use of data by 'free riders' fails to encourage further disclosure.
2. Where the user of information has insufficient data to distinguish between good or bad products, there will be an incentive for the sub-standard firm to oversupply goods (in this case investment opportunities), and the better firms will have to incur additional costs attempting to convince customers of their superior worth or withdraw from the market.
3. The potential users of information have differing levels of access to accounting information and resources to devote to its analysis. To the extent that costs incurred in analysis lead only to a redistribution of wealth through share trading and have no impact on the allocation of productive resources, this can be viewed as inefficient, and to the extent that analysts may have privileged access to accounting information it may also be deemed to be inequitable.

With all three possibilities of apparent market failure, there are conceivable scenarios which cannot accurately be described as failure, and most significantly where there are costs of contracting. It is quite possible that the costs of overcoming the market failure may be greater than those associated with the failure itself. Thus, it can be argued that even where it is agreed that market failure is occurring, some evidence would still be required that the alternative, a regulatory system, is preferable.

Thus every regulation introduces costs and benefits which may, or may not, be generally beneficial. Mian and Smith (1990a), in the first of two interesting papers investigating the effect of mandated full consolidation for all US groups, try to show how diversity in accounting regulation may be efficient in contracting cost terms. They investigate SFAS No. 94 which eliminated the option not to consolidate majority-owned subsidiaries whose affairs are materially different from those of the parent. The researchers reject the FASB's hypothesis that financial statement users seek uniformity in accounting methods across firms, and believe that the option not to consolidate had been used by firms for rational contracting reasons related to the firms' organisational structure (although the quotation from the FASB is quite explicit that off-balance sheet financing is the main motivation). They presume that the FASB's prescriptions will be damaging.

Organisational structure can range from total integration to complete separation. The accounting choice prior to SFAS No. 94 was whether to consolidate a majority-owned subsidiary. They believe that the accounting decision should reflect organisational choice as management accounts will drive financial accounts and be driven by organisational practices and they consider three cases where accounting practices may be driven by organisational realities.

1. Operating independence. Finance subsidiaries providing for the group are integrated whereas those that provide finance for customers are not. Manufacturer-lessors are seen as integrated whereas third party lessors are not.
2. Informational interdependence. Following ARB 51 Mian and Smith believe that finance firms should consolidate finance subsidiaries more often than manufacturers, manufacturing firms should consolidate insurance subsidiaries less often than financial firms, and foreign subsidiaries should be consolidated less often than domestic ones. They point out that consolidated accounts contain less information than the unconsolidated equivalents and that where this proprietary information is valuable to outsiders consolidation might be expected.
3. Financial interdependence. Where direct intra-group guarantees of debt are employed it is thought that consolidated accounts would be employed. Conversely indirect guarantees are thought to be associated with unconsolidated reporting.

Mian and Smith examine 484 firms of which 246 have finance subsidiaries and of these 98 consolidate no subsidiaries, 98 consolidate all, and 50 use a mixture. The results were broadly supportive of their hypotheses.

1. Operating interdependence. A description of the distribution of consolidated–unconsolidated subsidiaries does seem to confirm the operational links hypothesis. For example, 75 per cent of external financing subsidiaries are not consolidated whilst 92 per cent of internal financing subsidiaries are. Further subjective analysis of the mixed policy firms is also seen as supporting the hypothesis.
2. Informational interdependence. There is a marginally significant difference between the propensity of financial firms to consolidate and the others where unconsolidated accounts dominate. The 555 subsidiaries are separated by location and it is apparent that foreign subsidiaries are more likely to be consolidated than domestics.
3. Financial interdependence. Although the number of guaranteed firms is small subsidiaries which are guaranteed are considerably more likely to be consolidated than others. Direct guarantees are provided primarily to consolidated foreign finance subsidiaries, whereas indirect guarantees usually involve unconsolidated domestic finance and leasing subsidiaries.

In a multiple regression where the dependent variable is the consolidation policy five dummy variables were significant and of expected sign — foreign, non-financial parent, insurance subsidiary, direct parental guarantee, and indirect parental guarantee — and only the dummy indicating customer financing was insignificant, albeit marginally.

The FASB asserts that the attempt to mislead users concerning a firm's leverage is a motivation for avoiding consolidation. Mian and Smith respond that if this were the case other methods of off-balance sheet financing would also be employed by these firms but they find no evidence of this. It seems to be Mian and Smith's view that in this case regulatory prescription has failed to improve on the market's solution.

11.4.2 *Non-market rationales for regulation*

It should not be forgotten in the detailed arguments concerning the level or significance of any market failure, that there can be valid non-market rationales for disclosure. Groups within society that have no effective means of directly representing their need for information may still be deemed by society as a whole to have a right to accountability. Further, it may be felt that information should be supplied for educational purposes even where no apparent demand exists, and some groups, such as trade unions, have shown a willingness to bargain for information in a manner which is difficult to analyse in market terms.

It is also impossible to evaluate an extant system without consideration of the groups, in this case primarily the accounting profession, most directly affected by any change. The favourable economic and social position experienced by accountants is not only dependent upon specialist skills and an advanced capitalist society's need for these skills, but also on the mystique attached to their operation. This position is supported by the compliance of corporate management and the state as sponsors of the market for the profession's accounting and auditing skills (Willmott, 1986). In return the accounting profession manages the regulation of accounting and achieves considerable standing thereby. It need not be presumed that a protected market position is necessarily antisocial as the profession's actions to legitimise its role through training and enforcement of professional standards may be of value, though they also permit control over the supply, and hence the price, of accounting skills.

11.4.3 *Costs and benefits of regulation*

In the absence of demonstrable or quantifiable market failure some observers are unconvinced of the benefits of regulation and suggest that the imposition of standards increases the costs of information disclosure. Benston (1980) suggests that the imposition of standards increases costs for the following reasons:

1. Compliance with requirements above those that market characteristics imply will incur processing costs.
2. Attestation of these more complex requirements will increase auditing fees.
3. Competing firms may benefit from the disclosures made thereby imposing costs on the disclosing firm.
4. Even where a standard meets the level of disclosure that a free market would require, individual companies will wish to exceed or avoid such requirements.

It is difficult to evaluate the significance of any of the externalities and only limited evidence on this matter is available. Arguments that regulatory prescriptions will increase the costs of information production are intuitively convincing, but the potential benefits are less clear and less susceptible to quantification. This is particularly problematical for any regulatory agency which attempts to overcome the disadvantages inherent in market failure. Furthermore, the demand for information over and above that provided by the market is dependent on the varied economic circumstances of its potential users. Insofar as this is unknown, the regulatory agency can only estimate the incidence of benefits and costs.

Hence the cost for regulation is not proven by analysis which implies that we might expect market inefficiency or inequality, and closer evaluation of the costs and benefits is precluded by their indeterminate nature. However, the regulatory system in existence is a product of social, political and historical, as well as economic circumstances, and the scope for change is constrained by all four considerations.

Some papers have presented evidence of the costs of regulation. Mian and Smith's (1990b) second paper associated with changes in consolidated reporting requirements analyses the lobbying activity regarding SFAS No. 94 and the price impact of the regulation. Apparently the users the FASB expects to be helped by the change lobbied against SFAS No. 94. A small group lobbied for the changes for purely strategic reasons.

Mian and Smith examine whether non-consolidating firms (a) were more likely to lobby against SFAS No. 94, (b) suffered adverse price reaction on its adoption, and (c) took action to mitigate its effects. They analysed 232 submissions.

The costs of complying with sub-optimal accounting techniques and of recontracting suggest that non-consolidators will lobby against SFAS No. 94 and that consolidators would seek to keep options open; unless they have strategic incentives. The results clearly show that unconsolidated firms tend to resist SFAS No. 94. Of the nine who supported it none have relevant restrictive covenants, and the impact on their gearing is considerably less than on their competitors.

Mian and Smith calculate two-day market-adjusted returns around a number of relevant event dates. The only date with interesting results is 2/11/87 where the *Wall Street Journal* reported the FASB's decision and comments on the impact for a number of firms. Significant negative returns are observed for 169 firms with unconsolidated subsidiaries, for those firms that lobbied against SFAS No. 94, and for firms that were mentioned in the article.

Mian and Smith tabulated five activities which might be undertaken to mitigate against the effect of SFAS No. 94 — selling the subsidiary, closing it down, reorganising it, retiring debt with relevant covenants and selling securitised assets. The sample is those firms which lobbied the FASB. They find that those firms with unconsolidated subsidiaries and those that lobbied against SFAS No. 94 are much more likely to take avoiding action than other firms. This is a surprising result as firms are apparently taking costly action to avoid the simple requirements of an accounting rule and it would perhaps be wise to wait for corroborating evidence before relying on the final set of results.

In conclusion Mian and Smith are able to show that lobbying activity is dependent on firm characteristics, there is limited evidence of a negative price impact, and there seems to be remedial action taken. They suggest that:

> the FASB in reducing the accounting opportunity set has eliminated a valuable alternative . . . despite widespread use of the technique and strong lobbying against.

11.5   Decision criteria and accounting choice

11.5.1   *The difficulties of social choice*

While considerable time and resources have been expended on research into alternative accounting models, measurement rules and disclosure practice, no method of selecting the most socially desirable accounting alternative has been devised. The process of social choice entered into by the policy maker is based on the selection of an accounting theory which meets the policy maker's goals. However, while the FASB asserts that the aim of financial statements is to produce information to assist with economic decision-making, this does not constitute a goal through which accounting choice can be made. Alternative groups of users have different economic decisions to make and bear different costs. May and Sundem (1976) suggest that the appropriate decision rule should be the maximisation of social welfare and they further point out that if policy makers depart too far from this objective they are likely to be overruled by the legislature. Thus regulators set the task of producing quasi-legislation on the public's behalf.

However, it has been shown that even when making helpful restrictive assumptions (such as costless information production, dissemination and analysis), Demski (1973) has argued that:

> generally speaking, we cannot rely on standards to provide a normative theory of accounting. No set of standards exists that will always rank alternatives in accordance with preferences and beliefs — no matter what these preferences and beliefs are.

Here Demski is referring to desirable characteristics rather than the regulatory pronouncements when he uses the term 'standards'. Demski's argument is based on the finding that even costless information systems can only be ranked for preference for all users by the 'fineness' of the information presented, and that since alternative accounting systems cannot necessarily be evaluated by this characteristic no clear method of accounting choice is available. The reality of costly information systems only makes the comparison more invidious.

Cushing (1977) has suggested that Demski and others are overly pessimistic and that under certain circumstances, particularly in relation to partial accounting standards, rational choice theory can lead to optimal accounting standards. However, Bromwich (1980) has shown that the conditions favouring the possibility of partial accounting standards are narrow and, in particular, require limited interdependence between the standard under consideration and others in existence.

Despite these difficulties, systems of accounting regulation are universal and regulators appear determined to pursue the objectives they have set themselves. Where conflict arises in the utility of particular standards for differing groups the regulatory body has no option but to evaluate the case and make a social choice between the competing claims. However, Bromwich (1985) notes that as regards the evaluation of economic consequences,

> consideration of these matters is generally based on armchair empiricism and on assertions based on the experience of individual committee members.

The submissions to regulators in response to draft regulations confirm that choices between accounting options have been argued on an ad hoc basis, using normative models often founded in the 'accounting conventions' together with the 'true and fair' requirement. Consideration of the economic consequences seem to be constrained to the cost of information production and audit, the benefits to competitors of increased disclosure of commercially sensitive data, and the implications for the tax liabilities of firms.

11.5.2 *Economic consequences of accounting regulation*

It is reasonably clear that no simple decision rules are available to aid the choice between accounting alternatives and that even the economic consequences of alternative policies, although relevant, are not definitive.

Once enacted there may be the potential for assessing the decision relevance of disclosed information. The most frequent example of such work is the assessment of inflation-adjusted accounts, or other developments, as aids to shareholders' decision-making, by examining stock market reactions to new disclosure. However, this process is only available as an ex post exercise, requires some independent measure of relevance such as the reaction of an efficient market, and is susceptible to imperfections in the research methodology which may struggle to identify subtle reactions.

Selto and Neumann (1981, p. 317) review this limited focus of attention and note that:

> it would appear that most of the applied 'economic consequences' literature to date has focused on the effects on stock market prices. These effects, though important, are arguably only a small portion of what constitutes economic consequences.

Zeff (1978, p. 19) has suggested that interest in economic consequences of accounting standards was built up initially through the intervention of those external to the standard setting process and who resisted its pronouncements when they perceived them to be detrimental. As he notes, 'the very intervention by outside parties in the setting of standards appears to be due, in large measure, to their belief in the fact of economic consequences'. In the early days of these interventions to suggest that the policy makers should consider other than compliance with an objective model of good accounting and disclosure practice would have been unacceptable. However, the policy makers were forced to recognise the influence of certain third parties and the conflict between the Accounting Practices Board (APB) and the others lead to the demise of the APB.

Zeff (1978) records the catalogue of instances where third parties intervened or where the policy makers explicitly considered the effect of their actions on third parties. These included the discouragement of stock dividends, the case for replacement cost depreciation, the implications for the capital base of regulated utility companies, the perceived negating of investment incentives incorporated in US tax law, the information available to government departments for economic planning, the marketability of convertible debt, bad debt provisions in banking, the promotion or constraint of merger activity through 'pooling of interests' accounting, the valuation of marketable securities (primarily in the insurance industry), accounting for leases, and costing in the petroleum industry.

> On each of the questions enumerated above, outside parties intervened in the standard-setting process by an appeal to criteria which transcended the traditional questions of accounting measurement and fair presentation. They were concerned instead with the economic consequences of accounting pronouncements   (Zeff, 1978).

The stream of controversial issues has not ceased since the creation of the FASB to take over from the APB and again Zeff (1978) cites research and development, self-insurance, development stage companies, foreign currency fluctuations, leases, restructuring troubled debt, inflation accounting and exploration costs of the petroleum industry. The response of accounting bodies has been gradually to improve consultation procedures and extend the constituencies represented on the policy making boards to allow more explicit consideration of the economic consequences.

11.6 The political aspects of regulation

11.6.1 *The management of the political process*

Bromwich (1985, p. 6) notes that:

> the declared wish of standard setters to promulgate general all-purpose standards of utility to most users is an impossible task. Accounting policy makers therefore have to choose which sectors of society they wish to serve.

Yet if one section of society perceives that the ASC is not operating in its interest one might expect that sector to attempt to influence the ASC. There is some evidence that this does occur. The previous section cites Zeff's (1978) acknowledgement of the economic consequences which have persuaded various groups to participate in the political activity of the standard setting process.

Yet there is clearly a role for political activity to enable interested parties to express their views regarding the economic impact of considered changes.

11.6.2 *Positive accounting theory tests of political lobbying*

One of the most significant branches of accounting research was initiated, in part, by Watts and Zimmerman's seminal article (1978) 'Towards a positive theory of the determination of accounting standards' which is intended to 'provide the beginnings of a positive theory of accounting' and explores those factors likely to affect lobbying by management. Watts and Zimmerman view management activities as central in the determination of accounting standards. The full set of participants involved in standard setting include — the SEC, the Treasury, state regulation, public accountants, quasi-public bodies such as the CAP, APB and FASB, and management.

It is assumed that management act so as to maximise their own utility, without assuming congruence with shareholders, and without assuming an ability to manipulate share prices. In these models utility is constrained to future wages and incentives and the risk attached to those. These factors can make an impact through share prices or through compensation plans and are categorised as taxes, regulation, political costs, information costs, and management compensation.

1. *Taxes.* In the US, financial accounting is not directly tied to taxable profits but the adoption of a procedure for financial accounting increases the chance of it being adopted for revenue purposes.
2. *Regulation.* Where utilities profits are managed by a regulatory body the accounting determined costs will influence income.
3. *Political costs.* The government can effect wealth transfers through a number of processes. These are more likely to be disadvantageous where a firm, or industry, is seen to be making excessive profits. The impact of high profits on the political process is more obvious where the firms are large.
4. *Information costs.* This is simply the cost of producing and disseminating additional information, though it might equally be the competitive effect.

5. *Management compensation.* Most firms' management remuneration schemes include some element of incentives based on accounting income. Thus an increase in profits will increase compensation directly, but may also have adverse effects via the stock price impact.

Adjustments can be made to reverse a cosmetic change in accounting standards. Watts and Zimmerman suggest that there are incentives for non-executive directors to make an adjustment, but only weak incentives for politicians or regulators to do so. Hence management will have an incentive to lobby for income decreasing regulation where their firm is subject to political or regulatory costs, but the reverse where it is not.

They also conducted an empirical test of lobbying behaviour based on the 52 usable corporate submissions to the FASB in 1974 regarding a general price level (inflation) accounting proposal (see Table 11.2).

Watts and Zimmerman collected financial data, details regarding incentive plans, and estimated the effect of GPLA adjustments for each of the firms. Basic descriptive data clarify that smaller firms opposed GPLA and larger firms that expected a decrease in earnings supported GPLA. An attempt to incorporate a multivariate test was based on the following model.

The regressand is bivariate indicating support or opposition. Detailed results are given in Watts and Zimmerman (1978) — table 4.

$$p_i = \alpha_1 + \alpha_2 \frac{DEP_i}{MKTVL_i} + \alpha_3 \frac{NMA_i}{MKTVL_i} + \alpha_3 (SALES_i) CHG_i +$$

$$\alpha_4 \left(\frac{SALES_I}{TSALES_i} \right) CHG_i + \alpha_5 MCOMP_i + \alpha_6 REG_i$$

(11.1)

The first two variables are proxies for the GPLA impact on the firms' earnings and neither were significant, the third and fourth are supposedly indicators of political costs and the first of the two was significant, the fifth, a dummy variable which indicates the presence of incentive schemes, is negative but not significant, and the final regressor indicates regulated firms and is perverse, supposedly because of multi-collinearity. The only result of interest from the discriminant model is that size has a powerful effect. The model offers no other support for the theory put forward.

This paper is seminal. It is the first widely cited paper which explicitly studied accounting regulation from a positive accounting theory framework. The authors contend

Table 11.2 Median rank of firm size by regulation and position on GPLA

	Advocating GPLA	Opposing GPLA
Regulated	9(13)	9(10)
Unregulated	9(38)	25(92)

Number(rank)
Source: Watts and Zimmerman, 1978.

that they provide evidence of lobbying to enhance the utility of management, and particularly to avoid accounting practices which will encourage state intervention. The success of the paper in proving these points is debatable. Its influence is not.

Subsequently, Watts and Zimmerman (1990) reviewed the development of positive accounting research in 'Positive accounting theory: a ten year perspective'. They examine the evolution, accumulated evidence, and criticisms, and make some suggestions for the future.

Watts and Zimmerman feel that market-based accounting research has had little to say regarding accounting choice as value is thought to be independent of accounting in the finance literature. The introduction of debt and agency costs began to overcome this problem. This is a sub-set of the organisation analysis of the firm, and is not just an agency issue; hence the term contracting costs — including transaction, agency, information, renegotiation, and bankruptcy costs. Participants organise for maximum efficiency accepting that opportunistic behaviour will be normal. Thus the accepted set of accounting alternatives is agreed by the contracting parties for the sake of efficiency, and managers choose from that set.

The accumulated evidence from PAT studies shows that:

1. Stock price tests of the theory reveal some market reaction to mandatory accounting changes. Watts and Zimmerman regard these as weak tests of the theory.
2. Tests of accounting theory examine individual choice, sets of choice, or accruals. Explanatory variables are usually bonus plan, debt/equity, or political costs. In general the evidence supports all three but the operational variables are problematic.

Christie (1990) notes that:

> ... six variables common to more than one study have explanatory power ... managerial compensation, leverage, size, risk, interest coverage and dividend constraints ... the posterior probability that the theory taken as a whole has explanatory power is probably close to one.

However, it is important to note that the explanatory power of most of these studies is very low.

There have been a number of criticism of PAT research methodology which include:

1. *Model specification.* The models assume no change in opportunities and that no interaction between the explanatory variables is possible.
2. *Dependent variables.* The use of a single choice is limited, but using portfolios of decisions assume decisions can be cumulated, and accruals are noisy measures of choice.
3. *Independent variables.* Simplistic assumptions are made when measuring the existence or impact of bonus plans, restrictive covenants etc.
4. *Omitted variables.* Standard contracts correlated with included contracts, non-debt or compensation variables, and differences in the accepted set are all omitted from various studies.

Criticism focusing on alternative hypotheses suggests that there may be excluded variables which affect accounting choice and the explanatory variables, and there may be endogenous costs omitted from the model. The final source of criticism is based on the philosophy of science. These critics point out that positive theories are value laden or that PAT is a sociology of accounting not an accounting theory. Another branch asserts that PAT makes inappropriate use of rational economic theories and of the use of the term 'positive'.

Overall the contribution from PAT studies is that the research has documented regularities, and provided a framework for explaining accounting, it encourages relevant research, and emphasises the place of contracting costs. Watts and Zimmerman are concerned to encourage improvements in the links between the theory and the empirical tests. This includes better specification of the explanatory variables, development of alternative hypotheses, and, in particular, there needs to be an improvement in the measurement of political costs. They are also concerned with the link between choices of accounting processes and of other choices. This needs to be borne in mind and might be countered by intra-industry studies. Research studies described in earlier sections of this chapter have made use of, and advanced, the methodologies first advocated by Watts and Zimmerman.

11.6.3 *The visibility of the political process*

It is by now apparent to the reader that there is no one model of the desirable characteristics of accounting statements which can be used to determine the ideal form of accounting disclosures. If this fact is coupled to the presumption that the effects of different accounting policies are not trivial it will follow that users and preparers of accounting statements will mobilise their forces to influence the outcome in their favour. The power and politics of the choice of accounting options are matters of some interest and importance.

The influence exercised in the evaluation of accounting policy options can be apparent and emanate from the 'legitimate' authority conferred on individuals such as the members of the ASB, or may result from the 'competent' authority conferred on those whose experience or research gives them acknowledged insights. Less apparent but conceivably important will be the influence earned through manipulation, coercion and inducement. This latter group will tend to be well hidden and the lack of visible evidence renders any analysis of the effect of differing elements of influence problematic and unscientific. Hope and Gray (1982) point out that there are three dimensions at which political influence can be observed, as follows:

1. The behaviour of individuals or groups lobbying for results which can be ascertained to be seen to be in their interest.
2. Where groups or individuals prevent decisions being reached where an ascribable outcome can be seen to be in their interest.
3. Where groups or individuals or the institutional, social, political or economic environment prevent potential issues from being examined.

It is apparent that the first dimension will be relatively easy to observe and analyse, yet that analysis will only be partial. As the researcher progresses through to the third dimension the scope of the analysis broadens, but the ease with which it can be examined decreases. Indeed, it may be that considerable influence is being exerted to prevent an issue from arriving on the political agenda and yet no conflict or political activity may be apparent.

11.7 Conclusion

The choice between alternative accounting procedures and disclosure requirements can have a significant impact on economic efficiency and equality. Taxation liabilities and incidence, the price and availability of finance, monitoring and regulation of industry, wage negotiations and payments by results are examples of where economic consequences can flow from the accounting techniques adopted by firms. The material available to the financial analyst and the scope for exploitation of their special skills and privileged position are further considerations dependent on the system of accounting regulation. Furthermore, the economic and social standing of the accounting profession itself is influenced by the mystique surrounding complex and flexible accounting practices and is damaged by the inevitable failure of that system to produce financial statements which are consistently free from criticism. Dissatisfaction with the treatment of accounting for takeovers, off-balance sheet financing, extraordinary items, and brand valuations are recent examples of perceived failure of the financial reporting which will impact on the accounting profession's standing, not only with its principal markets, but also with the state whose patronage is crucial.

Some observers feel that a regulatory system dominated and funded by the accounting profession, with limited powers of enforcement and subject to political pressures, may be unable to maintain its credibility. Also where accounting rules can affect the distribution of wealth and income in society, it is unclear that the accounting profession has a mandate to make social decisions. Moreover, there is no resolution of the problems which accountants face in attempting to maintain their professional standing, and narrow the diversity of accounting practice whilst at the same time being pressured by their clients into setting broad permissive accounting standards.

Notes

1. Christine Cooper is a Lecturer in Accounting in the Department of Accounting and Finance at the University of Strathclyde.
2. Much of the next two sections follows Allen and Cooper (1993).

—————————————————— QUESTIONS ——————————————————

1. Discuss the contentions in the following submission to the ASC:
    (a) Accountants, particularly Chartered Accountants, are a responsible class of citizen.
    (b) Human progress depends on the exceptional person deviating from the norm.
    (c) Accounting Standards restrict the ability of the exceptional person to deviate from them; thus stultifying progress.
    (d) Accountants being responsible people, should be encouraged to experiment.
    (e) It is for the state to legislate, not private bodies of people.

2. 'Comparable financial information is necessary to ensure the free flow of capital at the lowest cost to the most efficient businesses.'
    (a) Despite this entreaty for international comparability, considerable diversity exists. Discuss the difference in international accounting treatment of three items and consider the impact that such diversity has on the analysis of financial statements.
    (b) Further diversity may reflect varied business practices or economic circumstances. Illustrate how such diversity will distort straightforward comparisons of accounting reports.

3. Discuss the argument that disclosure requirements such as those which regulate the contents of prospectuses are unnecessary, because a free market would provide the information which was desired by investors. (Society of Investment Analysts, Investment Regulation and Practice, November 1988)

4. Select a recent example of regulation by the accounting profession.
    (a) What were the alternatives available to the regulatory body?
    (b) What groups within society would experience economic consequences resulting from the regulation?
    (c) What evidence is there of any lobbying of the standard setters and to what extent has this been successful?
    (d) To what extent is this regulation consistent with IASC regulations and the regulations in other developed economies?
    (e) Can this example be demonstrated to be better than the regulations addressing the same issue in other developed economies?

5. Select an accounting regulation system from one country other than the UK. Briefly describe that system and contrast it with the British system described in this chapter. To what extent can the differences in the system be explained and to what extent can one system be shown to be 'better' than the other?

6. Provide definitions of the following terms as used in this chapter:
    (a) Legislative regulation.
    (b) Accounting standards.
    (c) Economic consequences.
    (d) Market failure.
    (e) Fineness.
    (f) Enforcement.
    (g) Flexibility.
    (h) Private sector regulation.

References

Allen, E. and Cooper, C. (1993) The representation of the accounting standard setting process, Working Paper, Department of Accounting and Finance, University of Strathclyde.

Benston, G. (1980) The establishment and enforcement of accounting standards: methods, benefits and costs, *Accounting and Business Research*, Winter, 51–60.

Bromwich, M. (1980) The possibility of partial accounting standards, *Accounting Review*, April, 288–300.

Bromwich, M. (1985) *The Economics of Accounting Standard Setting*, Prentice Hall International, Hemel Hempstead.

Choi, F. and Mueller, G. (1992) *International Accounting*, Prentice Hall, Englewoods Cliffs.

Christie, A. (1990) Aggregation of test statistics: an evaluation of the evidence on contracting and size hypotheses, *Journal of Accounting and Economics*, **2**, 15–36.

Cushing, B. (1977) On the possibility of optimal accounting principles, *Accounting Review*, April, 308–21.

Dearing, R. (1988) *The Making of Accounting Standards*, ICAEW, London.

Demski, J. (1973) The general impossibility of normative accounting standards, *Accounting Review*, October, 718–23.

Ebling, P. (1990) The ASB — time the talking stopped, *Accountancy*, August, 25–26.

Feroz, E., Park, K. and Pastena, V. (1992) The financial and market effects of the SEC's accounting and auditing enforcement releases, *Journal of Accounting Research*, Supplement **29**, 107–148.

Financial Accounting Standards Board (1978) Statements of financial accounting concepts No. 1, Objectives of financial reporting by business enterprises, FASB, Norwalk, Conn.

Griffiths, I. (1986) *Creative Accounting*, Waterstone, London.

Hope, A. and Gray, R. (1982) Power and policy making — the development of an R&D standard, *Journal of Business, Finance and Accountancy*, **9**, 531–58.

May, R. and Sundem, G. (1976) Research for accounting policy: an overview, *Accounting Review*, **I**, no. 4, 747–763.

Mian, S. and Smith, C. (1990a) Incentives for unconsolidated financial reporting, *Journal of Accounting and Economics*, **12**, 141–171.

Mian, S. and Smith, C. (1990b) Incentives associated with changes in unconsolidated reporting requirements, *Journal of Accounting and Economics*, **13**, 249–266.

Selto, F. and Neumann, B. (1981) A further guide to research on the economic consequences of accounting information, *Accounting and Business Research*, Autumn, 317–22.

Swaminathan, S. (1991) The impact of SEC mandated segment data on price variability and divergence of beliefs, *Accounting Review*, **66**, 23–41.

Watts, R. and Zimmerman, J. (1978) Towards a positive theory of the determination of accounting standards, *Accounting Review*, **53**, 112–134.

Watts, R. and Zimmerman, J. (1990) Positive accounting theory: a ten-year perspective, *Accounting Review*, **65**, 131–156.

Willmott, H. (1986) Organising the profession: a theoretical and historical examination of the development of the major accountancy bodies in the UK, *Accounting, Organisations and Society*, 555–80.

Zeff, S. (1978) The rise of 'economic consequences', *Journal of Accountancy*, November, 56–63.

Author Index

Abarbanell, J.   140, 144, 150
Adams, R.   334, 337, 355–7
Aharony, J.   310, 324
Alford, A.   229, 253
Alhabshi, M.   273, 275, 289
Allen, E.   382–3
Altman, E.   301, 304–7, 310, 324
Altman, I.   357
Antal, A.   333, 357
Argenti, J.   316, 324
Arnold, J.   46–7, 77–8, 82, 118, 150, 214, 218, 224, 296, 324

Ball, R.   34–5, 48, 124, 142, 150, 170, 184, 187–8, 190–2, 197, 224
Bank of England   324
Barbier, E.   357
Barnes, P.   105, 116
Beaver, W.   3, 45, 81–2, 125, 127, 147–8, 150, 188, 191–2, 194, 196, 199, 219, 221, 224, 228, 238, 247, 253, 301, 304–5, 310, 324, 398–9
Beecher, A.   109, 116
Belkaoui, A.   281, 289, 314, 324
Bell, P.   230, 253
Benesh, G.   203–4, 224
Benston, G.   329, 355, 373, 383
Benzie, R.   262, 277–8, 289
Bernard, V.   140, 150
Berry, A.   296–7, 324
Bhashar, K.   132, 150
Bhattacharya, K.   336, 355
Biddel, G.   202, 225
Biggs, S.   213, 224
Black, F.   165, 185, 187, 215, 224
Bougen, P.   349, 355–7
Bouwman, M.   86, 213, 224
Bower, D.   173–4, 184
Bower, R.   172–3, 183
Bowers, J.   79, 82
Bowman, R.   249, 253
Box, G.   105, 116
Brealey, R.   177, 184, 219, 224, 227, 251, 253
Brennan, M.   166, 183
Brickley, J.   271, 275–6, 289
Briloff, A.   202
Brodie, J   112, 116
Bromwich, M.   359, 375, 377, 383
Brown, G.   178, 184
Brown, L.   134, 138, 151
Brown, P.   142, 150, 187–8, 190–2, 197, 206, 224
Broyles, J.   272, 280, 289
Buck, J.   334, 355
Buckley, A.   354, 338–9, 340
Byrne, A.   258–9

Cakici, N.   273, 289
Capstaff, J.   136–44, 148
Carey, A.   328, 355

Carruthers, J.   113, 116
Cebenayan, A.   273, 289
Chadwick, L.   82
Chambers, A.   195–6, 224
Chapin, D.   328, 355
Chappell, H.   279–80, 289
Chen, K.   109, 112–15, 116
Chen, W.   173, 184
Cheng, D.   279–80, 289
Choi, F.   368–9, 383
Choy, A.   179, 184
Christie, A.   379, 383
Chugh, L.   213, 224
Citron, D.   296–7, 324
Clark, R.   191–2, 194, 224
Clark, T.   310, 324
Coase, R.   34, 45
Coates, K.   345, 355
Coggin, T.   134, 150
Cohn, R.   205, 225
Collins, D.   134, 144, 151
Collinson, D.   350, 357
Comiskey, E.   142, 151
Condoyani, L.   178, 183
Confederation of British Industry,   206–7, 224
Conn, R.   273, 289
Connell, F.   273, 289
Conray, R.   137, 151
Cooley, P.   281–2, 290
Cooper, C.   54, 326, 336, 356, 358, 382, 383
Cooper, D.   335–6, 350, 356
Corina, J.   343, 346, 348, 356
Cottrell, A.   333, 357
Courtis, J.   110–11, 116
Cox, D.   105, 116
Craft, J.   348, 356
Cragg, J.   134, 151
Critchfield, T.   138, 151
Cross, L.   179, 184
Cushing, B.   375, 383

Davis, J.   335, 357
Day, J.   118, 151, 218, 224
De Bondt, W.   140, 151
Deakin, E.   306–7, 324
Dearing, R.   370, 383
Dekker, H.   339–40, 356
Demski, J.   238, 253, 375, 383
Dev, S.   133, 151
Dhrymes, P.   173, 184
Diamond, H.   306–7, 324
Dietrich, J.   280–1, 289
Dimson, E.   79, 82, 169, 177–9, 184
Donnelly, B.   215, 224
Doukas, J.   272, 289
Draper, P.   153
Dukes, R.   196, 199, 221, 224
Dunn, J.   356
Dyckman, T.   138, 151

384

Easton, P. 236, 253
Ebling, P. 363, 383
Edey, H. 230, 254
Edminster, R. 306, 324
Edwards, E. 230, 253
Edwards, J. 226–7, 242, 253
Elgers, P. 248–9, 253
Elton, E. 134, 151, 169, 184
Eskew, R. 248, 253
Essex, S. 350, 356
Ezzamel, M. 109, 112, 116

Fama, E. 171–2, 168, 183
Feltham, G. 233, 253
Feroz, E. 62–3, 69, 82, 368, 383
Ferris, K. 132, 151
Finnerty, J. 274, 289
Firth, M. 177, 184, 188–9, 195, 223, 224, 271–2, 280, 289
Fogler, R. 173, 185
Foley, B. 349, 352, 356
Foster, G. 124, 151, 170, 184, 194, 197–9, 202, 206, 215, 224, 296, 308, 324
Fox, A. 343, 356
Franks, J. 272, 280, 289
Freeman, R. 144, 151
French, K. 172–3, 184
Fried, D. 134, 136, 139, 141, 151, 203, 224, 225
Friedman, M. 329, 356
Friend, I. 166, 173, 183, 185
Friskoff, P. 86, 116, 213, 224

Gentry, J. 315, 325
Givoly, D. 118, 134, 136, 139, 141, 151, 203, 224
Gomes-Casseres, B. 261, 289
Gragg, J. 138, 141
Grant, E. 195, 225
Gray, R. 9, 327, 330, 334, 356, 359, 380, 383
Gray, S. 77, 82
Griffiths, I. 364, 383
Gruber, M. 134, 151, 169, 184
Gultekin, N. 173, 184
Guthrie, J. 335, 356

Hagerman, R. 166, 185
Haldeman, R. 301, 306–7, 316, 324
Hamada, R. 248, 253
Hannah, R. 60–1, 82, 228, 232, 254
Harcourt, G. 238, 253
Harrigan, J. 314, 325
Harris, R. 137, 151, 273, 289
Harris, T. 236, 253
Harte, G. 335–7, 356
Hayes, C. 132, 151
Hecht, M. 272, 280, 289
Henderson, H. 33, 356
Hennart, J. 269, 289
Hessel, C. 289
Hines, R. 47, 78, 82, 336, 356
Hladik, K. 269, 289
Hope, A. 359, 380, 383
Hopper, T. 350, 356
Hopwood, W. 134, 151
Horowitz, B. 352, 356
Houghton, K. 297, 325
Hoymeyer, O. 335, 356
Hudson, J. 295, 325

Huizing, A. 339–40, 356
Hunter, J. 134, 150

Imholf, E. 137, 151
Ingo, W. 357
Institute of Chartered Accountants in Scotland 28, 45
International Accounting Standards Committee 56, 70, 73, 82

Jackson-Cox, J. 350, 356
Jacobs, B. 40, 45, 180, 184, 203, 217, 225
Jarrel, G. 271, 275–7, 289
Jarvis, R. 296, 324
Jensen, M. 178, 185, 256, 270–1, 274, 289
Jones, C. 310, 324
Jones, J. 253

Kagan, D. 335, 356
Kaplan, R. 202, 225, 314, 325
Kay, J. 226–7, 239, 242, 253
Keane, S. 78, 82, 177, 180, 185, 202, 205, 225
Keasey, K. 303, 315–6, 323, 325
Kettler, P. 247, 253
Kim, E. 166, 184
Kinney, W. 9, 327, 330, 334, 356–7
Klein, A. 138, 151
Knights, D. 350, 357
Kognt, B. 269, 289
Kothari, S. 170, 184

Lakonshok, J. 118, 138, 151
Lambert, R. 148, 150
Landskroner, Y. 166, 185
Laughlin, B. 334, 357
Lee, I. 274, 289
Leftwich, R. 124, 152, 235
Lev, B. 84, 86, 115, 116, 125, 132, 145, 151, 261, 265–6, 289
Levie, H. 348, 357
Levy, K. 40, 45, 180, 185, 203, 217, 225
Limmack, R. 272, 290
Little, I. 124, 151
Lloyd, A. 350–1, 357
Logue, D. 173–4, 184
Losq, E. 166, 185
Luchenbruch, P. 310, 325
Luckett, P. 238, 253
Lummer, S. 274, 290
Lyall, D. 346, 357

MacCalman, J. 333, 357
Magenheim, E. 274
Malkiel, B. 134, 138, 141, 151
Mandelker, G. 280–1, 290
Manegold, J. 194–5, 225
Markandya, A. 357
Mar-Molinero, C. 109, 112, 116
Marris, R. 278, 290
Marsh, A. 345, 357
Marsh, P. 79, 82, 169, 177–9, 184
Mathews, M. 334, 357
Maunders, K. 49, 329–30, 342, 352, 356–7
Maxwell, S. 335, 357
May, R. 375, 383
Mayer, C. 226–7, 239, 242, 253
McConnell, J. 274–5, 290
McDonald, B. 103–4, 116

McGowan, J. 239, 253
McKenzie, E. 178, 184
McNichols, M. 144, 152, 194–5, 225
McQueeny, J. 356
Meador, J. 213, 224
Meerjanssen, J. 82, 152
Menen, K. 317, 325
Mensah, Y. 315, 325
Merton, R. 171, 185
Mian, S. 371–2, 374, 383
Mingo, K. 113, 116, 314, 325
Mitchell, F. 350, 357
Modigliani, F. 164, 178, 184–5, 205, 225
Mohr, R. 248–9, 254
Moizer, P. 82, 118, 150, 296, 324
Monroe, R. 281, 290
Moore, R. 348, 357
Morris, M. 103–4, 116
Morris, R. 132, 150
Morse, D. 148, 150, 219, 224
Motyl, K. 337, 357
Mueller, D. 125, 147, 151, 215, 225, 274
Mueller, G. 368–9, 383
Mulford, C. 142, 151
Muscarella, C. 275, 290
Myers, S. 153, 219, 224, 251, 283–4, 290

Nantell, T. 275, 290
Narayanan, P. 301, 306–7, 316, 324
Neiderhoffer, V. 202, 225
Netter, J. 271, 275–6, 289
Newbold, P. 324
Newman, B. 376, 383
Nickell, S. 207, 225
Nobes, C. 76, 82
Noreen, E. 82, 206, 224
Norton, C. 315, 325

Ogden, S. 349, 355–7
O'Hanlon, J. 125–6, 140, 151, 179, 184, 226, 251
Ohlsen, C. 197–9, 224
Ohlson, J. 226–9, 230, 232–3, 253–4, 306, 308, 325
Ou, J. 142, 146, 152
Outram, Q. 355
Owen, D. 329–30, 335, 337–8, 350–1, 356–7
Owens, J. 274, 289

Papaioannou, G. 289
Pare, P. 137, 151
Park, K. 82, 383
Parker, L. 327–9, 331–2, 335, 356–7
Parker, R. 76, 82
Parker, T. 142, 151
Pastena, V. 82, 383
Patz, D. 137, 152
Paudyal, K. 148, 150
Pearce, D. 334, 357
Peasnell, K. 226–7, 230, 238–9, 254
Peel, D. 317, 325, 353, 357
Peel, M. 317, 325
Penman, S. 142, 146, 152, 195–6, 224, 228, 236, 254
Peterson, P. 118, 150
Pheby, D. 356
Pheby, K. 356
Pike, R. 46–7, 82, 118, 152
Pinches, G. 113, 116, 314, 325
Pogue, G. 164, 185

Poon, S. 151, 173, 185
Pope, P. 317, 325, 353, 357
Power, M. 336, 357
Puxty, A. 329, 332, 336–7

Queen, M. 310–11, 325

Ramakrishnan, R. 233, 254
Rappaport, A. 287, 290
Ravenscraft, D. 273, 276, 289, 290
Rayburn, J. 151
Rayner, A. 124, 151
Rees, W. 128, 148, 150, 152, 258, 273, 275, 289, 343, 346, 348, 356
Regan, P. 202, 225
Reger, U. 281, 290
Ricks, W. 202, 225
Roenfeldt, R. 281–2, 290
Rogers, R. 274, 289
Roll, R. 171–3, 183, 185, 202, 225, 310–11, 325
Rosewell, R. 345, 357
Ross, S. 173–4, 185
Rozeff, M. 134, 150
Ruback, R. 270–1, 274, 289
Rubinstein, M. 218, 254
Rudolph, S. 77, 82

Sammuelson, P. 40
Sams, K. 357
Saunder, S. 84, 115–16, 178, 185
Scherer, R. 256, 262, 274–6, 290
Schipper, K. 138, 142, 152
Scholes, M. 247, 253
Schwartz, K. 317, 325
Scouller, J. 259, 290
Selto, F. 376, 383
Sethi, S. 329, 332, 336–7
Shabahang, R. 352, 356
Sharpe, W. 215, 225
Sheffrin, S. 179, 185
Shevlin, T. 197–9, 224
Shimerda, T. 109, 112–15, 116
Shocker, A. 329, 357
Simkowitz, 281, 290
Singh, A. 278–9, 290
Smith, C. 34–5, 45, 371–2, 374, 383
Smith, R. 315, 325
Smith, T. 60–1, 82, 228, 232, 254
Solnick, B. 177, 185
Solomons, D. 238, 254
Sorensen, E. 280–1, 289
Stark, A. 239, 254
Steele, A. 133, 152, 241, 254
Stevens, D. 281, 290
Stewart, J. 103, 116
Storey, D. 316, 325
Strong, N. 236, 254
Sundem, G. 375, 383
Sutcliffe, C. 128, 152
Swary, I. 310, 324
Swiminathan, S. 359, 383

Taffler, R. 307, 323, 325
Tandon, K. 289
Taylor, S. 173, 185
Thaler, R. 140, 151
Thiagarajan, S. 145, 151

Thirkell, J.   356
Thomas, J.   233, 254
Ticker, R.   330, 357
Tinker, T.   326–7, 336, 357
Topham, T.   345, 357
Travlos, N.   272, 289
Trueman, B.   144, 152
Tweedie, D.   357

Urich, T.   169, 184
Urwitz, G.   314, 325

Varangu, L.   334, 357
Vergossen, R.   46, 82

Wadhani, S.   207, 225
Walker, M.   236, 254
Wansley, J.   281–2, 290
Ward, C.   178–9, 185
Watson, R.   303, 315–16, 323, 325
Watts, R.   41, 45, 124, 150, 152, 189, 225, 377–9, 380,
   383

Webb, M.   133, 151
Weinstein, M.   310, 324
Whidditt, R.   140, 151
White, P.   357
Whitford, D.   324
Whittington, G.   105, 116, 238–9, 254
Whittred, G.   317, 325
Willmott, H.   373, 383
Woodliff, D.   297, 325
Wright, F.   239, 254
Wright, W.   191–2, 194, 224
Wyatt, S.   274, 289
Wynarczyk, P.   316, 325

Yaanash, A.   151

Zavgren, C.   292, 301, 307–8, 325
Zeff, S.   376–7, 383
Zimmer, I.   317, 325
Zimmerman, J.   41, 45, 189, 225, 377–9, 380, 383
Zmijewski, M.   253

Subject Index

accounting
  beta 246–50
  vs. economics 62–3
  in financial analysis 55–6
  and inflation 68
  international 75–7
  measurement problems 56–9
  risk assessment 246–50
  statements, examples 15–20, 48–54, 89–91
  statements, ideals 56–9
  value 228–32
accounting rate of return and internal rate of return
  237–42
accounting regulation 358–81
  cost and benefits 373–4
  development of UK regulation 360–7
  Economic Union 370
  enforcement 62–3, 368
  France 368–9
  Germany 369
  Japan 369–70
  market for information 370–2
  non-market rationale 370–2
  political aspects 377
  positive explanations 377–80
  social choices 374–5
  USA 367–8
Accounting Standards Board 365–7
Accounting Standards Committee 362–3
  problems facing 363–5
accounting time series
  behaviour 118–28
  objectives 118–19
  structural change 121–23
acquisitions 225–87
agency theory and mergers 267
analysts 8
analysts' forecasts 3
analysts' report 246
annual report and accounts 278
arbitrage pricing theory 172–3
asset utilisation (turnover) 97–8
assets 59, 70–7
Associated British Foods 67
audit reports 31
  example 55
autocorrelation 124

balance sheet 58–9
bankruptcy (see financial failure)
beta 166–70
  accounting beta 246–50
  estimation 166–70
  reversion 169
bonds
  duration 210–11
  present value 207–11
  rating 312–13
  spot rate 210

  yield to maturity 208–9
bootstrapping and mergers 267
BP plc 337–8, 340–1
buy-outs 257

Cable and Wireless Plc 65
capital asset pricing model 164–73
  evidence 171–4
capital markets 154–6
capital market efficiency 174–82
capital structure 99
Carrefour SA 67, 89–91
cash flow statement 75
  market reaction 196
causal models of earnings 124
chair's statement 34
  example 47
Chief Executive Officer's (MD's) statement 54
collective bargaining and information disclosure 347–53
  constraints 348–9
  empirical evidence 352–3
  impact of 349–50
  international comparisons 351–2
  use of 350–1
competition and earnings behaviour 126
competitors 6
concentric mergers 265
consensus forecasts 134–5
conglomerate mergers 265
corporate social reporting (see social reporting)
correlation 108
creative accounting 59–69
  market reaction 199–200
credit rating 313
cross sectional analysis 92
current ratio 98
customers 6

debentures (see bonds)
defensive strategies against takeovers 276–7
depreciation 65
deterministic time series 124
discriminant analysis 302–10, 317–21
diversification 36, 162–3
divestments 262–3
dividend discount models 215–18
Dragados y Construcciones SA 122
DSM NV 48–54, 63
duration, bonds 210–11

earnings behaviour 119–28
  and competition 127
  determinants of 127–8
  empirical evidence 124–6
  and firm size 127
  and gearing 127
  and product type 127
earnings forecasting (see forecasting)
earnings forecasts and share prices 202–4
earnings per share 99–102

economic consequences of accounting regulation 375–6
efficient frontier 163
efficient market hypothesis 40, 78–80, 173–81
  size effect 179–80
  tests of weak form 176–7
  tests of semi-strong form 177–8
  weekend effect 178–9
empirical research 39–40
employee reporting 342–7
  and human relations 343
  and industrial democracy 343–4
  and political motivations 345
  and technological change 344–5
  practice of 345–7
employees 6
environmental reporting 332–42
  BP example report 337–8, 340–1
  current practice 337
  Netherlands 338–9, 342
  opponents 336
  sustainability 334–6
event studies 189–94
expenses 74
exposure drafts 361
Extel Financial Services 10–23
extraordinary items 66

financial analysis 2–3
  demand for 4
  ten commandments of 3
financial databases 39
  example 10–23
financial analysts' forecasts (see forecasts)
financial failure 291–317
  capital market 310–11
  cash flow 315
  conditional probability models 308
  debt rating 311–14
  financial variables 297–302
  history 293–5
  inflation accounting 314–16
  information used 295–97
  multivariate analysis 302–10
  multivariate example 317–21
  small firms 316–17
  univariate analysis 298–302
financial statements 69–75
  definitions 57, 73–4
firms
  incorporation 33
  and contracting 34–5
  ownership and control 35–7
forecasts (earnings)
  accuracy 136–8
  analysts 134–47
  bias 138–40
  concensus 134–5
  and fundamentals 144–7
  management 133–4
  and market expectations 141–3
  rationality 140–1
  and share prices 142–4
functional form of ratios 102
fundamental (accounting) beta 246–50

gearing (leverage) 99
gearing and earnings behaviour 127

Gordon growth model 212
government 7
  local 7
  revenue 6
group accounting 284–6

Hanson plc 76
horizontal mergers 265

income 73–4
incorporation 33
inflation
  and accounting 68
  and failure prediction 314–16
  and market values 205
information disclosure (see collective bargaining)
initial public offers 258
insolvency (see financial failure)
intangible assets 66
interim accounts 28
  market reaction to 195
intermediaries 8
internal rate of return and accounting rate of return
    237–42
international accounting differences 75–7
International Accounting Standard Committee 57–9
investors 45

joint ventures 257
  motives for 269–70
  performance of 273–5

kurtosis 108

late disclosure and market reaction 195
leverage (see gearing)
liabilities 70–79
liquidation costs 301
liquidity 78

management
  forecasts 30
  labour market 38
  objectives 37–8
  product market 38
  and shareholders 37
  and takeovers 37
market portfolio 163–4
market rate of return 171
market reaction to accounting announcements 187–97
  cash flow figures 196
  delayed disclosure 195–6
  interim accounts 194
  small firms 195
  unexpected earnings 193–4
matching (accruals) 64–8
media (financial) 9
MEPC plc 313
mergers
  accounting for 284–6
  asset utilisation 277–80
  characteristics of participants 277–80
  defensive strategies 276–7
  history of 259–62
  investing in targets 280–3
  impact on economy 264
  managerial motives 265–9, 275

performance record 270–3
predicting 280–3
target undervalued 268
types of 265
valuing 283–4
waves 262–3
Moody's Investment Services 313
myopic markets 205–7

net asset turnover 98
net profit margin 97
normative research 41

ownership vs. control of firms 35–7

political aspects of accounting regulation 377
political considerations 42
portfolio theory 159–64
positive accounting theory 41–2, 377–80
post earnings drift 197–201
price/earnings ratio 214, 218–21
  diversity 218–21
  valuation 214–15
privatisations 259
product type and earnings behaviour 127
profit and cash flow 64
profit and loss account (see income)
profit maximisation 36
prospectus 28
public 8

quantitative non-financial information 30
quarterly data 124–5

random walk 123
ratio analysis
  and accounting 93–4
  basic analysis technique 95–101
  bench-marks 86
  choice of 112–13
  cross sectional analysis 92
  decomposition 100–1
  distributional characteristics 106–9
  examples 84–5
  example computation 95–9
  in formal decision models 86
  international differences 85
  inter-relationships between ratios 109–13
  negative numbers 84
  non-linearity of ratios 102
  selection 92
  size standardisation 88
  small divisors 94
  statistical properties 101–6
  summary statistics 85
  transformations 106–9
  and unsynchronised data 93
recognition (of income/expenses) 64–8
regulation 7
residual income and value 232–5
return on capital employed 96
return on equity 95
return on investment 157
return on sales 97
risk
  aversion 155

of investment 157–8
and return 157–65
Rolls Royce Plc 135

satisfying behaviour 37
Scottish Hydroelectric Plc 68
Securities and Exchange Commission 28
share price charts 29
share prices and earnings forecasts 142–4
share valuation models 211–3
shareholders 4–5
Sharpe, Albert E. 24–6
Siemens AG 10–23
size maximisation 36
skewness 108
small firms and market reaction 195
social reporting 328–32
  accountability 329–30
  case against 331–3
  standards 331
social theories 42
sources of information 9, 27–33, 46–7
spot rate of interest (bonds) 210
standard deviation 107
standard setting process 360–7
strong form market efficiency 177–8
subsidiaries 284–6
suppliers 6
synergy 265
systematic risk 164

takeovers 255–87
targets 255–287
Tarmac Plc 24–6, 121, 129–30
technical analysis 29
theory, the role of 38–9
time series (see earnings behaviour)
Tobin's Q 279–80
trade unions 6
transactions (number of) 68

unexpected earnings 189–94
union competence and information disclosure 348–9
US accounting 76
users (of financial analysis) 4–9

validation (holdout) sample 309–10
valuation models 207–21
  debt 207–11
  dividend discount models 215–18
  equity 211–13
  practices 213–18
  price-earnings based 214–15
  and price earnings ratios 218–21
Value
  book value and earnings 236–7
  clean surplus earnings 228–32
  forecast residual income 232–5
  to owner 242–6
vertical mergers 265

weak form EMH 176–7
weekend effect 179–80

yield to maturity (bonds) 208

Z-score 302–7